Macmillan History of Europe

Eighteenth-Century Europe

HISTORY OF EUROPE

PUBLISHED

Early Medieval Europe, 300–1000 (second edition)
Roger Collins

Sixteenth-Century Europe
Richard Mackenney

Seventeenth-Century Europe, 1598–1700
Thomas Munck

Eighteenth-Century Europe (second edition)
Jeremy Black

FORTHCOMING

Nineteenth-Century Europe, 1789–1914
Alan Sked

Twentieth-Century Europe
Richard Vinen

History of Europe
Series Standing Order
ISBN 0–333–71699–X hardcover
ISBN 0–333–69381–7 paperback
(*outside North America only*)

You can receive future titles in this series as they are published by placing a standing order. Please contact your bookseller or, in the case of difficulty, write to us at the address below with your name and address, the title of the series and the ISBN quoted above.

Customer Services Department, Macmillan Distribution Ltd
Houndmills, Basingstoke, Hampshire RG21 6XS, England

Macmillan History of Europe

Eighteenth-Century Europe

Jeremy Black

Second Edition

First edition 1990
Second edition 1999

MACMILLAN PRESS LTD
Houndmills, Basingstoke, Hampshire RG21 6XS
and London
Companies and representatives
throughout the world

ISBN 0–333–77336–5 hardcover
ISBN 0–333–77335–7 paperback

A catalogue record for this book is available
from the British Library.

This book is printed on paper suitable for recycling and
made from fully managed and sustained forest sources.

10   9   8   7   6   5   4   3   2   1
08   07   06   05   04   03   02   01   00   99

Published in the United States of America by
ST. MARTIN'S PRESS, INC.,
Scholarly and Reference Division
175 Fifth Avenue, New York, N.Y. 10010

ISBN 0–312–22539–3 (paper)
ISBN 978-0-312-22539-1

Transferred to Digital Printing 2009

Contents

List of Maps

Chronology

International relations

1759	Britain's year of victories. Fall of Québec
1761	Third Family Compact: France–Spain. First two in 1733 and 1743
1763	Peace of Paris and Treaty of Hubertusburg end Seven Years War
1768	Outbreak of Russo-Turkish war. France purchases Corsica
1772	First partition of Poland
1774	Treaty of Kutchuk-Kainardji: ends Russo-Turkish war
1776	American Declaration of Independence
1778–9	War of Bavarian Succession
1778	France enters War of American Independence
1781	Austro-Russian alliance against Ottoman Empire
1783	Russia seizes Crimea. Treaty of Versailles ends American war
1786	Anglo-French commercial treaty
1787	Turks attack Russia. Prussians intervene in the United Provinces
1788	Gustavus III of Sweden attacks Russia
1790	End of Austro-Turkish and Russo-Swedish hostilities. Anglo-Spanish Nootka Sound Crisis
1791	Ochakov Crisis between Britain and Russia
1792	Treaty of Jassy ends Russo-Turkish conflict. Outbreak of the French Revolutionary war
1793	Britain joins Revolutionary war. Second Partition of Poland
1795	Third Partition of Poland

Britain

1701	Act of Settlement establishes terms of Hanoverian succession
1707	Union of England and Scotland
1714	Whigs replace Tories following accession of George I
1715–16	Jacobite rising
1716	Septennial Act: elections only necessary every 7 years
1720	South Sea Bubble bursts
1721	Walpole becomes chief minister
1733	Excise Crisis
1742	Walpole falls after 1741 elections
1745–6	Jacobite rising
1754	Death of Henry Pelham inaugurates period of ministerial instability

1757–61	Pitt–Newcastle ministry
1770–82	Lord North chief minister
1781	Surrender of army at Yorktown
1783	William Pitt the Younger becomes chief minister
1788–9	Regency crisis

France

1713	Bull *Unigenitus* condemns alleged Jansenist doctrines
1715	Accession of Louis XV. Orléans regent until 1723
1720	Collapse of Law's financial schemes
1726–43	Cardinal Fleury chief minister
1749	New tax, the *Vingtième*, imposed
1751	First volume of *Encyclopédie* appears
1758–70	Duc de Choiseul chief minister
1764	Expulsion of the Jesuits
1771	The 'Maupeou Revolution': reorganisation of the *parlements*
1774	Accession of Louis XVI, fall of Maupeou, recall of *parlements*
1774–6	Turgot controller-general of finances
1787	Assembly of Notables meets. Calonne replaced by Brienne
1788	Assembly of Notables fails. Estates General summoned. Brienne replaced by Necker
1789	Estates General meets. Fall of the Bastille. Estates General becomes National Assembly. Declaration of the Rights of Man and the Citizen
1791	Flight to Varennes. New constitution
1792	Monarchy abolished
1793	Louis XVI executed

Habsburg Territories

1703–11	Rakoczi rising in Hungary
1711	Hungary revolt ended by Peace of Szatmár
1713	Pragmatic Sanction issued
1753–93	Kaunitz chancellor
1781	Religious liberty granted to non-Catholic Christians
1782	Pius VI visits Vienna

Prussia

1722	General Directory established
1740	Frederick II accedes and invades Silesia
1744	Acquisition of East Friesland
1766	New excise introduced

Russia

1700	Battle of Narva: Peter I defeated by Sweden
1703	Building of St Petersburg begun
1708	Revolt of Ukraine
1710–11	Conquest of Baltic provinces
1711	Creation of the Senate
1718	Murder of Tsarevich Alexis. Creation of administrative colleges (ministries) begun
1722	Table of Ranks issued
1730	Leading nobles fail to impose restrictions on Anna
1741	Coup by Elizabeth
1762	Accession, deposition and murder of Peter III. Abolition of compulsory state service for the nobility
1767	Legislative Commission meets
1773–5	Pugachev serf rising
1775	Reform of provincial administration
1785	Charters to the nobility and the towns issued

Other States

1720	New written constitution greatly reduces power of Swedish monarchy
1747	Orangist revolution in the United Provinces
1750–77	Pombal chief minister in Portugal
1759	Jesuits expelled from Portugal
1759–76	Tanucci chief minister in Naples
1765–90	Grand Duke Leopold ruler of Tuscany
1770–2	Struensee reforms in Denmark
1773	Dissolution of the Jesuit Order
1786	Synod at Pistoia

Rulers of the Major States

Austrian Dominions: Habsburgs

Leopold I	1657–1705
Joseph I	1705–1711
Charles VI	1711–1740
Maria Theresa	1740–1780
(Joseph II co-regent	1765–1780)
Joseph II	1780–1790
Leopold II	1790–1792

France: Bourbon dynasty

Louis XIV	1643–1715
Louis XV	1715–1774
(Regency of duke of Orléans	1715–1723)
Louis XVI	1774–1793

Great Britain

William III	1689–1702
Anne	1702–1714
George I	1714–1727 ⎫ Hanoverian
George II	1727–1760 ⎬ dynasty
George III	1760–1820 ⎭

Prussia: Hohenzollerns

Frederick I	1688–1713
Frederick William I	1713–1740
Frederick II 'the Great'	1740–1786
Frederick William II	1786–1797

Russia: Romanovs

Peter I 'the Great'	1682–1725
Catherine I	1725–1727
Peter II	1727–1730
Anna	1730–1740
Ivan VI	1740–1741
Elizabeth	1741–1762
Peter III	1762
Catherine II 'the Great'	1762–1796

Spain: Bourbons

Philip V	1700–1746
Ferdinand VI	1746–1759
Charles III	1759–1788
Charles IV	1788–1808

Sweden: Vasa

Charles XII	1697–1718
Ulrika Eleonora	1718–1720
Frederick I	1720–1751
Adolphus-Frederick	1751–1771
Gustavus III	1771–1792

United Provinces (Dutch Republic): stadtholders

William III	1672–1702
No stadtholders in major provinces	1702–1747
William IV	1747–1751
William V	1751–1795

Popes

Innocent XII	1691–1700
Clement XI	1700–1721
Innocent XIII	1721–1724
Benedict XIII	1724–1730
Clement XII	1730–1740

Benedict XIV	1740–1758
Clement XIII	1758–1769
Clement XIV	1769–1774
Pius VI	1775–1799
Pius VII	1800–1823

Frederick II of Prussia is referred to in the text as Frederick the Great to distinguish him from Frederick II of Hesse-Cassel.

Preface to the Second Edition

'Not enough on Rousseau. Too much on Russia.' 'Too much on Russia. Not enough on Rousseau.' If it is impossible to write a general work that will satisfy all, that has become even more the case as the scholarly agenda has widened. It is no longer acceptable to offer simply what one scholar unfairly reviewing an earlier general work on this period referred to as 'comfortable old chums like "The Rise of Great Britain", "The Decline of the Dutch Republic" and "The Emergence of Prussia"'. The selection of material entails the risk of bias. How is the teleological challenge posed by the French and industrial revolutions to be faced? Is what happened in Prussia more important than developments in Piedmont? As there are no obvious criteria by which such questions can be answered those interested in this period can benefit from the varied approaches of different scholars. This book is thematic rather than chronological or national in its organisation. For those who prefer the latter approaches there are a number of excellent surveys available.

I owe thanks to a number of institutions and individuals. By asking me to produce an expanded edition of this book Jonathan Reeve provided me with the opportunity of undertaking a very interesting project. Two chapters are entirely new and all the others have been extensively revised. My research was helped by those institutions which, in supporting foreign archival work, gave me the opportunity to work in libraries after the archives were shut. Furthermore, the book benefits from my work in Austrian, British, Dutch, French, German and Italian archives since 1978. The use of original examples enlivens this study and, more significantly, a grounding in eighteenth-century archival sources has provided a grasp of the uncertainties and compromises of the period. This contributes to a feature of this book, an emphasis on the difficulty of offering sweeping explanations. Instead, there is a stress on the contrasts of the age, the variety of developments and the complexity of analysis. In place of traditional preconceptions and easy explanatory antitheses, such as despotism and revolution, *ancien régime* and new order, privilege and protest, tradition and progress, stability and strife, liberty and order, authoritarianism and affection, high and low culture, there is a concern with detail in order both to show the vivid concreteness of the age and to suggest interaction as well as tensions within the eighteenth-century world. There is also a stress on the protean, adaptable character of the old order.

Wendy Duery provided crucial secretarial support. Matthew Anderson, Nigel Aston, Edward Corp, Malcolm Crook, Bill Gibson, Sheridan Gilley, Jan Glete, Nick Henshall, Murray Pittock, David Sturdy and Peter Wilson helpfully discussed aspects of the new edition, which was written in the summer of 1998. The preface to the last edition closed: 'The book was begun in 1983, two homes ago. I thank Sarah for everything.' Now, it should read three homes. The thanks are the same.

JEREMY BLACK

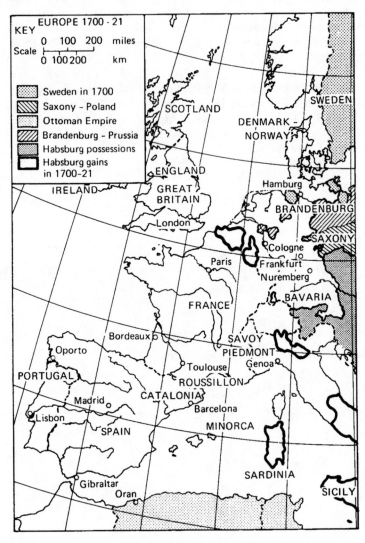

Map 1   Europe 1700

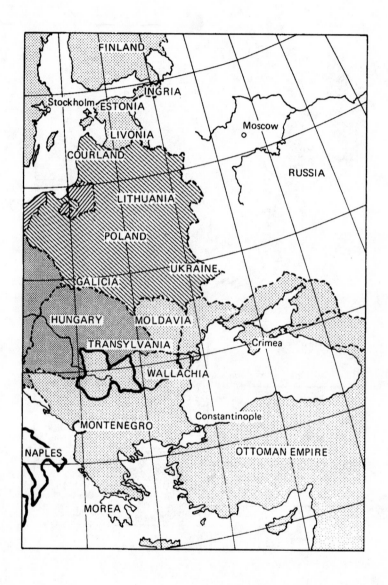

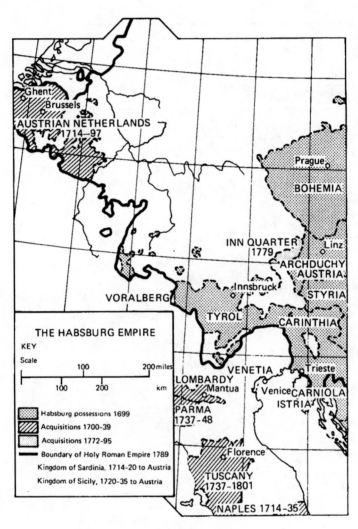

Map 2   The Habsburg Empire

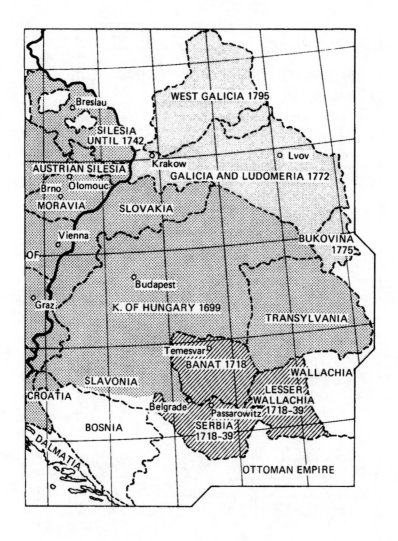

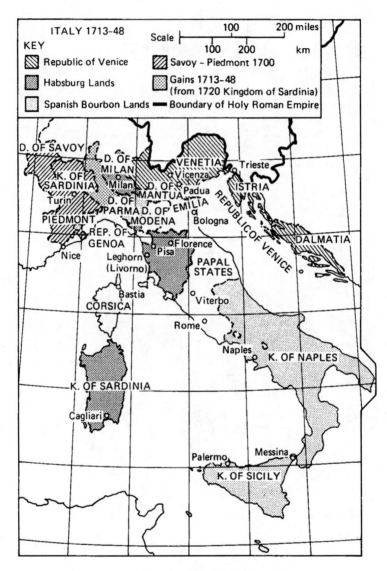

Map 3   Italy 1713–48

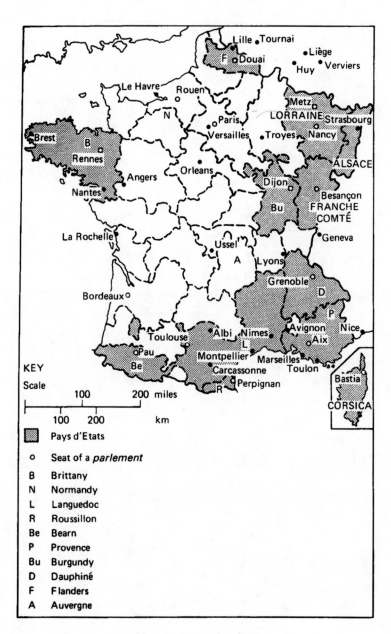

Map 4   France in 1789

1 Hostile Environment

There is an unphilosophical story of a woman brought to bed the other day at Paris of two young lions after having been to see a lion baited; that is believed at court, and generally through all France, and will probably make as great a noise as our rabbits.
(Robert Trevor, Haute-Fontaine, 1729, referring also to the belief that Mary Toft, a Godalming woman, gave birth to rabbits)[1]

The lives and activities of individuals of all social groups were governed in Europe by a hostile environment. Many of the difficulties are still familiar today, particularly in the Third World, but modern familiarity with such problems as disease or adverse weather conditions should not blind us to their significance. They affected not only the experiences and actions of individuals, but also their attitudes, and it is necessary to consider the latter in order to understand the impact of facts of life and death.

Demography, disease and death

The pre-modern demographic (population) pattern was usually static, and essentially procreation-postponing, with low illegitimacy, and with late marriages linked to job opportunities. However, the general movement in population in eighteenth-century Europe was upward, particularly after the early 1740s. The European population rose from about 118 million in 1700 to possibly 187 million a century later. As with so much in a period for which diversity was the keynote, this general increase concealed significant variations, in terms both of the rate of growth and of its chronology. Unfavourable demographic and economic regimes could produce a decline in population, as could catastrophes such as serious warfare. In such circumstances the fall in population often owed much to emigration and, in the case of towns with death rates higher than their birth rates, to a failure to sustain immigration. In a century when the availability and accuracy of statistics were, and are, limited, most population figures should be taken as approximate. Nevertheless, there are clear signs of a drop in some areas. The Danubian principalities, Moldavia and Wallachia, now in modern Romania, suffered a substantial decline that owed much to repeated wars between the Turks and

1

the Christian powers and to emigration. War also helped to reduce the population of the electorate of Saxony from 2 million in 1700 to 1,600,000 at the end of the Seven Years War in 1763, a war that had cost Prussia, through death and flight, 10 per cent of its population. In contrast, despite being besieged and captured, Antwerp owed its population decline from 67,000 in 1699 to 42,000 in 1755 largely to adverse economic circumstances, as did Ghent.

Stagnation characterised the population figures of many areas for much of the century. The population of Rheims was stable at 25,000 from 1694 until 1770, before beginning a period of growth that was to take it by 1789 to 32,000, but that was only a return to the figure for 1675. At a smaller scale, also in France, the population growth in the community of Duravel in Haut-Quercy was insufficient by the end of the century to reach the figures that had preceded the 1693 famine. Economically stagnant Venice, bereft of the trade that brought prosperity to so many Atlantic ports, had a population of 138,000 in 1702, 137,000 in 1797. Stagnant population figures were not necessarily a problem. It could be suggested that, in part, a stable population reflected a desire to benefit from higher per capita incomes by limiting population, as much as a response to poor economic conditions. Many areas that witnessed population growth, such as the Dutch province of Overijssel and Ireland in the second half of the century, encountered difficulties.

Nevertheless, the general trend was for a rise in population, and this affected both areas that were clearly experiencing significant economic growth and others that were not. In the latter category, the population of the kingdom of Naples on the mainland nearly doubled to over 5 million, that of the island of Sicily rose from 1 to 1.5 million, while the Portuguese figures rose from 2 to 3 million and those of Norway from 512,000 to 883,000. Economic activity was not the sole factor. Territorial gains, especially from Poland in 1772–95, helped to push Russia's figures from 15 million in 1719 to 35 million in 1800, a figure that put her ahead of France whose population had risen, again partly due to annexation, from 21.9 million in 1675 to 22.4 million in 1705, 24.6 million in 1740 and possibly close to 30 million in 1800. The latter rise again illustrated the diversity of the age, for it concealed both periods and areas of slack growth, such as the 1740s, 1780s, and western France, and others of marked increase, such as Burgundy and Alsace. Elsewhere in Europe, the population of Poland began to rise in the 1720s, after a period of war and epidemics, while that of the German duchy of Württemberg rose from 428,000 in 1734 to 620,000 in 1790, although this increase was exceptional within Germany and does not reflect the less dramatic overall trends. The process of population growth in Spain accelerated after 1770, but most of the eighteenth-century growth occurred in peripheral and coastal provinces such as Valencia, rather than in the poorer agricultural central regions. Discrepancies in growth rates become more marked as the range of geographical focus narrows and, in particular, as the towns are considered. Though the Italian population rose from 13 to 17 million during the century, that of Turin, a government centre (for Piedmont) with little industry, rose from 44,000 to 92,000. Urban growth was greatly dependent on immigration. While the general rate of increase in the Rhineland over the century was 30 per cent, the population in Düsseldorf and the nearby villages doubled between 1750 and 1790 thanks both to a higher birth rate and to immigration. Berlin, the capital of Prussia, witnessed a jump from 55,000 in 1700 to 150,000 in 1800.

Detailed variations in population movements provide some clues to the reasons for change at the same time as they make a general thesis more difficult to devise. Birth control, including higher ages of marriage, restricted the numbers born, disease and malnutrition were the principal limiting factors thereafter. The average age at which women married for the first time, a crucial source of differences in demographic growth, varied greatly, but there are signs that it reflected an awareness of economic opportunity. In eastern Europe, where population densities were low, labour was generally in demand and overpopulation was less of a problem, the age was commonly 17–20, and most women married. The contrasting figure for north-west Europe, with its higher densities and population pressure, was 23–27.

Economic adversity structured demographic activity, creating and altering norms of behaviour and producing great pressure on individuals. In the Tuscan village of Altopascio the average age on marriage rose from 21.5 prior to 1700 to 24.17 between 1700 and 1749, and was matched by a decline in the average number of children per couple. This probably owed much to the depressed incomes that paralleled the fall in the price of wheat at the beginning of the century. The adverse economic situation in the village of Bilhères in the French province of Béarn, a community whose population pressed on its limited food supplies, helped to produce an average age of women at first marriage of 27 and very few remarriages. The comparable figure between 1774 and 1792 in the village of Azereix in the French Pyrenees was 26 and the average gap between births was long, suggesting contraceptive practices. The slight decrease in the French birth rate after about 1770 has been attributed in part to the latter, particularly coitus interruptus. A Church conference on marriage in 1715 had insisted that women must perform their conjugal duties, but it was left to the parish clergy to try and enforce it. Sermons dwelt on the theme. There are signs that more enlightened priests by the 1770s were handling these awkward moral issues with a new sensitivity, tacitly allowing contraceptive practices. As the prosperity of the Austrian Netherlands declined towards the end of the century, the marriage rate fell.

There are therefore clear signs that birth rates were in some areas related to an awareness of economic opportunities. Until the late 1760s marriage rates at Strasbourg followed the movement of prices. The cycles in the silk industry of Krefeld in the Rhineland were mirrored in the local marriage figures. The 1755 census in Brabant revealed that the marriage age for peasants was later than that for artisans, who generally had greater possibilities for earning money and achieving independent status earlier in life. Economic opportunities could lead to significant increases in population, due to immigration, higher birth rates or both. The rise of the British population has been attributed to a lower age of marriage and more fertile marriages rather than to a declining death rate, and the former may owe much to rising real wages, as in Yorkshire. The population of England and Wales, in millions, rose from 5.18 in 1695 to 5.51 in 1711, 5.59 in 1731, 6.20 in 1751, 6.97 in 1771 and 8.21 in 1791. The population of Castres in France rose 50 per cent between 1744 and 1790 in response to the recovery of the town's textile industry. It has been suggested that proto-industrialisation, the development of industrial activity in certain rural areas, led to demographic growth in these areas. These areas then in effect used their wealth to export their malnutrition to the peasantry of agricultural regions, such as Hungary and Galicia in eastern Europe, by importing food from them.[2]

However, population growth was not simply a matter of rising birth rates reflecting economic growth. Population did not only rise in areas of such growth, and it has been argued that a declining death rate was a more significant feature of the European demographic regime. Life expectancy was not high by modern European standards. In the Bohemian town of Pilsen, the rate of deaths prior to a fifth birthday was 52 per cent, but towns were particularly unhealthy. The comparable figure for the Moravian village of Poruba was 36 per cent, but this was still harsh. The mean age of death in Poruba in the first half of the century was 27 for men, 33 for women, figures that improved to 54 and 55 for those who survived to 15: surviving childhood was the key to achieving a reasonable age. In the second half of the century the figures were actually worse, due to the famine of 1772.

Even where they occurred, increases in average life expectancy could not counter individual fear, particularly given the readily apparent fallibility of contemporary medicine. The situation was harsh at both ends of the social scale. Frederick II (the 'Great') of Prussia succeeded his father Frederick William I in 1740 because his two elder brothers had died, both before the age of one. Three-quarters of the infants left at the Hospital of the Innocent in Florence in 1762–4 who were not reclaimed by their parents died before reaching adulthood. The comparable figure for the General Hospital of Amiens in the 1780s was two-thirds dying by the age of five. Institutionalisation helped infection. In Walloon Brabant, part of modern Belgium, 20 per cent of those born died in their first year, and the life expectancy was less than 40. Nevertheless, the population still rose, and at an annual rate of 0.69 per cent in the second half of the century.

The plague

Disease was a significant killer both as a constant presence and through dramatic epidemics. Plague could have a terrifying impact. The plague epidemic that began in the late 1700s decimated the population of eastern Europe. Hungary lost about 10 per cent of its population, Livonia over 125,000 people. It also disrupted economic, political and cultural activities, bringing closures such as the Austro-Hungarian frontier in 1709–14 and the university of Königsberg in 1709. A plague epidemic that ravaged the Ottoman Empire, Hungary and the Ukraine in the late 1730s and 1740s killed about 47,000 in Sicily and Calabria in 1743. A savage epidemic at the beginning of the 1770s affected Russia and the Ottoman Empire. Over 100,000 people died in Moscow, where rumours spread that doctors, secretly in alliance with the nobility, were spreading the disease instead of fighting it. In Kiev, where 18 per cent of the population died, the obscurantist clergy refused to approve the burning of the clothes of the dead, a necessary measure in order to fight the disease.

In one perspective, the plague was in retreat. In Scotland the last major epidemic ended in 1649, in England in 1665, in Spain in 1685, in France in 1720, and in Italy in 1743. The situation looked less favourable, however, in eastern Europe, where significant epidemics affected the Balkans in the 1710s, 1720s, 1730s, 1740s, 1770s and 1780s. Furthermore, the general attitude was one of fear and vigilance not optimism. Europe was bisected by a plague cordon, a network of quarantine officials, posts and regulations that were intended as a barrier to resist the effects of the hostile environment. It was most apparent on the European borders of the Ottoman Empire. Vigilance, always constant, rose to a frenzied pitch during epidemics. Venice sent warships into the Adriatic to prevent the arrival of ships from infected areas in 1743 and that winter prohibited trade with the rest of Italy. Her regulations did not respect rank and the duke of Modena was forced into quarantine. In response to epidemics, troops were used to close frontiers in eastern Europe, as in 1753 and 1770, and naval patrols were established off the Neapolitan coast in 1778. Western Europe was not free of anxiety. An outbreak of fever in Rouen in early 1754 was falsely identified as plague, and three years later the disease was reported at Lisbon. In 1781 the Sardinian government took major precautions to prevent the spread of plague from the Balkans.

The potential effectiveness and ruthlessness of eighteenth-century measures for the control of the plague were well demonstrated in the moves to limit the spread of the Marseilles outbreak of 1720. Without the *cordon sanitaire* which isolated the city in 1720 the epidemic might rapidly have spread throughout France. Quarantine regulations were arguably the government activity that was of most benefit to the people of Europe, but, as with so many other aspects of state activity, their effectiveness is difficult to assess. The practice of quarantine was well-founded, since, if isolation could be achieved, the chain of infection would be broken.

However, eastern Europe lacked the bureaucracy to police the disease effectively, and it is arguable that public health measures were less significant in limiting the outbreaks of plague than mutations in the plague parasite and changes in its more common hosts, the rat and flea population of Europe. Barriers against disease were flimsy, and reactions to it clumsy and erratic, due to prevailing attitudes and the limited nature of medical knowledge. It is possible that the chances of infection in western Europe were reduced by the alterations in human habitat characterised by construction with brick, stone and tile, for example the move away from earthen floors, although these remained common in the dwellings of the poor. Whatever the causes of the change in western Europe, they were of no comfort to the peoples further east, where plague neither disappeared nor diminished in virulence. In the Ukraine, and Russia more generally, bubonic infection came from ground-burrowing rodents, and the spread of agriculture southwards led to increased occupation of lands occupied by these rodents. However, ploughing also restricted the natural habitats of the rodents, and, thanks in part to the greater availability of food, the population rose.[3]

The fight against smallpox

The plague was by no means the only serious human disease, although the quantification of disease patterns is hindered by the imprecision of many eighteenth-century medical terms. Decline and palsy were really conventional terms for symptoms preceding death, while ague and flux were very imprecise labels, diagnosed with an unknown extent of variability. Smallpox was a serious killer, especially of children, and was responsible for mortality crises in Milan in 1707 and 1719 and in Verona in 1726. It was endemic in Italy in the 1750s and in Venetia in the early 1760s, and was the principal killer of infants in Vienna in 1787. It was also no respecter of rank. Pedro II left Lisbon for the countryside in January 1701 in order to avoid it. Louis XV died of it in 1774 and three years later it claimed the king of Naples' brother, leading the monarch to have his children inoculated.

The disease was difficult to conquer. Resistance to inoculation against smallpox, frequently on the grounds of tempting divine providence, was not always uninformed. The Reverend Norton Nicholls wrote from Rome in 1772, 'The smallpox has raged like the plague here and made dreadful havoc. They are much prejudiced against inoculation, and have a ridiculous notion that the disorder may return again so, but not after having had it in the natural way.'[4] In fact, the spread of inoculation in Italy after 1714 might be related to the higher frequency of smallpox, as inoculated persons, when not isolated, were a source of infection. Inoculation in Britain became safer after the Suttonian method of inserting only the smallest possible amount of infectious matter was widely adopted from about 1768. Vaccination, rather than inoculation, played a major role in defeating smallpox, but it was not first performed, by Edward Jenner, until 1796. It was introduced into France in 1800 and it has been estimated that within a decade 50 per cent of French babies were being vaccinated.

Other diseases

Typhus, typhoid and relapsing fever were endemic in Europe and could become epidemic. Influenza was a serious problem, with major European epidemics, as in 1733, 1742–3 and 1753. Bacillary dysentery was always common in rural Europe and the primitive sanitation and poor nutrition of the period helped to make the disease a killer. Epidemics of dysentery had savage effects in France in 1706 and the Austrian Netherlands in 1741; another, known as the Red Death, affected the Low Countries in the 1770s. In Sweden pulmonary tuberculosis was endemic from the mid-century, and the 1770s and 1780s were periods of severe crop failures and dysentery epidemics. Malaria was a significant problem in certain Mediterranean areas, such as the island of Sardinia, while syphilis was another common disease. The absence of antibiotics and the limited use of condoms ensured that venereal disease was a constant concern of the period. In addition, a whole host of illnesses and accidents that in modern Europe can be tackled successfully were killers.

In 1768 an allegorical ballet entitled *Prejudice Overcome* was staged at the Russian court. Two opposing temples, of Ignorance and Aesculapius, the god of medicine, were presented alongside a character Ruthenia, representing the Russian people, worrying about smallpox. Minerva, symbolising the Russian ruler Catherine the Great, who had herself been recently inoculated, emerged from the Temple of Aesculapius and agreed to be inoculated, whereupon Ruthenia followed and a dance of hope began, celebrating the expulsion of Superstition and Ignorance, two characters in the ballet, from the kingdom. Reality was otherwise. The trickledown theory was limited by a lack of interest from many rulers, such as Catherine herself, in the situation of the people, and by popular resistance to new ideas, whether the attempt to prevent burial inside churches in Brittany or to implement the sanitary reforms devised by the government of the Austrian Netherlands in 1779. Church authorities often failed to provide new consecrated burial grounds.

Nevertheless, there was a greater understanding of some of the problems that contributed to disease. A French royal declaration of 1776 declared that cemeteries in built-up areas that endangered 'the salubrity' of the air must be moved wherever possible, and that only bishops, priests, patrons and seigneurs could be buried inside churches. Town planning revealed a preference for public spaces that were ordered, airy and well lit. French plans for the ideal market sought to offer air, space and water, to consider the physical safety of customers, the control of smells and the cleanliness of the building. It is possible that some success in the struggle against disease should be attributed to the efforts of local institutions, whether by providing more hospitals, supplying clean water or, as with the Basque Society of Friends of the Country after 1771, campaigning in favour of inoculation against smallpox.

The virulence of eighteenth-century diseases, however, was also a product of the circumstances of the age. Trade and migration spread them. In 1730 a Spanish squadron from the West Indies brought to Cadiz the first European cases of yellow fever. Armies were mass transmitters and victims of illnesses, helping bridge different disease regions and thus exacerbating problems in areas with limited immunity to particular illnesses. The diseases that raged in the Russian camp at Narva in 1700 infected the Swedes when they seized it. Austrian troops brought illness to the Upper Palatinate in 1752 and from Hungary to Silesia in 1758, while the Russian troops operating in the Balkans during the 1768–74 war with Turkey spread typhus to Russia. In addition, migrants seeking food or work were widely regarded as a source of infection. This helped to encourage a hostile response to them. The Bavarian envoy in Vienna wrote in 1772 of the Bohemian poor bringing death on their lips.

Sanitation and diet

Sanitation and diet were clearly problems. The housing conditions of the bulk of the population, in particular the habit of sharing beds, were conducive to a high incidence of respiratory infections, an apparent consequence of the lack of privacy that was produced by the limited nature of the housing stock. Sanitary practices and standards of personal cleanliness were important, particularly in communities with a high density of population. Louse infestation was related to crowding, inadequate bathing facilities, and the continual wearing of the same clothes. Cleanliness was associated with wearing clean shirts and linen, rather than washing, but both were only possible for a minority. There were few baths or lavatories. Whatever their wealth, humans had few defences against a whole range of the natural world from lice, bed-bugs and fleas to tapeworms.

The habit of washing in clean water was perforce limited, while the proximity of animals and dunghills was unhelpful. Europe was a society that conserved rather than disposed of its excrement. Animal and human waste were gathered for purposes of manure. This manure stored near dwellings was dangerous and, once spread, could contaminate the water supply. Effluent from undrained privies and animal pens flowed across streets and on and beneath the surface into houses through generally porous walls. Typhus was one result. Clean drinking water was absent in most of Europe, particularly in large towns, coastal regions and lowland areas without deep wells. River water was often muddy while pump water could be affected by sewage. This accounted for the importance of fermented drinks.

Poor nutrition also contributed to the spread of infectious diseases, by lowering resistance. Furthermore, malnutrition limited sexual desire and activity, hindered successful pregnancy, and, if chronic, delayed sexual maturity and produced sterility in women. Problems of food shortage and cost ensured that the bulk of the population lacked a balanced diet, even when they had enough food. Diet varied by area and social group and substitution was possible; for example, in Russia fish, berries and honey could provide nutritious substitutes for meat and sugar. In general, fruit and vegetables were expensive and played only a minor role in the diet of the urban poor, who were also frequently ill-clad. Much of this group was affected by declining real wages as prices rose and a larger population led to labour surpluses.[5] The European peasantry consumed little meat and ate the less desirable cereals.

In some areas there are signs of a deterioration in the diet. In Austria, per capita meat consumption fell in the second half of the century. In Sweden the quantity of animal products consumed per capita fell. Evidence from military archives on the height of Bohemian, Hungarian and Swedish males suggests that boys growing up towards the end of the eighteenth century suffered some degeneration of health and nutrition and that their growth was inhibited accordingly.

Poor hygiene and nutrition appear to have played a major role in the spread of epidemics. In Strasbourg until the 1750s periods of food scarcity were accompanied by epidemics. Hunger was associated with dysentery in the Brabant countryside. Across much of Europe the rise in cereal prices in 1739–41 was followed by an upsurge in epidemic diseases; although this also coincided with very bad weather. The Italian famine of 1764–8 may have been responsible for the fever epidemic that hit central Italy in 1767. Conversely, in the late eighteenth-century Rhineland, good harvests were matched by a relative absence of epidemics.

The impact of disease was not solely affected by nutrition. Climatic factors were also of great significance, particularly in weakening resistance. Epidemics of fatal respiratory disease became rife in France during the early 1740s, probably due to hypothermia. Savage climatic conditions were exacerbated by shortages of firewood and by the damp, cold, cramped and insanitary nature of much accommodation. Nevertheless, the state of the food supply was clearly of major significance, not only in preventing famine, but also in affecting general health and morale.

Famines

Famines could bring massive mortality, about a quarter of the Finnish population in 1696–7. Nearly a quarter of a million people died of starvation and disease in East Prussia in 1709–11. Famine led to a sharp rise in the death rate in Bari, Florence and Palermo in 1709 and in the kingdom of Naples in 1764. The last led Ferdinando Galiani to write *Dialogues sur le commerce des blés*

(1769), a strong attack on free trade in grain. In 1771–2 about 170,000 people, 7 per cent of the population of Bohemia, perished in a subsistence crisis. The local impact could be savage and prolonged. The number of deaths registered in the French town of Albi jumped from 280 in 1708 to 967 in 1710, the births slumping from 357 to 191 and the marriages from 100 to 49. Recovery was slow. Economic activity remained low, municipal debts high and houses abandoned. By 1750 Albi had still not regained its population of 1700. Not all famines had such dramatic effects, but they could serve to exacerbate the impact of disease. The bad Swedish harvests of 1717 and 1718 led, in regions where both salt and flour were in short supply, such as Dalecarlia, to illnesses connected with undernourishment, causing a sharp rise in the death rate. In Tournai in the Austrian Netherlands the famine of 1740 led to few deaths, but paved the way for the virulent epidemic of 1741.

It is unclear how far the general rise in the European population in the eighteenth century was due to success in the battle with famine. This battle took two principal forms, an increase in agricultural production, and communal and government attempts to improve the distribution of food and to deal with the direct effects of famine. Aside from the general conviction that the strength of a state was relative to the size of its population, a conviction that reflected the importance of numbers for both the army and agricultural work, famine was also a serious political issue. It often led to riots, whether in Istria in 1716, Paris in 1725, the United Provinces in 1740, England in 1766, Normandy in 1768, Palermo in 1773, Ireland in 1778 or Florence in 1790. In Paris in the 1750s seditious comments often cited the high price of bread and the general misery of the people as reasons why Louis XV should be killed. Fears of famine prompted popular disturbances in the Austrian Netherlands in 1767–9 and 1771–4, revealing popular alertness to rumours of famine. The widespread nature of such disturbances helped focus the concern of governments and political writers on the food supply. In addition, poor harvests seriously disrupted economies and threatened revenues by reducing the potential tax yield and focusing consumption on the supply and price of bread.

There are signs of an improvement in the situation during the century. In 1740–2 Scandinavia and Ireland were the sole regions where mass famines occurred. Elsewhere, public welfare and relief programmes served to limit deaths, despite food shortages and a rise in cereal prices. The possibilities for effective government action were revealed in Prussia. A network of royal granaries already existed, and despite a bad harvest, the onset of war (the

War of the Austrian Succession) and adverse climate, the Prussian government proved reasonably successful in preventing increases in destitution and unemployment, itinerant vagrancy and riots.

The Prussian system remained effective for the rest of the century. The grain stocks available in the public granaries, the grain policies of Frederick the Great, and the social control exercised by landlord and government minimised the social responses to dearth, such as migration, that helped to cause higher mortality figures. The Prussian government believed in preparation and firm action to deal with food shortages. A general edict in November 1740 called upon all nobles and lessees of crown land to sell their grain stocks in the markets within two weeks on pain of confiscation, at a price set by the government. In 1770–1 the effect of crop failures in East Friesland, a Prussian possession from 1744, was limited by the use of the royal depots. Frederick's system acted as a model for Hesse-Cassel, and helped minimise the extent of starvation arising from the serious crop failures of 1770–1.[6]

There were also significant improvements in Denmark. Before the 1770s the Danish annual death rate had displayed very wide variations, partly due to epidemics and limited resistance following crop failures. The Danish agrarian reforms brought a general rise in the standard of living, including new and better housing. From the 1770s mortality figures fell alongside a certain levelling out of variations in the number of deaths, although significant rises linked to epidemics continued to occur.

Public action to counter disease and famine was taken in much of Europe, particularly in cities, the location of most acute food-supply pressures and the places where disturbances were most serious. It was, however, easier to issue regulations or construct edifices, such as granaries, or the Aqueduct of Free Waters for Lisbon built between 1729 and 1744, than to establish comprehensive relief systems or alter attitudes. By 1740 public granaries had been built in Besançon, Lyons, Marseilles and Strasbourg, but most of the French population was still exposed to grain shortages. In addition, the terrible Italian famine of 1764 revealed the inadequacies of public relief and provisioning systems in the peninsula.

The food supply

Success in combating famine was not simply due to public initiatives. There was also a significant improvement in agricultural production. In Brabant, a province in the Austrian Netherlands where the population doubled between 1709 and 1784, the potato was introduced towards 1710 and after 1740 was spread widely. By the second half of the century, famine there did not lead to significant mortality, and life expectancy was higher. The introduction of maize in Altopascio in Tuscany in 1710 may have been responsible for the weakening of the mortality crises there after 1717. The supply of foodstuffs into Copenhagen indicates that a distinct improvement in nutrition took place during the 1750s, whether reckoned according to the quantity of calories or of proteins. From the 1780s, potatoes began to be introduced there. In Burgundy and Picardy in France there was both agricultural improvement and a rise in population. Ireland suffered massively in 1741, though it was able to absorb population pressure later in the century due to increased reliance on the potato. Expanded international trade in food may also have helped in the tackling of subsistence crises. Improved medical provision may also have been a factor, particularly in the towns. The rise in the birth rate and decline in infant mortality in Strasbourg may have owed something to improvements in midwifery. However, as the real killer of babies was puerperal fever, whose cause was not understood until the following century, it is not surprising that medical provision appears to have had little effect on infant mortality.

In other regions the situation was less favourable. In south-western France major subsistence crises in 1746–8, 1769–72 and 1785–9 helped to weaken the population and to ensure that during the major epidemics of 1772 and 1787–9 death rates exceeded birth rates. In much of the region there was no surgeon and the sick had to rely on the priests. Similarly there was no new demographic regime in the Languedoc area of southern France. In the French Pyrenees there was no sign of an agricultural revolution. The diffusion of the potato was very slow; though found in the market of Foix from 1778, it was not sold officially in that of Tarbes until the 1790s. There were regional demographic crises in 1746–7, 1759 and 1769. In the town and hinterland of Ussel in the Massif Central in France the economy remained depressed and there was no increase in population. A high rate of infant mortality was combined with serious crises of mortality which produced a high incidence of broken families. In Duravel in the Quercy region of France the cultivation of maize had spread in the first half of the century, but after 1765 the good agricultural lands had been exhausted and, as the limited agricultural techniques did not allow any increase in production by more intensive cultivation, food shortages became a serious problem. In the 1760s deaths exceeded baptisms and the demographic situation remained poor until the spread of the potato early in the next century. In the Rhineland town of Koblenz, despite peace from 1763 to 1792, there was little sign of a good late eighteenth century replacing an unfavourable earlier period, as there was in some other regions. Agricultural production failed to match the pressure of Koblenz's population. Despite the good will of the authorities, progress in hygiene was limited and the old town, where the artisans lived, remained particularly unhealthy.

More generally, the persistence of disease ensured that weak sections of the community remained especially vulnerable. There was only a slight decline in the high infant mortality figures in the suburbs of Bologna. In the poor quarters of Toulouse, birth and death rates were high and many children were abandoned. In contrast, in the wealthier centre of the town, a new and more favourable demographic regime developed with lower birth and death rates. Similarly in Geneva and Rouen the mortality rate among the children of the local notables was lower than average. In the village of Rosny-sous-Bois near Paris poorer families had higher mortality rates for both infants and adults than their wealthier counterparts.[7] Subsistence crises were not simply the result of exceeding the amount of food available, but also had their roots in the unequal distribution of resources, and in the limitations of governmental action.[8]

Conclusions

Although in some areas and among certain groups there were moves towards a more favourable demographic regime, this was by no means general. Famine remained a constant fear and a continual preoccupation of government. In many areas the quantity of surplus foodstuffs was slight and the balance of subsistence could be wrecked by any sudden adversity. This was most likely to take the form of severe climatic developments, or the military moves, such as the build-up of Austrian troops in Hungary in late 1787, that led to food shortages and fears of a famine. The generally peaceful conditions in western, central and southern Europe between 1763 and 1792 may have played a significant role in helping the growth of population. In contrast, areas that experienced serious warfare tended to face demographic crisis, not so much because of deaths in combat as because of the spread of infection, the seizure and destruction of crops and the disruption of the rural economy caused by flight and requisitions, particularly of draught animals and seed corn. Between 1695 and 1721 around 60–70 per cent of the population of Estonia and northern Livonia died as a consequence of disease and the

Great Northern War of 1700–21. War also hit communications and trade, making it far harder to move food to areas of shortage.

In western Europe as a whole the situation both became more favourable and remained fragile. What was still a relatively static agrarian society had to cope with demographic fluctuations, not just growth. Downward trends in the death rate were interrupted by crises, as in the early 1740s. About 13 per cent of the population died of fever and starvation in Ireland in 1739–40. Mortality peaks due to subsistence crises did not end. As late as 1816 a major subsistence crisis associated with dearth and disease sent mortality rates up in Switzerland, Italy, Austria and Ireland. Thus the general rise in population did not free communities from anxiety. Instead, it put greater pressure on food supplies, including in areas where these increased. It is significant that food featured prominently in utopian works, such as those of Fénelon and Morelly, as well as in popular fantasies. The distribution of food reflected most obviously the nature of the socio-economic system, but fears about the consequences of subsistence crises ensured that even those who were never short of food had to consider its supply.

The general rise in population had many consequences. It led to increased pressure on the economic system as more sought land, employment, food and relief. The pressure on the land was a serious problem, because the primitive state of agricultural techniques and technology ensured that in much of Europe the area under cultivation could not be greatly increased. Overexploitation of what could be farmed led to environmental degradation, as in parts of Denmark.[9] Throughout Europe, areas of 'waste' lands not hitherto cultivated were farmed, largely as a result of private initiative. In Alsace, whose population and cultivated area had fallen greatly due to conflict, there was a re-population of the countryside that owed much to migration from Switzerland, so that by 1789 the rural population was three times that of a century earlier.

Across much of the continent, especially in western Europe, land hunger became a major factor, encouraging emigration. In the second half of the century the population of the Scottish Highlands showed a dramatic increase, raising pressure on a tiny and finite amount of arable land, while in France demographic growth forced younger sons and poorer sharecroppers to abandon their hopes of acquiring independent peasant status. The general rise in population led to an increase in the number of day labourers, the most economically vulnerable section of the workforce, in areas such as Majorca, Catalonia and southern Spain, and to growing rural pauperisation. As the population rose, poverty became more general in many areas of Europe. It was a particular problem in regions that enjoyed little economic growth, such as Calabria in southern Italy or eastern Overijssel in the Netherlands, but it also affected those with a more favourable economic regime, such as much of France and the Rhineland. In the latter, food prices rose and land hunger led to the subdivision of holdings and an increase in the number of landless labourers. As undernourishment was no longer so commonly eliminated by early death it became the permanent condition of more people. Population growth disrupted local economies, leading to a greater concentration on the production of cereals at a time when, in general, insufficient attention was devoted to the raising of animals, the principal source of manure.

The rise in population thus became part of a more hostile environment. At the individual level, disease and malnutrition, if not starvation, were still constant presences. The consequences of demographic pressure were the principal determinants of the circumstances of the rural population in western Europe, although less so further east where the ratio between land and people was more favourable. In the towns unemployment and mendicity (begging) became more serious problems as people migrated from rural poverty. There was little by way of social welfare to ease the lot of individuals, and it is not surprising that some responded with despair, particularly as new births tested the family's ability to survive. The dramatic fate of a Viennese publican harassed by debts, who cut the throats of his pregnant wife and 9-month-old infant and threw himself into the Danube in February 1774, was less typical than the sorry records of the abandonment of children. In the second half of the century, there was a very substantial increase in the number abandoned in Italy, particularly of girls. A widespread preference for male over female babies was an aspect of the male-centred nature of society. In the 1780s the average rate of abandonment of children monthly was 160–70 in Lyons and over 650 in Paris. At the personal level, the demographic regime, whether old or new, was too often a cause of fear and misery.

Calamities and conservatism

Human vulnerability was not only displayed in the face of demographic pressures. The full range of calamities that could affect individuals and communities revealed in this period the fragility of personal circumstances and the weakness of communal responses. Non-epidemic illnesses could be a crushing blow to sufferers and there was little that could be done either to cure the illnesses or to alleviate the pain. Opium and alcohol were the only painkillers or dullers and cheap laudanum, a preparation containing opium, was a widely used panacea. There was little to ease the pain of dying, except opiates. Childbirth was often a killer, disrupting families.

Agricultural labour was arduous, generally daylight to dusk in winter and about 6 a.m. to 6 p.m. in summer. Fishing was dangerous. Industrial employment was arduous and frequently dangerous. Many places of work were damp, poorly ventilated and/or badly lit. Many occupations involved exposure to hazardous substances, such as lead and mercury. The presence of explosive gas in mines made the use of candles there very dangerous. Apart from numerous accidents, mining also led to respiratory diseases due to dust and gas. Miners were affected by pneumoconiosis, mystagmus, rheumatism, the arduous work of heaving coal, and premature ageing, and they had a short life expectancy. Millers worked in dusty and noisy circumstances, frequently suffered from lice and often developed asthma, hernias and chronic back problems. Construction work was very dangerous.

In 1705 the first English edition of the *Treatise of the Diseases of Tradesmen* by Bernardino Ramazzini, professor of medicine at Padua, was published. Ramazzini had investigated the relationship between illness and occupation, and his book revealed the serious consequences of employment in an age when there was little understanding of health and safety at work. He pointed out that disorders could result from the strain of unusual physical demands or postures, such as those required of tailors and weavers. Ramazzini's account of the occupational illnesses of chemists, fishermen, bath attendants, vintners, tobacconists, washerwomen, of the phthisis acquired by stonemasons and miners, the eye trouble of gilders and printers, the sciatica of tailors and lethargy of potters, reveals the hazardous nature of industrial activity before the development of the factory system. Nevertheless, the notions of health and safety at work were barely understood.

Medical care was of limited assistance in dealing with these and other problems, as medical knowledge was often deficient and skilled practitioners were unavailable. Doctors were concentrated in the towns, and though France had one doctor per 10,000 inhabitants, in many areas they were a rarity, even if their services could be afforded. Medical treatments, such as blistering or mercury, were often painful, dangerous or enervating, and some patients refused treatment. Surgery was primitive and performed without anaesthetics. There was no effective medical treatment available for typhus, typhoid and dysentery.

Medicine was scarcely more efficacious in the case of animal diseases. These could have serious economic consequences and they revealed the limited options available to governments. The primitive nature of veterinary science ensured that the response to disease could not be preventive. Instead, animals had to be slaughtered, their movement prohibited. The outbreak of disease in the Italian territory of Lucca in 1715 led Florentine troops to close the border to livestock trade. In 1747 the Venetian army made similar moves. In late 1751 the Estates of Holland sought to prevent the spread of the cattle disease raging in Friesland, which had also broken out in Holland, by prohibiting the import and export of cattle and banning their movement within the province without proper authorisation. The effectiveness of these measures varied. Success against bovine disease in Flanders in the 1770s may reflect the determination of the Austrian government to enforce its policy of killing all ill or suspected animals and offering compensation, thus ensuring a degree of compliance, against the wishes of the local government and population. However, the Austrians could not prevent an epidemic carrying off many of their cavalry horses in Hungary in 1788.

The economic impact could be significant, in both the short and the long term. The epidemics of rinderpest that hit the cattle-breeders of Friesland and Groningen in the northern Netherlands led some to shift to grain production. In late 1749 the losses by the peasants of Groningen made it difficult for them to pay their taxes. Outbreaks of cattle disease could cripple local agriculture, as in Holstein in 1764 and Béarn in 1774, as well as driving up distant meat prices, thus indicating the developing economic links between distant regions. Meat prices in Bratislava and Vienna were driven up in 1787 by animal mortality in Hungary and Transylvania. Again the situation at the level of the individual proprietor was of a hostile and unpredictable environment, of forces that could be neither prevented nor propitiated, of the effort of years swept away in an instant. The line between independence and calamity, between being poor and falling into pauperdom, could be crossed easily and fast.

The climate presented a similar challenge. In general, the climate may have become more favourable, with warmer and drier summers improving crop yields. The 'little ice age' of the seventeenth century came to an end. The rise in average August temperatures may in part have been responsible for a decline in deaths due to bacillary dysentery. Yet the weather continued to have a major impact on economic life.[10] At the level of the individual, the capriciousness of the climate could be a major problem and the limited capacity of communal action could be all too apparent.

An obvious instance was flooding, both coastal and riverine. Across much of Europe, rivers had not been canalised and their flow was unregulated by any system of dams or reservoirs, while coastal defences were often inadequate or non-existent. Flooding could interfere with transport, along and across rivers, and with fishing, disrupt the activities of industries, such as milling, that were dependent on water power, and damage the most fertile agricultural areas. Coastal areas such as Friesland were vulnerable, and the location of most major towns on the coast or on major rivers had serious consequences. Florence and the lower valley of the Arno were heavily flooded in 1740, at the cost of many lives. When the Rhone rose in December 1763 two-thirds of Avignon went under water. Rural areas tended to be less well defended against flooding than towns, and there is little evidence that the situation improved during the century. Thousands of cattle died when the Dutch dykes were breached in the winter of 1725–6. In the winter of 1787–8 heavy rains and serious flooding washed away much of the seed grain in Saxony.

Drought was another problem, hitting water supplies, agriculture, river transport and waterpower-based manufacturing. It threatened famine, as in Geneva in 1723, and particular crops, such as in 1778 the vineyards of Burgundy. Water-power was also vulnerable to the ice of winter, which prevented mills from operating, causing unemployment and flour shortages. As the water mills were frozen up in early 1748 the Poles were forced to resort to hand mills in order to grind the corn, a far more arduous process. Because of ice, the working year of the Dutch towboats was only 300 days, and their labour force, largely unskilled and hired for casual rather than long-term employment, suffered if the winter was particularly harsh and the working year was curtailed. An alternative source of energy to water was wind, but windmills were affected by storms.

Agriculture was naturally vulnerable to the weather. There were few improved crop strains, and rainy winters produced diseased and swollen crops, while late frosts attacked wheat. The frosts of 1709 killed most of the lemon trees near Genoa, ending the export of the product. Many other aspects of the human environment were also vulnerable. Houses were affected by lightning and also susceptible to fires, such as the terrible fires at Rennes in 1720, Vyborg in 1738, Moscow in 1753 and Madrid in 1790. Straw-thatched buildings provided attractive environments for numerous pests and were also fire hazards, not least because they often lacked chimneys. Difficulties faced attempts to drain malarial lowlands in southern Europe, and in much of the area habitation was restricted to the hills and avoided the highly cultivated valley bottoms and their often stagnant waters.

Another aspect of the hostile environment was the confrontation between man and other beasts, both real and imaginary. Wolves and bears, which could attack humans and their farm animals, were a problem and not only in mountainous areas. In 1699 near Abbeville in France wolves regularly attacked sheep. They were a serious threat near Senlis, north of Paris, in 1717, and in south-western France in 1766. In the bad winter of 1783–4 the *Journal de Physique* reported numerous deaths in France from marauding wolves. In mountainous areas the conflict was more constant, and the wolves' heads and bears' paws displayed in areas such as Savoy were a testimony to an often bitter struggle for the control of alpine grazing areas.

Other animals could also pose problems. The absence of pesticides and the difficulties in protecting crops and stored food exacerbated the situation. Though the emperor Joseph II enjoyed hunting, he ordered the destruction of all wild pigs on account of the damage they did to peasant property. Mice and rats destroyed a lot of food and crops, plagues of mice having disastrous effects on the harvests in East Friesland in 1773 and 1787. Worms damaged the Dutch dykes in the 1730s and those in East Friesland in the 1760s. When locusts advanced towards Vienna in 1749 they were seen as a manifestation of divine wrath and public prayers were ordered to avert this.

The threat from real animals was joined in the hostile environment by the anxieties aroused by imaginary creatures. Strange beasts that attacked human beings were reported. One such, near Saragossa in Spain in 1718, was described as ox-sized, with a head like a wolf, a long tail and three pointed horns. Another savage creature was described on several occasions in the Gévaudan region of France in the mid 1760s. Popular folk tales, the support of biblical and classical authority and the continual discovery of gigantic bones in the earth led to a belief in giants that was supported by many clerics.[11]

Fear of witches persisted.[11] Although the last recorded witch trial in England occurred in 1717, the high point in witch-hunting in the Polish province of Mazovia in the early modern period was the first quarter of the century. Distinctions between heresy, blasphemy, sorcery and necromancy were often blurred, torture was employed, and witches were burned, a practice that was not declared illegal in Poland until 1776.

A sustained debate over witches, magic and vampires took place in the middle years of the century, particularly in Italy and France. Scipione Maffei's *Magic Arts Annihilated* appeared in 1754. Eight years earlier the French cleric and scholar Augustin Calmet had published a book on vampires. George II of Britain believed in vampires. The belief in vampires was attacked in the *Encyclopédie*, the repository of liberal learning and fashionable views launched in France in 1751, in an article that appeared in 1765. Calmet's book was also criticised and cited as an instance of the impact of superstition on the human spirit. In 1772 the leading liberal French intellectual Voltaire condemned Calmet's work and queried how it was possible after the work of the English philosophers Locke and Shaftesbury, and during the period when the French liberal intellectuals d'Alembert and Diderot were active, to write a book on, or believe in, vampires. On this, as on so much else, Voltaire's righteous scorn was a misleading guide to popular attitudes. Witch-hunting, with only a few exceptions, did die out, but there is little sign that belief in vampirism abated, and panics occurred in Hungary, Bohemia and Moravia in the 1730s, 1750s and 1770s. A variant of concern about vampirism could also be found in the centre of European consciousness, Paris, in 1749–50. It was widely believed that children were being seized and killed in order to provide blood for baths to help Louis XV combat leprosy. This concern about an institutionalised vampirism subverted the notion of the monarch as a sacral healer. Vampires and the supernatural also played a role in literature, for example the influential ballad *Lenore* (1773) by Gottfried Bürger.[12]

Vampires were not alone in the taxonomy of the dark side of Enlightenment Europe. An anonymous German writer of 1782 claimed that the uncertainties of agricultural life fostered in the peasant a true humility and a sense of his dependence upon factors over which he had no control. In comprehending or assuaging these forces, traditional astrological and occult beliefs and practices appear to have played a large role, particularly in rural areas. It was an animistic world and one inhabited by spirits, with death no necessary barrier to activity, experience and intervention. In his *The Life of my Father* (1778), Nicolas Restif de la Bretonne (1734–1806) recorded that in his parental milieu, that of a wealthy French peasant near Auxerre, shepherds told tales of the transmigration of souls to animals and werewolves. The enlightened Baden bureaucrat Johann Reinhard (1714–72), growing up in a Calvinist home in the German principality of Nassau, encountered a world peopled largely by witches and ghosts, where the devil was omnipresent. As the devil played a major role in Christian consciousness, it was scarcely surprising that many invested him with a panoply of supporters and acolytes who lived not in any separate world, but in a sphere that enabled them to intervene directly in human affairs. In 1727 Cardinal Fleury, the leading French minister, expressed his belief that the devil was able to thrash his human subjects. At the end of the century, belief in sorcery and witchcraft was still widespread among the rural population of the German principalities of Jülich and Mark. More generally, there was a widespread belief in fairies. They were seen as having a capacity for good or ill, and it was necessary to propitiate them, for example by offering food and drink. Hostile external forces were blamed for intractable illness. The world outside people's dwellings, especially after dark, seemed more hostile and mysterious than is comprehensible to modern people who are accustomed to using electricity for illumination. In the absence of the moon, the night was pitch dark, especially in rural areas. Within houses it was shadowy when the candles were lit and dark when they were snuffed.

Popular religious beliefs, however removed from the teachings of the churches, did not amount to an alternative religion. Pagan practices were not the same as paganism. Instead, such beliefs and practices co-existed or were intertwined with Christian counterparts, with little sense of any incompatibility, especially among ordinary lay folk in rural areas.

If old superstitions had lost little of their hold in rural areas, it could be suggested that the cultural gap between popular and elite beliefs had grown wider than in the previous century, that views and activities hitherto general, such as belief in astrology, had been driven down the social scale. Many of the wealthy and well-educated appear to have lost their faith in magical healing, prophecy and witchcraft. This oft-stated argument has to be employed with care. Clearly fashion played an important role in elite culture, increasingly so as the growth in the quantity of printed works spread knowledge of what was judged desirable. It is difficult, however, to assess the significance of the changes in fashion. The popularity of miraculous medical cures and the vogue, in the France of the 1780s, for the theory of animal magnetism advocated by the Austrian doctor Mesmer, who advanced a complicated post-Newtonian cosmology, suggest that it is dangerous to regard the culture of the elite as in some way better-informed. It was rather the case that their superstitions were faddish.

At all levels of society, there was a wish to understand the hostile environment and to cope with the fears that it inspired and the unpredictable gamble that was life.[13] There was a search for stability in an essentially unstable world, an attempt to reconcile divine justice with human suffering, and to order experience in a way that reflected the hard and arbitrary nature of life. The religious world view provided the most effective explanatory model, the best psychological defences and the essential note of continuity. In Russia, Peter the Great's policies were understood by many in the light of beliefs that he was an un-Russian evil substitute or antiChrist. His denial of the divine identity of traditional Russian monarchy, his blasphemy, his theft of time from God when he changed the calendar, and his sacrilegious violation of the image of God in man, when he forced people to cut off their beards, could be understood by presenting the world as a battleground between God and the devil. In Spain manuals of piety, religious tracts and sermons that stressed the transitory nature of life on earth and the spiritual dangers facing the rich were very popular and frequently reprinted.

Faced with calamities, communities and individuals turned to the church. God was seen as providing means to cure all ills, if only they could be discovered. It was common to ring church bells against thunder and lightning. In 1775, a month after Joseph Priestley's chemical experiments were exhibited at the Academy of Dijon, the local church bells were rung to drive away a storm. Individuals and communities sought the support of interceding powers. In 1725, when Paris was threatened with flooding and a bad harvest, the reliquary of the local patron saint, Geneviève, was carried in procession in the hope of stopping the heavy rain, as in 1696 it had been deployed against drought. The following year a crude engraving with an explanatory text was produced. In 1755 the Venetian authorities, faced with a lack of drinking water, exposed a statue of the Virgin Mary. Communal dedication and good conduct were both sought. In 1756 Charles Emmanuel III of Sardinia and his family participated in the celebrations in the cathedral of Turin to give thanks that the city had survived a recent earthquake relatively unscathed. Pope Clement XIII responded to Italian famine in the 1760s with prayers and ceremonies. In January 1765 all public diversions were suspended in Florence and public prayers held for the return of good weather, as they were in Milan in 1765 and 1766. In Terracina in central Italy, a miraculous image of the Virgin was carried in procession in April 1769 attended by great crowds in the hope of securing better weather. At the beginning of 1788 a violent gale on the north-west coasts of France was met by solemn processions to the churches and night-time services.

The hostile environment was understood in terms of retribution, with the possibility of gaining remission by good actions, either in terms of religious services or by satisfying the demands of the occult and spirit world. It was thus possible to construct a cosmology that was acceptable in both Christian and non-Christian terms. For many people, Christian and non-Christian were not alternatives, but rather closely related beliefs and habits of thought.

In some circles there was questioning of the notion of divine intervention. Nearly all the writers in the Austrian Netherlands who discussed the Lisbon earthquake of 1755 interpreted it as a divine judgement. Most came to a similar conclusion about the bovine pest that affected the Austrian Netherlands in 1769–71, but a distinct minority disagreed. Similarly the prediction that Naples would be entirely destroyed by an earthquake in March 1769 threw some, but not all, of the population into confusion. At the beginning of the century care of the handicapped was a preserve of the clergy, and deaf-mutes were thought to be possessed by the devil. This did not prevent Jacob Pereire (1715–80) from seeking to rehabilitate them, although his development of this unknown skill and subsequent cures were understood by many as miracles. Understanding of handicaps and compassion towards the handicapped do not appear to have greatly increased during the century.

The search for divine support did not necessarily lead to worldly passivity, particularly on the communal level. If the environment was understood as hostile, there was, nevertheless, much activity aimed at coping with the consequences. This was by no means new. Whether clearing the waste, or draining Dutch polders and Mediterranean malarial swamps, there was clear continuity with the previous century, and in many areas a resumption of activity after the serious wars of the period 1688–1721. In some areas progress was definitely made. Science was beginning to transform the relationship between man and the environment: some buildings were better constructed, lightning was tamed by lightning conductors, and a few illnesses were mitigated. Ironically, there were also signs of a problem that was to become more urgent in the nineteenth century: the human and environmental costs of urban and industrial development. In 1714 the French envoy in London complained repeatedly about the effect on his breathing of the coal smoke that enveloped the city.[14] During the course of the century much of the Black Forest suffered deforestation in order to provide timber in particular for the Dutch shipbuilding industry. The denuded slopes suffered serious erosion.

Nevertheless, one of the most obvious features of the eighteenth century is the limited progress that was made in dealing with the hostile environment and the catastrophes that affected individuals and communities so grievously. Those communities whose population grew tended to face serious problems as pressures mounted on food supplies and living standards. The limited progress that was made in improving the condition of man and the human environment is understandable in light of the restricted technology of the age and the scanty resources of government. It also reflected the dominant attitude of the period. Despite the confidence of some in the possibility of human progress through communal action, the majority of the population lived in a precarious fashion, fearful of the future and possessing only limited aspirations. This popular conservatism was to play a major part in hindering government plans for change.

2 Economic Framework

Agriculture

Agriculture was the principal source of employment and wealth, the most significant sector of the economy, the basis of the taxation – government, ecclesiastic (tithes), seigneurial and proprietorial (rents) – that funded most other activities. Land and its products provided both the structure of the social system and the bulk of the wealth that kept it in being and provided the opportunities for social change. The vast majority of the population lived in the countryside and agricultural activity dominated the lives of the people of Europe. In 1789, 74 per cent of the active population in the Vivarais region in France were employed in agriculture, a fairly typical figure.

Furthermore, the impact of agriculture was not restricted to rural areas. There was no hard barrier separating town from countryside, industry and trade from farming, workers in industry from agricultural labourers. In regions such as Bohemia (in the modern Czech Republic) much industrial production took place in rural areas and many industries such as the metal trades, glass-making and pottery, even textiles, were to be found in the coal-mining areas, which, as yet, were also still agricultural. In areas such as French Flanders many of those who worked in rural industry also tended plots of land or were members of a family economy in which another member was a part of the agricultural workforce.

In some areas of Europe, such as Sicily, a surprisingly high percentage of the population lived in towns. However, this was a reflection of traditional settlement patterns, rather than of a functional response to urban activities, for, in much of Mediterranean Europe, agricultural workers lived in towns or substantial villages rather than in dispersed settlements. To a certain extent this was true of all of Europe. Towns tended to be surrounded by areas of intensive agriculture, rather than the suburbia of the modern age, and in addition, agricultural activities, such as horticulture, were common within town walls, there being no zoning system to prohibit them or any sense that agriculture was in some way functionally incompatible with urban status.

The links between agriculture, industry and trade were close. The limited advances in the state of technological and scientific knowledge ensured that manufacturing was based on natural products. The age of synthesised products had not yet arrived. Most manufacturing involved the processing of agricultural goods, particularly if forestry is regarded both as a variant on such extensive agricultural activities as animal husbandry and as a source of casual or seasonal employment for the agricultural workforce. The staple industrial activities were concerned with the production of consumer goods – food, drink, clothes, shoes and furniture – that relied on raw materials produced in the countryside. Though some processing involved agricultural products produced outside Europe, such as cotton, West Indian sugarcane and North American tobacco, the source of most goods was European and often local: thus woollen and, even more locally based, leather industries were found almost universally throughout Europe. Thus industrial activity, whether urban or rural, was closely involved with the agricultural hinterland. For example, the town of Niort in western France, where animal skins played an important role in the local economy in the 1720s, depended on receiving large numbers of goat kids from the surrounding countryside. Trade was also closely involved with agricultural products, processed or unprocessed, and this was as true of distant as of local trade.

As the bulk of the population lived in rural areas and engaged in agricultural activities, it is not surprising that the prosperity of these activities played a significant role in determining the nature of the purchasing power in the communities of Europe. Rural wealth created a market both for industrial goods and for expensive agricultural products, such as meat. Conversely poverty, the commonest state for the bulk of the rural population, acted as a permanent limitation on both. Any rise in the cost of agricultural products, particularly cereals, affected the urban population, reducing purchasing power, both in the towns and among much of the rural population, and restricting the market for manufactured goods. Alterations in the prices of agricultural products were a constant feature, essentially for seasonal reasons, the price of foodstuffs generally rising to a peak in the early summer as last year's harvest was used up. Harvest variations dictated additional price changes that were often very sharp. The consequences of these contributed to a sense of uncertainty and helped to focus official awareness on agriculture.

The eighteenth was the last century when Europe had to feed itself. Food imports from outside Europe were still essentially luxury goods, such as sugar, that could bear the transportation costs of a trading system that relied on small wind-powered ships lacking effective refrigeration and storage facilities, although fish was imported from Newfoundland and rice from the Carolinas. The following century was to witness the opening up of food sources in North America, Argentina and Australasia, with refrigeration, the steam-powered iron ship and effective European control in these areas arguably helping, as much as any developments on the continent itself, to free Europe from the Malthusian equation of population size and limited resources.

Before the late nineteenth century, Europe had essentially to be self-sufficient, and as a result, land in 1800, as in 1700, was the principal source of national and individual wealth. The prevailing systems of farming did not produce enough to create a reliable margin of safety in the event of harvest failures and few regions produced a sufficiently large marketable surplus to help areas where cereal crops failed. Slow and expensive transport limited the effect of those which did. As a result, movements in agricultural prices were not essentially restricted by intra-European trade. In addition, although food imports could help to alleviate the consequences of harvest failures, when sharply rising prices justified transport costs, they could neither enable government to ignore the state of agriculture, nor permit any general regional curtailing of agriculture in order to specialise in different economic activities. The need for food in an agricultural regime characterised by low productivity and uncertain production forced all sections of European society and all areas of Europe, however unfavourable they might be for food production, to devote attention to agriculture. Furthermore, agricultural regions had to concentrate on cereal production to an extent often disproportionate to their capabilities. Grain had to be produced even in areas best suited to animal husbandry.

The reality of social life was not the clean, healthy, plump peasants of the painter Boucher's idyllic landscapes, without spots or blemishes, their activities framed in a lush, sunny and clean countryside inhabited by animals as healthy and plump as the people, but a harsh agricultural and social regime. For the bulk of the population, the harvest was the key factor in individual and communal fortunes, the only other developments proving of comparable potential importance, epidemic disease and warfare, being episodic. This situation did not alter during the century, which puts into perspective the limited impact of the peacetime actions of government in both the economy and other spheres of life, and also explains the popular reluctance to consider new ways to organise the food supply, and the appeal of paternalist landowners.

Recognising the importance of agricultural production and distribution, governments and intellectuals devoted attention to ways in which the situation could be improved. Motives might vary, from national strength to an improvement in the lot of the peasantry, but, alongside the continual interest in developing manufacturing and oceanic trade, there was an awareness of the need to help agriculture. Fénelon, the leading clerical critic of Louis XIV, linked economic prosperity to the cultivation of the soil in his *Télèmaque* of 1699. The French economic writers of the mid-century known as the 'physiocrats', Quesnay, Dupont de Nemours, Mirabeau, Mercier de la Rivière, argued that any increase in wealth in the manufacturing and commercial spheres could only take place on the basis of prior increases in the amount of raw materials extracted from nature. They claimed that the land was the sole source of real wealth, that manufacturing simply changed the form of its products and that trade only moved them. The physiocratic call for more investment in agriculture was combined with proposals designed to increase its profitability. The argument that grain must be allowed to rise to its natural price level and that restrictions on its sale, such as export prohibitions, should be reduced, was intended to transfer more of the benefit of grain production to the rural community. Within this community the physiocrats wished to prevent the peasantry from being burdened by high rents in order to increase their incentive for work, and to ensure that funds were available locally for agricultural investment. They wanted taxes to be kept low in order to increase the return to the landlord.

Interest in agriculture was not restricted to the physiocrats. The Dutch 'Patriot' writer Schimmelpennick argued in 1784 that a republic was undoubtedly a viable form of government if the energy of the population was directed towards agriculture, which he suggested, in common with other writers such as the American Thomas Jefferson, was the guarantee of equality and virtue.

State interest was always present as a result of the social, economic and political costs of food shortage, but it was further increased for fiscal reasons. In a society where the bulk of employment, revenues and national production stemmed from agricultural activity, it naturally followed that such activity was the principal fiscal resource of the state. Fiscal interest grew in areas where agriculture had moved from self-sufficiency or a barter economy to market relationships within a cash context. Such a development made it easier for the state to derive fiscal benefit from agriculture. In Russia the growth in agricultural exports led to an increase in government fiscal interest. As the European agricultural economy in part became increasingly integrated and crops or animal husbandry for cash sale became more significant, the potential direct tax benefit from government intervention in agriculture rose. This played an important role in the second half of the century in government policies for the relief of the peasantry from various burdens, as the benefit to be derived from a well-motivated agricultural workforce appeared the easiest way to raise the national fiscal yield. In 1788 the Bavarian government rejected an Austrian offer to purchase 2000 horses with the argument that, although the money would benefit poor Bavaria, the true wealth of the state lay not in money, but in agriculture, for which the horses were required.

There were some signs during the century of an improvement in agricultural production, the dissemination of new ideas and techniques and the increasing integration of European agriculture, as specialisation, commerce and the cash economy developed. There were, however, equal signs of continuing conservative practices, and local economies scarcely affected by change elsewhere. Farming was diverse and possibly less improved than the signs of and interest in agrarian change would suggest. As the situation of local agricultural economies was of crucial importance to the health and prosperity of the population, it is necessary to consider the reasons for the diverse responses to the possibilities for agrarian change.

New lands cultivated

An obvious approach to the problem of increasing agricultural production was the traditional method, the extension of the area used for agrarian purposes and, in particular, the cultivated area. In order to transport the food produced to the European markets, this had to take the form of an increase in the cultivated area in Europe rather than in the overseas colonies. The most significant European increases took place as a result of the actions of the two states that extended themselves through territorial colonisation into neighbouring areas, Russia and Austria. Between 1680 and 1720 both powers pushed their frontiers forward either into areas hitherto Turkish, such as Hungary, or into those that had essentially served as buffer-zones with the Turkish Empire, principally the Ukraine. In the case of Russia this expansion continued after 1720, at the expense of the Turks and of other non-Russian peoples to the south of Russia. These gains offered tremendous opportunities for an increase in agricultural production. Some of the areas, such as the black-soil region of the Ukraine, were naturally fertile and many, such as the central Hungarian plain, had not had their fertility denuded by cereal cultivation, having been hitherto essentially zones of animal husbandry.

Not all of the schemes for colonisation and agricultural improvement were successful, but there is no doubt of an appreciable increase in the area devoted to cereals. The Ukraine and river Don regions of Russia both became significant grain-exporting areas, and a major reason for the strong interest displayed during the 1780s in the development of trade with southern Russia through the Black Sea was the wish to exploit what was perceived correctly to be a significant likely source from which to feed Europe. The Volga area possessed enormous economic possibilities, with tobacco as a promising cash crop. If, for western Europe, colonialisation was essentially trans-oceanic, in central and eastern Europe the opportunities were not seen to be so distant. 'You may look upon Hungary as a new World,' wrote one diplomat in 1736;[1] and if, by the second half of the century, this aspiration was largely centred on southern Russia, it was, nevertheless, an important one that helped to create a sense of change and opportunity.

This feeling played a major role in one of the most significant of the population changes in the century, the move of a large number of people to the Austrian and Russian zones of colonisation. Some of this migration was internal, the movement of Austrians and Russians from areas of high population density and limited economic opportunity to lands that were essentially open. Part of the settled population of the new lands was indigenous, people who had been forced or encouraged to exchange for cereal cultivation a nomadic or semi-nomadic life and/or one devoted to animal husbandry. In the case of the Austrian Balkan frontier lands a significant percentage of the population were Slavs, particularly Serbs, who had fled Turkish rule in the 1690s. About 40,000 Serbians led by Arsenije IV, the Patriarch of Pec, had moved in this period. Migration in the Balkans owed much to warfare, since opposing armies viewed people as a resource to be denied to their enemies.

A large number of the migrants to the new lands were from central or western Europe, and formed part of the tendency of people to move in search of agrarian opportunity within a continent where the possibility of acquiring land varied greatly, and agriculture was the principal source of employment and wealth. The second Russian census, begun in 1744, showed that over the previous quarter-century the steepest percentage increases in population had occurred in increasingly-settled frontier or peripheral areas, such as the lower Volga, the northern Urals and the Ukraine.

For some, the new lands were in America, particularly the British colonies in North America, which placed fewer restrictions than the other American colonies on the immigration of non-nationals and offered opportunities in an agricultural and climatic regime that was not too dissimilar from large areas of Europe. Many Germans went to Georgia, and between 1760 and 1775 at least 12,000 German immigrants entered the port of Philadelphia. Of the approximately half a million people who emigrated from south-west Germany and Switzerland in the eighteenth century, about 40 per cent went to North America, the rest to Hungary, Prussia and Russia. Similarly, Rhineland emigration was shared by North America, Hungary, Prussia, Russia and Galicia, part of Poland that was acquired by Austria in 1772.

The key to the development of most 'unproductive' lands, whether marginal land neglected by settled communities or newly colonised, was the establishment of an adequate population in these regions, although this was very much the perspective of the colonisers. Immigration was actively encouraged by rulers for this reason. Frederick the Great followed his father's policy of seeking migrants and by 1780 about 5 per cent of the Prussian population were immigrant rural settlers. Laws were relaxed for them, people being more desirable than the policy of uniformity. In 1772 a Prussian edict permitted foreigners who wished to settle in the province of Magdeburg to retain non-Prussian legal codes. Catherine the Great devoted considerable attention to the colonisation of southern Russia. Her proclamations of 1762 and 1763 offered significant privileges to foreigners settling in Russia, and she spent vast sums, between 5 and 6 million roubles, on the settlement project. Most of the immigrants were Germans. During Catherine's reign about 75,000 foreign colonists arrived, over 25,000 of them settling on the Volga between 1764 and 1775. Large numbers of migrants also moved into the eastern areas of the Austrian Empire. In early 1771 it was reported that over 20,000 people had left famine-stricken Lorraine for Hungary. The continuing migration into Hungary and Galicia was by 1787 principally from the western regions of Germany. Emigration was regarded as a sufficient threat to national strength to lead several states to take moves to prevent it. Danish regulations sought to limit the internal mobility of the common rural population and in 1753 Denmark prohibited emigration.

The migration to the new lands in eastern Europe was not always a success. Many immigrants became disenchanted, and a trickle returned to their original homes, such as the Lorrainers who came back from Hungary in 1752 feeling cheated, as it had not turned out to be the land of opportunity, wealth and security that they had been promised. A similar disappointment affected many of those who went to Russia. Despite much expenditure, the government was unable to fulfil the grand vision of Catherine and the help provided for the migrants was limited. The frontier zone lacked amenities, the indigenous population was not welcoming, and schemes, such as that for Volga tobacco-growing, took longer to come to fruition than had been anticipated. Nevertheless, these developments were of considerable importance, offering Europe a potential escape from the Malthusian dilemma. It could be suggested that for Russia the economic development of the steppe lands was as important as the conquest of Sweden's eastern Baltic provinces in 1710–11, not least in helping to make her politically a great power by increasing the resources at her disposal.

Less spectacular than the bringing of more intensive agriculture to the frontier lands of Austria and Russia was the process of internal colonisation elsewhere in Europe. It was a common theme of agrarian activity throughout the continent, although, in the absence of comprehensive detailed statistics for agricultural production, it is difficult to say whether increases in production were due largely to an extension of the cultivated area or to improvements in technique. The extension of the cultivated area in Europe, whether achieved through the digging of irrigation ditches, the clearing of trees or the removal of stones, was essentially the product of labour-intensive methods. This was due to both the technology of the period and the nature of the available resources.

In much of Europe, internal colonisation enjoyed government support. A French declaration of 1766 granted exemption from tax and tithe to land abandoned for at least 40 years that was brought into cultivation. In areas such as parts of Spain and Hesse Cassel hitherto without settled agriculture, villages were created thanks to government initiative. The attitudes held gave a clear preference to settled communities and intensive agriculture. Uncultivated areas were regarded as waste lands though in fact they might support a long-settled population living on forestry, semi-nomadic animal husbandry and 'cut-and-burn' shifting cereal cultivation. This stance was associated with the suspicion with which such peoples were often viewed both by governments and by the population of intensively-farmed lowland areas.

Internal colonisation was not solely due to government encouragement. With the exception of Prussia, which faced particular problems of underpopulation after the famine of the early years of the century and the mid-century wars, it is arguable indeed that this encouragement was of limited effect and importance. Colonisation was a direct product of land hunger, whether it took the form of clearing the waste, as in France in the 1760s, or of alterations in the use of land already within the agrarian system. In Wallachia and Moldavia the land was commonly unimproved, and there was a general reduction in the amount left as forestry and pasture, in order to make way for the spread of grain cultivation. The principal stimulus was export of grain to Constantinople and further afield. On the contrary, demographic pressure, rather than economic opportunities, helped to account for the clearing of some of the forests of Béarn in south-west France, and the spread of the cultivated area in Lombardy. In Sweden, the increase in agricultural production was largely a matter of internal colonisation. Demographic pressure increasingly ensured that marginal arable land was brought under the plough, particularly in south-east Sweden. Feeble agrarian growth contributed to the relative decline of east-central Sweden. The more vigorous growth that took place in west Sweden and in Scania rested upon an expansion of the cultivated acreage, rather than on any significant improvements in productivity. In contrast the opportunities for breaking new ground were more limited in the east-central regions, where, in addition, many settlements were dominated by large estates and there were restrictions on the establishment of new farm households. Similarly, in late seventeenth-century Sicily, increases in wheat production were achieved only by continuously extending the area of land under cultivation, and crop sizes were maintained only by sowing on tilled fallow. The tilling itself was done by hoes that barely scratched the surface of the soil.

New methods

There were also qualitative advances in agriculture. As some of the changes in agrarian practice called for by agricultural reformers did not demand specialised knowledge or equipment, it was possible to improve farming without costly changes. Such improvement was pressed forward by a sizeable number of activists. Model farms were established by landlords, such as the Saxon Johann Schubart, who advocated the cultivation of clover and was ennobled by Joseph II.

Practical advice was offered by agricultural literature. There was a marked increase in the literature of agricultural improvement, particularly in western Europe, where authors such as Jethro Tull and Duhamel de Monceau argued the case for new techniques. Though Tull's *Horse Hoeing Husbandry* (1733) appeared earlier, most of the significant works dated from the second half of the century, as did their republication and dissemination. Whereas no Polish publications on agriculture existed in 1700, about 300 appeared in the half-century after 1750. A journal devoted to agriculture was founded in Parma in the 1760s, and the ducal government was well aware of the possibility of extending agricultural knowledge through publications. It was not until the 1770s that the real introduction of agricultural innovations into Hungarian literature took place. The first significant work was written by Lajos Mitterpacher, a Jesuit scholar, who, after the dissolution of the Order, became professor of natural history and agricultural science at the University of Buda. His three-volume *Elements of Agriculture* appeared between 1777 and 1794 and was written in Latin, still the *lingua franca* of education, science, politics and public life in most of eastern Europe. The book contained extensive scientific discussions which both sought to throw new light on agricultural problems from the perspectives of biology, physics and chemistry and drew on the work of British scientists, such as Priestley. A basic source of the work was Arthur Young's account of his travels in northern England in a German translation published in Leipzig in 1772. Whereas in the first half of the century, books published in nearby Halle had spread Pietist ideas throughout eastern Europe, in the 1770s Leipzig disseminated Young's views on turnips. An earlier more specialised work on bee-keeping had a similar history. John Geddy's *English Apiary* of 1675, reprinted in 1722, dealt with a method whereby honey could be taken out of the hive without first killing off the bees by fumigation. A German translation was published in Leipzig in 1727, and a Hungarian translation of this, not of Geddy's original, appeared in 1759.

Alongside the literature, agricultural societies appeared throughout Europe. They played a major role in publicising change. In 1759 the Academy of Besançon organised a competition for the discovery of a vegetable substance capable of replacing bread in case of need. It was won by the young Antoine Parmentier, the populariser in France of the potato, with a chemical examination of that plant. Agrarian improvement became a cult for considerable numbers of gentlemen farmers. This reflected the traditional desire of landowners to benefit from their holdings, but also, in part, a determination to exploit the often exaggerated and only partially grasped opportunities that agricultural change appeared to offer. The instructions of wealthy Russian nobles to their stewards in the early years of the century indicate a new concern for efficient record keeping, improved yields, the systematisation of rent obligations and increased cash profits. The instructions for one of the Sheremetev estates in 1703 suggested that the peasantry provide money in place of their customary offerings of supplies for the landlord's table. In Denmark, land ownership was no longer an indication of noble status, even if in practice it still conferred social position, and a more utilitarian approach to land developed during the century, with a move towards large-scale farming, enclosure and rural reform in the second half. In southern Italy in the 1780s the Calabrian landlord and aristocrat Domenico Grimaldi demanded a state loan for new presses for the olive oil industry. He proposed that the king should appoint instructors to tour the countryside demonstrating the use of the new presses, which, in fact, caught on among the surrounding large landowners. Agricultural improvement became fashionable with many British landowners, who often took pride in being painted alongside bulky bullocks and other signs of agrarian progress.

Aristocratic interest was matched by government concern. Many of the Rhineland princes sponsored agriculture, improving grazing and appointing commissioners to promote stall-feeding and selective breeding. In Transylvania, where the rudimentary level of agricultural technology was associated with a two-field, two-year rotation – one year cultivation, one year fallow – the government tried to encourage a shift to a three-field, three-year rotation with fallow every third year only, a way to enhance production. In 1752, the new king of Sweden, Adolphus-Frederick, ordered the provincial governors to encourage the peasantry to cultivate tobacco and plants that were of use for textile production, such as dyes. Tillot, the leading minister in the Italian duchy of Parma in the 1760s, encouraged the cultivation of hemp, flax, sainfoin, potatoes, mulberries and vines and the improvement of animal breeding, and sponsored the publication of a work on bee-keeping. Sir Benjamin Thompson, who as Count Rumford, played a major role in the Bavarian government between 1784 and 1795, was a keen advocate of the potato and maize, which he believed to be nourishing and cheap, and sought to use the army to introduce agricultural improvements. He established military gardens with the object of publicising new agricultural methods and crops, particularly the potato. In France agricultural improvers, supported by the government, sought to introduce rice, a move, however, greeted with popular anger and, in the Auvergne, rioting, as it was regarded as a cause of disease.

The impact of the agricultural improvers is open to question. It is easy to point to failures, such as the numerous but ineffectual Italian agricultural academies or, in France, the marquis de Turbilly, who published a work in 1760 on the reclamation of land for cultivation, only to have his own success queried by Young. Many innovations had only a limited effect, such as the artificial incubator developed by Dominique Chazotte in Parma in the 1760s, or the potato-processing machine tested in the same town in 1762. Regulations were often neither observed nor enforced. It was claimed in 1765 that the Parmesan laws on the harvesting of silk cocoons and the spinning of silk and the 1760 law on the plantation of mulberries were not being enforced.

There are, however, signs of a qualitative as well as a quantitative improvement in agriculture, and these signs were not restricted to the areas that are commonly associated with eighteenth-century agricultural improvement, namely England, the Low Countries and Catalonia. In these, particularly the first two, improvement did not begin or methods alter significantly with the eighteenth century. The reason for agricultural development in these areas is difficult to isolate, and possible causal links have to be assessed with care. The presence of substantial local markets was doubtless significant, but these did not have comparable effects around Naples or Constantinople. The presence of a large local labour force aided projects of land reclamation and improvement, such as irrigation, drainage and reclamation from the sea, and facilitated intensive techniques of cultivation, such as deep ploughing, planting in rows and regular weeding. Yet other areas with a comparable labour force, such as Sicily, did not witness similar changes. The mutually beneficial relationship, not least in terms of manure, between cultivation and animal husbandry was significant in England, the Low Countries and Catalonia, but agrarian growth was clearly not simply a factor of manure production, as is demonstrated by Hungary, an area of extensive husbandry. It is possible that tenurial practices were more important. In all three regions much useful land was owned by the cultivators and they benefited directly from raised productivity, whereas in much of Europe such land was often the more marginal areas. Continuity among the farming population, either through the inheritance of family farms, as in Catalonia and some of the Low Countries, or through regularly renewed leases, as in England, was crucial in assisting the development of the land's potential. Different attitudes towards the land were important in encouraging the spread of agricultural improvement.

In England, Catalonia and the Low Countries, it is possible to point to obvious signs of qualitative improvement. The spread of fodder crops, such as clover, coleseed and turnips, helped to eliminate fallow and to increase the capacity of the rural economy to rear more animals, sources both of crucial manure and of valuable capital, for animals were the most significant 'cash crop' in the economy. The spread of convertible or 'up and down' husbandry, in which land alternated between pasture and arable after a number of years, was also of importance, resulting in increased yields when the land was cultivated, and improved grass at other times. A measure of agricultural specialisation was also apparent, Catalonia producing wine and brandy, the Low Countries horticultural or industrial crops, such as flax and hemp.

These changes, particularly those entailing specialisation, were aided by the practice of enclosing land. Consolidated, compact and enclosed holdings were not an innovation of the period, but their presence increased, particularly in England where, by 1700, around half, and by 1800, most of the cultivated land had been enclosed. Enclosure did not necessarily increase efficiency, and there are examples of unenclosed areas that witnessed agricultural improvement. It appears, however, to have made it easier to control the land, and enclosure was often accompanied by a redistribution of agricultural income from the tenant farmer to his landlord, a step that may have encouraged investment. Enclosing landowners often alarmed the rural population. They created wide disruption of traditional rights and expectations, common lands and roads. However, being labour- rather than capital-intensive, processes like enclosure and emparkment also entailed much employment on tasks such as hedging and ditching.

Areas that had already experienced agricultural improvement in the seventeenth century witnessed further development in the succeeding period. This was particularly the case in the Low Countries and England. Much of the Austrian Netherlands was more productive than France, and the eighteenth century saw a continual increase in the cultivation of potatoes. Provinces such as Hainault were already very productive by 1700. The following century was characterised by the spread of crop rotation, the end of fallowing and the use of new tools, so that, despite its high population, the Austrian Netherlands ceased to be a net grain importer and became instead a net exporter. Specialised crops, particularly flax and tobacco, spread. In French Flanders, an area influenced by the Austrian Netherlands, agricultural growth began in about 1690, decades ahead of the rest of France. Both total and per capita production rose as a result of more intensive agricultural methods, such as the stabling of cattle.

There was also considerable improvement in the United Provinces. Dutch drainage methods became more sophisticated. In the Dutch province of Drenthe, though the increase in the cultivation of rye, the principal cash crop, took place essentially within the framework of traditional farming practices, there being a growth in the area devoted to it, farming methods became more intensive and manuring increased. In the more fertile Dutch provinces of Utrecht and Gelderland, a lot of tobacco was grown by smallholders, and the continual population growth of the period suited what was a labour-intensive type of cultivation requiring little capital investment. Far from displaying a conservative resistance to change, the local peasantry readily adapted to new farming techniques. From the 1730s snuff manufacture developed alongside the cultivation of a new type of tobacco. The cattle-breeding gentlemen farmers of the Dutch province of Friesland were interested in selective breeding.

Though in general the Low Countries and Britain enjoyed crop yields that were larger than those of the rest of Europe, they were not uniformly areas of agricultural improvement. As with so much else, variety was the keynote. While in Flanders the late eighteenth century saw an intensive agriculture of crop rotation, new fertilisers, crops such as potatoes and tobacco and improvements in livestock breeding, the Walloon areas of the Austrian Netherlands were more traditional in their methods, with the continuation of common pasture and less rotation. In addition, specialisation was not always successful. The area of commercial horticulture and attendant processing that had emerged in Gelderland and east Utrecht in the seventeenth century declined in the eighteenth. The diffusion of new methods of cultivation and agrarian organisation was uneven, and these methods were not always appropriate. Furthermore, they did not necessarily solve the problems of demand or respond adequately to changes in it. In the 1730s England was a significant grain exporter and domestic grain prices were generally low. This placed a strain on the grain producers, who therefore welcomed the rise in domestic demand associated with the mid-century growth in population. However, they failed to maintain their export markets and to satisfy the new demand, for by the 1760s England was importing significant quantities of grain.

Agricultural improvement was not restricted to England, the Low Countries and Catalonia, and though the first two of these regions were most prominent in the field of agricultural literature and were the most developed countries in terms of agricultural methods, it could be argued that in the eighteenth century the most important advances occurred elsewhere, not least in terms of the general increase in production. Possibly the most significant improvement was the spread of new crops, particularly potatoes and maize. Both produced large yields, though, without manure, they posed the problem of soil exhaustion. Potatoes became particularly important in Ireland and across the North European plain, especially in Germany. They did not require much investment or particular new skills, and they were thus suited to peasant cultivation. The potato's cultivation was not restricted to northern Europe. In the Sault region of Languedoc, cultivation by the peasantry began in the early 1720s. In the Vivarais the peasantry adopted the potato and its production soared in the 1750s.

Maize was more popular in south-west France and northern Italy. It played a major role in helping the large growth of population in south-west France, but its diffusion was patchy. Maize was not adopted in the Armagnac region. In that of Bigorre it was introduced at the end of the seventeenth century but, for a while, played only a secondary role, not starting to replace millet until the 1750s. By the end of the century it had spread throughout the area around Toulouse. Europe was starting to move toward a situation in which, as a rough guide, one can draw a line across a map from Bordeaux eastwards, i.e. along the 45th parallel. North of that line the potato was to be the crucial crop, and south of it maize. There were exceptions – maize flourished in the Loire valley and parts of northern France, for example – but the 45th parallel is the dividing line at which the climatic changes affecting the viability of the two crops mainly occur.

The cultivation of new crops was evidence of the willingness to change traditional practices, and the increase in the variety of crops cultivated in a given area diminished local vulnerability to crop diseases and climatic disasters. In Duravel, though the potato did not spread until the start of the nineteenth century, the cultivation of beans began a half-century earlier. Chestnut trees were planted by the peasantry of the Vivarais, their living standards threatened by the local rise in population. The increase in the Corsican production of chestnuts, which could be converted into flour, favoured demographic expansion on the island.

Certain other areas of Europe witnessed obvious improvements in agriculture. In Prussia there was a general introduction of lupins, sainfoin and other high-grade fodder crops. In general, however, Frederick the Great sacrificed agriculture to industry. In order to reduce industrial costs and thus make exports more attractive, the king prohibited price rises of raw materials. The producers of flax, leather and tobacco complained without success. An unwillingness to offend the nobility and possibly a lack of sufficient royal interest ensured that Frederick's plans for agricultural improvement had only a limited effect. Frederick supported the ending of common pasture by peasants, abolishing it in Silesia in 1771, in order to improve pasture care and enable each peasant to keep more animals. Though Frederick implemented this policy on some of his own domains, very few nobles followed his example. Frederick also supported the consolidation of the scattered strips worked by individual peasants. This policy was largely a failure and it was particularly unsuccessful on noble estates.

Further west, the rise in the population of the Rhineland led both to geographical spreading of traditional forms of agriculture and to qualitative improvements. Fodder crops, particularly clover, spread; fallow was ended, and the stall-feeding of animals increased. The numbers of livestock rose. By 1750 potatoes were widely grown in the Rhineland and the subsistence crisis of 1771–2 encouraged their cultivation. Wine was exported to the United Provinces.

In south-west Germany potatoes, cash crops such as flax and tobacco, and fodder crops, such as clover and turnips, spread, particularly in the second half of the century. Meadowlands were improved, better breeds of animals were imported and livestock numbers rose, thus improving the supply of manure. In the duchy of Baden an attempt was made in the 1760s to abolish the three-field system by planting soil-renewing crops on the fallow.

In Germany as a whole the principal achievements of the agricultural reformers occurred towards the end of the century. Little progress was made in consolidating holdings, though much success was achieved in increasing the cultivation of products to be used as fodder, in particular clover and turnips, thus enabling the rearing of more animals. The spread of iron mouldboards across the North European plain increased the possibility of deep ploughing, though, in most other respects, there were few improvements in agricultural implements. Even in the more marginal and remote agricultural areas there were signs of improvement. In the hill regions of the Eifel and the Hunsrück between the Rhine and the Austrian Netherlands slash-and-burn clearing and transient cultivation practices were still found, but, by the end of the century, potatoes and clover were also being cultivated.

Further south in Lombardy, a naturally fertile agrarian region, rice cultivation increased from the 1730s, partly as a result of the activity of the leasehold farmers and partly because there was sufficient local capital to support the necessary irrigation. In the second half of the century there were clear signs of Lombard agricultural expansion, particularly in the rise of rice, silk, cheese and butter exports. There were also significant improvements in Venetia, where maize spread widely. However, in general, the Italian position was bleaker, substantially a matter of traditional methods and extensive cultivation rather than agricultural changes and intensive methods. The mixed farming of the Lombard plain, with animals providing manure and milk, made little progress elsewhere, and efforts to encourage the cultivation of the potato had little impact. The principal problems, harsh terrain, denuded soil, poor water supplies and communications, and a lack of investment, still dominated the peninsula in 1800, and the major cause of increased production was the expansion, particularly from mid-century, of the cultivated area. Though commercial farming spread in most of Italy in the second half of the century, and common lands were enclosed, subsistence agriculture was still the norm.

It is clear that agricultural improvement cannot necessarily be regarded as a development forced by reformers on unwilling peasants. Far from clinging to traditional practices, many peasants were willing to experiment with new crops. In the Vivarais in France it was the peasants who increased the production of potatoes and chestnuts without the assistance of provincial officials. In Sweden the consolidation of strips made possible by a law of 1757 was not simply a reform imposed from above by economic theorists. The reform appears to have met no significant peasant opposition, and the minutes of the Estate of Peasants for 1765–72 provide no suggestion that the reform was unpopular or unwanted. Instead, the Estate complained about delayed or inefficient surveying and of the time taken at the county courts in granting approval to consolidation schemes.

The role of peasant enterprise in increasing European food production is impossible to quantify. It could be suggested, however, that it was of great importance, understandably so in light of the peasantry's role in production. Possible enterprise among peasants, however, may have been lessened by a lack of a capital and as a result of tenurial regimes that gave them insufficient benefits and independence. If so, this would complement the effects of a socio-educational environment that denied many with talent the opportunity for advancement and thus deprived society of their abilities. Illiteracy limited receptiveness to agricultural innovations. In several respects, the situation of the peasantry was arguably a cause not only of their hardship, but also of general social impoverishment. The peasantry, of course, was neither geographically nor socially a homogeneous group. It was, however, affected generally by the rise in European population which both provided greater market opportunities, exercising a powerful 'pull' on local agrarian economies, and exacerbated local relationships between supply and demand, production and dearth. At this level, local enterprise appears more significant than the activities of the champions of agricultural improvement, who tended to concentrate their attention on gentlemen farmers rather than the peasantry.

New markets

The rise in the European population was of questionable benefit in terms of agricultural specialisation. Though it led to larger markets for areas producing surpluses of food and materials required for industrial purposes, it also increased local demand throughout most of Europe, leading areas that could have derived more benefit from cash crops to stress cereal production. However, an obvious feature of the century was the increased role of distant markets in agriculture with the consequent opportunities for interdependence and specialisation. The social and cultural consequences of any decrease in subsistence agriculture, the fall in auto-consumption by individuals and families, are open to debate, but it could be suggested that it lessened the parochialism that was such an obvious characteristic of rural life.

The integration of agricultural regions producing different products was not a new feature in agrarian society. Transhumance, the seasonal movement of livestock often over very long distances, had long been a crucial aspect of agricultural activity throughout Europe. Man's domination of upland pasture zones was only seasonal. The cattle left the Savoyard mountains for the valleys every year on 10 October. At about the same time, the sheep of the Mesta, the Spanish wool monopoly, set off on their march from their open summer grazing lands in central Spain to the lowlands, the largest annual migration of animals in Europe. Pasture was the principal benefit derived from mountainous zones, and it linked regions: the Apennines to the Emilian plain, the Abruzzi mountains to the plains of the Capitanata near Foggia, Transylvania to the Wallachian lowlands. In areas of animal husbandry the bulk of production had always been for the market, rather than for auto-consumption. Traditionally animal products were sold, or often bartered, in order to obtain cereals from nearby areas of grain production. But such products could also be sold to distant markets, and there are signs that this increased during the century.

Many towns were surrounded by lowland grain-producing areas and obtained their animal products, with the exception of milk, from more distant farming regions that were unsuitable for grain production, usually due to their terrain and climate. These regions were not all mountainous. In the absence of widespread drainage, marshlands and areas prone to flood were used, as was much of southern Europe where irrigation had not been introduced. Before refrigeration in the late nineteenth century, animals were driven to market, an inefficient method that involved a significant weight loss. Towns were the biggest market. Sheep were driven from Roussillon to Barcelona, cattle from Piedmont to Genoa and from Wales to London, geese from Norfolk to London. Such movements were often part of a sophisticated system linking upland grazing areas to lowland fattening-up regions nearer to urban markets.

The distances animals were moved were frequently considerable. Lean cattle were driven to the principal urban markets in France, particularly Lyons and Paris, from the mountainous Auvergne region in central France. In mid-century many of those destined for Paris were sent for fattening to Lower Normandy, a grazing region, whence they were moved to Poissy, the market from where Paris was supplied with live bullocks. Warsaw was supplied with beef cattle from the Ukraine and Little Poland. Hungarian sheep, cattle and oxen were exported to Germany. The Dutch cities received beef cattle from north-west Germany and Denmark, while traditional cattle areas in the United Provinces increasingly specialised in dairy produce.

There were important changes in the long-distance movement of animals, particularly in the second half of the century. Wallachia and Moldavia, where scant qualitative improvements in agriculture took place during the century, developed their agricultural exports in the second half. Aside from grain exports to Transylvania and Constantinople, cattle were moved to Silesia and horses in large numbers, up to 10,000 annually, to central Europe.

The mid-century wars involving Austria opened up new markets for Hungarian agriculture, as did Austrian and Bohemian industrial development and growing governmental interest in purchasing Hungarian products for the Austrian army. Exports rose, and in the 1770s and 1780s there developed a layer of the nobility dealing with large agricultural exports, which, as regards their needs and aims, went beyond the average level of the nobility. Knowledge of market relations increased, linked with a spread of newspaper reading and of correspondence. There was to be a further boom in Hungarian agricultural exports to Austria during the Napoleonic wars. In Hungary the rise in agricultural exports was both the prime source of economic development and a significant influence on aristocratic conduct.

Long-distance trade was not restricted to animals. Grain exports were of particular importance, to both producing and importing regions. Hungary and the Ukraine were important sources. However, the biggest remained the Baltic, though the importance of Baltic grain supplies declined, both in relation to general grain movements and with regard to Baltic exports, which by the end of the century were increasingly dominated by other products, principally timber, flax, tar and hemp. In

1784–95, the largest markets for Baltic rye were the United Provinces, Norway and the west coast of Sweden.

There was a significant increase in Russian grain production for export. Large Russian landowners were particularly interested in expanding their estates into the more fertile territories of southern Russia and there producing grain, flax and hemp for the European market. They were aided by the pacification of the Ukraine and improvements in communications. In the mid-1730s the completion of the new transport system linking the new market of St Petersburg with the river Volga led to a fall in transport costs and a decline in grain prices in the capital, as supplies increased from the new producing areas of the northern steppe and along the Volga. In spite of the rapid growth of St Petersburg during the 1740s and 1750s, the high productivity levels of the new lands provided an abundant supply of grain at low prices for its population. In the 1760s rising international grain prices, caused by the growth in the European population, led to a geographical extension of Russian production. In the early 1760s Catherine II, a keen supporter of agricultural development, backed the policy of her adviser Gerhard Linke to relieve the grain trade from restrictions and allowed the free export of grain from several Baltic ports.

Food exports were not limited to basic foodstuffs. The century saw increased trade in a range of agricultural products with consequent developments in specialisation. For its size, Europe, particularly its western half, had a very varied topography and climate, and this naturally encouraged agricultural specialisation and trade. The vine was an important cash crop in Mediterranean Europe, and in the eighteenth century it spread in a number of areas, including Friuli and Portugal. There was significant urban investment in the vineyards of the Beaujolais and Lyonnais and large-scale viticulture responded to growing demand. Wine or wine products were often moved a considerable distance: from Portugal to England, or from south-western France to the United Provinces. The opening of the Col du Tende pass at the southern end of the Alps to wheeled traffic led in 1780 to hopes in Piedmont and Savoy that wine could be exported to England via Nice. An important element of the economy of Orléans was the transhipment of Languedoc and Anjou wine from the Loire for movement to Paris and Rouen. In Languedoc the growth of the provincial market was crucial for the development of local wine and grain production.

The development of the vine as a cash crop provided a valuable source of employment and wealth, but the potential market in France was restricted by the cost of transportation, tariffs and limited purchasing power. Overproduction led the government in 1731 to prohibit the planting of new vineyards without special authorisation. Wine production fell in Duravel both because of the need to grow more cereals and because an edict of 1741 forbade the entry of Quercy wines into the Bordeaux region prior to Christmas. Local wine prices were very sensitive to the distant market and fell in consequence.

The vine was not the sole cash crop. Fruit and horticultural produce appear to have increased, possibly with valuable consequences for nutrition. The lemons and olives exported from the Genoese town of St Remo in the 1770s were sold to foreign merchants, the local community controlling the price in order to ensure that all the crop was sold. Though European demand for Ottoman products did not become significant until the nineteenth century, cotton and tobacco were cultivated as cash crops in the Balkans.

Cash crops were often the most progressive and developing sector of agricultural economies. In southern Italy, grain production remained very much a part of the traditional subsistence agriculture which still prevailed in many parts of the interior. Except for Naples, its markets were generally local. In contrast, the production of olive oil in Apulia and Calabria was highly commercialised and export-oriented. In the Vivarais the production methods used for grain and livestock were substantially unchanged. However, viticulture spread in the north of the region, while many mulberry trees were planted in the south. With the encouragement of the local Estates and *intendants*, the production of raw silk and silk thread in the Vivarais and Languedoc expanded rapidly from the mid-century. The general effect of the increase in cash crops was greater trade and a more integrated European agricultural system. Cattle from Hungary blocked the roads near Frankfurt-on-Main in the 1780s. Olive oil, wine and fruit from the south of France were moved up the Rhône to Lyons and thence by land to Roanne and, along the Loire, Canal de Briare, Loing and Seine, to Paris.

Market links transmitted demand and helped in the diffusion of new ideas. The dependence of the Drenthe farmers on the price their rye could command on the international markets ensured that Drenthe rye prices closely followed those of Prussian rye on the Amsterdam corn exchange. State activity underlined the demand caused by rising population. Larger armies had to be fed, granaries filled. In the 1750s the Austrian government contracted with the Styrian peasantry for its artillery horses.

Yet it is necessary not to exaggerate the direction or scale of agricultural changes. Much agriculture remained subsistence, the diffusion of improvements was limited, areas of potential demand and supply often poorly integrated. In Poland, a traditional grain-exporting region, the market phenomena of pricing affected only a small percentage of national production and consumption. In effect there was a dual economy. Poland's role as a grain exporter had not led to an export-oriented agricultural revolution. The degree of agricultural specialisation was very low, with self-sufficiency in all products an important goal for estate economies. Grain yields were lower than in the early seventeenth century and grain exports fell. Agricultural techniques appear to have degenerated, and it is probable that the population consumed less in food and other products, with obvious consequences for local industry. The nature of the Polish political and tenurial system ensured that much of the product of the land went to the landowners not the labourers, lessening the incentive for peasant initiative.

The attitude and role of the landowners were problems elsewhere in Europe. Portuguese agriculture was very backward, the aristocracy preferring to seek wealth through colonial and court appointments. Marquis Domenico Caracciolo, viceroy of Sicily in 1781–6, blamed the aristocracy for the poor state of local agriculture. In southern Italy the aristocracy was essentially parasitic, diverting rural rents to urban expenditure. The serfs of Transylvania had little incentive to work hard, and their productivity was very low. In the Loire valley small peasant holdings were acquired by bourgeois and noble engrossers whose grain-growing and cattle-raising estates farmed by *métayers* (sharecroppers) were not characterised by improved farming methods.

Tenurial relationships were not the sole issue. Improved methods spread unevenly. Insufficient numbers and quality of animals and inadequate manure remained a general problem. A scarcity of livestock in northern France was matched by a lack of fodder, which ensured that weak animals pulled the poorly constructed ploughs, producing an inadequate seedbed. Weeds had to be pulled out by hand, field drainage was inadequate. With livestock essential for ploughing, harrowing and harvesting, poor animal stock meant gruelling human labour. In Altopascio the plough used in the region produced only a shallow upheaval of soil. The real soil preparation was achieved by the use of shovels. If the lack of manure, whether in Brittany or Transylvania, was still a problem, the spread of new, particularly fodder, crops was also limited. In much of Europe it is impossible to point to technological changes introducing any significant rises in productivity. In his utopian novel *L' An 2440* (1770) Louis Sébastien Mercier looked forward to regulated wheat production, adequate grain stockpiling and the improvement of crops and livestock by hybridisation and selective breeding. In 1800 this prospect was still far distant. Many regions of Europe had witnessed no agricultural revolution, but the principal impression both within and between regions is one of variety. If Piedmont in the latter half of the century witnessed a deteriorating agricultural regime, with undernourished workers and declining numbers of cattle, orchards and fodder crops could be found on the Savoyard shores of Lake Geneva. The stress, whether on change or on conservatism, could be and was placed differently by commentators.

In combination with a European rise in population the general impression is one of an agriculture that failed to keep pace with demand. The clearest indication of this was a general rise in European food prices. This varied by region and product and in time, but the general chronology is clear. Superimposed on seasonal and annual fluctuations, that varied according to the state of the harvest, there was a general price stability in the first half of the century, corresponding to demographic stagnation, and a marked rise thereafter. In Drenthe, rye prices betrayed substantial variations, but the general picture was one of depressed prices between 1650 and 1750. Decennial averages reveal price falls in the 1700s, 1710s and 1720s, rises in the 1730s, a near static position in the 1740s and 1750s, followed by rises in the 1760s and 1780s, with the 1770s generally static.

General European agricultural production did not rise sufficiently either to free the population from malnutrition, or to release a large section of the agricultural workforce for industrial employment and for migration. Nevertheless, the increase in the amount of land cultivated, combined with a partial spread of new crops and techniques and limited improvements in transportation, seem to have provided sufficient extra food to aid population growth and support consequently a higher rate of economic activity. If agricultural changes were generally quantitative, and therefore less disruptive of traditional practices, rather than qualitative, they were still of importance. The agricultural improvers had less impact than they sought, but, across much of Europe, the peasantry and the landowners produced more. This was particularly apparent in certain regions of eastern Europe, especially Hungary and the Ukraine, and is arguably related to the greater international strength of Austria and Russia.

Industry

The manufacturers of eighteenth-century Europe were not to know that their activities would subsequently be scrutinised by scholars searching for the origins and causes of the period of industrial growth generally termed the Industrial Revolution. The term is not an appropriate description for the century, for the phenomena commonly understood by it such as steam-driven power and specialised factories, and associated social changes such as widespread urbanisation, were atypical in this period. Nevertheless, it is foolish to present the century in terms of a failure to achieve an Industrial Revolution. That was not what industrialists sought. There was no cult of industrial development comparable to that for agricultural innovation. Instead, industrialists were primarily interested in achieving profits by using traditional techniques. New markets were sought more than new methods. However, industrial growth did occur in many regions of Europe and in some areas there was a substantial shift in the occupational profile of the population, even if variety is again the keynote that emerges from any consideration of economic change in the century.

Manufacturing was affected by factors of supply and demand. Demand was principally influenced by European population growth, purchasing power and consumer attitudes. Though manufactured goods were increasingly exported, both to colonists and to non-European people, most industrial production was for the European market. As foodstuffs formed the largest portion of the average budget and also fluctuated widely in price, the market for industrial goods and craftsmen's services was vulnerable. The bad harvests at the beginning of the 1740s pushed the price of grain up at Aachen, Leipzig and Nuremberg, leading to cuts in the price of textiles. Purchasing power was also affected by the general wealth of the population, the poor state of the Rouen cotton industry in 1769 being blamed on general poverty, and by the extent to which a market economy had developed. There were problems in Russia in developing salt production as the product was intended for the general population and rural areas had been only poorly integrated into the market economy. Governments, however, provided a demand that was both more resistant to harvest difficulties and part of the market economy. The armed forces were the leading sector of government demand. Munitions, uniforms and warships were of particular importance. The main Russian state arsenal at Tula produced between 1737 and 1778 an annual average of nearly 14,000 basic infantry muskets.

Demand was in no way fixed and most industrial production was able to serve existing and developing demands profitably without seeking to alter its supply-side capability. However, supply factors were also of significance. These included the quality of entrepreneurship, the supply of skilled labour, technological developments, and changes in industrial organisation and location that permitted the cutting of costs. The last is commonly associated with the controversial thesis of 'proto-industrialisation',[2] the development of rural regions in which a significant portion of the population became dependent on income from the industrial production of goods for inter-regional or international markets. This has been seen as the consequence of the expansion of traditional rural domestic craft production without any major technological advance. It was commonly organised by urban entrepreneurs who used their capital and knowledge to supply the raw material, control the manufacturing and market the product. This has traditionally been termed the 'putting-out' system; it was most common in linen and worsted textile production, and co-existed with other forms of domestic industry, and with early industrial plants such as ironworks, potteries and breweries.

There is no doubt that rural industry was important. Much was traditional, a matter of household production for family use, of clothes in particular. Market production was well developed in a number of European rural regions. There were a number of reasons for this development. Urban manufacturing suffered from the restrictive practices and related higher wages of town workers who used their organisation into guilds to exercise some influence in the manufacturing process. The guilds, which were run by masters (senior skilled workers), limited the role of women and children, both sources of cheap labour. In rural areas the absence of alternative non-agricultural employment and of a tradition of organised labour, and the presence both of grinding poverty and of a low income from farming, produced a lower wage economy. Low wages encouraged urban entrepreneurs, offsetting the disadvantage of transport costs to markets. In Bohemia workers in the glass and linen industries cultivated smallholdings and therefore needed lower wages. This helped to ensure low prices for Bohemian glass and linen. A similar dual economy of small-scale landowning combined with industrial work such as weaving or metal-working could emerge whenever there were urban merchants willing to buy the products. In some areas energy costs may have been significant. Water-power was easier to utilise in areas of rapid flow, and wood supplies were more plentiful in the countryside, as, in coal-mining regions, was coal.

The crucial element in rural industrialisation appears to have been demand, for despite the general availability of cheap rural labour, most rural areas did not become important centres of industry. Demand reflected the presence of markets, and entrepreneurial activity was crucial in producing a symbiotic relationship between rural activity and urban funds, markets and, often, stages in manufacture. Entrepreneurial activity was necessary to enable rural industry to move from the stage of direct sale by domestic craftsmen to that of sale to distant markets. There was no clear conflict between urban and rural sectors. Rural industries competed with each other as much as with the towns.

Textile production lent itself readily to rural industrialisation. Power could be supplied by rivers, traditions of rural domestic textile manufacture were strong, wheels and looms could be found in the countryside and textiles could be transported without much risk of damage. The rural and urban aspects of textile manufacturing were intimately linked. Finishing processes were usually concentrated in towns. The woollen and linen industries led to much rural activity, particularly in West Yorkshire, the Low Countries, Silesia and Württemberg.[3] In the Low Countries textiles dominated rural industry, but the latter was concentrated in certain regions. The less populous and less urban east of the United Provinces had a smaller amount of rural industry than Flanders where nearly half the rural population was occupied in weaving linen and spinning flax. Flanders benefited from proximity to markets and there was also a large rural population to support. These activities were also common in several other areas, such as Overijssel and northern Brabant, and particularly in regions lacking alternative employment.

In the area of Ban de Herve east of Liège there was a fruitful combination of pastoral agriculture and domestic textile production that pre-dated the century. Grass occupied up to 90 per cent of the land on some farms, a degree of specialisation permitted by ready markets for butter and cheese in Liège, Verviers and other nearby towns. Smaller holdings could be sustained only by income from the spinning and weaving of wool, which by 1800 occupied half of the region's population. Land ownership was substantially local and small-scale and there was a fairly active land market with over 50 sales annually in a region of 10,000 acres with about 2000 landowners. Economic activity benefited from a system of land ownership that ensured a good return for the local population, and the active land market was a further indication of a region that was well integrated into the cash economy and far from stagnant. Rural industry enabled the maintenance of levels of population that were excessive by the standards of local agriculture. It was thus often associated with very small farms, as in the region of Comines-Warneton in the Austrian Netherlands, where the revenues of the peasantry depended on the development of a local cloth industry which benefited from the absence of corporate regulations.

The extent to which growth in rural industry in the Low Countries was a result of the absence of these regulations is unclear. In the third quarter of the century there was serious guild opposition in Flemish towns to the development of the rural textile industry. Possibly more significant was the presence of urban capital and markets seeking inexpensive rural production. Thus the development of the weaving of fine linen fabrics (lawn and cambric) in the country around Cambrai and Valenciennes in French Flanders operated to the prejudice of urban weavers, but owed much to the activities of urban merchants. Other aspects of the economy were conducive to the development of rural industry. In 1635–59 and then again in the late 1660s, 1670s, 1690s and 1700s, the Low Countries had been one of the leading battlegrounds of Europe, a handicap shared by the Rhineland, Lombardy and Hungary. However, between the end of the War of the Spanish Succession in 1713–14 and the invasion of the Austrian Netherlands by the army of revolutionary France in 1792, the Austrian Netherlands was only once directly involved in war, between 1744 and 1748. France and Austria negotiated a neutrality agreement for the territory in 1733, thus avoiding local conflict during the War of the Polish Succession (1733–5), and the Austro-French alliance of 1756, part of the so-called Diplomatic Revolution, kept the region at peace during the Seven Years War (1756–63). Peace alone was not enough to produce significant industrial growth in eighteenth-century Europe, as Denmark and Portugal, both of whom enjoyed long periods without war, illustrate, but it was generally associated with higher levels of economic activity.

The attitude of the aristocracy in the Austrian Netherlands was also significant. They developed coal mines, invested in the iron and steel industry and brought new lands into cultivation. Arguably the limited local possibilities of the last encouraged aristocratic investment in industry. In Hainault members of the de Croÿ and Aremberg families played an important role in coal-mining. This was significant because, aside from requiring a favourable political and legal context, rural industrialisation also needed capital. In the provinces of Hainault and Namur the coal mines, iron forges and blast furnaces were mostly owned by abbeys and nobles who generally invested insufficient money to enable the businesses to expand. The average blast furnace employed only seven or eight workers. However, from the 1770s coal-mining increased as a result of mechanisation made possible by fairly large investments made by a few enterprising aristocrats.

Aristocratic enterprise was also important in Russian rural industry. Most Russian manufacturing was dispersed and domestic. Industries apparently characterised by big concerns, such as the Tula metalworking area, often consisted of dozens of separate units of production. Coarse woollen cloth was produced on aristocratic estates or in villages of state peasants that had been acquired by merchant entrepreneurs early in the century. Peter I allowed merchants to purchase serfs for industrial labour, and a law was passed in 1721 permitting merchants to buy entire villages for their enterprises. This practice was prohibited in 1762, and the second half of the century witnessed significant production of a number of goods, including paper and woollen and linen textiles by serf labour on manorial estates. In parts of central Russia, the shift after about 1760 from labour services to payment in cash or kind was associated with a sharp rise in domestic industrial production. In western Europe, aristocratic enterprise was important, but merchants played a larger role than in Russia.

In Italy there was a modest expansion of rural domestic textile production, silk and wool remaining the basic industries in most of the country. Velvet manufacture in the villages round the city was organised by Genoese merchants, the rural workers putting in long hours and being obliged to keep their looms in repair. By the end of the century there were signs of change. In the Upper Veneto certain sectors of the domestic-based textile industry changed from 'putting-out' to more centralised factory-based, mechanised production.

Merchant enterprise was also most significant in Switzerland and western Germany, both regions of rural industrialisation. The production of ribbons near Basle was organised by merchants from the town. In Württemberg a trading company of merchants and dyers based on the town of Calw organised the weaving of wool in the duchy, while cotton-printing developed in mid-century in the Sulz area and came to employ over 1000 rural workers.

In 1779 the French government gave in to merchant pressure and relaxed restrictions on the rural production of cloth. As a result, greater quantities of lower-quality cloth were produced by relatively unskilled rural workers, while wages and prices were kept low. In Picardy in the 1780s, thousands of looms in the wool, linen and hosiery industries were supplied with yarn by the spinning of numerous peasant women.

The development of rural industry was generally a response to the merchants' demand for inexpensive labour and the peasants' for employment. It should not necessarily be seen as a sign of qualitative development, a transition to 'full' industrialisation. 'Proto-industrialisation' is a term that is used often with the implications of development and growth, yet in many senses rural industrialisation was a stabilising factor. It made it possible to deal with the demands of a rising consumer population without increasing costs excessively and thus squeezing demand. It also brought more prosperity to rural zones, supporting marriage at an early age, limiting emigration and, possibly, the pressure to increase agricultural production, and stabilising communal life.

Most rural industry was not mechanised to any significant extent, and over most of Europe the predominantly wooden textile machinery in common use changed little before 1800. The wide range of wool-growing and of wool and flax spinning formed the basis of a scattered textile industry. However, often products were for a local market only, techniques were limited and the capacity for innovation low. Only the larger markets and the more substantial capital of major entrepreneurs could lead to experimentation in, for example, dyeing and new technology. For the ordinary small man with perhaps a smallholding and his weaving, the local product done in the traditional way was all that he had time to produce. Such areas in England – Devon, Essex and Norfolk for example – did not advance in the way that the more specialised and faster-growing regions did.

For rapid industrial growth, the essentials were capital, transport, markets and coal. Coal, a readily transportable and controllable fuel, was useful even in the preparatory stages of traditional manufacturing methods, such as soap-boiling, let alone with factories. Coal was critical to the concentrations of population and production which could build up the pools of skill and specialisation. These were as important as new machinery. Wood, with its greater bulk for calorific value and less readily controllable heat, was a poor basis for many industrial processes, as well as for the development of large new industrial populations, with their attendant demand for bricks, pottery and all the other fuel-consuming ancillaries of towns. Coal without transport was not sufficient, as South Wales before the railway demonstrates. However, coal with transport tended to create buoyant mixed-industrial regions with large pools of labour and demand, and of specialist services.

If household weaving was more typical of the age, signs of technological development were more important for the future. The technological level of most industries was fairly low and innovations often spread only very slowly. The first Bohemian mechanised mill for spinning linen yarn was not built until 1836. Much industrial plant was primitive, prone to climatic disruption, a particular problem with mills, and dependent on an often poorly-educated labour force. The provision of fuel was often erratic, fuel economy limited, and mechanical working parts prone to break down. Poor communications affected industrial efficiency. Industrial units were often very small, with little specialisation either in machinery or in labour. Most mines had a very small labour force. There was a general disinclination to innovate, understandably so in a culture where training was largely acquired on the job and where tradition determined most industrial practices. The apprenticeship system did not encourage new methods. Artisanal mentality included a sense of the importance of traditional values and communal stability.

The limited and precarious financial resources of most enterprises also discouraged innovation. Most contracts were short-term, hindering the development of a relative security that might encourage often expensive investment in new plant. This ensured that investors with substantial funds were of great importance.

Most plant was fairly simple and there was rarely an opportunity or need for the costly retooling that might have encouraged innovation. In most areas technological developments were limited and industrial activity was characterised by many problems and often poor products. It was estimated in 1757 that many Russian muskets could not fire six times without danger of breaking. In areas such as construction, machinery remained very primitive. More generally, man- and horsepower remained the key. Skilled labour was often in short supply, its loss, as in the Brussels paper manufacturing industry in 1728, sometimes serious. It was at a particular premium in Russia. Aware of this shortage, governments competed to obtain skilled labour, often bribing workmen to migrate from other countries, such as Britain. In mining and metal-working in particular, skills were not readily transmissible except by acquiring the men who had them; books or blueprints would not suffice.

These attempts, combined with industrial espionage, indicate a realisation that change was possible and that benefits would accrue to those who seized their opportunities. In some spheres, such as mine drainage, technology offered the possibility of extending activities in hitherto closed directions, for example by sinking deeper pits; in others, such as textiles, of producing goods more rapidly or in greater quantities though most gains probably came through the simpler build-up of skills due to specialisation.

Most power generation at the end of the century was still traditional. If water was still a major source of power, whether for saw-mills at Berne or silk-works at Bologna, so also was wind.

A traveller observed in 1787 the common form of industrial activity: the processing of agricultural products. 'The first thing which strikes the eye on approaching Lille is the immense number of windmills whirring perpetually in the environs. These are principally employed in grinding the grain of the colza, a species of cabbage cultivated in this country, from which is extracted an oil used in various manufactories.'[4] However, the introduction for mining and manufacturing purposes of the steam engine at the beginning of the century in England offered an alternative source of power. Steam engines were expensive and not free from problems and were best suited to enterprises such as large mines, where substantial quantities of energy were required for a long period. They were particularly useful for pumping water out of mines and were also used for winding and, by the end of the century, for driving machinery. Use of steam engines was concentrated in Britain, where in 1769 James Watt patented an improved machine that was more energy-efficient and therefore less expensive to run, although more expensive to buy. The use of steam engines also spread to continental Europe. The first steam engine to pump water from the coal mines of the principality of Liège was introduced in about 1725, enabling deep-mining operations to be carried on which were the most advanced in continental Europe.

Technological innovation was not restricted to energy provision. Significant developments occurred in metallurgy where the smelting of iron and steel using coke rather than charcoal freed an important industry from dependence on wood supplies: mineral replaced organic sources of power. Britain led the way but the technology spread. In Parma in 1762–5, Tillot supported experiments on new methods for iron and steel production, schemes opposed by those keen on traditional practices. In Liège in 1770 coke replaced charcoal in the manufacture of high-grade iron. Friedrich von Heinitz, head of the Prussian mining department after 1776, built the first Prussian coke furnaces and introduced many innovations based on scientific principles. In 1779 the first steam pump for mine drainage in Prussia was installed.

Textiles were another sphere that witnessed technological development. John Kay's flying shuttle of 1733 increased the productivity of handloom weavers by making it possible both to weave double-width cloths and to weave more speedily. It was introduced into the Austrian Netherlands in the 1740s and led to significant growth in the local linen industry, a major exporter, but it was in general use in Yorkshire only in the 1780s and was only slowly spreading elsewhere in England 20 years later. It was still almost unknown in Prussia and Switzerland after the Napoleonic wars.

In England the 1760s, 1770s and 1780s saw a series of developments that produced machine-spun cotton yarn strong enough to produce an all-cotton cloth, particularly Richard Arkwright's water frame (1768), which applied the principle of spinning by rollers, and Samuel Crompton's mule (1779) with its spindle carriage. Arkwright and his partners built a number of water-powered cotton mills in Lancashire and the Midlands, the first in Derbyshire in 1771, that displayed the characteristics of the factory system, including the precise division of labour and the continual co-operation of workers in the different manufacturing processes. In 1790 Arkwright erected a Boulton and Watt steam engine in his Nottingham mill.

These developments spread. In 1776 the first modern cloth-making machines were introduced into Portugal from Britain. The first mechanised textile factory at Düsseldorf was opened in 1783, the following year the framework knitters of lower Champagne began to make use of cotton yarn spun *à la mécanique* and the mechanisation of cotton spinning began in the Norman town of Louviers. However, the majority of European spinning was still on the hand wheel by 1800, despite 30 years of the jenny, and its adoption in some regions.

Though technological innovations were particularly associated with the fields of steam power, metallurgy and textiles, they were not restricted to it. A widespread interest in technological innovation is apparent in a number of spheres in the last decades of the century. There were developments in ceramic technology as well as style. Hard, high-fired British china drove majolica products from the Dutch market after 1770. Josiah Wedgwood turned a craft into an industrial process, creating a major export industry. The spread of mining led to greater interest in railroads. Sophisticated engineering was developed by the innovations of men such as Matthew Boulton. The Montgolfier brothers, using heat as their motive power, invented aviation with their hot-air balloon.

Innovations were not always welcomed by the workforce. The guilds in the French cloth-making town of Troyes, who demanded the suppression of rural manufacturing at the time of the Revolution, also attacked the spinning jenny for causing unemployment. In the same period the industrialists of Verviers, favoured by the local government, were divided from their workers and opposed to the revolution in Liège. The miners in the Røros region of Norway were hard hit by the change in extractive technique introduced in the second half of the century, when gunpowder replaced wood and they lost their incomes from carting timber.

Mechanisation was expensive and demanded a concentration of goods and labour. It was associated in branches of the textile industry, such as the production of printed calicoes, with the division of labour, quality control and factory-type production systems and buildings. However, in Russia large enterprises were frequently due to the difficulty of organising a serf workforce. The factory serfs of the Urals were brutally treated by the manufacturers, who forced them to neglect their agricultural pursuits and to purchase provisions from factory stores at high prices.

The tension in the Urals, which was to lead to violence in the early 1760s and during the Pugachev rising of 1773–5, was but one instance of the stress caused by industrial activity, much of it related to issues of economic regulation – evidence of the actual, potential and perceived role of government, national and local, in industrial matters. Different interests took up conflicting positions on regulation. In Brussels in 1761, J. L. T'Kint, a merchant seeking to set up in cloth production, argued that monopolies were harmful and challenged the local economic corporations who defended their privileges. The role of water-power in Louviers pitted millers against dyers, manufacturers against riverside dwellers.

There was often a close relationship between government and industry. Aside from the role of the former as a market, it could also provide privileges. These took essentially two forms, domestic privileges and protection against foreign rivals. In the former case, industries sought freedom from unwanted regulation, such as guild restrictions, as well as specific positive benefits. In the 1760s Tillot, seeking to boost local employment in Parma and cut imports, founded enterprises for the production of earthenware, textiles and mirrors. In Prussia, the Potsdam porcelain factory was given free firewood from the royal forest and protected from imports, while the highly efficient Silesian glass industry was not allowed to sell its products in the other Prussian provinces lest their smaller producers suffer. Privileged establishments were not necessarily inefficient producers. In France many were at the forefront technologically. Government support most commonly took the form of moves against foreign products. High tariffs or outright import prohibitions were used. In 1719 the Spanish government decreed that only Spanish cloth should be used for military uniforms; in 1757 it prohibited the import of Genoese paper and silk products. A depression in the Nîmes silk-stocking industry in 1786 was blamed on a Spanish import ban. In 1731 the Papal States put a heavy tax on Venetian wax imports in order to encourage local production.

Economic regulation for the benefit of local industry was a constant feature throughout the century though it appears to have reflected in part the fiscal consciousness and needs of government. Governmental intervention in industry was essentially designed not to obtain technological innovation, but to secure local production. A good instance of this was the sugar-refining industry. Frederick the Great awarded the Berlin refinery a monopoly of the Prussian market, while Maria Theresa encouraged the growth of the industry in Antwerp and Brussels, thus restricting imports from Hamburg and the Dutch Republic respectively.

State intervention did not alter the general pattern of industrial change, one that mirrored agricultural change in largely increasing production through spreading activity rather than innovation. As in agriculture, one of the striking features was the growth in eastern-European production. Though the mineral workings in northern Hungary were among the most advanced in Europe, it was generally the case that eastern-European industry witnessed little innovation, in either technology or organisation. Aristocratic enterprise played a major role in the region. When in the early decades of the century the Habsburgs encouraged the development of Transylvanian industries, such as glass, paper and potash, much of the development took place on aristocratic estates using serf labour with merchants supplying additional capital. In the 1750s Count Joseph Kinsky built mirror factories in Bohemia and acted as an entrepreneur in textile production. In 1761 Kinsky asked the government to ban the import of mirrors, arguing that his own factories were able to supply the home market. A ban was imposed on imported Nuremberg mirrors, and by 1767 half of Kinsky's mirrors were exported to Poland, Russia, Denmark, Spain, Portugal, Turkey and the United Provinces. In the same year a commission of the Bohemian government reporting on the grievances of local glass-workers noted that they complained of irregular pay, the enforced purchase of goods, such as clothing, from their employers, and 'that they were treated with blows like dogs'.

In eastern Europe there was no correlation between areas of agricultural and industrial development. Hungary, Wallachia and Moldavia did not witness industrial growth comparable to that of their agriculture. Most Polish industry was small-scale, and the country did not experience development comparable to that in neighbouring regions such as Bohemia and Silesia. The Polish grain trade did not produce skills, techniques and forms of organisation that would aid industrialisation and it led to little manufacturing activity bar milling. However, within Poland there were areas of growth. Though Cracow exported relatively little, it enjoyed an economic revival in the 1740s, thanks to its solid regional market. Artisanal production increased, as did immigration to the town. In the 1750s Cracow's commercial activity increased and the following decade witnessed industrial growth. The nearby rock salt mines were the largest industrial enterprise in Poland.

Nevertheless eastern-European industrial growth was largely found in Russia and in the area of east-central Europe comprising Bohemia, Saxony and Silesia, a region fought over in mid-century. Though the domestic Russian market was limited by the poverty and heavy tax burden of the peasantry, the state provided a significant market for several industrial sectors, particularly metallurgy. The copper and iron deposits of the Urals served as the basis for a major growth in local industry, particularly of iron foundries, and the region became the principal foreign supplier of iron to western Europe, supplanting Sweden in that position. In other respects, Russian industrial developments were not striking. Russian goods were frequently poorer in quality and higher in price than imports, and Russian merchants often found it hard to sell them. The coal and iron of the Ukraine were not worked on a scale comparable to the Ural metal deposits. The value of the unskilled compulsory labour that was widely used was limited. Many industrial establishments, such as those that produced cloth for the army, did not become foci for urbanisation or further industrialisation. However, compared with her principal political rivals, Sweden, Poland and Turkey, Russia achieved significant industrial growth. If it was regionally specific, that was little different from the situation elsewhere in Europe. Most Russian enterprises, such as the hat, stocking and rope factories at Saratov in the 1770s, did not produce goods for export, but that also was in no way exceptional.

Industrial activity was a more marked feature of western than eastern Europe. It was most pronounced in England, where it has been estimated that in 1688, 44 per cent of the population were employed outside agriculture and produced 63 per cent of the national income, though many were not industrial workers. Progress in England took many different forms. There was a marked increase in the number of patents issued from 1759. Industrial development led to more specialisation, division of labour, and the growth of capital. There were important changes in the experience and intensity of work, the organisation of labour, and in material conditions. There was a greater emphasis on the need for constant and regular labour: new working practices and technology required a more disciplined workforce. Although by the end of the century fewer than 2000 steam engines had been produced in England, they each represented a decision for change. The cumulative impact of often slow and uneven progress was impressive by the end of the century, and, by then, the rate of industrial growth had risen markedly.

Both in England and elsewhere in western Europe, there were areas, such as Vendôme and its region in France, where industry was nearly absent. There were also spheres of industrial decline, such as the Dutch shipbuilding industry. The reasons for decline are indicative of the problems that manufacturing encountered, not least volatility of demand, variability in economic regulation and the difficulty of ensuring consistent investment. The economy of Huy on the Meuse in the bishopric of Liège declined, the victim of disinvestment, weak local demand, municipal indebtedness, protectionism and the rigidity of the corporate regime. The southern French cloth town of Clermont de Lodève suffered from the low status of entrepreneurship in French society. Production there was dominated by a privileged mercantile elite who responded to mid-century economic difficulties by disinvesting and transforming themselves into a *rentier* class. In Clermont, declining local industry pressed particularly hard on the propertyless wage-earners, many of whom became unemployed. However, elsewhere, both in Languedoc and in the French textile industry, decline was avoided. In mid-century Carcassonne, growth in the cloth industry brought a lot of wealth and manufacturers played a dynamic role in the town.

Diversity was, as ever, the key both in France and further afield. Though Toulouse had a cloth industry it was not a major industrial and commercial city, while Marseilles, in the second half of the century, contained cloth, sugar, glass, porcelain and soap factories. The contrast in their industrial structure owed much to their differing roles as trading centres. In Troyes, where a large portion of the working population was employed in the cotton industry, raw cotton was imported from the West Indies and cotton cloth exported to Italy, Spain and southern France, the industry being run by merchants, not clothiers. In the less international and capitalised Rheims, woollen cloth industry clothiers played a larger role. International trade played a major part in the location of industries processing colonial products and of shipbuilding in towns on France's Atlantic coast such as Bordeaux. However, French industrial growth was less characterised by technological innovation than its British counterpart. The flow of technology indicated that French industrial production methods were inferior. There were relatively few large-scale units processing raw materials, such as iron foundries or spinneries in northern France. In 1789, Paris still had very few factories, and her revolutionary movements were not the achievements of factory workers, although the Reveillon riots in April 1789 centred on a small factory and were an important harbinger of later mob activities in the capital. Only in her northern suburbs were there a few large textile manufactories employing between 400 and 800 workers. One-third of Parisian workers were employed in the traditional building trade.

The situation was little different in Italy and Iberia. In Lombardy in 1767 only 1.5 per cent of the population were industrial workers. Lombard industry was poorly developed and, with the exception of silk production, did not grow significantly. Nevertheless, Como in 1769 had 25 establishments producing woollen goods with a total of 180 workers, 155 for other fabrics with about 2000 workers, four dye-works with 78 workers, three tanneries with 80, four soap factories with 23, two hat-works with 12, eleven looms for cotton goods with 20, and two looms for knitted stockings with 120. In nearby Locco, 500 women were employed silk-making in 1774, while that year Bellagio on Lake Como contained six soap-works and seven looms for knitted cloth. Italian industry was hampered by a weak domestic market, inadequate capital, poor communications, active foreign competition and backward techniques.

Similar problems afflicted Iberian industry, though in both Spain and Portugal efforts were made to increase production. In the late 1760s the rapid exhaustion of alluvial gold production in her Brazilian colony limited Portugal's ability to pay for British manufactured imports. The Pombal administration responded in 1769–77 by setting up hundreds of small factories for sugar-refining, metallurgy, textiles, hats, pottery, glass and paper production. Only the textile factories prospered. Campomanes actively supported industrial activity in Spain in the 1770s and, though many of his schemes failed, the last decades of the century witnessed the spread of the putting-out system and the emergence of new types of industrial production relying upon wage labourers.

At the end of the century industry in most of Europe was still much less important than agriculture as a source of wealth and employment. Most of the problems confronting industrial activity were still apparent. If poverty, transportation costs, poor communications, and tariffs restricted markets, a general lack of capital and the limited pool of skilled labour were still significant constraints. Possibly equally important were the psychological rigidities.

Technological possibilities were not grasped in many sectors and areas. These ranged from the Imperial Free Cities, which on the whole failed to keep pace in production technology, to the

Swedish metallurgical industry. In the French flour-milling industry, millers opposed the combination of mills into larger units which would have reduced costs, bakers hindered changes in milling methods that limited their freedom of action, and were reluctant to adapt to new sorts of grain that required different handling, kneading and baking techniques, and the public authorities resisted changes in milling that might lead to popular disquiet. By prohibiting the introduction of certain practices, such as grain purchase on speculation, the authorities impeded the modernisation of the industry. By the Revolution most mills were still not like factories. Though some groups supported change, with the physiocrats advocating economic milling, conservative attitudes were paramount. As in the previous century, most state-protected industrial enterprises produced luxury goods for limited and usually competitive markets and many, such as Frederick the Great's Berlin silk industry, enjoyed limited success. Established producers frequently resisted innovations, the Augsburg cloth-making and dyers' guilds opposing vigorously the establishment of cotton-bleaching and -printing factories. The general economic situation was not sufficiently favourable to encourage a positive response from those whose livelihood was put at risk by technological innovation.

Industrialisation was a highly regional process. Contemporaries were certainly aware of the pace of change in those regions. It was linked to highly competitive international markets, with nations keen on tariffs, impeding the exports of machines and plans. However, as yet technological transformation was selective and change slow, firm size was small and organisation personal, labour markets local, outwork common and factories rare, even in Britain.

3   The Wheels of Commerce

Communications

Agricultural and industrial development depended on a number of factors, but one of the most significant was the nature of the infrastructure. Without effective transport systems, regions could not benefit from improvement. Economic activities had different requirements, and improvements in infrastructure did not necessarily benefit all, particularly if the two-way flow of improved communications led to competition from better or cheaper products. However, problems with communications were of general importance. There was significant demand across eighteenth-century Europe for both agricultural and industrial products. That this demand did not produce commensurate growth was due in part to structural difficulties in the economic system. In his memorandum of 1763 on commercial policy Nikita Panin linked his proposals for increasing Russia's exports to the improvement of transportation within the empire and called for the construction of roads and canals to help move goods to market.

Communications were a serious problem, whether in terms of the movement of people or of goods, of transport with speed or in bulk. Poor communications magnified the effects of distance and imposed high costs on economic exchanges. Without metalled roads or mechanised transport, land communications were generally slow. The quality of the roads reflected the local terrain, in particular drainage and soil type, and the ability and determination of governments and local communities to keep the roads in good repair. The resistance of the road surface, generally loose and rough, to bad weather or heavy use was limited. Narrow wheels chewed the roads into ruts. Rain and frost damaged road surfaces. The rainy summer of 1708 made the Russian and Lithuanian roads very soft, hindering the Swedish invasion of Russia.

The need for constant repair was expensive in terms of money, manpower and government effort, and it is easy to appreciate why road construction or improvement might be seen as a poor investment. The most important Russian road, that between St Petersburg and Moscow, was laid out by Peter I in the first two decades of the century. The roadbed consisted of tree trunks, with piles driven into the marshes and low-lying soft spots. Covered with a layer of gravel, sand or dirt, such a roadbed was supposed to provide a firm and relatively smooth surface, but the rotting of the wooden base, erosion of the surface and gradual subsidence of long stretches into the soft, marshy soil, kept it in a permanent state of disrepair. Important Russian secondary roads lacked any roadbed and were simply a cleared expanse on which construction and cultivation were forbidden.

The absence of any standardisation helped to ensure great variety in European roads. In the kingdom of Naples land communications were so bad that it was easier to ship olive oil than to take it across the country by cart. In contrast, the roads in the Austrian Netherlands were both relatively good and well maintained. In France the transportation networks were substantially denser and more interconnected north of a line stretching from Geneva to St Malo than south of it. There was no integrated French national framework, although there was a substantial improvement in the road system after 1750 and journey times were reduced.

Poor roads led to long and unpredictable journeys that strained individuals, damaged goods and tied up scarce capital in goods in transit. The bad Portuguese roads ensured that the 350 km journey between Lisbon and Oporto took about a week. The newly crowned Adolphus-Frederick of Sweden, when touring his territories, was forced in 1752 to abandon his plan to return from Finland along the shore of the Gulf of Bothnia, because of the difficulty of crossing the rivers, the bad state of the roads and the impossibility of finding sufficient horses. In 1775 another new king, Louis XVI, had to alter his plans for touching for scrofula in Champagne because the roads were impracticable and the passage of the rivers uncertain.

Freight encountered difficulties with the road surface and the provision of draught animals. A wagon drawn by four horses pulling 4000 lb could rarely cover more than 20 miles daily. Poorly constructed roads often enforced the use of light carts and only two horses, increasing the number of carts necessary to move a given load and the consequent cost in manpower and forage. Still more often, burdens were limited to 2.5 cwt (280 lb) or so, which could be carried in panniers on a horse or mule, against the 10 cwt (1120 lb) which could be drawn by a single horse over good roads. Pack-horses were still very common in Britain's advancing areas even in the 1800s and the construction of good roads could therefore offer a fourfold increase in loads.

Often wagons and carts afforded merchandise only inadequate shelter, and the methods of packing and of moving heavy goods onto carts were primitive. Draught animals were affected by the weather and the availability of forage, and their supply was often limited. The land transportation of coal was restricted by the supply of mules and horses. In 1748 Venetian contractors were unable to find the 5000 mules required by the Austrian arms, in Italy.

These problems faced road transport over favourable terrain; in difficult terrain there were additional hazards. Road construction and maintenance techniques were of limited effectiveness in marshy regions or areas with a high water table, and mountainous terrain increased the need for draught animals and limited the speed of transport.

Some road improvements were made. A powerful incentive was governmental, with the need to move instructions, officials, armies and monarchs more swiftly. The improvements made on the St Petersburg–Moscow road between the death of Peter I (1725) and the 1760s, including the construction of bridges, reduced the journey time over its 825 km from five weeks to two. A critical commentator observed in 1772: 'The road from Naples as far as Barletta is very good, for which the public is obliged to the King's liking the chase of Bovino; as it is obliged for the road from Naples to Rome, to His Majesty's being married; Kings in these regions are not Kings of the People but the People, People of the Kings.'[1]

It is clear that economic motives also lay behind much road improvement, particularly when, as in northern Italy, different states would gain from any shift in trade routes. In 1748 over 500 labourers were employed in building a new road from Bologna to Florence which it was hoped would improve trade between Lombardy and Tuscany. Six years later, the Austrian government was worried about the effects on their possession of Milan of Genoese plans to build a major road from their port of Sestri to Parma. Philip V began a star of wagon roads radiating from Madrid to the various coasts of Spain, a scheme designed to foster political centralisation and to bring economic benefits. In the 1770s the Neapolitan government tried to build roads to open up the provinces.

Aristocrats were also aware of the economic advantages of better communications. In 1753 the Bavarian Baron Haslang pressed for the routing of the new road to Ingolstadt via his estate. The construction of a good road between Ath and Halle in the Austrian Netherlands in 1765–9 was due to the efforts of the duke of Aremberg. In 1779 Governor Sievers reported that the local inhabitants were happy to build a section of a highway that passed through a remote section of Novgorod province, because it promised to double or even treble the value of their produce.

By the end of the century there were signs of improvements in areas such as Spain, France (particularly Languedoc) and Savoy. The École des Ponts et Chaussées established in Paris in 1747 was partly responsible for the development of French bridge-building in the second half of the century. However, in general, road transportation was still bad. Main roads were often still primitive, that between Verviers and Aachen in 1785 being still in part 'a narrow sandy lane'.[2] There were major gaps, such as between Provence and Genoa, that prevent any depiction of an integrated system. The general stability in regional transportation networks and inter-urban spatial relationships reflected the limited construction of new routes. The enormous effort that was required for those that were built helps to explain the relative absence of significant change: the mountain road over the Col de Tende between Nice and Turin, finished in the 1780s, was the first complete opening of an alpine pass to wheeled traffic. It had taken 17 years to build. In Britain the government played a far smaller role. A sizeable network of 'turnpikes' was created, radiating from London by 1750 and from the major provincial centres by about 1770. By then, when there were 24,000 kilometres (15,000 miles) of turnpike road in England, most of the country was within 20 kilometres (12.5 miles) of one. The main impetus for this came from trade and the desire of local merchants and manufacturers for growth. Road improvements were also encouraged after the inauguration of the Royal Mail coach services from 1784. Turnpike roads were constructed by turnpike trusts authorised by Parliament to raise capital for such purposes and to charge travellers on the roads. Thus the road system came in part to reflect the degree of dynamism of individual trusts and the ability of particular routes to generate revenue.

The difficulties and cost of road transport helped to ensure that much was moved by sea or river. A Tuscan government enquiry in 1766 found that it cost as much to move goods overland from Pescia to Altopascio as on the water route from Altopascio to Livorno, which was six times as far. Water was particularly favourable for the movement of heavy or bulky goods, such as building stone from Savoy to Lyons. In 1703 the Swedes used the Vistula to move their heavy baggage and artillery in Poland.

However, the river system was not always helpful: many rivers were not navigable, transport was often only easy downstream, and many rivers were obstructed by mills and weirs. Furthermore, rivers did not always supply necessary links. This was clear in the case of St Petersburg, separated by the nearby continental divide from the Volga and Dnieper river systems that provided much of the rest of western Russia with a good network of trade routes. Instead the natural hinterland of the city was confined to a smaller and less developed area based on rivers draining into Lake Ladoga.

The canalisation of rivers and the construction of canals was the response to problems with the river system. It represented a determined human attempt to alter the environment and make it operate for the benefit of man. Canal construction was affected by considerations of terrain and political support: it was notably absent in the Balkans, a region whose infrastructure scarcely developed during the century; a factor which affected its ability to benefit from greater European trade. Political support and finance were crucial for canal development in France, Prussia, Russia and Spain. In order to increase industrial activity in central Spain, the government of Charles III planned a series of canals to link this region to the sea and thus overcome the centrifugal effects of geography upon the Spanish economy. The canal of Aragon, built in the 1780s alongside the Ebro, brought activity to the upper Ebro valley. In Prussia, Frederick the Great built a number of canals partly in order to move grain to the state granaries. In 1780 the river Ruhr was made navigable and exports of local coal rose. Four years later the Slesvig-Holstein canal between the North Sea and Kiel was opened.

Though there was some canal construction in Poland in the 1770s, nothing in eastern Europe compared to the level of Russian activity. Peter I was well aware of the importance of water transport between ports and the interior. His original intention was to profit from his conflict with Turkey in the 1690s in order to develop the port of Azov, near the mouth of the Don. In order to increase the commercial potential of his conquest, Peter ordered the construction of canals between the Don and the Volga and Oka. Forced to return Azov in 1711, Peter switched his attentions to the potential presented by his Baltic conquests. In 1709 the passage of a caravan of boats across the continental divide at Vyshnii Volochek, in a canal built by a Dutch expert to link the Neva and Volga systems, marked the first successful use of an artificial waterway in Russia. Further improvements led to the amount of freight passing through the waterways at Vyshnii Volochek rising from 2166 tons annually between 1712 and 1719 to a maximum of 216,000 tons annually in the 1750s. Additional improvements to the system later in the century included the extension of the aqueducts supplying additional water for the canals, the rebuilding of the reservoirs and locks in stone and the construction of sluices and dams on subsidiary waterways. In 1778 permanent staffs of officials were assigned to supervise the movement of boats through each part of the system and to improve navigation by removing rocks and other hazards. The number of boats passing through the canals at Vyshnii Volochek rose from 1707 in 1769 to 3958 in 1797. By 1811 Russia had one of the most extensive networks of inland waterways in the world.

A comparable canal and river improvement boom occurred in Britain, characterised by private enterprise and finance. By 1790 the rivers Trent, Mersey and Thames were linked by a canal network. There was no comparable expansion elsewhere, but nevertheless, canals were dug. In 1777 the Martesana canal from central Milan to the River Adda and then to Lecco was opened.

Canals were not free from problems. French schemes were affected adversely by government apathy, the hostility of vested interests, technical problems and a lack of capital. Of the three schemes for major canals advanced during the reign of Charles III of Spain, that for a canal linking Segovia to the Bay of Biscay was overambitious while the plan for one from Madrid to the Guadalquivir above Cordoba, linking central Spain to the Atlantic, remained at the planning stage. The Vyshnii Volochek system was affected by low water levels. However, canals clearly brought economic benefits, particularly to Russia and Britain. If the development of such a costly and inflexible transport system reflected the difficulties of moving bulky goods cheaply by road transport, it also increased the comparative economic advantage of particular regions, or interests within them.

There was little improvement in the condition of European marine transport during the century. It still remained heavily dependent on the weather, as Charles XII of Sweden discovered when a storm disrupted the movement of troops from Sweden to her Baltic provinces in October 1700. The seasonal variation of insurance rates reflected the vulnerability of wind-powered wooden ships, which had not yet reached their mid-nineteenth-century levels of design efficiency. Sea travel was very slow compared with what it was to become in the following century. However, it was the cheapest method for the movement of goods and the sea brought together regions, such as south-western Scotland and eastern Ireland, or north-western Spain and western France, whose road links to their own hinterlands were poor.

Changes in transportation were limited during the century. Exciting technical developments, such as the hot-air balloons of the 1780s, and railroads, had scant impact, although recent industrial archaeological activity in north-east England suggests that railway development as early as the 1780s should not be underestimated, with rails used for speeding up horse-drawn traffic in collieries and on wharfs. Relatively few new European transport routes were developed, and road construction usually followed existing routes, as in Languedoc. The balance between water and land transport did not alter significantly, the major changes coming only in the following century. Poor communications had obvious economic consequences. By making the land transport of bulky goods expensive they helped to limit regional specialisation.

Yet, where they were constructed, canals and improved roads were clearly of considerable importance in shrinking distances and developing intra-regional links. New and improved transport routes required large amounts of capital and led to increased employment. Transport costs were reduced, thus helping to increase and extend consumption and markets. The increased speed and frequency of deliveries also improved the integration of production and consumption and furthered the development of the market; it became easier to dispatch salesmen, samples, catalogues, orders and replacements.

This was not the situation across much of Europe. In Portugal, for example, the bad state of the roads and limited number of navigable rivers protected local industry from imports. In Europe as a whole, the dense network of local routes changed very little during the century, in quality, direction or use, though levels of use appear to have increased.

Money, standards and credit

The currency and credit systems of Europe also limited economic activity. In the case of currency there were problems with standardisation and supply. The circulation of different types of coin within individual states was but part of a more general problem of varying standards. One such affected time. Different calendars were in use in Europe: New Style dating, used by the bulk of Europe, was eleven days ahead of Old Style and it was only in 1700 that the division of the United Provinces into two calendar zones ended. In 1700 Russia shifted to Old Style from 7208, the supposed number of years from the creation. Between 1700 and 1712 Sweden was one day ahead of Old Style. In 1752 Britain switched from Old to New Style calendar, to be followed by Sweden, but not Russia.

Weights and measures also varied greatly, not just in Europe but inside individual states. The diversity of legal codes within states was also a hindrance to economic activity. In France, despite the calls of many writers, including the physiocrats and encyclopedists, for a rational system of uniformity in weights and measures, the government judged the situation too complex and delicate to reform, and new standardised measures did not come until the metric units of the 1790s: on 1 August 1793 the National Convention accepted the idea of what were presented as natural units: the metre, kilogram and litre. The decimal system was also adopted in the new calendar that was decreed on 24 November 1793. Months were to be of equal length.

In Naples tariff reform was intertwined with the question of the diversity of weights and measures. It would have been impossible to introduce a uniform duty on the export of olive oil, as the reformers wished, without first establishing a uniform measure and no such progress was made. In Prussia, in contrast, the 12 different ways of measuring length in common use were standardised in 1773, whereas in Britain throughout the century each region had its own variants on such customary measures as tons, chaldrons and bushels.

In the case of coinage, governments tried, in general, to achieve standardisation. France possessed a common coinage and in 1718 coins were struck simultaneously in the major regions of Spain. Moreover, currency within Britain had differing values. The Irish pound was worth less than the English; from 1701 the official value of the Irish pound was £108 6s 7d to £100 English (or 13 pence to the English shilling). An additional problem with coinage in the Empire (Germany) was that substantial sums were lost in *agio*, the costs of exchange between the different legal coinages in circulation. The livre used in Savoy was separate from the Piedmontese lira, the former following the movements of the French money market, the latter those of Milan and Genoa. Nevertheless, in 1755 Charles Emmanuel III, king of Sardinia, ruler of Savoy-Piedmont, issued an edict to regulate the coinage that also extended to Savoy. A general shortage of specie was a significant problem for the European economy. It led to the circulation of coins in foreign countries, with Portuguese gold and Spanish silver coins circulating in England and Austrian and Spanish silver coins in the Turkish Empire. Spanish dollars, overstruck as worth 4s and 9d, were common in Scotland in the second half of the century.

Despite the growth of Portuguese gold supplies from Brazil and the production of Russian silver in the Amur valley and the Altai,[3] there was an insufficient supply of bullion to meet the coinage needs of Europe. Much of the American production of silver and gold was lost to areas with which Europe had a negative trade balance, principally China and India. Bullion was also reduced through use in non-monetary forms and through the continuous loss of metal from coins due to processes such as wear, reminting and fraudulent clipping.

Most of Europe was on a silver standard, but there were inadequate supplies to meet demand. This situation helped to lead to recoining, as in Prussia in 1767, and debasement, as in Prussia during the Seven Years War. It also led to shortages of coinage, as in Vienna in 1786 when silver coin was in very short supply. These shortages necessitated the use of paper money, introduced, for example, in Austria in 1761 to help pay for the Seven Years War. The use of negotiable paper was not new in Europe, the bill of exchange already being a common medium of mercantile transaction. The eighteenth century witnessed the spread both of banking and of banknotes. However, the precarious nature of most banking firms and institutions and their close relationship with government and state finance created difficulties.

State manipulation of financial mechanisms in order to obtain credit limited confidence in paper money in much of Europe, a situation compounded by relatively limited experience of national banking, related credit markets and currency mechanisms. The absence of a state bank in France owed much to the oscillations of national credit in the first two decades of the century. Delays in the striking and delivery of new coins by the Paris mint led in 1701 to the issue of certificates, known as *billets de monnaie*, to the owners of old coins and bullion delivered for recoinage. These were overissued and consequently depreciated in value. Inadequate tax revenues led to the need to finance the War of the Spanish Succession (1701–14) by borrowing and, in addition to the *billets de monnaie*, bills were issued on other agencies involved in royal finance, such as the Receivers-General and the General Tax Farmers. By 1708 the total had reached about 800 million livres and Desmaretz, who became controller-general of finance that year, partially repudiated the *billets de monnaie* by converting the 800 million into 250 million livres of *billets d'état*. However, confidence in the new *billets*, as in their predecessors, was limited by the government's refusal to accept them as payment for taxes, though it used them to pay bills. The fluctuating value of these units of paper currency hampered trade, and general confidence was further lessened by the government's capital debt, which was sufficiently large for several economic advisers after Louis XIV's death in 1715 to suggest a default. The deflationary policy pursued by Desmaretz from 1713 led to a reduction in the availability of cash and a consequent fall in commercial activity as coin was hoarded. The small reserves of undercapitalised Parisian banks helped to ensure bankruptcies in 1715.

The duke of Orléans, regent for Louis XV, who had succeeded to the throne at the age of 5 in 1715, became increasingly involved with John Law, the Scot who in 1716 was authorised to establish a private bank. Law believed in the demonetisation of specie and its replacement by paper credit. Arguing that the circulation of money was a source of wealth, Law was a supporter of an expansionary monetary policy that would lower interest rates, with banknotes serving to stimulate the economy, particularly underutilised agricultural resources. Increased circulation of money would thus, he hoped, improve the income of community and king. Orléans' support allowed Law to implement some of his plans. In 1717 he founded the Mississippi Company to exploit the economic potential believed to be present in the fledgling colony of Louisiana. In 1718 his bank became the state bank, owned by the king, and in 1719 the Mississippi Company, renamed the Company of the Indies, absorbed all the other French oceanic trading companies.

Already in control of a monopolistic commercial empire, Law moved to tackle national fiscal problems. In 1719 he acquired the sole right to coin money, and the Company of the Indies took over the national debt and became responsible for collecting direct and indirect taxes. The merger of bank and company in February 1720 created a commercial monopolistic company that was also the sole issuing bank. Law, created controller-general, hoped that confidence, colonial profits and economic growth would keep the system buoyant, but it fell victim to speculation in the shares of the company and a massive increase in the amount of paper money issued by the bank, neither of which was related to its bullion reserves. Public confidence and the value of the shares collapsed in the spring, Law was dismissed and the bank closed. By November 1720 banknotes could not be given or received in any financial transactions; the system of paper currency had collapsed.

Law's system brought some benefits to France in 1716–19, including a measure of economic growth and a certain redistribution of wealth. However, its crash in 1720 sapped confidence in the idea of national financial institutions and ensured that public banking played little part thereafter in pre-revolutionary France. The discount bank established in 1776 was a relative failure partly because it was compelled to make excessive loans to the government.

Similar problems of confidence affected other European attempts in public banking. The Spanish government's project of 1749 to establish a general bank that could deal in letters of exchange with all of Europe ran into problems as the merchants were willing to borrow money from it, but not to provide money in return for its letters of exchange. This exacerbated the general problem of the export of Spanish coinage. A negative trade balance with France led to French towns like Toulouse becoming important centres for dealing in Spanish coin.

A visitor to Rome in 1768 noted that the taxes there were heavy, that coin was both bad and scarce and 'that both bankers and shopkeepers are forced to receive and pay, if the sum be considerable, in paper: and this very paper, however authorized by the public banks, is, when carried thither, refused to be paid in cash'.[4] Experiments with public banks were not always successful. The relationship between new financial devices and the fiscal needs of government could reduce confidence. The barrier to a significant increase in the Swedish money supply was removed in 1745 when the government started to print paper notes. This led to the danger of serious inflation, which was realised when the value of the Swedish currency could not be sustained during the major expansion of the money supply that accompanied participation in the Seven Years War. The economic consequences of the mid-century changes were serious for Sweden. The rate of exchange on Amsterdam, the price of the Dutch rix-dollar expressed in Swedish coinage, remained singularly stable around parity in the years 1740–55. In 1755 the rate began to rise significantly and the situation deteriorated during the Seven Years War. The rate of exchange was then forced down rapidly during the deflationary crisis of 1765–8, only to climb again from 1769. The devaluation of 1776 brought a measure of stability that lasted until 1789. As Swedish commerce and industrial production were dependent upon Dutch credits, largely because Dutch rates of interest were lower and capital more plentiful, these changes created difficulties. During the deflation of 1765–8 prices fell faster than the costs of production, causing economic losses and a rise in debt. The change in the value of the Swedish coinage in 1776 caused further confusion.

Russia was affected by a chronic shortage of capital that obliged the government to play a major role. The Exchange Act of 1729 legalised the use of bills of exchange and set up a network of exchange offices around the country. The effectiveness of the legislation was limited by the law's prohibition of peasant endorsement of bills and by the lack of sufficient legal guarantees for commercial operations. The situation was exacerbated by the absence of deposit banks and the rapid depreciation of financial paper. In mid-century the government sought to establish formal institutions of commercial credit. The first Russian banks, the Nobles' Bank and the Bank for the Improvement of the Trade of St Petersburg, were founded in 1754, the Astrakhan Bank a decade later. The St Petersburg Bank closed, however, in 1782 with depleted reserves. Although these banks did help in the financing of foreign trade, they did not develop into a significant system of commercial credit and they played little role in the development of the financing of domestic trade.

Finance remained a problem for Russian merchants who, in the absence of established credit institutions, had to rely on private credit, usually offered at very high interest rates because of the number of defaults. Similarly, private mercantile capital and aristocratic resources both played a large role in the development of Russian industry. The high rate of interest hindered economic expansion. Catherine II was concerned about the economic consequences of the financial system. In 1764 she complained to the procurator-general Viazemsky that there was an insufficient quantity of money in circulation. The Russian manifesto of 1768, explaining the decision to establish an Assignat Bank and print paper money, argued that it was necessary to overcome the effects of distance and the weight of copper coins in order to improve the circulation of money and thus encourage economic development. The absence of local banks that might aid in the turnover of private capital and issue financial paper was responsible for the setting up of the Assignat Banks. An issue of 3.5 million roubles was anticipated, but by 1796, 157 million were in circulation, helping to produce depreciation and inflation. Further difficulties in Russia were created by the fact that the hard currency area of the rouble did not cover all of the country. The Baltic conquests continued to have a different local currency.

Public financing of economic activity was important in other areas of Europe as well, the state intervention in the economy, termed mercantilism, in part being made necessary by the weakness of the financial system. Governmental foundation of industrial enterprises often reflected the absence of sufficient capital accumulation in private hands or an unwillingness to invest. This was the case in Austria, Prussia and Savoy-Piedmont. Prussian schemes in the 1730s for the establishment of an East India Company based at Königsberg, Stettin or Lentzen were handicapped by the unwillingness of Hamburg merchants, the principal source of north German mercantile capital, to invest in Prussia. In 1765 the Berlin Discount and Loans Bank was founded by the government to provide loans to merchants and manufacturers. Prussian provincial governments formed credit institutions to help keep estates intact. Much of the credit finance system in neighbouring Poland was handled by periodical assemblies held to conduct financial transactions; these became the meeting place of the local gentry. The risks of investment in Poland were such that many enterprises were feasible only for great aristocrats whose manufacturing activities were based on their own resources.

In France, credit was provided by private individuals or consortia. Most was urban in origin. The bankers of Montpellier were recruited primarily from among the local wool merchants, clothiers and financial officials. Regional credit was often used substantially for land purchase and fiscal arrangements related to state finance, rather than for commercial enterprises. This was the case in Montpellier. Despite diversification, land overwhelmingly remained the priority for elite investment. Significant commercial activity tended to look for its credit, as for its political support, to Paris, thus helping to increase its dependence on the vicissitudes of national credit. While Mediterranean commerce at the beginning of the century remained largely a monopoly of Marseilles, Parisian financiers were significantly involved in or actually dominated almost all the other commercial companies. In the 1780s merchants in the French ports relied on Parisian financiers for credit and basic banking facilities. French interest rates varied greatly. Government borrowing drove up the cost of credit. In 1786, interest rates of 10 per cent for commercial loans to French merchants were normal.

The nature of the French financial system had harmful economic effects. Financiers' investments were generally short-term, while investment in the economy, in large-scale manufacturing plant, in canals, and in schemes of agricultural improvement, such as irrigation, or in oceanic trade, required longer-term commitments. Much of the French economy was undercapitalised. In the 1780s many of the Bordeaux merchant firms trading with France's West Indian colonies were financially weak with a limited margin of security and little liquid money. Most fixed capital sums needed for manufacturing were comparatively modest as there was little need for specialised buildings and they could often be adapted from corn or other mills. The machinery was mostly simple. However, glass-, iron- and pottery-works could be very costly, especially where investment in infrastructure was involved. As a result, the proposals late in the century for economic flour-milling called for loans to millers from regional and local institutions for conversion purposes.

Britain and the United Provinces had a more sophisticated credit system. The Dutch had the most highly developed financial institutions in the world, including futures markets and an important maritime insurance industry. The Bank of Amsterdam, a municipal institution, had substantial reserves and a large number of depositors. The generally high level of financial confidence helped to keep interest rates low, and to encourage

Amsterdam's role as an international financial centre. The economic consequences of the latter are ambiguous. Much Dutch money was invested abroad, particularly in London and Paris, and frequently in government borrowing, rather than commercial enterprise. Such loans were not always a good investment, as they could be affected by international developments and since many governments did not deserve a good credit rating. In 1770 the Russian government found little interest in Amsterdam in its proposals for a new loan as the lenders on the last one had lost money. It is unclear how far the sophisticated Dutch financial system siphoned wealth abroad. It has been held partially responsible for the Dutch failure to industrialise, but other factors, such as high wage rates and the protectionist policies of potential markets, have to be considered. Continued Dutch commercial strength owed much to the Dutch financial system.

In Britain the Bank of England, founded in 1694, operated successfully as a source of government credit and this helped to bring relative stability and growth to the banking system. Banking houses, single-unit partnerships with unlimited liability for their losses, developed in London and the provinces, especially in the second half of the century. By the end of the century there were several hundred provincial banks, highly local in their operation, helping to keep the money supply buoyant and circulating and to spread credit. These developments were not without their problems, as a growth in the role of credit helped to make the economic system more vulnerable to international financial problems, such as the speculative boom in Britain, France and the United Provinces at the end of the 1710s and the widespread crisis in state liquidity in the late 1760s and early 1770s.

One sign of greater European financial awareness was that the traditional clipping of coins was increasingly matched by the counterfeiting of paper currency. Turin was overrun with counterfeit bank bills in 1762. As with so much else, the financial situation and its economic consequences varied widely in Europe. If the currency of the Austrian Netherlands, Liège and much of the Empire was reasonably stable in the first half of the century, that of France was not between 1689 and 1726. In Nantes in July 1715 there was a general complaint of an absence of money and trade and many merchants were close to bankruptcy. Merchants would not sell their substantial stocks of wine and brandy, refusing both money and bills, because they were anticipating an alteration in the coinage. In general, the century witnessed increasingly complex commercial mechanisms with the growing use of bills of exchange, *bourses*, multilateral transactions and sales on commission. However, credit and currency difficulties remained a significant problem for economic activity, particularly commerce. If the spread of the money economy played an important role in integrating European trade, problems with the supply and reliability of money and credit restricted this development.

Trade

The volume of European trade rose during the century. Figures are most extensive and reliable for distant and, in particular, international trade as that presented governments with the greatest opportunities for taxation. Smuggling reduces the reliability of statistics, while the usefulness of individual series is affected by changes in international relations and shifts in the patterns of economic activity. Nevertheless, the general picture is of a significant peacetime rise in trade. The average annual traffic on the Rhine between Mainz and Strasbourg, a crucial route, grew by 70 per cent between the 1740s and the 1780s, the rise becoming especially marked after 1770, in common with so many other economic indicators. Reasonably good statistics exist for Baltic trade. In 1730 about 4000 ships annually paid the dues for passing through the Sound, another very important route. In 1784–95 inclusive, 118,933 ships sailed through the Sound both ways and were registered in the Sound Books, a numerical increase that was accompanied by a rise in tonnage and in international commercial transactions in leading Baltic ports, such as St Petersburg.

Colonial and trans-oceanic trade was another major area of expansion, and imports of colonial and trans-oceanic goods rose markedly. Whereas in 1660 Marseilles had imported only 19,000 quintaux of coffee, of Yemeni origin, from Egypt, in 1785 it imported 143,310 quintaux, of which 142,500 came from the West Indies, in other words from a region of European colonial control. Introduced to Martinique and Guadeloupe in 1725 and Saint-Domingue in 1730, French West Indian coffee was more popular than that produced by the Dutch in Indonesia, and it swiftly became the principal global source: 350,000 quintaux were produced in 1770 and over 950,000 in 1790: most went to France and much was then re-exported, from Marseilles principally to the Turkish empire.

Not all goods enjoyed comparable growth or made such an impact. However, increases in sugar, tobacco, cotton and rice imports were marked. They were principally obtained by the western European powers and their re-export became a significant source of wealth to ports such as Le Havre, Nantes and Bordeaux. Bordeaux's imports of sugar, indigo and cocoa from the French West Indies tripled in 1717–20, the beginning of a massive increase in re-exports to northern Europe. At Bordeaux the colonial trade was conducted by French merchants, but re-exports were largely controlled by foreign firms established in the town. At the beginning of the century most were Dutch, but by 1730 there was a significant German presence. The outbreak of the fourth Anglo-Dutch war in 1780 led to a rise in Antwerp's importance. European involvement in slavery and the slave trade was a very harmful facet of the marked growth in trans-Atlantic trade.

As in the previous century, the opportunities apparently offered by trans-oceanic trade encouraged other powers to attempt to gain a share, principally by the foundation of char-tered trading companies. The Ostend Company, based in the Austrian Netherlands, the Prussian East India Company, based at Emden in East Friesland, and the Swedish East India Company were only the most prominent examples of a more general interest. The Swedish company, created at the start of the century, received a royal charter in 1731. Initially it was heav-ily dependent, like the Emden and Ostend companies, on for-eign capital, contacts, expertise and shipping. The first four ships of the Emden company were purchased in Amsterdam and England. The Swedish company traded with China, exporting Spanish silver coins obtained at Cadiz and importing tea, porce-lain and silk. Investors received high dividends and the trade of the company increased from an annual average of 1,600,000 rix-dollars in 1738–40 to one of 2,290,000 in 1744–6. The new companies competed for European markets and helped to depress prices, making goods from the Orient more affordable. Attempts to continue the activities of the Ostend company, after it was suppressed in 1731 as a result of Anglo-Dutch pressure, threatened British tea sales in Hamburg, one of the leading European markets for colonial products. In 1753 the price of tea at Hamburg fell as a result of sales there of cargoes imported by Danish, Prussian and Swedish companies. Colonial products stimulated internal European trade as they were transported to consumers, and increasingly so as they became less expensive. Towards the end of the century Milanese merchants brought cof-fee, chocolate, sugar and spices to Switzerland, purchasing the muslins of St Gall and Zürich in return.

Trans-oceanic areas were not simply a source of products. They also became a significant market for European goods. This was not so much true of the Orient, where the taste for European manufactures was limited, as of the western hemisphere. There colonies with a large European population and relatively high

wage rates were willing and able to purchase European manufactured goods in return for their bullion and their plantation
crops. The struggle to supply goods to the Spanish empire was,
especially in the first half of the century, as sharp as that to sell
colonial goods to Europe, the two being intertwined. In mercantile and, increasingly, in political circles, international disputes,
such as the War of the Spanish Succession, took on the appearance of a struggle to control markets. These were especially
important to Britain and France. In 1741–2 Bordeaux exported
over 8 million livres' worth of produce to the French West Indian
colonies annually, principally wine and textiles. The comparable
figure for 1753–5 was over 10 million. For French manufacturing
towns, such as Elbeuf, Spain and the Spanish empire were an
important market.

However, while France, thanks partly to cheaper sugar from
her new West Indian plantations, increasingly beat Britain in the
European re-export trade, Britain was more successful in obtaining colonial markets for her manufactures. This was partly due to
political factors. The French were disappointed by the unwillingness of their Spanish allies to open up their empire to French
commercial penetration. In contrast, in the first half of the century, Portugal and its Brazilian empire took significant quantities
of British products, particularly textiles, paying for them with
Brazilian gold, which helped to keep the British financial system
buoyant and to finance British trades that showed a negative balance. Financial buoyancy was particularly important in long-
distance trade in which new ships lasted only for two or three
voyages, financial returns were delayed, and merchants needed
to obtain long-term credit on favourable terms. French defeat in
the Seven Years War (1756–63) was also significant, particularly
in India, where British predominance was ensured, and in North
America, where the threat of French encirclement of the market
occupied by British colonists was ended. In 1763 France lost
Canada to Britain and Louisiana to Spain, neither yet well populated or a significant market, but both possessing considerable
potential. Whereas British trade with Asia rose to a significant
percentage of her total trade, France's did not.

British trade with her North American colonies was upset during the American War of Independence, but, thereafter, in defiance of traditional mercantilist assumptions that linked commerce
to politically controlled markets, trade rose. The newly independent state was populous and lacked the range of British industrial
production. This was particularly fortunate for Britain, as the
1780s witnessed difficult industrial and commercial conditions in
western and central Europe which provided added incentives for

the expansion of foreign trade to cope with temporary industrial over-expansion or the contraction of internal markets. The French were particularly hopeful of Russia, with whom they signed a commercial treaty in 1787. However, although trade with Russia grew, she did not become a leading commercial partner. This was but part of a more general disappointment experienced by Austrian and western European merchants who had hoped to create new markets. The small population of the Ukrainian hinterland, poor communications, the over-extension of credit to Russian buyers and the rarity of 'sound money' in Russia were serious problems, though more significant was the outbreak of a major Balkan War in 1787.

Trade regulation

War was not the only way in which governments affected trade. Economic regulation was also significant. This took two linked forms, attempts to influence production and trade for industrial and commercial reasons, and fiscal policies both to secure these ends and to raise revenues. The pressure for regulation varied by country, period and activity, but it commonly represented a symbiotic relationship between government and certain economic interests. It would be inaccurate to regard regulation as something imposed by government on the economy, or as stemming simply from ministerial ideas. Instead regulation was central to most forms of agricultural, industrial and commercial activity and was present at most levels of the economy, whether in the form of guild restrictions on manufacturing practices or of agreements over the use of common lands or regulations over markets. Regulation was rooted in both elite and popular attitudes, and reflected cultural notions of order and stability.

Government, whether seigneurial, municipal, provincial or national, entailed the regulation of economic activity and this was actively sought by interested parties. In the case of the Krefeld silk industry, an alliance between the Prussian government and a small number of silk enterprises suppressed entrepreneurial initiatives which arose outside the circle of the small number of Krefeld producers. French commerce in the first decade of the century was regulated partly in accordance with the views of the Council of Commerce established in 1700. Far from advocating free-trade policies the deputies of the Council, selected by the leading commercial towns, were protectionist in outlook and their pleas for liberty were based on the traditional support of rights and privileges. Believing in the importance of the balance of trade and of maintaining large reserves of bullion, the deputies sought to achieve these objectives collectively through a symbiotic relationship between government and commerce, and individually by obtaining state support for specific privileges. More generally, the ambiguities latent in any symbiotic relationship were exacerbated by the continual struggle by interested parties for privileges. This was accompanied by a degree of uncertainty in many governments as to how best to attain agreed economic objectives. Differences of opinion over general policy and disputes over specific privileges combined to produce disputes over how best to regulate economic activity.

The stress on state action was particularly marked in the first half of the century, and was characteristic of the economic thought known as mercantilism. Mercantilism was not so much a common body of economic thought, since much writing involved special pleading, as, more often, a set of characteristic biases. Most writers did not favour the competitive market mechanism as the basis for the allocation of investment. There was little appreciation of the free market as an automatic adjusting mechanism, partly because the pursuit of private profit was not applauded, but seen rather as self-interest and opposed to communal prosperity. By regarding the individualistic pursuit of profit as hostile to the public interest, writers revealed and strengthened their bias in favour of control and regulation.

Further stress on state activity was provided by the belief that economic activity was both naturally and actually competitive. This was particularly appropriate in the fields of colonial activity, oceanic trade and bullion where the objects of competition were felt, with reason, to be essentially limited. Most of the policies loosely termed mercantilist were, in their intention, aggressive. In a context where one state pursued such policies it was necessary for others to reply in kind. Calls for free trade and criticisms of protectionist commercial systems and such devices as monopolistic national trading companies and colonial policies, such as those advanced by the Glaswegian economist Adam Smith in his *Wealth of Nations* (1776), were intellectually satisfying as indicators of how much better the world might be organised. However, it did not follow that any of the individual states would have done better unilaterally to abandon its protective tariffs, trading companies and colonies. The alternative to mercantilist policies was not free trade but, in many instances, no trade. The trading areas not colonised by one power were going to be colonised by another. Even Great Britain, where belief in a degree of economic freedom (laissez-faire) grew in the second half of the century, did not abandon many of its protective policies until the mid-nineteenth century.

The concentration in economic thinking on long-distance trade, rather than on agriculture, accentuated the stress on government activity. Such trade was felt to require state assistance, military, political, financial and regulatory. The heavy investment required to finance distant trade and to develop such features as colonial trading stations was best secured by granting monopolistic privileges. Trade played a large role in the economic thought of government. The economic development and financial strength of Britain and the United Provinces were a powerful spur in this direction, as was the sense of opportunity associated with exploration and the anticipation of new markets and sources of supply. This was particularly marked in the case of the Pacific at the beginning of the century, the sense of opportunity playing a role in British and French keenness to develop trade to the 'South Seas'. Economic writers, entrepreneurs and speculators pressed governments to take a role in the economy. Geronimo de Ustariz, the author of *The Theory and Practice of Commerce and Maritime Affairs* (Madrid, 1724), was an admirer of Louis XIV's minister of the marine, Jean-Baptiste Colbert, who had supported state activity, and emphasised the need to use the government's power in order to help Spain catch up in the race for economic growth. Ustariz saw overseas trade as the key to development. Similarly, Frederick II, in his *Essay on the Forms of Government*, argued that it was essential to maintain a favourable balance of trade.

The first half of the century saw much government activity in the shape of new national trading companies and of conciliar bodies for the encouragement of trade. In Russia in the 1700s the liberties previously enjoyed by merchants and manufacturers were replaced by detailed state regulation and by monopolies. A college (ministry) for commercial affairs was set up in 1718. A commerce commission was established in Russia in 1758 which concentrated on methods for increasing trade, reducing restrictions and appointing more honest and well-informed officials. As was common with economic councils elsewhere, it devoted its attention to industry and trade rather than agriculture. Conquered areas were forcibly integrated with the Russian economy. Ukrainian merchants lost their freedom to trade wherever they wished and in 1714 were ordered to shift their business to Russian ports. Their loss of trade routes to Poland and Turkey helped cause the decline of the Ukrainian economy. In 1719 the export of Ukrainian wheat was forbidden so that the Russian government could buy it for its own use at a very low price. A stringent system of import duties was created to prevent the import of finished products, and Russian merchants were given preferential treatment in the export of goods to the Ukraine, forcing many local merchants out of business.

Conciliar bodies were seen as important to the Danish economy. In 1704 Frederick IV revived the College of Commerce that had operated from 1670 to 1691. It declined after 1711, but, in the meantime, played a valuable role in regulating trade and industry, though its proposals for a monopolistic joint-stock company to handle trade with the Danish possession of Iceland and for a bank in Copenhagen failed. An Economic and Commercial College was set up in 1735 and it was responsible for a number of major measures aimed at easing the serious crisis in the Danish economy.

Much government activity took the form of action to redirect the channels of commerce. This generally entailed restrictions on rival products, trade and traders, and moves to encourage native activity. Prohibitions and tariffs were commonly used. Particular effort was directed to ensure that foreign traders did not play a role in native commerce. In the Prussian town of Königsberg in 1716 foreign merchants were prohibited from trading both with non-local people and with nearby ports such as Danzig, Elbing and Memel. The town was an important supplier of salt to Poland and the government supported local attempts to limit foreign participation in this trade by banning the storing of salt by importers. In 1724 Sweden prohibited trade between Swedish ports in the ships of other powers. In 1747 Frederick the Great interrupted Saxon trade with Hamburg by making all ships on the Elbe unload at his town of Magdeburg and the goods move overland through Prussia before being loaded on Elbe ships again.

Economic regulation was not restricted to international trade. Internal tariffs and prohibitions were common and one of the principal strengths of the British Empire was the relative lack of such devices and their total absence within England. In contrast, states such as France, Prussia and Russia limited internal trade by their systems of regulation. There was a complicated system of internal customs barriers in France. French cider-based liqueurs could only be sold in Normandy and Brittany lest they compete with the wine brandies which alone could be sold to Paris and the French colonies. Mid-century Norman requests for permission to sell to the colonies were rejected. French wine was taxed at the entrance to major towns such as Lyons and Paris. To help the Berlin silk industry, Prussian officials tried to protect it from competition. In 1749 imports of velvet to Prussian territories east of the river Weser were banned, including that produced in the Prussian town of Krefeld. Similarly in 1768 a general import embargo on manufactured goods produced in the Rhineland and Westphalia harmed some Prussian producers.

In the second half of the century contradictory attitudes to economic regulation can be discerned. The most striking was between policies of continued regulation and, in particular, the protection of native industry and commerce by prohibiting foreign rivals, and the call for free or freer trade. There was, however, a distinction between internal and international commerce. The former received less regulation in the second half of the century. In 1748 free internal trade in the Papal States was introduced. In 1775 a common customs tariff for the Habsburgs' German hereditary dominions was introduced. A general customs tariff was advocated in Poland. In 1765 the domestic trade in Spanish cereals was freed, while in 1778 the regulations limiting Spanish trade with the Spanish colonies in America were eased.

However, the easing of regulations on domestic economic activities was not supported by all. Many had benefited from regulations such as monopolies and sought to maintain them. As in international trade, there was a symbiotic relationship between government and certain economic groups and, just as restrictions on international competition were maintained and privileges sought, so there was also pressure for a comparable position in the domestic economy. The existence in countries such as France of a vast network of interests, institutions and corporative regulations made it necessary for industrial and commercial concerns, particularly new ones, to seek privileges. Such pressure revealed divisions of opinion within government as well as within the economic community. In general, there was greater support for the relaxation of regulations governing domestic economic activities than for taking steps to permit competition from foreign goods. In 1747 Jean-Claude Vincent de Gournay became *intendant* of commerce in France and began to press for free trade and the ending of government regulation of industry. In 1755 he suggested that the Company of the Indies lose its monopoly of France's oriental commerce and argued that this would lead to a growth in French trade. Gournay suggested that, in place of 12 ships making the annual voyage to the Orient, there would be 100. A decade later Nicolas Bacon, a councillor responsible for commercial affairs in Brussels, pressed the provincial government to reduce regulations and curtail the powers of the guilds.

Guilds and protection

A particular butt of criticism were the guilds, corporative institutions which regulated much urban industry and commerce, and

were an aspect of workers' efforts to protect their pay and conditions. The weakness of guilds as a regulatory device was a
dependence on urban government at a time when national governments were taking an increasing role in economic regulation
and were the most effective allies of those seeking support, as
oceanic trading companies appreciated. Guild regulations fulfilled a vital function in providing quality controls and legal
codes in many areas of economic activity, but they, also, served to
restrict the numbers of those engaged in particular trades and
hindered the spread of innovative techniques and practices. In
the early decades of the century, for example, the bakers of the
town of Enghien in the Austrian Netherlands passed statutes to
protect their privileges from newcomers and rivals. Guilds in
eighteenth-century Ireland were an important agency of Protestant supremacy. Those, predominantly Catholics, who practised
trades with which the guilds were concerned but who were unable
to become members were obliged to pay quarterage.

More generally, the guilds often appeared to have little interest in the fate of other producers. The ordered economic world
that guilds sought to defend and police could be regarded as
inimical to economic growth. Many governments adopted a hostile attitude to corporate groups that regulated economic activity,
particularly if this regulation appeared to be independent of central governmental control.

Peter the Great was opposed to privileged mercantile corporations. He felt that their stress on privilege was bad for the economy and that the expanded bureaucracy that was a significant
product of his reign made their service function of advising the
sovereign unnecessary. Peter established craft guilds to regulate
the relationship of masters and apprentices, hitherto left to custom, but they were a creation of government, lacking special
privileges, and their membership was not an exclusive right
passed on by inheritance. Elsewhere in Europe, guilds were
brought increasingly under government control. In the Empire,
governments greatly mistrusted the guilds because of their inter-
state links, such as the organisation to look after travelling journeymen. In 1732–5 Frederick William I reorganised the guilds,
retaining them for regulatory and training purposes at the same
time as they were made responsive to government interests. In
1772 the town of Bruges attacked the privileges of the largely
hereditary corporation of butchers and allowed whoever wished
to do so to sell meat on two days a week. This led to a fall in the
price of meat. Joseph II's ordinance of 1786 ending the guilds'
monopoly of trade encouraged cottage industries.

The effects of the moves against guilds varied. In the Austrian
Netherlands the monopolistic control of guilds over trade and

industry was significantly lessened. In addition, the balance between guilds and government in the initiation of economic regulation was shifted towards central power. Much depended on the nature of the individual industry or trade. By the 1780s the guild structure in the cotton industry in Troyes in France had begun to collapse as a result of the extension of the putting-out system into the countryside and the influx of new workers. Mechanisation did not require traditional skills, and non-guild labour, such as children, could be used. In Rouen, in contrast, the guild structure continued, the manufacture of woollen cloth requiring greater skills.

On the whole, government attitudes towards guilds can be best understood in terms of co-operation on ministerial terms rather than suppression. This was in accord with the widespread attitude towards both privilege in general and economic matters in particular. The task of governments was one of balancing between competing needs and contrasting interests while bereft of the administrative structure that would enable an effective assessment, let alone supervision, of the economy.

In some countries, the second half of the century witnessed a continued attempt by governments to intervene directly in a traditional fashion in the regulation of domestic activity. In general, government knowledge of economic affairs and of the economy of particular states increased. Some rulers displayed a marked interest in such matters. Karl Friedrich, margrave of Baden-Durlach, founded an Economic Society in Karlsruhe in 1763 and in 1772 wrote a *Summary of the Principles of Political Economy*. Nevertheless, government control of economic life remained limited, if only because of administrative weaknesses, a limitation masked often by the firm language of government regulations. There was a continued dependence on advice and on the regulatory assistance of others. During the reign of Catherine II the merchants of St Petersburg elected some of the local customs officers. The relationship between government regulation and particular economic privileges frequently matched that between government supervision and reliance on the administrative assistance of others. This relationship probably eased the burden of regulation and may have helped to foster a certain incoherence in government policy, as regulation in one sphere contrasted in intention and/or method with the situation in another. In the case of the Neapolitan silk industry the attitudes of the reformers betrayed a considerable degree of inconsistency and mercantilist and laissez-faire views co-existed uneasily.

There was a general ambiguity in the concept of economic freedom. Liberty was commonly seen not as a rival of royal authority, but as a result of its support for economic activity, particularly in the form of privilege, which could be regarded as a distinguishing mark of economic freedom that did not deny liberty to others. In a society organised on a corporative basis, initiatives could often flourish best under the protection provided by exemptions and privileges. This attitude did not mean that everyone necessarily accepted the disposal of privilege. To stimulate coal production in Languedoc in the 1770s, the French government granted regional monopolies of exploitation to individuals or syndicates who bid for privileges. The resultant protests from landowners left local officials reluctant to enforce these monopolies. Similarly, when in 1777 a group of merchants sought to obtain a monopoly to supply the city of Naples with olive oil for ten years, it was claimed that this would certainly ruin the cultivation of the product and trade in it.

Disputes over the allocation of privileges and the regulation of particular activities were not, however, the same as fundamental criticism of the role of government. There was little of the latter, although it could be argued that public enterprises were an obstacle to economic growth, both as hindrances to private initiative and as a possible waste of public money. The mercantilist ethos remained dominant, particularly in issues of international trade. This was fostered by the continual pressure for privileges from mercantile groups, by the specific benefits flowing from protection, such as the vital outlets for the cloth exports of the Austrian Netherlands provided by concessions in the Austrian hereditary dominions, and by the strong belief that the state should intervene in this sphere. This could be regarded as part of the traditional obligation on monarchs to care for their subjects. Concepts of the common good and of national power were identified with economic prosperity. This attitude made regulation a duty and a necessity, rather than a matter for intellectual debate. In France the impact of the Revolution and Napoleonic rule was to release, energise, direct and, in part, expropriate national resources, as national legal frameworks lessened or transformed sectional privileges, for example in water control, drainage and irrigation.[5] Guilds were abolished in 1791.

Protectionism and trade

The impact of eighteenth-century government intervention is open to debate. It could be suggested that only rigorously enforced import restrictions enabled the development of a wider industrial base in states such as Denmark, Prussia, Sardinia and Sweden. The weakness of indigenous industrial and commercial circles was clearly a problem in these states, particularly in raising capital and organising foreign trade. However, possibly more benefit would have been derived from investing in agriculture and from permitting foreign capital to take a major role in economic activity. The former would not have been easy, given the limited capability of the administrations of most states, particularly in rural areas. Nevertheless, there were many spheres, not least communications and rural credit, where the infrastructure of agricultural activity was open to improvement. Clearly the benefit of protection varied by region and sector. In general it hindered trade.

National protectionist policies were one hindrance to trade. Another was the fiscal burden of transit duties. These could be found throughout Europe, particularly at trans-shipment points, such as sea and river ports. The most famous individual set of duties was the Sound Tolls paid by shipping passing the Danish port of Elsinore. The economic burden that such duties represented varied. The best known difficulties attended river transport in the Empire (Germany). On the Weser between Bremen and Minden there were 21 toll stations, on the Rhine between Basle and Rotterdam, 38. These tolls had an effect. The Oder–Spree canal, finished in 1668 and its sluices rebuilt with stone in 1702, was designed in part to facilitate trade from Silesia to Hamburg, to help link an inland industrial zone to Germany's leading port. However, a commentator noted in 1716 that the tolls removed the cost advantage of water travel: 28 tolls were charged, besides the boat money paid at weirs, sluices and bridges. Conferences of representatives from states along the route, held in 1685 and 1711 to lower the tolls, failed. In 1716 there were 19 tolls for Danube traffic between Regensburg and Vienna, helping Silesian cloth, which travelled overland, to undersell cloth shipped from Regensburg. In 1740–1 excessive toll charges on the Aire and Calder Navigation in Yorkshire led local traders to protest and to create a series of turnpike roads to bypass the waterway. High Austrian, Dutch and Prussian tolls in the early 1750s on the middle stretches of the Meuse drove trade from the river to land routes. In 1749 the Dutch proposed a common customs house for the three powers and the sharing of the revenues, but the proposal came to nothing.

Tolls could play a major role in influencing trade routes. The mid-century switch in Austrian trade from traditional routes to the Baltic and North Sea towards the Adriatic owed something to the loss of Silesia to Prussia, but was also influenced by tariffs and tolls. The heavy tolls on rivers such as the Rhine were clearly a significant cost for transportation on such routes, discouraging the movement of low-cost items and therefore inhibiting regional specialisation.

Tolls were not the only regulatory hindrance that commerce had to face. They were matched by regulatory prohibitions. In 1700 only six French ports were allowed to trade with the French West Indies. The Dutch port of Veer enjoyed exclusive free trade in several articles with Scotland and therefore opposed the mid-century Dutch free port scheme. Such specific privileges were often expressed through differential tolls and tariffs. At the beginning of the century Bordeaux's sugar refiners enjoyed the right of transporting their product to much of France without paying many of the internal tolls of which their rivals in La Rochelle, Marseilles and Nantes complained. The negative role of tariffs and tolls helps to account for the importance attached to free ports. Livorno's prominence as a trading centre owed much to its designation as a free port in 1675. Other Italian rulers sought to emulate this achievement. Messina became a free port in 1728, Ancona in 1732. When in 1719 Austria wished to boost her Adriatic commerce, Trieste and Rijeka were given this status.

The (limited) development of free ports was one aspect of a shift in commercial organisation designed to facilitate commerce. Another was the ending or limitation in some trades of monopolistic rights, particularly of oceanic trading companies. However, in general, commercial organisation did not change very much. Two obvious signs of an essential conservatism were the continued predominance of family concerns and the role of fairs. As trade was dominated by families it is not surprising that it was undercapitalised, or that many merchants had only a limited commitment to commerce, regarding it as a means to accumulate wealth that would permit the establishment of the family as landowners, their money invested in the safer equity of land with its valuable yield of privilege and respect.

The trade of La Rochelle, a major French Atlantic port, was dominated by family-based businesses. Family firms and partnerships were crucial, as were kinship networks. They served as a means of capital accumulation and circulation, providing a valuable bond of confidence in a precarious financial situation. As with monarchs, so with merchants, dynasticism was central, not only as an objective, but also as a means of operation. In La Rochelle, dowries served as a means to redistribute capital between generations and families. The risky nature of colonial trade encouraged only limited specialisation. La Rochelle's colonial trade was affected by the wild fluctuations in slave-trade profits, as well as by wars and attendant colonial losses. As a result merchant families limited their business endeavours neither to maritime trade nor to any one branch of it, and balanced their investments between commerce and *rentes*. Similarly in Russia, where native merchants were largely restricted to the domestic market, most constituted single-owner firms and did not specialise in any particular line of goods.

Another aspect of limited specialisation was the persistence of fairs. They reflected what was essentially for many an intermittent commercial system. Periodic fairs were related to episodic, often seasonal, needs for contact with the market, that differed markedly from those catered for by the development of village shops. In Russia, the rural population needed the market economy only in the spring to sell winter handicraft products, and in the autumn to sell the harvest. Besides the major international fairs, such as Beaucaire in France and Lvov in Poland, there was a dense network of local fairs. The lower Auvergne region in France had 344 in 1743, 407 in 1777. Vital components of such fairs in meeting local commercial needs were pedlars, who brought both new and familiar goods to remote settlements. They were as much the cutting edge of the market economy, as the landlords who sought to substitute cash rents for payments in kind. Local fairs were also used by peasants to exchange goods, often without merchant intermediaries.

Pedlars were frequently not members of the local rural community. As with many itinerants, they were often viewed with suspicion, regarded as independent and thieving if not criminal in a wider sense: spreaders of heretical and seditious opinion or literature, or participants in occult practices. This alienation was one that was shared in some degree by many merchants. They were often members of minority ethnic or religious groups. In much of eastern Europe a large number of traders were Jews, in the Ottoman Empire, Armenians, Greeks and Jews. The most conspicuous type of this separatism occurred in the case of international trade. This was often conducted by small communities of foreigners, British in Portugal and Russia, Dutch in Russia and Sweden. The British communities in Lisbon and Oporto were protected by treaty and enjoyed a special legal and religious status including their own courts. Their entrepreneurial skills, political protection and access to capital allowed them to penetrate large areas of the metropolitan and colonial economy of Portugal, directly in the case of the wine trade or indirectly as with the Brazilian economy. Russia's Baltic trade was controlled by British and Dutch merchants, and other countries, such as France, were forced to use them as intermediaries. The Dutch organised the supply of French luxury goods enjoyed by the Russian aristocracy and of the naval stores required in France, transported the commodities and financed the trade. Much of the export trade of Naples was controlled by Genoese and French merchants.

Alongside this dominance by foreign merchants, there was also often a disproportionate role for particular national groups. The economic development of northern Sweden was closely linked to its staple products, iron, tar and timber, which could be moved, economically and practically, solely by water. Even though the legal restriction on sending ships abroad was lifted in 1766, by the 1780s only about 10 per cent of all staple products were shipped directly to the crucial foreign markets. The lack of capital in the hands of the townspeople of northern Sweden ensured that the export trade still largely remained in the hands of wealthy Stockholm merchants: northern Sweden remained a pre-industrial peripheral zone, her economic progress hindered by a lack of capital.

The economic and social significance of trade and merchants was no doubt diminished in much of Europe by the 'foreign' nature of the mercantile community. The local impact of struggles between competing groups, such as Jewish and French merchants in Salonica in Greece in 1722, was therefore lessened. The alien nature of many merchants reduced both their emulatory appeal and their possible role in local society. Their separation limited their economic impact, frequently – though with significant exceptions – discouraging their investment in local concerns. The restricted role of trade did not stem simply from this separation. Some products and ports were only poorly integrated with the surrounding economy. This was particularly the case with ports serving colonial trade, which often acted only as transshipment points. Ports such as La Rochelle or Whitehaven, lacking prosperous hinterlands and developed interior networks of communications, did not serve as dynamic forces in their regional economics. In contrast, ports such as Glasgow, Liverpool, Rouen and Bordeaux had a closer economic relationship with changes in their hinterlands.

Certain changes in commercial organisation can be perceived in this period. Though it varied in scale, where change occurred there was a general shift towards a money economy. This affected a wide range of activities, ranging from the mid-century publishers of Saxony, and of Leipzig in particular, who abandoned the traditional practice of trading on an exchange basis in favour of payment in cash, to the numerous Polish peasants who found their labour services commuted into cash payments. Though family business organisations remained dominant, joint-stock companies played a significant role in some areas. The relatively unspecialised nature of the economic system in, for example, cargo ships, ensured that disinvestment could take place nearly as easily as investment. However, there were increased signs of permanence. In La Rochelle, company structure evolved in the direction of more permanent and complex organisations.

A major shift was the developing role in international trade of the merchants of countries not hitherto regarded as major commercial powers. This was particularly the case with various German states, Sweden and the Austrian Netherlands. In the late 1760s merchants from the last developed a transit trade, Ostend serving as an intermediary between Britain and the Empire and Lorraine, to the detriment of the Dutch. By the 1780s certain Brussels merchants, such as Frédéric Romberg, were major traders owning numerous ships. The fourth Anglo-Dutch war caused a trading boom in Brussels in 1780–3.

Baltic traders also became more prominent. In 1767, of the 6495 vessels that passed the Sound, 2779 were Swedish or Danish. The Hansa ports, particularly Hamburg, and the Danish port of Altona enjoyed a rise in activity. From mid-century on, Hamburg, Bremen and the Prussian port of Stettin supplanted the Dutch increasingly in the trade between Bordeaux and the Baltic. A comparison of the olive oil exports from Gallipoli in Apulia in 1744 and in the 1780s reveals that the old-established markets, such as Britain and the United Provinces, had declined and that neither was used any longer as an entrepôt, while there had been a considerable growth in exports to Hamburg, Stettin and the Baltic in general.

These developments were to be interrupted by the Napoleonic wars and the accompanying disruption of trade, as Britain dominated oceanic commerce and France developed continental routes. However, there is little doubt that by the 1780s there had been an appreciable growth in the commercial activity of a number of states outside western Europe. This was accompanied by a measure of industrial growth in certain regions and by competition with western European products. Dutch and Silesian competition led to a fall in British cloth sales to Königsberg around 1715. In the following two decades French dominance of the Spanish linen market was broken by Silesian linens shipped from Hamburg. This trade was sufficiently valuable for Bremen to move into it during a dispute between Spain and Hamburg in 1752. The Brno Fine Cloth Factory in Moravia went bankrupt in 1789 partly because the Austro-Turkish war had closed a major export market. The number of workers employed in 'commercial crafts' in Lower Austria rose from about 20,060 in 1762 to over 180,000 in 1790, figures that can be matched in Bohemia and

Moravia. By 1780 there were significant structural changes in the economy of these regions as larger, more concentrated enterprises began to take a more important role.

Bereft of the spectacular benefits of colonial trade, there were, nevertheless, signs of appreciable developments in the commerce of the non-colonial powers. This owed much to the importance of European goods traded only on short sea routes. Though the value of trans-oceanic goods in Europe was high, profits were lessened both by the risk and cost of the trade and by the delay in recouping investment. In contrast, European trade was larger in volume and more secure, requiring a smaller investment and less political and military protection. Thus, whereas chartered trading companies, large consortia or wealthy merchants dominated ocean trade, generating much contemporary discussion, many records and a lot of scholarly attention, the converse was the case with the bulk of European trade. As a result the economic importance of this commerce has been under-rated. Much of it centred around the movement of unprocessed products from areas of production to those of processing and consumption.

In 1778–80, 14.6 of the 18 million roubles of Russian annual exports were naval stores (hemp, flax, tallow and canvas), timber, iron, grain and caviar. The Sound Toll accounts for 1784–95 reveal that the goods most frequently exported westwards out of the Baltic were hemp (for rope), tallow (for lighting, lubricants, soap manufacture and tanning) and iron, these going mostly to Britain; linseed (for dyes and soaps), mostly to the United Provinces; flax (for linen), mostly to Britain and Portugal; wheat, rye, potash (for bleaching), soap and glass, mostly to Britain, France, the United Provinces and the Austrian Netherlands. The principal goods moving east were wine, brandy, sugar, coffee, tobacco and salt, the last from Cheshire, western France, Setubal in Portugal, Alicante in Spain, Ibiza, Cagliari in Sardinia and Trapani in Sicily. Between 1770 and 1790 cereals, timber and forestry products made up between 80 and 90 per cent of exports from Danzig (now Gdansk), this leading Polish port importing coffee, wine and salt. Sweden annually purchased large quantities of Polish, Prussian and Russian grain. Salt in the 1780s was the largest Swedish import from Iberia and the Mediterranean, linking Sweden and Denmark to the island of Sardinia, whose leading export it was. Exports of basic products were important for many regions: horses from Holstein or silk from Piedmont, 78.7 per cent of the latter's exports in 1752.

Travellers referred frequently to signs of extensive trade, aspects of what has been presented as a consumer revolution fuelling economic growth. Taking the Mt Cenis route between Lyons and

Turin in 1770, Lady Miller found mules carrying rice coming from Italy, the same essential beasts of burden carrying jewellery and expensive cloth in the opposite direction.[6] The economic impact of such commerce varied clearly by area. In some regions it was vital. Norway exported timber, fish and metals, the peasantry, directly or indirectly, being deeply involved in production for export, which is thought to have formed about 30 per cent of the country's aggregate production around 1801.

Trade was clearly of considerable importance to the European economy, and yet it is necessary not to exaggerate either its role or the changes it underwent during the century. In many respects, commercial organisation and trade routes and products changed surprisingly little. Significant hindrances to trade existed, both those ostensibly designed to affect it, such as tariffs and prohibitions, and those that served to inhibit it, such as the lesser prestige of merchants as compared with landowners. Both were of importance, though it is fruitless to speculate as to what would have happened had they not existed. Arguably the biggest hindrances were the limited sophistication and restricted development of agriculture and industry, and the restricted purchasing power of the bulk of the population.

A changing economy

The question of commercial change is thus linked to the general problem of assessing the economic situation in Europe. This is a serious topic, as economic performance, in both per capita and aggregate terms, conditioned both the living standards and expectations of the people of Europe and the fiscal capacity and, therefore, policy capabilities of their governments. To suggest that the situation was one of both change and continuity, innovation and conservatism, is to draw attention to the variety in economic activity and regional fortune that characterised Europe. There are major problems both in measuring activity and in assessing how far change was feasible. The former posed difficulties for contemporaries, as it has done for modern scholars. In part, despite the efforts of governments and intellectuals, most eighteenth-century Europeans were not strongly conscious of the value of statistics; in part the surviving figures are incomplete and pose as many problems as they solve. This is of course a characteristic of all statistics, but, nevertheless, a glimpse at surviving figures provides some measure of the problem.

The size of the population was of importance to government, for its revelation of the nature of the state's potential power in terms of numbers of taxpayers and soldiers. Demographic data also provided information on producers and consumers. The quest for population statistics was often linked to specific schemes. The census carried out in Aragon in the mid-1710s had a fiscal purpose. During their rule of Little Wallachia (1718–39), the Austrians reorganised the fiscal system, which necessitated the establishment of fixed levies and, for the first time, an accurate census. The landowners sought to evade it and to conceal the number of their peasants, leading to variations in the local census figures for the 1720s. When direct taxation was introduced into the Ukraine in 1722, the collection was uneven, as a result of the absence of precedents, co-operation and information. After the collapse of the Pugachev rising, a census of the Yaik Cossacks was taken as a preliminary to reorganising them under strict government control. In order to provide a reliable basis for intended fiscal reforms, the government of Lombardy was ordered in the 1750s to update an earlier census. In 1786 the population and house ownership of Namur were assessed in response to a project for the reorganisation of the parochial system conceived by Joseph II.

Given the common fiscal consequences of censuses, it is not surprising that they were unpopular and evaded where possible. One source of the unpopularity of the Russian parochial clergy was their obligation to provide information on the population. There were significant problems of reliability, not least because of the shifting nature of some of the European population and the role of seasonal migration. The Sicilian census of 1747 took 23 years for the Deputation (permanent committee of the Estates) to compile.

The general achievement was varied. A Swedish census was taken in 1749, the first Danish one in 1769 and the first official Spanish censuses of individuals in 1768 and 1787. A census of Savoy-Piedmont, planned in 1700, was finally carried out in 1734. In Britain, however, no census was taken until 1801, while the information available on the Balkan and Polish populations was limited. A similar variety characterised information on land ownership, while that on agricultural productivity was very limited. Information about ownership was essential if agrarian wealth, the bulk of national resources in most countries, was to be taxed fairly.

Charles XII of Sweden wanted a land register as the basis for a reformed land tax. The Swedish Pomeranian Survey Commission of 1692–1709 was designed to provide the basis for a new tax system. Frederick William I introduced a uniform land tax in East Prussia, payable alike by nobility and peasantry, based on the land assessment rolls and the productivity of the soil. Frederick the Great introduced a similar tax to Silesia in 1740 and to West

Prussia in 1772. A systematic tax survey and mapping of Silesia was carried out for Frederick, including a careful assessment of the productivity of the land. Detailed land surveys of Piedmont and Savoy, establishing the ownership and value of land, were completed in 1711 and 1738 respectively. Lombardy was mapped in the late 1710s. Such schemes were a measure of the strength of many states, revealing an ability to execute new schemes in the face of opposition from those who enjoyed privilege and upon whose co-operation government relied.

However, land surveys encountered considerable difficulties. As with much else, they suggest that government power, or possibly co-operation from the landowners in novel proposals, increased during the century, particularly after 1748, but only to a limited extent. The land register inaugurated in the Papal States in 1777 was hindered by landowner opposition. The attempt by the duke of Courland to conduct a survey of his own estates was bitterly opposed by nobles seeking to transform leases of ducal lands into legal titles of ownership. During the Hungarian revolt of 1789 the registers of titles which were to have served as the basis of the reform of land tenure were destroyed.

Landowner resistance was serious, because land surveys tested the capacity of national administrations. The Russian College of Landed Estates was supposed to record all transfers of landed property in a land register, but, as transactions could be registered only in St Petersburg or Moscow, many were not recorded, while the register anyway suffered from poor record-keeping. The imposition of the death penalty in 1766 for interference with the activities of land surveyors was little substitute for the necessary administrative structure and for general political support. Russian options in taxation and local government were limited by the absence of an accurate land survey. In the Baltic provinces the nobility refused to accept a new survey by the Russian government.

Information on economic activity was also fairly limited, although governments often stipulated that such information should be collected. In Sicily, Victor Amadeus II ordered censuses of mulberry and olive trees in the 1710s. The Danish poverty ordinance of 1708 laid down guidelines for the assessment of each parishioner's ability to contribute according to the needs of the parish as a whole. Under the Danish compulsory state fire insurance scheme introduced in 1761, in order to arrive at the appropriate insurance cover, every building had to be described, and the valuations were supposed to be revised every decade.

Governments sought information for a variety of specific purposes, because it was held to assist government activities, and in response to a widespread interest in classification and enquiry on the part of influential intellectuals.[7] Victor Amadeus II tried in the 1710s to build up a register of roads and bridges in Sicily, while the succeeding Austrian administration used army engineers to prepare the first detailed map. Following the suppression of the 1745 rebellion, a military survey of Scotland served as the basis for more accurate maps. A major military survey of Bohemia was begun in the 1760s and completed under Joseph II. Lower Austria was surveyed from 1773 and a major survey of Hungary finished in 1786. In Saxony, where a new standard mile was introduced in 1715, the geometrician Adam Zürner carried out a cartographic survey, completing 900 maps, which formed the basis of the Electoral Postal Map, first published in 1719. He discovered that many of the milestones on Saxony's major roads between Dresden and Leipzig were missing or placed at the wrong distance.[8]

Frederick William I sought regular reports on Prussian harvest yields, price fluctuations and cattle breeding. However, only his personal domains kept exact records, while Frederick the Great's attempts to obtain methodical reports and statistical information were limited by the use of different provincial criteria, which made it difficult to establish comparable data, a common problem in Europe given the general absence of standard measures.

A Swedish national bureau of statistics was established in 1749, while, from mid-century, the government of the Austrian Netherlands began to collect industrial statistics regularly. In the last years of Louis XV's reign there was a marked French government interest in enquiries and statistics, under the impulse of controllers-general such as Terray (1770–4) and with the support of certain dynamic *intendants*. In order to make his *dirigiste* policy effective Terray sought to establish a system to gather information on the grain supply that would permit him to manage the market in order to lower prices and end shortages.

The attempts to gain information were dangerously dependent on the co-operation of others. Sometimes this was reasonably successful. The French Council of Commerce played an important role in the collection of data through the *Bureau du Commerce*, which it helped to establish in 1713. However, much information presented to governments by merchants was designed to serve particular ends and was of questionable reliability. This difficulty was general in a society where it was difficult to check reports, where record-keeping was often fairly primitive and where accounting techniques were limited. The Neapolitan government found itself unable to procure an accurate notion of the state of its woods, because of unreliable and contradictory reports. Terray's scheme was thwarted not only by bad harvests, but also by the failure of many *intendants* to supply necessary information, by slow communications and by the inability of eighteenth-century bureaucracy to deal with imperfectly understood economic forces. In 1774 Turgot abandoned the demands for information on the harvest prescribed in 1773 by his predecessor, Terray. In 1776, as a result of recommendations from Du Pont and the marquis de Mirabeau, Charles de Butre was ordered to survey every village in Baden in order to be able to calculate an equitable, single, direct tax. By 1789 he had surveyed only 58 villages.

It is difficult to assess what change took place. It is similarly problematic to establish what change was feasible and to use this in the discussion of the balance between change and continuity. To point out the discrepancy between aspirations for change and/or innovation and limited achievements, whether in economic, political, social, religious or administrative matters, is not to deny that change took place. The balance varied clearly by region. To take one region of obvious change, central Scotland, there was a clear expansion in economic activity in the mid-century, especially in industry and banking. Though sugar and tobacco trading were enclave activities at Glasgow, the profits gained from them acted as stimuli for other sectors of the economy as did the Seven Years War. A certain amount of mercantile capital was spent on the purchase of landed estates, but the local business mentality and the tax system did not encourage any wholesale transfer of funds from industry and trade. The investment of profits from the tobacco trade substantially funded the development of the chemical industry in west-central Scotland. Similarly, the liquidity of banks such as the Edinburgh-based Royal Bank was increased by the profits of the tobacco merchants. The early 1760s witnessed the appearance of provincial banks in Aberdeen, Ayr, Dundee, Glasgow and Perth. Several industries saw considerable growth. Whereas only seven Newcomen steam engines appear to have been in operation in 1759, increasing numbers were used in coal-mining thereafter and the industry grew in the 1760s. From the early 1750s there was a build-up of forge and foundry establishments, particularly around Glasgow. By 1761 the Carron Company at Falkirk, a leading metallurgical enterprise, had 615 employees and was an example of the increased amount of capital being invested in industry and the consequent larger size of industrial concerns. Four new paper mills were established in 1750–6, while the printed-linen industry grew from 1753. The Scottish chemical industry developed using coal in the mid-century, with sugar-boiling in Dundee and a vitriol (sulphuric acid) works opened at Prestonpans in 1749. The period was also marked by the growth of scientific and intellectual enquiry; the Select Society, founded in 1754, being one of several Scottish professional clubs and institutions promoting advances and improvement. Agricultural improvements were actively pursued, the potato being introduced as a field crop in 1743. After a visit to Edinburgh and Glasgow in 1760, Joseph Spence wrote of the road programme:

> they laid a map of the whole country before them; first marked lines of communication from the most considerable towns to the capital, and to one another, for the benefit of commerce and travelling; made a fund of £30,000 by a subscription; and began at once with nine roads from Edinburgh, which are already branched out into above thirty. I went no farther than Glasgow ... all [the roads] very good, and mostly made so within these eight years. Agriculture is greatly improved too, wherever I went; and through Berwickshire (and our neighbouring county of Northumberland) greatly even with these two years.[9]

Significant as these developments were, it is important to recognise the continued backwardness of the Scottish economy. This was particularly marked in agriculture and finance. Agricultural prices remained dangerously susceptible to variable harvests, with consequent problems for other areas of the economy. There were also problems with credit. In 1761 the Scottish credit system was revealed to have an inadequate cash basis, while the 1760s were marked by an exchange crisis between England and Scotland.

Nevertheless, the growth in the economy of central Scotland showed what was possible in this period and could be mirrored elsewhere. Growth naturally exacerbated regional economic differences, but these were not a novelty of the century. As with previous periods, the contrast was not between growing urban industrial zones and stagnant rural agricultural areas. Instead, some industrial areas declined, many towns were not significant productive centres and a great deal of industry, including much developing industry, was rural. The fundamental division was between areas that were economically developing, interdependent and integrated to the market economy and those where such interdependence and integration were limited.

In general, the century was marked by greater economic interdependence. In 1788 John Thomson wrote from Constance: 'The effects of our English speculations are felt even here – in Zurich I am told two thousand tradesmen have been discharged in one week as the raw cottons and silk in Spain and Piedmont have been entirely bought up by our merchants.'[10] Trade interacted with changing domestic demand, especially the growth in consumption of goods designed to stimulate: groceries such as sugar, caffeine drinks – tea, coffee, and chocolate – and tobacco. This was very much consumerism: none of these goods was 'necessary'. There were also more material goods, a rising demand for all types of goods, and a slowly changing material fabric of life. All encouraged the spread and intensity of the money economy.

The causes and consequences of interdependence were various. Improved postal services played an important role. The postal network spread. In 1693–4 the Saxons inaugurated a weekly post from the United Provinces and improved the service with Hamburg so that a reply could be received in eight days. A new service to Nuremberg was opened in 1699. Portugal signed postal conventions with England in 1705 and Spain in 1718: by 1763 about 12 kilograms of mail a month were being handed over to Spanish postal officials.[11]

The spread of the money economy, state fiscal demands and the problems and opportunities created by population growth clearly facilitated the drive towards interdependence. In stressing the continued dominance of agriculture and the limited extent of improvement, however, it is necessary to underline the changes that did occur. If general European economic growth failed to keep up with the rise in population and therefore living standards were depressed, significant regional growth did, nevertheless, occur.

4 Society

I sincerely pity them, they are such slaves as I have heard the Negroes in the West Indies described. No uncommon sight to see them threshing corn, driving waggons, hoeing turnips, mending the highways.

(Adam Walker on the women he saw between
Füssen (Bavaria) and Innsbruck (Austria), 1787)[1]

Eighteenth-century European social relationships and attitudes reflected a clear cultural inheritance and a prevalent economic and technological environment. The Judaeo-Christian inheritance, clearly enunciated in the laws and teachings of the churches, decreed monogamy, prohibited marriage between close kin, stipulated procreation as a purpose of matrimony while condemning it outside, denounced abortion, infanticide, homosexuality and bestiality, made divorce very difficult, enforced care of children on their parents, while demanding reverence and obedience in return, venerated age, and ordered respect for authority, religious and secular, legal and law-enforcing. The environment was technologically unsophisticated and predominantly agrarian. Economic productivity was low, there was little substitute for manual labour and the value accrued through most labour was limited. Most of the population neither controlled nor produced much wealth. The principal means of acquiring wealth was by inheritance and most inheritance took place within the family. It is not surprising that the dominant ethos was patriarchal, hierarchical, conservative, religious and male-dominated.

Women and families

It would be difficult to guess from many textbooks that women made up half the population; indeed that the gender balance in the population was frequently weighted towards women. They are often not deemed worthy of mention and seldom appear in indexes. It might be suggested that, as they faced ecological challenges similar to those of men, any additional consideration is superfluous. However, women's biological role brought specific problems, while their treatment by society differed from that of men. The women ploughing in the fields near Lyons and Abbeville in 1787 or dragging boats upstream to Mainz in 1789

102

faced gruelling labour and debilitating diseases identical to those of the men at their sides, but they were also in a society that awarded control and respect to men, and left little independent role for female merit or achievement. The economy of the poor was such that employment was the essential condition for most of the women in the population. The arduous, restricted and restrictive nature of the work available to women, usually domestic service or agricultural labour, and the confining implications of family and social life, together defined the existence of the vast majority of women.

The basic unit of society in much of Europe, especially in much of north-western Europe, such as England, was emerging as the nuclear family, a married couple and their generally non-adult children. However, circumstances varied geographically, socially and by individual family. In other regions, such as the hinterland of Ussel in Limousin (France), the extended family was the norm. Extended families persisted among the farmers around Salzburg, but declined among the cottagers, while in the city itself, family types common in modern cities, single-person, incomplete and residual households, increased in importance. Because of the question of safety in an insecure and often violent society, isolated individuals could be in a vulnerable position. In Languedoc it was common for a married eldest son, his wife and his children to live with his parents in an extended family. In Altopascio in Tuscany nuclear families appear to have been preferred, but family combinations were encouraged by the lack of land, the effects of death and the family-based economic system. Labour dues influenced household size in Courland, frequently necessitating more than a simple nuclear family.

Individual family structure was of course not constant. Birth, ageing and death ensured that the life-cycle of families was continually changing. It was necessary to adapt in order to survive periods when the family altered to include dependants, young children and invalid adults. As these groups consumed without working, they posed a challenge to the economy of individual families, just as they created formidable problems for society in general, and many other functions like education. The standard response was to avoid the problem, so far as it was feasible. Governments generally left the responsibilities of social welfare to families, communities, and private and religious charity. Individual families coped with the problem of feeding children by getting them to work as far as possible and in so far as it was necessary. Many children were found tasks as soon as was feasible or were used to assist in begging. Many agricultural and industrial tasks could be accomplished by children. At Altopascio 4- and

5-year-olds tended livestock. In Languedoc children progressed from looking after chickens and ducks to cattle, via sheep and goats. In the mines of the Cévennes 12- to 15-year-old boys were used to push wagons, girls of the same age washing the ore.

The concept of childhood, as a distinct stage in life and individual development, was far weaker than was to be the case in the twentieth century. Governments and publicists approved of child labour, arguing that it prevented idleness and begging, educated children to useful employment and accustomed them to work. Most families, however, needed no such encouragement. Their problem was to find employment for the children and to feed them until they were able to work.

The availability of land and the manner in which it was worked played an important role in the nature of family organisation. Where land was plentiful, as in much of eastern Europe, and tenurial relationships permitted, it was possible for young men to marry, leave their parents and set up a separate household. Conversely, where land was in short supply this process was more difficult, and children might continue to live in their parents' household until quite late in life. In Altopascio, where there were many extended families, the head of a household had an official description – *capo di casa*. Most of these were over 38 and all who were not heads were legally dependent. Designated as *figlio di famiglia* (child of the family), they could not contract for land or enter into any other form of contractual relationship. In Languedoc the legal rights of men were limited until the age of 25. In areas where land was farmed collectively, extended or complex family structures, such as fraternal communities, appear to have been common. Demographic chance, in particular the relatively high mortality rate among young women, often in childbirth, and the frequency of remarriage by widowers, also affected family organisation. It ensured that many children were brought up by stepmothers, a relationship that was not always an easy one. Though its significance is open to debate, stepmothers featured often in a poor light in popular tales. The children's game *Belle-mère* recorded by Restif de la Bretonne opposed a vicious stepmother to a mistreated stepdaughter.

Whatever the nature of the family, the employment of as many of its members as possible was essential not only to its well-being but also to its very existence as a unit. Aid from the community for the less fortunate was limited by modern Western standards, in large part because of the pressures created by widespread poverty. Nevertheless, such aid – the kindness of neighbours – was more welcome than institutional charity, which, in so far as it existed, offered little to families. It was often specific by age or sex.

Individuals, not families, were taken into care and institutional charity was therefore generally the last resort of families. Families who could not cope left children to foundling hospitals. Similarly, unmarried mothers turned often to abortion and infanticide, both treated as serious crimes, and the former hazardous to health. The women, often very young, who were punished as a result of these desperate acts suffered from the generally limited and primitive nature of contraceptive practices, as did those exhausted from frequent childbirth. That unwanted children were not only an economic liability, but also, when born to unmarried mothers, the source of often severe social disadvantages, moral condemnation and legal penalties, made the situation worse. In a society where women sought marriage as a source of precarious stability, the marital prospects of single mothers were low, with the significant exception of widows with children of a first marriage, particularly if they possessed some property. As a result, unmarried mothers frequently were treated as prostitutes or were forced to turn to prostitution.

Thus social and economic pressures helped to drive women towards matrimony and also towards employment, whether they were unmarried or married. A common form of work for unmarried women, as for unmarried men, was domestic service. In a society where household tasks were arduous and manual, the technological contribution minimal, service was the life of many. Jobs such as the disposal of human excreta were unpleasant. Water-carrying, generally a female task, could cause physical distortion. Cleaning and drying clothes involved a lot of effort: the dirt had to be trampled or scrubbed out and early mangles required a lot of muscle power. Many servants were immigrants from rural areas, and generally not members of collective groups, and lacking guilds, they were largely at the mercy of their employers. It was possible in the hierarchy of service to gain promotion, but, in general, domestic service was unskilled and not a career. Wages were poor and pay was largely in kind, which made life very hard for those who wished to marry and leave service, as married servants were relatively uncommon. For girls saving for a dowry, domestic service was far from easy, and they were often sexually vulnerable to their masters.

Service was not only domestic, though that was the field in which female labour was most important. Agricultural servants were also vital. Generally living with their employers, they gave many nuclear families the quality, in part, of an extended family. Domestic and agricultural service was responsible for the approximate figure of 168,000 servants out of a Bavarian population of 1,052,000 in 1770. The comparable figure for Norway in 1801 was 95,000 out of 883,000. The need for both men and women to go into service, and also the need for servants, varied geographically, seasonally and socially, and the contradictory needs produced difficulties such as dismissals and migration in search of employment, producing a labour market filled with uncertainties.

Another important source of female employment for both married and unmarried women was domestic manufacturing. Clothing was the biggest, though not the sole, form of employment in this area. Spinning-wheels featured frequently in British household inventories. Women played a major role in the Lyons silk industry, in the spinning of yarn for the Picardy cloth industries, in the Normandy town of Elbeuf's woollen industry, where the normal working day for women and children was 15 hours, and in the developing French cotton industry. The married and unmarried women of the Pays de Caux spun for the nearby Rouen cotton entrepreneurs. In mid-century Montpellier most of the young girls found employment in sewing. In Altopascio the textile workforce was almost entirely female. Those of the rural poor did the spinning while the women of the lower artisan class did the weaving. The very poor women spun flax.

Domestic manufacture could be an important contribution to family income, especially in areas where agriculture was poor and in households that had limited agricultural resources; either the women formed part of a family in which all members worked in domestic manufacturing or they supplemented income derived from other activities. As the value added by their work and that of children was generally greater than that derived from comparable labour in the fields, women and children generally made a greater contribution to family incomes if they engaged in domestic manufacturing. However, their opportunities were limited by the restricted nature of market-orientated domestic manufacture in many areas, and, to a lesser extent from the second half of the century, by the growth of factory-type employment which, by taking the worker out of the home, made it difficult to care for children. Particularly if combined with the move of manufacturing, this change destroyed the basis of the family economy and lessened the chance of married women obtaining remunerative labour. It has been suggested that these economic changes had social consequences, including a rise in divorce and separation.

The most striking aspect of the female contribution to the labour force in this period was its variety. Although in general women had little significant role in the church, save in charitable works and female education, and less in the armed forces, they were found in most spheres of employment, including arduous physical labour such as mining, portering, refuse collection and agriculture. In Languedoc for example, many women were involved in the sale of food, serving in the towns as butchers, fishmongers and greengrocers. Female pedlars, such as the coffee-women of Paris, were a common sight in the towns. Women were generally given the worse-paid jobs. In many industries, such as glove-making, women were given the less skilled jobs or their employment was defined as less skilled and therefore lower paid.

Female employment did not always reflect the expediency economy of the poor, though arguably female opportunities were limited as much by poor education as by legal restrictions. Literacy rates were commonly low for both sexes and lowest for women. In western French towns literacy declined among domestic servants, while in the Vivarais, whereas 20–30 and 30–40 per cent of men could sign their name in 1686–90 and 1786–90 respectively, the comparable figures for women were 3–4 and 8–11 per cent, although these were still significant increases. In north-west Germany, where literacy rates were high, there was a large gap between male and female achievement. The illiteracy of rural women, the direct result of an almost total lack of schooling and a general neglect by educational reformers, changed only slowly. In Austria the reformer Gerard van Swieten opposed Joseph II's wish to abolish all payment for tuition in elementary schools, as he felt that this would be too expensive. The resulting compromise left girls to pay, while boys were let in free. Nevertheless not all women were confined to poor jobs, even if few reached posts as impressive as Madame de Maraise, a businesswoman who acted as the financial and commercial manager of the important Oberkampf calico-printing company in 1767–89. In the Breton building industries some women profited as entrepreneurs, while others toiled in workshops. Many worked with their husbands by, for example, managing the accounts.[2]

In some spheres job opportunities for women increased. Some women benefited from the expansion of the commercial economy. Women were also of great importance as consumers, and the need to satisfy their demands and fashions comprised a major aspect of what has been termed the 'consumer revolution' of the period. At the top of the scale, a tiny minority of women were not prevented from following interesting careers. The Italian Marie Agnesi was an important mathematician, her compatriot Laura Bassi studied electricity and air compression, Caroline Herschel was an astronomer, though very much her brother's assistant, and Angelica Kauffmann and Elisabeth Vigée-Lebrun were highly sought-after portrait painters.[3] Bassi (1711–78), the first woman to graduate from the University of

Bologna and the first to hold a university teaching position, faced restrictions on her public teaching and university voting privileges, and her position as a role model was short-lived.

Female legal rights were not always inferior to those of men; for example, in Poland noblewomen enjoyed the same rights of property and inheritance as noblemen. More generally, marriage contracts usually protected female property rights by defining the jointure between the bride and her husband, with all else remaining her personal possessions, and not legally at the disposal of her husband. Marriage contracts also specified that, if there were no children by the marriage, the personal possessions and property of the bride would revert to her family on her death (and would not be inherited by her husband, who retained only the jointure). Prevailing patterns of inheritance custom were important for the status of women.

However, in general, women suffered legal disadvantages, especially in the ownership and disposal of property, and social and political discrimination. This was true at all social levels. The image of justice might be female, but its formulators and executors were all male. The life of women in court society could be bleak. Particularly if brought up in convents, they often had limited experience of men of their own age and rank, were married off with little attention to their wishes, commonly ignored by their husbands and sometimes in effect separated. Mary Magdalene was sung by the soprano Margherita Durastanti at the first performance of Handel's oratorio the *Resurrezione* in 1708. A complaint by Pope Clement XI that a female singer had been allowed to take part in a sacred work led to her replacement by a castrato for the second performance.

Legislation tended to reflect these divisions in society, as did the churches. When, in response to pressure from manufacturers, the Danish government limited the length of the period of mourning in 1752, widowers were given liberty to remarry after six months, widows only after one year. In general the outlets for female piety were important but limited in comparison with those for men. Nevertheless, there were growing opportunities for women, even if the female preaching among the Salzburg Protestants was exceptional. In France devotional literature for women sold well. Confraternities, such as those dedicated to the Rosary, the Sacred Heart and Saint Catherine, were the bedrock of female piety before the Revolution, and they played no small part in ensuring that women played a key, independent role in the survival of Catholicism during the Revolutionary crisis. New orders such as the Sisters of the Christian Doctrine (founded 1694) and the Sisters of Saint-Anne (1709) sent three or four sisters into villages to form miniscule convents that could fulfil every form of practical task, winning them the names of 'Houses of Charity'. Such institutes of *filles séculières* scattered around the French provinces played a vital part in sustaining women in their faith throughout the Revolution. No less important were the *béates*, usually a widow or spinster with just enough education herself to teach lace-making to the village girls while they recited their catechism.

It has been suggested that the French Catholic Jansenist tendency implicitly sought to find a role for women in the church. The enthusiastic female response to certain charismatic religious movements, both Protestant and Catholic, is notable. There was a large female role in the outbreak of Catholic religious zeal in 1730–2 that accompanied the convulsions in the Parisian cemetery of Saint-Médard. A few women became Protestant preachers. The relationship between women and the church was generally not that experienced by Catherine Cadière, whose alleged seduction by a Jesuit confessor led to a sensational trial in France in 1731. In Italy, religious foundations for single women who did not wish to become nuns were intended to protect women whose virtue was endangered by the absence of adequate family protection.

The use of the household as the basis for social organisation necessarily stressed the role of men, who were regarded as heads of households when they were present. In Elbeuf, population statistics were calculated by numbers of households, not numbers of people. The standard way of counting serfs after the introduction of the Russian poll tax in 1722 was by the number of males over 15. In Altopascio, as elsewhere, the responsibility of the head of the household for its members extended into moral and social spheres. More generally, female roles and tasks owed much to the position of male heads of households. In the Lauragais region of south-west France sharecroppers' wives and daughters were expected to act as unpaid laundresses and housemaids for landlords.[4]

Yet it would be mistaken to imagine that women lacked political consciousness. A large number took part in the Paris bread riot of 1725. In Bayonne in 1750 women attacked troops assisting tax collectors, while women frequently participated in English riots. These actions may well have reflected the crucial role that women played in the purchasing of foodstuffs and the sense that women would receive more lenient punishments than men, but they also argue for a degree of female political awareness. If this took the form primarily of hostile responses to changes in the price or availability of foodstuffs that were believed to be unfair, that was the politics of the poor in general. During the French Revolution, the subsistence grievances of Parisian women were frequently expressed in a pointed political fashion.

Poverty was also an experience to which women were particularly vulnerable. This was different from that of men for a number of reasons, particularly the responsibility of women, both unmarried and married, for children. It was women who were commonly held responsible for the birth of illegitimate children, while married men had a greater propensity than their spouses to abandon their families. In the French city of Carcassonne the legal declarations by abused unmarried women complained most commonly that they had been abandoned by men who had courted them. They had also often, in the apt phrase of the period, suffered the injury of an infant. They complained that their lovers, in fleeing their paternal responsibilities, had left them in a difficult social and financial situation. They sought marriage, as the only way to repair their personal and family honour. Judicial assistance was a poor second choice. In Carcassonne the position of such women deteriorated during the century. Until 1747 the burden of proof rested on the accused men, frequently heads of households alleged to have seduced their servants, girls who had migrated from the countryside. Claims that wealthy men were being accused, rather than the true fathers, led the judges thereafter to demand proofs from the women, a judicial shift that accompanied a change in social values. Pity for the forthcoming children appears to have diminished, and male honour to have supplanted that of women in the order of priorities. Men were less frequently condemned for breaking promises to marry. Seeing their legal position deteriorate, unmarried mothers in Carcassonne took great care to keep their pregnancies secret.

In England, where newborn child murder was a capital offence for any mother convicted, women played a decisive role in the legal process. They were important both in bringing a suspect to the attention of the authorities and in playing a part in determining her culpability under the statute of 1624. A 'Jury of Matrons' was used to ascertain whether the suspect had given birth or not. These women were helping to define what made for acceptable female behaviour in their communities.[5]

The absence of an effective social welfare system and the low wages paid to most women ensured that prostitution, either full- or part-time, was the fate of many. Accounts of town life in government records make it clear that prostitution was a common feature. In his series, Scenes of Paris Life, painted in the 1750s, Étienne Jeaurat depicted the detection of prostitutes in 'The

Arrest of Disorderly Persons' (1755). There were, however, too many to arrest for any length of time, and demand, both for sex and for its income, was too great to bring any lasting success to the attempts to suppress prostitution, such as those made in Austria by Maria Theresa and Joseph II. Prostitution was prohibited in France as well as many other countries, and denounced by the Church, moralists, medical men and physiocratic economists. It was seen as a threat to morals, both male and female, to population growth, and to venereal health. Government action itself was episodic, and directed principally at any threat to public order. In 1778 the Parisian clandestine trade was attacked in a regulation which in effect unofficially licensed brothels. However, with a total force of 1500, the *lieutenant de police* was unable to make this policy work. Arguably there was little that could be done about prostitution, an economic necessity for many, even if seen as a social problem for the community, but the fight against it revealed the limited resources of governments. As the attempts to deal with prostitution were essentially repressive, and there was no general policy of providing alternative paid employment, as indeed was scarcely possible, it is not surprising that governments failed. The diseased prostitute, her hair and teeth lost in often fatal mercury treatments, was a victim of the social-economic and cultural circumstances of the age. Her fate was more grisly than that of lower-class Italian women forced into institutions when their love affairs ignored social barriers, or of married women caught in adultery, but the situation was essentially the same. An economic system that bore down hard on most of the population, irrespective of gender, was nevertheless linked to a social system in which the position of women, whether fortunate or unfortunate, was generally worse than that of men. The breakdown of marriage and desertion by the spouse frequently featured in accounts of women vagrants.

It has been argued that the eighteenth century witnessed the rise of a pattern of family life that placed more weight on the wishes of individual members and in which affection rather than discipline, emotion rather than patriarchalism, bonded families together. This shift has been explained in part by demographic changes: an increase in the life expectancy of children and women encouraging a greater degree of emotional commitment. These changes have in turn been linked to a range of developments, including the rise of distinctive fashions and the toy industry for children, the literary cult of the sentimental family, and new pedagogic fashions that placed greater weight on the individuality of children and the need to socialise them without treating them as embodiments of original sin.

These suggestions produced a vigorous debate among historians in the 1970s and 1980s, and broad agreement has emerged.[6] It is not possible to answer many of the questions that have been raised, particularly if the field of enquiry is extended to much of Europe and to the overwhelming majority of the population who did not keep journals, leave correspondence or feature in relevant social records, other than in legal actions where their opinions were generally represented in the terms used by those who controlled justice. Furthermore, it is far from clear how one assesses, let alone measures, affection and changes in it. It is important not to mistake changes in style, such as modes of address within the family, for changes in substance. If marital experiences and expectations were related to economic circumstances, then it is difficult to see much reason for major change.

In addition, recent work on sixteenth- and seventeenth-century family life has revealed that many of the suppositions supporting the ideas of subsequent periods as different were actually false. The idea that romantic love was an invention of the eighteenth century, whether a consequence of 'modernisation' or not, has been rejected, as has the notion that children were brutally treated as a matter of course. Rather it seems clear that in the eighteenth century, as earlier, parents of all social and religious groups loved their children and that, in bringing them up, they saw the need to teach them basic skills, but regarded this, correctly, as for the benefit of children as much as parents. This was particularly the case when children were to follow the occupations of their parents, a tendency that limited education and opportunities (a restricted number of different jobs by modern standards), and inheritance practices made desirable. French millers were generally apprenticed within their families or with family friends, while their families frequently helped them to find brides, many of whom were the daughters of bakers.

The fact that families lived together in close proximity led to a need for co-operation and mutual tolerance. This necessarily affected the nature of patriarchal authority. Adult figures may have remained external role models in peasant society, as has been suggested. In the southern Massif Central peasants continued to live in a world of patriarchal authority, authoritarian families inculcating deference, discipline and piety. However, this does not mean that affection played no role in relationships, or that families were not the economic partnerships that they had to be were they to survive.

Typical of the writings that denigrated women was *La Morale du Temps*, written by a priest, that appeared first in Valenciennes in 1700 and presented women as inferior and unbearable beings, who provided an opportunity for sin. Female sexuality, often believed to be voracious, and male sexuality, inspired by women, aroused concern in many writers. Rousseau was not alone in fearing female sexuality. These fears were related to the double standard for sexual conduct, which rejected adultery as grounds for separation of a wife from a husband, but not a husband from a wife. Women, but not men, were expected to be virgins when they married and chaste thereafter. If the traditional depiction of women with its obvious Christian roots, that, for example, led the Russian Old Believers to oppose the rule of women, was negative, many of the arguments suggested by intellectuals were little better, and were 'progressive' often only in the sense that they made the debate a secular one.

Given, however, the proprietary pattern of authority between husband and wife, the general legal assumption that women needed the constant protection of a superior male sex, many of these arguments did constitute a challenge to dominant views. Most of the writers of the French Enlightenment condemned customs that limited women's role in society. Their attempts to make a new, supposedly 'rational', analysis of institutions like marriage and the family, such as Montesquieu's examination of marriage in a cultural context, conflicted with the universal assumptions of monogamy and patriarchalism made by the Church. Though the writers did not challenge the viability of marriage as an institution, the validity of certain practices, such as arranged marriages, was contested. Many *philosophes* called for legal changes which, in effect, would have secularised marriage, permitted divorce, which was not to be introduced in France until 1792, and limited paternal power, but, by modern standards, their attitude was generally anti-feminist. Diderot, Helvétius, Montesquieu and Voltaire all supported divorce, but not equal status for women. Condorcet was an exception. D'Holbach praised women's capacity for sentiment, but did not view marriage as a partnership of equals, because he thought that women's weaker 'organs' made them incapable of intense or intricate thought. Diderot thought them incapable of great concentration or displays of genius. Arguing, as the *Encyclopédie* put it, 'that women's destiny is to have children and to nourish them', many of the *philosophes* defined this role in a manner that challenged traditional patriarchalism, while, nevertheless, leaving the woman's role as essentially domestic, a solution that was inappropriate for the economic position of most women.

The call for a new marital relationship, based on sentiment, did not entail a concept of equality. Sentimental literature romanticised domestic life and love, offering a code of values in which affection replaced adultery. Voltaire's *Enfant Prodigue* (1736) and Diderot's *Père de Famille* (1758) advanced this view in the theatre, while Rousseau's novel *Émile* (1762) expounded the value of the relationship it presented between the mother and Émile, the child she had breast-fed. The work was condemned in a number of countries, including France, Geneva and Russia, though for its religious rather than its pedagogic content. The appeal to mothers to suckle their own children was anyway inappropriate for those who had to go to work. While Émile was to be educated in accord with 'nature', this was not to lead to liberation for his wife Sophie, who was to develop her 'natural essence' of motherhood and dependence on man. Opposed to sexual equality, Rousseau also advocated a domestic role for women in his *Discourse on Inequality*. Though Rousseau had a decidedly restrictive view of women, he did write about several who were fully rounded people.

A contrast between women's emotional and physical appeal and their intellectual shortcomings underlay the attitude of most of the *philosophes*. Women might, according to the Chevalier de Jaucourt in the *Encyclopédie*, constitute the principal ornament of society, but this led many writers to regard them as ornaments for the pleasure of men, as well as mothers. Rousseau, who felt women to be incapable of original thought, argued that they should learn the arts that pleased men. The playwright Pierre Marivaux had a more positive attitude to women and in his *La Colonie* (1750) discussed the possibility of a society organised on the principle of sexual equality, including female control of many senior and administrative positions. The thrust of the suggestion was, however, weakened by the comic nature of the play, in which the women eventually divide in accordance with their social origins and send for the men to fight against an alleged invasion, while the fantastic nature of the story, located on an imaginary island, gave it a utopian character. A more progressive writer, Abbé Riballier, in a pedagogic work of 1785, argued that women were naturally equal and should learn arts, sciences and philosophy to the level of men. The popularity of Sarah Scott's *Millennium Hall* suggests that some women members of the elite fantasised about taking complete control of their lives. More generally, there was a growth of female interest in print culture.

The position of women was also debated in Germany, opinions varying considerably. Whereas in 1767 the Baden bureaucrat Johann Reinhard described a utopian world in which public heroes, both men and women, were honoured, the conservative writer Ernst Brandes argued 20 years later that the blood of women was chemically different, that because they had weak brain nerves (a widely held belief), they could not see connections between different ideas, that these anatomical and psychological facts were supported by the historical evidence of male domination, and that women possessed their own distinctive and important functions for which nature had predestined them by giving them the appropriate qualities. Brandes claimed that the rise of a female reading public was dangerous as it would lead them to neglect their domestic obligations.

Brandes' tone was defensive, necessarily so in the face of developments he disapproved of, such as female journalism. Women's journals written by women began in Germany in 1779, 18 years after the strident Madame de Beaumer took over the Parisian *Journal des Dames*, hitherto edited by men. Probably the most popular of the German journals was Sophie von La Roche's *Pomona*, which argued for female education and considered the happiness of individual women at the same time as it stressed an ideology of service for them. In contrast, Marianne Ehrmann in her journals adopted a more critical stance and thought men partly responsible for women's current inferiority. Though the magazines did not call for fundamental alterations, they accepted change, both for individuals and for women in general, as a possibility and suggested that women should assert themselves, a position also found in the English writer Mary Wollstonecraft's *Vindication of the Rights of Women* (1792). Wollstonecraft pressed for equality in education and legal rights, in order to give women a proper role and status. The dilemma facing many women had been earlier represented by the German female playwright Luise Gottsched, in whose first play (1736) the heroine Luisgen, not daring to defy her mother and marry her fiancé, has to resign herself to await her fate, while her wicked sister Dorgen laughs at her concern with parental wishes. Luisgen is rewarded when her father overturns her mother's wishes, while Dorgen is promised a husband when she agrees to behave. The issue of parental authority was similarly evaded in Johann Schlegel's (1746) treatment of the sentimental heroine Amalia, whose beloved turns out to be her father's choice in disguise.

For the philosopher Immanuel Kant women had other problems than the choice of spouses. In 1784, he argued that they were failing to become enlightened, because they were supervised by those who did not wish them to become independent and, accordingly, exploited their timidity and need for comfort. Kant's friend the Prussian civil servant Theodor Gottlieb von Hippel, who had in 1774 produced a conservative treatment of marriage, stressing the subordination of women, in 1792 published a study of women in which he argued that they were equal, adducing theoretical and empirical evidence, including the observation that among the lower classes women, like men, carried out heavy labouring tasks. Claiming that marriage was a technique for social control of women and that enforced ignorance kept them unable to compete with men, Hippel called for equal education, while arguing that equality of the sexes did not imply indistinguishability. His work is an example of what is sometimes seen as the increasingly politicised and fragmented late Enlightenment when many writers attempted to extend its benefits and sympathetic concern to previously scorned or ignored groups, including the poor, women and slaves. Stating that the continued suppression of women might lead them to rebel, Hippel also argued that they had been disappointed by the French Revolution. Indeed the latter, while asserting the civil rights of women, had done little to improve their condition.

The position of women in revolutionary France underlines the question of the practicality of change. Hippel himself observed that among the lower orders the condition of wives was hardly different from that of their husbands, lives of crushing and precarious poverty that limited the opportunities for reflection. Hippel's audience was the middling orders, where circumstances permitted change, including the education of women. The position was possibly not as bleak as he argued. A number of German states had ordered the establishment of local schools and the enforced attendance of both boys and girls. They included Waldeck (1704), Eisenach (1705), Saxony (1724), Württemberg (1729), Hesse-Darmstadt (1733), Holstein-Gottorp (1733–4) and Wolfenbüttel (1753), all Protestant states that were followed in the 1770s and 1780s by several Catholic territories, such as Würzburg. The decrees seem to have been implemented, at least in Württemberg, Prussia and Saxony, where nearly every hamlet had an elementary school by the end of the century. Not all children attended, not least because of their need for immediate employment, but the availability of public elementary schools offered many German peasant women the opportunity to receive a basic education. It is unclear, however, that this had much impact on their lifestyle.

The French proclamation of 1724 ordering every parish to have a male and a female teacher and all parents to send their children to school, was widely ignored and, where there was education for girls, it often consisted of only the catechism and reading. Few French treatises on educational reform included women in their programme, and female education was generally seen as a process of character training, rather than training of the intellect. The structures and programmes of German female education, both elementary and specialised, directed girls to household tasks. Only a small number of women were given an intellectual education. German educational writers of the second half of the century, the so-called philanthropists, called for educational improvements, but emphasised the need for a different education for girls in order to prepare them to act as wives and mothers. These male writers argued that men and women should be equal in marriage, but that such equality came from their naturally different contributions to it, contributions that education should aid without obscuring the differences. Johann Campe's *Fatherly Advice for my Daughter* (1788–9) not only saw marriage, children, and home as the proper destiny for women, but claimed that the unfavourable conditions of women in human society derived from the divine plan for humanity.

Attitudes to the position of women clearly varied. There was no universal patriarchal code or set of conventions. Further contrasts can be discerned if attention is directed away from France and Germany. Though some writers called for dramatic changes in the treatment of women, they were a small minority. Equality was increasingly approved of, but the general notion of equality was one of respect for separate functions and development, and the definition of the distinctive nature of the ideal female condition was one that, by modern standards, certainly did not entail equality. It has been argued that male attitudes to women softened and became more sympathetic to female feelings in the period as a crucial part of the process by which more 'polite' and genteel social norms were encouraged. Yet any stress on this politeness and on restraint in attitudes and behaviour has to address the question as to how far it was deliberately inculcated, to foster moral improvement, social order and Christian manners, in order to cope with a very different way of life and expression. Similarly, the contemporary emphasis on separate spheres was in part a response to the concern of many moralists that numerous women were not conforming to conventional roles. Gender relations were more fluid and flexible than much public debate might suggest.

To a certain extent eighteenth-century debates about their position and goals were meaningless for most women. Even if elementary education could be extended to them, their circumstances were generally bleak, because of their economic condition and the nature of medical knowledge and attention: Wollstonecraft died in childbirth in 1797 at the age of 38. It was to be changes in the last two factors over the following century and a half, rather than legal reforms, that improved the position of most women.

The orders of society

[At] the balls ... the company is of diverse sorts from the first nobility to the poorest countryman, for at paying only about the value of a shilling you are at liberty to enter ... notwithstanding the liberty given to everyone to enter, there is a little more regularity within, the nobility dancing separately, for a citizen is not permitted to dance with a lady of nobility nor even to ask her, so that they are obliged to dance in another apartment or not at all.

(Joshua Pickersgill on the Turin carnival, 1761)[7]

The weight of the past was never more apparent in eighteenth-century Europe than in the distribution of wealth, status and power within society. The influences that affected this distribution were similar to those of the previous century and there was little change in the methods by which the social position of individuals was determined or could be altered, although there was also considerable and increasing diversity of views about the nature of hierarchy. Nevertheless, social control by the elite was a fact, not an issue, in politics. Heredity and stability were regarded as intertwined. Snobbery was common. Furthermore, certainly in comparison with the following two centuries the rate of social change was, particularly at the upper levels, relatively slow and rigidly governed by a variety of devices, including marital strategies, inheritance practices and government patronage, although that does not imply that there was little social change across the century.

The terminology used to describe society was and is frequently misleading or applicable only in some local circumstances. The social context of privilege was not constant. Attitudes and practices, legal definitions and government regulations varied and the assessment of wealth and status was not the same throughout Europe. Whether one considers the economic position of the peasantry or the legal rights of nobles, the reality was one of variety within Europe: an essentially similar agricultural system, the production of goods with relatively low productivity per worker and inegalitarian landownership patterns, being offset by different tenurial relationships and varying social customs.

Within peasant society, there was a major distinction between regions of dispersed settlement and those with stronger communal traditions. In certain parts of Europe the peasantry enjoyed particular political privileges as well as a reasonable social position and an economic regime that was not too unfavourable, as for example, in the Tyrol and in the neighbouring Vorarlberg where the Diet was dominated by the peasants. In Sweden, where the peasantry owned 31.5 per cent of the farmland in 1700, compared with 33 per cent owned by the nobility and 35.5 per cent by the crown, there was a peasant Estate. However, though few Swedish nobles owned much land, many of the peasants owned very little land. In most of Europe the distribution of land ownership was obviously inegalitarian and was matched by readily apparent differences in status and position. The figures vary but they always point to marked differences in landed wealth. For instance, 41 per cent of the lands of the village of Ittre in Brabant in the Austrian Netherlands belonged to the nobility, 8 to the church and 51 to the peasants and bourgeoisie; the major proprietors, nearly all of them nobles, possessed large estates on the most fertile land. The three parishes that made up the community of Duravel in south-western France had a population of about 2300. In the last decades of the century 54 per cent of the families worked on the land, while 27 per cent engaged in artisanal activity closely linked to agriculture and 8 per cent can be defined as nobles and bourgeois, the latter often difficult to distinguish from the well-off peasantry. While 75 per cent of the proprietors of land owned less than 5 hectares, and 90 per cent less than 10, six nobles owned 23 per cent of the farmed property.

Status and power were linked to wealth although not always identical with it. Although in both Catholic and Protestant countries the higher clergy had a rank and privileges similar to those of the nobility, the clerical order was still seen as distinct. Its special character was obvious in the clergy's sacramental powers, corporate identity, wealth and, though only in part of Europe, special clothes and coiffure, and celibacy. Within the nobility, wealth was not the sole basis of status, for birth, connections and government service were all important. Patents of nobility frequently stressed the services of families that were ennobled.

The very existence of social distinctions was seen as obvious, as arising from the natural inequality of talents and energies, and egalitarianism found favour with few writers on social topics, though some thinkers, such as Mably, were willing to propound a radically different type of society. D'Holbach, who discussed a society of classes structured on utilitarian principles, nevertheless accepted the need for a hierarchical structure. Rousseau's project for the government of Corsica revealed a preference for administration by an aristocracy of merit and a hierarchical society. The regulations both of the central governments and of other institutions distinguished between members of particular social groups, as did the conventions that governed their working practices. Legal rights were often socially specific. Noble Russian landowners received full police powers over their peasants, the right to send the latter to hard labour being given them in 1765, while two years later peasants were forbidden to address complaints to the sovereign against their owners, a situation that already existed in Poland. Noble privileges in Russia extended to a particular sensibility, and it was an offence to use offensive words in public before the well-born.

Social differentiation was reflected in a range of activities and spheres, such as sport. Hunting regulations were an obvious field for the implementation of privilege in order to raise local standing, the frequent consequence being a lowering of the living standards of the peasantry or an exacerbation of tension. In Sicily hunting became a perquisite of the wealthy, their methods – falcons and dogs – being accepted, while those of the poor – netting and traps – were prohibited. In order to protect the monopoly of hunting by the Norman nobility, the peasantry were prohibited from possessing arms. Under a regulation of 1766 a simple denunciation by a noble could lead to a peasant's house being searched and the culprit jailed for three months without recourse to the ordinary courts, a situation that led to protests in the *cahiers* of 1789.

As the legal system of most of Europe, whether customary or codified on a national basis, was generally dependent on noble officials for its implementation, noble privileges stood a better chance of being enforced than new government regulations. Legal institutions were not distinct from the rest of the social system; they encapsulated and sustained privilege. Patterns and practices reflected social distinctions. It was rare for members of the elite to suffer execution or imprisonment unless involved in treason, while aristocratic debtors similarly escaped the imprisonment for debt that was a frequent consequence of the role of credit in society. Whether regalian rights had been surrendered or not, the enforcement of the law was generally dependent on those who wielded social power, even if they acted in this capacity as officials of the crown. The Welsh squirearchy was far from alone in abusing the law and courts in order to get their way in disputes with tenants. In many areas, such as Hungary, the legal system was one of private jurisdiction based on local custom rather than a national legal code.

Regulations were generally socially specific. A Tuscan edict of 1748 greatly cut back the ceremonies to be observed in burials and mournings, an example of the determination of many governments to control religious practices and to limit expenditure on them. Nobles who had died were to be exposed in churches upon a pall with twelve wax candles around their corpse, citizens being permitted only six candles. Non-citizen commoners were denied funeral ceremonies and were to be carried to their graves with four flambeaux only. Education was another field in which regulations differentiated between social groups. Though the rules banning commoners from the High School of the St Petersburg Academy of Sciences subsequently lapsed, four prospective students were banned on these grounds in 1734. Noble children were strictly segregated from those of the bourgeoisie in the Karlsschule founded by Karl Eugen of Württemberg in 1771. Throughout the century, Polish nobles in their local assemblies regularly and vainly demanded the enforcement of old sumptuary legislation directed against upstart commoners.

However, it was not solely government regulation that was socially discriminatory. Institutions, whether Spanish religious confraternities or French army masonic lodges, reflected the values of the social hierarchy. The seating arrangement in churches, and the treatment of the dying and their corpses, also reflected social status and differences. Sumptuary legislation, regulating people's clothing, was generally effective because it conformed to social expectations. In the German Imperial Free City of Augsburg women's clothes varied strictly according to their social position. The right to wear a sword in public was restricted in Poland to the nobility, and poor nobles who could not afford one carried a wooden sword. The three Estates in the French Estates General of 1789 dressed very differently.

Attempts to improve the position of groups prior to the Revolution were marked not by any levelling of social distinctions, through the destruction of privileges that they did not possess, but by allowing them to acquire these privileges. When Pombal sought to improve the status of Portuguese merchants, he gave them the right to wear swords, hitherto enjoyed only by the nobility. In contrast, during the Revolution there was in France a demand for simplicity and equality in dress, as noble fashions were rejected as the garb of privilege.[8]

Discrimination in dress was matched in other fields where the benefits of status lent force to a sense of exclusiveness which played a major role in defining social position. Modes of address helped to define status, the nobility possessing an exclusive right to certain forms, such as *Fräulein* for unmarried young ladies in the Empire. It was the continual reiteration of exclusiveness that was crucial to status in a world where members of different social groups lived together and where a failure to maintain position could be regarded as having detrimental consequences.

Marriage was both an opportunity to enhance and maintain the social position of individuals and their families, and also a threat to it. When in 1766 Johann Wöllner, an estate administrator who was the son of a cleric, married the only daughter of General

Itzenplitz, the members of the general's old noble family persuaded Frederick the Great to annul the marriage as a violation of established social barriers. Wöllner was accused of winning the girl's hand improperly. The threat that socially mixed marriages were believed to present was partly responsible for the exclusiveness of many social arrangements. In Frankfurt-on-Main, the merchants and principal citizens constituted a social world that was separate from that of the nobility, who would not admit them into their assemblies. Social distinctions, such as separate education or graded seating at any gathering, whether religious, political or social (the public concerts in Frankfurt for example), defined and protected the world of hierarchy. Those who infringed it could be punished.

The orders into which society was divided were not uniform all over the continent, while the importance both of the orders and of their division varied greatly. Hungarian society was legally stratified, with four estates possessing political privileges: the prelates (higher clergy), the titled nobility, the lesser nobility and the burghers of the royal free towns and mining cities. The Hungarian lesser nobility had the same legal status, but differed much in their wealth; a small group owned several villages and had generally received some higher education, whereas others owned only a little land, and the majority, known as the slippered nobility, possessed no land. In much of Europe the ownership of a significant amount of land was no longer, and had sometimes never been, an indication of noble rank, even though in practice it gave social status. This was the case, for example, in Britain and Denmark.

The extent to which the notion of orders conformed to any social reality was a contentious issue in the period and wealth was potentially an important solvent of other social distinctions, though the capacity of the society of orders to facilitate social mobility and assimilate its consequences should not be under rated. There were obvious disparities in wealth within the first two orders of most of Europe: the clergy and the nobility. Furthermore the wealth, particularly when expressed in the form of landed property and seigneurial jurisdiction, of non-nobles, whether urban or not in origin, was a significant challenge to any notion that the nobility was identical with the major proprietors of land.

The willingness of the nobility to accept new members varied. As wealth was not the sole criterion used, recruitment to this order was not necessarily an incorporation of wealthy non-nobles only. In some areas there was a relatively open social system. In the county of Nice, an adaptive and open society permitted a major role for wealth and talent. In Sweden during the 'Age of Liberty', 1719–72, where the nobility was, in general, open to talent, noble land was acquired by the peasantry through purchase, mortgages and collusive arrangements. Although ennoblement was not valid in Poland unless the *Sejm* (Diet) agreed, in fact significant numbers, often the clients of great nobles, joined the nobility by surreptitious ennoblement or by court judgements 'confirming' their noble status. The new articles of war of 1767 restricted officers' commissions in the Polish army, hitherto open in theory to applicants from all orders, to the nobility, with the exception of the artillery, where the twin pressures of technical need and social derogation encouraged different criteria. Though the regulations were not always enforced, commoners, as in many other armies, were prominent in the technical services and middle, but not higher, ranks.

In Poland it was assumed that ennobled commoners came from the bourgeoisie, an assumption that was common in much of Europe as members of this group enjoyed the wealth that permitted them to purchase landed estates. In Russia, however, social mobility was linked more directly to the notion of service. Not all of those who occupied the top four grades of the Table of Ranks in 1730 enjoyed considerable wealth. But even though wealth was not a precondition for these positions, there were no sons of serfs and free peasants, both specifically banned, or of priests and provincial nobles. However, only 62 per cent of Russian officers in the 1720s were of noble origin and the Petrine period was one when both social mobility via military service was a real possibility and the non-landed element in the officer corps was substantial. As the century progressed, such upward mobility became more difficult and fewer non-nobles achieved commissioned-officer status and therefore noble rank. This trend matched the success of the nobles in prohibiting non-noble industrialists from acquiring serfs. It also mirrored the Russian decrees of 1737, 1739 and 1742, which attempted to limit the ability of local administrators to advance commoners in their service to noble rank.

In Prussia, where the purchase of estates by commoners was hindered, the situation also became more restrictive. Under Frederick I (1688–1713) the granting of titles had been fairly common, and under his son Frederick William I (1713–40) the majority of officials, including those of senior rank, were of non-noble stock. However, Frederick the Great (1740–86) sought to end the granting of titles for money and was generally unwilling to confer them on commoners, believing that the nobles were the natural support of the administration and the army. Far from buying noble land, Frederick ensured that no noble estates could be sold without his permission, and in the 1770s rural credit institutes were established to help landowners in difficulties and to provide investment capital. The *Académie des Nobles* was founded in Berlin in 1763 to train young nobles as administrators and officers.

In France a number of criteria determined status. The *capitation* tax introduced in 1695 divided French society into 22 classes. Classification was in terms of birth, governmental position, wealth, and consideration or personal connections. The importance of royal service was indicated by the first class, which included ministers and leading tax farmers, but not princes and dukes who were not close relatives of the king.[9] In France, it was possible to acquire nobility by purchase of a variety of offices that conferred this status and its attendant privileges. The absence of restrictions on the purchase of land by non-nobles further helped to blur social distinctions. Though certain *parlements* sought to exclude commoners, this process had not begun in the eighteenth century and many commoners, or those only recently ennobled, were still being admitted to other *parlements* in appreciable numbers during the reign of Louis XVI (1774–92). There was no great change in the social composition of the *parlements* during the century. The percentage of commoners entering the *Parlement* of Paris remained constant at about 10 between 1715 and 1771.

Ennoblement in France was relatively easy for those with money. The ennoblement of merchants represented a social recognition of the economic benefits of commerce. Though all *intendants*, the key agent of the central government in the localities, were nobles, an increasing number came from recently established families. Ennoblement was not without political benefits, including the more willing integration of important groups in territories recently conquered.

If it is difficult to measure, there is none the less little doubt of the existence of tensions in eighteenth-century society. However, it would be misleading to suggest either that there was widespread criticism of the existence of a hereditary hierarchical society or that tensions were only apparent between, as distinct from within, social groups. The peasantry and the nobility, far from being uniform, were generally legally defined groups characterised by internal differences. Nobles vied with one another for local political power and social eminence, a process matched by that of peasants within their own communities. The peasant who sought to plant whichever crops he judged most profitable, and thus challenged the communal solidarity necessary for common farming, was as much a source of tension as the artisan who defied guild regulations.

Such disagreements were not novel. The theory, and practice, of communal activity had always had to co-exist with the conflicting aspirations of individuals, and it is by no means clear that this became a significantly greater problem throughout Europe during the century. It has been argued that the corporate social structure of France declined in the last decades of the *ancien régime*, as traditional social units, such as extended families, guilds, towns and provinces, ceased to satisfy the aspirations of the population. However, it is by no means apparent how novel or general this trend was and recent studies on peasant communities, towns and guilds suggest that it was far from common. Neither is it certain that economic development and wealth acted as a solvent of traditional notions of social organisation and behaviour. Fashions and opinions were shaped by the nobility, became important and successful if they adopted them, and thus were emulated by other groups. Notions of social status overwhelmingly stemmed from the nobility.

In Mercier's *L'An 2440* a painting was described that illustrated the eighteenth century. The century was represented by a woman whose beautiful head was weighed down by extravagant ornaments. In each hand she grasped apparently ornamental ribbons which concealed chains that bound her tightly, while allowing her enough room to frolic about. Her smile was forced, her captivity disguised, her rich dress torn and dirty at the bottom. Through holes in her dress it was possible to see thin little crying children feeding on a scrap of black bread. In the background of the painting, magnificent *châteaux* surrounded by poorly cultivated fields filled with piteous peasants were depicted. Mercier captured the contrasts of the period, the poverty and hardships that the privileged sought to keep at bay. Those whose wealth challenged the traditional society of orders did not generally wish to destroy the world of privilege. The seigneurial life of Voltaire, whose wealth came from the most decided rival hierarchy, that of talent, awoke him to the extreme plight of the peasants, and his landed investments made him a philanthropist. By contrast, most aspirants to status wished simply to live in the *châteaux* and to have their consequent position awarded due rank and deference. The large number of poems produced to commemorate the death of the Duke of Brunswick, who drowned in the river Oder in 1785 while attempting to rescue two peasants being carried away by flood waters, was a testimony to a heroic model of true nobility and individual bravery, not a suggestion that the elite ought to sacrifice themselves for the poor.

Nobility

It is not surprising that Europe's power and wealth was concentrated in the hands of a relatively small number of families. The hierarchical nature of society and of the dominant political systems, the predominantly agrarian nature of the economy, the generally slow rate of change in social and economic affairs, the unwillingness of monarchs and their commonly noble-dominated governments to challenge fundamentally the interests of the nobility or to govern without their co-operation, and the inegalitarian assumptions of the period, all combined to ensure that the concentration of power and wealth remained reasonably constant.

Most nobles were neither particularly powerful nor especially wealthy, even if, in comparison with the bulk of the population, they would be fairly placed in these categories, but those who enjoyed power and wealth tended to be nobles by birth or creation. The character and position of the nobility varied greatly, both across Europe and within individual countries, and they cannot be said to have possessed a united view on affairs. The nobility's attitudes were crucial to the reception and success of government policies and many of the central social and political questions of the period, such as changes in the nature of taxation and in the position of the peasantry, revolved around their likely and actual response. This was influenced by a mixture of precedent, privilege, self-interest, the interplay of traditional and novel views, and the political context. Governments sought the consent of the nobles, sometimes through constitutional necessity but, more commonly, because of their reliance on nobles as the effective administration in the community, and also because co-operation was seen as desirable as well as essential, a source of legitimacy as much as of implementation. Successful government initiatives were generally those that the nobility were willing to support, acquiesce in or at least not actively seek to thwart.

Towards the end of the century this general co-operation over privileges, the disposal of patronage and policies was placed under great stress, first in the Habsburg lands, where Joseph II proved unwilling to adapt the nature and pace of his changes to noble susceptibilities, and secondly in France where the attempt in the late 1780s to produce a programme of reforms that would enjoy adequate support from the nobility failed. Though some nobles were willing to surrender many of their privileges, most of their representatives were not. It proved impossible to create a satisfactory political consensus, and, in the volatile atmosphere of the summer of 1789, the nobles saw most of their privileges abolished by legislative fiat. Outside the National Assembly, most French nobles were no more enthusiastic about their loss of privileges than their counterparts in the territories of Joseph II, although there were important regional differences, with Normandy, western France and the Massif Central proving more conservative than the Paris basin.

Numbers

It is scarcely surprising that the percentage both of nobles and of their ownership of land varied greatly by country, given the marked differences in definition that characterised their position. In England, where special privileges, and relatively few of those, were attached only to the peerage, its numbers were very small. At the beginning of 1710 there were only 167 male peers, and the plentiful creations of the 1780s took the number up to only 220 in 1790. The small size and relatively closed nature of the peerage helps to make nobility too narrow a specification for any analysis of the English elite. Throughout Britain it was the major landowners who constituted the most appropriate comparison with the continental nobilities.

The relative size of the continental nobility varied enormously. In Venice and its mainland possessions, where the appeal and ease of ennoblement were limited, there were about 10,000 nobles in mid-century, 0.7 per cent of the population. The 795 noble families in the duchy of Savoy in 1702 constituted just over 1 per cent, while the figure for Piedmont was slightly larger. At the end of the century, there were about 2500 titled aristocrats in Sicily, while in the province of Luxemburg in 1766 there were 424 noble families, their loss of fiscal privileges and the province's poverty and infertile soil being possibly responsible for their low birth rates. France had about 110,000 or 120,000 nobles in 1789 in about 25,000 families, of whom 6500 had become noble during the century. Some estimates for the number of French nobles are, however, far higher. In Bohemia there were 228 families of princes, counts and barons in 1741, and 303 of knights, a noble rank. In contrast to the countries with a relatively small percentage of nobles, a list that also included Austria, Sweden and Tuscany, several possessed proportionately large numbers. In Transylvania (8–9 per cent) the ownership of land was substantially restricted to the nobility, in Poland at least a comparable figure claimed noble status, a figure that rose to over 10 per cent for north-west Spain, while in Hungary the percentage was also appreciable.

The figures did not remain constant during the century. Attempts to regulate the position of the nobility, by, in particular, scrutinising claims to this rank, helped to depress figures in some countries. In Spain the majority of the nobles were poor *hidalgos* and the measures taken to restrict their numbers led to a fall in the size of the nobility from 722,000 in 1768 to 400,000 (4 per cent of the population) in 1797. In 1773 poor *hidalgos* were ordered to take up manual work. This did not, however, entail any attack upon the existence of the nobility. With the exception of Ferdinand VI, the Spanish monarchs of the period were prepared to grant a significant number of promotions to the senior ranks, at the same time as very few new *hidalgos* were created. In the absence of an interventionist monarch, the largely self-governing nobility of Russia's Baltic provinces acted in mid-century to resist access to the nobility. The compilation of new registers of the nobility in Estonia in 1743 and Livonia in 1747 and the approval of new regulations from the Diets in the late 1750s limited Diet membership and office-holding there to registered nobles who possessed manors, a move that handicapped non-registered nobles, who had acquired status through service under the tsars, as well as landholding townspeople. The registers of the corporations of the nobility of Estonia, Livonia and the island of Ösel comprised only 324 families.

The partitions of Poland (1772, 1793, 1795) were followed by the partial regularisation of the position of the Polish nobility, as governmental control limited aristocratic pretensions. The Sarmatian ideology, based on the myth that the nobles were descended from the people of ancient Sarmatia, had stipulated the equality of the Polish nobility, but had scant appeal for governors conscious that the majority of the large number who claimed noble status and privileges were poor and poorly educated. Count Pergen, the first Austrian governor of Galicia, had as little sympathy with his charges as many of the English officials sent to Ireland had for theirs. Most of the privileges of the nobles, including exemption from direct taxation, were abolished, while the introduction of new titles and the accompanying regulation of the local nobility ensured that the privileges of only about 700 nobles were recognised in the 1780s. As had been the case prior to the First Partition, the majority of the nobles were poor and in debt, but the small number of families who owned most of the land became proportionately more numerous. Whereas Russia had gained relatively small additions to her nobility when she acquired Estonia and Livonia and encouraged the leading Cossacks of the Ukraine to assume hereditary noble status, her gains from Poland ensured that as late as the 1850s the majority of the Russian empire's nobility were Polish. In contrast to the figure of 150,000 nobles for all the Greater Russian provinces in 1795, about 600,000 individuals claimed nobility in Lithuania, western Ukraine and eastern Belorussia (White Russia, Belarus), although the Russian government was reluctant to accept some claims, particularly by nobles who were tenants.

Falls in the number of nobles were not due to positive government action alone. A failure to permit sufficient ennoblement could have comparable effects, as it did in both Genoa and

Venice. Though the demographic decline of the nobility of the latter has been blamed in part on the infertility produced by gonorrhoea, for which there was no reliable cure, the marital strategies of the nobility were important. The stress on obligations to the family over individual inclination, common to the nobility throughout Europe, produced in this context a pressure for younger brothers and sisters to remain unmarried, in order to avoid a dissipation of family resources. In Britain a comparable effect, as far as the numbers of the nobility were concerned, was produced by the inheritance of noble status by the eldest son alone. Other children were not released destitute into the world, but the combination of primogeniture and the restriction of noble status was largely responsible for the relative absence of poor nobility in Britain, and particularly England. There were, however, poor gentry.

In contrast most of the European nobility was poor. Of the approximately 2500 Sicilian titled aristocracy at the end of the century, 142 of whom were princes, marquises, dukes and barons, only about 20 were particularly important and prosperous. Only 42 noble families ran Venice. In the 1740s there was marked tension between the wealthy Venetian nobles and their more numerous poor colleagues. In 1762, 51 per cent of Russian serf-owners had fewer than 21 male serfs over the age of 15, whereas 1 per cent owned over 1000. In Belorussia, 26 owners possessed one-third of all the serfs. Nine of the Bohemian counts declared incomes over 50,000 florins in 1741, 94 incomes of less than 10,000. An enquiry into non-demesne holdings in the Trans-Danubian region of western Hungary in 1767 revealed that 28 lords, 5 of them ecclesiastical, controlled 47.6 per cent of the area, while 943 lay lords controlled only 6.1 per cent.

Differences in wealth were not the sole distinctions within the European nobility. Nobles were also divided by rank, date of creation, and privileges. There were about 350 families of German Imperial Free Knights, exercising authority over about 1500 small territories with a combined population of about 350,000. Though generally no wealthier than most German nobles, and sharing a similar lifestyle, they possessed sovereign rights, such as those of levying taxes, conscripting troops and decreeing capital punishments in their courts. Unlike most German nobles, who were subordinate to particular territorial princes, the Imperial Free Knights had a collective right to sit at the Imperial Diet and were answerable only to imperial authority. Distinctions within the nobility could create tension, as in Brittany, where the exclusiveness of the older nobility was not welcoming to those recently ennobled. However, client relationships could serve to unite wealthy and poor nobles, particularly where there were many of the latter and relatively few opportunities for state service, as in Poland.

Definition and role

A significant source of tension in some countries was the attempt to redefine nobility by altering its purpose and/or composition. This sometimes derived from obvious political intentions. The parliamentary representation of the Scottish peerage was limited to 16 chosen by them every election after the Act of Union with England was passed in 1707. Twelve years later the Peerage Bill sought to change this to 25 nobles who were to inherit the position at the same time as the size of the English nobility was to be fixed. The measure was defeated, not least because of the heavy representation in the House of Commons of gentry who aspired to ennoblement. The Bill was a British variant on the standard agenda of monarchical politics. It had been designed to limit the options of the heir to the throne, the future George II, who was bitterly opposed to his father's ministers. In Scotland, in another political measure, heeditable jurisdictions were abolished as part of the attempt to increase governmental control of the Highlands after the suppression of the 1745 Jacobite uprising.

In other countries attempts to make changes in the nobility were more obviously administrative than political. Tables of Ranks issued in a number of countries, including Sweden (1696), Denmark (1699), Prussia (1705) and Russia (1722), made it clear that social and political privilege derived from monarchical approval on a continuing basis. In Russia the Table provided a set of regulations by which those who already had nobility could be ranked on criteria favourable to the ruler, while noble status could be awarded to those who achieved high rank in his, or her, service. All officials who reached at least rank 8 received hereditary noble status and thus at least legal equality with the hereditary nobility.

Nobility of birth was also recognised in the Russian Table of Ranks, which stipulated the grant of a coat of arms to those who could demonstrate at least 100 years of noble status, despite their failure to serve, though Peter the Great also decreed that a born nobleman who did not serve and therefore had not achieved rank in the Table was to be regarded as inferior to a ranked commoner. The Table did not take the place of the genealogical considerations that played such a major role in European regulations concerning nobility and lists of nobles, but it supplemented it, crucially so in a society where monarchical favour was central to political prominence and important for gains in wealth.

Social tension between 'old' and 'new' nobles had been common in much of Europe for a long period, and was exacerbated as a political issue when monarchs could be regarded as going too far in favouring and/or creating new nobles. The purpose behind an institutionalised service nobility, defined in a Table of Ranks was to ease this tension, for, while lessening the basis for the exclusiveness of the 'old' nobility, it simultaneously provided them with a social system that they could hope to dominate anew, as, indeed, was generally intended and for which their aptitudes fitted them. The senior ranks of the Russian Table were dominated by members of old noble families.

The idea of service as central to status and privileges was stressed more in eastern than western Europe. In Poland, the increasingly unrealistic idea of the special role of the nobility, particularly in military affairs, backed up by an intense stress on the service and self-sacrifice of virtuous ancestors, was used to justify their legal privileges. In western Europe distinctive noble status was harder to define, other than with respect to the past: the individual past of noble birth and the collective past of grants of privileges in return for services. In such a system, ennoblement could cause more tension, though in France the continuous role of the idea of service was represented in the ennobling quality of many offices, some of which were, however, sinecures. The relationship between status and service in France focused on access to governments.

Much of the western European nobility performed no obvious service, particularly in periods of peace, while the service that was offered was not always on acceptable terms. The writer and official Gaspar Melchor de Jovellanos hoped that the Spanish nobility would become a bureaucratic elite, but they saw no reason why they should change their destined role. In 1756 the prince of Conti's claim that he had been dishonoured by not being granted command over the army that was preparing to move into Westphalia, led Louis XV to note that he was receiving too many similar complaints and that they infuriated him. The same views were voiced by other monarchs. Charles XII of Sweden, who abolished the difference in rank between noble and commoner members of the High Court and appointed commoners to important posts, thought, like Peter the Great, that officers should serve an apprenticeship as common soldiers. In 1706 he rejected a suggestion that a nobleman should be exempted from this process, with the observation that rank had nothing to do with merit. Frederick II of Hesse-Cassel generally ignored family petitions for preferment in his bureaucracy, maintaining his resistance to noble pressures that were directed against the merit system helping to preserve the professional standards of his officials.

Though the rulers of Prussia and Russia might not be happy with the nature of the service they sometimes received, most of their adult male nobles appear to have served as officials or officers. The contrast with the position in western Europe may have owed something to the greater average wealth of the nobility in the latter, outside Spain. The general poverty of the rural economy in eastern Europe encouraged most nobles to seek state office, in which gains could be considerable. The landed estates of the Russian monarchy were nearly halved by Peter the Great's grants to the service nobility. The poverty of many nobles in countries where this option was less common indicated the potential value of state service. In Transylvania most nobles struggled on small estates, unable to support the lifestyle judged essential for the maintenance of their status. In Poland, where the relatively large proportion of nobles would have created a strain on any system of state service, many nobles welcomed the opportunity to serve either their wealthy fellows or foreign rulers, a large number joining the Prussian forces.

In western Europe many nobles sought to enter state service, though this was neither as general as it was in Russia, nor expressed in a Table of Ranks. In France, the 'old' nobility opposed the entry of newer nobles into the army. Possibly the decline in the size of the French army from its highpoint in the latter years of Louis XIV's reign, and the general peacefulness of western Europe in 1763–92, played a role in reducing the opportunities for noble service in France, with arguably serious political consequences. Contemporaries stressed the pressure for war from the nobility at the time of France's entry into the wars of the Polish (1733) and Austrian (1741) successions. The Corsican *principali* (notables) sought in 1730 to restrict to themselves access to the major posts in the administration, army, church and judiciary. Deploring the confusion which they discerned between '*nobili e ignobili*' they called for the institution of an order of Nobili Regnicola, in which the most ancient and illustrious families could be inscribed. Definition and information were to serve the cause of status. In Britain the growth in employment in the armed forces, the bureaucracy, law and medicine between 1680 and 1725 can be seen as opening up major opportunities to the gentry, at least those who were Protestant, and in helping to provide the social context of stability. No comparable expansion has been discerned elsewhere in western Europe. In Spain the *grandees* (most senior nobles) displayed little enthusiasm for military or civil employment, though sinecures were welcome.

The attitudes of the corporate society were still very much alive in the 1780s. In some circles the distribution of privilege and status was under challenge, but, in general, the notion was as uncontested as its hereditary form. The willingness of some nobles to renounce their privileges at the time of the Revolution reflected the impact of critical views, but they were in a minority. In France the National Assembly abolished noble titles in 1790. In Hungary that year counts Mihály Sztáray and János Fekete renounced their titles and joined the lower chamber in the Diet, the former speaking French as an expression of his political views. Most of their colleagues were unmoved. On 1 January 1791 the order was changed for the usual march of the Chevaliers du Saint Esprit in Paris, from one of birth and quality to one of length of membership in the Order. The attack on the nobility was not the least of the reasons why the French Revolution had so little appeal elsewhere. The redefinition of noble membership and status decreed in some countries over the previous century had been accepted, if, at times, only partially. Destruction was, however, a different matter. The European societies of Orders, whatever their weaknesses, did not collapse before revolutionary and Napoleonic France. They had to be conquered and then assimilated.

Power and government

The power of the nobility was not simply a matter of their social status and assumed role in society. They were also collectively extremely wealthy, a situation maintained in some countries by their inheritance practices and by legal restrictions on land purchases by commoners. As most wealth was inherited or acquired by marriage the relevant laws and their implementation were important. Entails to maintain estates intact were obtainable in Italy, Spain and much of the Empire, while the 'strict settlement' in England limited the ability of a landowner to alienate his family estates. Not the least irritating of Joseph II's proposals was his attempt to end entail and his determination to give every child an equal right to the succession. Across Europe, most land lost by individual noble families was not lost from the nobility. Losses by marriage or sale were generally to other nobles, or to those who were ennobled. Discussion of poor and declining noble families has sometimes ignored both the presence of wealthy and ascending noble families and the continual changes in relative wealth brought about by demographic chance, economic fortune and political success.

Possessions, particularly land, were the basis of noble wealth. The extent to which nobles personally exploited them varied. Much European agriculture was starved of capital and arguably of managerial expertise, but it would be misleading to suggest that nobles were especially bad landowners. In many areas of Europe, such as Prussia and south-west France, they were energetic and efficient estate managers. The Salers and the Escorailles, nobles in the agriculturally stagnant Upper Auvergne in central France, actively invested in local agriculture and depended heavily on market-oriented dairy production. The nobles most prominent in the Rakoczi rising in Hungary (1703–11) were actively engaged in agricultural production for the market and in mining and metallurgy.

The extent of noble commercial and industrial activity varied greatly. If nobles in Overijssel in the United Provinces sought a monopoly of wine and brandy sales in 1725, those in Russia owned half the registered woollen mills in 1773 and the marquis de Castries received mining concessions in France in 1777, it was nevertheless true that most European nobles took no part in these activities. However, though the mass of French or Polish nobles were agrarian, provincial in every sense of the word, and not wealthy, this does not diminish the importance of those of their wealthier colleagues who were more active and varied in their investments.

A certain degree of noble wealth derived from seigneurial rights. The ownership, nature and significance of rights of overlordship varied. In Britain such rights were scanty, but in much of Europe they were considerable, particularly in the field of jurisdiction. Though in some countries, such as France, it was not necessary to be a noble to enjoy such rights, in most of Europe they were enjoyed only by nobles. Additional, though frequently related, to their ownership of land, they could bring considerable profit and power, particularly over the peasants of the area. Judicial decisions had often to be paid for, while the monopoly services of the manor, such as milling and baking, could be enforced through the seigneurial courts. In Sicily, where seigneurial rights increased after the Bourbon acquisition of the island in 1735, peasants were forced to use nobles' mills and olive presses, and were prevented from competing with them. Such dues could play a major role in the agricultural economy. Seigneurial revenues accounted for about one-third of the total income from the estates of the Salers and the Escorailles. In the Rouergue region in France taxes on the use of ovens and mills, tolls and market duties were evidence of the continued vitality of feudal fiscalism. Seigneurial powers could also help in the erosion of common rights. The nobles of Artois thus acquired 40 per cent of the province's common land in 1759–89.

These powers were, however, not only condemned by many writers, such as the future revolutionary Lebrun, who in 1769 urged the chancellor Maupeou to abolish seigneurial justice in France, but also viewed with disfavour by many officials who resented this limitation of royal powers and queried the way in which they were implemented. The existence and practice of seigneurial jurisdiction was attacked in several countries, though these attacks were resisted. A commission formed in 1736 to investigate the matter in the kingdom of Naples saw its proposals shelved in 1744 as a consequence of noble opposition. The French government reversed their 1780 transfer of police powers of the seigneurial court of the duchy of Elbeuf to the local *intendant* when the seigneur, the prince de Lambesc, complained. It was not until 1788 that the powers of French seigneurial courts were curbed. Though in 1790 seigneurial justice was abolished in Portugal, and the administration of justice thus unified, no such progress was made in Spain. Marquis Domenico Caracciolo, viceroy of Sicily 1781–6, however, launched a determined attack on noble jurisdiction. Blaming it for poor law and order and for weakening the economy by oppressing the peasantry, he required proof for baronial claims to jurisdiction, forbade the substituting of baronial insignia for those of the king, attacked landlords who forced tenants to use their mills and sought to defend local authorities against the claims of the nobility. Though Joseph II did not abolish manorial jurisdiction, seigneurial courts were reduced in number, while their officials had to take an oath of allegiance to the ruler and, though chosen by the noble, had to be approved by the local court of appeal. In Denmark the nobility's right to exercise judicial rights on their own lands met growing opposition by the 1780s and the administrative role of local royal officials was expanded accordingly.

While the existence and role of noble jurisdiction aroused the hostility of some ministers, noble domination of high positions in the church led to less criticism and action. In some countries, noble claims to preferment were formalised in regulations that excluded the claims of others. This was particularly the case in the Empire where appointments to the senior positions in most bishoprics, abbacies and chapters were exclusive to the nobility. The prebendaries of dioceses such as Olomouc had to prove their nobility, while the chapter at Münster required that all its members be legitimate and of the imperial feudal nobility to the fifth degree, that is each of the 16 great-great-grandparents of the candidate had to be thus qualified. Such provisions obviously encouraged marriage within families that fulfilled this requirement. Noble influence was not restricted to Catholic principalities in the Empire. Prussian nobles received monastic and collegiate prebends from the government. In England and Ireland there was no noble monopoly of senior clerical posts, though the proportion of noble bishops rose through the century, as it did in France where the percentage of noble bishops rose to 97 by the beginning of 1789. Furthermore the average longevity of the familial noble status of the French bishops increased appreciably. If, in France, the nobility did not have a legal right to a monopoly of episcopal office, they did not suffer as a consequence. Noble dominance of senior French ecclesiastical posts was not limited to the bishops, but extended through most of the clergy, both regular and secular. It was not solely in the chapters of Guyenne that there were few from a mercantile or peasant background. Similarly in Hungary and the Austrian Netherlands, senior dignitaries were of noble origin.

Noble influence was not restricted to the composition of the upper ranks of the clergy. Both as clergy and laity, nobles controlled much church patronage. About 12 per cent of English church livings were at the disposal of the peerage in the 1720s, a figure that had increased to about 14 per cent by 1800. Though the legal basis of noble nomination to livings varied in Europe, it was a reality in many areas. Nobles could also feel confident that their status would be recognised in the world of religion, as in the ceremonial of religious services and processions, the seating arrangements in churches or the size and location of funerary monuments.

Nobles dominated the senior ranks of Europe's governments as well, if only because many non-noble administrators, such as Pompeo Neri, were ennobled; 25 per cent of those Hesse-Cassel officials occupying key middle- and upper-level positions in 1760–85 whose fathers were not born into the nobility became nobles, either in recognition of their own work or through the ennoblement of a civil servant father. The political sphere most dominated by the nobility was the court. This was where they most wished to shine and where social rank could be most readily transmuted into offices of prestige, power and profit. Though not all monarchs regarded themselves as, in some way, the 'first' of the nobility, most tended to see the senior nobility as their natural social companions, a tendency encouraged by the presence among them of cadet branches of the royal family. All the Portuguese dukes claimed kinship with the monarch. Far from living in the provinces, nobles were expected to hold posts at court. Karl Friedrich of Baden and Frederick the Great, who excluded bourgeois councillors from high office, were not alone in regarding nobles as a biologically superior group.

In much of Europe central government was in part an extension of the court, although there was a gradual movement of government away from the court after mid-century. This was a reflection of new demands for expertise in administration that nobles could not supply. Court ceremonial remained, but it was less an expression of power than of social prestige. The court nobility, with their social eminence and favoured access to the monarch, benefited from royal patronage. Sometimes this aroused the envy and hostility of the poor provincial nobility. In France there was a certain degree of animosity directed accordingly towards the court and the more prominent noble groups and milieux. Similar tendencies could be found in other countries, sometimes exacerbated when the court nobility was associated with a foreign monarch, such as the Saxon kings of Poland, or a monarch who could be conceived of as foreign. However, clientage relationships could serve to link court and provincial nobilities, as could a sense of common identity in an inegalitarian society, a sense in which a shared history and status compensated in part for distinctions in wealth and for frequently limited social relations.

Many nobles entered full-time government service. The cosmopolitan nature of much of the European nobility, particularly in its senior ranks, and the strongly developed tradition of entering the service of foreign rulers, particularly in the Empire and Italy, where nobles might own possessions in different territories, ensured that individual nobles could seek posts under several rulers. Furthermore, many rulers welcomed foreign nobles as officials, a process eased by the foreign origin of several dynasties, such as the Spanish Bourbons. Numerous German nobles entered Russian service, though many of them were from the conquered Estonian and Livonian provinces and from Courland. Italians flocked to Austria and Spain. At the higher levels, administrative posts were not closed by entrance requirements with formal qualifications of competence or an ability to handle the native language. Count Joseph Gabaléon de Salmour, a Piedmontese noble, whose mother was Polish, entered Saxon service in the 1780s. It was not simply a matter of monarchical favour overcoming obstacles, for republics were also keen to appoint foreigners, particularly to military posts. William VIII of Hesse-Cassel and William of Hesse-Philippstal were not the only German princes to gain posts in the Dutch army, while William Graeme of Bucklivie served in the Dutch before transferring to the Venetian army. Military service was preferred by many nobles: 35 per cent of the old Danish nobility and 17 of the new were in military service in 1700, compared with only 6 and

8 per cent respectively in the civil service. In 1765 the percentages for Sweden, where in accordance with the definition of noble privileges in 1723, all senior official and military posts were reserved for the nobility, were 73 and 14. Military posts sometimes entailed the governorships of strategic fortresses or provinces.

Possibly the importance of noble officership should be related not only to the prestige of service in the army, but also to the relatively underdeveloped nature of most central administrations. There were few posts for nobles in the poorly developed fields of central government administration of economic and social welfare affairs. However, nobles tended to be represented disproportionately in the senior ranks of government, such as the Privy Council and General Directory in Hesse-Cassel. Over 74 per cent of the French ministers of 1718–89 possessed nobility older than the third generation. It was the custom to appoint only nobles to the presidencies of the colleges (ministries) in Baden, while all members of the senior ranks of the Portuguese nobility had the right to at least the title of councillor of state, and membership of the comparable institution in the Austrian Netherlands was reserved to nobles.

The attitude of nobles to their posts varied greatly. Many wished to serve only in accordance with their own conception of their role. In 1727 the highly-intelligent duke of Richelieu confessed to an intimate that he had been led to accept the French embassy at Vienna only because he wished to improve his situation by holding an official post and to convince himself that he was capable of serious affairs. He admitted that many diplomatic issues did not interest him and that he sought a post 'which frees me from the tyranny of the Secretaries of State and leaves me to read tranquilly what I want, to amuse myself with my friends and help them with the king...or a governorship that would allow me to lead the life of a small king, that is to do whatever I like from dawn to dusk'.[10] Thirty years later, the marshal-duke of Belle-Isle had to be persuaded that he would not compromise his social position if he became secretary of state for war. The disdain of the French nobility of the sword for bureaucratic tasks and qualities was pronounced.

The co-option of members of old noble houses, the ennoblement of non-noble officials and the promotion in the aristocracy of low-ranking members who held important offices, helped to sustain noble dominance of central government. In Portugal Pombal wished not to destroy the old nobility, but to revive it by an infusion of new blood and thus create a governing group open to new ideas and aware of the value of trade. Such attempts, however, were not free from disagreement, for, aside from differences over policies and patronage, there were tensions within the nobility, revealed by criticism, such as the hostility to new blood expressed in France by the duke of Saint Simon, that was focused when favours were given to those who were felt not to deserve them.

The balance between the employment of nobles, old and new, high rank and low ranks, and commoners varied by country and ruler, but the diminution in civil conflict in most countries, compared with the previous century, possibly helped to remove the principal hindrance to the employment of the nobility. Domestic political stability encouraged stability in the employment of nobles in central government, and was, in turn, encouraged by it. This could be compromised when issues of monarchical succession arose, as in Spain during the War of Succession, Bohemia in 1741 or Scotland in 1745, when nobles were most prominent in declaring their allegiance to one or other claimant, but such issues became increasingly uncommon. Furthermore, another important barrier to the employment of noblemen was lessened by the gradual move towards elite religious homogeneity that had been pronounced in the previous century, with, in particular, the widespread conversion of noble houses in France, Poland and the Austrian Habsburg lands to Catholicism. This continued in the eighteenth century.

Whatever the position in central government, local government tended to be dominated by the nobility. This appeared natural to most monarchs, as well as being the practical current solution to an issue that many wished to ignore or did not see as a problem, the power of the nobility in the localities. Noble dominance of local government took two forms: control over the relevant posts, and the allocation to the nobles of many responsibilities, that might otherwise have fallen into the public sphere, a process that was readily apparent where they enjoyed seigneurial jurisdiction. In some areas, central control of the localities definitely declined. This was particularly marked in the Balkans where a new group of provincial rulers commonly known as *ayans* (notables) emerged with a local power base. Effective local administration was frequently provided only by them. Powerful local families dominated Albania, central Greece and the Morea with the aid of private armies. Bosnia was run by the beys, a strong local, Muslim, semi-independent nobility, who spoke the local language and understood local traditions, while the power of the Turkish governor was often very restricted. The sale of state land to rich officials in much of the Turkish Empire did little to increase central authority. The weakness of the central government forced it to co-opt many of the *ayans* into the provincial administrative system and, particularly in periods of difficulty, they were granted official appointments. At other times determined leaders sought to curb *ayan* power, the energetic grand vezir Halil Hamid Pasa launching one such attempt in 1785 which was, however, abandoned when war broke out with Russia two years later.

It was not only in the Balkans that the relationship in the localities between government and the nobility could be ambiguous. The control of coastal smuggling in Brittany was complicated by the participation of many nobles. The prince of Conti's opposition, as seigneur of Étampes, to measures to stop illicit grain-dealing in 1738 was not the sole occasion when seigneurial privileges and interests clashed with the regulation of the grain trade by the Paris police.

In the Austrian Netherlands, where many nobles depended on positions at the court in Brussels, provincial governors were invariably nobles, though during the reign of Maria Theresa (1740–80) the higher nobility found their influence in the central government of the Austrian Netherlands decline. Provincial governors in France were nobles, certain families enjoying such posts for many years. The dukes of Aumont were governors of Boulogne from 1622 until the Revolution. The French provincial governors could control considerable patronage, and they were also politically important, remodelling the provincial *parlements* for Maupeou in 1771. The following year, Frederick II of Hesse-Cassel created 10 provincial governorships, all of which were to be filled from the nobility as a result of consultation between them and the landgrave. In Denmark landlords had a responsibility in rural tax collection and military conscription, being personally answerable for the land tax and conscript quota of their tenantry. Here, as in much of Europe east of the Elbe, government obviously relied on a partnership between rulers and landlords who performed many basic public functions. The rural commissioners responsible for the execution of administrative regulations appointed in Silesia in 1742 were royal appointees, but they were chosen from the local nobility and regarded by them as their delegates.

In the early years of the century the government of Morea in southern Greece, conquered by the Venetians in 1685–7, provided poor Venetian nobles with posts and opportunities to plunder the local population. The loss of this territory was blamed for an increase in noble crime and vice in Venice. Poor nobles were also sent as governors to Venetian possessions in Dalmatia and the Ionian islands. In the Baltic lands conquered by Peter the Great, however, there was no attempt either to displace the local nobility or to remove their control over local government. When insecure at the beginning of her reign, Catherine II confirmed the rights and privileges of the local nobility. Until 1786 the *de facto* government of rural Livonia was a committee comprised of representatives elected by the local Estates, which were dominated by the nobility and, in turn, set the rules for entry into their ranks. Many Baltic nobles were unhappy with the later reforms of Catherine II, and they referred to the 'judicial despotism' of her new courts. Nevertheless, though personal and hereditary noble status in the Baltic provinces was determined now by the Russian Table of Ranks and the Charter to the Nobility, not by the membership rolls of noble corporations, noble status remained a condition for responsible positions.

Peter the Great's attempt to develop Russian provincial government was hindered by the difficulty of finding suitable nobles or of persuading them to go to their posts, and this remained a problem for his successors. Outside the conquered provinces, the nobility lacked a corporate organisation and elected representatives. How best to use the nobility in local government was debated. Catherine II did not pursue proposals put to her in the early 1760s to associate elected noble representatives with local administration, but the reform of the latter in 1775, with its multiplication of offices and devolution of responsibility, spread the benefits of office to more of the provincial nobility, who were elected to some local judicial and administrative posts.

If office was often a privilege of nobility, it was not the sole one. Privileges varied, but whatever their value, they represented the principle of hierarchy that was crucial to social status. Privilege was valuable because not enjoyed by others and because it denoted membership of an exclusive group. Privilege often took the form of exemption, such as the exemptions of the French nobility from militia service, billeting and some taxes. Not all nobles shared the partial tax immunities of those of, for example, Hungary and Sweden. British peers paid land tax, Bohemian nobles paid appreciable amounts of tax, and Frederick the Great suggested in 1752 that Maria Theresa would need all her charm in order to overcome the impression made by new taxes on her nobles. Frederick largely abolished noble tax privileges in Silesia. The exemption of the majority of French nobles in most areas of France from the *taille*, the most important direct tax, did not extend to their lands when they rented them out, or to new taxes such as the *capitation* (1695) and the *vingtième*. The preamble to the *vingtième* edict (1749) stated that the tax would be levied on all ranks of society in proportion to their ability to pay, though this did not in fact occur. The role of nobles in the assessment and collection of taxes, however, enabled many, such as those of

Sicily, to minimise their liabilities. The Land Tax in Britain was heavily affected by under-assessment. Russian nobles, responsible for the collection of poll tax from their serfs, ensured that their own feudal dues were paid first and many senior officials were tax debtors.

Privilege also entailed the enjoyment of rights over others, particularly the exaction of labour services. The value of privilege can be seen in the attempts made to defend it. New fiscal demands, such as the attempt by the duke of Mecklenburg in 1751 to increase taxation from free tenants of the local nobility, were resisted. The deliberations of the Legislative Commission, an attempt in 1767 to create a new Russian legal code, revealed that while the nobility sought to obtain immunity from torture and corporal punishment for itself, rights already enjoyed by most of the European nobility, it did not feel that this privilege should be granted to others, but instead, regarded torture as an effective weapon against brigands.

The continued determination of the European nobility to protect their privileges was on the whole successful. Though the legal position of the nobility, both as a special caste and as the controllers of peasant labour, was compromised with, in the latter case, serious implications for the finances of some nobles; and though the position of the poor nobility tended to deteriorate, being accompanied in some areas, particularly Poland and Spain, by the loss of individual noble status; the domination of society and the agrarian economy, and the control of government by the nobility remained a pronounced feature of European life on the eve of the French Revolution. Aspects of noble life were criticised both within and without the nobility, but there was little sense of any lack of confidence in their purpose or future. Whatever the complaints about their privileges, the continued existence of a powerful nobility seemed as obvious as that of the monarchy and the Church.

The middling orders

It would be misleading to present society in terms of an elite and the bulk of the population, if that detracts attention from those who can be variously termed the middling orders, middle class or bourgeoisie. The bulk of this group lived in the towns and can best be considered under that head in the next chapter. There was also a middling order in rural society: the agents of landlords and, where they existed, tenant farmers. The middling orders as a whole were a distinct social group, but many of the factors already discussed in terms of the structuring of society, such as concern with hierarchy, the role of birth, and snobbery, also played a major role for them, and there was a widespread aspiration among them to rise in landed society. The emerging concepts of politeness, gentility and sociability that were associated with the middling orders were also shared by the bulk of the nobility, and distinguished both from the more traditional emphasis of a 'warrior' nobility.

Yet the middling orders also emphasised values and practices of professionalism, specialism and competence that helped to define their social presence, and were reflected in their choice of clothing, especially a more sober costume than that favoured by the nobility.[11] The expansion and profitability of the commercial and industrial sectors of the European economy led in particular to a growth in the urban middling orders, who were especially difficult to locate in terms of a social differentiation based on rural society and inherited privilege.

Peasantry

Serfdom

Many European peasants, especially in the west, were not serfs, but serfdom demands attention, first, because it is now unknown and thus requires explanation, and secondly, because it was the aspect of peasant life that most excited contemporary debate and government action. Serfdom was a system of forced labour based on hereditary bondage to the land. Its purpose was to provide a fixed labour force and the legal essence of it was a form of personal service to a lord in exchange for the right to cultivate the soil. It was distinct from slavery, which was relatively uncommon outside the Turkish parts of Europe and was used for direct personal service, rather than to provide the mass agricultural labour force produced by serfdom. Serfdom, however, also entailed restrictions on personal freedom; indeed, in its most severe form, it was akin to slavery.

Most aspects of serfdom varied greatly, for its nature was influenced by legal codes and jurisdictional and tenurial practices. As in other spheres of eighteenth-century European life there has been a tendency to adduce a line of 'development' from north-western to Mediterranean and eastern Europe. England had had no serfdom since the sixteenth century and it had been banned in the 1660s; France had less than Austria. In practice, the real picture was more patchy and specific to regional societies and traditions. The existence of bond salters and colliers in Scotland was deplored by Adam Smith as a regional survival of serfdom. Serfdom was characteristic of eastern and some of central Europe, though not all the peasants in these areas were serfs. In Transylvania in 1767, 21 per cent of the population, excluding the major urban centres, were free peasants, while in Poland–Lithuania in 1791 the figure, including the towns, was 11 per cent, in comparison with figures of 40 for noble serfs, 10 for church serfs and 9.5 for royal serfs. In Russia one category of the state peasantry, the *odnodvortsy*, who comprised 5 per cent of the population in the 1760s, though more than half that of the provinces of Belgorod and Voronezh, was allowed to own serfs, though only a tiny minority did so. Nevertheless the majority of the peasantry east of the Elbe were serfs. In addition serfdom could be found throughout much of the Empire (Germany), though its character was not generally as harsh as in eastern Europe, as well as in regions that had formerly been part of the Empire, such as Franche-Comté and Alsace, where French serf-dom was concentrated, and in several other areas. The varie-gated nature of peasant conditions was such that individual monarchs ruled areas where serfdom existed and others where there was none. Savoy had serfdom, Piedmont none.

Serfs were subject to a variety of obligations, the principal being those to their landlord, and generally, though not invari-ably, also the lord who exercised personal authority over them. Their dues commonly took the form of labour services which had sometimes been commuted into payments in cash or in kind, although many simply entailed cash payments. East of the Elbe labour services were generally performed for landlords, west of it for the ruler. Labour services were not solely demanded from enserfed peasants. Free peasants in eastern Europe had obliga-tions, the *odnodvortsy* having to serve in a frontier militia, while in France the roads were maintained by forced labour, the *corvée*. The work could be onerous and the peasantry were often mis-treated. Labour service in the Empire among the peasantry could be considerable. In Hesse-Cassel it was owed to the land-lord, the community and the sovereign, and it could be substan-tial, up to half the peasant's available time. Although in Upper Austria *robot* (forced labour) was only obligatory on 14 days in the year and in Tyrol and Further Austria it was also light, in Lower Austria 104 days could be demanded, a figure confirmed in 1772, while in Styria a maximum of 3 days weekly was not imposed until 1778.

Labour service was not the sole obligation placed on the peas-ant in the Empire, but his position depended on his personal legal status, whether he was free or a serf, and the rights of tenure he had on his land. There were a few independent proprietors, free of all rents and dues, and they were chiefly found in the north-west. In East Friesland most land was allodial and not held under feudal tenures and there was no tradition of serfdom. All those possessing a small amount of land in freehold or tenancy or a certain capital could attend community assemblies and elect deputies to the Diet, where there was a third Estate of independent farmers. Though the peasantry of nearby Friesian West Holstein and Dithmarschen were also in a strong position, elsewhere in the Empire the situation was less favourable. However, as ever, generalisation is dangerous. In the Prussian territory of Minden three groups of peasants were distinguished in 1753. Alongside those tied to the soil by local custom and the serfs, there were free peasants exempt from labour services, while in East Prussia (not itself in the Empire), there was also a free farming class known as the *kölmer*. In Hesse-Cassel the type and extent of peasant obligations varied regionally and within the same community. The peasants there were not bound to the soil, but could leave the estate on paying a small fee, while, like many German peasants, they enjoyed in practice hereditary tenure of the land they cultivated.

Peasants in most of the Empire owed dues payable to their lord on a variety of occasions, including marriage and death. These dues reflected their personal dependence as serfs. In addition dues were paid to the landlord for the land that was cultivated. The impact of these demands on the peasantry in the Empire varied, not least depending on the willingness of the lords to forgo benefits at times of poor harvests, but the condition of the peasants, whether serfs or not, was generally better than those of their counterparts further east.

Eastern European serfs were not universally worse off. The principal difference for the individual peasant was possibly the arbitrariness of serfdom. The succession of a new lord could transform the tolerable into the merely survivable. The tithe tended to be less of a burden in eastern than in western Europe, where it was considerably resented in, for example, parts of France, England and Ireland. Furthermore, their lords had a powerful incentive to protect them not only from the demands of the state, such as military service and taxes, but also from the effects of adverse economic and environmental circumstances. It would be foolish to argue that a Transylvanian serf was necessarily worse off than those further west, whether a sharecropper in the Sologne, a crofter in Drenthe, or the appreciable and growing numbers of landless labourers in Saxony, Thuringia and Westphalia. Of the agrarian working population in Saxony in 1750, 30 per cent had little or no land and were dependent on wage labour.

Land hunger, in contrast, was not a problem in most of eastern Europe and the labourer unable to find land to rent was a less common figure than in the west. Landlords in the east sought to prevent the flight of their serfs not only because they were a source of wealth, but also because the size of the agrarian labour force had to be maintained. If the central problem in peasant conditions is seen as population pressure and its consequences, then the eastern European peasant was arguably better off, with the important exception of periods of poor harvests, such as the early 1770s. Indeed when peasants were emancipated, as in Sicily in the 1780s, this did not necessarily produce any real improvement in their lot.

If land hunger was not much of a problem in eastern Europe, the profits of the agricultural economy there did not reach the serfs to any worthwhile extent. In part this was due to the low productivity of much of eastern European agriculture. In Poland agricultural yields appear to have fallen in the aftermath of the Great Northern War (1700–21), though there was a definite recovery after about 1750. The benefits to be derived from export crops were reduced by the cost of transporting them considerable distances, placing a premium on regions with good river systems. Short of labour and unable or unwilling to pay wages for it, landlords used serfdom in order to provide a cheap and reliable labour force. *Robot* obligations were generally extensive. They were also increasingly regulated during the century. The first step towards government prohibition of serfdom was the regulation of the demands that it entailed, but in the eighteenth century this process of regulation was not always favourable to the peasantry. In Transylvania, where serfs were allowed to cultivate only very small plots of land, the Diet of 1714 established high limits for serf obligations, 4 days manual labour weekly or 3 with animals. Moreover serfs had little recourse, short of violence, against more labour being demanded. In 1766 the Moldavian nobility forced the *hospodar* Grigore III Ghica to raise *robot* to 35–40 days a year, and in 1775 labour obligations were again increased. In addition, many formerly free Moldavian peasants became serfs. In Wallachia, in contrast, many serfs worked less than the required 12 days. In the western Ukraine, however, *robot* increased and the position of much of the peasantry deteriorated, leading to rebellions.

Labour services were often assessed in terms of what the peasant could offer. In Poland, where they were heavy, a peasant who used his own plough and draught animals for service, had to perform proportionately fewer days. Furthermore wealthy Polish peasants hired poorer villagers to discharge their obligations, while those of the latter were often heavier in proportion to the size of their landholding. In Galicia there were no restrictions on *robot*, a serf being obliged to provide 6 days weekly in the summer, the time when his labour was most useful on his own, as well as the lord's, land, and 2 in winter. *Robot* in Bohemia had been restricted to 3 days weekly in 1680, a limit repeated in 1717, 1738 and 1775. The royal patents gave peasants a right to appeal to the crown against abuse, but the dominance of local administration by the Estates made this of little value. In Moravia in 1748 *robot* demands amounted to an average of 40 days annually. These obligations were made more onerous by the length of the days worked. Though this varied with local circumstances and the season, one among many examples of dependence on the environment, it was generally long. The definition of the working day as 10 hours in some of the Habsburg dominions in 1775 represented a decrease for most. Obligations could also be made more onerous by setting a norm for the serfs to achieve on each day that they worked and obliging them to continue working if they did not achieve it. Very high, indeed often unrealistic, quotas tended to be imposed.

Just as it would be mistaken to suggest that all eastern European peasants were serfs, so it is untrue to suggest that *robot* was the prime obligation of all serfs. Money rents could be common, as they were in the western Ukraine at the beginning of the century. In eastern Belorussia money rent, not *robot*, was the most common form of peasant obligation to landowners, and peasant holdings were of great importance in producing for both local and export markets. Money rents became more important in Poland, especially western Poland. Yet, even if their *robot* was low, serfs were subject to a number of other burdens. Though they varied, they all reflected, and in turn sustained, the strength of the landlords' position. In Bohemia and Galicia serfs who had not purchased the right to do so could not sell their land, incur major debts, or designate an heir, and they were liable to be moved from their existing land to other land. All Bohemian serfs, even those with a hereditary right to their land, were obliged to seek their lord's permission, which was generally granted only in return for payment, before migrating, marrying, or having their children educated or apprenticed outside the manor.

Such extensive local powers produced in the community a dominance by the lords greater even than their formal rights. The obligation to buy from or sell to the lord could be onerous. It could also entail prohibitions on the production of goods that might compete with those of the landlord. They benefited the landlord, whereas in France the most notorious example of such an imposition, the *gabelle*, a salt tax by which, in part of the country, the *pays de grande gabelle*, a fixed annual minimum amount of salt had to be purchased irrespective of need, served a royal monopoly. Limitations on personal mobility were a significant restriction that reduced the serfs' bargaining power within the labour market by essentially preventing the development of such a market. Such limitations did not arise simply from formal prohibitions. Though Balkan peasants retained a number of privileges and did not become serfs, the effect of their retention of legal freedom was lessened by the terms of their relationship with their lords. Most of the latter owned not only the peasants' dwellings, but also their tools. Seed, animals and cash were loaned and peasants, obliged therefore to produce crops, were in no position to migrate, even where better earnings were available in rural industry. Similarly, in order to prevent a shortage of agricultural labour in Prussian Silesia in 1769, work in the mines was made dependent on the written consent of the lord of the manor. When Catherine II introduced the poll tax in the Baltic provinces, peasants were registered in the name of their lord, while the many unattached individuals who could not register as townsmen and thus enjoy the benefit of that status, were obliged to register as serfs or state peasants.

Another major hindrance to any attempts by peasants to improve their position was the restrictions placed on their acquisition of land. The absence of significant peasant land ownership was a central problem, whatever their legal status. It obliged peasants, whether they were serfs or not, to serve landlords on their superior's terms. Legal controls over property transmission and, in particular, rules of entail, were important in restricting the amount of land that could be acquired by the peasantry, as was mortmain, the inalienability of most ecclesiastical land. Until such laws were abolished the prospect of peasants acquiring much land was very limited in the settled parts of Europe. It has been argued that 'serfdom's true end in Hungary and Transylvania came not with the edict by which Joseph II untied serfs from the land in 1785, but with the 1848 abolition of entail'.[12]

Legal restrictions on peasants acquiring land were important, but more significant was the absence of purchasing power among most of them. Individual peasants increased their wealth, not least by careful marriage strategies for their entire family, but the potential financial power of the peasantry was dissipated by their numbers, their precarious living standards and the range and weight of their dues and other obligations. Many Polish serfs were in debt. Royal taxes and lords' dues, split roughly one-third and two-thirds, took an average 35 per cent of peasant income in Moravia, 45 per cent in Lower Austria, 50 per cent in Inner

Austria.[13] In Bohemia, ordinary peasants paid 41 per cent of their gross income. These burdens were greater than those borne by other members of the community.

The list of serf obligations could be extended with ease. *Robot* could be increased at harvest time, children be required to do household duties for the lord. Cartage was often a major burden, entailing the transport of seigneurial goods for long distances. Peasants were expected to make such journeys with their own carts and horses. As serfdom was a series of diverse arrangements, rather than a consistent system, duties varied, as did their fulfilment and commutation. Agreements between lords and peasants defining obligations were based on local circumstances, as was their implementation. However, whatever their obligations, peasants in general suffered from the low productivity of eighteenth-century agriculture as it was exacerbated by a harsh fiscal regime.

Discussion and action over the position of the peasantry

In Johann Reinhard's *Ein Traum*, his utopian society's agriculture was cultivated by proud yeoman farmers, not poor peasants. In pastoral paintings, such as those of Boucher, plump and handsome peasants, very different from those described by tourists, lived in an idyll disturbed only by their mutual longings. Other manifestations of this illusion were the cottages inserted as a 'rustic' note in landscape gardens, where a 'peasant' could be paid to live, as in the duke of Newcastle's grounds at Claremont, Surrey, and Marie Antoinette and her friends dressed as milkmaids and labourers in *Le Hameau* specially built at Versailles.

Such conceits did not imply any interest in the position of the peasantry. However, though many commentators did not praise the views and character of peasants in intellectual circles, there was little articulate defence of their oppression. Nevertheless, traditional notions of human capabilities based on inherited capacities were scarcely favourable to the peasantry, whose poor status and arduous circumstances could thus be explained.

Advanced views were hardly more helpful. The prevalence of the notion drawn from sensationalist psychology that environment formed character led to a harsh view of the peasants, for their surroundings were seen as degrading. On the rare occasions when peasants featured in heroic roles in the artistic works of the period they were generally their social betters in disguise. In fashionable intellectual circles peasant conservatism led to criticism, and it was widely believed that the masses could never be educated or weaned from superstition.

More serious for the peasantry was the determination of most landowners to preserve their privileges. This was based on self-interest and a sense of innate superiority. Suspicious of the serfs, Prince Mikhail Shcherbatov denied them any positive role in Russian life and opposed any attempt by government to act on their behalf. It would not be excessively unfair to say that the attitude of the defenders of the status quo was to treat the serfs like beasts of burden. Serfs might be Christian and have souls that required saving, but they were also regarded as inhuman or subhuman, needing firm discipline. In the mid-1760s, when the newly founded Russian Free Economic Society held an essay competition on the theme of peasant property, the majority of the essays offered a negative assessment of peasant capabilities. And yet other commentators believed that it was important to improve the position of the peasantry and necessary to do so through the agency of government action, which should redefine the rights and obligations of the peasantry and establish them legally. The sources of concern for the peasantry were varied. An important theme was traditional Christian solicitude expressed especially by many clerics.

Anxiety about the agricultural economy was also significant. Agricultural improvement did not necessarily entail any benefit for the peasantry. It was not simply that the profits generally accrued to landowners and major tenants, immediately or eventually, particularly if the land was worked by serfs, day labourers or those with insecure tenure. It was also the case that new practices could entail heavier burdens on the peasantry. Polish peasant petitions suggest that they led to stricter supervision, the extension of labour services to hitherto exempted areas of the estate, such as fallows, and the matching of the level of services more closely to more precisely measured tenements.

However, many writers on agricultural matters argued that improvements required a free peasantry owning the land they cultivated, or at least benefiting from increased yields. Wealth for all was to flow from incentives for the peasantry. A buoyant agrarian economy would, it was hoped, not only yield more taxes, but also lessen migration, crime and disorder. Physiocrat writers such as Quesnay, believing that land was the sole source of value, proclaimed the social and economic benefits of prosperous peasant proprietors and tenants. Necker in his *Eloge de Colbert* (1773) stressed the need for the French government to act to free peasants from arbitrary assessment by officials. Antonio Genovesi, professor of political economy in Naples 1754–69, argued that large estates would be more productive if divided among numerous proprietors. The Hungarian Baron Lörintz Orczy maintained in 1761 that the serfs' great possibilities could be realised if they were given their freedom. Some of the advisers of Joseph II, such as Joseph von Sonnenfels, professor of political science in Vienna, had an idealised view of the peasantry. In the 1750s and 1760s pastor Johann Eisen and certain officials of the Financial Office for Livonian, Estonian and Finnish Affairs, pressed for changes to protect the serfs of those areas from the arbitrary actions of their landowners. Eisen suggested that if the peasants owned the land they cultivated, this would be in the economic interest both of the government and the nobility.

In the Empire public discussion of agrarian issues and the position of the peasantry became more pronounced from the 1770s. The Osnabrück administrator and publicist Justus Möser argued that improving the position of the peasantry by reducing the penalties for indebtedness would have long-term economic benefits. His recommendation that all leaseholds by both freemen and serfs should become hereditary, in order to increase peasant commitment to profitability, was thwarted by opposition from the nobility. The Agrarian Society of Hesse-Cassel informed the government in 1782 that agricultural productivity would not increase significantly until manorial obligations were eliminated. Such essentially pragmatic arguments for the improvement of peasant circumstances, entailing a commutation of their dues and obligations for higher profitability as well as money rents, were accompanied in the 1780s and 1790s by claims for peasant emancipation on the basis of natural rights. These claims had earlier had an impact on Austrian legislation. The chancellery official Franz von Blanc, who had served on the *robot* commissions for Austrian Silesia and Bohemia, had a powerful commitment to natural rights.

In the first half of the century there is little sign that arguments for improvements in the lot of the peasantry, still less their emancipation, had much effect. There were well-established reasons why governments should protect peasants from their landlords if they wished, for example to maintain their tax yield. Cameralist writers had been concerned about the position of the peasantry and in the first half of the century the protection of the peasantry against excessive taxation and noble exactions had been advocated by a number of writers including Christian von Schierendorff, imperial treasury secretary under Joseph I and Charles VI, and French thinkers who hoped that the accession of Louis XIV's eldest grandson, the duke of Burgundy (a prospect cut short by smallpox), would usher in a period of agrarian peace and plenty. However, the period witnessed scant improvement in the legal position of the peasantry. Proposals for significant reforms tended to reflect episodes of political turmoil, prefiguring the situation at the time of the French Revolution. In Valencia, where there had been a major peasant rising in 1693, the peasantry were offered in 1705 by supporters of Archduke Charles, claimant to the Spanish throne (the future emperor Charles VI), freedom from service obligations and taxes and the promise that the lands of his noble opponents would be divided among them. Similarly in 1742 Charles Albert of Bavaria, the emperor Charles VII, fighting the Habsburgs in Bohemia, sought the support of the local serfs with the offer of emancipation. This was, however, a measure of Charles's desperation.

The first half of the century saw few improvements and, in some areas, a definite deterioration. Peter the Great's unpopularity with the peasantry was indicated by their tendency to imagine him as antiChrist or a changeling rather than as a peasant tsar, and by the failure of later pretenders to claim his name. If he allowed the peasantry to retain their traditional customs and beards, it was because he was fundamentally only interested in the elite that he wished to mould. The peasantry was designated for the service of monarch and nobility. Peter turned down suggestions that the nobility should not be rewarded with land, and that, instead, the state should be financed by peasant taxes, because he felt that officials should own land as a matter of course. During the reign of Elizabeth (1741–62), the Senate consistently supported landowning nobles in their disputes with the peasantry, while the granting to the Ukrainian Cossack nobles of equality of status with the Russian nobility extended their rights over the peasantry. The process continued under Catherine II.

From mid-century, governments increasingly intervened in the sphere of landlord – peasant relations in eastern Europe. The most influential Phanariot *hospodar* Constantine Mavrocordat responded to the problem of widespread peasant flight by persuading a noble assembly in Wallachia in 1746 to end personal bondage, a measure adopted in Moldavia also in 1749. Peasants were allowed to buy their freedom. *Robot* was fixed at 12 days in Wallachia, 24 in Moldavia. The reforms ended the distinction between serfs and free peasants who worked land belonging to nobles on an agreed basis. It proved, however, to be difficult to enforce in the face of noble opposition, particularly after Mavrocordat had been replaced. In the Empire a number of rulers sought to improve the position of the peasantry. In Bavaria Max Joseph III and Karl Theodor supported the commutation of *robot* into cash payments, a process begun in Hanover in 1753 and nearly complete by the 1790s.

In his *Essay on the Forms of Government and Duties of Sovereigns* (1777) Frederick the Great argued that rulers should imagine themselves in the position of peasants or artisans, while, in practice, he passed a number of decrees and issued instructions entailing improvements for the former. In 1748 he limited *robot*, a measure that led in 1750 to complaints by the Hither Pomeranian Estates which demanded the continuation of noble rights to unlimited services. In 1749 striking peasants with sticks was made an imprisonable offence; in 1763 serfdom in Pomerania was abolished with the agreement of the Estates, and *robot* in Silesia was limited. The following year, measures were taken to protect peasant landholdings throughout the entire state, while in 1773 serfdom in East and newly annexed West Prussia was abolished. However, except on the royal estates, little was done to enforce these laws. Thus, for example, the abolition of Pomeranian serfdom was limited in practice.

Frederick II of Hesse-Cassel was cautious in pushing through change. When in 1763 he decided that hunting and forest labour services were being exacted too arbitrarily, he limited rather than abolished them and did not extend the decrees to noble estates. Indicative of the increasing role of money in peasant life and peasant–landlord relations was Frederick's decision to pay peasants who were still recruited for these services. In the 1770s *robot* was commuted for cash payments on the landgrave's estates, labour being recruited by payment. However, as in Prussia, the pace of legislation was not matched by comparable implementation. An investigation into the conditions of the peasantry in 1782–3 revealed extensive abuses. Despite the decree of 1773 that *robot* could not be required, even if paid for, whenever the peasant needed the time for essential work, this practice had not ended. The major reform of Danish rural conditions was initiated by government legislation.

The dramatic changes in mid-century Austrian government affected peasant rights. Haugwitz's new fiscal system of 1748–9 entailed a reduction in the share of taxes paid by the peasantry. He was also aware that their ability to pay taxes required protection. This involved restrictions on the lord's ability to burden the peasantry, and the inverse relationship between *robot* and taxes was referred to explicitly. Joseph II was personally committed to easing the peasant's lot. When he visited Transylvania in 1773 he received 19,000 petitions complaining of *robot* abuses. A number of decrees were issued to limit *robot*. As that of 1747 for Hungary had been rendered ineffective by noble opposition, in 1767 the Council of State issued an *urbarium* (set of regulations) without the consent of the Diet. The need to lessen lords' exactions in order to increase peasant taxable capacity had been stressed in the government's discussions and, therefore, the enforcement of the regulations was entrusted to a special state commission, rather than to the noble-dominated local administration. By 1780, when conditions in Croatia and the Banat of Temesvar had been regulated, the *urbarium* had been applied to the whole of the kingdom of Hungary. Similar, though not identical, edicts were issued for other Habsburg dominions. *Robot* decrees were issued for Austrian Silesia in 1768 and 1771, Lower Austria in 1772, Bohemia and Moravia in 1775, Styria and Carinthia in 1778 and Galicia in 1774 and 1784. The principle of regulation was far from novel, the 14 days annually worked in Upper Austria deriving from an edict of 1597, but the scale of intervention was. The decrees were designed to complement rather than replace voluntary agreements reached between lord and tenant. However, there was no doubt that the emphasis was on reducing compulsory labour and thus the decrees fitted in with the attempt by the government to encourage a trend towards money rents and paid labour, such as that seen on Maria Theresa's private estates in the late 1770s.

Habsburg policies represented the most sustained effort by any major state to improve the position of the peasantry. They reflected a widespread tendency, but their timing owed much to the crisis of the early 1770s when poor harvests and malnutrition led to the death of about 250,000 in Bohemia, a serious blow not only to the reputation of the Habsburgs, but also to their revenues and their attempt to increase their strength relative to that of Prussia. The threat that Habsburg policies posed to the position of the nobility explains why other major states with serf economies were reluctant to follow suit. It was claimed that the poorer Hungarian nobles suffered badly as a result of the regulations of 1767, and it has been estimated that all Bohemian manors suffered a loss of at least a quarter of the income they had received from *robot*.

The changes did not simply affect peasant labour. Thus in Galicia, tenures were guaranteed and private ownership introduced when feasible. Local officials were ordered to stop the oppression of the peasantry. The election of peasant jurors to manorial courts was decreed, while the officials of these courts were ordered to meet specific qualifications. Given such consequences, it is not surprising that the limitation of *robot* was not popular with much of the eastern European nobility. In 1765 the changes in the position of the Latvian peasantry decreed by the Diet amounted to little. Rather than producing detailed regulations for *robot*, these were left to the discretion of the landowners. In 1780 the Polish *Sejm* (Parliament) rejected improvements in the legal status of serfs proposed by a substantial landowner, Andrzcj Zamoyski, who instituted comparatively favourable treatment for his own serfs. The Polish constitution of May 1791 proclaimed the right of the peasantry to the 'protection of law and the national government', but revealed that this was to be extended only to voluntary agreements between nobles and peasants. The insistence of the Prussian nobility led to the confirmation of serf services in the *Allgemeines Landrecht*, the lawcode of the Prussian state, of 1794. Catherine II's Charter to the Nobility of 1785 did not reduce the nobles' power over their serfs.

It would, however, be misleading to suggest that the position of the peasantry in eastern Europe outside the Habsburg lands was uniformly bleak. Marginal improvements can be noticed. In the 1780s there is evidence that the peasantry of Russia's Baltic provinces had a measure of confidence in new police and judicial institutes and took to them disputes with nobles over *robot* and poll tax allocation. It appears that they were often able to obtain justice from the courts.

Attempts to alter *robot* were not the sole moves that affected the peasantry. In a number of countries there were moves to abolish serfdom – hereditary bondage to the land, which was seen both as economically negative, as it limited peasant incentives, and as morally abhorrent. Edicts of 1762 and 1771 enfranchised the Savoyard peasantry. However, opposition by the landed proprietors led to the suspension of the emancipation decree in 1775–8, and the process was not completed until after the French invaded in 1792. The personal restrictions of servile status were abolished in the Bohemian lands (1781), the Austrian lands and Galicia (1782), and Hungary (1785). By the measures of 1781, seigneurial jurisdiction was limited, peasants were permitted to leave their home villages, provided they had a certificate from their seigneur stating that they had met all their obligations, seigneurial permission to wed was no longer required and peasant children were freed from compulsory labour service.

These moves had effects elsewhere. Fearing peasant agitation, margrave Karl Friedrich of Baden abolished serfdom in 1783. Serfdom for most Danish peasants was abolished in 1788. Abolition reflected humanitarian sentiments, as in the Swiss canton of Solothurn in 1785, but was not determined by them. Charles Emmanuel III of Savoy-Piedmont, the first of the royal emancipators, was not noted as an enlightened ruler, while Karl Friedrich had resisted suggestions from intellectuals among his advisers that he free the peasantry.

As important was the fashionable view that gains would derive from freeing the bulk of the population from seigneurial control. The duke d'Aiguillon's motion for the abolition of seigneurial rights, presented to the National Assembly on 4 August 1789, claimed that they harmed agriculture and desolated the countryside. When in 1787 Frederick Karl, archbishop-elector of Mainz, announced his intention to abolish serfdom, for which the necessary regulations were not issued until 1791, he stated that the payments due when a serf died or moved were too heavy and that, as a result, the economy and the lot of individual serfs suffered. However, his decision was not without its costs for the peasants. Dues had to be redeemed at a rate of 20 times the average annual sum paid by any community. Though the redemption rate in Savoy was low, its existence was responsible in part for delays in emancipation. Joseph II sought to enable peasants to contribute more to the government. On 10 February 1789 a patent appeared that was to have become effective later that year, but never did so. It decreed that all populated land, whether held by lord or peasant, had to pay an annual tax of $12\frac{2}{9}$ per cent of its assessed value, while the dues and services that the peasant had to pay his seigneur were commuted into a cash rental not to exceed $17\frac{7}{9}$ per cent of the peasant's annual gross income from his holding. Though this was intended for the wealthier peasantry only, it is clear that Joseph's policy towards the peasantry cannot be divorced from the tax reform proposals that arose from his fiscal difficulties. As the agrarian sections of the economy produced the greatest share of gross national product and taxation in all of the countries of eastern and central Europe, it was obvious that peasant issues had to be addressed in a fiscal context.

Initially changes in France, where the abolition of serfdom was the topic for the poetry prize of the Académie Française in 1781, conformed to developments elsewhere. Louis XVI, apparently influenced by criticism of serfdom as an offence against natural liberty, abolished it on royal manors in 1779. The decree condemned serfdom, but declared that respect for private property precluded any general abolition. Louis expressed the hope that other serf-owners would follow suit, but the *Parlement* of Franche-Comté, where most French serfs lived, refused to register the decree, until compelled to in 1787. Two years later, serfdom was abolished in France, but it was not until July 1793 that all obligations to seigneurs were ended without any indemnity. The armies of revolutionary France brought emancipation or lessened serf obligations to conquered areas such as the Rhineland and Switzerland. The abolition of serfdom did not necessarily lead to any improvement in peasant conditions, particularly if, as in Moldavia, where *robot* increased, it was associated with a rise in peasant obligations.

In much of Europe there was no emancipation of the peasantry. In most of the Empire, the abolition of labour services and the granting of hereditary tenure to peasantry did not come until the following century. In Russia, hundreds of thousands of state peasants saw their position deteriorate during Catherine II's reign as they were converted into private peasants. The character of Russian serfdom was bitterly criticised in Alexander Radishchev's *Journey from St Petersburg to Moscow* (1790). He denounced the arduous work and poor living conditions of serfs, and the right of lords to sell serfs, and to flog them. The radicalism of the book led to Radishchev's arrest and banishment to Siberia. Most nobles did not share his views. The value of serfdom to landowners, whether Russian or not, was such that they generally resisted change. French seigneurs either rarely consented to surrender their rights or demanded large payments for so doing. In the face of such opposition, rulers were not prepared to push through emancipation.

Rural unrest

Peasant political representation was limited. In the Empire the approximately 20 principalities where peasants were represented in the Estates were mostly very small, though in Württemberg and the Palatinate, since urban deputies sat for the rural districts surrounding their towns as well, the peasantry were technically represented. In Sweden the Estate of the Peasantry represented the independent taxpaying landowning peasantry, as well as crown tenants, and such individuals, freely elected, were its delegates. Electors were not allowed to be 'dependent' on a member of another Estate and suitably qualified women were granted the franchise. The peasantry who were tenants of the nobility had, however, no representatives in the Swedish Diet. The Swedish Estate of the Peasantry was treated as inferior and excluded from the Secret Committee and thus from the centre of government, but it was not politically quiescent. In 1742 their attempt to appoint members to the Committee was seen as a means to end the war with Russia.

There was little interest in Europe in extending peasant political representation, though Leopold II considered bringing the peasantry into the Styrian Estates in 1792. Intellectual circles tended to display little interest in the political views of the peasantry, which were generally believed to be either non-existent or primitive, and though peasant sensibility was depicted artistically, there was little pressure to establish peasant Estates or emulate the constitutions of Sweden or the Vorarlberg. A relative lack of interest in peasant views, though not in their circumstances, characterised rulers such as Joseph II and different political groups. Very few peasants were members of the early Jacobin clubs in revolutionary France, and these clubs displayed little interest in the redistribution of land to the peasantry.

Most peasant political activity was not national, nor targeted at questioning the established order. It was commonly centred on their community, which was often responsible legally for a wide range of public functions including the allocation of taxes, law and order, the upkeep of roads and churches and poor relief. In Poland village communal assemblies were responsible for the performance of all labour dues and obligations, the payment of tithes and taxes and the maintenance of order. In Russia their responsibilities included organising agricultural work, settling disputes between peasants and taking care of orphans. Peasant communities also enjoyed certain rights, particularly over common lands, and in some areas, such as Württemberg, Prussia and parts of France, there were strong communal rights and nearly autonomous villages.

Negotiation between landlords and village communities over obligations was a constant feature of rural life. In the event of disputes they generally resorted to one of two frequently linked methods, litigation and the appeal to the agents and institutions of government. In Russia village assemblies drew up petitions expressing their grievances and sent representatives with them to local and central authorities. In Poland appeals were made, for example, to landowners against their officials and leaseholders, while peasants on crown properties appealed to a special court. In France it was common to take legal action against seigneurs. In Quercy, widespread opposition to seigneurs and tithes in the 1770s and 1780s was expressed through judicial action, not violence, until the spring of 1789.[14] The increase of legal action in eastern France in the second half of the century has been related to a supposed cultural transformation of the peasantry, compounded of increased mobility and literacy, an alleged loss of respect for traditional authority and a greater willingness to resort to legal remedies. In Germany, peasants' use of the imperial court system to press complaints has been put forward as an explanation for the relative lack of violent protest.

The frustrations, tensions and conflicts of rural life did not lead only to legal action. They were reflected also in a failure to perform obligations adequately and in a reluctance to consider new demands. In Poland and Russia 'to work as you work on the demesne' described indolence. More generally, demands considered excessive were commonly not fulfilled, and outright malingering was widespread. Flight – illegal migration – was another response to adverse circumstances. The attempt to prevent it by harsh laws was weakened by the willingness of many landlords and rulers to receive runaways.

Violent unrest was generally small-scale, such as the killing or maiming of the landlord's animals, or the destruction of his property. Peasant grievances were frequently expressed through arson, while the destruction of fences and hedges was a reply to attempts to enclose common land. Anger over the damage done by game and hunters led sometimes to the wholesale slaughter of game, an act of collective fury that could supplement the peasant diet as usefully as the more commonplace attrition of seigneurial privileges wrought by poaching. Most peasant violence was local, the response to specific grievances directed against particular landlords who were felt to be abusing their position, and a consequence of the essentially local, specific and varied nature of landlord–peasant relations. The beating up or killing of officials and sometimes landlords that occurred was often related to rural crime, but rural terrorism directed against harsh and, in particular, innovating landlords could also be important. In England violent opposition to the Game Laws was linked to Jacobite political protest. In Ireland movements such as the Whiteboys of the 1760s centred on the defence of traditional peasant rights.

The violent nature of rural life may also have played a role in supporting a level of violence that made attacks upon landlords and their officials seem less surprising. In 1764–9 at least 30 landowners were slain by their serfs in the province of Moscow alone. Feuds between villagers and between villages were common in much of Europe, though not generally with the intensity of those in Corsica. In much of eastern Europe serfs were beaten for real or alleged misdemeanours, while landlords' torture chambers were not unknown. The different racial, linguistic and religious background of landlords and peasants could also be a source of tension. In east Galicia relations between the Polish nobility and the Ruthenian peasantry were poor, while in Ireland Catholic peasants were in the grip of an Anglican and English Establishment.

Most violence was small-scale and directed against property, more akin to theft and insubordination than insurrection, a limited rebellion in the world of the manor rather than in that of the realm. However, there were regions and episodes where the situation was more serious. Frontier regions in eastern Europe were particularly prone to disorder. In the western Ukraine, attempts by Polish landlords to extend labour services, impose serfdom and convert forcibly to Catholicism in a volatile frontier region led to significant levels of violence. The revolt of Semen Palij at the turn of the century was followed by serious uprisings in 1734–7, 1750 and 1768. Peasant risings were in part due to, and in turn made more serious by, breakdowns in political and judicial order, as in the Polish civil wars associated with the Great Northern War (1700–21), the War of the Polish Succession (1733–5) and the formation of the Confederation of Bar in 1768. In a similar fashion, the major French peasant disturbance of the century, the 'Great Fear' of 1789, was associated with the disruption of the revolutionary period, specifically rumours that aristocrats were trying to suppress the peasantry and ruin the harvest.[15]

The situation in the western Ukraine was made more serious by the weakness of the Polish army, but the willingness of Russia to extend its role in Polish politics to the suppression of peasant risings proved crucial to the successive failures of those revolts. The savagery of the 1768 rising was genocidal. The 'Golden Charter' ordered the killing of Poles and Jews, a task carried out in a number of massacres. Other frontier areas, such as the Carpathian foothills in Poland and also the Lower Volga, witnessed serious peasant unrest. In a major rising in Transylvania in 1784 peasants slaughtered landowners, priests, townsmen and government officials and advanced radical demands, including the abolition of the nobility and the distribution of their land to the peasantry. As so often in eastern Europe ethnic tensions surfaced, with the rising eventually pitting Greek Orthodox Romanian peasants against Hungarian Calvinists, both noble and non-noble.

The Transylvanian rising also involved two other common features of major peasant risings, heightened excitement created by an anticipation of major reforms, and a linked belief that the rebellion served the interests of the monarch. Joseph II's redefinition of landlord–peasant relations elsewhere in his dominions had made these relations appear precarious and dependent on monarchical wishes in Transylvania, and, at the beginning of the rising, the rebels claimed to act in Joseph's name. Similarly in Bohemia in 1775 the government's attitude to peasant conditions had made them a volatile issue of more than local significance, and the rebels claimed that an imperial decree, suppressed by the nobility, had freed them from their obligations. A large force had to be deployed to prevent the rebellion spreading to Moravia and to suppress it. The desperation that the rising revealed, with its suppression followed by emigration, some peasants asking the soldiers to kill them, and others burning grain that they were obliged to cut, played a major role in encouraging Joseph to press on with the amelioration of peasant conditions. In some instances peasants were clearly aware that change was possible, changes were occurring. In 1786 those on the estates of Prince Liechtenstein on the Moravia–Lower Austria border sought to transfer themselves to the emperor and their attacks on Liechtenstein's property had to be suppressed with troops.

Rumour was central to the political world of *ancien régime* Europe, a necessary consequence of a monarchical system extremely dependent on the personal wishes of monarchs operating in a milieu in which communication was heavily oral. If courtiers and diplomats, scrutinising the entrails of court life, considered the significance of royal frowns and smiles, peasants heeded rumours of royal support. A conviction both of monarchical support and that this support would bring improvement played a major role in the largest European rising, that of Pugachev. However, rather than claiming to interpret the wishes of a live monarch such as Joseph II, Pugachev, a Cossack adventurer, claimed in 1772 to be Peter III, a claim advanced by at least ten other pretenders since Peter's murder in 1762. Pugachev's rebellion stemmed from another frontier region. Just as Stenka Razin's rising against Tsar Alexis in 1669–71 and Bulavin's rising against Peter the Great in 1707–8 had been based in the Lower Volga and among the Don Cossacks respectively, so Pugachev found support among the Yaik Cossacks, suffering from internal disputes and concerned about the suppression of traditional rights such as free access to the fisheries of the river Yaik. He was also supported by serfs who worked in factories and by many Bashkirs, a frontier tribe which had risen unsuccessfully in 1708, 1735 and 1755. The rebellion began in 1773 and government attempts to suppress it then were defeated. Pugachev set up his own court modelled on that of Catherine II, Cossacks and Bashkirs were promised their traditional way of life, including the freedom of lands and water, and, though he suffered a number of setbacks in early 1774, in July of that year he managed temporarily to seize Kazan, a major city where, according to one contemporary, 'those in German dress and without a beard' were killed.

Pugachev's rising was now specifically directed against serfdom. He called on serfs to overthrow it by seizing the land and the response was a widespread slaughter of the nobility in the Volga region. There was also a religious element in the rising, namely support for the Old Believers and a strong cultural antipathy to the westernisation of Russia. However, Pugachev's appeals were increasingly unsuccessful as his arrival brought chaos and fighting and as the resilience of the government became more apparent. The summer of 1774 saw Pugachev unsuccessful in raising the Don Cossacks, and also a Russo-Turkish peace that promised to release Russian forces to deal with the rising. Those who were already pursuing Pugachev succeeded in defeating him in August and in the following month he was handed over to the government by disillusioned supporters.

A rising such as Pugachev's was exceptional; none such was to occur thereafter in eighteenth-century Russia, though there was another wave of risings in the 1790s. It was exceptional not only in its radicalism, scale and ready resort to violence, but in its duration and the degree of its initial success. The risings that enjoyed most success were those, essentially in frontier regions, where the issue at stake was as much the survival of a traditional culture as the condition of the bulk of the population, and where, as among the Cossacks, the rebels were familiar with military life, and their way of life lent itself most readily to conflict.

It would be inappropriate to regard Pugachev's rising as typical of peasant activity in either methods or objectives. Most peasant unrest was specific in its causes and limited in its objectives, thus conforming to the general patterns of political activity in *ancien régime* Europe. Opposed to innovations, such as new obligations, and to what were construed as abuses of authority, much peasant action aimed at conservative redress through direct action that would elicit a sympathetic response or favourable royal intervention. The situation was similar in other areas of the world. In Japan there were permissible methods for remonstrating against grievances and there was considerable legal petitioning. As in much of Europe, popular tales of protest personalised injustice as the wrongdoing of unfair aliens, while the 1780s were a critical decade when governmental authority was badly shaken and popular protest thereby facilitated.[16]

Conclusion

The lot of the European peasantry was far from easy, but it would be inaccurate to present them as living in similar circumstances throughout the continent or in any one area. The fatalism that was such a marked characteristic of peasant consciousness reflected, however, one common feature of peasant life. Though peasants were affected differently both by the economy of proprietary wealth, the system built around rent and poor remuneration for labour in the context of a markedly unequal distribution of land, and by governmental intervention, they were all dependent on the environment. In the twentieth century it is difficult for a predominantly urban readership to understand a world in which the calamities of environmental mischance were matched by the incessant pressures of trying to scratch a living (a reasonable remark given the nature of the ploughs of the period) in adverse circumstances. Electricity, the internal combustion engine and selective crop and animal breeding had not yet conquered the countryside and transformed both agriculture and agrarian life. Power was limited to human and animal muscles, with milling performed by the aid of wind and water. Furniture, utensils and foodstuffs were basic and rough, crop and animal breeds improved only by the watchful care of generations. And everywhere the awful and unpredictable extremes of climate and disease could always lessen or annihilate the prospects of crops, livestock and the humans who depended on them.

5   Towns

Don't you think that the overgrown size of our metropolis is one great cause of the frivolousness, idleness and debauchery of the times; I have often wondered that the Legislature has not long since labour'd to put bounds to its increase, for it is really too big for the good observance of the Law or the Gospel... a weak Police can lay but little restraint upon such multitudes.

(Joseph Yorke concerning London, 1763)[1]

Any discussion of the importance and growth of towns is made difficult by problems of defining what a town was. The legal definitions of the period paid only limited attention to size or function. In the region of Aix-en-Provence in southern France all built-up areas surrounded by walls and provided with royal justice were defined as towns, irrespective of their size or function. In Poland towns were legally incorporated institutions, again irrespective of size or function. Settlements without owners were defined as towns in Russia, and though they differed greatly in age, size and other factors, they were all subject to the same laws and regulations and contrasted legally with settlements that were the property of an individual or an institution.

Such definitions were of limited value. They classified as towns settlements that were functionally villages and conversely, though less seriously on the whole, ignored important settlements. Part of the problem with terminology therefore is that there was no agreed contemporary functional definition of a town, as well as no legal classification that was valid across the whole continent, and it is dangerous to impose modern notions. To follow one modern definition, that of the town as a creator of effective space, a nexus whose most crucial export was control and the locus of a characteristic urban lifestyle, is to ignore the large number of very small settlements, classified as towns, whose inhabitants engaged primarily in agrarian activities. This was the case, for example, in Poland. The only large town in mid-century Denmark was Copenhagen, while in Sweden–Finland no more than 10 out of the more than 100 towns had a population greater than 7000. Many would be defined as villages today.

The use of eighteenth-century legal classifications is complicated further by the frequent failure to define one urban area as only one town. As urban status was essentially a matter of legal

164

privilege, rather than population size or economic function, there was no particular reason why this status should be rationalised in accordance with contiguous urban areas so that they were treated as single towns. Enclaves of distinct status frequently existed within contiguous urban areas. Urban status was a particular problem in the case of suburban or extra-mural (outside the walls) developments. For example, Castelviel, the western suburb of Albi in southern France, was an autonomous community of over 700, outside the town's ramparts and with its own consuls and administration. It was not united with Albi until the Revolution. Conversely, urban status extended often also to rural areas outside town walls.

If towns present problems of definition, the size of their populations is also not always easy to assess, particularly as many population statistics were calculated in terms of households, not people. Though there are signs of urban growth, particularly in the second half of the century, Europe was not unique in its degree of urbanisation. Of the 19 cities of the world believed to have had a population of over 300,000 in 1800 only 5 were European: London (3rd), Constantinople (8th), Paris (9th), Naples (14th), St Petersburg (17th).[2] The extent of urbanisation within Europe varied. In some regions it was relatively low. Well below 10 per cent of the Russian population lived in towns: those registered in the censuses of 1762 and 1782 as being in the urban estate were 3.04 and 3.07. Mid-century Savoy-Piedmont had a population of 1,774,000, but only two towns, Turin and Alessandria, had more than 20,000 people. About 10 per cent of Norway's population was urban in 1801.

Other areas had more marked urbanisation. Of the 1.1 million inhabitants of Austrian Lombardy in the 1700s, 130,000 lived in Milan, although the next three towns had a combined population of only 54,000. Of the 2.3 million inhabitants of the republic of Venice in 1766, nearly 300,000 lived in the six leading towns. The 260,000 inhabitants of Lisbon, capital of an empire, in 1755 constituted about 10 per cent of the Portuguese population. The population of Amsterdam was nearly twice that of the provinces of either Friesland or Overijssel.

Growth or decline

It is difficult to relate urbanisation to economic activity or growth. Large towns were as obvious a feature of relatively stagnant Mediterranean Europe (Constantinople, Naples) as of growing north-western Europe (London). Many urban activities had only a tenuous relationship with economic growth. Though the figures given in 1726 by a contemporary, of 70,000 licensed prostitutes and 60,000 living by the law in Naples, may be questioned they underline the variety of activities that helped to make towns centres of consumption and service industries as much as of commercial and industrial activity.

Clearly a sense of opportunity played some role in urbanisation by encouraging migration to the towns. The percentage of the French population living in towns did not rise markedly during the century, and in 1789 only about 7.5 per cent lived in towns of 20,000 or more. There were very few new towns.[3] However, Bordeaux's population grew from 45,000 in 1700 to 111,000 in 1790, a higher rate of growth than in the other major French cities. As the crude birth rate in Bordeaux was about 3 per thousand per annum lower than the crude death rate in 1735–89, this was only achieved by an immigration that reflected Bordeaux's commercial growth and the high population density of certain nearby rural areas. Such immigration was responsible for the growth of most large towns.

Towns that grew tended to be areas of opportunity, if only sometimes in terms of social welfare and/or in contrast to regions of rural poverty, rather than a dynamic economy. Nevertheless, the economic pull was often marked. Bordeaux's attraction stemmed from, and was reflected in, a major wage differential between town and hinterland. Rural nominal wages in the hinterland, and indeed, more generally, in western Europe, rose little in the second half of the century and real wages fell as bread prices rose. In contrast, wage rises in Bordeaux often surpassed price rises. Economic growth played a major role in the growing population of other towns. Some, such as Liège and Verviers in the area of the middle Meuse valley, were also located in regions of relatively prosperous agriculture. The growth of other towns reflected government activity. The naval base of Karlskrona was the third most populous town in Sweden in 1700, Vienna had grown to 205,000 by 1790; while many towns, such as Helsinki, benefited from their garrison status.

Not all towns, however, grew in size. In Germany many of the Imperial Free Cities, which owed obedience to no ruler bar the emperor, declined, in part due to a lack of political strength vis-à-vis the consolidating territorial states, such as Prussia and their protectionist economic policies, in part due to the strength of their guilds. This was true of both Aachen and Cologne. Throughout Europe, many of the older towns suffered from the growth of rural industry and from their hostility to immigration. In contrast new industrial centres grew in size, as did most capital cities. In 1740 Stockholm controlled over 60 per cent of

Sweden's foreign trade, four times that of its closest rival Gothenburg. However, after 1750 the capital suffered from economic and demographic stagnation. Its commercial and industrial importance declined under the impact of the growth of industry in Norkoping and trade at Gothenburg, which enjoyed the most significant Swedish commercial growth during the century.

Urban growth and decline were not a random matter, though chance played a significant role, in terms both of war damage and of natural disasters, such as the silting up of estuaries and rivers. Several trends are apparent. The vast majority of towns did not enjoy any marked growth. Many appear to have been economically and demographically dormant market centres, such as Aurillac in Auvergne. Though the European economy was in general growing, much of the profit and of the consequent growth accrued to a relatively small number of towns, particularly capitals and major trading centres. Atlantic trade was one of the most important factors stimulating the growth of some towns. Towns such as Bordeaux and Glasgow flourished.

Small towns helped to form the commercial and fiscal infrastructure that sustained more dramatic and substantial cases of growth, but the latter were a minority and sometimes owed much to political considerations, particularly in the case of capital cities. It is true that the rise in the number and size of large towns was not necessarily related to state plans or policies, and therefore reflected the dynamism of sections of the European economy. This was particularly apparent in Atlantic Europe, especially Britain. However, governments' attitudes towards particular towns and to urban life in general were often of considerable importance.

Jan de Vries has suggested that a significant shift occurred in mid-century, that in place of a situation where large cities, particularly ports and capitals, grew most and small towns stagnated or declined, the growth of large cities came to an end over most of Europe. For a century urbanisation was to be caused by the expansion of smaller towns leading to a relative displacement of urban population from the largest cities.[4] As his study is, understandably, based on a small number of towns, those with a population of over 10,000, it is not clear that its findings are more widely applicable. What is clear is that not all emigration was to major cities, and that rural population growth acted as a powerful stimulus to emigration. Both primogeniture and the subdivision of rural landholdings increased the appeal of emigration at a time of population growth. More research is required on the relative position of major and minor towns. The former attracted most contemporary attention, as they posed the greatest problems of social welfare and law and order. Large towns were also more significant in influencing notions of urban life.

The divergent fortunes of towns were not unrelated to their rivalries. Towns within a state competed for economic and other functions and this helped both to reduce their autonomous political strength and to increase their often symbiotic relationship with government. Rivalry was apparent in a number of spheres. Rather than fearing government, most towns actively sought the location of administrative or political functions. In north Italy, Reggio was angry that the Este had their court at Modena, a view echoed by Piacenza with regard to Parma. It was estimated in 1785 that the move of the Palatine court from Mannheim to Munich, upon the extinction of the Bavarian Wittelsbachs in 1777, had led to the former losing a third of its population. There were bitter urban rivalries in France in 1790 when new local government agencies were created. There was intense lobbying of the National Assembly as so much hung on the outcome. Thus Clermont and Riom were rivals to become capital of the new Puy-de-Dôme department. In 1792 Marseilles used force to bring the administrative and judicial functions of the department from Aix. Similar ambitions and tensions were replicated in Revolutionary politics. The Jacobin clubs of leading provincial cities, such as Bordeaux and Marseilles, sought to bring nearby clubs into line with their policies, while all clubs were in theory affiliated to the Paris club.[5]

Economic rivalry between towns was constant. Towns sought to retain their economic independence, Elbeuf, for example, seeking to keep clear of Rouen's orbit. Such rivalry was most apparent when fiscal or political privileges were at issue. The discussion of the plan for a free port held in the Estates of Holland in April 1753 revealed vociferous opposition from the manufacturing towns of Leyden and Haarlem. In 1754 the possible redirection of Meuse trade pitted Amsterdam and Arnhem against Dort, Nijmegen and Rotterdam. In West Yorkshire in the second half of the century, competition between textile towns led to the building by subscription of six large halls in different towns for the more convenient marketing of cloth.

Alongside these rivalries, towns were affected by more general economic shifts. The rise of rural industry diverted investment, employment and immigration from many of the older manufacturing towns, though it also helped those towns best placed to service or control such rural industry. The fortunes of particular regions and industries were also of importance. Dutch manufacturing encountered problems, but shipping remained strong and in government finance especially, and financial activity in general, the second half of the century was a period of substantial growth for the United Provinces. The development of specialisations and of regional disparities during industrialisation affected particular towns. In eastern Switzerland, particularly in St Gall, a very dynamic bourgeoisie with a wide commercial span was replaced in mid-century, after a crisis in the local linen industry, by a new generation of businessmen with narrower horizons. Shifts in commercial routes and relationships also affected towns. Albi's industries declined as a result from the 1680s, Cracow's from the first half of the seventeenth century.

The principal economic functions of towns were as centres of production, trade and consumption. Some industries had little significant rural competition, for example Cologne producing tobacco and eau-de-Cologne; Morlaix tobacco and paper. Others were able to compete successfully, or to retain control of the more skilled and profitable sections of the manufacturing process. This was particularly the case in textiles, and many European towns regained their economic vigour during the century, while some, such as Valencia with its silk industry, enjoyed massive growth.

As centres of trade, towns benefited from their dominance of the transportation and financial networks. Their success in developing as commercial centres varied. Poor hinterlands that were unable or unwilling to purchase manufactured goods were a problem in much of eastern Europe, particularly Russia, Poland and the Balkans. Limited mercantile resources helped to restrict the indigenous merchants of northern, central and eastern Europe. In 1726, as a result of pressure on the Danish Board of Trade from Copenhagen merchants, who were opposed to foreign middlemen and determined to control all Danish trade, the government awarded the merchants a monopoly of the maintenance of bonded warehouses and gave them control over the importation of wine, spirits, salt and tobacco. However, as the merchants lacked the necessary resources, the policy proved a failure and was abandoned in the early 1730s.

Urban commerce was generally most successful when it was local, requiring limited investment and political assistance, and when it served a long-established need, such as the supply of salt from Königsberg or the servicing of Swedish mining by Vasteras. The majority of towns also found their commercial function to be similar to their administrative one, linking localities to distant centres of power, production, consumption and finance. The growth of Turin as a market for the Piedmontese economy led to a measure of growth for the smaller towns of the region as they became intermediaries between the capital and the countryside.

Their functional subservience was reflected in migration, as rural migrants were most likely to move permanently to Turin.

Towns as centres of privilege and control

The hierarchy of administrative organisation was not identical with that of economic control, but in many regions it was close to being so. This was the aim in Russia, where an attempt was made to create an urban structure. The provincial reform of 1775, dividing Russia into provinces and counties, required the existence of a town in each to serve as the centre of administration. To this end, 216 towns were founded by 1785. Though some did not develop as commercial centres as had been hoped, others did, such as Odessa which was founded in 1793. Throughout Europe, there were examples of towns lacking any significant commercial or industrial activity that, nevertheless, were of importance as administrative centres or still enjoyed a degree of prosperity. Toulouse lacked Bordeaux's commercial and industrial prominence, but was a centre of provincial government, with a *parlement*, a university and a population of nearly 60,000 in 1789. Nearby Auch was described by the British traveller Arthur Young in 1787 as 'almost without manufactures or commerce, and supported chiefly by the rents of the country'.

Government administration, both lay and ecclesiastical, was essentially urban in its organisation. This was the case with the law, fiscal administration and the armed forces. Whether soldiers were billeted or housed in barracks, they tended to be based in towns. Location in towns was not solely, however, a matter of urban-based organisations, for institutions that did not need to be in towns were often found there. This was the case with Russian monasteries and nunneries, while, though the bulk of the income of the Spanish church was derived from rural rents and tithes, both regular and secular clergy congregated in the towns, leaving many rural parishes unattended. Many monasteries were located in French towns and small cathedral cities. They could be an important element in the local economy, and this was a major worry when the National Assembly legislated against monasticism in 1790. Much of the tithe income from Roussillon in southern France went to support the local bishop, chapter and seminary, all located in Perpignan, thus lending a geographical perspective to local disputes.

As education was generally controlled by the clergy, it is not surprising that it was concentrated in the towns, where demands for educated labour and interest in learning were strongest. Urban seminaries were a long-standing Counter-Reformation strategy largely complete by the early eighteenth century. As part of his reform programme, Joseph II established seminaries in Prague and Olomouc in 1783 to educate priests under state supervision. Towns were cultural as well as educational centres. The Royal Bohemian Society of Sciences was established in Prague in 1770, and the town had 15 printers in 1781. The Enlightenment itself was markedly urban in nature. The dependence of cultural interchange upon communications furthered the importance of towns, where newspapers, publishers, learned societies and coffee-houses were to be found. Indeed historians frequently mean urban culture when they write of provincial culture. In the English Midlands the Enlightenment was centred as much on new towns like Birmingham as on older centres like Lichfield. In some parts of Europe, the urban concentration of secondary education and modern cultural activity had linguistic consequences. In Bohemia the towns were the centres of German language and culture, while Czech was strongest among the peasantry and those who attended elementary schools. A similar linguistic contrast existed in both Languedoc and Lithuania, where respectively the French and Polish of the elite were opposed to the *langue d'oc* and Lithuanian of the bulk of the population.

The role of towns as centres of administration varied. Government was most important to capital cities that lacked significant economic activity, such as Berlin and Munich. St Petersburg, which became the capital of Russia, was a new city founded by Peter I; Karlsruhe, which became the capital of Baden, was founded in 1719. Such towns derived considerable power from their political position, becoming major centres of consumption. It has been estimated that of the 2,750,000 lire of taxes collected by Savoy-Piedmont in 1700, about 1,500,000 were sent to Turin. The importance of ruler and government in capital cities was symbolised by the central location of palaces and offices and their prominent position in urban townscapes. Building in such towns was often influenced by the ruler, with urban and suburban palaces or *places royales*, as in Nancy, the capital of Lorraine.

In most towns government was less exalted. However, administrative functions could still be significant sources of employment, income and power over the surrounding region. It was not without reason that Russian provinces and counties were named after towns. European towns were often dominated socially by those who derived their position and wealth from administrative and judicial posts. Lawyers, for example, dominated Besançon, a town in eastern France with a *parlement*, and also its surrounding region. They and their families constituted about 6 per cent of the urban population there and were its leaders in economic and cultural terms. Rennes, the seat of the Breton *parlement* and a regular meeting place for the provincial Estates, was a good example of a French regional political centre.

If relations between towns and states, townsmen and central government, varied it was principally in the field of politics that the central government was most obtrusive. There was a general hostility to urban attempts to display or maintain political independence, particularly in the areas of military strength and foreign policy. Government policies towards towns, however, were far from uniform. In much of Europe there was a tendency towards greater control by central governments, often related to an attack upon urban privileges, particularly upon the role of the guilds. The initiative for change tended to rest with central government, which, on the whole, obtained its ends without violence or formal opposition.

Urban independence tended to be strongest in western Europe, where privileges were generally most deeply entrenched and respected. Though in 1699 the office of lieutenant-general of police (chief police magistrate) was extended to all major French towns, the official gaining much of the judicial authority formerly held by the town council, French urban administration was largely a matter of co-operation. Towns such as Bordeaux, Orléans and Paris had special privileges in militia matters. The British government was forced to accept frequent political criticisms from the elected political institutions of major British cities, particularly London, and to resort to techniques of management – patronage and persuasion – in order to defend their position.

Rebellion was atypical; an element of central government coercion was, however, present in some towns. In Florence in the 1720s military precautions were taken against the threat of trouble over high taxes. In 1766 the Spanish government reacted firmly when the elite of Lorca, which controlled many municipal offices and was opposed to the royal reforms being implemented by the governor, took advantage of and exacerbated popular concern over the price of grain in order to drive out the governor and seize power. It was rare for urban privileges to play a role in wider struggles, though after the successful siege of Barcelona during the War of Spanish Succession, Philip V confiscated all the revenues of the town and limited its privileges, as he did those of the province of Catalonia. For Spanish towns, Philip's victory led to the diminution of municipal autonomy, by the nomination of a *corregidor*, an official representing royal authority.

A peaceful loss of rights was more common. In the towns of Bohemia and Moravia, royal officials oversaw both town finance and public order. In 1706 royal officials were appointed in

Bohemia to manage town finances. Similarly the position of the towns in the Estates (provincial representative assemblies) was limited. By 1709 urban representation in that of Bohemia was restricted to the three towns of Prague. The delegates of the seven royal towns of Moravia could attend the Estates, but, until 1711, they had to stand during the proceedings. In both Estates the urban representatives had only a single joint vote, and were therefore equal to only one aristocrat. Under Frederick William I many of the powers of the old Prussian town councils were transferred to agents of the central government and royal officials came to administer police and judicial functions. However, as in much of Europe east of the Elbe, most of the towns had already been fairly weak and Frederick William's changes often amounted to replacing aristocratic domination, rather than urban independence. Peter I attempted in 1721 to introduce municipal self-government to Russia, but he also saw town councils as an essential support for central government. Heavy taxes and administrative duties, particularly tax collecting, imposed on Russian municipal institutions contributed to serious fiscal difficulties. In so far as there was any municipal organisation, it generally looked after part of the town only, as large sections of towns were directly subordinated to the central government, the church and individuals. The function of the 'municipal' sector was in large measure to serve the state. In some towns councils were never set up, in most they were weak, and the consequent administrative crisis led to a reversal of Peter's policies in 1727 and the subordination of towns to local governors. Russian towns remained heavily dependent on government, a situation facilitated by the importance of central government in communications, commerce and the economy, and the significant role of the military in many towns, such as St Petersburg.

Rulers keen to enhance their power sought to limit municipal rights. Joseph II transferred control of the police in Habsburg territories from town councils to central government. The heavy indebtedness of the communities in the county of Nice and the absence of a general assembly helped to ensure that they were in no position to resist central government, whose local agent, the *intendant*, intervened vigorously in municipal elections. Municipal reforms, designed to codify laws and centralise government, culminated in a general regulation of 1775 for Piedmont and the county of Nice which ended much of the municipal independence in Piedmont. Urban councils were placed under the control of *intendants*, deprived largely of initiative and responsibility and charged with the execution of instructions. Government changes were sometimes matched by social legislation that restricted the rights of townsmen. The contempt with which they were held by some rulers and by much of landed society is revealed in the Table of Ranks drawn up by Duke Eberhard Ludwig of Württemberg, in which army lieutenants preceded the mayors of the leading towns in the duchy, Stuttgart and Tübingen.

And yet relations between towns and central governments were not always poor. Central government influence or control was often preferable to that of the local aristocracy. The latter enjoyed considerable powers, both legal and otherwise, in many towns. A large number of European towns belonged in the feudal sense to aristocrats. This was not only the case in eastern Europe. In France, the mayor of Albi was chosen by its seigneur, the archbishop, while the royal right to choose the mayor and councillors of Angers was given to a royal prince, the count of Provence, in the 1770s. Montargis belonged to the duke of Orléans. The prince of Condé, sovereign prince of Charleville, exercised extraordinary influence over the school that replaced that of the Jesuits.

In much of eastern Europe aristocratic privileges ensured that towns looked to central government for support, and this was also the situation in much of Mediterranean Europe. The legal rights and economic activities of landowners were a problem for towns, particularly in eastern Europe. Russian landowners encouraged their serfs to engage in manufacturing and commerce and so helped to prevent the concentration of these activities in towns. Jakob Sievers, the reforming governor of the province of Novgorod, failed to persuade Catherine II to allow serfs to purchase their freedom and enrol as townsmen and to ban peasant traders from the towns. Russian landowners wanted to encourage the commercial activities of their peasants in order to increase their revenues and they got their way, the Charter to the Towns of 1785 allowing peasants to engage in handicrafts and to sell their products in the towns. Only one of the Polish provincial Estates, that of Royal (Polish) Prussia, included urban representatives, and the Polish landowners enjoyed privileges that hindered urban economic activity.

Many towns and townsmen benefited from, and sought, government assistance. Wealth and employment frequently derived from government-granted privileges and support, particularly those denied to others, and lobbying, the best way to obtain them, was frequent. Economic benefits flowed from such government support. The Catalan city of Mataro enjoyed considerable growth in the first two decades of the century, partly due to fiscal exemptions from which its trade benefited, leading foreign merchants and even some from Barcelona to move there. Government support, however, often entailed upsetting other towns or particular urban groups. For example, the Portuguese minister Pombal supported large merchants in their disputes with their smaller competitors, because he saw the latter as commission agents for foreign merchants whom he hoped to displace with the assistance of the former.

The divided nature of many urban communities, particularly over economic matters, ensured that regulations would not be free from dispute. The support of urban institutions either for established economic practices or for change could create difficulties and controversy. In 1719 the burghers of Danzig (Gdansk) complained to Augustus II that its commercial decay was due to concessions made by the magistrates to Anabaptists, Jews and other non-burghers residing in the suburbs and neighbourhood. Concerned in 1784 about the supply of firewood to Paris, the *Parlement* of Paris criticised the responsible wood merchants, making clear their opposition to what they considered excessive profits. Louis XVI replied that the best way to supply Paris was to enable the merchants to make a profit.

Because of their role in commerce and administration, vulnerability to war, the presence of a relatively literate population, and the tradition of seeking state support, towns were more open to governmental activity than most of the countryside. The detailed impact of this activity varied clearly. If Dresden was dependent on the Saxon court for its wealth, Warsaw was transformed in 1795 from a national capital into a Prussian provincial centre as a result of the actions of the partitioning powers. Governments could be physically creative or destructive. The French built Versoix on Lake Geneva in order to limit the trade of Geneva, while many of the houses in Breslau were destroyed in 1749 when lightning hit the Prussian gunpowder magazine. However, as administration was primarily urban in location, if not ideology, it is not surprising that, with the exception of the expression of political views, the relation between towns and government was generally close.

Town and country

The economic and administrative role of towns caused problems in urban–rural relations. It is easy to see signs of clashes of interest and views between town and countryside. These were particularly marked in economic affairs. Economically dependent on their hinterlands, towns sought to control both the activities in these zones and the terms of their relationship with them. Particular attention was devoted to ensuring an adequate supply of food.

The Venetian tariff system was mainly designed to control the supply of foodstuffs for the capital. One writer observed in 1748: 'As to Lyons, you well know with what art and authority they can here manage their police, so as to prevent any appearance of scarcity in their great cities, however it may show itself in the country villages'.[6] Touring Sweden in 1768, the future Gustavus III wrote to his brother from the small settlement of Avesta, 'At Stockholm where one lives in plenty it is impossible to imagine the condition of these poor people.'[7] Rural poverty, unemployment and famine were, however, of scant interest to townspeople, who in general restricted their assistance. Toulouse was typical in posting guards to keep out work- and charity-seekers during the hard years of 1709–13, 1747–8 and 1773.

Influence in agriculture was not limited to foodstuffs, for towns provided the crucial outlets for goods that entered the market economy, and tended to control processing and marketing. The Spanish Jesuit Pedro de Calatayud in 1761 attacked the merchants of Bilbao for exploiting the small rural sheep-owners in the purchase of wool for export and for forcing them into usurious contracts, and criticised merchants in general. The provision of cheap olive oil for Naples had detrimental effects on provincial production. This city's influence was often expressed through the extension of urban credit and the purchase of land was matched by a determination to restrict rural industry. In order to limit the latter, which was largely tax-exempt, a Prussian edict of 1787 allowed only one carpenter, one blacksmith, one wheelwright and one tailor in each village. Such restrictions angered rural communities, particularly as population growth increased the appeal of rural industrial employment.

Fiscal privilege frequently accompanied urban economic privilege. Many tax systems discriminated against the rural population. The commercial sectors of agriculture were often taxed heavily, as in the kingdom of Naples. In Württemberg the oligarchs dominating the powerful municipal governments of such cities as Stuttgart and Tübingen had every reason to champion the traditional tax structure since it placed a heavy burden on the villages.

Tax structures varied. Urban elites protected their interests by taxes on food, which hit the poor most heavily. Excise duties fell more on those who bought what they consumed, classically townsmen, than on peasants who supplied much of what they consumed. In Sicily the flour excise was the easiest tax to collect; politically acceptable as it fell on the poor. Equally, land taxes or taxes on production hit the rural sector hard. They were, in the shape of the tithe, the basis of taxation for the Church. In

England at the beginning of the century the rural community felt that it contributed more, in the shape of the land tax, towards the War of the Spanish Succession, than the towns.

Across Europe as a whole many of the taxation schemes advanced during the century, such as poll taxes, and attempts to extend direct taxation to the aristocracy, bore most heavily on the rural community. Russia introduced a poll tax in 1724, fixed at 74 kopecks per registered individual, a figure obtained by dividing the projected cost of the army by the number of people listed in the 1719 census. Nobles did not pay the tax, though they were responsible for its collection from their serfs. In 1783 the Russian government introduced the poll tax into Estonia and Livonia, a measure that led to social unrest. An attempt to introduce a poll tax on all subjects was rejected by the Bavarian Estates in 1746, while Karl Eugen of Württemberg's 1764 proposal for a graduated property tax, based on an inventory of assets, failed.

There was considerable success in ending tax exemptions. The Bohemian nobility began paying taxes seriously in 1706. At the opening of the 1718 campaign in the Great Northern War, Charles XII of Sweden decreed a capital levy of 6 per cent on everyone as a civilian contribution to the war effort. In 1722 direct taxation was introduced into the Ukraine, the higher clergy and gentry being made subject to it. Frederick William I brought in a uniform land tax in East Prussia, payable alike by nobility and peasantry, based on the land assessment rolls and the productivity of the soil. Frederick the Great introduced a similar tax to Silesia, abolishing the tax exemptions of nobility and clergy and declaring that all should contribute, since the state extended its protection to all subjects. In 1772 the tax was extended to Prussia's gains from Poland. The French edict of 1749 introducing the *vingtième* provided that the tax would be proportional to the revenues of taxpayers. In the preamble, Louis XV stated that he preferred this mode of taxation, because the *vingtième* could be levied on all ranks of society in proportion to their ability to pay. However, the government climbed down in practice. The clergy did not pay, the nobility underpaid and in 1789 the privileged orders still paid very little in direct taxation. In 1756 the first *vingtième* was prolonged and a second introduced for the duration of the Seven Years War despite the opposition of the Paris and provincial *parlements*.

The effect of these fiscal changes on the percentage of taxation paid by the rural community is difficult to assess. Very little work has been done on the subject. Part of the problem is the extent to which new tax demands on aristocracy and clergy were passed on to the peasantry in the form of higher rents. It has been calculated that French agricultural production rose on average by up to 40 per cent during the century down to the Revolution, but ground rent rose by over 60 per cent, and tithes by 10 to 20 per cent, producing heavy rural indebtedness. The tax paid to the state, however, was stabilised, if not in real terms, at least in the percentage of the total gross agricultural product. This stabilisation was not jeopardised until the 1780s, when taxation increased in the aftermath of French intervention in the American rebellion. This may well under-rate the extent of taxation passed on in the form of rents. In this light, taxing the landowners was a relatively effective means of increasing the fiscal yield from the bulk of the population for a society that lacked a substantial bureaucracy or reliable information on its own resources. It was, however, dependent on the co-operation of the landowners. Clearly the relationship between tax and rent was such that any tax increase on a section of the rural community would not be limited in its effects.

The susceptibility of many governments to urban opinion appears to have made them wary of pushing up excises. Urban demonstrations about excises, as in London in 1733 and Tournai in 1739, were difficult to ignore. Frederick the Great's attempt to push through a new excise in his Swiss principality of Neuchâtel in 1766 was abandoned in 1768, after riots, and ancient rights were guaranteed. Popular clamour greeted an edict of 1777 announcing the cutting of subsidies on olive oil for the citizens of Naples, and, fearing riots, the authorities suppressed the edict. Unwilling for political reasons to increase urban taxes or to cut urban subsidies, such as those on bread in Naples, many governments pushed up rural taxes. The often violent response to such increases suggests not only a disinclination to pay higher taxes, but also that they created difficulties for the rural community. In Brittany sporadic tax revolts against the *capitation* in 1719–20 inspired government fears of another tax rising, abetted by the provincial nobility. As a result, the *vingtième* was only established in the province after compromises with the local Estates. The population of Berne in Switzerland was lightly taxed, but the town used its control over the surrounding region, and in particular the Pays de Vaud, to raise revenue from these areas, leading to serious disaffection. In 1788 there was a serious revolt by farmers near Oudenaarde in the Austrian Netherlands against the levying of taxes on livestock and rents.

If revolts against rents are seen, in part, as risings inspired by the attempts to pass on tax increases, then it is possible that tax-related disturbances were more common than is often realised.

How far they should be attributed to an explicit intention to increase the rural share of the tax burden is unclear, though there are some signs of such an attitude. When in 1754 Amsterdam, supported by Haarlem, Leyden and Rotterdam, proposed in the States of Holland that the tax on houses be cut by half, the largely rural northern section of the province complained that such a move would favour the urbanised southern half, and demanded a reduction in the land tax. In the end, the house tax was cut in half, and a tax on beer reimposed, a move that was unwelcome to the brewers. This led to a cut in the quality of beer in Rotterdam, provoking a disturbance there that summer, thus indicating the divergent interests of the urban population.

Urban influence was also expressed in other fiscal spheres. The relative shortage of credit in Europe, accompanied by the concentration of credit facilities in towns, posed problems for the rural sector. Rural indebtedness increased urban control over aspects of the rural economy. Warsaw and Danzig dominated Polish credit transactions, helping to enlarge these towns' role in the economy. Taxation and rent income in the kingdom of Naples were the channels by which wealth was transferred from the agricultural sector to the population of the capital. About 10 per cent of the population lived in the capital and their employment depended upon this movement of wealth. As capital accumulated there credit was easily available at low rates of interest (3 per cent). In the provinces credit was harder to find and interest rates higher (8+ per cent). While there were banks in Naples, there were none in the provinces, where the need for credit, in the face of heavy tax and rent demands, was constant.

Economic tension between town and country was sometimes linked to cultural rivalry. In many areas there were also ethnic differences between urban and rural populations. Balkan cities, divided into quarters, each inhabited by a different group of the population, had a disproportionate share of the Muslim population. Muslim administrators, estate owners, many of whom were absentee, and officers preferred to live in towns. In western Poland there were many Germans in the cities, and the rural population was largely Polish, while in east and south Poland the townspeople were largely Polish and Jewish, the rural population Lithuanian or Ruthenian.

Even where urban and rural inhabitants were ethnically and religiously homogeneous, there were clear cultural differences between town and countryside. Literacy was more common in urban areas, while in regions such as Languedoc, crime was a more pronounced feature of rural life. There were differences in religious sensibility, in terms of, first, adaptability to Reformation and post-Reformation reforms, both Protestant and Catholic, and later, response to secular tendencies.

It has been suggested that in both Protestant and Catholic Europe the seventeenth and early eighteenth centuries witnessed efforts by the dominant urban groups to cement their superiority over the largely rural lower orders, as well as over their urban counterparts. The ideological aspect of this was a morality that condemned indolence, sexual licence, insubordination and disorder, and that praised deference and order. This was disseminated by the newly trained parochial clergy supported by devout laymen. The response of rural areas to this campaign was mixed, but often unenthusiastic, as was the rural response to Enlightenment tendencies, which were in many respects an encapsulation of progressive urban culture. In the towns of western France there were signs of secularisation towards the end of the century, while the countryside remained strongly clericalist, so that socioeconomic clashes between town and country were paralleled by a cultural clash. Under the strain of the French Revolution, this cultural clash in 1793 became a military one in the Vendée, a clericalised area in which the Counter-Reformation had been extremely successful.

The relationship between town and countryside was not solely one of urban initiatives and influence. Indeed it is not always helpful to pose the question: urban or rural? This is particularly so when it comes to the influence of nobles possessing landed estates who lived in the towns, which was the general pattern in much of Europe. Many towns, as in Italy or Russia, were controlled by these nobles. The influence of the urban-based nobility was not always preponderant. There were towns, such as Aurillac in France, where many nobles lived, but were less influential than in the countryside, because of the presence of an important bourgeoisie. In some areas, the nobility had a more apparent pernicious effect. In Poland, besides possessing an exclusive right to exploit the timber, potash and minerals of their estates, nobles were able to buy properties in towns and use them for economic activities, without paying municipal taxes. In 1763, when preparing an appeal to the Polish Diet (Parliament), Old Warsaw expressed distrust of courts dominated by the nobility, opposition to their possession of city estates, and suspicion of their unregistered acquisitions of land within the city. Similar complaints were made regularly by most Polish royal towns.

Given these tensions between town and countryside, it is not surprising that relations were often cool. In some areas this was expressed in institutional and constitutional forms, with long-standing disputes over economic regulation, the allocation of fiscal obligations and political issues. In the Dutch province of Groningen there was a traditional hostility, fought out in the Estates, between the town of Groningen and the surrounding region, and new issues, such as the conflict in 1708–10 over the appointment of a stadtholder (provincial governor), reflected this dispute. Other regions lacked similar institutional and constitutional opportunities for the expression of disputes. In Roussillon there was hostility towards the principal town, Perpignan, where the clergy, tax farmers, lawyers and grain merchants lived. It was seen as rich and privileged by the rural population and was also the main centre of French language and culture in a region where the major language was Catalan. In disputes the *intendants* supported Perpignan against rural interests. The drawing up of lists of grievances (*cahiers*) in early 1789 in preparation for the meeting of the Estates General provided an opportunity for the expression of these rural grievances. These complaints concerned the grain merchants, clergy and tax farmers, the slowness and formalism of legal procedures, the monopolistic position of the Collège de Perpignan and the absence of rural education. The most insistent of the rural demands was for the suppression of the judicial and fiscal privileges of the citizens. At times such urban–rural tensions took a violent form. The Corsican rising against Genoese rule in 1730 took the form of a struggle between the countryside and the towns, where many Genoese lived, both competing for the control of the fertile alluvial plains. The towns were seen as the domain of usurers and merchants. In 1790 the Flemish countryside rose against the urban-based notables of the Austrian Netherlands.

And yet, it would be a mistake to present town and countryside simply as rivals. The clashes between them were not always as clear as they might seem, or regarded as town–country antagonisms. In many cases, there were strong links between them in economic affairs. Successful rural textile manufacturing areas, such as the Austrian Netherlands, or the Elbeuf area in Normandy, were dependent on urban commercial and financial services.

Furthermore, although migration from the countryside did not destroy the traditional nature of urban culture, it affected the social and cultural character of towns. Migrants did not always benefit from the opportunities presented by urban life. They often occupied the more marginal jobs and housing and suffered higher rates of unemployment. Integration into the urban environment was difficult, though it was easier when there were large numbers of immigrants and this helps to account for their propensity to congregate together. Many immigrants moved, often through necessity, on to the seamy side of enterprise. In Bordeaux they figured disproportionately in cases of prostitution and theft. Others, however, found more steady employment, such as the Corsican and Swiss troops stationed in Genoa in the 1730s. Whatever their individual fortune, immigrants, particularly if they were seasonal workers, served to link town and countryside.

Cultural links also existed. Peasants flocked to towns not only to go to market, but also to attend fairs or religious ceremonies. Conversely, the reception of urban initiatives was not always hostile. The diffusion of urban ideas was assisted by the presence in the countryside of men who by their functions played an intermediary role, particularly clerics. In Languedoc, midwifery courses designed for rural women were established in four towns. These helped to alter rural practices, and urban postures for giving birth were adopted generally. Wet-nursing provided another instance of co-operation. It was primarily a rural service and source of income. In France working women, particularly in Paris and Lyons, sent their children to peasants' wives in areas that lacked rural industry.

Aside from areas of co-operation, the impact of tension was limited by the divided nature of urban and rural interests. While the poor of the Corsican town of Bastia when it was attacked by the rebels in 1730, did not support them, preferring communal solidarity to any perception of shared social interests, the clan structure of Corsican society divided the rural interest. In Roussillon the clash between Perpignan and the countryside was confused by divisions in both camps. Pastoral farmers, their animals competing with vineyards, were opposed to cultivators, while the poor of the Perpignan suburbs were neither citizens of the town nor closely identified with its interests. As with so much else, links and tension between towns and rural areas were intertwined, symbiotic relations producing stresses, as well as benefits, and at the individual level conclusions are difficult, often a matter of perception. The indebted peasant was both the victim and the beneficiary of the market economy, and the struggling immigrant found hardship, as well as opportunity, in the towns.

Towns and social hierarchy

Towns shared in the inegalitarian and hierarchical nature of European society. Their individual social and administrative structures varied in accordance with their function, historical and political circumstances and the nature of their hinterland. As with the rest of society, the terminology used to describe social ranks, whether legal or economic, varied widely and was often inconsistent. The relationship between legal and economic classifications was imperfect. Just as the terms aristocracy, nobility, gentry and land-owners confuse as much as they describe, particularly when applied on a continental scale, so those of bourgeoisie, burghers and middle class are often unhelpful.

The inegalitarian nature of European society, urban as well as rural, and the economic functions of towns ensured that most towns had a common social structure, however defined in legal terms. The smallest group were the wealthy and prominent, their power expressed in, and deriving from, their ability to organise others, generally economically and often politically. Their strength extended into the rural hinterland, where they would enjoy influence as a result of their power as a source of credit, tend to own estates and, if merchants, control rural industry. Within the towns, this group might be employers or landowners, but, more commonly, would enjoy political power as a result of social status and its control over the institutions of urban govern-ment. Some members of the group would possess noble rank, though the importance of that varied greatly. Most derived their income from trade, official, particularly judicial, positions, and the profits from wealth invested in land or in interest-paying loans.

The largest urban group were the poor. They tended to lack political weight and often were not citizens of the town in any legal sense. Their poverty stemmed from the precarious nature of much employment in even the most prosperous of towns and the absence of any effective system of social welfare. Most lacked the skills that commanded a decent wage and many had only seasonal or episodic employment. A large number were immi-grants. As a result of their poverty, the poor were very vulnerable to changes in the price of food and generally lived in inadequate housing. As they could not afford much fuel they were often wet and cold in the winter and the circumstances of their life made them prone to disease.

In between these two groups, though not separated rigidly from them in economic terms, was a third one enjoying a more settled income than the poor. Many in this group were artisans, their economic interests and social cohesion often expressed through guilds or other fraternities of workmen. They frequently played a political role, their participation in town government institutionally and constitutionally defined, even if the effects were frequently circumscribed by the oligarchic tendencies of the town notables. The consistent pattern of tight intermarriage within socio-economic groups (endogamy) made entry into the elite of merchants and magistracy very difficult.

The extent to which towns conformed to this pattern largely depended on their urban functions. The government and social composition of a garrison town were generally very different from those of a maritime port. Urban functions affected the character of towns as well as their social composition. The administrative activities of Koblenz, the capital of the Electorate of Trier located at the confluence of the Moselle and Rhine, played a major role in creating the great economic and intellectual gulf between the small number of wealthy, high-ranking lay and clerical officials, a largely endogamous (intermarrying) elite open to new ideas and keen to reform the town's economic and welfare policies, and the merchants, artisans and petty bureaucrats with their conservative and protectionist views. The third section of Koblenz's society, the economically vulnerable and, often, socially isolated day-labourers, servants and paupers, were a common feature of urban society.

The nature and privileges of the urban wealthy and prominent varied. In particular, the source of their wealth differed, as did their legal and social position with regard to the aristocracy. In some towns, merchants played a major role, in others officials. Genoa was dominated by noble bankers, Carcassonne by textile manufacturer–merchants, Toulouse and Béziers by large landowners. The larger Polish towns were run by oligarchies controlling both public offices and commercial enterprises. The smaller ones tended to be dominated either by the owner or by royal officials. Figures compiled in the French town of Montpellier in 1753–6 revealed that of the 1490 houseowners, 73 per cent possessed only one house or a part of one, 17 per cent owned two, and 10 per cent three to eight, the last group owning in total nearly a quarter of the town's houses. Expressed socially, the clergy, nobles, merchants and senior officials owned 27 per cent of the houses, concentrated in the wealthiest sections of the town, the lesser officials and professionals 35.5 per cent, and the artisans and peasants 36.5 per cent. In terms of rent from Montpellier buildings, the first category held 54 per cent, two groups of officials in this category alone owning 14 per cent of the houses and taking 29 per cent of the rent.

The relationship of the nobility to the bourgeoisie varied. There were signs of tension, but they tended to be overlaid by shared interests and the desire of the latter to emulate aristocratic culture. The nobility of the Austrian Netherlands had considerable difficulty in keeping the bourgeoisie from usurping its privileges, but this, itself, was evidence of nobility's prestige in the eyes of the latter. The local nobility owned less land than the bourgeoisie, though there were fewer nobles. The purchase of landed estates by the bourgeoisie played a significant role in underlining the common aspirations of both groups, though on the individual level it could create tension. Intermarriage further facilitated the links between aristocracy and bourgeoisie, though it was usually a matter of merchants' daughters marrying noblemen's sons, transferring wealth and creating links without compromising social position. Public office was a common method of ascending the social scale. The legal boundary dividing noble and bourgeois cut across merchants and officials, but its flexibility varied. Many individuals encountered opposition to social mobility. In 1772 the acquisition of a senior municipal post in Béziers in southern France by someone who had been a hairdresser led to complaints that it would threaten the social order.

The definition of the bourgeoisie is far from easy, particularly as its legal character varied according to national and local statutes. A French edict of 1765 on urban administration distinguished merchants from bourgeois living nobly, that is wealthy *rentiers*. In Poland the burghers were mainly those Christian taxpayers who enjoyed full civic rights. The Parisian bourgeoisie was defined as those who had lived in Paris for a year and a day, were neither employed as domestics nor lived in rented lodgings, and who shared in the common tax assessments. In return, they enjoyed legal and economic privileges, including the right to sell some goods duty free.

Russia was unusual in making urban status a matter of wealth alone. Decrees of 1775 divided urban dwellers into two broad groups: merchants and *meshchanstvo*. Merchants were organised into 'guilds', not by type of business, but according to the amount of capital they possessed, those lacking sufficient capital for membership in even the lowest guild being enrolled in the *meshchanstvo*. Movement from guild to guild or between the merchant group and the *meshchanstvo* was automatic, a response to a change in wealth. These distinctions based on wealth had status consequences. In 1785, under legislation that was part of a plan for society as a whole, all merchants were freed from compulsory state service and allowed to purchase an exemption from military conscription, while the first and second merchant guilds were granted immunity from corporal punishments and permitted to use certain status symbols such as coaches. Russian zoning regulations welcomed the wealthy to town centres.

Whatever the definition, the size of the bourgeoisie was commonly limited. In the larger Swedish towns the burghers were a clear minority of the adult male population. Of the total population of the French town of Chartres in 1766, 5.6 per cent, representing 8.3 per cent of the number of households, had the title of bourgeois. Of the 352,000 inhabitants of Hungary's royal free towns and mining cities in 1782 only 20,000 (5.7 per cent) were burghers, and, as a group, they possessed little capital and scant sense of common interest.

The character and political power of the bourgeoisie differed. They shared a determination to preserve their privileges, but these, again, varied greatly. While, for example, the 'middle bourgeoisie', of professionals and sometimes merchants, had some access to municipal power in Languedoc, the petty bourgeoisie lacked this. Exemptions freed the nobility, lawyers and most merchants from service in the Bordeaux militia in 1722, but they did not extend to all who would have been considered bourgeois. The predominantly official, rather than mercantile, character of the bourgeoisie across much of Europe possibly played a part in their relative resistance to new men. They were all too aware that the number of official posts had to be limited if their prestige and value were to be retained, and, as a result, they shared the general hostility of the guilds to innovation. Most bourgeois were traditionalist in their aims.

The bourgeoisie did not usually want economic or political change. Rather than seeing themselves as the flag-bearers of a putative rising middle class, the bourgeoisie displayed little sign of what would later be termed class consciousness. The political process may generally have been closed to any demands for greater power for them, but there is little sign that they sought it. Though the bourgeois individually might be profiteers from greater flexibility in rural society and the partial liquidation of features of the traditional 'feudal' regime by, for example, buying land in regions such as Savoy, there is scant sign that they saw it as a collective aspiration or achievement. Economic interests divided them. Thus in Lille manufacturers and merchants differed in their response to government economic regulations.

It has been argued that there were some signs of a new ethos. The French bourgeoisie in the 1770s and 1780s read works that portrayed a way of life emphasising the value of industry, discipline and professionalism, a conscious alternative to aristocratic values, but it is important not to exaggerate the significance of such ideas. They were neither new nor politically pointed, and their impact on social mores appears to have been slight.

Bourgeois conservatism was shared by the artisans. It reflected, in part, the world view held by most townspeople, and, in particular, the opposition to outsiders. Though immigration existed, it, and its effects, were generally resisted by artisans keen to protect the value of their skills. In the German manufacturing town of Nördlingen 58 per cent of a sample of grooms at first marriage in 1701–3 followed the same occupation as their father. The adults in the town were divided into citizens and non-citizens.

The former were economically independent heads of households and only they could belong to a guild and carry on a craft. Non-citizens were socially and economically subordinate, mostly apprentices, journeymen, servants and casual labourers, and few were married, most living in the homes of their employers or in special hostelries for journeymen. While the son of a citizen enjoyed a hereditary right to that status, a non-citizen had to apply for membership. The nature of the community and the potential labour force was also controlled in Nördlingen by the regulation of marriages. Special permission was required for a man under 23, or a woman under 20, to marry, and outsiders wishing to marry into the community were expected to meet property qualifications.[8]

Restrictions on new entrants were a common feature of European guilds, and progress within them to a mastership was often difficult. The high fees expected from new masters in Elbeuf helped to ensure that the average worker had scant hope of rising so high. The elaborate system of guilds reflected, in part, the economic insecurity of artisans, but it was also a product of their communal and social aspirations. The initiation rites of guilds and other fraternities acted as a secular counterpart to religious ceremonies. Polish guildsmen not only took oaths of loyalty to the guilds, but also worshipped together in guild chapels, served in the militia in guild units and frequented the Guild House with their family. Irish guilds had a sociability based on Protestantism and therefore included those whose meagre propertied status might have excluded them if the confessional base had been wider. Merchant confraternities were often very similar to guilds.

The conservative response of artisans to new industrial techniques and organisation thus reflected not only economic interest, but also a determination to protect the existing social order and way of life, that derived from a sense of the importance of traditional values and communal stability and continuity. Free market conditions were viewed with suspicion, and public authorities received appeals from artisans threatened by them. The lace-makers of Valladolid in Spain complained about the effects of putting-out arrangements. French hat-makers resisted the impact of cheaper hare or rabbit furs on traditional working practices and structures.[9] Artisans could also react with violence to threats to traditional practices. New machines were sometimes attacked, as in Rouen in 1789. From 1725 to 1755 the Imperial Free City of Aachen had a regime based on the guilds, which was opposed to schemes for mercantile change. Imports of competing goods, such as rough needles, were prohibited. In 1755–6 this government was brought down by the merchants and 'mob', supported by a nearby ruler, the elector Palatine. The guilds took over again in 1763, only to lose power in 1786.

The corporate organisation of many urban artisans, and their defensive attitude, were understandable in the light of the inadequate nature of public social welfare and consequent need to combine to provide it, and of the limited support that guilds enjoyed from other urban groups. The corporate and hierarchical social structure of eighteenth-century Europe tended to express itself in terms of exclusion, such barriers being the counterpart of privilege, which was valuable only if restricted. In February 1788, and again a year later, the town council of Narbonne in France rejected pressure from artisans for their entry to the council. Spanish municipal government and military orders excluded artisans, and in the Spanish province of Galicia tanners could not hold public office, obtain membership in a guild or religious confraternity or aspire to the priesthood. In 1783 Charles III of Spain issued an edict declaring artisans fit for municipal office and their trades 'honest and honorable'. This alteration of the traditional hierarchy of honour, however, appears to have had little effect, and Spanish municipal governments remained dominated by landowners. That of the town of Horche, east of Madrid, resisted royal orders to elect manufacturers to office from 1781 to 1794.

Towns and political strife

In many areas of Europe, particularly the Empire, struggles over the nature of municipal government were not new, and artisan aspirations to political influence were traditional. They made little progress for much of the eighteenth century, most of which, compared with the sixteenth, was quiescent in this respect. Whereas, for example, artisans had played a role in the town governments of Languedoc in the earlier period, they were excluded from it in the later one until the Revolution.

Urban unrest over political issues could be serious. In some towns, such as London, Geneva, certain Imperial Free Cities and those in the province of Holland, there was a marked tradition of often violent political activity. In others, such as Madrid, it was more episodic. As with peasant uprisings, violent action and radical demands were not restricted to areas of economic difficulty. The desperation that fuelled food riots could be found in towns that were usually prosperous, while articulate political demands seem to have reflected traditions of communal action generally. During the Genoese rising of 1746 the reform of the 1576 law, which had consolidated the power of the oligarchy, was demanded, while the pre-oligarchy Assembly of the People was revived. The magistracy and the middling orders of Danzig (Gdansk) clashed over the town's government in 1752. In 1707, the 1730s, 1760s, and 1781-2 there were disturbances in Geneva, a town governed by a few wealthy families. The basic issue broadened from government actions, such as taxation without consent, to the location of sovereignty. Whether the general council was sovereign or merely to be consulted became a major issue, and in 1781 a visiting Saxon, Karl Küttner, described a general obsession with rights and political arguments that extended to women as well as men.

Many episodes of civic violence, such as those in Geneva, Genoa and the United Provinces, were characterised by an appeal to lost, often mythological, communal liberties and marked by communal action, such as the formation of popular militias and the demand for elected officers and officials. Sometimes there were also political dimensions to urban unrest that was sparked off by other issues, and it is apparent that the ostensible motives of such unrest could be misleading. Sicilian urban disorders in 1778 arising from the grain trade monopoly had political connotations.

Most civic violence stemmed from industrial disputes or the price of grain. Employment problems and food shortages often coincided and exacerbated each other. There was a major food riot in Rheims in 1770 during a depression in the textile industry. In Liège in 1739-41 and 1767-8 there was a clear element of economic conflict; difficulties in the textile and metalwork industries in the former case and in metalwork in the latter leading to wage cuts and strikes. In Lyons social tension was related to poor relations between merchants and handicraft workers.[10]

The presence of political or quasi-political institutions in major cities, not least princely courts, and their potential interaction with popular urban tension could also serve to increase urban political volatility. Disturbances in London were linked to parliamentary opposition in 1733 and again during the Wilkite troubles in the 1760s. Bread riots in Madrid in 1766 were exploited by courtiers keen to overthrow reforming ministers. It was not surprising that most rulers, mindful of seventeenth-century uprisings in cities such as London, Paris, Moscow and Constantinople, regarded their towns, particularly their capitals, as serious political risks. As Arthur Young suggested in July 1789, 'Without Paris, I question whether the present revolution, which is rapidly working in France, could possibly have had an origin. It is not in the villages of Syria ... that the Grand Signor [the Sultan, ruler of the Ottoman Empire] meets with a murmur against his will; it is at Constantinople that he is obliged to manage and mix caution even with despotism.'[11] Revolutionary and anti-revolutionary crowds emerged from the crowded, difficult lives of the urban poor.

The urban environment

Towns were not simply a potential political problem. They also, particularly the major ones, constituted the living space of the most articulate and informed members of European society. Furthermore they appeared to be one of the principal products of human activity, the section of the environment most amenable to action, of society most open to regulation. Town planning, whether achieved or only an aspiration, revealed the views about urban organisation held by some of the intellectuals of the age. Urban planning was not a novelty of the century; witness the rebuilding of Genoa after it was shelled in 1684 on the orders of Louis XIV. Paris, in contrast, received from the same monarch several major buildings, whose construction he supervised, two squares designed to magnify the ruler, an urban plan, and edicts regulating the paving and cleaning of the streets, the avoidance of fires and public health.

Similar moves were made in many major towns in the following century. Lyons at the beginning of the century had been dominated by its numerous monasteries, but the urban works carried out under the impulse of Soufflot between 1740 and the Revolution gave the town a new aspect, reflecting the views of writers such as André Clapasson and Ferdinand Delamonce who condemned features of the town that they found irregular and bizarre and the excessive prominence of churches. Legislation in England authorised Improvement Commissions to oversee urban improvements. In 1721 Peter I instructed Russian town magistrates to establish hospitals and houses of correction and to support schools. Town planning, building inspection and the enforcement of safety standards were ordered. Some successes were achieved. The authorities of Astrakhan initiated an effort to rebuild the town and straighten and widen its dusty streets in 1746, some other towns following. The new towns in southern Russia reflected contemporary trends in town planning. However, in general, government hopes were not realised. St Petersburg developed in a haphazard manner, most of its streets muddy and crooked, and most of the housing still traditional wooden structures, despite fears about fire. Most other Russian towns conformed to this pattern.

By contrast, after the 1755 earthquake, Lisbon, which had been a labyrinth of alleyways, was reconstructed as a planned town.

Concern with air and light, public hygiene and open spaces, led to the construction of wide streets and huge squares in the town, and the introduction of pavements, attention to drains and street cleaning. It also encompassed the idea of supplying water to every house and the creation of cemeteries, in place of the former habit of burial in church. These priorities reflected common themes in most major towns. In Poland the real improvements came after 1765, with the establishment of Improvement Commissions in Warsaw and other major Polish towns. In Warsaw the streets were paved, drains laid, footbridges built over streams, and in 1767 the town was incorporated into a single municipality. New cemeteries were built in many European towns, in Palermo, for example, in the 1780s.

The creation of a regulated environment was not simply functional in its rationale. It also reflected an intellectual plan based upon a moral vision, an attempt to create harmony upon earth, a spirit of change that was in some respects as traditional in aspiration as it was progressive. The specific manifestations of this concept ranged from new drains to larger police forces, but the need for conscious direction and improvements to the urban environment was widely accepted. The impetus behind them often came from central government, though many municipal councils shared similar aspirations. Much action derived from the scale of the problems facing urban communities. Poverty and crime were concentrated in towns, as were problems of sanitation and health. Few people could drink water in Paris: there were more than 10,000 inhabitants per public fountain. The nature of urban life, with a relatively large number of people living in marginal circumstances, often in disrupted family circumstances and outside established patterns of hierarchical control, all problems exacerbated by the very growth of towns and by immigration, posed a significant problem for government. The inflexible nature of much municipal government and the simple problem of resources further impelled intervention.

Crime was a major problem of urban life in towns such as London. The urban concentration of people provided criminals with opportunities for recruitment, crime and concealment, and they were responsive to economic and financial developments. In 1777 Viennese extortionists, threatening poison if not paid, were prepared to accept payment in bank bills. Municipal police forces were frequently unable to cope with the level of crime and central governments often felt obliged to intervene. In 1760 Pombal completely reformed the Portuguese police system, creating an office to oversee it. Paris acquired a strong, permanent force of municipal police, including a detective section to gather intelligence and investigate crime. The city was well policed, local criminals not being strong enough to confront the force, and on learning of the breakdown in public order in London during the Gordon Riots in 1780, Mercier suggested that similar unrest was impossible in Paris. Refuse removal was another major and growing problem that became the object of attention and planning, as was poverty.

Poverty and social welfare

The poor and the ill were still left largely to themselves, their families and the churches, but there were more signs of government intervention, generally concentrated in the towns. This was often expressed in the construction of buildings to house some of the poor and ill, a civic counterpart to the granaries built to store grain. The institutionalisation of unfortunates was supported by intellectuals. The Italian writer Ludovico Muratori recommended public education and the construction of hospitals, foundling homes and welfare institutions. In 1780 a Rouen essay contest on how to wipe out beggary in Normandy was won with the proposal for a social insurance plan to which workers would contribute while employed, public works, projects for able-bodied beggars and the establishment of workhouses and hospitals for children and the aged. However, care for the weak was but one of the many fields in which the achievements of eighteenth-century states, however 'absolutist' their constitutions apparently were, fell short of their own aspirations, let alone those of some outsiders. At the beginning of the century, much poor relief was organised by the church, and the stimulus behind provision of relief by institutions and individuals was generally religious. In an age when morality was an expression of religious beliefs and teachings, such a situation was regarded as proper. Social welfare was seen as an adjunct of spiritual care, not a substitute for it, and a universal provision of such welfare by government institutions would have been not only impracticable, but a breach of the standard precept of care, that it should discriminate between the deserving and the undeserving. This religio-moral principle tended to be applied on grounds of age, health and sex, rather than on socio-economic criteria relating to income and employment. The sick, elderly, young and women with children were the prime beneficiaries of relief, while the able-bodied, whether in low-paid employment or unemployed, were denied it. There was scant understanding of the problems posed by unemployment and underemployment, and such hardships were wrongly treated as self-inflicted and thus deserving neglect or punishment. Despite experiments with new forms of poor relief, across much of Europe attitudes towards the poor changed very little during the century, a testimony to the resilience of traditional views and to the scale of the problem posed by poverty.

In rural areas the parochial clergy played a major role in poor relief, distributing alms and frequently arranging medical assistance. Religious fraternities often provided the structure of social welfare and both elicited and organised charity. In Spain, workhouses to confine beggars and vagabonds proliferated after 1750. They were paid for out of endowed revenues held by religious confraternities and by 1798 they had been founded in 25 towns. However, there were never enough and most lacked the financial resources necessary to implement projects for helping the poor. There are some signs that a willingness to provide charitable bequests decreased towards the end of the century in parts of France and this has been linked to an alleged tendency towards 'de-christianisation', with people ceasing to view the world, social organisation and personal morality in Christian terms. In Aix-en-Provence the traditional, religiously-motivated private charity, on which the poor had for so long been dependent, was in relative decay from about 1760. The percentage of citizens leaving charitable bequests in Montpellier fell and in the diocese of Bordeaux the decline of such generosity in the second half of the century helped to cause the ruin or weakness of ancient charitable foundations. However, it is by no means clear that declining charity was a problem throughout all of Europe, or even in France, and therefore the signs of greater interest in state intervention cannot be explained in terms of a response to such a decline.

Possibly more significant was the rise in urban poverty due to falling real wages, a substantial and only partially employed labour force kept up by demographic growth, much of which stemmed from immigration, and the disruption caused by economic change. This increased the numbers of able-bodied poor, workers exposed to shifts in the economy.[12] In the second half of the century begging was a constant problem in the French linen-manufacturing town of Amiens, the town's dependence on the textile industry making the poor particularly vulnerable to economic crises. The gap between rich and poor there widened in the difficult 1770s. Brussels had a major problem with able-bodied unemployment, which appears to have played an important role in local crime rates. Paris could not provide enough jobs for immigrants, responding to the general rise in population and the worsening conditions of life in the rural areas in the Paris basin, and this helped to cause a decline in real wages. The effects of this decline were exacerbated by price rises covering most of the budget for the majority of townspeople: rent, bread and fire-wood. Economic difficulties did not create hardships for the poor alone, though the generally inaccurate view that unrest stemmed from the poor, rather than the artisanal groups who feared descent into poverty, helped to increase government and munici-pal sensitivity about the destitute.

Municipal social welfare increased during the century. Much welfare was directed at the price of grain. At the beginning of the century for example, the town council of Albi organised the pur-chase of grain from elsewhere. However, throughout Europe both lay and ecclesiastical help remained very selective, with repression and no pity for vagabonds and able-bodied beggars. In the Austrian Netherlands each town, parish and village was expected to be able to maintain its poor residents who were unable to work, with the income furnished by local boards of charity, who could be supported by a poor tax. Regulations of 1734 prohibited the able-bodied from begging; the possibility that their unemployment was involuntary was ignored.

The scale of the problem encouraged a response by national government in some areas. In 1775 Charles III of Spain instituted compulsory military service for men between the ages of 17 and 26 who lived in idleness. Conscription was ordered for all those caught sleeping in the streets, young men admonished by their parents for idleness, and artisans who abandoned their work. This was more than simply an attempt to fill the ranks. At the same time, other decrees were issued against gypsies, itinerant salesmen and all who lacked visible means of support. In 1774 Charles ordered the creation of schools in Galicia and Asturias to teach the population how to make linen at home; in 1786 a gen-eral decree ordered the establishment of spinning schools in all the towns and villages of the kingdom. Count Rumford cleared Munich of beggars, inaugurating a system of workhouses and poor relief. Dividing Munich into 16 districts, he appointed to each a respectable citizen, called a commissary, who was aided by a priest and some medical assistants. Applications for relief could be made only through the commissary, who ensured that appro-priate assistance was given. A workhouse was established and on 1 January 1790 the Munich beggars were moved to it.

Such constraints were hardly an attractive feature of the age, but governments rarely considered the opinions of the poor. The principal limitation on any policy of incarceration was the absence of sufficient resources, rather than any concern for the views of the poor. Social welfare was seen by government as for the benefit of society as a whole, not its constituent members.

Constraint played its part in France. In 1749 a diplomat reported from Paris:

> The Lieutenant de Police in this Town has just done a thing which gives me a great opinion of his alertness and diligence; 'till within this month the streets of this capital swarmed with beggars and vagabonds of all sorts, that it was impossible to stop one's coach an instant, in any part of the town, without having ten or twenty about you immediately, on a sudden a proclamation in the king's name is published, and a small reward given by the magistrates of the city for apprehending them, and you may now go from one end of Paris to another without seeing one; they are all put into workhouses and places where they are made useful, except those that are too infirm, and they are provided for in the Hospitals: I wish some such scheme could take place in London, it would be the likeliest way to prevent the frequent disturbances that happen amongst you.

It subsequently emerged that some of the vagrants had been sent to French Guiana, their captors being paid a bounty, and that some who were outside the scope of the declaration had been seized.[13] The following May the detention of children led to riots in Paris.[14] French policy was rarely thus dramatic, although rumours arising from the expulsion of vagrants from Paris had also led to riots in 1720; but central government activity increased during the century. Several important shifts of opinion occurred, but the general tendency was one of coercion. Pressure for the use of general hospitals (institutions not necessarily for the sick) to restrain and assist poor beggars led to legislation in 1724, which, as interpreted by local hospital administrators in the province of Champagne, in practice provided assistance either to the urban resident poor who were old or infirm or to children. Reflecting a harsher climate of opinion which appeared after 1750, and saw the professional beggar and vagrant much more as a social menace, a wave of French government initiatives in the 1760s and early 1770s was more repressive in character. It may have arisen in part from the social problems created both by the growth in population and poverty and by demobilisation after the Seven Years War (1756–63). This released adult men habituated to violence and usually unskilled onto a labour market that was unable to take them. There are indications in other parts of Europe, such as Surrey, that crime also rose with peacetime demobilisation.

In France in 1764 the arrest of vagabonds and of beggars without regular employment was ordered. In 1767 a network of *dépôts de mendicité* in each *généralité* was established for the incarceration of beggars and vagrants. The government directed and funded the operation through its local officials. The *dépôts* in part came to be regarded as institutions for the systematic study of society.[15] They were certainly used to try to control it. In Champagne, a region without Estates and therefore more exposed to central government, officials followed orders without modification, arrests and convictions varying in accordance with royal directives. Judicial decisions often displayed great severity. The Châlons-sur-Marne *dépôt* began as a place of detention for old and disabled beggars and vagrants. The Turgot ministry (1774–6) converted it into a prison-like structure for the imprisonment of beggars and vagrants seen as troublesome. In the 1780s the Châlons *dépôt* evolved into a coherent institution with the goal of 'correcting' inmates and creating a respectable poor. Turgot had ordered an archbishop, Loménie de Brienne, to review policies towards poverty in 1774. Brienne argued that the sole remedy was a comprehensive programme of reform that would require a major investment in institutions. He urged the establishment of a permanent network of workhouses, that could serve to regulate short-run fluctuations in the demand for labour. Brienne wanted the new system to extend down to the parish level and to direct all charitable funds.

In practical terms, it proved impossible to create an adequate system in France. Many *intendants* feared that resources were inadequate, and both government action and the level of urban poor relief were inconsistent. Vagabonds were harshly treated by the legal authorities in Toulouse in the 1780s. Begging and vagrancy were seen as proof of criminal intention. In Amiens unemployed workers pressed for the opening of workhouses, but begging remained a major problem. Nothing was done in Elbeuf, a plan for a workshop-hospital being rejected for lack of funds. In the *généralité* of Caen the government sought to suppress begging, mainly through confining the dependent poor and those judged deviant, first in the municipal hospitals and later in the workhouses. Despite the efforts of the 1760s and 1770s, there was in France in the 1780s a feeling of despair about the problems posed by poverty and a growing fear of the poor, with much anxiety about crime, including arson and vandalism. As the poor constituted the bulk of the urban population, this tempered the enthusiasm of some about towns. As far as the bulk of the population was concerned, this situation was more important than court factions and their policies.

The Revolution encouraged a view of the poor as virtuous, and brought a rejection of *ancien régime* poor-relief strategies, especially of hospitals, which were anyway threatened by hostility to ecclesiastical institutions. The *Comité de mendicité* and the *Comité des secours publics* held numerous meetings in 1789–92, encouraging the idea that poverty was a national responsibility. Home-relief was seen as the solution, with support for state retirement pensions for the elderly poor. Funding, however, was inadequate and the replacement of the *ancien régime* system of social welfare was pursued less energetically than its rejection. The combination of wartime pressures and the reaction against Revolutionary radicalism led in 1796 to an abandonment of novel schemes. Instead, by modern standards, an inadequate provision for poverty remained the case and the poor were probably worse off than before the Revolution. In areas conquered by France the poor also suffered from disruptions to poor-relief systems.[16]

The situation was difficult throughout eighteenth-century Europe. In Russia, a few workhouses were established in the 1770s, but the position of the poor was bleak. In the Austrian Netherlands the relief of the poor proved deficient even in years without high grain prices and high unemployment, and the exacerbation of this situation in hard years helped to lead to vagrancy, disturbances, begging and looting as in 1739–40. In Liège poor relief was inadequately funded and ineffective and neither poverty nor begging were brought under control, despite the principality's participation in the 'Great Confinement' of the poor. By the 1770s the system was under criticism from those worried about its cost, or the creation of competitive low-wage labour, or the assault on individual liberty. Fears about the last were also voiced by Spanish writers such as Valentín de Foronda and Francisco Cabarrús. In Denmark, by way of contrast, a regular system of poor relief, financed by compulsory contributions, was introduced after 1784. In Britain a relatively flexible and well-established system of poor relief was available through the Poor Law, though growing public concern about it led the House of Commons to establish committees of enquiry into the state of the poor in the 1770s and 1780s. In Ireland the situation was less favourable. City corporations of the poor in the charge of workhouses were created in Dublin (1703) and Cork (1735). They were supported by local taxes and donations. Legislation of 1772 extended these corporations to the entire country and decreed that they were to be supported by local rates. The impotent poor were to be maintained and the deserving poor were to be licensed to beg, but begging without a licence was made a criminal offence. However, the Act of 1772 was in general inoperative. In Italy progressive intellectuals called for reform by public action, but progress was slight, particularly in southern Italy and Sicily. More was done in northern Italy. The government of Milan followed the policy of incarceration.

The general problem was the same everywhere, an absence of resources to deal not only with the poor *in situ*, but also with problems posed by migration. There was neither the wealth nor the tax income sufficient to provide a widespread welfare system, and local initiatives, if attractive, only invited immigration, despite attempts to restrict them to locals. However, as governments were not seeking to abolish poverty, but, instead, to alleviate the fears created by their depiction of the poor, it is possibly anachronistic to criticise them for failing to create an adequate system or for treating the effects of poverty, rather than dealing with its causes. The latter was arguably unwanted as well as impossible. Had governments really been concerned about poverty, they would have incurred more debts to cope with it, or evolved more coherent and consistent policies and an accompanying effective infrastructure. At the national level, only a fraction of the effort devoted to military affairs and foreign policy was expended on matters of social welfare. The poor as a menace were less serious than the Prussians, or other foes.

The extent to which urban life had distinctive cultural and behavioural effects is open to debate. In some respects it offered freedom. Such a claim might have appeared ridiculous to those in the orphanage and prison of Pforzheim in the Empire, whose compulsory labour was used by the local woollen industry from the 1750s; to the 10,200 textile workers unemployed in Troyes in October 1788; to the citizens of Angers struggling for a measure of self-government; or the families living each in a single room in Paris. Furthermore, there was considerable cultural and intellectual ambiguity in attitudes towards towns, whatever the utopian views advanced in town planning. French prose fiction tended to glorify Paris until the 1760s, but thereafter, the provinces were eulogised. The article on towns by Antoine-Gaspard Boucher d'Argis in the *Encyclopédie* stressed their corruption and vice. Rousseau emphasised the moral and social dangers of large cities such as Paris. The Neapolitan progressive economist Antonio Genovesi had a very negative view of Naples.

Yet if towns did not offer equality of opportunity, they did provide opportunity, and the sustained migration to them that characterised the demographic history of the period was a testimony to this. Each migrant represented an individual decision that life might be better in a town. For many this proved illusory: rural penury translated into urban poverty. Nevertheless, social control was laxer, because harder to enforce, in the towns. Breaches in sumptuary legislation occurred in towns. It was easier to obtain an education there. The guide who in August 1789 took Samuel Boddington up Mont Blanc had spent six years in Paris and told

Boddington, when asked if he believed in the devil, that Voltaire had said that bad men were the devils. Urban populations were not on the whole radical in their politics or beliefs, but town life did provide the context for most new ideas, both elite and popular, and also offered new experiences. It was also easier to bridge the divide between elite and populace in towns, whether in the abandonment of dark and heavy clothing, initiated by the former, or in the dissemination of new political views.

The concentration of people in towns, their higher rates of literacy and more marked traditions of political improvement helped to foster, at least in part, a consumer society that was restricted neither to goods nor to economic services. The potential and actual dangers this posed were sensed by clerics worried about irreligion and rulers fearful of sedition. In 1715 the prince-bishop of Liège, Joseph Clément, claimed, 'it is absolutely necessary that the citadel of Liège remains a fortress capable of holding the common people of Liège in awe. Without this restraint there will be no security for honest men, only murder and brigandage.' He later wrote of the need 'to prevent the evil schemes of the majority of the Liégeois who would like to become a republic and to join the United Provinces as another province...the burgomasters and other men of that quality wish to see themselves on chairs of velvet and be received with the salutes of cannon...only troops and fortresses can hold them to their obedience.'[17] His response was a somewhat hysterical one, an after-effect of wartime defeat and disruption. Most towns did not seek legal independence and their interest in running their own affairs was tempered by a desire for government support and protection. However, Joseph Clément was correct in sensing the difficulties that urban life presented for government.

6   Faith and the Churches

He was very free with abuse on the archbishop of Lyon for taking away from the watermen their tutelar saint St Nicholas, and putting a stop to their processions. They had nobody, he said, now left to pray to. To be sure there was the bon dieu still, and after him he knew there was the Virgin Mary; but it was a very bad thing to take away the watermen's own saint; and the archbishop would not have done it, if he had not been to get something by it. Then since the Jesuits were expelled, the poor went totally uneducated: nobody would take the pains to instruct them; the other religious orders ate and drank and did nothing.

(Account of a Rhône boatman, 1776)[1]

In December 1789 the Austrian chancellor Count Kaunitz told the French ambassador that it was not true to say that there was nothing new under the sun, as the impiety of some was unprecedented.[2] To the casual observer of today the eighteenth century may not appear a particularly religious age. The mocking scepticism of writers such as Voltaire or the doubts of intellectuals and scholars such as Hume are most often remembered. The abhorrence of 'Enthusiasm', in its superstitious, Methodist or any other guise, was strong in educated people committed to the middle way. Eighteenth-century urban building is generally visually not recalled for its chapels, any more than the painters of the period are remembered for religious works. Religious warfare is seen as largely something of the more distant past, whereas the eighteenth century is viewed as one of growing toleration and 1773 saw the dramatic dissolution of the Jesuits, the religious order that had played such a major role in the Catholic (Counter-) Reformation. The eighteenth century is seen as a period of enlightenment, and the Enlightenment as a secular movement. Faith, it is believed, was sustained by inbred conservatism or irrational religious enthusiasm.

Though such views are not found in most scholarly works, they are still widely believed; and there are genuine problems of definition and methodology. What was the quality of the religious experience of the lower orders and the source and depth of their faith? This is a particular problem, because in recent years considerable attention has been devoted to the thesis that the second half of the century witnessed a de-christianisation of much of the population of certain areas, particularly several regions of France.

200

This has been linked to an alleged de-sacralisation of monarchy, and thus an ideological world has been mapped in which the mutually sustaining relationship of Throne and Altar was drained of meaning and strength. In the space of a chapter it is only possible to sketch a few themes, such as the vitality of eighteenth-century religion, the political importance of ecclesiastical issues and the buoyancy of faith. De- or non-christianisation was a characteristic only of special groups.

A divided continent

There was little change in the official religion of particular states between 1700 and 1789. Catholicism was the official faith in Iberia (Spain and Portugal), France, the Italian territories, Poland, some of the Swiss cantons and certain German states, most prominently Bavaria, and also in the Habsburg dominions, though the position in Transylvania and Hungary was complex. Protestantism was the official religion in the rest of western, northern and central Europe, though different types of Protestantism predominated: Lutheranism (Scandinavia and much of north Germany), Anglicanism (England, Wales and Ireland), Calvinism (Scotland, the United Provinces, Switzerland, several German territories). In Russia the Orthodox Church was dominant; in the Balkans Islam was the state religion.

These divisions fuelled some of the religious animosity of the century. Competing states were supported by antagonistic churches. Religion was used to define and test loyalty. Contemporaries perceived links between some religions and particular forms of government. Many of the conflicts of the period generated confessional zeal, the churches offering support, not least financial assistance. This was true of the principal religious divide in Europe, that which separated Christendom from Islam. In Islamic thought the realm of the Turkish ruling House of Osman existed solely to fulfil God's will on earth by spreading Islam, and preserving the power and prestige of God's shadow on earth. In the 1720s clerical opposition to Sultan Ibrahim, which helped cause the Istanbul uprising of 1730, arose largely from his failure to carry out his divine mission, and in particular his treaty of 1724 with Russia and his war with the Muslim Persians.[3]

Similar attitudes were present in Christendom, increased in the Catholic faith by the incentive of indulgences (remissions of punishment in the afterlife) attached to meritorious worldly acts. Following the Spanish capture of Oran in 1732, the British envoy reported, 'there is scarce a Spaniard who does not think himself half way to his salvation by the merits of this conquest'.

Throughout Europe, religious hatred was sustained by accounts of atrocities, and men were exhorted to suffer in God's cause. Wartime accounts, such as the description in the *Vienna Gazette* of 29 December 1759 of Prussian atrocities in a Bohemian monastery, including the desecration of altars, images, crucifixes and the host, were matched by the steady pressure of peacetime indoctrination with a creed of suspicion and hatred. Visiting Rheims in 1754 Lord Nuneham heard a sermon 'which ended with an account of heresies in Great Britain, in which we poor wretches were miserably clawed and abused'.[4] Whatever the faith of certain intellectuals in the future, the people of eighteenth-century Europe continued to live in the past. Their collective memories were those of Reformation and Counter-Reformation Europe: wars, insurrections, massacres and conspiracies that had been and were presented in religious terms. Their interpretation of the past offered both a corporate identity and a set of warnings. Vigilance was as necessary for the Swiss peasant, of either faith, as it was for the ruler. Christianity, Islam and Judaism, the three European religions of the period, were all historical faiths, but their followers looked back to a recent as much as to a distant past.

Religious antagonism was made more dangerous because Europe was not composed of confessionally homogeneous states. Many states contained dissident communities or the memory or perceived threat of them. In the Balkans this did not trouble the Turks, who engaged in limited proselytisation. Elsewhere tension was more acute. The Balkans were not the sole region where the religion or church of the majority was not that of the state or that which was most privileged. In Ireland and parts of the southern United Provinces the majority were Catholic, in the Morea (Peloponnese region of Greece), ruled by Venice 1699–1718, the majority were Orthodox. In Prussia the majority of the population was Lutheran, though their monarchs were Calvinists. In eastern Poland and western Russia the Uniates, a branch of the Orthodox which acknowledged papal authority, were strong.

Elsewhere, dissident minorities could be important: Episcopalians and Catholics in Scotland, Catholics and Dissenters in England, Protestants throughout the Habsburg lands, in Poland and in France (the Huguenots). In Ireland both the Catholic majority and the mainly Presbyterian Dissenter minority were subject to penal laws; the established church was itself a minority faith.

There were three large zones where there were few members of minority communities. One was Catholic: in Iberia and Italy Protestantism had made little impact and had been largely extirpated during the sixteenth-century Catholic Reformation. Protestantism made little progress in this zone during the eighteenth century. The Genoese Huguenots were expelled in 1747, and though Tuscan commercial policies retained Protestants in Livorno, they were unpopular. The principal dissident communities in this zone were foreign merchants, such as the Anglicans in Lisbon, and Jews, established in ghettos in several major Italian cities, particularly Rome and Venice.

In Iberia alleged crypto-Judaism was the principal target of the Inquisition. The Jews having been expelled, the Church doubted the integrity of those who had become converts, the New Christians. Inquisitorial activity in this field diminished during the century: 51 people were executed as a result of the Portuguese Inquisition in 1734–43, 18 in 1750–9; 1761 witnessed the last case of capital punishment in Portugal and in 1768 the distinction between Old and New Christians was abolished. The Inquisition was not directed only against alleged Judaism but also against Protestants and crypto-Muslims. In Granada in Spain in the 1720s, 250 people were sentenced by the Inquisition for being the latter. Nevertheless, Philip V did not assist the Spanish Inquisition in its financial difficulties and the institution appeared increasingly redundant from mid-century.

The treatment of dissidents in Iberia contrasted with that of Jews in many Italian territories. In the Papal enclave of Avignon and the Comtat Venaissin in southern France Jews lived in four ghettos. Though they were marked out and humiliated by being obliged to wear yellow hats and to attend Christian sermons, and at a time when Jewish guilt for the death of Christ played a prominent part in the liturgical season of Lent at least, their treatment by the administration was reasonable by the standards of Catholic Europe. As with many tolerated minorities in Europe, for example the Jews in Poland or the Protestants in Transylvania, they were largely self-governing, a policy that accorded with the corporatist ideology and practice of the period. In the Papal territory of Avignon there was a Jewish system of poor relief and self-taxation, and signs of increasing Jewish prosperity. This, however, appears to have provoked rising popular hostility that led to more strictly enforced 'ghettoisation' and consequent emigration. Despite legal handicaps and popular prejudices, in favourable circumstances Jews could achieve a certain degree of prosperity. The Sephardi Jews of Gascony were markedly better off than the Ashkenazi Jews of eastern France.

The second zone with few dissidents was firmly Lutheran: Scandinavia and Brandenburg. In Sweden the clergy had an elected Estate in the Diet, every beneficed cleric having a vote.

They were rigidly orthodox, shocked by the negotiations of the governing Hat party with the Turks in the late 1730s and described by a hostile Frederick the Great as living in the tenth century. The Swedish Conventicle Act of 1726 was passed to check the growth of religious heterodoxy, especially Pietism, a Protestant movement. The first clause of the Swedish constitution of 1772 declared: 'Unanimity in religion, and the true divine worship, is the surest basis of a lawful, concordant, and stable government.' Every Swedish regiment had a pastor and chaplains, and hymns were sung before battle. Not until 1781 did non-Lutheran foreign Christians enjoy the right in Sweden to build churches and worship according to their own rites, and then only on condition that they did not attempt to proselytise. Jews were not allowed legally to settle and build synagogues until 1782.

The third zone was central Russia. In conquered regions there were significant minorities: Protestant in the Baltic provinces, Catholic, Uniate and Jewish in the Ukraine and former Polish territories, Muslim on the southern frontier, animist in Siberia. When he conquered Livonia, Estonia and Russian Finland, Peter I guaranteed the maintenance of Lutheranism as the official religion, though the position of the Orthodox was also protected.

Elsewhere in Russia the Orthodox were dominant. Although in 1702 Peter I had enacted general religious toleration, effectively limited to Christians, all forms of non-Orthodox proselytisation had been forbidden. This prohibition was repeated in 1735. Mixed marriages with Catholics had been authorised in 1721, but only on condition that there was no conversion of the Orthodox party and that the children were brought up as Orthodox. A 1727 regulation expelling the Jews from Russia was not implemented, but a second one in 1742 had more effect, denouncing them as the 'enemies of Christ'. In 1738 a Jew, together with a Christian whom he had converted, was burnt alive in St Petersburg.

However, this zone of relative Christian homogeneity was riven by schism, for as a result of late seventeenth-century disputes over theology and quite small issues of observance, such as the means of making the sign of the cross, the Orthodox Establishment and its imperial protectors were confronted by the Old Believers, a substantial, though divided group. They were regarded as opponents of the state and decrees were issued against them, as for example those in 1730 and 1733.

The three zones of relative homogeneity were not without their disputes and paranoias. They also excluded most of Europe, where significant minorities challenged the monopolistic pretensions of established churches and were believed to threaten the relevant faiths. This was the position in the Habsburg territories, Poland, the Empire, Switzerland, Britain, the United Provinces and, to a lesser extent, France. The Peace of Westphalia of 1648, the settlement that had brought to an end the Thirty Years War and, with it, the last of the major Wars of Religion, had guaranteed the established position of Calvinism, Lutheranism and Catholicism in particular territories in the Empire, at the same time as it had left Protestants in the Habsburg territories without protection. The Peace had not brought religious peace. Religious tension is not easy to assess, still less to measure. In terms of violence there were few disputes, in the Empire or elsewhere, that were exclusively religious in nature, for one of the principal features of such confrontation was the role of religious differences in expressing a wide range of tensions. This was a product of the importance of religion as a focus of identity and a means of definition, the interpenetration of religious affiliations and political, cultural, social and economic connections and values and the significance of religious settlements as the basis of wider arrangements.

However defined, there is little doubt that religious differences were related to much violence. Indeed if the 'official' hostilities of territories at war are discounted, religious conflict was probably the most significant category of organised violence in much of Europe during this period. Hostile acts were frequently directed against minorities, such as the riots against Dissenters in England in 1710 and 1715, against Catholics in Hamburg in 1719, Edinburgh in 1779 and London in 1780 (the Gordon Riots), or against Jews in Corfu in 1788. A host of disputes could lead to religious confrontations. For example, the Protestant desecration of a Jesuit chapel in Thorn (Törun) in Poland in 1724 and Catholic reprisals caused an international crisis. Disputes were not always so violent or sustained, but religious differences and identities were the common currency of much popular tension.

Riots reflected popular animosity, but they were not its sole product. Religious tension is difficult to measure, because its classic product was not the violence that might attract judicial and military attention, but the prejudice that was expressed in endogamy, discriminatory political, social, economic and cultural practices and the acid of hatred, fear, abuse and insult. In 1754 the French envoy in the United Netherlands complained about a poster in Amsterdam proclaiming that the French were to send troops to back a Catholic rising and the destruction of all Protestants.[5]

Religious minorities cohered not only in order to practise their faith, but also for protection, employment and the maintenance of their identity. Endogamy (marriage within the clan) also served to preserve their strength, and minorities censured inter-marriage strongly. Whereas in the twentieth century European religious groups generally face the challenge of the assimilation of their members into predominantly secular cultures, in the eighteenth century the challenge was from other religious groups, especially from established churches. Many of the dramatic out-bursts of religious revival had their roots in fears of assimilation. There were also new religious movements such as Pietism and Moravianism which sought to go behind church divisions. Con-version, if away from the established church, was generally illegal and often incurred serious penalties.

Religious groups had to consider more than just the attitudes and actions of other groups. Their position was defined legally, and affected by the attitudes of governments to established churches and to other faiths. Europe was divided into Church-states, countries where the government defended the established church and the church preached a doctrine of obedience to the ruler. Government was supposed to serve a moral purpose, the state to possess and propagate a religious identity. This obviously created problems for those who differed from the established church. Coronations were religious ceremonies. When crowned, monarchs swore to protect the Church and generally, as in the case of France, to extirpate heresy.

The identification of Church and State led to the Church con-stituting a branch of government, though this was pictured dif-ferently in different states. In contrast to secular administrations, the actions of established churches were more widespread, their representatives present generally in every parish. The need to offer a cure of souls gave these churches a territorial structure and presence generally lacking in secular governments. Though eighteenth-century churches have been criticised for concentrat-ing their personnel and resources in towns, they nevertheless sought a comprehensive rural presence. In contrast, secular gov-ernment agents were commonly overwhelmingly urban. As with their secular counterparts, established churches as systems of government were far from uniform and the degree to which they responded to the wishes of the territorial ruler varied. However, they commonly served as a sphere of patronage, a source of funds, a means for disseminating propaganda and an ideological support. Peter I's principal clerical agent, Feofan Prokopovich, archbishop of Novgorod, asked in his *Russian Primer*, a catechism written in 1720, 'What doth God require in the fifth com-mandment? He commands us to honour and obey our parents, a name which includes our Sovereign, our spiritual pastors and civil governors, our teachers, benefactors, and elders.' Besides inculcating obedience, the established church was also to instruct in new regulations, Russian parish priests serving as agents of central government. In 1720 they were ordered to announce in church all decrees about new taxes. The use of the church in this way was common throughout Europe and suggests the state's dependence on the church as a means of communication and of conferring legitimacy. Joseph II required priests to announce regulations on such matters as the banning of corsets and the servicing of peasants' mares by imperial stallions. In addition, the parochial clergy were the major collectors of government statistics in much of Europe.

It was therefore not only a duty for rulers to defend the established church and thus maintain true religion, but also a political necessity. Rulers and ministers were convinced of the power of the clergy over the people, and therefore sought to control and defend them. If this brought them into conflict with apparently disobedient laity and clergy within these Churches, it also entailed both ensuring devotion and respect from those who were ostensibly believers and controlling the activities of members of other religious communities. Established churches prescribed a moral code, and ecclesiastical and secular power joined in promulgating and enforcing it.

Those who were not members of the state religion were not necessarily seen as disloyal. However, whatever the loyalty of dissidents, most rulers sought to advance their established churches. Catherine II financed church-building in Cossack territories, the Orthodox Church being seen as a central instrument of ideological and political influence. Maria Theresa, who would not permit the Protestants in the Austrian Netherlands to hold civil offices, erect churches or have public ministers, decreed in 1760 that the Transylvanian Romanians were not at liberty to renounce the Uniate faith in favour of Orthodoxy. Though the Polish constitution of 1791, which is generally considered one of the more 'progressive' political documents of the period, granted toleration to all faiths, apostasy from Catholicism was still considered a felony and Catholicism was confirmed as the state religion.

The protection of established churches generally entailed restrictions on the public worship of other groups. Furthermore, members of the latter encountered limitations on their political rights and on their ability to hold offices. In France the legal position of Protestants was poor, apart from in Alsace where the Lutherans enjoyed full civil rights, as a consequence of the terms on which the rulers of France had been ceded control in the seventeenth century. Elsewhere public office and the professions of law, medicine and midwifery were closed to Protestants. In law all the French were Catholics, the only valid marriages Catholic ones and the children of Calvinist marriages were bastards. Attendance at open-air services could lead to imprisonment. Though these laws were systematically applied only in 1724, 1745 and 1750–2, the position of Protestants in other periods was unpredictable and sometimes extremely difficult. Protestantism had long been broken as a political force in France, but the resistance of the faith posed a challenge which was met by sectarian aggressiveness on the part of the Catholics. An annual religious procession was held to celebrate the expulsion of Protestants from Toulouse in 1562 and during the wars of the period there were fears of a Protestant rising there as late as 1745 and near Montauban in 1761. It was not until the 1760s that *de facto* toleration was practised in the Cévennes. Early in the previous decade Louis XV had devised a plan to reduce Protestantism by encouraging the performance of marriages and baptisms in the Catholic church and using troops against those who disobeyed. The plan had to be abandoned when the Seven Years War diverted military resources.

Despite the opposition of much of the French clergy, *de facto* toleration appears to have increased in France as the political impotence of Protestantism became more apparent. The legal bastardisation of Calvinist children slackened. Many law courts had found devices by about 1760 to prevent collateral Catholic heirs from appropriating inheritances from the widows and children of dead Protestants. Despite clerical complaints, the judges were intimating that public recognition of a marriage over a period meant that there was no need to produce a certificate to say there had been one. In Angers, where Protestantism was largely destroyed by the revocation of 1685, tolerance increased during the eighteenth century. In turn, in place of the millenarianism of the Camisards of the Cévennes and of certain of Louis XIV's opponents, such as Pierre Jurieu, who had predicted the end of Catholicism for the 1710s, with the second coming following, Protestants became less restive.

Disputes within the French Catholic Church and between clerics and secular authorities were both more politically contentious than those involving Protestants and also influenced their treatment. In 1765 the Jansenist priest Louis Guidi claimed that Jansenists, in contrast to Jesuits, preferred persuasion to force. In some circles intolerance had become deplorable as well as unfashionable. In 1767 *Bélisaire*, an historical novel condemning religious persecution, by Voltaire's protégé, Jean François Marmontel, a contributor to the *Encyclopédie*, was a sensational success. By 1770 the *parlements*, no longer seeing Protestantism as a danger to civil society and the identity of France, stopped enforcing the laws against Protestant marriages. The already existing passive tolerance of unobtrusive Protestant worship was increasingly matched by a willingness to extend civil rights to them. In 1785 William Bennet noted in his journal at Bordeaux, 'The Protestants are still numerous in the Southern Provinces, and Government connives at without tolerating them, only now and then hanging an old priest by way of checking their progress and of late has omitted even this too sanguinary method of pleasing the bigoted Catholics.'[6] The Edict of 1787 on the rights of non-Catholics freed Protestant infants from the need for Catholic baptism if they were to gain civil status, but, besides this status, only freedom of conscience was guaranteed. Protestants were still specifically banned from organising as a corporate entity and from legal and educational positions. They were allowed no churches, no public clergy and no entry into the professions. On the eve of the Revolution, French Protestants were not emancipated, and still faced widespread opposition. The 1787 reforms had been particularly strongly criticised in Languedoc. Full legal toleration did not come until the Revolution: in 1790 Protestants were granted the right to worship publicly.

In other countries too, the position of Nonconformists was often poor. In general, legal codes tended to permit freedom of conscience and private worship, but limited or prohibited public worship, education and political power. In England few offices and professions were open to Dissenters, and particularly not to Catholics. Instead of a Protestant cultural consensus, tension between the Church of England and Nonconformity was a basic political, cultural, religious and ideological division, and one that interacted with tensions within the Church of England. Protestant identity was a contested area. Although their numbers were relatively small, Dissenters were important and they prevented the success of the attempt to base a unifying doctrine of the state on the Church of England. The Corporation Act (1661) and the Test Act (1673) obliged members of borough corporations and office-holders under the crown to receive communion in the Church of England. Under the Toleration Act (1689) Dissenters who took the Oaths of Supremacy and Allegiance and made the Declaration against Transubstantiation were allowed to worship in their own meeting-houses, although these had to be registered with a bishop or at the Quarter Sessions. Though the Occasional Conformity (1711) and Schism (1714) Acts, designed respectively to prevent the circumvention of communion requirements for office-holding and to make separate Nonconformist education illegal, were both repealed in 1718, attempts to repeal the Test and Corporation Acts failed. The Whig Party had traditionally been associated with Nonconformists, but the Whig administration of Sir Robert Walpole (1721–42) was unwilling to tamper with religious fundamentals, not least because of the considerable groundswell of opinion in defence of the Church. Government control of ecclesiastical patronage brought the senior ranks of the Church of England closer to the Whigs. Though Walpole obtained indemnity acts, protecting the Nonconformists from malicious prosecution each year, bar 1730 and 1732, moves to repeal the Test and Corporation Acts were defeated in 1736 and 1739. The Jewish Naturalisation Act of 1753, which made it easier to be naturalised by private Act of Parliament, dropping the phrase 'on the true faith of a Christian' from the Oaths of Supremacy and Allegiance, was repealed in the face of a vicious press campaign of anti-Semitic hatred, with popular backing, although it had shown the liberalism of the English Establishment. Parliamentary attempts in 1787–90 to repeal the Test and Corporation Acts were unsuccessful. The identification of Religion and State in the form of government protection for the Church of England was reaffirmed.

Catholic aspirations in England were curbed by William III's successful invasion in 1688; in Ireland they were ended by William's troops in 1690–1. The Anglican ascendancy had then been confirmed. Under the Banishment Act of 1697 hundreds of Catholic clerics had been banished under pain of execution if they returned. The castration of Catholic clerics was subsequently considered. Under the penal statutes passed in the first half of the eighteenth century, Catholics were prevented from acquiring or bequeathing land or property, disfranchised and debarred from all political and legal offices. It has been estimated that the percentage of land in Catholic hands fell from 22 in 1688 to 14 in 1703 and 5 in 1778, though some of the Protestant ownership was only token. The Penal Code was designed essentially to destroy the political and economic power of Catholicism rather than the faith itself, although it was also an attempt to erode Catholic belief and practice. The ability of the Anglican Establishment to proselytise in Ireland was limited by its general failure to communicate with a still largely Gaelic-speaking population. In contrast, the Catholic colleges stipulated a knowledge of the language as a requirement for the mission. The Catholic percentage of the population did not diminish, because the Catholic clergy continued their work, sustained by a strong oral culture, the emotional link with a sense of national identity, and by hedge-school teaching, and serious repression was episodic. If it had been possible to implement the religious clauses of the Penal Code and if a persistent attempt had been made to do so, then Catholicism might have been seriously challenged, though the military forces in the island were not large and the result in 1715 and 1745 might have been Jacobite insurrections in favour of the Catholic Stuart claimants to the throne as serious as those in Scotland. Catholic clerics in Ireland still prayed for the Stuart claimant 'James III' in the 1730s and the draconian wartime legislation of 1697, 1703–4 and 1709 was inspired by fears of Catholic disloyalty and links with France. Persecution usually slackened in peacetime, and for most of the century vicious confessional action was infrequent.[7] Nevertheless, long-standing religious grievances helped to exacerbate political disaffection in the 1790s.

More generally in Britain the idea of religious assimilation as a route to nation-building could not work for contingent reasons. These included the need for the reconstruction of the Church of England after the Restoration of the Stuarts in 1660, the crucial role of the Dissenters in the opposition to James II and the Whig regime, the degree to which the Church of England was compromised by the succession crisis of 1688–9 and, thereafter, by Jacobitism; and the plain inefficiency of the Church. The Church of Scotland was given the task of assimilating the Highlands to Lowland religion and the English Bible and, against the odds, largely succeeded. The Church of England was given the task of assimilating Wales, Ireland and the Dissenters in the American colonies, and failed in all three. In Wales, the effort of assimilation was energetically pursued, but encouraged a religious revival which was Welsh, evangelical and dissenting. In Ireland, when lethargy was eventually shaken off, the policy of assimilation provoked a Catholic revival. In America, where the policy proceeded under greater difficulties, it materially helped to provoke civil war in the shape of the War of American Independence.

Legislation, administrative action and prejudice against legally disadvantaged religious groups could be found throughout Europe. In Poland the decline of a numerically strong Protestantism continued, the sole remaining Protestant member of the Diet being expelled in 1718. In the United Provinces the political rights of the substantial Catholic population were severely restricted. Jews were discriminated against everywhere. Ceilings on the number of Jewish families in Moravia and Bohemia were lowered in 1725 and 1726 respectively. In France, particularly Lorraine, Jewish merchants had to be protected by the government against widespread hostility, especially by those hoping to exploit anti-Semitism in order to achieve the cancellation of personal debts to money lenders. The worst cases of non-, rather than de-christianisation were those of subject races not catered for by their rulers. However, efforts were made to deal with these. A serious attempt was made in the early decades of the century to tackle Estonian paganism. Shamans began to employ the forms of Christian rites and to use Christian terminology, but the peasants found it difficult to abandon ancestor worship.

Violence, emigration and quietism were responses to discrimination. Habsburg catholicisation policies were a significant cause of tension and instability that frequently led to violence. Protestant discontent at Leopold I's attempt to limit their rights played a major role in inspiring the Rakoczi uprising in Hungary (1703–11). Force was used against Protestant communities throughout the reigns of Charles VI and Maria Theresa. Transylvanians resisted the attempt by the Habsburgs to push the Orthodox into the Uniate Church by risings in 1744 and 1760. There were Protestant revolts in the Habsburg hereditary lands in 1713–14, 1732 and 1738, and unrest in Carinthia in 1738–41.

Religious emigration was also an important element during this period. The Huguenot diaspora was large and extensive: over 70,000 to the United Provinces, 50,000–70,000 to England, 44,000 to the Empire. An Irish Catholic diaspora formed substantial communities in France and Spain. Discontent with Habsburg policies resulted in Protestant emigration to Saxony and Prussia. The expulsion of all Protestants over 12 in 1731 by Baron Leopold von Firmian, prince-archbishop of Salzburg, cost him 30,000 subjects and provided Prussia with 20,000 settlers and Protestant Europe with an object lesson in the continuance of religious animosity. If the experience of oppression could lead to a deep sense of alienation for groups such as the English Quakers, or produce millenarian fantasies, such as those of the Catholic cleric Charles Walmesley who, in his *General History of the Christian Church* (1771), predicted the end of Protestantism for 1825, persecution also allowed those excluded from state service to concentrate on commerce, the creation of strong communities and private worship, as Huguenots in western France, Catholics in Ireland and Jews throughout Europe sought to do. Many proscribed communities, however, found their options seriously limited by governmental restrictions and popular hostility.

The relationship between established churches and governments varied greatly. In ecclesiastical principalities – the Papal States and also an appreciable portion of the Empire – the government was controlled by a cleric. The Papal States, directly ruled by the pope, covered a wide swathe of central Italy. Ecclesiastical principalities in the Empire were ruled by three of the eight electors, the archbishops of Cologne, Mainz and Trier, and a number of other clerics, including the archbishop of Salzburg and the bishops of Trent, Passau, Brixen, Freising, Augsburg, Bamberg, Würzburg, Fulda, Liège, Münster, Paderborn and Hildesheim. In the Balkan principality of Montenegro, an independent territory which the Turks claimed as a subject province, secular authority was exercised by the Orthodox archbishop, an office that had descended since 1697 in the house of Petrovíc-Njegos.

Elsewhere established churches had to turn to secular authorities for support. This created difficulties and suspicion when these were of a different religion. A number of German princely families, including the electors of Saxony (1697), the electors Palatine and the dukes of Württemberg, converted to Catholicism. Though they could no longer change the religion of their churches, there was considerable unease, not least because of the experience of the Palatinate after the accession of Catholic electors. The conversion to Catholicism of Frederick, the heir to Hesse-Cassel, in 1749 led his father, William VIII, to consider excluding him from the succession, and to force him and his subjects to swear to a succession agreement restricting Frederick's ability to appoint Catholics, removing confessional matters out of his hands and compelling him to separate from his wife and children. The restriction of rulers' rights to alter the religious character of their countries, even in Protestant Europe, where there was no external focus of loyalty and source of orthodoxy comparable to the papacy, was a fundamental limitation of their authority.

In addition, several dynasties ruled collections of territories where different churches were established. From 1689, when Presbyterianism replaced Episcopalianism (Anglicanism) as the established church in Scotland, this was the position in Britain. The Calvinist Hohenzollern rulers of Prussia were particularly tolerant. Though Frederick the Great continued his father's policy of stirring up Protestant opposition in the Habsburg territories, he respected Catholic rights in his conquests of Silesia and West (Polish) Prussia, obliging the Protestant minorities to continue paying tithes to the Catholic clergy. Frederick also gave refuge to the Jesuits and allowed a Catholic church to be consecrated in Berlin.

However, in much of Europe, toleration, where it existed, was the product of military stalemate and political compromise, rather than humanitarianism. It was for this reason that it was generally partial, restricted to specific religious groups, frequently limited geographically and carefully demarcated, rather than granted universally. Despite contacts across confessional boundaries, schemes for the union of Catholicism and Protestantism, such as those of Gottfried Leibniz, were as unrealistic as those of William Wake, archbishop of Canterbury 1716–37, for closer Anglican relations with Orthodoxy, the French Catholic Church and continental Protestantism, or schemes for Protestant reunion, for the conversion of the Jews, or for the conversion of Russia to either Protestantism or Catholicism. Instead, compromise, where it existed, was generally a matter of expedient political arrangements reflecting historical developments, rather than a confessional agreement. This was the case in the Empire after the Peace of Westphalia. The prince-bishopric of Osnabrück alternated between Catholic and Lutheran Hanoverian rulers. In several imperial cities, such as Augsburg, where the Protestants were generally wealthy, the more numerous Catholics poor, authority was also divided. In Transylvania there were the four recognised religions of the gentry and the towns, Lutheranism, Catholicism, Calvinism and Unitarianism and one tolerated one, Orthodoxy, the faith of most of the peasantry. The treaty of Szatmár (1711) that ended the Hungarian rising ensured freedom of conscience to the Protestants.

Across much of Europe such compromises had not been reached or were partial or resented, and the situation was often perceived as precarious. Rumours of conspiracies, both international and domestic, were believed in, and gave rise to anxiety, as in the anti-Catholic panic in the United Provinces in 1734. These fears were not without reason. Bohemian and Silesian Protestants appealed to Charles XII of Sweden for support. The Pietists of Halle, supported by the Prussians, sought to maintain Protestantism in the Habsburg territories, sending both preachers and scores of thousands of books. The Habsburgs, promising freedom of religion, successfully instigated a revolt of Serbs against Turkish rule in 1737. The Austrian government blamed foreign emissaries when many peasants in Upper Austria and Styria declared themselves Lutherans in 1752.

It was scarcely surprising therefore that governments regarded those outside the communion of the established church as possible traitors, particularly when their co-religionists wielded political power elsewhere. Military success was sometimes turned to religious advantage. The Protestants proselytised in Lille in 1708–13 after the British captured it from Louis XIV. Governments acted on behalf of co-religionists. The Russians intervened on behalf of the Orthodox in Poland. The British interceded on behalf of Protestants in Austria, France, the Palatinate, Piedmont and Poland, the French on behalf of Catholics in Britain. Awareness about the plight of co-religionists was well developed, and the Papacy and the international Catholic religious orders played a major role in disseminating such an awareness in Catholic Europe. Clement XI, responding to a request from the Spanish bishop of Majorca in 1714, persuaded Louis XIV to press Britain about the condition of Catholics after her recent acquisition of Minorca. In Protestant Europe refugee communities, newspapers, diplomats and clerics followed developments in other countries. The Salzburgers benefited from collections throughout western Europe. The English Society for the Propagation of the Gospel in Foreign Parts (SPG), founded in 1701, was very active in British America, but it was also concerned about the position of non-Anglicans in Europe.

Growth of toleration

Religious tension is difficult to assess, but it is often said to have diminished in the second half of the century. The advance of Catholicism in central Europe that had been such a pronounced feature of the period 1620–1719 had stopped. Prussia had taken over the defence of Protestantism in this area from Saxony and Sweden. The Jacobite challenge in Britain, which had aroused considerable anxiety in much of Protestant Europe, was crushed and France humbled in the Seven Years' War (1756–63) by Britain and Prussia. Catholic Europe appeared not less conscious of religious issues, but increasingly divided over Catholic ones, with the relations of Church and State more obviously contentious and the international foci of Catholicism, the Papacy and the religious orders, increasingly shunned by rulers determined to adopt an interventionist attitude to ecclesiastical matters.

A measure of toleration was introduced in many countries, not least as a measure to strengthen states in a situation of acute international competition. Much was a matter of practice, rather than legislation. After the mid-century wars, the large number of crypto-Protestants in Moravia were allowed *de facto* toleration, no persecution in return for no public profession of faith. In the frontline religious state of Poland, the Catholic authorities were not strong enough to impose uniformity, and the government was both unwilling and unable to do so. Major administrative and legislative changes occurred in the second half of the century in a number of states, including Russia and Austria. In 1764 Catherine II abolished the Office of the Converted, a body designed to govern Islamic communities and established in 1731, which had destroyed mosques, kidnapped children and forcibly christened adults. The Muslim Tartars of the Volga and the Urals were invited to send deputies to the Legislative Commission in 1766, while in 1773 the construction of mosques was permitted and religious persecution of Muslims formally abandoned. The following decade brought the construction of many Muslim mosques and schools; in 1786 the latter were placed under the Commission on National Schools and in 1788–9 a Muslim Spiritual Assembly was established to supervise religious life throughout the Russian empire. The senior officials were given noble status. In common with the 'nationalisation' of religious life that characterised Church–State relations over much of eighteenth-century Europe, continuing an obvious characteristic of the previous two centuries, Russian Muslim clerics and teachers were acceptable, but entry was prohibited for those from Central Asia and the Turkish Empire. The latter were seen as disloyal.

Catherine had defined her religious policy in 1773, when she declared that she would emulate God in tolerating 'all faiths, tongues and creeds' and thus ordered the ecclesiastical authorities to leave matters concerning other faiths entirely to civil regulation. In 1786 the civil equality of the Jews was legally established, as were the requisite privileges and obligations. Catholics were allowed freedom of worship, though the first Partition of Poland was followed by a reorganisation of the Catholic Church in the territory acquired by Russia in which papal prerogatives and views were ignored. Within Russia, the Old Believers were treated with increased tolerance. They were no longer forced to wear distinctive clothing or prohibited from painting icons according to old models, and in 1785 public office was opened to them.

Joseph II sought to dismantle the confessional state. In 1781 he granted religious liberty to his non-Catholic Christian subjects. In the Austrian Netherlands the clergy tried to stir up the Estates in opposition and the nuncio (Papal representative) also inspired criticism, but Joseph ignored it. In 1782 he abolished the Inquisition in his dominions and sought to integrate the Jews into Austrian society. Hitherto they had been segregated, as many European minority communities were. Under the Austrian regulations of 1764 severe restrictions on Jewish economic and religious life had been imposed. They were not allowed to buy real property; religious services were restricted to the home. In 1782 Jewish sumptuary obligations, the requirement for married men and widowers to wear beards and their prohibition from places of public entertainment, were abolished. However, Jews were now obliged to pay what was termed a toleration tax, faced new and increased taxes on marriages, holy candles and kosher meat, were not to be admitted to provinces from which they had been hitherto excluded, and no synagogues were permitted in Vienna. For Joseph toleration, though never promoted without Catholic scruples, was a means to free society, and the economy, from unproductive restrictions. Tolerated Protestants in Ostend were to regenerate the port. Jews were to be prohibited from using Hebrew for non-religious purposes and this would, it was hoped, help make them useful citizens. In 1785 and 1788 the judicial autonomy of their Bohemian and Moravian communities was abolished.

For Joseph, a practising and believing Catholic, religious hostility was a pointless legacy of the past. However, toleration did not entail the granting of complete freedom, but simply the removal of specific restrictions, and a state composed of Catholic believers, who would attain salvation, remained his personal ideal. In decreeing a measure of equality, however, rulers left little scope for religious groups such as the Old Believers and the Jews, whose wish to maintain a separate identity led them to seek more than freedom to worship. Many of the former rejected Catherine II's reforms. The Jews found that Josephist toleration entailed the destruction of self-rule, their autonomous institutions being seen correctly as barriers to integration. Jewish emancipation was felt to entail not only the end of legislative restrictions, but also that of traditional practices. As a result Joseph's schemes had only limited success. Attempts in Galicia to force all Jews, except rabbis, to abandon their traditional clothes failed, as did the introduction of secular 'German-Jewish Schools' and efforts to ban Jews from innkeeping. Greater success attended the plan to assign western surnames. In the religious sphere what was believed by some to be progress could entail the legislative weakening of the corporate distinctiveness and legal separation of particular communities. Toleration of Jews was inexstricably linked to the possibility of Christianisation for protagonists of emancipation.

The revolutionaries in France were in no way exceptional in their policy in this respect. Though the abbé Maury, a royalist member of the National Assembly to whom the otherness of Jews was ineradicable and should be admitted by the state, argued that Jews should be allowed to retain their own corporate institutions, including their civil courts, and be treated as protected aliens, this idea was rejected. Instead, Protestants received full civil rights in 1789, Jews in 1791. The corporatist religious freedom of eighteenth-century Poland, of Jewish communities that disciplined themselves, and were essentially self-governing, held no appeal for those who wanted to use the state to change society, whether it be Joseph II or the revolutionaries who executed his sister.

It is certainly true that the pace of agitation for toleration and legislation markedly increased in the 1780s. The policy of rulers varied. Clemens Wenzeslaus, the archbishop-elector of Trier, granted limited toleration to Protestants in 1783, although insisting that their clerics and places of worship were to be inconspicuous, while Karl Friedrich of Baden provided funds to build a Catholic school and church in Karlsruhe. In 1783 Gustavus III called upon Pope Pius VI and attended a Christmas Mass at St Peter's to publicise his toleration of Catholics in Sweden. However, not all rulers changed their attitudes, those of Iberia and Italy seeing little reason to emulate Joseph II.

It is difficult to assess the effectiveness of legislation and literature proclaiming the virtues of toleration. In general, it could be argued that the issue provided yet another illustration of the contrasts between aspiration and achievement, legislative or intellectual fiats and reality, that are such a marked feature of the period. The sense of opportunity and threat that legislative change encouraged probably helped to increase tension. The revolutionary period was to witness an upsurge in confessional violence within and outside France. In 1795 the Orange Order was founded in Ireland to reassert the Protestant ascendancy against the views of the United Irishmen. It would also be mistaken to suggest that religious tension disappeared as a factor in international relations. It remained significant in relations between Poland and Turkey and their neighbours. Religious tension continued to be important in the Empire, its complex constitution providing numerous occasions for disputes. Speculation about Joseph II's intentions, in the light of the apparent resurgence of Austrian expansionism in the 1780s, produced Protestant anxiety, while, as emperor, Joseph was the recipient of complaints about the condition of Protestants, for instance those of the Palatinate in 1786. The increasingly nationalised Catholic Church might appear less credible as a source of international conspiracy, but government policies of active or passive toleration could not dispel prejudice and concern about the local aspirations of members of other faiths.

De-christianisation?

Religious tension is intertwined with belief and observance. Certain practices, such as the taking of communion or participation in pilgrimages, can be quantified, but their significance as a measure of faith is open to debate. It has been argued that in the eighteenth century a 'cycle of faith', associated in particular with the Catholic Reformation (often termed the Counter-Reformation), came to an end and that this led to a decline in religious sentiment. Alternatively, a change in the nature of religious belief and practice has been discerned. Several historians have used the term 'de-christianisation' to denote either such a change or an effective lapsing of religious commitment. Others have claimed that the impact of the religious movements of the previous two centuries was more superficial than has been appreciated and that signs of irreligion or limited dedication during the eighteenth century do not amount to anything new. The subject is complex methodologically, with different interpretations being placed on changes in various indicators of religious activity. It also suffers from the patchy nature of the research on it, with most attention having been devoted to France.

In 1714 Cardinal de La Trémoille, the French envoy in Rome, suggested to Louis XIV that the dispute between Clement XI and Victor Amadeus II of Savoy-Piedmont, who had recently been granted Sicily in the Utrecht peace settlement, was having a detrimental effect on Catholicism in the island. La Trémoille claimed that the use of papal interdicts, which had been placed on Sicilian bishoprics, would cause the people, 'otherwise ignorant of the principles of religion', to forget them entirely, and alleged that he had witnessed the same process in the diocese of Sorrento, south of Naples: the people no longer troubling themselves, not attending Mass nor taking the sacraments.[8] La Trémoille's view was a common one among both Protestant and Catholic divines. Without clerical endeavour, a missionary zeal by a church able to reach all, the people would sink into irreligion and superstition. The church was in this view the barrier against a loss of faith among a populace whose religious faith was superficial.

In this perspective it was possible to assess irreligion in terms of a failure to participate in the services and sacraments of the church, and to treat popular religious practices, such as local saint cults, as superstitious. Throughout the century there was no shortage of clerics willing to adopt such a view. Clerical complaints centred on three issues, intellectual scepticism, popular superstition, and the defiance or ignoring of religious moral standards. There is some evidence of an increase in the last in parts of France. Illegitimacy rates rose in a number of towns, including Lyons and Grenoble. Traditional religiously motivated charitable bequests declined in Aix-en-Provence, particularly after 1760, and in Montpellier, and this has been associated with the spread of indifference to religion, and also, in part, to a spread of lay charity. The decline in charitable bequests increased financial difficulties for ecclesiastical charitable institutions in towns such as Grenoble and helped to lead to their gradual laicisation, as in the diocese of Bordeaux. Certain pilgrimages lost their popularity, such as that to the chapel of the Virgin at La Balme in the

1770s. Many dioceses witnessed a decrease in ordinations after about 1760, and a vocational crisis has been discerned, although a revival in vocations in the 1780s has also been detected.

These developments have led some historians to write of de-christianisation or de-sacralisation in France. Other changes have been cited as evidence for the same process, such as the increasing number of paintings in the 1770s and 1780s that drew on the ancient world for morally exemplary subjects, and the progressive ascendancy of secular history painting over religious art in the Salons of the period. Similarly, some historians have also discerned a laicisation of social and political attitudes. The Paris police, for example, ceased to regard sodomy as a sin, renamed it pederasty, and treated it instead as a threat to social order, though in Britain it remained a capital offence.

It has been argued, furthermore, that these changes had political consequences. It has been suggested that patriotism replaced religion as the principal source of moral values. A de-sacralisation of the French monarchy has been discerned under Louis XV and the process is seen as culminating in the Revolution when Church and monarchy fell simultaneously. In 1789 the National Assembly voted to place church lands 'at the disposal of the nation'. In the French Revolution aggressive anti-clericalism was followed by the prohibition of Christian practice and worship, the closing of churches, the replacement of the Christian calendar by a Revolutionary one and the introduction of new religious cults, centred on Reason or the Supreme Being.

Outside France a measure of de-christianisation has also been observed. From 1743 the theologian Concina argued that Venetian society was de-christianised and in 1756 he claimed that theological debates no longer excited interest. A decline in voluntary support for the indigent (poor), always a prime religious duty, has been discerned in Spain and Italy. In the Austrian Netherlands, popular religion continued in the seventeenth-century pattern until about 1770, with nearly universal attendance at Mass and taking of the sacraments, enormous support for processions, cults of the saints and the Virgin, confraternities, pilgrimages and relics, and an active clergy. From about 1780, however, increasing signs of indifference have been discerned with a rise in illegitimacy and a fall in priestly vocations.

In both France and elsewhere historians have pointed to increasing scepticism and attributed it to the influence of Enlightenment intellectuals. There is no doubt that some writers challenged the fundamentals of Christian belief and ecclesiastical activity. Voltaire clashed with Jesuit missionaries in Colmar in the 1750s, attacked the Bible in his *Dictionnaire Philosophique* (1765), and made repeated jokes about eating and excreting one's God, which represented his challenge to the eucharist from the perspective of rational scrutiny. In a mandement of 1763 ordering a Te Deum at the end of the Seven Years War, Christophe de Beaumont, archbishop of Paris, complained of 'this arrogant philosophy which, little by little, undermines the foundations of the altar and the throne by inspiring the people with contempt for authority, divine and human'.

In the *Encyclopédie*, condemned by Pope Clement XIII in 1759, Diderot claimed, 'when the people perish from hunger, it is never the fault of Providence, but always that of the government', a denial of the divine role. Scientific observations and methods could be used to challenge Christian cosmology and history. The discovery overseas of new species made it difficult to envisage all animals as issuing from the Ark and, by mid-century, most explanations of the distribution of plants, animals and men no longer referred to biblical sources.

In response, the underground Jansenist Parisian periodical the *Nouvelles Ecclésiastiques* attacked Buffon's biological classification as contrary to Holy Writ (1754), condemned the *Encyclopédie* as irreligious and castigated Helvétius, Rousseau and Voltaire. Adeodato Turchi, who became bishop of Parma in 1788, attacked toleration, the *philosophes* and the eagerness to read prohibited books. These condemnations arose partly because many of them made a head-on attack on miracles. Karl Bahrdt (1741–92) described Moses as an experimenter in explosives whose efforts on Mount Sinai were mistaken for divine thunder, and ascribed Jesus's miracles to secret medicines and stored foodstuffs. Anacharsis Cloots (1755–94), a Prussian émigré who later sought to internationalise the French Revolution, published in 1778 his play *Voltaire Triumphant, or the Priests Deceived*, and in 1780 claimed that revealed religions were false, miracles and prophecies contrary to reason, and science the foe of superstition, and argued that the microscope provided proof of the falseness of the eucharist. Belief in the devil was in some circles the casualty of scientific work. Revelation and the miraculous were banished by some writers to the realms of the irrational and the imagination.

If certain writers, such as Diderot, became atheists, more were deists. Deism was not a clear intellectual position or a movement, for it had neither creed nor organisation; it was a vague term used by polemicists that had a wide range of religious connotations. Eschewing the notion of a God of retribution, deistic writers suggested a benevolent force that had created a world and a humanity capable of goodness, and a God not intervening through revelation or miracles. The universe therefore had origins, order and purpose, but there was no need for a priest-hood. Non-Christian religions could have value; morality was superior to revelation. The English writer Joseph Addison argued in 1712 that the excellence of faith consisted in the influence it had on morality. This was not necessarily a deist argument, though it contrasted with otherworldly doctrine, for it emphasised life on earth.

It would be misleading to suggest either that most intellectuals were sceptical or that there was any dichotomy of enlightenment and faith, the secular and the religious, scientific and mystical, progressive and archaic. If William Young, later an MP and colonial governor, could write in 1772 of 'the Light of Knowledge now universally breaking on the world',[9] many clerics could welcome this. Many French parish priests praised Montesquieu, Voltaire and Rousseau, differentiating their commendable arguments from their anti-clericalism. The clergy were major purchasers of the *Encyclopédie*. Neither were Protestant preachers necessarily opposed to Enlightenment ideas. Similarly, many intellectuals found much to praise in religion and even in the church. The Encyclopedists were not alone in believing that, by seeing reason as a divine gift, theology and philosophy could be seen as in harmony. In *Les Cabales* (1772) Voltaire attacked those *philosophes* who tolerated the expression of atheism. Yet, for the Encyclopedists theology as taught by the Catholic Church required recasting and a recognition of error by the Church.

The impact of new ideas is far from clear. When Andreas Lamey, a German born in the prince-bishopric of Münster who had studied theology in Strasbourg, visited Paris in 1751, he was struck by the difference between Catholicism there and in Mediterranean Europe. He reported that though the poor did not mock the pope, purgatory, the invocation of saints and priestly celibacy, as their wealthy fellow citizens did, they were less superstitious and less interested in relics than Catholics elsewhere. Furthermore, there were always some groups which seemed resistant to religious notions and some individuals who were willing to steal the host. Certain mobile occupations, such as those of soldier, boatman and valet, tended to be particularly associated with scepticism. Despite the regulations, organised worship seems to have been neglected in mid-century British warships, though not in the armies of German states.

The notion of de-christianisation can be challenged both by suggesting that changes in religious sensibility should not be mistaken for its decline, and by arguing that the available evidence indicates that scepticism, though present, was marginal and that what was more common was a buoyant popular Christianity, often unresponsive to the proddings of reforming clerics. It is not inconsistent to argue both that there were changes in religious sensibility and that popular practices were generally traditional. The range of religious practice within particular faiths was vast. Literacy, relative wealth and an urban environment enabled some to respond to new intellectual and spiritual currents, though it would be wrong to suggest that rural religion was necessarily unchanging. Changes in certain habits, such as French testamentary practices, suggest that, for some, personal conviction was being stressed at the expense of the public piety that had been so significant. Religious practice was not, however, simply a matter of adherence to or disobeying the strictures of unchanging churches. Far from being static or exhausted bodies, the churches of the period witnessed a number of developments that offered the believer the possibility of fresh spiritual and moral renewal. Faith did not have to exist in a wilderness of enthusiasts, nor were clerics simply concerned with their institutional, doctrinal and ecclesiological position.

There is copious evidence both of massive observance of the formal requirements of the churches and of widespread piety. Just as much of the evidence for de-christianisation comes from France, so also does much that points in the opposite direction. Though peasants protested against the tithe and Masonic lodges were founded in Toulouse, in that diocese the percentage who did not take communion at Easter was minute. In the parish of Tournefeuille, until the Revolution, the demand for an early morning Mass was made repeatedly and the local confraternity remained strong. Though fewer girls were sent to convents, there is little evidence of de-christianisation in Provence. Far from assimilating or becoming indifferent, the Protestants of La Rochelle sought to maintain their faith and clandestine baptisms were common. The Catholic Church appears to have benefited from a wave of evangelism in rural France, its revival possibly owing something to the central role of the church in the spread of rural education. Pilgrimages were generally popular, and the Cult of the Sacred Heart – approved by the hierarchy and popular with the faithful – was one of the religious success stories of the century.

Catholic belief was buoyant not only in rural France, but also in the Catholic states of Germany where the populace adhered tenaciously to the 'Baroque piety' that had been encouraged during the previous century. There was little doubt of the intensity of popular religiosity, and this was true also in towns such as Koblenz, Cologne, Mainz and Munich, religious life being characterised by numerous services, processions, pilgrimages and confraternities. Charles VI and Maria Theresa encouraged the veneration of the

Bohemian saint John of Nepomuk with considerable success, statues and confraternities springing up accordingly. Viennese fraternities grew in popularity under Maria Theresa, and Joseph II's attack on them was far from popular. When Pope Pius VI went to Vienna in 1782 to remonstrate with Joseph about his religious policies he was unsuccessful. However, on this, the first meeting between a pope and an emperor since 1530, the pontiff was given an ecstatic reception by the bulk of the population; 100,000 people greeted him on his entry to Vienna, his public papal blessing on Easter Day saw a demonstration of intense devotion, and he was given a rapturous welcome on the rest of his journey, particularly at Munich, Augsburg and in the Tyrol. When Frederick the Great abolished several of the numerous Catholic and Protestant feast days, he was forced to moderate his policy because of strong Silesian opposition. In much of Catholic Europe, piety remained centred on local saints and their shrines, as in southern Italy, or on numerous shrines of the Virgin each with their miraculous icon, as in Poland. In Russia popular spiritual poetry developed, the material apocryphal, biblical, liturgical and oriented towards the Orthodox church year.

In Protestant Europe religious renewal was not restricted to the German Pietists and to new movements such as Methodism. Despite the claims of other Protestant groups, the established Protestant churches were not devoid of energy, their congregations not sunk in torpor. These churches ministered to their flocks and were not averse to religious campaigns, such as that waged in Wales in the early decades of the century by the Anglicans and the Dissenters, against Catholicism, drunkenness and profanity and for salvation and literacy. In London strong popular piety led to the growth of weekday services, and of morning and evening services. The religious texture of social life persisted. An English tourist noted at St Goar in the Rhineland in 1785, 'The watch proclaim the hour by blowing so many times with a horn, and making a little pious address to the people who are all Protestants, to thank God for giving them another hour.'[10] The century was also in some ways a high point of Christian civilisation. In Catholicism it was the era of the great South German and Austrian pilgrimage and monastery churches and libraries, in Protestantism the era of Bach's masses and Handel's oratorios.

Considerable religious fervour was displayed by evangelical groups and by those accused of 'Enthusiasm', a claim to a personal, private revelation, a charge that was not accepted by those so accused. Judaism, a religion characterised by relatively independent communities, was seriously divided as a result of one such group. A Ukrainian faith-healer, Israel ben Eliezer (1700–60), attacked what he claimed was the formalism of orthodox Judaism and, stressing divine omnipresence and the possibility of direct communion with God, urged the bypassing of rabbinical intercession and authority. His revivalist arguments were not intended initially to inspire a new movement, but, eventually, his followers formed a separate congregation, the Hassidim, whose leaders were excommunicated in 1772.

Protestant Enthusiasm took a number of forms. Millenarianism was not unimportant, though it appears to have varied in response to confessional and political circumstances. The expulsion of the Huguenots and the War of the Spanish Succession witnessed an upsurge in a number of areas, such as Württemberg, where the 'Inspired' condemned the established church as corrupt, and among the Huguenots themselves. The French Prophets, a group of survivors of the Cévennes rising, arrived in London in 1706, announced the coming millennium, and, finding a surprising degree of support, inspired a minor outbreak of religious enthusiasm. From there, they spread to America, the United Provinces and the Empire, creating a considerable sensation, and arousing significant opposition among the established Protestant churches, whose sober and rationalist character has been attributed to their confrontation with Enthusiasm. They had little time for popular millenarianism, neither did the Pietism of Halle nor the Methodism of Wesley. Millenarian trends during the century are still largely uncharted territory. They can be found in France, among the convulsionaries of Saint-Médard and in works such as the *Dissertation sur l'époque du Rappel des Juifs* (1779), among the Old Believers and among the English Unitarians. Both Joseph Priestley and Richard Price expected the millennium to follow the downfall of authority.

Pietism, a late seventeenth-century north German development, was an attitude rather than a creed. Seeking to revive German Protestantism, it called for the development of spiritual gifts among the flock. Philip Spener (1635–1705), court chaplain in Saxony and then a refugee in Berlin, argued that faith had to be dependent on an active piety. Pietists stressed the role of preaching and education, particularly of the poor, and emphasised the importance of individual conversion. Pietists presented the state as an institution designed to discipline and improve society, and this contributed to the particular political culture of Prussia, one that made a morality of state service.[11]

Individual conversion was also crucial to John Wesley (1703–91) who began an evangelical campaign in England in 1738. Wesley combined concern for the church Establishment with first-hand contact with continental Protestants, particularly the revived Moravian Brethren based at Herrnhut, a Saxon religious community developed by the Pietist count Zinzendorf, and derived from the Hussites. Methodism, initially intended by Wesley as a means to reawaken Anglicanism, was thus part of the 'Great Awakening', a widespread movement of Protestant revival in Europe and North America. Seeing his mission as one of saving souls, Wesley urged men to turn to Christ to win redemption and promised they would know that they had achieved salvation. Wesley offered an eclectic theology that was adapted to a powerful mission addressing itself to popular anxieties. His belief in religion as an epic struggle, with providence, demons and witchcraft all present, and his willingness to seek guidance by opening the Bible at random, all found echoes from a growing popular following. This was facilitated by the energy of the preaching mission, the revivalist nature of Methodism, with its hymn-singing, watchnights and love feasts, and by Wesley's flexibility. He was well aware of the value of print, producing many tracts and much serial material. Strongly anti-Catholic, and thus scarcely tolerant, Wesley, nevertheless, was flexible, accepting men and women of all denominations for class membership, and, from the mid-1740s, using lay preachers, because he could not obtain enough support from ordained ministers. This helped to increase clerical opposition, as did unease about Wesley's theology.[12]

Jansenism

In his *Enthusiasm of Methodists and Papists Compared* (1749–51), George Lavington, bishop of Exeter, claimed that Methodism imitated the enthusiastic excesses of medieval Catholicism, with visions, exorcisms and healing. Twenty years earlier, Paris had witnessed a comparable episode when the tomb of a Jansenist deacon in the cemetery of the Parisian church of Saint-Médard became the scene of apparently miraculous cures and of people in convulsions, claiming to be inspired by the Holy Spirit. As with Methodism, this aroused ecclesiastical concern. By 1732 reports of the spreading 'fanaticism of Saint-Médard' had been received from dioceses all over France, including Bordeaux, Chartres, Marseille and Tarbes.[13] The cemetery was shut, resulting in private domestic services, still very common in Paris in the early 1760s, where convulsions played a major role in expressing a sense of spiritual liberation. To a certain extent this episode, like Protestant revival, indicated both the strength of religious feeling of a section of the population, in which women were prominent, and the limited ability of established ecclesiastical organisations, centred on a parochial clergy administering the eucharist, to meet this need.

The events at Saint-Médard dramatised the possible serious consequences of Jansenism among the populace. Many labels used for eighteenth-century religion are unhelpful or fraught with difficulty – Evangelicalism, for example, creating problems if applied to Anglican, Wesleyan and Dissenter revivalism in Britain at the end of the period – but few are as slippery as Jansenism. Originally an early seventeenth-century theological movement, it acquired a host of meanings, ecclesiastical, theological, cultural and political. If in France the persecution which Jansenism suffered from secular and ecclesiastical authorities led to its being seen by outsiders and adherents as a clearly delineated group, this was not the case elsewhere, and French Jansenism itself was far from homogeneous. Theologically, Jansenism restated Augustinian notions and called into question the ability of man to achieve salvation by his own efforts. The Jansenists insisted that the church was necessary and their argument that 'divine grace is not something to be worked for and won along a path which is already revealed to us, but rather a gift in the hands of a God whose criteria are beyond our understanding, expresses the new awareness of a world in which there is no necessary relationship between the ways of men and the will of God.'[14]

It is not surprising that Louis XIV, who sought uniformity in French religious life, was unhappy both about a belief that denied the ability of secular and ecclesiastical authorities to represent God's will infallibly and about division within French Catholicism. In 1704 Louis's grandson, Philip V of Spain, referred to the need to destroy a 'sect so pernicious to the state and the church'.[15] Action against the Jansenists was stepped up in the 1700s. This aroused opposition both in the French church and in the *Parlement* of Paris, each of which defended national 'Gallican' privileges in the face of the universal legal pretensions of the papacy, and even, briefly, fuelled notions of union with Archbishop Wake's Church of England. In 1703 Louis and Clement XI cooperated to seek the suppression of Jansenism as a movement and an issue. Fearing opposition if he attempted to register it in the *parlements*, Louis sent the papal bull to each bishop, with a letter from a secretary of state announcing that it represented an accord between king and pope for maintaining the integrity of the faith. When several bishops interpreted the letter as an order to publish the bull and did so, the *Parlement* of Paris intervened to show the irregularity of this conduct and Louis, unwilling to provoke a dispute at a time of great national strain, allowed the *Parlement* to proceed against the bishop of Clermont. In 1713 Louis persuaded Clement to issue the bull *Unigenitus*, which condemned 101 alleged Jansenist propositions. With the end of the

War of the Spanish Succession in sight, Louis sought to force the *parlements* to register *Unigenitus*.

This touched off a dispute that helped to divide the French Catholic Church-state for decades. The Church, the government and the *parlements* were divided, and not all who defended the Gallican position and were therefore termed Jansenists adopted the theological position associated with Jansenism. The nature and intensity of the division varied, but Jansenism provided a battleground for a Catholic country more concerned about the nature of papal, episcopal and *parlementaire* authority than the challenge posed by weak French Protestantism. Most bishops attempted to use *Unigenitus* and their own authority to browbeat dissenting *curés*. Many of the latter, particularly in Paris, were influenced by Richerism. Based on the writings of Edmond Richer (1559–1631) and the Jansenist Pasquier Quesnel (1634–1719), whose views were condemned in *Unigenitus*, this suggested that, just as bishops were the spiritual heirs of the apostles, so priests were the successors of the disciples of Christ, and thus not dependent on the former for their position. The right of the priest to administer the sacraments, irrespective of episcopal authority, was asserted. An wish for improvement in the status and position of the parochial clergy thus became a view associated with Jansenism, though not all *curés* dissatisfied with their share of the tithe, or with bishops and the regular clergy (monks, friars and nuns) adopted Jansenist theological positions.

It has been suggested that the disputes arising from and related to Jansenism played a significant role in disturbing the constitutional consensus of the French state and weakened the monarchy, not least by reducing the effectiveness of the political support that the church could provide and challenging the shared consensus of received values, symbols, and myths. Jansenist issues certainly led to a challenge to royal authority on a number of occasions, particularly in the mid-1710s, the early 1730s and the early 1750s. However, one must not assume that disputes in a political system comprising a number of institutions with well-developed senses of identity and pretensions were proof of a serious crisis. Having rediscovered the importance of symbols and myths some historians possibly exaggerate their significance. There is a tendency to neglect the 'political' dimension of pre-revolutionary European states and churches, to under-rate the importance of differences of opinion and institutional and factional disputes. Royal policy, papal pretensions and episcopal views had scarcely gone unchallenged over the previous two centuries. Far from seeing the *ancien régime* as a stable, if not static, series of churches and states increasingly challenged in the eighteenth century, the challenges producing stress and finally revolution, it is more appropriate to note that the churches and the states of the period developed continually, that the differences this reflected and gave rise to were not proof of instability, and that the institutions of the period were able to sustain a substantial amount of tension and disagreement. Consensus and myths neither required nor led to inertness and silence.

If Jansenist issues posed serious political problems in France in certain periods, in others, such as 1733–48 and after the 1750s, they did not. From the late 1740s police action against the Jansenist newspaper the *Nouvelles Ecclésiastiques* became sporadic. If the political crisis of the 1750s was more sustained than that of the 1730s, that owed much to the difference in political skill between the vacillating Louis XV and the more adroit cardinal Fleury, who, as first minister (1726–43), had successfully reduced tension. The struggle between the *Parlement* of Paris and the ecclesiastical authorities was scarcely new, but it was now much more intense. By 1758 the *Parlement* had won ultimate judicial control over the public dispensation of the sacraments. Clerical remonstrances in 1758, 1760, 1762 and 1765 were ineffective, and in 1765 the *Parlement* nullified the decisions of the General Assembly of the Clergy of France, which had sought to increase clerical independence.

Jansenist ideas were not restricted to France or to those who can clearly be defined as Jansenist. They were also influential in Italy from the 1730s where they were propagated by Muratori and his pupils and supported by rulers and ministers opposed to papal pretensions. In his works, one of which was dedicated to Charles VI, both Holy Roman Emperor and, for part of his reign, ruler of half of Italy, Muratori argued in favour of simple worship and against Baroque piety, and criticised the papacy and the regulars. Jansenist ideas circulated in Tanucci's Naples and Tillot's Parma in the 1760s, and Jansenist bishops and priests were influential in Lombardy in the 1770s and 1780s, when the government restricted the rights of the papacy and the regulars, enacted toleration, suppressed the confraternities and the ecclesiastical courts and decreed that in future all parish priests should study at the seminary of Pavia, now reorganised under Jansenist clerics. Joseph II personally gave gold medals to leading Jansenists there in 1784. In Tuscany Joseph's brother, Grand Duke Leopold, supported the reforms of Scipione de'Ricci, the Jansenist bishop of Pistoia and Prato. However, the attempt to simplify liturgical practice, reorganise the church in order to increase the power of the parish priests, and attack the regulars led in 1787 to opposition from most of the Tuscan bishops and riots in Prato, and Leopold withdrew his support.

Jansenist influences in the Austrian Netherlands played a role in the government regulation of church activities and in moves against papal influence. Jansenism had originated in the area, but by the eighteenth century it was concerned less with doctrinal issues and more with the ending of religious practices regarded as incompatible with those of the primitive church. The idea of a purified and more austere religion, with ceremonial trimmed as much as papal authority, was propagated. To that end, many Jansenists supported both popular education, as vital for a proper knowledge of Christianity, and a vernacular Bible. *Unigenitus* opposed this loosening of established controls by condemning the notion of the laity's right to read the vernacular Bible and to participate actively in the liturgy.

Ideas and clerics from Italy and the Austrian Netherlands influenced Austria. In 1752 John Joseph von Trautson, the archbishop of Vienna, stressed the superior value of preaching for the instruction of the people, compared with theatrical rites and ceremonies. Count Christoph Migazzi, archbishop of Vienna, sponsored Jansenist confessors for the imperial family, and from 1757 until 1767 he opened clerical training to Jansenist influences and broke the Jesuit monopoly of theological higher education. Numerous Jansenist-influenced bishops introduced a number of changes with the support of Maria Theresa. Count Herberstein, bishop of Ljubliana, criticised confraternities. Count Spaur, bishop of Brixen, reduced the veneration of images.

Not all Austrian clerics supported the attitudes and policies that have been described as Jansenist. Migazzi himself later turned against the reformers, and criticised some of the teachers of theology at the University of Vienna. He complained about Joseph von Sonnenfels's attacks on celibacy, and in 1777 censured Ferdinand Stöger, who, in his lectures on ecclesiastical history, had criticised papal authority and the Inquisition. In addition, not all 'Jansenists' approved of the royalist ecclesiastical policies of the Habsburg monarchy. Some who maintained the theological tradition, such as Karl Schwarzl, argued that Joseph infringed rights that were integral to the church, and claimed that his vision of the church was military rather than apostolic. On one point, at least, the two strands were united: in Austria as elsewhere in Europe, Jansenist ideas and regalism combined in opposition to the Jesuits.

The fate of the Jesuits

The suppression of the Jesuits was both the most dramatic example of State power over the Church prior to the French Revolution and an obvious proof of the divisions within Catholicism. As an international Order with a special oath of loyalty to the papacy, the Jesuits had long symbolised in Protestant Europe the united purpose and ambitious schemes of international Catholicism. They were believed to wield considerable secret power as royal confessors throughout Catholic Europe. Many of them did indeed seek to do so, Augustus III's confessor Ligerit intriguing against his leading minister, count Brühl, in 1748. In Catholic Europe the Jesuits had enemies, in Rome, at Catholic courts, and among the secular clergy and other orders. Their loyalty was distrusted, their wealth (both real and rumoured) and position envied, their beliefs and practices criticised, particularly by Jansenists, for excessive flexibility. It would be misleading, however, to represent the Jesuits' fate as a simple triumph of State over Church. They were also weakened by clerical criticism and opposition. In 1704, 1715 and 1742 papal condemnations ended their effort to convert the Chinese governing class, by prohibiting the expedients by which the Order had sought to adjust Christianity to Chinese beliefs. Under Benedict XIV (1740–58), Jesuit influence in Rome declined.

Nevertheless, the decisive challenges to the Jesuits were mounted by secular governments. The first came from Portugal, where the leading minister, Pombal, suspicious of Jesuit intentions in their Paraguay mission and concerned about their power in Portugal, became convinced that they had to be destroyed. Earlier, as a diplomat in Vienna, he had been influenced by Jansenist ideas. In 1758 he was able to trump up charges implicating the Jesuits in an attempt to assassinate Joseph I, and, the following year, they were expelled. Regalian works denounced Jesuitical subversion. In 1761 the Italian Jesuit Gabriel Malagrida, a preacher who had been regarded as a prophet and a saint in Portugal and who had attributed the Lisbon earthquake to divine anger with the Portuguese government, was publicly garrotted and burnt.

Attacks on the Jesuits were frequent in France in the 1750s, and they were blamed, without cause, for the attempted assassination of Louis XV in 1757. Jesuit financial problems led the *Parlement* of Paris in 1761 to investigate their constitution and to decide that their obedience to a foreign superior-general posed a political danger. They were ordered to close their colleges and their special religious vows were declared null and void in 1762. Louis XV and most of the bishops sought to avoid their expulsion and to Gallicanise the Order in France. Initially, most French Jesuit leaders favoured such an arrangement, but it failed in the face of the intractability both of the *Parlement* and of the superior-general, Lorenzo Ricci. In 1764 the Jesuit society in France was suppressed.

Accused of responsibility for riots in Spanish cities in 1766, they were suppressed in Spain and Naples in 1767. Clement XIII sought to protect them, but his successor Clement XIV was bullied by the Bourbon rulers, who seized the Papal enclaves of Avignon and Benevento, into abolishing the Order in 1773. This reflected the declining prestige of the papacy. The Order was then suppressed in the remaining Catholic states, principally the Habsburg dominions, Poland and parts of the Empire, while Ricci died in a papal prison in 1775. Some Jesuits found refuge in Prussia and Russia, neither of whose monarchs was willing to promulgate the papal prohibition. Pius VI fruitlessly pressed Catherine II to dissolve the Order, but impressed by their educational talents, she protected it.

The suppression of the Jesuits was unpopular both in certain ministerial circles and with many of the people. Maria Theresa had misgivings about the Order, but made no attempt to suppress it until Clement acted. The anti-Jesuit legislation of the *Parlement* in Paris in 1762 was not emulated by the sovereign courts of Alsace, Artois and Flanders, and Franche-Comté. The moral and intellectual prestige of the Jesuits in Béarn ensured that they were openly defended by the nobility in the local Estates. The *Parlement* of Pau feared that their educational role would be difficult to fill. The Palatine minister Baron Beckers anticipated similar difficulties in education, preaching and the confessional. Sympathetic bishops in France appear to have helped some Jesuits take up new ecclesiastical positions. Popular opposition to the suppression was voiced in a number of areas, including parts of the Empire and Italy. This was particularly the case where they had fulfilled a pastoral mission, as in Béarn, or Poland, where they had been active in preaching and catechising in the late 1760s. In the Tyrol the cult of the Sacred Heart of Jesus, fostered during the Jesuits' popular mid-century missions, was to be suppressed during the Josephist campaign against 'Baroque piety' in the 1780s, but its popularity led to its revival after 1790. The Jesuits' educational and pastoral roles were largely taken over by other bodies, both secular and religious, but the delight expressed by Jansenists and Enlightenment writers was not shared by all. The suppression of the Order reflects little credit on those who carried it out. Many of the Jesuits were brutally treated, particularly in Portugal, and many useful institutions were destroyed or harmed. The college of Malines was not alone in having its library sold. Two Hungarian ex-Jesuit poets, Ferenc Faludi and David Szabó, saw the suppression as the death of a culture that was a symptom of the decline of European society. Maria Theresa made huge loans to aristocrats from the money gained, while the Order's chief house in Vienna became the seat of the war department.

Church–State relations

A clear-cut division between Church and State was essentially a legacy of the French Revolution. Before that time, no government had broken with organised Christianity, even if it had had disputes with clerics or the papacy. The societies of *ancien régime* Europe were bound to the churches not only through belief and the need to express and fulfil it through collective and sacramental worship, but also through the churches' role in a host of activities, particularly education and social welfare, and the joint use of the churches' revenues. Church and society were linked not only at senior levels, but also at that of the parish. Local notables frequently played a formal or informal role in the appointment of the local clergy, and their support was often vital for the latter. However, much of the revenue of the church benefited the laity. In England one-third of tithes were held by lay impropriators, 53 per cent of church patronage was controlled by private individuals and 10 per cent by the crown. English church properties were rented on favourable terms. Most tenants were too powerful to be exploited and resistance to episcopal rent increases was effective, although the Church of England did become richer after 1750, thanks to increasing agricultural output. Many Prussian benefices were converted to lay preferments for long periods and granted to the nobility. Lay influence was also exercised in senior Prussian church appointments. In Wallachia and Moldavia, where the Orthodox Church was a major landowner, exempt from taxation, it was dominated by the local elite. Equally, governments called on clerical assistance. In Spain there was a long tradition of clerics in senior government posts, nine of the twelve presidents of the Council of Castile in 1700–51 being clerics, while both Aragon and Catalonia had clerical viceroys in the 1700s. Neither were all church lands exempt from taxation. The Austrian church was taxed and, like secular landowners, subjected to the heavier Contribution (direct tax) introduced by Haugwitz in 1749. Though the French church retained its right of self-taxation, General Assemblies of the Clergy were expected to grant substantial sums, 16 million livres being offered in 1755. In general, clerical taxation increased during the century as a result of government action.

Many rulers were personally pious, and, as religion was seen as a social necessity as well as a personal experience, rulers, governments and landlords sought to foster religious observance.

Charles XII read the Bible every day of his life. Elizabeth of Russia's faith has been described in terms of fits of religious mania. Ferdinand, duke of Parma, who was excommunicated by Clement XIII in 1768 after suppressing the Jesuits, heard Mass twice daily. The imperial family closely identified itself with the Catholic Church and participated prominently in services and festivals. The empress dowager served 15 poor people at table at the feast of St Joseph in 1709, and under Maria Theresa, Easter ceremonies were always attended in common by the whole court. Joseph II, however, cut the number of times the court attended church.

Landlords were expected to influence local religious life. Peter I continued the policy of his predecessors in allowing only those foreigners who converted to Orthodoxy to own estates with Orthodox serfs. The instructions of Russian landlords to their stewards reveal a concern with the moral life of the peasantry. Custom and legislation protected the established churches. Blasphemy and infringement of the sabbath were illegal. Danish legislation of 1676 included regulations against swearing, drinking and trading on holy days. Religious costumes were forbidden at Italian masquerades.

Custom and legislation also expected much from the clergy. Whether in Protestant Baden or Catholic France, the parochial clergy were responsible for registering baptisms, marriages and burials, they supervised schools, organised and dispensed charity, introduced new farming methods and attended the sick. These relationships of mutual support and the shared function of fostering the moral and spiritual health of the people remained central throughout the disputes between rulers and clerics. These were not new. Uniformity of opinion over ecclesiastical issues had rarely been present over the previous century, and just as political loyalty co-existed with constitutional disputes, so belief was not shattered by ecclesiastical conflicts. The flexibility and resilience of *ancien régime* institutions and beliefs should not be underestimated.

The central theme in Church–State relations was the determination of rulers to secure and maintain control over the religious life of their territories. As we have seen above, this entailed discouraging religious dissidents and could also involve action to increase power over their churches. In 1753 Frederick the Great informed the Catholic Order of St John that it would retain the privileges of its Silesian commanderies only on condition that they be conferred on Prussian subjects and made independent of the Grand Priory of Bohemia, which was located in Habsburg territory. Opposing this, Kaunitz insisted that if the Order agreed, Austria would insist on a similar preference for her own subjects.

In Catholic Europe the ecclesiastical system and doctrinal orthodoxy were dependent on an international body, the papacy. The manipulation or ignoring of papal authority was scarcely new and the rifts of the eighteenth century arose out of traditional causes of dispute. Victor Amadeus II clashed with Clement XI from the beginning of the century over preferments and regalian rights, jurisdictional questions, clerical immunities and suzerainty over Papal fiefs. A bitter conflict, that involved disputes in Savoy-Piedmont, Sicily and Sardinia, was not settled until the concordat of 1742, when the papacy yielded on most issues. John V of Portugal broke with the papacy over his demand for a patriarchate in Lisbon, diplomatic relations being severed in 1728–32, as they were to be again in 1760–9 when Pombal was dissatisfied with Clement XIII's support for the Jesuits. The concordat of 1753 gave Ferdinand VI control over the Spanish church.

In international negotiations the papacy was also increasingly ignored, and rulers, such as the Emperor Joseph I in 1709, were still prepared to use military force in disputes with the popes as temporal rulers. Papal representatives, injunctions and jurisdictional pretensions were frequently ignored or denied, and much anti-papal activity arose from the determination of several popes to maintain their authority. Clement XI, who had disputes with all the Catholic powers, pressed papal claims to suzerainty in Italy. The excommunication of Ferdinand of Parma later in the century led to reprisals by the duke's Bourbon relatives. The wide-ranging nature of clerical pretensions inevitably led to disputes. Benedict XIV condemned Tuscan funerary legislation in 1748 for infringing clerical jurisdiction. From the 1760s a determined anti-papal offensive imbued with a regalist ideology gathered pace in a number of states, one cardinal writing in 1776:

> the war that the courts of Vienna and Naples wage on the Papacy seems to get worse daily. Nearly every courier brings bad news of the plans and the innovations that the two courts daily make to the prejudice of the rights and authority of the Papacy and the Church. His Holiness has resigned himself to await for Providence and altered circumstances.[16]

Other international Catholic bodies also suffered. The power of the Inquisition was limited or destroyed. Governments challenged the authority of foreign diocesans, for example that of the archbishop of Salzburg over clerical taxation in Bavaria in 1789. The regular clergy were increasingly subjected to the authority of local rulers. Charles III followed this policy in Spain, creating Spanish congregations, as for the Carthusians in 1783. In 1776 Tanucci sought to separate the Neapolitan Carthusians from their French superior. Arguing that the Carthusian constitution infringed the authority of the sovereign, Neapolitan ministers in 1778 considered using the Order's wealth for government schemes, such as naval construction, and pensioning off the monks. More than authority was at stake. Monasticism was widely rejected in intellectual, government and some clerical circles in Catholic states as an immoral and unnatural waste of resources. Praying for the souls of the dead seemed less important than the care of those of the living. The success of monks in fulfilling their vocation varied. Despite the claims of critics, not all were sunk in ignorant indolence, and some, such as the Benedictines of Kremsmünster, helped to spread Enlightenment ideas. If some monks, such as the Benedictines of Saint-Hubert or the Cistercians of Paix-Dieu en Hesbaye, enjoyed a comfortable life, that did not necessarily contrast with the parish clergy. The long survival of the monastic ideal was matched by the large numbers still involved. This was another institution of the old order capable of soaking up criticism. Many French monks were reluctant to abandon the contemplative life when they had the chance in 1790. The female religious orders in France were in particularly good health.

The immunities and tithes enjoyed by the regulars aroused the envy of many seculars, and their wealth excited the interest of ministers. In the Austrian Netherlands, where Joseph II suppressed 163 monasteries, they were great landowners, 11 per cent of Brabant belonging to them. The Assembly of the Clergy pressed for the reform of French monasteries in 1765, and Louis XV, determined to control the process, established a commission of reform in 1766 directed by Loménie de Brienne; 426 houses were suppressed, the legal age for taking vows was raised and new constitutions for religious orders were issued. This gave French monasticism a new lease of life. The French monasteries began to attract more vocations in the 1780s, after a period of decline. Nevertheless, monasticism was still unpopular with many writers and enjoyed little support in the culture of print. This had its effect in the Revolutionary crisis. In October 1789 religious vows were suppressed and the contemplative orders dissolved. Only those involved in education, hospitals and charity were spared for the time being.

Some other countries followed a similar policy. The Calabrian earthquakes of 1783 led to the suppression of a number of monasteries for the benefit of the sufferers. Attempts were made to reduce the number of friars in Spain. Sicilian monasteries were ordered to open free schools for the poor. Maria Theresa accepted the advice of Paul Riegger, a professor of canon law with Jansenist leanings, that the crown had the right to exercise control over monasteries. In 1765 Joseph II wrote of the need for reforming some monasteries and employing 'them for pious purposes which would be at the same time useful to the state, such as the education of children'.[17] After he achieved sole power in 1780, the contemplative orders were suppressed and about 700–750 religious houses were dissolved in the Habsburg dominions as a whole. The property was put to a variety of uses, some educational and charitable, but some religious, including new dioceses and several hundred new parishes. In Ghent former monasteries were turned into barracks. Monastic libraries were dispersed, books by authors such as Jesuits who were disapproved of, being sent to be pulped. The Hanoverian Protestant writer Ernst Brandes, who had little sympathy for monasticism, nevertheless criticised the harshness of Joseph's policy, especially the cruelty towards individual monks and the contempt for tradition. The impact of dissolutions on local communities was great. The continuity of religious life was broken. In Russia monastic wealth was also secured to the state. Monasteries were assigned the task of caring for disabled soldiers in 1722. In 1764 church lands in Great Russia and Siberia were secularised and their management transferred to the College of Economy. In all, 411 out of the 572 monasteries were suppressed and the remainder were granted a fixed establishment.

In a number of countries, the clerical role in censorship, education and marriage was reduced. The secular authorities took over control of censorship in a number of states including Tuscany (1743), Lombardy (1768) and Portugal (1768). This did not necessarily entail a weakening of the Catholic position. In Portugal, for example, clerics continued to play a role and non-Catholic doctrines were still censored. In the 1750s Maria Theresa allowed Gerard van Swieten and the Censorship Commission to establish more secular criteria for censorship. Montesquieu's *L' Esprit des Lois* was allowed entry, though Maria Theresa would only permit the admission of Protestant books in special circumstances, and the censorship became less liberal after van Swieten's death (1772). Nevertheless, ecclesiastical authority was not reimposed. In 1774 the censors in the Austrian Netherlands were forbidden to approve any work concerning religion, whoever was the author, without consulting the government. In England, where pre-publication censorship had lapsed in 1695, an attempt by Archbishop Tenison to revive it in 1702 failed.

Marriage was another sphere in which church authority was reduced. In 1721 Peter I legalised Protestant–Orthodox marriages.

A Russian ordinance of 1702, abolishing the penalty for the non-fulfilment of contracts of engagement concluded between the families of the parties concerned, encroached on the sphere of ecclesiastical jurisdiction. The minimum age for marriage was fixed in 1714, the length of the marriage service cut in 1723. The role of the Church and the civil power in marriage was bitterly contested in the mid-century Austrian Netherlands, the validity of the marriage of minors without parental consent being challenged. In 1783, despite clerical hostility, an Austrian edict established the principle that marriage was essentially a civil contract. Civil marriage was introduced in the Austrian Netherlands in 1784 and the legality of divorce for Catholics accepted.

Education was similarly brought increasingly under secular supervision. This entailed essentially controlling, not dispensing with, clerical participation, though certain circumstances, particularly the suppression of the Jesuits, and the policies of individual rulers, especially Joseph II, led towards lay control. In Russia clerical schools were instructed to fulfil the temporal needs of society. In Protestant Hanover and Brunswick the clergy successfully retained control over education and resisted attempts to turn them into essentially a branch of government. In the 1780s Brunswick failed to remove education from the control of the clergy and to place it under a special organisation.

In Catholic Europe secular control became more of an issue from the 1760s. In Parma, where in 1755 the College Lalatta was founded and Tillot brought in teachers with new ideas, it became necessary in 1768 to have government permission to found schools. Subsequently medical and legal studies in the duchy were reformed and scholasticism downgraded in theological studies. Higher education was reorganised in Austria in the 1750s. In 1759 Pombal forbade the use of Jesuit manuals and methods of teaching and reformed the educational system. An enquiry in 1770–1 castigated the Portuguese university of Coimbra, where Descartes, Gassendi and Newton had still been judged unacceptable in the 1740s, as backward, and in 1772 new statutes were issued. The university became more secular. Colleges for mathematics and science were founded, laboratories established and foreign teachers introduced. In Spain there was talk of secularised education and in 1766 Campomanes proposed a general reform of the universities. In combination with reformers within the university a new plan of studies was issued for Salamanca in 1771:

> Before 1770, the full cloister had dispatched its affairs by meeting a leisurely two or three times a month. Now it found itself summoned

three or four times a week, sometimes every day, to deal with piece-meal royal orders affecting tenure, salaries, university finances, internal government, examinations, and nearly every other aspect of univer-sity life.[18]

In the Austrian Netherlands the university of Louvain was seen as a conservative force and in 1768 Kaunitz pressed the need for reform. In response to it an Imperial and Royal Academy of Sciences and Literature was founded at Brussels in 1772. Stressing technology and economic development, the Academy helped to foster a government-supported lay scientific culture. In 1776–7 education in the Austrian Netherlands was reorganised and a separate ministry founded. In the Rhineland clerical influence decreased in the schools and their curriculum became more prac-tical. Similarly, in the reformed universities of Mainz and Trier and the new foundation of Bonn, theology declined in import-ance while more weight was given to modern languages and sci-ences, though in Cologne the traditional curriculum and methods remained dominant. In the Empire there was considerable inter-est in the educational ideas of Johann Basedow (1723–90). He founded the *Philanthropin* at Dessau in 1774, a school which stres-sed the spontaneous development of children's benevolent and rational faculties, rather than conventional religious education.

In France reformers greeted the suppression of the Jesuits with the hope that a national state-controlled educational system could be created, with teaching by laymen or seculars in practical subjects. Their hopes were not fulfilled. Jesuit schools were handed over to local boards, there was no drastic change in teaching methods or curriculum and the vast majority of teachers remained clerics. Pressure for change had been dissipated in the face of popular conservatism, an absence of necessary motivation among the teachers, a lack of government interest, and conflict among authorities claiming to control the schools: *parlements,* the royal administration, local authorities and the clergy. In the Habsburg dominions the government was more interested in education and more determined to achieve its objectives. Maria Theresa sought to elicit co-operation from the clergy and was hesitant about uni-lateral action. The expulsion of the Jesuits obliged the govern-ment to take action. The universities were encouraged to train civil servants, not scholars, the objective of education becoming knowledge useful for the secular state. The government strictly supervised intellectual life and established a system of approved examinations. In 1774 compulsory school education was intro-duced, while in the training of clerics stress was laid on the idea of 'pastoral theology', emphasising their pastoral rather than their spiritual or scholarly role.

The wealth as well as the financial and judicial immunities of the Church also inspired government action. Though many individual clerics and ecclesiastical institutions were poor, their collective wealth was considerable. At the beginning of the century, 22 per cent of Lombardy, the region that provided the initial stimulus to Habsburg monastic reform, belonged to the Church, and in the kingdom of Naples ecclesiastical income was as great as or greater than state revenues in the 1720s, though the Church probably had to support more buildings, personnel, institutions and social welfare. In Castile the Church owned about one-seventh of the grazing and farmland, the rise in agricultural prices and rents helping to keep clerical wealth buoyant. In Bavaria in 1764 the Church owned 56 per cent of the land, the elector only 15 per cent. Governments sought to prevent the churches acquiring more wealth and to tax them more effectively. The further extension of mortmain, the inalienable possession of land by the Church, was prohibited in a number of states including Bavaria (1704, 1764), France (1749), the Austrian Netherlands (1753), Austria and Venice (1767) and Naples (1769–72). In England the regulations were tightened up in 1736.

Concordats limited the fiscal privileges of the clergy. In many countries the clergy and their possessions were brought into a tax system more direct than that of voluntary or coerced corporate grants. The Russian church was particularly subject to government authority. When Patriarch Adrian died in 1700 his see was not filled, and, under the Spiritual Regulation of 1721, the Patriarch's authority and that of the church councils was vested in the Holy Synod, a clerical body under government control. In Catholic Europe claims for control in ecclesiastical matters were supported by traditional regalist arguments in, for example, France and Portugal, but the issue was not simply one of Church versus State. Many of the changes introduced by the state, such as the reduction of the number of feast days in many countries, including Austria and Naples, were advocated also by clerics, particularly those described as Jansenist. In 1780 the archbishop of Tours brought the Breton bishops together to co-ordinate the suppression of some local festivals. The interpenetration of Church and State, the far from unified nature of their respective corporate bodies and the great variety of issues debated ruled out any rigid institutional and ideological divide. The Catholic clergy were divided on Church government. 'Febronius', J. N. von Hontheim, vicar-general of the archbishop of Trier, in his *Present State of the church and the legitimate power of the Roman Pontiff* (1763), presented a limited view of the power of Rome. At Koblenz in 1769 and in the so-called Punctuation of Ems in 1786 the three German archbishop-electors challenged the authority of the papacy. Echoing traditional themes, they asserted that only a general council could wield supreme legislative and judicial power. Many clerics, while supporting the idea of a close Church–State relationship, had no rigid view of its practical nature, and aware of the fluid nature of ecclesiastical life in the second half of the century, they were prepared to accept significant changes.

In Catholic Europe there was a widespread aspiration for what was regarded as rational progress through practical religious and social action. It was argued that traditional and contentious delimitations of secular and ecclesiastical authority could be discarded in favour of a more sympathetic symbiosis of Church and State. In directing attention, in the modern phrase employed by scholars 'Enlightened Despotism', to the relationship between governments and secular intellectuals, many of whom were anticlerical, it is important not to ignore the relationship between 'reforming' governments and clerics, and the attempt to adjust the ideologies and practices of Church–State co-operation to new aspirations and circumstances. This was placed under considerable strain first by Joseph II and secondly by the Revolution. Religious issues and the Church played a major role in creating opposition to Joseph in the Austrian Netherlands and inspiring revolution there in 1789. The strength of the Church there was considerable, but so also was the extent to which Joseph's boldness and determination defeated attempts at compromise and made them appear increasingly implausible.

In France, clerics had played an important role in the political changes of the late 1780s. The *prélats politiques*, such as Brienne, portrayed themselves as supporters of generally beneficial reforms. The last General Assembly, that of 1788, supported the call for the summoning of the Estates General, and commitment to fiscal equality was very evident across the First (clerical) Estate in the spring of 1789. Religion was not a central issue in the *cahiers*: only 10 per cent called for the abolition of the tithe, 4 per cent for that of the regular clergy and 2 per cent for the sale of all church land. Many of the bishops held liberal political sympathies and were prepared to co-operate in the National Assembly's work of constitutional reform. The breakdown of the relationship between those who sought both reform in the Church and to make traditional teaching and practices relevant to a new age, and the secular reformers belongs to the history of the Revolution. However, the belief that clerical views must be subordinated to those of government was well developed before the breakdown occurred.

The Christian mission and the churches

The religious history of the period is not simply one of struggle and strife: conflicts with government, other ecclesiastical institutions, different faiths and those whose beliefs and practices did not accord with the views of the clergy. It is also necessary to draw attention to the general success of the churches in succouring their flocks and to the changes that they made in order to enable them to do so better. Administrative reorganisation was less significant than the education of the clergy. Outside Russia, the former was relatively insignificant in pre-revolutionary Europe. Dioceses and parishes remained very different in size, population and resources. However, there were some important changes, most obviously in connection with diocesan reorganisation. In Catholic Europe this was more a feature of the Habsburg dominions and Portugal, than of France, Italy and Poland. Vienna was raised to a metropolitanate in 1717, while the number of sees in Bohemia and Moravia was increased in 1754, and in Hungary in 1776–81. Joseph II did not share Maria Theresa's hesitations about consolidating the Galician bishoprics. Five new bishoprics were founded in Portugal in the 1770s. Four were founded in Spain to try to rationalise archaic boundaries.

The nature of property right in tithes and presentations made it difficult to envisage any major alterations in parochial structure. However, the principal weaknesses of the latter were often eased, as in Austria, by the activities of the regular clergy. Their missions played a particularly important role in Spain. The parochial structure was extremely archaic in Italy and Spain. In contrast, more than 800 new parishes were founded in the Austrian lands of the Empire with the proceeds of Joseph II's attack on the monasteries. The pace of ecclesiastical change before rising population was slowest in England. When the Commission for Building Fifty New Churches in London and Westminster, established in 1711, was abolished in 1758, owing to the inadequacy of its principal source of funds, the coal duty, it had authorised the construction of only 12 churches.

Much effort was devoted to improving clerical standards. In the 1730s Tsarina Anna founded 17 theological seminaries. In the second half of the century, particularly under the impetus of increased episcopal control, a major attempt was made to raise the standards of the Russian priesthood. Seminary education was developed, clerical drunkenness attacked. Elsewhere in Europe, much depended on the energy and views of individual bishops. The Council of Trent had required every bishop to establish a seminary, but many had not done so. Some rulers also played a role, the Habsburgs being prominent in this field. In 1733 every Hungarian bishop was instructed to establish a seminary. Whereas at the beginning of the century Hungarian priests were ordained after only one year's training, by mid-century four years were required. Under the educational reforms of 1777, which imposed a uniform structure on Hungarian education, decreeing the presence of an elementary school in every village and bringing all secondary schools and universities under the control of the Education Commission established in 1776, seminaries remained under diocesan control, but their curricula had to be approved by the Commission. In Spain, seminary education was inadequate, though the situation was improved after reforms ordered by Charles III in 1766, when new ones were founded and existing ones improved. Whereas there were 28 seminaries in 1747, there were another 18 fifty years later. In Galicia after the First Partition of Poland both Maria Theresa and Joseph II sought to raise the educational standards of the Catholic and the Orthodox clergy. The improvement of the seminary system was not sought only by secular rulers. Muratori advocated and Benedict XIV encouraged the foundation of new seminaries, as did the French bishops. In Poland a system of diocesan seminaries was established in the first half of the century and attendance at them was made compulsory for all candidates for the priesthood. Seminaries were supplemented by periodic spiritual conferences for the clergy, which were promoted in a number of countries, including France and Spain.

The quality of the parochial clergy varied enormously, as did their relations with the laity. In some areas, such as Alsace, there is evidence that the seminary system succeeded in improving the parochial clergy. In others, however, such as Portugal, standards appear to have remained low. Whatever the social origin of the priesthood, and few came from the peasantry, particularly the poor peasantry, their education and calling obviously differentiated them from their flock. A different background could cause tension, as in the diocese of Lyons, where the clergy sought to do away with some forms of popular religious activity, but a different social, geographical and educational background did not necessarily have this effect. It is easy to present a picture of a populace alienated from the clerical Estate by both the background and the financial prerogatives of the latter, and particularly, but not only, in Catholic Europe, by the consequences for popular religious practices of the clerical ascetic Christianity. There is no doubt that tension and disagreements existed. Not all complaints about tithes were directed against bishops, monasteries, chapters and the laity. The tithe and disputes over fees attached to church services, such as funerals, caused friction between numerous priests and all or some of their flocks. Tithe resistance could be widespread, as in the French diocese of Comminges in the 1780s. Equally, throughout Europe, attempts to regulate or limit traditional practices, such as images, pilgrimages, festivals and confraternities, led to protests, non-compliance, law suits and sometimes, as in Florence and Livorno in 1790, violence. Despite opposition, the peasants of Bresse in France persisted in their celebration of Midsummer's Night, combining the Catholic liturgy with pagan customs.

However, rather than reifying popular religion and contrasting it with that of the church, it is necessary to note the relative adaptability and amorphousness of the former. Furthermore, the individual churches were less rigid in practice than they might appear in precept. In leading their flocks and enforcing religious teaching over difficult issues, such as usury, contraception and Sunday observance, priests were accustomed to exercising discretion. Many were keen to encourage popular religious feeling and practices. Catholic use of the vernacular increased. In Slovakia the church used Slovak for the less understood parts of the Mass, as well as peasant instruments and peasant melodies. The pastoral experience of the clergy – isolated individuals, who wished to lead their parishioners – was more important than the denunciation of 'superstitious' practices by intellectuals and some of the clerical hierarchy. Furthermore, many pilgrimages, cults and holidays were not suppressed. In Alsace pilgrimages and old cults, such as that of St Odile, the patroness of the region, continued, a populace that was far from de-christianised being served by a clergy that was little interested in Enlightenment ideas. Popular culture continued its long and varied interaction with Christianity, more successfully so than the attempt in the 1790s to create a religion from the utopianism of the French Revolution.[19]

The criticisms advanced by reformers, enthusiasts and *philosophes* were not without substance. In most parts of Europe the established churches appeared unable to overcome weaknesses in their ministry. Areas of expanding population, as in England, and rural regions where parishes lacked incumbents, as in Spain, sometimes posed insuperable problems. Much church wealth was not applied to the cure of souls. Reforming clerics who co-operated with rulers often found that the latters' conception of the purposes of reform was secular. The very nature of established churches that sought to minister to all, in an age when religion was a social obligation as well as a personal spiritual experience, posed problems for some of those, both clergy and laity, who decried anything that might compromise this spiritual experience. Believers sure of their faith could find the compromises of national uniformity abhorrent. Dissatisfaction, however, reflected the importance of religion, the churches and the clergy. Few believed that they could or should be dispensed with. Disputes and criticism should not distract attention from their context, the symbiotic relationships of faith and reason, Church and State, clergy and laity, religion and the people.

7 Enlightenment

There is not a Sicilian in the polite circle, but can ask you how you do in three languages, talk of Newton and Descartes; tell you that Theocritus was their countryman, and Palermo once called Panormus; but this their knowledge is to such a wonderful degree superficial ... the men seem universally to affect a tone of society foreign to their real characters, their dress, their manner, their conversation ever put me in mind of poor tinselled strolling players, who were delivering a speech of fustian or humour, with all the affectation of outrageous theatrical grimace, the meaning of which they themselves understood not.

(Sir William Young, 1772)[1]

Much of the eighteenth century is often referred to as the Enlightenment or the Age of Enlightenment. Frequent reiteration does not make these terms any easier to define. This has become more difficult as attention has turned away from a concentration on the writings of a small number of French thinkers to an assessment of the situation throughout Europe. The political, social and religious setting varied in different states, and it is not therefore surprising that statements advanced with reference to prominent thinkers in France are inappropriate for Italy and Scotland, Russia and the Empire. Even in France the views of those generally classed as Enlightened were far from uniform. Furthermore, Enlightened thinkers were generally challenged by writers who would rank as intellectuals but who did not share their views.

The Enlightenment could be described as a tendency, rather than a movement, a tendency towards critical enquiry and the application of reason. However, though questioning of assumptions and practices was an obvious characteristic of those deemed Enlightened, it is also the case that, as with others who proclaim the value of reason, *a priori* assumptions played a major role and the conclusions to which reason should lead were generally circumscribed by the intellectual preferences and methods of the reasoners. These varied in accordance with individual views and national circumstances.

Reason was a goal as well as a method of Enlightenment thinkers. They believed it necessary to use reason, uninhibited by authority and tradition, in order to appreciate man, society and the universe and thus to improve human circumstances, an objective in which utilitarianism and the search for individual happiness could combine. Some thinkers, especially Frenchmen and members of some religious minorities, believed that existing authorities were an active restraint on the quest of reason and adopted critical views accordingly, but such a clash was untypical. Reason was believed to be the distinguishing mark of man, the insane therefore being generally regarded as a form of monster and treated like wild beasts with the discipline of the whip. Reason was believed to be a characteristic not only of the human species, but also of human development and social organisation. Though Rousseau argued that society multiplied man's problems, it was commonly argued that man and the human mind had progressed. The savage mind was held to be wild, enveloped in lurid fantasy and obsessed by a world of terror, in which monstrous anxieties were projected onto nature. Thus, the furies and gorgons of ancient Greece could be seen as the product of men with undeveloped reason. In the eighteenth century, it was believed that reason had freed men from unnecessary fears and could continue to do so. Newton had demonstrated that comets were integral to nature, not portents. The historical development of man through reason was held to be a continuing process, but it could also be shown through the education of wild men, children living in the wild, or 'savages', who could be thus civilised. In his pioneering anthropological study which influenced Rousseau, *Customs of the American Savages Compared with the Customs of the Earliest Times* (1724), the French Jesuit Joseph Lafitau, who had spent some of the 1710s among the Iroquois, presented the American Indians as a living model of human society in its primitive form. It was argued that reason aided human development by helping man to explore, understand and shape his environment, and that this was facilitated by a reliance on objective fact, scepticism and incredulity.

Theoretically this was a radical position, and some thinkers advanced claims that indeed challenged views that were widely held, not least by prominent members of the Enlightenment. The existence and radicalism of an Enlightenment movement were discerned by critics. In 1759 the *Parlement* of Paris was informed by the attorney-general, Joly de Fleury, that there existed 'a Society organised ... to propagate materialism, to destroy religion, to inspire a spirit of independence and to nourish the corruption of morals'. This was blamed on works such as the *Encyclopédie*, whose privilege was accordingly revoked by the government. However, a striking feature of the writings of most Enlightenment figures was their ability to reconcile their theoretically universalist and subversive notions of reason with the particular circumstances of their countries and positions and with the suppositions of traditional authorities.

Religion proved an obvious instance of this. The prerogatives, pretensions and personnel of the churches were criticised by many. The clergy could be seen as the intellectual heart of a conspiracy dedicated to limiting human progress and the views of Enlightened thinkers. The Middle Ages, generally condemned as sunk in ignorance due to the dominance of the church, were held to substantiate this view. Nevertheless, much of the criticism of clerics and of ecclesiastical practices and pretensions should be placed in the perspective of vigorous debates among believers about these matters. If Enlightenment figures attacked the Jesuits, so did the Jansenists. Reason led few to attack Christianity itself. Instead, Reason was believed to support the established procedures of Christianity, not least in opposition to the claims of religious enthusiasts, such as the French Prophets. Clergy were often at the forefront of Enlightenment thought. Reason could be used to confirm revelation. If the Scottish philosopher David Hume, in his *Essay on Miracles* (1748), challenged their existence, Thomas Sherlock, an Anglican bishop, was able, in his *Trial of the Witnesses of the Resurrection* (1729), to come to an opposite conclusion. The limited impact of scepticism was indicated in 1751 when widespread anxieties arising from English earthquakes led Hume's publisher to delay the second edition of his *Philosophical Essays*. Most intellectuals shared the view of the English radical and rationalist philosopher John Locke (1632–1704) that a rational appreciation of man's situation would lead people to be Christians. By treating reason as a divine gift and the universe as a divine creation, they established a framework in which observation need not be viewed as hostile to faith. Far from being compromises with tradition and religion, these views reflected the attempts of pious men in a religious society to comprehend the achievements and possibilities of scientific discoveries.

Some radical thinkers adopted materialist and psychological notions that left little role for divine action. It was also possible to advance ethical views that owed little directly to Christianity. The rejection of the idea of original sin in the name of original goodness by, for example, Rousseau, challenged the notion of divine grace. However, such challenges to Christian teaching, as opposed to Christian teachers, were few, and though the optimism of some Enlightenment figures might appear to suggest ideas of the perfectibility of man, it was far from widespread. Certain writers believed in progress. Others, impressed by the fall of Rome, propounded cyclical theories. Few had any interest in such Christian ideas of history as millenarianism, but, in this, they were little different from many, though by no means all, church leaders. In addition, if Enlightenment figures propounded the possibility and virtues of secular improvement their optimistic hopes were centred on the action of national institutions and laws, rather than on the mass of the population who were regarded by most thinkers as mentally unimprovable.

The contradictions among Enlightenment figures, indeed in the writings of particular individuals, are readily apparent. If there were pessimistic and optimistic strains, there were also humanitarian, liberal, moral and totalitarian dimensions. This diversity makes it doubtful whether the search for the origins or chronology of Enlightenment is particularly helpful. The origins have been found in a reaction against Louis XIV among English, Dutch and French writers, in a reaction against the baroque, in the scientific revolution of the seventeenth century, and in a crisis of conscience at the end of that period. As the Enlightenment was a far from uniform tendency, rather than a movement, it is not surprising that a variety of sources operating over a long period can be discerned. The attempt to date and define a cause or set of causes is made even more difficult when the complex nature of seventeenth-century thought and culture is appreciated. Far from representing a reaction against a monolith, as some of its polemicists claimed, the Enlightenment reflected the diversity of earlier thought. As with so much in the eighteenth century, continuity in change is apparent.

Continuity was eased by the unsystematic nature of much Enlightenment thought. The crusading zeal of particular campaigns, for example against torture and against the Jesuits, was not matched by a consistent code, other than one expressed in generalities, such as tolerance and reason. These views were endorsed by writers propounding a range of often conflicting views. The political recommendations of prominent Enlightenment figures varied greatly, Voltaire's support for monarchical authority being greater than that of Montesquieu. Diderot's response to political problems varied considerably.

If the amorphousness and contrasts of Enlightenment thought made it easier to accommodate to varied circumstances, the role of personalities had a similar effect. In France, where the Enlightenment was a very public phenomenon, it was not so much ideas that were debated as those who propounded and denied them. The personal integrity of thinkers was a matter of great moment, and gossip was a central means for the creation and destruction of reputations. The particular intensity of the French Enlightenment owed much to the prominence of this public sphere and the consequent need to appeal for public support.

Bereft of the patronage of the crown, French writers had to seek that of the public. In doing so, they helped to call that public into existence and to define its identity.

It was in France that the search for public support and the belief that man could better understand his environment combined to produce the controversial scheme for a published compendium of knowledge. The *Encyclopédie* launched by Diderot and d'Alembert in 1751 was originally a project to translate Ephraim Chambers' *Cyclopaedia, or an Universal Dictionary of Arts and Sciences* (1728). It was transformed into a work of reference that was also a vehicle for propaganda for the ideas of the *philosophes*, the French thinkers who presented themselves as progressive and Enlightened. In his article *Encyclopédie*, Diderot wrote that by helping people to become better informed, such a work would at the same time help them become more virtuous and happier. The *Encyclopédie* was the most famous product of the French Enlightenment and an indication of the major interests of many of the *philosophes*. The last volumes of text were printed in 1765. Much of the *Encyclopédie* was written by Diderot, d'Alembert and the chevalier de Jaucourt, but a large number of writers contributed, including d'Holbach, Morellet, Rousseau, Turgot, Quesnay and Voltaire. Some of its articles might seem subversive, particularly in religious matters, though they were far less dangerous than much of the clandestine political literature circulating in this period. In *Autorité Politique*, which appeared in the first volume, Diderot advanced the principle of government by consent,

> No man has received from nature the right to command others. Liberty is a present from Heaven. ...If Nature has established any authority, it is paternal power. ...All other authority derives from some other origin. ... Power which comes from the consent of people supposes necessarily conditions which make its use legitimate, useful to society, advantageous to the republic and which restrains it within limits.

Like many major publishing ventures the first edition was produced by subscription. The process of subscription helped to enhance the collective nature of the project. It was not produced in response to a government's commission, though equally it was not sold to an anonymous mass market, such as bought the subsequent cheaper editions. The cost, equivalent to £50 in the British currency of the period, was such that the 3931 subscribers were necessarily fairly affluent. Later editions were less expensive, publishers exploiting a demand for a cheaper version by producing one with a smaller format, on paper of poorer quality and with fewer plates. The majority of the purchasers came from the traditional urban elite of professional men and officials, especially lawyers, rather than from merchants and manufacturers.

Increasing sales and new editions might suggest a gradual diffusion of the Enlightenment from the world of the Parisian Salons. However, it is clear that much book purchasing was eclectic and that the impact of the writings of the *philosophes* should not be exaggerated. They do not appear to have been read deeply by the Bordeaux *parlementaires*, whose libraries consisted largely of traditional works in law, history, theology and literature. Among the nobility of the Charolais, a rural part of Burgundy, some were aware of the world of Enlightenment, reading fashionable books and supporting advanced ideas, but the majority remained faithful to traditional notions, and displayed little interest in change, a preference reflected in their reading.

It would also be wrong to exaggerate the radicalism of the *philosophes*. They wished to Enlighten society, not to revolutionise it, and their Enlightenment was designed to realise the possibilities of man as a social creature by ending past practices that limited his usefulness and happiness and thus the efficiency of society. The attitude of most of the *philosophes* to the common people was harsh. They were concerned with their interests, but sought to improve their views, rather than heed or trumpet them. The people were often presented as ignorant, their beliefs the very antithesis of those of an Enlightened man. The lot of the peasantry was to be improved, in order to realise their capabilities and make them more useful and society wealthier. The peasantry would thus be happier, both more prosperous because of their improved efforts and free from primitive terrors because they were better educated. The call to better the position of the peasantry was not therefore akin to such other aspects of agricultural improvement as the selective breeding and care of animals, but the views of the peasantry were similarly of little interest. The language used to describe them was that used to discuss children or animals. Mercier de la Rivière presented the *peuple* as living in habitual delirium or madness. In *Émile*, Rousseau rejected the mores of the uneducated poor.

There was more interest in the poor from the 1760s. This was part of the turning of attention to domestic problems that followed the mid-century wars, but it also reflected growing concern about economic and social problems, especially agricultural productivity and poverty, and the reconsideration of educational goals and methods after the expulsion of the Jesuits. Frederick the Great was expressing a common theme in 1770 when he wrote of the need in Silesia to 'raise the common people from their stupidity and savagery'.[2] As with children, they were assumed to require guidance, stimulation and control, but they were believed capable of limited development only and this was thought to be all that was desirable. Joseph II wanted a literate population, but he wanted their education to be directed towards what was immediately useful. In France education was seen as a means for occupational training, economic utility and social control. Like Joseph II, the *philosophes* wanted education compatible with the prospects of its recipients, and these prospects were conceived of within the notion of a fundamentally unchanging society where the bulk of the population must live as poor workers. This education was to consist of vocational training, writing, reading and arithmetic, moral teaching and physical exercise. Entry to the upper levels of the educational system was to be restricted. Education that might undermine social harmony was considered dangerous and there was little notion of education as a right.

Thus writers who advanced ideas of community and popular sovereignty, and who saw natural law as justifying man's right to be free, were not democrats. Egalitarian ideas were advanced in utopian works, but Enlightenment writers, responding to their social environment, offered what appeared to them to be plausible. Their theme was essentially improvement, not radical change. Economic and social practices were to be made more productive and useful. The religious and political counterparts of this were toleration and the rule of law. Enlightenment writers wished to end the arbitrary nature of power and therefore pressed for virtue on the part of rulers and the rule of law. Liberty to them was obedience only to the legal actions of legally constituted authorities. All were to be equal before the law, but social inequality was regarded as natural and necessary. Property was seen as a right. The division of society into orders was regarded as natural. Few thought it illogical that Hungarian nobles or Virginian gentlemen should press for their liberties and employ the language of liberty, while maintaining what they saw as a benevolent tutelage over their serfs and slaves.

However, it would be misleading to suggest that Enlightenment views on political matters were uniform and that their impact was limited. The redefinition of just rule and a useful society which the *philosophes* sought, though with varying conclusions, had radical possibilities. So also had the satirical manner of some writers such as Voltaire, their campaigning causes and methods, and their criticisms of privileges such as feudal dues, which were attacked by Condorcet though collected by Voltaire.

This potential was not realised during the early decades of the French Enlightenment. Louis XIV's wars were followed, during the regency of the duke of Orléans (1715–23), by an upsurge in intellectual speculation and cultural vitality. Paris attracted talent and new works became fashionable. While the intellectual curiosity and energy of Parisian circles were maintained, different ideas and authors attracted attention during the century. The period up to the 1760s saw the *philosophes* grow in influence, with Voltaire's popularisation of Newton in the 1730s, Diderot's deistic works of the 1740s, and the *Encyclopédie*. By the 1760s the intellectual style of the *philosophes* was dominant in fashionable Parisian circles and the institutions of metropolitan culture were under their influence. Defined as a fashion and a clique, the French Enlightenment and the *philosophes* reached their peak in the 1760s. Their pretensions, real and supposed, offended many. In 1768 the young Genevan academic Horace Benedict de Saussure wrote of Marmontel, 'I recognised in him what I had been warned to expect in Parisian *beaux esprits* – a very arbitrary tone, a habit of speaking of his set as the only one to be called philosophic, and of despising and making odious insinuations against those who did not belong to it'.[3]

If the cliquishness of the *philosophes* offended many, not least the rising generation of writers who envied their position, their ideas were under challenge by the 1770s from new intellectual trends. To term these 'anti-Enlightenment' would be to confer a false unity on the Enlightenment, and to ignore the extent to which some of these trends were prefigured during the middle decades of the century. Moral nihilism and sentimentality had already been expressed by writers generally regarded as Enlightenment figures. New trends were apparent in the 1770s, especially the pre-Romanticism that appeared to reject balance, and the varied beliefs that did not accord with conventional rational expectations. However, they were less a stark challenge to the Enlightenment, than the product of the diverse and often incompatible ideas that had been given a false coherence by the cult of reason. Some of the new ideas represented a return to past notions, such as the revival in France in the 1780s of the belief that monsters were the product of maternal fantasies, an example of the decade's resurgence of interest in the power of the imagination.

Many of the *philosophes* died or their activities lessened in the 1770s and the new generation of writers and thinkers that rose to prominence, often with different interests, did not so much reject the arguments of the *philosophes* as adapt them to new circumstances, including an increasing sense that the French state would have to alter. This adaptation was helped by the very amorphousness of the Enlightenment. Such amorphousness aided the diffusion and adaptation of Enlightened notions, at the same time as they made it difficult to define.

In France the earlier criticism by the *philosophes* might be limited in its goals and muted by their close relationship with the upper reaches of society, and their prime assumptions – of the need to obey the Laws of Nature and to understand them through the use of natural faculties – might have little obvious political (as opposed to religious) import, but the *philosophes* were seen as critics by much of the old order. When the French government itself seemed to move towards new ideas in the 1770s with the policies of Maupeou and Turgot, ministerial policies aroused unease among many intellectuals. What appeared to be the physiocratic legal despotism of the government in 1771–4 clashed with liberal and radical positions that could also look to the central premises of the Enlightenment.

By the reign of the uncharismatic Louis XVI (1774–92) some Enlightenment figures were closely linked with the government, a process eased by the abandonment of the policies of the early 1770s. However, both they and the leading literary figures were attacked by a new generation of critics who, fired by poverty, envy, the absence of opportunities and their analysis of Rousseau, produced often lurid works that attacked established authorities and demanded change, without explaining how it was to be achieved in the absence of authority. The dissatisfaction which these critics expressed and exacerbated helped to accentuate the volatility of the 1780s. Like the *philosophes*, they exaggerated the possibilities of education and of man's social nature and neglected the difficulties of turning aspirations into policies, the problems of government, the vitality of popular religiosity and the disinclination of men to subordinate self-interest and their own notions of a just society to the self-righteousness of others. This neglect helped to produce confusion and frustration among many writers during the early years of the Revolution and to engender an attitude in which the creation and defence of a just society through terror seemed necessary. The roots of the Reign of Terror can be traced in the radical thought of the 1780s.

If the *philosophes* were commonly critical of the actions of established authorities in France, in most of Europe the relationship between the Enlightenment and authority was far closer. Governments sought the services of intellectuals. Many acted as officials or as academics in state educational institutions. Intellectuals sought to influence government policies. The extent to which this relationship developed varied by state, and it was not without its difficulties. Rulers might reject advice, intellectuals propound schemes that were impracticable. In addition, the relationship was not static, but was constantly redefined in the light of changing circumstances and the altering expectations of both rulers and intellectuals. For example Joseph II's arbitrary and autocratic methods produced disillusionment in the Habsburg dominions in the mid-1780s. Nevertheless, in much of Europe there was what has been described as the corporatist or state Enlightenment. This was especially the case in the Empire and in parts of Italy.

In the Empire the Enlightenment is known as the *Aufklärung*. This was defined by the Prussian philosopher Immanuel Kant (1724–1804) in 1784 as man's realising his potential through the use of his mind. This definition would not have offended the *philosophes* and they would have applauded the German stress on education. However, the close relationship between German intellectuals and governments would have surprised many Frenchmen, as would the relative absence of anti-clericalism. Kant stressed the creative role of the monarch, calling the Enlightenment 'Frederick's Century', a reference to Frederick the Great. In Catholic Germany, anti-clericalism centred on the distant papacy and to a lesser extent on the monastic orders. The secular clergy and religious belief itself were rarely scorned, and many of the prince-bishops were in the forefront of the movement for reform, not least in terms of the employment of intellectuals. This was true, for example, of the three ecclesiastical electorates in the 1780s, one of which, Cologne, was ruled by Joseph II's youngest brother Max Franz. There was little anti-clericalism in the German Protestant Enlightenment, the Church being seen, like the State, as a means of reform and education. Thus, the centre-piece of the Enlightenment in the electorate of Hanover, the University of Göttingen, which opened in 1737 with an emphasis on concrete subjects such as medicine and natural sciences rather than metaphysics, and with a library that was seen as performing a central function, owed much to support from the government and from officials. Protestant intellectuals stressed the role of the state. The mathematician and philosopher Gottfried von Leibniz (1646–1716), who became founder-president of the Berlin Academy of Science in 1700, and, believing in the unity of knowledge and the need for power to be guided by an intellectual elite, hoped to discover a universal scholarly language and to create harmony through mathematical and symbolic logic, was a Hanoverian official and publicist. Although in theory he believed in rule by the wise, in practice he supported hereditary monarchy and severely limited the right of resistance to it. Christian Thomasius (1655–1728), professor of jurisprudence at Halle from 1690, sought authority enlightened by reason. He condemned torture and trials for witchcraft and pressed for laws based on reason, but also argued that individual liberties were to be enjoyed only at the ruler's discretion.

Academics and officials played a major role in the German Enlightenment, helping to make government appear the crucial pivot of social activity. The large number of opportunities presented by the numerous governments of the Empire helped to provide employment for intellectuals. Intellectual capability and government service led to social advancement and state recognition in the Empire to a degree unknown in France. Not all intellectuals were equally satisfied and satisfactory. In the 1780s some of Kant's religious essays were refused publication by the Prussian censor, while at the time of the French Revolution he stressed the value of individual freedom and argued that serfdom was illegal. However, Kant was opposed to ideas of popular sovereignty and the general will and he accepted both the inegalitarian social hierarchy and the idea that dependants such as servants should not enjoy political rights. Because the accommodation of the Enlightenment to the authorities of the Empire was easier than in France, it is not surprising that German ideas proved influential in eastern Europe.

Catherine II was interested in the *philosophes*. In 1762, the year of her accession, she invited d'Alembert to take charge of the education of Grand Duke Paul, an invitation he refused, and she offered to allow the printing and publication of the *Encyclopédie* in Riga, though she rejected the suggestion of an edition in Russian. Voltaire corresponded with Catherine and presented her as a champion of the struggle with barbarism, ignorance, clericalism and the Catholic Church. Diderot received a pension from Catherine and visited her in 1773–4. However, Catherine sought publicity from the *philosophes*, rather than direction. She discouraged Voltaire from visiting Russia, and when Mercier de la Rivière met Catherine in 1768, he was disabused of his idea that he should serve her as a leading minister. Diderot unsuccessfully sought to persuade Catherine to implement his ideas and to keep the Legislative Commission in being as the 'depository of the laws' in Russia. His ideas did not provide the basis for realistic policies, even if Catherine had been willing to support them.

When they looked at foreign states, the *philosophes* tended to search for philosopher kings to provide patronage and implement their ideas. Voltaire saw Frederick the Great in this light. They were generally disappointed, a natural result of the failure to appreciate the views and circumstances of the monarchs they discussed. Frederick maintained political censorship. The naïveté of theorists was mocked. In his comedy *Damocles* (1741), the abbé Poney de Neuville presented a philosopher who had written the *Art of Reigning*, and believed that only a philosopher could govern wisely, that peace and happiness should be fostered and wars and taxes dispensed with. Given a chance to rule, he is a failure. The state is swept by war while Damocles curses the human race for opposing his plans.

The naïveté thus depicted reflected the gap between aspiration and the discussion of detailed policy that characterised many of the *philosophes*, in part because of the censorship restrictions that they had to consider when writing material for publication. Too often they ended up applauding what they would have criticised in France. In 1762 Diderot praised Pombal for his reforms and for his opposition to the Jesuits. The arbitrary and brutal nature of his policies was ignored.

In Italy intellectuals found support only under some rulers. Savoy-Piedmont (the kingdom of Sardinia), the Papal States, Tuscany under the last of the Medici, and Genoa were centres neither of new intellectual ideas nor of the employment of intellectuals in the service of the government. In 1737 Clement XII tried to prevent the erection of a mausoleum to Galileo in the Florentine church of St Croce. The centres of *Illuminismo* (the Italian Enlightenment) were Naples, Milan, Tuscany under Leopold and a number of the smaller states, especially Modena and Parma. Much depended on particular intellectual traditions and political and cultural circumstances. Interest in new philosophical ideas and a measure of anti-clericalism characterised many of the thinkers. The development and application of new ideas in practical spheres, such as the economy, penal reform and education, attracted attention, with writers such as Beccaria, Galiani and Genovesi prominent. Other writers tackled more theoretical topics. Both Muratori and Vico discussed the nature of historical development. Giambattista Vico (1668–1744), professor of rhetoric at Naples, emphasised the historical evolution of human societies in his *Scienza nuova* (*New Science*, 1725) and advanced a cyclical theory of history.

The sense of continuity with the past in the historical theory of Vico formed an obvious contrast with the attitude of many of the *philosophes*. They both disparaged much of the past, the Middle Ages for being barbaric, the age of the Reformation for being fanatical, and the reign of Louis XIV for its supposed obsession with *gloire*, and found that history could not provide the logical principles and ethical suppositions that were required to support the immutable laws they propounded. However, Vico's interest in history was in no way exceptional. Historical research was well developed in England where scholars studied both the Anglo-Saxon period and the more recent past, the seventeenth century being a particular focus of discussion and research. In the Empire historiographical traditions of imperial reform, imperial history and Latin humanism were very much alive. The Sicilian clergyman Rosario Gregorio used scholarly methods to challenge false views of the medieval past of the island. In Sweden, Olof von Dalin wrote a scholarly *History of Sweden* which was commissioned by the Estates and refuted the Gothicist myths of Sweden's early history. Sven Lagerbring introduced a criticism of source material into Swedish history. Alongside the notion of history as *belles-lettres* or 'philosophy teaching by example', propounded by Voltaire and Bolingbroke, there was a strong interest in the idea of an impartial enquiry into the past. This left little role for divine intervention. In France historians replaced the customary view of Clovis as a miracle-working royal saint by that of a royal legislator.

Many of the great British writers were historians. The Scottish cleric William Robertson (1721–93) acquired a European reputation with his works, which were praised by Catherine II, D'Holbach and Voltaire, he being elected to academies in Madrid, Padua and St Petersburg. Robertson was a thorough researcher, noting in the preface to his *History of the Reign of Charles V*, 'I have carefully pointed out the sources from which I have derived information.' David Hume (1711–76), who argued in his *Treatise of Human Nature* (1738) that only impressions definitely existed and that it was impossible to prove the existence of the mind and the nature of causality, was best known in his lifetime as the author of a *History of England*. Edward Gibbon (1737–94), the author of the *Decline and Fall of the Roman Empire* (1776–88), attributed the fall in large part to the rise of Christianity. The degenerate empire was contrasted with the vigour of the barbarian invaders. The notion of the inexorable fall of a great civilisation was pessimistic, but the work was a masterpiece of scholarship and scepticism. The great critic of the French Revolution, Edmund Burke (1729–97), wrote an unpublished *Essay towards an Abridgement of the English History* (1757–60) which ascribed the development of human society to Providence's role in providing suitable conditions.

This strong interest in the past reflected a sense that it had shaped the present, and a concern with organic development that is not always associated with Enlightenment thinkers. Though many writers advanced theoretical ideas from general principles, whether in the fields of philosophy, politics or psychology, there was also a concern with the social context and with the relationship between theory and practice. Thinkers were as much concerned with discovery, whether through exploration, observation or historical study, as with speculation, and though the nature and closeness of the relationship varied by individual and subject, it was crucial to the development and application of Enlightenment ideas. A sense of the transforming possibilities of time invited attention not only to the past, but also to the prospect of future change.

Publications were the main channel through which new ideas were diffused. The book trade and the network of correspondents that lay behind scholarly journals provided the channels for ideas, and both became more active. The corollary of the publications were the societies, ranging from the informality of coffee-houses to organised academies, that discussed ideas. Informal networks of learned sociability preceded institutions. Clubs and institutions, from the subscription concert to the Masonic lodge, were a popular feature of cultural and intellectual life, the corporatist spirit being central in many spheres of eighteenth-century society. The great metropolitan academies were copied by provincial academies, which were especially numerous in France. French provincial academies sponsored essay competitions on topical subjects that attracted numerous entries, such as Grégoire's on Jewish emancipation for the Academy of Metz in 1787. The Royal Academy of Science, Inscriptions and Belles-Lettres of Toulouse, founded in 1746, offered courses for the general public and published several volumes of *Mémoires*, besides possessing a botanical garden and an observatory. Though it devoted most of its energy to assimilating and disseminating knowledge reported from elsewhere, principally Paris, it gave a major secular impetus to the intellectual life of the region, enabling the local elite to adapt to new ideas and informing the public of scientific developments, such as the principles of Newtonian physics and the discoveries in astronomy. Its members were 27.5 per cent nobles, 18 per cent clerics and the rest bourgeois, especially doctors and lawyers. This was no rising capitalist bourgeoisie. In the Empire and the United Provinces, scientific and literary societies and reading clubs helped to foster a cultural identity among their members. Many admitted members without regard to rank or religion. Not all the societies founded lasted or served more than social purposes, though the idea that sociability should be linked to the furtherance of knowledge was itself important. Many German societies failed to outlast their founders. The Societas Incognitorum Eruditorum, founded in 1746 in Olomouc in Moravia by Joseph Baron Petrasch for the propagation of learning, failed because of a lack of sufficient local government support. Where national cultural institutions and foci were weak or absent, as in Wales, the spread of new ideas was also hindered. Whatever the nature of the cultural institutions, the limited literacy of the bulk of the population necessarily restricted the spread of ideas through print. The ability to sign one's name as an indication of literacy is a poor guide. Two more detailed surveys carried out in the areas of Arras and St Omer in northern France in 1802 and 1804 revealed that hardly 35–40 per cent of the men were reckoned as knowing how to read and write and fewer than 5 per cent of the rural population were considered well educated. It appears that the ability to read and write was considered a skill necessary to some but useless to most, who required only the capacity to sign.

But the spread of new ideas was not simply a matter of the existence of the necessary channels of communication. The vitality and applicability of traditional views and their capacity for development were such that in much of Europe the Enlightenment can best be seen either as the import and sometimes grafting of new fashions, or, indeed, as largely the product of the development of indigenous thought. Enlightenment has been discerned in a variety of countries, such as Portugal and the lands of modern Romania, in a manner that would have surprised the *philosophes*. It is more appropriate in some cases to note the coincidence and in some spheres congruence of new and traditional ideas and to be cautious in regarding the former as necessarily alien to the latter or as defining an Enlightenment. If Enlightenment is taken to mean new secular ideas, specifically the application of reason to knowledge, then the term could be applied across the continent, but it becomes so devoid of specific meaning as to be unhelpful as a term of analysis. In the United Provinces, the centre of European publishing and the country where many of the works of the *philosophes* were printed, the local Enlightenment was essentially a continuation of the erastianism and relative political and religious toleration of the previous age, but one that was illuminated by a continued belief in Christian revelation which led Diderot to present the Dutch as superstitious. There were few Dutch Deists and most of the scientific advances were presented within a framework of natural theology. Books regarded as attacks upon religion were banned, such as Diderot's *Pensées Philosophiques* (1746), a deistic and sceptical work that defended the passions, attacked superstition, preferred reason to revelation and cast doubts on miracles, and La Mettrie's *L'Homme Machine* (1748), which denied that man had a soul. La Mettrie, already exiled from France, was expelled from the United Provinces in 1748 and went to Berlin where he was welcomed by Frederick the Great. There was little new or distinctive about the Dutch Enlightenment and it is not clear that the phrase is a particularly helpful one.

The same is true of Spain, where French influences and the writings of a small number of intellectuals, several of whom were officials, had only a scant impact. The Swedish envoy Count Creutz claimed in 1765, 'most of Europe wallows still in shameful ignorance. The Pyrenees in particular are the barriers to the enlightened world. Since I have been here it has seemed to me that the people are ten centuries behind.'[4] Though this jaundiced view scarcely did credit to the efforts of Charles III (1759–88), and though the succeeding decades were to see a growth in secular intellectual activity associated with officials such as Campomanes and Jovellanos, it was, nevertheless, the case that Spain had neither the sophisticated reading public and density of unofficial cultural institutions of France, nor the integration of intellectual and official activity of the Empire. The Spanish church was far more hostile to new ideas than many French and German clerics and some of the leading Spanish preachers attacked them bitterly.

New ideas were most successful when adopted by officials and thus related to prevailing political, social and intellectual circumstances. In Poland it was the Catholic priest Stanislaus Konarski (1700–73) who was probably most instrumental in encouraging change. In 1740 he organised in Warsaw the *Collegium Nobilium*, a school for the nobility which prepared its pupils for public office and where the idea of political and economic reform was discussed. With papal permission, he later extended his programme into all schools maintained by the Piarist Order. After Stanislaus Augustus Poniatowski became king in 1764, Konarski's views became more influential. In 1773 a Commission of National Education was established, the first European state agency in charge of education. Textbooks which accommodated new ideas were produced. The *Introduction to Physics* (1784) by the German mathematician, physicist and geographer Johannes Hube presented science as a means to enable man to exploit the earth's natural resources. Hube advocated experiments as a basic part of instruction and of testing the presented information. Hube's *Mechanics* (1792) explained physical laws on the basis of experimental and rational premises.

A special characteristic of the Polish Enlightenment was the establishment of new educational and political institutions, though caution is necessary in attributing much to a distinct Enlightenment. Many of the nobles who were prominent in their support for new intellectual tendencies were opposed to political change, and the roots of educational reform can be traced to two religious orders, the Piarists and the Jesuits.

Indeed the source of much that is described as Enlightenment can actually be traced to religious institutions and movements, many of them deriving their impetus from seventeenth-century developments. More generally, the importance of seventeenth-century thinkers for eighteenth-century thought is readily apparent whether Jansenism, the German Natural Law tradition, Lockean psychology, Newtonian physics, international law, or Deism are considered. Conscious of a shift in early eighteenth-century France from the dominance of Cartesian thought and the assertiveness of Louis XIV, the *philosophes* under-rated the continuity in French and general European thought. If some writers, especially in France, Scotland and Naples, defined their concepts in reaction to the past, most did not, and those who stressed change often used the ideas of the past.

The situation in Poland and the varied perceptions of it by intellectuals in other countries are a reminder of the problems attending the use of the term Enlightenment. Ideas and intellectuals were not distinct from society. The cosmopolitan nature of the Republic of Letters, and the similarity of metaphors such as *lumières* and Enlightenment, encouraged both contemporary and modern commentators to exaggerate the role of common traits and to under-rate the importance of distinct national characteristics and intellectual traditions. In essence, it is the diversity of eighteenth-century thought that is really impressive. People asked different questions, used various methods and arrived at different answers. The process of questioning and answering may be referred to as Enlightenment, but only if its diversity and the difficulty of too closely defining it is appreciated. Yet, if a shift is to be discerned it is towards an increasing interest in change. This rested on a sense that stability itself was not a cause of happiness, but rested also on an increasing view that the process and consequences of change were themselves valuable and could be planned, moulded and forwarded by mankind. The future was seen as open-ended, the ultimate goal of history defined for many in secular terms rather than with reference to paradise.

8 Culture and the Arts

Any summary of the rich variety and complexity of European culture in this period encounters the problem of describing changes in style, particularly since these developments can be perceived fully only through an appreciation of specific texts, objects or performances. The most common approach is to discuss developments in terms of a shift from baroque to rococo soon after the beginning of the century, with a subsequent neoclassical reaction against rococo and baroque from the 1760s onwards, and a little later in Scandinavia and the Empire, especially southern Germany. In addition, elite and popular culture are generally defined in contrasting terms, while different sources of cultural and stylistic influence, whether particular nations, or social, intellectual or religious groups, are seen as competing.

There was certainly a rhetoric of competition and an occasional polemical war of styles, but, in general, it would be mistaken to stress conflict. The co-existence of different influences and styles is more apparent than their clashes, even though public criticisms were part of the establishment of an identity for newer styles, while the appropriateness of the accepted stylistic vocabulary in describing the wide variety of European cultural activity is open to question. A vocabulary or chronology that might suit Parisian portraiture is not necessarily appropriate for Venetian opera, and it is not simply a matter of suggesting that some countries, arts or artists were in advance of others. If common themes can be discerned in some fields it is more appropriate to write in terms of stylistic tendencies, rather than to suggest that distinct uniformities can be discerned. The tentative nature of much writing on cultural matters, particularly on the subjects of artistic influences and intentions, inspires additional caution.

Patronage

It is possible to discern several important sources of patronage and artistic market-places, though it would be inappropriate to suggest that they were necessarily distinct and unrelated. The situation varied not only by artistic form, the churches featuring as patrons of music but not of novels, but also by area. In western

Europe, where political units, with the obvious exception of Ireland, tended to be relatively homogeneous, linguistically and religiously, the middling orders quite large, education relatively widespread and literacy rates comparatively high, the various sources of patronage were more closely related than they were in eastern Europe, where education and literacy were less widespread, the middling orders smaller, and ethnic, religious and linguistic differences more pronounced both between different social groups and within individual regions.

Courts and aristocracies

The greatest individual patrons were the monarchs. Royal and court patronage of the arts was of considerable political significance. Monarchs created for their courts settings of splendour and elegance that were designed to enhance their prestige, and were also significant patrons in other fields. Royal interests and activities inspired many artists. Traditional triumphalism was particularly associated with military victories. In 1734 Johann Sebastian Bach (1685–1750), *cantor* at the Thomasschule in Leipzig (Saxony) from 1723 until his death, produced cantatas to commemorate the Polish victories of Augustus III. The Parisian painter Charles Parrocel (1688–1752) served for a year in the French army, and having followed Louis XV on his 1745 campaign, exhibited the following year ten paintings of Louis's victories. Aleksandr Sumarokov (1717?–77), appointed director of court music and theatre to Catherine II in 1769, wrote an ode that year which stressed the human cost of the Russo-Turkish war, but by 1775 was offering extravagant praise of Catherine's military success. The palace of Peterhof, built for Peter the Great after the plans of the French architect J.-B. Alexandre Le Blond (1679–1719), was altered in the 1770s by Iuril Fel'ten to provide a setting for sixteen paintings depicting Russian naval victories in the Aegean in 1769–72, the work of the German Philipp Hackert (1737–1807) and the Briton Richard Paton (1717–92). Though not connected with a military victory, the comte d'Angiviller, appointed Directeur Général des Bâtiments in France in 1774, planned to turn the royal palace of the Louvre into a grand public museum designed to encourage national patriotism.

Architecture was a major field of royal patronage, the desire of monarchs for a range of buildings, including impressive palaces, hunting lodges, opera houses and military and government buildings, being matched by an ability to command the necessary funds, labour and artistic skill. Emulation played an important role. Louis XIV's palace of Versailles, a display of and stage for monarchical power,[1] also indicated the opportunities offered by building on open land, rather than in a city. It was followed by a large number of palaces, including Schönbrunn, near Vienna, begun for Leopold I in 1695; the town palace of Stockholm, begun in 1697 to replace the recently burnt down royal castle; and Berlin, begun in 1701 to mark the new royal status of the House of Brandenburg. Other rulers followed, Augustus II of Saxony beginning the Zwinger palace at Dresden in 1709, while, following French style rather than the Habsburg models that had influenced his predecessors,[2] Max Emanuel of Bavaria rebuilt Nymphenburg outside Munich. The prince-bishop of Würzburg began an enormous Residenz in 1719. The Sicilian architect Filippo Juvarra (1678–1736), who had been brought to Turin in 1714 by Victor Amadeus II, rebuilt the Piedmontese palaces of Venaria Reale and Rivoli, made additions to the royal palace in Turin, and in 1729–33, built a pleasure palace and hunting seat at Stupinigi outside the capital for Victor Amadeus. Aside from the construction of new palaces, monarchs also rebuilt old ones, their changes frequently reflecting stylistic shifts. For Victor Amadeus's mother, Juvarra produced a superb façade with a grand ceremonial staircase across the front of the old Palazzo Madama in Turin (1718), a prototype for later work in central and eastern Europe. George I had Kensington Palace expanded. In the 1780s Friedrich Karl of Mainz rebuilt the interiors of his palace at Mainz and his castle at Aschaffenburg in the latest style.

Monarchs seeking to beautify their palaces patronised a range of arts, including landscape gardening, painting and the production of splendid objects. Much effort was devoted to palace grounds. The formal gardens of Versailles were the dominant, though not the only, model. When in 1701 Max Emanuel began to lay out the gardens at Nymphenburg he summoned a Parisian expert, Carbonet, followed by another, Girard, in 1715. From 1769 onwards Max III Joseph of Bavaria added statues on classical themes and large marble vases at Nymphenburg. Towards the end of the century the English landscape garden became fashionable, Friedrich Karl of Mainz creating one around his *château* of Schönbusch.

Townscapes were also created or altered to add impact to palaces. The avenues of the town of Versailles converged on the palace, and a similar effect was achieved for Karl Wilhelm of Baden-Durlach's new palace at Karlsruhe, begun in 1715, and for the Spanish palace at Aranjuez. Magnificent without, palaces were also intended to be splendid within. They provided opportunities for a large number of craftsmen, who produced bronzes, frescoes, medals, furniture, tapestries, mosaics, ivories and porcelain, as well as more transient products and performances, such as clothes, festivals and theatrical productions and sets. Giambattista Tiepolo (1696–1770) and his son Giandomenico painted for the Würzburg Residenz the Kaisersaal, for which they received the enormous sum of 10,000 Rhenish florins, as well as painting the fresco over the great staircase in 1750–3.

The interest of rulers in the arts varied greatly. It has been argued that 'the artistic taste of Louis XVI would scarcely sustain a thesis'.[3] It is certainly true that Louis did not devote personal attention comparable to that of Louis XIV, though this was, in part, compensated for by the efforts of the relevant officials, the activities of government being too varied to depend on the constant attention of one man. Even when monarchs were not noted for their artistic interests, the established routine of court festivities and embellishment of palaces helped, in general, to ensure that portraits were painted, furniture and porcelain purchased, operas and theatricals staged. Royal events, such as accessions, were commemorated and celebrated. When a dauphin was born in 1729 the French ambassador in Rome held a fête, and a concert that was in turn painted by Giovanni Paolo Pannini. When Joseph II was married in 1765 Christoph Gluck (1714–87) wrote an opera and a ballet, both on classical themes. Handel produced and conducted the coronation anthems for the coronation of George II, Mozart played his Coronation piano concerto at the coronation of Leopold II. Conversely, artistic life suffered during royal absences or periods of mourning.

Many monarchs were great patrons of ecclesiastical art, architecture and music, John V of Portugal expending great sums on the monastery-church of Mafra, while Victor Amadeus II began work in 1717 on a huge church at Superga to commemorate his victory at nearby Turin in 1706. Behind the church, which dominates the Turin skyline, a monastery was built that was designed to serve as the mausoleum for the dynasty, the monks offering perpetual prayers for their salvation. The basilica, consecrated in 1727, was a triumph for Juvarra. Though the building of great churches, which served as the setting for major royal events, particularly coronations and weddings, was the most obvious example of royal patronage of ecclesiastical art, many monarchs were also generous patrons of existing foundations, and, for example, commissioned much church music. A shift in religious sensibility in some Catholic courts away from the exuberant, ostentatious religiosity of the late seventeenth century had artistic consequences. Not all the Catholic monarchs of the 1780s would have been eager to commission a reliquary to hold a saint's skull, as Cosimo III of Tuscany had done in 1703 for Saint Cresci, though Maria I of

Portugal, who ruled from 1777 until her son John assumed power in 1792 as a result of her insanity, built a basilica at Estrela. More generally, cultural patronage was an example of the influence of religion among the elite.

Many members of the royal circle were also active patrons of the arts. Philip duke of Orléans, regent in 1715–23 for the young Louis XV, had close links with prominent men of letters, several of whom, including Voltaire, he sponsored. Voltaire's epic poem the *Henriade* was designed to appeal to Orléans, both because Henry IV was Orléans's esteemed ancestor and because the poem offered a parallel between the situations of the two men, while praising enlightened and monarchical rule and condemning fanaticism and aristocratic anarchy. Orléans also supported the royal library and was closely associated with the development of what was to become known as the regency style, the French rococo, an essentially ornamental, elegant and light style. The move from Versailles to *hôtels* in Paris was a trend set by Orléans which, in turn, promoted investment in quality rococo interiors among the aristocracy. Madame de Pompadour was another great patron from 1745, when she became royal mistress, until her death in 1764. She supported the pastoral painter François Boucher (1703–70) and sculptors such as Étienne-Maurice Falconet and Jean-Baptiste Pigalle. Her brother, later the marquis de Marigny, as Directeur des Bâtiments (1746–73), was an active sponsor of the arts, giving Claude-Joseph Vernet (1714–89) the royal commission to paint the ports of France. In these mid-century works, reproduced in engravings, Vernet introduced the world of work into court art. In 1748 an art school, the École Royale des Élèves Protégés, was established with royal approval.

It was not only in France that rulers and their favourites were prominent patrons. This was particularly the case in small states where the court had greater proportional social influence, both in the Empire and in Italy. Frederick II of Hesse-Cassel launched a major building programme in Cassel after the Seven Years War, rebuilding the palace and endowing it with a French garden and Chinese and classical Greek motifs, as well as building a new opera house. By the late 1770s, 70 different operetta productions, using many Parisian and Italian performers, were being staged every year. In both content and form, the particular character of the Florentine baroque was mainly the consequence of the interests of the Medici. Cosimo III sent artists to Rome for their training, while his elder son Ferdinand (1663–1713), a sensitive patron of the arts, was very keen on opera, supporting Handel and Alessandro Scarlatti. In 1740 the Teatro Regio was opened by Charles Emmanuel III in Turin. Designed for opera, it was reserved for the court and privileged individuals.

Another sphere in which monarchs were important patrons was the institutionalisation of secular culture. Academics either required or sought royal patronage, whose importance derived often from the privileges that could be offered. Many monarchs, keen to act and appear as patrons, were willing to offer sponsorship. The Danish Royal Academy of Art was founded by Frederick V in 1754. In 1786 Gustavus III both reorganised the Academy of Letters, founded in 1753, and founded a Swedish Academy devoted to Swedish language and literature, himself selecting the first members, including the leading poets of the period.

If the role of monarchs as sources of money and privileges furthered their cultural influence, there were several other spheres in which they were important without necessarily dominating the activities in their countries. Large-scale musical works, both vocal and instrumental, required numerous performers, and if these were to be professionals, this could be expensive. The chapel of Joseph-Clément, archbishop-elector of Cologne, included ordinarily between 1716 and 1722, 17 or 18 vocalists and 18 instrumentalists, a total number that rose to 50 for important occasions. Aside from 23 trumpeters, drummers and hautboy players the British court included 24 musicians and a 'Master of Musick', while George I's subscription to the Royal Academy of Music, founded in 1719–20 in large part with his assistance, was £1000 annually. The German composer George Frederick Handel (1685–1759) received a salary of 1000 taler on his appointment in 1710 (after four years of study in Italy) as kapellmeister to George as elector of Hanover. He was awarded £200 annually for life by Queen Anne of Britain as a reward for his birthday ode of 1713 and his thanksgiving ode for the Treaty of Utrecht. Karl Eugen of Württemberg built the largest opera house in Europe at Ludwigsburg in 1750, patronised musicians, such as the Italian violinist-composer Pietro Nardini (1722–93), and in 1750 founded a court opera company, with a substantial orchestra, under the directorship of the Italian Nicolo Jomelli. Creative artists in music, architecture and landscape gardening could not break away from patronage, as writers and artists – at least in some genres – could.

If music, particularly opera, was an established form of court entertainment, so also was drama. Actors in Madrid were expected to perform at court at a moment's notice.[4] The Viennese theatres during the reign of Maria Theresa were royal property, and in 1776 Joseph II sought to help German drama by ordering that the Burgtheater in Vienna was to be used exclusively for it and would be called the Nationaltheater. Catherine II wrote a number of works, including a comic opera satirising Gustavus III, which she had performed in her private theatre in 1788, and an operatic ballet performed in 1791, which implied that she was the heir to a Russian prince who had led a successful attack on the Byzantine Empire in 900. The secular Russian theatre was a creation of the mid-century, after the failure of attempts made under Peter the Great, and it benefited from royal patronage. In all countries and arts where censorship operated, as in the Russian theatre, the patronage or at least approval of the royal government was important, and court politics often played a role in such matters.

The role of the greater nobility in artistic patronage was often similar to that of the monarch. The world of privilege, whether positive, as in academies or permissions to produce or publish, or negative, as in censorship or the exclusive policy of privileged bodies such as theatres enjoying royal licences, derived largely from royal or ecclesiastical authority, but great nobles displayed, often consciously, a regal taste in their artistic patronage. The essential requirement was considerable wealth, particularly in the case of architectural patronage. Prince Eugene of Savoy (1663–1736), the leading Austrian general of the early decades of the century, was a great patron of architecture, but Vienna was not alone in witnessing major private architectural commissions. Under the Regency there was considerable development in the western suburbs of Paris, the proximity of the court being a factor, as it was for the comparable development in London's Westminster. Important commissions established reputations. Princes of the blood had what were in effect courts of their own and these included architects and artists. Jean Aubert, the court architect of the Bourbon-Condé family, helped to build the Bourbon palace in Paris (1724–9) and also built the stables at their rural seat at Chantilly (1721–33), which surpassed their model, the royal stables at Versailles, and were the most monumental buildings of the 1715–23 period. In Britain too a large number of stately homes and their accompanying gardens were constructed and remodelled by the nobility. Architects such as Sir John Vanbrugh (1664–1726), the exponent of the English baroque, who built Blenheim, Castle Howard and Seaton Delaval, displayed a degree of spatial enterprise similar to that of the architects of princely palaces on the continent.

As with royal palaces, great aristocratic houses served as bases for the patronage of a host of decorative arts. The British architect and interior designer Robert Adam (1728–92) rebuilt or redesigned numerous British stately homes, including Harewood House, Kedleston Hall, Kenwood, Luton Hoo, Osterley Park and Syon House. His work is a testimony to aristocratic wealth. The fact that he was so often engaged in redesigning interiors, or harmonising extensions with existing buildings, freed him to evolve an extensive repertoire of interior motifs and colour schemes, and to develop the use of delicately moulded stucco forms on ceilings and walls. Adam's work was redolent with classical themes. Landscape gardening, inescapably linked to wealthy landed patronage, flourished in this period. The architect William Kent (1684–1748) developed and decorated parks (grounds of houses) in order to provide an appropriate setting for buildings. The greatest exponent of British landscape gardening was Lancelot 'Capability' Brown (1716–83), who designed houses as well as reshaping many of the great English parks. Rejecting the rigid formality associated with continental models, Brown contrived a setting that appeared natural, but was, nevertheless, carefully designed for effect. His landscapes of serpentine lakes, gentle hills and scattered groups of newly planted trees swiftly established a fashion, in a world where the small number of patrons and their interest in new artistic developments permitted new fashions to spread swiftly, while their wealth enabled them to realise and develop the new fashions. After Brown died his ideas were developed further by Humphry Repton, in accordance with the concept of the 'Picturesque', which stressed the individual character of each landscape and the need to retain it, while making improvements to remove what were judged blemishes and obstructions and to open up vistas. This essentially pictorial remoulding of landscape, vividly shown in Repton's 'red books' giving before and after views of a potential client's park, was a testimony to aristocratic wealth and visually informed taste. Though parkland was not without economic value, the labour required to excavate basins for artificial lakes or to create hills was considerable. British landscape gardening reflected and created a new aesthetic, initially private, but one that was to become public, gaining public financial patronage and thus achieving permanence. It would be foolish to advance a general psychological explanation for this interest in nature, albeit an altered nature, but, though the new fashion entailed stylistic conventions, it was less rigid than the previous fashion, and this permitted a more personal response to the tamed natural environment that was presented. If a greater interest in nature was to be one of the major themes of late eighteenth-century culture, this sensibility was to be one that stressed the personal response, although it was also an aesthetic that derived from artistic models. In the

Empire from mid-century there was also a new emphasis on more 'natural' irregular garden layouts.

Wealthy nobles were also important patrons of painting. For numerous painters such patronage was crucial. Furthermore, patrons generally determined the subject of the work and often influenced its composition. Count Nicolo Loschi, who commissioned Giambattista Tiepolo in 1734 to decorate his villa near Vicenza with frescoes, wanted a complex set of didactic allegorical illustrations. Portraiture was another field where their patronage was very important. The role of the nobility in the courts of Europe ensured that their patronage often led to or stemmed from royal favour, as it did with Johann Zoffany (1733–1810), the German painter made popular in Britain by George III's wife Charlotte, and Francisco Goya (1746–1828), who became painter to Charles III of Spain in 1786. Jean-Baptiste Pierre (1713–89) became *Premier Peintre* first to the duke of Orléans (1752) and then to Louis XV (1772). Noble patronage was not restricted to the decoration of palaces and portraiture. Many nobles were keen collectors of paintings and, though this frequently involved the purchase of old masters, living painters too were patronised, thus serving to retain and foster links between artists and the tastes and interests of individuals. An important theme was aristocratic recreations, particularly hunting, while the classical interests of patrons and artists combined in the depiction of classical landscapes and stories, the heroes of ancient Rome being suitable companions for the portraits of modern aristocrats. The Orléans collection attracted international interest when it came onto the open market in the 1790s as a result of dispersals during the French Revolution.

A similar mix of leisure and classical sentiment can be found in the drama that aristocrats patronised. Private theatrical performances were very popular with the aristocracy, frequently marking, as at royal courts, major events such as the marriage of the duke of Orléans in 1770. Many aristocrats took part in such performances themselves, as at Blenheim in the 1780s and 1790s. Furthermore, the aristocracy was a major source of patronage for the public theatre. Their sponsorship helped to bring a new troop of French actors to Vienna in 1775 and to pay in 1738 for the return to France of another troop, prevented from acting on the London stage by a populace that carried their xenophobia to the point of a riot at the Haymarket Theatre. In 1753 nearly all the theatre posters displayed in Paris were found in the aristocratic districts.[5] Their role as patrons and leaders of fashion, and their influence, both in courts and in major towns, ensured that the wealthy nobility played a crucial role in the artistic world.

If the less affluent nobility could neither emulate their patronage nor share in their role, they were nevertheless still of considerable importance in rural Europe. Their influence has received insufficient scholarly attention, not least because they could not afford to patronise major artists. However, they were arguably a central means by which new styles, whether in clothes or portraits, buildings or gardens, were disseminated.

Religion and the Church

The Church was also a great patron, as religion continued to be a major theme of the arts. However, it could also be obstructive to artistic events. What was judged immoral or sacrilegious was frequently condemned, and the role of clerics in censorship made this condemnation a serious matter. The Spanish Inquisition sought actively to prevent the circulation of corrupting works, particularly French books, and the Spanish clergy has been blamed for mid-century restrictions on the theatre. In 1753 actresses were forbidden to wear trousers. The Spanish clergy was able to restrict the spread of the theatre outside Madrid, plays being banned in Granada in 1706 and Seville in 1731. The general view that relaxation had to be circumscribed led to the closure of many European theatres during Lent and on Sundays and days decreed for prayer. Hostility to the theatre was not limited to Catholic Europe. Many of the German Pietists were critical of both theatre and secular literature, and in 1771 the abolition of Danish censorship was seen by some as a concession to irreligion. Frederick the Great wrote to his sister, the queen of Sweden, condemning the Swedish clergy for being scandalised by the introduction of the French theatre and claiming that French tragedy inspired more morality than the clergy. The Scottish church effectively prevented the setting up of provincial theatres in Scotland before 1750.

It would be misleading to see the clergy entirely as opponents of culture. The churches were great patrons and if some religious figures had views on the place of art in society and the disposal of patronage, both their own and that of others, they did not differ from many lay figures. It would be unreasonable to condemn clerical critics of opera while accepting Hogarth's criticism of Italian influences in British culture or Diderot's hostility to what he saw as the self-indulgence of much French art. One of the greatest royal critics of the church, Joseph II, on his visit to Ghent ordered clothes to be painted on van Eyck's triptych of Adam and Eve. What many clerics shared with lay commentators on the arts was a sense that they should serve a didactic purpose, inculcating morality by inspiration and example. The lay critics lavished considerable praise on the French painter Jean-Baptiste Greuze (1725–1805), when in 1755 he exhibited at the Salon (Parisian picture exhibition) a group of pictures including the *Père de famille expliquant la Bible*, which displayed the sort of moral ideas favoured by Diderot and Rousseau.

A large number of painters tackled religious themes. In France there was a strong tradition of religious art. Louis de Boullongne (1654–1733), who in 1725 was appointed *Premier Peintre* and ennobled, painted religious pictures for the chapel at Versailles and in the 1700s scenes from the life of Saint Augustine, including his apotheosis, for the Parisian church of Saint Louis des Invalides. Painters such as Jean-Baptiste van Loo (1684–1745) produced many works for churches and his brother Charles-André (Carle) (1705–65), one of the leading mid-century Parisian painters, produced enormous religious pictures on such topics as *St Peter curing a Lame Man* (1742) and *St Augustine disputing with the Donatists* (1753). As in the previous century, most French painters were not restricted to either religious or secular subjects. Strong compositional similarities between certain genres allowed shifts of subject quite easily. François Lemoyne (1688–1737), who rose to be *Premier Peintre*, painted both the *Transfiguration* in the choir vault at the church of St Thomas d'Aquin and the *Apotheosis of Hercules* for Versailles.

Throughout the Christian and especially the Catholic world the need to decorate churches, chapels, monasteries and religious foundations such as almshouses ensured that there was plentiful demand for religious paintings. Pierre Subleyras (1699–1749), a southern French painter who lived from 1728 in Italy, principally in Rome, was patronised extensively by the pope, the cardinals and the religious orders. His most famous work, the *Mass of St Basil*, was commissioned by the pope for St Peter's. Pompeo Batoni (1708–87), best known for his portraits of tourists visiting Rome, also painted many altarpieces, including the *Fall of Simon Magus* for St Peter's. Goya, whose admission piece for the Academiá de San Fernando was *Christ's Crucifixion* (1780), painted the fresco of the Virgin for one of the domes in Saragossa cathedral in that year. Many clerics, such as Pope Clement XII (1730–40) and Giuseppe Martelli, archbishop of Florence (1722–41), were great individual patrons. Religious paintings were also produced in Protestant countries. In London the paintings commissioned for the court room of Captain Coram's Charity depicted religious scenes and were designed to incline the viewers' hearts to charity. More generally, art was a medium of religious thought.

Religion also provided patronage and themes for music, while the churches offered training and employment for many musicians. Alessandro Scarlatti (1660–1725), one of the founders of the Neapolitan School of opera, provided the music in 1703 for the annual celebrations of the Feast of Our Lady of Mount Carmel at the church of Sta Maria di Monte Santo in Rome, a task Handel was commissioned to perform in 1707, the year Scarlatti was appointed choirmaster of Sta Maria Maggiore in Rome. Georg Philipp Telemann (1681–1767), who had been a church organist in Leipzig, while music director and town *cantor* of Lutheran Hamburg from 1721 until his death, produced 46 settings of the Passion. In 1786 Haydn composed his *Seven Last Words*, a commission for Cadiz cathedral based on Christ's seven last words. Until late in the century serious music in Poland was dominated by the Catholic Church, the first public performance of a Polish opera not occurring until 1778.

Throughout Europe much energy was devoted to hymns and carols, both Catholic, such as those of the Pole Franciszek Karpinski (1741–1825), and Protestant, such as those of Bach, of the Dane Hans Brorson and of the English Methodists, Charles Wesley (1709–88) writing over 6000. Religious drama was also important, frequently staged at particular periods of the year, such as Corpus Christi in Spain. Tsarina Elizabeth, who had a taste for such drama, liked to have uplifting works performed at court during Lent. The English traveller Richard Creed found numerous puppet shows depicting religious themes in Roman churches in 1700. If the Christian drama was primarily performed in church, many theatrical plays propounded Christian morality, as did popular passion and miracle plays.

Religious literature was of varying importance. In some publishing centres, such as London and Vicenza, the percentage of works published on religious and theological topics declined. Until mid-century religious literature dominated the publishing of French books, both in translation and bilingually, in Poland. In the 1750s and 1760s this dominance was challenged, and from the 1770s there was a rapid growth in lay literature. In other areas, religious literature remained more important. This was true of Spanish presses, such as those of Valladolid, and of those in Moldavia and Wallachia, where the printers were under episcopal or monastic direction. In Transylvania, where Greek Uniate priests were laying the foundations of what was to become Romanian national culture, a printing press, which published its first book in 1753, was established at their educational centre in Balj. It was to produce liturgical and pious writings in their language. Seeking to establish a press that could serve its Serbian and Romanian subjects and achieve political and economic goals, the Austrian government had in 1770 awarded the Viennese printing house of Joseph Kurzböck a twenty-year privilege to print books in the Cyrillic script, and this press published religious and school books. The *Bibliothèque bleue*, the inexpensive works produced for the French popular market, included numerous saints' lives, sermons and canticles.

Religious patronage was most apparent in architecture. Numerous monastic houses were rebuilt in whole or in part during the century, particularly in central Europe, where monasteries were major landowners. Their wealth eventually brought government hostility and expropriation, but it also financed much artistic and craft activity. Architects such as Jakob Prandtauer, the Asam brothers, the Dientzenhofer brothers, the Zimmermann brothers and Balthasar Neumann created majestic buildings with splendid interiors on spectacular sites. The costs were often considerable. The Benedictine monastery at Melk in Austria, whose reconstruction under Prandtauer began in 1702 and took 47 years, cost 25,000–30,000 florins annually with a normal daily complement of 100 masons, apprentices and labourers during the building season. At the monastery of St Florian about 12,000 florins was spent annually on reconstruction.[6] Many churches were built and rebuilt throughout Europe, although the eighteenth century is not popularly associated with church construction. This was true both of Protestant countries, such as Britain, and Catholic states, such as France, where Jesuit churches were built at Épinal, Verdun and Langres between 1724 and 1760.

Church architecture reflected a variety of styles, from the baroque and then the rococo of the central European monasteries and churches to the neo-classicism that became increasingly important in Paris, as with Nicolas Nicole's Madeleine (built 1746–66) and Germain Soufflot's St Geneviève, now the Panthéon. The primacy of the classical 'look' in France in the second half of the century led to the altering of many gothic churches, by giving the bases and capitals of pillars a classical appearance and by removing gothic ornamentation judged hideous, such as the altars, rood screens and choir stalls of Saint-Germain l'Auxerrois (1756). Churches were also often whitewashed and stained glass removed to let in more light. The French Revolution led to much vandalism, directed at buildings, fittings and decoration, both within France and in areas overrun by French forces. Networks of patronage were destroyed and the expropriation of clerical wealth left fewer resources available for ecclesiastical cultural activities, such as church choirs.

The middling orders: patronage by the public market

Protesting at the way in which noble characters were glorified at the expense of their bourgeois counterparts in comedies performed at the Comédie Française in Paris, Louis-Sébastien Mercier noted, nevertheless, that the bourgeoisie in the audience did not react unfavourably. In arguing that the patronage of the middling orders was of growing importance this does not imply that their tastes were necessarily very different from those of the nobility. In numerous spheres the bourgeoisie shared noble tastes, which was not surprising, as the permanent or seasonal urban sojourns of, in particular, the wealthy nobility helped to provide a model for behaviour. Similarly important was the impact of royal courts on major towns, while the pattern of cultural transmission was generally from capital cities to smaller towns. There was, nevertheless, a significant expansion in the patronage of the arts by the middling orders. Unable individually to provide sustained patronage, they participated through public performances of works and public markets for the arts and these expanded considerably during the century.

In Mercier's book *L' An 2440* all the citizens were able to decorate their walls with scenes depicting examples of heroism and virtue thanks to the reproduction of all the masterpieces of painting and sculpture in engravings. His vision of a culture centred on the mass-production of didactic art was clearly located in the future, but the eighteenth century witnessed an increasing dissemination of new cultural works. Most of the means of diffusion, such as engravings, newspapers and books, were far from new, but there was a definite expansion in the scale and variety of the culture of print during the century. The reproduction of paintings for wealthy collectors had usually taken the form of having individual copies painted, but the eighteenth century saw a considerable increase in their mass reproduction. The Gobelins tapestry factory commissioned the French painter Jean François de Troy (1679–1752) in 1742 to produce seven large compositions on the legend of Jason and Medea. These were used for tapestries that sold well. A large number of the paintings of the period were reproduced in engravings. The moral satires of William Hogarth (1697–1764) were a considerable success. His engravings of his six paintings *The Harlot's Progress*, the latter purchased by a wealthy collector, sold over 1000 sets, and were much imitated. Pictures by Hogarth that depicted depravity were produced from within a Christian view of vice and morality.

The public sale of paintings and production for such sales, rather than in response to a specific commission, was far from novel, being particularly well developed in the United Provinces in the seventeenth century. The following century, however, brought a considerable expansion in this field in a number of cities, including London and Paris. Paris became the centre of the European art trade in the first half of the century. Large-scale purchases of French artistic products were made by foreign rulers, such as Max Emanuel of Bavaria (1662–1726). From 1748 Karl Eugen of Württemberg retained a Parisian agent whose only task was to supply all new French publications, court circulars and manuals of architecture and decorative style. Matching the activity of private patrons was an increasingly organised Parisian art market, which helped to heighten interest in French art. Picture sales became more frequent, attractively printed and compiled auction catalogues illustrating the manner in which the growing culture of print fostered developments in other arts, as it did with the increasing availability of sheet music. Parisian picture sales for which a catalogue was printed rose from an annual average of 3 in the early 1750s to one of 30 for 1774–84. By the mid-1770s, 60 picture and print dealers were operating in Paris, while by the end of the 1780s there were 4 major sale rooms. The ambience became more clearly commercial and impersonal. Whereas, in mid-century, catalogues had often begun with a pan-egyric of the collector or a statement of the pleasures of collecting, later in the century the investment opportunities in buying paintings were presented more clearly.[7]

The growth in the public sale of art in Paris was matched by a growth in the public viewing of art. This developed as a result of the exhibition of pictures in the Place Dauphine on Corpus Christi Day and more significantly, of the public exhibitions in the Salon Carré of the Louvre palace held in 1667, 1673, 1699, 1704 and 1725, regularised in 1737, and then held either annually or biennially. Known as the Salons, these exhibitions were controlled by the *Académie Royale de Peinture et de Sculpture*, whose members enjoyed the sole right to submit their work. The Salons both offered the opportunity for a wider public to view art and encouraged the development of artistic criticism. Furthermore, the idea and the importance of public taste were advanced. Salon criticism began in 1747 when Étienne-François de La Font de Saint-Yenne published his thoughts on the 1746 salon.[8] Related to the underground *libelles*, which expressed liberal notions in satirical forms, salon criticism was vigorous, as in Diderot's 1765 attack on Boucher, newly appointed *Premier Peintre*, but castigated for being a proficient purveyor of moral corruption. It has been argued recently that class did not determine the cultural priorities of the Parisian picture-viewing public, that the creation of and response to stylistic change was not class-based, not least because the Academy displayed an eclectic taste.[9] However, while it is inappropriate to talk of a bourgeois art, the growth of a wider public gave rise to bourgeois patronage that, while not necessarily distinct in its tastes, fostered particular interests and trends. Art journalism was not restricted to France. In Britain towards the end of the century the social role of the art critic was stressed and reporting was heavily influenced by political considerations.

Though many musical productions were still private, the musical world was also becoming more public. If many opera houses were very much for the court, others were open to the public. When La Scala was completed in Milan in 1778, it was capable of holding 3600 people. The lavish opera house constructed in Bordeaux in Louis XVI's reign was a testimony both to the city's affluence and to provincial appetite for high culture. Public concerts became more frequent. Telemann's oratorios were performed repeatedly in the Hamburg Drillhaus from the 1720s, 'the first regular public concerts in North Germany'.[10] It was stated in London in 1737 that 'Music has engrossed the attention of the whole people: The Duchess and her woman, the Duke and his position, are equally infected'.[11] The Austrian composer Joseph Haydn (1732–1809), who spent from 1761 to 1790 in the service of Prince Esterhazy in Hungary, living in the servants' quarters of his palace, came to London to give public concerts in 1791 and 1794. Haydn benefited from the growth in music-publishing.[12] Instrumental music did not pose the financial demands upon patrons that opera claimed, and it was far easier for amateurs to participate in. Chamber and solo works thus enjoyed considerable popularity and both music and manuals, such as François Couperin's *Art de toucher le Clavecin* (1716), were produced accordingly. The *Principles of the Harpsichord* by Monsieur de Saint Lambert (1702), which has been described both as the first genuine harpsichord method and as the first book about practical music that is comprehensible to readers with no prior knowledge of the subject, recommended the instrument in practical terms that could be expected to appeal to genteel readers.

Musical journalism developed in response to this increase in public interest, and provided a forum for a stylistic debate that opposed new operatic forms to the dominant *opera seria*, a world of classical mythology, serious heroism and solemn music brought to life by Italian composers and singers. In London the ballad opera, exemplified by John Gay's *Beggar's Opera* (1728), offered popular tunes and songs and scenes from low life, in a deliberate attack on the Italianate operas patronised by the cosmopolitan court and composed by, among others, Handel. These operas were driven out of fashion. Handel produced his last in 1741, but, the following year enjoyed a considerable success with his *Messiah*, an oratorio that revealed the commercial possibilities of sacred music. Such music had always been public, but now it increasingly served commercial, rather than liturgical purposes, being performed at concerts. In Italy the challenge came from the lighter *opera buffa*, one example of which, *La Serva Padrona* of Giovanni Pergolesi (1710–36), caused a great stir in Paris in 1752. Related, though not identical, trends led to the development of the *opéra comique* in France, the *tonadilla* in Spain and the *Singspiel* in Austria. Russian comic opera appeared in the 1770s, using settings in rural or peasant life and receiving powerful stimulus from specifically Russian needs and conditions. In contrast to the cosmopolitan nature of *opera seria*, these novel forms tended to offer entertainment in the vernacular.

Bourgeois patronage was important in the theatre, crucial to the development of a secular, public theatre in countries such as Poland, and in the foundation of theatres outside capital cities. A new public theatre was opened in Copenhagen in 1747. In the Empire, state-supported theatre was used to encourage a bourgeois consciousness equally opposed to indulgence, whether decadent 'aristocratic' mores or popular ignorance and vice. Colley Cibber, George Colman, George Lillo and Oliver Goldsmith offered similar moral and sentimental works to London audiences. Much of the British theatre propounded a morality similar to that of many novels. Virtue and moral conduct were closely associated with religious notions in the theatre. The etiquette of the period condemned dishevelment and slovenliness in clothing, and self-indulgent behaviour. Lower down the social scale religious moral plays and domestic scenes were performed by strolling entertainers.

To some commentators the eighteenth century, in areas such as urban England, witnessed the commercialisation of leisure. Since this can be seen as a triumph of bourgeois culture, it is appropriate to stress that there was no necessary antipathy between that and the culture of the court and greater nobility. If morality was increasingly prescribed and indulgence proscribed from mid-century this represented not a bourgeois reaction against noble culture, but a shift in sensibility common to both. For every decadent aristocrat depicted on the stage in the second half of the century there were several royal or aristocratic heroes. The role of the bourgeoisie was largely one of patronising both new and traditional artistic forms rather than developing or demanding distinct styles. This was true of architecture. Urban growth and prosperity and increasing demand for public buildings, such as theatres and libraries, did not really lead to a distinctive style.[13]

The rise of the novel can be seen as an important instance of the embourgeoisement of culture largely only if that is regarded as a matter of patronage rather than content. In Britain novels created and responded to a large readership, Henry Fielding's *Joseph Andrews*, for example, selling 6500 copies in 1742. The growth of proprietary and subscription libraries as well as the serial publication of books permitted those who could not afford to purchase them to read them. Far from conforming to a common tone, form or intention, novels varied greatly, a trend encouraged by the size and diversity of the reading public. Thus Richardson's first novel *Pamela* (1740), a very popular book on the prudence of virtue and the virtue of prudence, was countered by Fielding's *Apology for the Life of Mrs Shamela Andrews* and his *Joseph Andrews*.

Throughout Europe the publishing of books increased. It was most restricted in the Balkans. Although there had been short-lived presses in Istanbul for the printing of Hebrew, Greek and Armenian, religious views had prevented the introduction of Turkish and Arabic printing and it was not until 1729 that secular Turkish works began to appear. Ibrahim Müteferrika, a Hungarian by birth, who had become a court steward, was permitted to publish 17 works, historical, geographical and scientific, mostly in editions of 500. This was dependent on western expertise: the second book, a geographical work, was seen through the press by an apostate Spanish monk, while the plates were engraved by a Viennese workman. However, after Ibrahim's death in 1745, no books appeared for 14 years and no more than 8 in the following 40, publishing only reviving seriously in the next century.

Elsewhere, publishing increased, growing particularly towards the end of the century, in the Empire in the 1770s and 1780s. Over 70 per cent of all the books produced during the century in the East Slavic territories were printed in the last quarter. Peter the Great had sought to substitute books for scrolls in government, but it was only during the reign of Catherine II that handwritten culture ceased to be the basis of literary life. In her instructions on the codification of Russian law Catherine decreed that it should be in the vernacular and produced in a low-priced book.

Not all books published were for commercial sale. Particularly in areas where there was relatively little publishing, printing for governments was important. However, in much of Europe publishers and booksellers sought to create a public market. As the period witnessed little technical innovation in publishing, profitability depended on increased sales, and publishers producing sizeable editions, such as Strachan in London and Panckoucke in Paris, had to be sensitive to the market. While some German intellectuals argued that the reader must be trained to think independently and responsibly, rather than simply to follow the author's views, publishers were all too aware that the consumer dictated the content of the book market. The growth of the reading public affected literature. In the field of British history authors such as David Hume and hack writers such as Richard Rolt were able to write for a large and immediate readership, producing a clearly commercial product, in contrast to the classical model of history for the benefit of friends and a posthumous public. In 1731 Voltaire brought dramatic near-contemporary history to a huge readership, his *Histoire de Charles XII* being printed ten times in its first two years. His *Siècle de Louis XIV* and his *Histoire de la Guerre de 1741* were similarly successful.

Authors sought to make their writings as comprehensible as possible to the anonymous expanding literate population. Books, magazines, newspapers and dictionaries assisted the spread of new ideas. They helped to transmit to the general reading public the grand themes of artistic and intellectual life. Throughout Europe this was easiest in an urban setting, the principal context of cultural patronage by the middling orders. Many cultural institutions, learned societies, periodicals and theatres helped to create a cultural climate more sensitive to new ideas. In Toulouse academic publications, almanacs and the reports of the Academy of Floral Games spread these ideas. In Norwich, where there was a very active musical life, both public and performers were ready to accept quite rapid change, and at the end of the century concert-goers were able to hear the latest British and German works. However, the impact of such institutions was not uniform. If some French provincial academies, such as those of Bordeaux, Châlons and Dijon, were major centres of intellectual life, others were not. The Academy of Pau, founded in 1718, held meetings and concerts and created a library open to the public, but it had a narrow socio-cultural base, most of the local bourgeoisie not participating, and its relations were limited regionally and nearly non-existent internationally. Elsewhere much of the new mechanism of bourgeois patronage was missing. There were no public libraries in Greece until the next century.

In France, the Revolution led, alongside much vandalism, to an increase in the accessibility of art. Much art was expropriated during the Terror, catalogued by the government, and allocated to the national and provincial public museums that were founded in order to provide cultural opportunities for the citizenry. The decline of aristocratic patronage in France also accentuated the role of the public market and thus of the commercialisation of art.

The populace: distinct and oppressed?

High and popular culture are frequently sharply differentiated and then presented in terms of a 'battle of cultures'. A recent study of Parisian musical entertainment claims that

> there was a clear distinction between classical and popular musical entertainments with respect to form, style, and content...the two cultures appealed to different public tastes in part because they appeared in very divergent physical settings...throughout the eighteenth century, low musical culture struggled to survive the repeated attacks of the privileged theatres who were determined to drive popular entertainment from existence, or to control it.[14]

Popular culture is presented often as being under assault from the moral didacticism of the secular and ecclesiastical authorities and middling orders. 'A broad evangelical assault on late eighteenth-century popular culture'[15] has been discerned, not only in England. Traditional popular celebrations, often characterised by an unrestrained exuberance, were suppressed or tamed in much of Europe. In Toulouse the authorities reduced a carnival activity parodying the monarchy, organised by the Basoche, to an innocent official parade, before ending it in 1776.[16] Between 1778 and 1786 many French rural fêtes and carnivals were prohibited.

It is not only in the artistic sphere that this tension has been discerned and that the analysis and presentation of relationships has been coloured by the use of words and phrases such as 'oppressive', 'control' and 'protective mechanisms'. Indeed the discernment of artistic duality is but part of a wider sense of cultural conflict, of different *mentalités*, of worlds in collision, which has influenced the assessment of popular religiosity. This clash has been approached from a number of angles including urban–rural tension and the supposed destruction of a seventeenth-century common culture: 'by 1800 the elite had withdrawn from the culture of the people'.[17] New intellectual and artistic fashions and codes of behaviour are held to have corroded the loyalty of the upper and middling orders to traditional beliefs and pastimes and it is claimed that Protestant and Catholic religious revival, the Scientific Revolution, the Enlightenment and the cult of sensibility marginalised the common culture and pushed it down the social scale.[18] Given such an analysis it is unsurprising that attention has been devoted to the contrast between popular and elite culture and that this is held to have inspired initiatives such as campaigns by intellectuals, governments and the middling orders to 'reform' popular practices through legislation and education. 'We can cure the people of superstition. We can, by speech and pen, make men more enlightened,' wrote Voltaire, referring essentially to religious beliefs. In 1791 the *Leeds Intelligencer* printed a letter attacking bull-baiting as 'a disgrace to a civilized people' that produced depraved manners rather than amusement, 'Tis pity, then, but those who make this a practice merely from *custom* would reflect upon the cruelty of it, and, by substituting any harmless diversion in its stead, do themselves a most permanent credit, and render a true service to the rising generation.'[19] Other English newspapers of the period attacked such popular practices as wife-selling, gambling, the shooting of street lamps for fun, boxing, swearing and cruelty to animals, although, bar wife-selling, all of these were popular with the aristocracy also.

Nevertheless, considerable caution is necessary in dealing with this subject. Archival sources are elusive, methodological problems numerous and scholarly research still patchy. It is by no means clear that popular culture is a valid concept that can be readily studied. Oral rather than written communication remained of great importance, oral culture being not simply a consequence of illiteracy. Much of the evidence for the views of the bulk of the population comes from outsiders, literate commentators who contrasted their beliefs with a world they depicted as irrational and unfashionable. This would suggest that there was a distinct folk culture that was readily apparent, even if located beneath a veneer of civilisation. Nevertheless, it could be argued that the idea of a sharp distinction between the culture of the elites and that of the bulk of the population is misleading. Aside from the fact that there was a mutual interchange of ideas, it is by no means clear that there were two contrasting *mentalités*. Voltaire's obsessive preoccupation, for example, in his *Dictionnaire philosophique* (1764), with religious issues, and especially the church, church history and the authority over people's minds enjoyed by scriptural texts, was that of a man seeking not only to scoff at the masses, but also to win over or subvert the educated who still largely shared this outlook. The concept of a de-christianised and enlightened Europe is increasingly questioned. It is not simply that the Enlightenment can be seen to have had a dark side, such as a preoccupation with the occult, but rather that the culture of the elite was still generally Christian, that new fashions included emotion and sensitivity in the arts, ancient ruins, distant and mysterious places, peoples and cults. As the process of de-mythologising the Enlightenment continues and as attention is increasingly directed to countries where the elites cannot satisfactorily be analysed in conventional terms, so it is possible that the idea of a common culture, albeit one with different styles, will be revived. In Spain where Charles III's reforming minister Pedro Campomanes sought to use the press to diffuse new writings, particularly advances in economics, science and technology, these never enjoyed a wide circulation, the general reading public at all social levels preferring to read almanacs. These were also very popular in other countries, including Britain. Rather than advancing two conflicting *mentalités*, it is more accurate to suggest that performers and the public sought to investigate and express common problems and emotions, to make sense of a common world in a number of different styles and formats. If the traditional repertoire of amateur actors in the Austrian Netherlands was often derived directly from medieval mystery plays, audiences in England were willing to turn out in large numbers for Handel's sacred music on biblical themes. There was noticeable overlap between the amusements of the 'best people' and the rest in such places as the Paris theatres at the successive fairs held there which were frequented by the nobility as well as the lower orders. The same was true of entertainments such as bear baiting and cock fighting.

In part the relationship between sections of elite and popular culture derived from the greater interest in popular culture displayed by artists and intellectuals enjoying elite favour during the century. Considerable effort was devoted to collecting peasant tales and songs, M. Chulkov making a large collection of Russian popular and Cossack songs. Aleksandr Ablesimov (1742–83) used folksongs in his three-act comic opera *Mel'nik*, first performed in Moscow in 1779. The work enjoyed a considerable success. In the 1760s and 1770s 'the peasant and his culture made their appearance as serious subjects for literature, journalism and art'.[20]

It is, however, true that when rural life was presented, it was often idealised, as with Boucher's shepherdesses presented as allegorical figures, or the stylised charm of Gainsborough's cottages, and attention was concentrated on areas where it was possible to present a positive image of virtuous rural folk, as in America or the Alps. By the 1770s and 1780s there was more interest in their supposed lifestyle, a process that matched growing fascination with the sublimity of wild, particularly mountainous, landscapes. In comparison the flat lands lacked interest, while the routine grind and miseries of peasant life were generally ignored. Those, like Greuze, who wished to use peasant life for sentimental effect and didactic purpose, had little interest in exploring its problems; though his peasant interiors are often crowded, it is for dramatic effect, not a matter of social realism. And it was still the case that the folk tales of the peasantry were of less interest than those of ancient times.

Considerable attention was devoted to peasant folk tales in what is sometimes termed the pre-romantic period, which stretched from the 1760s and 1770s to whenever the Romantic period is held to begin. To the antiquarian tradition of interest in ancient literature, such as the Anglo-Saxon studies of the English clergyman Edward Lye (1694–1767), was added a fascination with the ancient 'folk' literature, which was presented as offering an imaginative perspective as capable as Chinese philosophy or the noble savage of reviving European culture. James Macpherson (1736–96) published poems which he claimed to have translated from the Gaelic of a third-century Highland bard called Ossian. His *Fragments of Ancient Poetry collected in the Highlands* (1760) brought him fame, being followed by *Fingal* (1761), dedicated to George III's favourite, the earl of Bute, the preface of which proclaimed the superiority of Celtic to Greek heroic poetry, and also by *Temora* (1763). These works, in part his own creation, in part based on genuine Gaelic poems and ballads, enjoyed a phenomenal success. Endowed with a primitivism that appealed to fashionable pre-Romanticism, they were translated into several European languages, including French (1777) and Russian (1792), and were to influence Byron, Coleridge, Goethe, Schiller and Napoleon, among others. Impressed by Macpherson, Thomas Percy (1729–1811), a grocer's son who sought to show his descent from the medieval dukes of Northumberland, published *Five Pieces of Runic Poetry, translated from the Icelandic* (1763) and *Reliques of Ancient English Poetry* (1765, 4 editions by 1794), an edition of old ballads which promoted a revival of interest in the subject. The German philosopher Johann Gottfried Herder (1744–1803), court preacher at Weimar from 1776 until his death, was also impressed by Ossian. He published several collections of German folksongs which he believed important as the root of poetry and a source of national consciousness.

If the peasantry was less interesting and uplifting as an artistic topic for elite culture than ancient Greeks, Celts and Goths, it was also the case that very few peasants became artists who were patronised in that culture. However, it would be as misleading to suggest that popular and elite culture were autonomous as it would be to imply that they were uniform or that the former was unchanging. Far, for example, from 'art' and 'folk' music being distinct and antithetical, the folk music being conservative and transmitted almost solely in oral tradition, there is considerable evidence of inter-relationship and change, both thematic and stylistic. There were striking changes in elite culture, such as the development of string-playing by Corelli, Antonio Vivaldi (*c.* 1675–1741) and Giuseppe Tartini (1692–1770), the new tuning system of equal temperament championed by Bach, and the invention of the piano in about 1709 by Bartolomeo Cristofori and its popularisation in the 1770s by Mozart and Muzio Clementi. Nevertheless, popular culture was not therefore static. If for most of the European population music meant ballads, hymns and primitive instruments, that does not mean that popular music was necessarily unsophisticated or unchanging.

Popular culture is a subject that poses serious conceptual and methodological problems.[21] The questionable nature of generalisations about peasant conservatism, or cultural borrowing from the elite, is apparent. There is need for far more work on the topic if the cultural world of the bulk of the population is to be rescued from simplifications. In particular, the effects of migration, urbanisation, commercial change and economic developments require examination. At present it seems reasonable to suggest that, alongside the evidence for varied elite cultural forms and changes and a diversity of stylistic changes, it is necessary to appreciate that popular culture was also changing, and by no means hermetically sealed off from 'high' culture.

Changing styles

The definition of styles for any particular art form is a matter of controversy. Definitions vary, as do attributions of individual artists or works to specific styles. The subject is made more difficult if the discussion of style is broadened from one particular art form to the full range of cultural activities and even to the social and political setting. If it is difficult to define rococo architecture, it is even harder to decide how to apply the description to literature or to performing style in music. Rather than assuming the existence of defined, rigid and exclusive styles, common to all art forms in all countries in a particular period, it is more appropriate to suggest that these styles should be regarded as tendencies and that they were not specified in universally accepted ways, or completely compartmentalised. Stylistic pluralism was common in the work of individual artists or particular periods and countries, and there was a considerable degree of overlap on the continental scale. So, for example, in Portugal the baroque style was dominant until mid-century, at a time when its influence had faded north of the Alps. Traditional themes continued to be addressed, old genres survived and old methods were used at the same time as new developments and insights advanced.

Several different styles have been discerned. It is commonly agreed that at the turn of the century the most important was baroque, to varying degrees emanating from Rome, that in the second quarter of the century rococo, which can be regarded as an offshoot of the baroque, was influential, that a conscious neo-classical style developed in reaction to it, and that towards the end of the century interest in the ideas of sensibility and the value of nature combined in early Romanticism. Such a description is open to extensive qualification, and it excludes other developments such as the neo-gothicism that affected some English architects in the second half of the century, or the vogue for Chinese motifs and artefacts which went alongside both rococo and neo-classical styles. Furthermore, linear periodisation is by no means always accurate, and it is far from clear how the work of individual artists is to be related to particular styles.

The magnificence and geometrical strength of the baroque were influential in the early decades of the century. The Viennese architecture of the period and the majestic theatrical spectacles produced there by Ferdinando Galli-Bibbiena exemplified the baroque. The vogue for painted ceilings remained strong, and in the early eighteenth century there was a growing tendency to give added splendour, particularly in the form of fresco decoration, to churches, monasteries and palaces. Pellegrini's fresco work for Lord Manchester at Kimbolton was an example of artists moving easily between countries and cultures, and of the importance of diplomats in facilitating the process.

The relationship of what has been termed the rococo to the baroque is open to debate. Rococo is a term commonly associated with painting and interior decoration. Charles-Nicolas Cochin, who first used the term in a critique of 1755, referred to it as a style of furnishing and interior decorating. The latter was characterised by mirrors and wall panels in carved wood, asymmetry, flowing curves and shell and leaf patterns. The term rococo may have been derived from *rocaille*, the rock-like watery and shelly substance used for artificial caves, and *coquille* (shell). It has been applied to other art forms, such as the chamber music of Stamnitz or the poetry of Christoph Wieland, whose *Musarion, oder die Philosophie der Grazien* (1768) was a literary *fête galante*. Related shifts can be detected in other spheres. French organcases, for example, became less academic and architectural in design, more elegant, flowing and nuanced. Rococo is often approached as a delightful decorative style, exquisite, fragile and intimate. The rococo aesthetic was one of a man-made environment of and for pleasure:

> tendency to avoid profound emotions is an integral portion of the eighteenth-century attempt to achieve the greatest possible pleasure by living in harmony with the laws of nature. Harmony is based upon the geometry of balance, and balance *will* be upset by profound emotion ... the ornamentation of the *Rococo* style was a glorification of that maximum variety compatible with harmony.[22]

If an underlying order lay behind rococo ornamentation, it was nevertheless the case that the ornamentation was apparent. This expressed two features of rococo art, intimacy and pleasure. A sensibility stressing both became more prominent in the early decades of the century. In Paris, for example, there was a discernible shift in taste from large history paintings to smaller genre scenes.

In the last two decades of Louis XIVs reign French painting changed. Controversies over purpose and style helped to lead to *Rubénisme*, a stress on nature and colour. Jean-Antoine Watteau (1684–1721) created the genre of the *fête galante*, artificial, fanciful and poignant drawings after nature. Watteau's influence was sustained by the publication in four volumes of engravings of his drawings and paintings. Thus a painter who had been patronised by a small group of wealthy collectors became the object of unprecedented sustained reproduction. One artist who participated in this engraving and was greatly influenced by Watteau was François Boucher (1703–70). Boucher offered a rich decorative style, a sense of elegance and wit, and a light eroticism that appealed to his sophisticated Parisian and court patrons. One possible indication of the growth of the interest in the individual to which the century contributed was the increased willingness to paint informal portraits of women.

The criticisms of the rococo related essentially to painting and decoration. It was an attack not so much on the quality of the work as on its purpose, or apparent lack of it, for artist and patron. Mid-century critics, such as Diderot, found art for pleasure inadequate. Instead, they sought a didactic art capable of arousing sentiment and morality, rather than of confirming comfort. Diderot criticised Boucher's work as full of affectation and a corrupting influence and in the *Salon de 1763* he praised Greuze, whose works might also strike the modern viewer as affected, because 'the genre pleases me; it is moral painting. After all, has not the brush been consecrated to debauchery and vice long enough? Ought we not to be pleased to see it vie at last with dramatic poetry in moving us, teaching us, correcting us, and inviting us to virtue?'[23] The German painter Anton Raphael Mengs (1728–99), a friend of Winckelmann's who did much of his work in Rome and was much favoured by the Spanish court, argued in his *Gedanken* (1762) that artists should imitate the essential nature of the objects they perceived, arouse praiseworthy passions and instruct the mind. He had no time for the alleged frivolity of baroque and rococo art, and had his work preferred at Madrid at the expense of that of the elderly Tiepolo. In his *Discourses* as president of the Royal Academy, Reynolds propounded a purposeful view of art. In 1770 he claimed that a true painter 'instead of endeavouring to amuse mankind with the minute neatness of his imitation... must endeavour to improve them by the grandeur of his ideas'. Two years later, in his *Considérations sur le gouvernement de Pologne*, Rousseau carried a belief in the power of affirmative art so far as to recommend that all the arts be used to create a Polish national spirit.

The argument about the need for a moral culture was neither new nor restricted to painting. The cult of 'sensibility', of sentiment and fine emotion, had a considerable influence on the theatre and newly emerging novels of the period. In the Empire, the theatre was subject to clerical criticism as a corrupt influence promoting loose morals, adultery and prostitution. A secular counterpart, called 'reform' theatre, sought to offer improving plays. Reform theatre, as demanded by the leading German writers of the second half of the century, was intended to improve spoken language and banish coarse humour. The sentimental novel enjoyed considerable popularity in Europe. Dealing with recognisable individuals and, by the standards of *fêtes galantes*, realistic backgrounds, novels offered improving thoughts, entertainment with a moral. The new moral simplicity also influenced other genres, such as opera. In his *Orfeo* (1762) Gluck, a friend of Winckelmann's, offered a stern and simple work with self-consciously simple arias and only three soloists. In the dedicatory epistle to his opera *Alceste* (1767), Gluck pleaded for a 'noble simplicity' and condemned 'superfluous ornament. Music was to express the drama and sentiments of the story'.[24]

The art to which these attitudes gave rise is generally described as neo-classical, though that was not a term used in the period, the 'true style' being the favoured description. The 'true style' was an austere style in conscious reaction against frivolous eroticism. Turning to classical history for its sources, it inculcated virtue and its greatest master was the French painter David. Classical antiquity, as portrayed principally by Winckelmann, was the stylistic criterion by which the rococo was found wanting or castigated. Winckelmann's ecstatic portrayal of the wonders of

Greek art made the rococo appear mere empty frivolity. Neo-classical theories accorded with many of the suppositions of the period. The idea that culture should be exemplary had never been lost. History painting, a public, demonstrative and declamatory art, proclaiming noble and elevated ideals and depicting the actions of heroes at moments of moral or historical significance,[25] remained at the top of the French academic hierarchy of subjects. It could be suggested that once a major public debate about the purpose of art and the artist developed, it was likely that it would have taken the attitude, critical of the rococo, that was adopted in mid-century. The exclusive court and aristocratic circles that patronised the rococo were not especially interested in public debate. However, if anti-rococo polemics were often directed against the allegedly trivial, corrupt and expensive nature of artistic patronage, that did not mean that neo-classicism was the art of the bourgeoisie. A class-based analysis of eighteenth-century artistic movements is subject to too many empirical and methodological qualifications to bear close examination.

No one category is adequate to cover the variety of artistic developments from mid-century until the Revolution. If the Romanticism of the early nineteenth century is associated with the individual emotions of the artist, often at variance with social and cultural conventions and inspired by the intoxicating power and wildness and the ravishing beauty of elemental natural forces and a world fractured by revolution, then there were harbingers in the pre-revolutionary period. There was a strong interest in landscape painting, a new appreciation of the 'sublime' qualities of savage landscape. The anguish and isolation of the Romantic hero had been foreshadowed in several paintings, such as that of *Milo of Croton* by Jean Jacques Bachelier (1724–1806) exhibited at the 1761 Salon, and in much of the writing of the German *Sturm und Drang* movement. This literary movement, increasingly influential from the 1770s, saw nature as a creative force, not as a pleasing and inconsequential landscape, the human soul as a seat of passion, rather than harmony, the feeling man of action as superior to the reflective scholar. In his novel the *Sorrows of Young Werther* (1774), Johann Wolfgang von Goethe (1749–1832) provided a complex hero driven to suicide by unrequited passion and the terrible power of total feeling. Romance ceased to be a game, as in many French novels of the period, or an opportunity for sentimental poses, as in their English counterparts, and became a cruel mistress. *Werther* had a great impact and was much imitated. Rousseau's emphasis on sensibility and spiritual awareness was also very important in forming proto-Romantic taste.

Other art forms were changing in the pre-revolutionary period. Karl Philipp Emanuel Bach (1714–88), the second son of Johann Sebastian Bach, had little time for his father's contrapuntal style and was one of the originators of the sonata form. In his numerous concerti, he followed the doctrine that music must touch the heart and arouse strong emotions. He influenced both Haydn and Mozart, who was also affected by Karl Philipp Emanuel's younger brother Johann Christian (1735–82), who had played a major role in replacing his father's style by the *galant* style. Mozart (1756–91) also benefited from the dynamic orchestral range of the Mannheim composers, and he transformed the piano concerto from a work of limited forms and devices into a dramatic interplay of piano and orchestra. Mozart brought melodic richness to his orchestral and operatic compositions. In 1778 he composed the music for the ballet *Les Petits Riens* for Jean-Georges Noverre (1727–1810), who was changing ballet extensively, demanding more expression and a clearer story. Noverre wished to replace the old formal dances and became the founder of *Ballet d'Action* (Dramatic Ballet), which used mime extensively.

Though changes were clearly occurring, it would, however, be misleading to think simply in terms of linear progression. Reynolds's successor as president of the Royal Academy, the American painter Benjamin West (1738–1820), whose style was greatly influenced by that of Mengs when he visited Italy, produced history paintings on modern themes, such as the *Death of Wolfe* (1771), while another painter encouraged by Reynolds who spent eight years in Italy, the Swiss Johann Heinrich Füssli (Henry Fuseli) (1741–1825), offered visions of horrific fantasy, comparable to some of the contemporary 'gothick' novels. Influenced by reading Rousseau, Füssli was a precursor of Romanticism, who argued that the individual and society, art and morality, were in conflict. In his *Remarks on the Writings and Conduct of J. J. Rousseau* (1767) he claimed that the arts were a divine gift which elevated man by their force, impact and terror. Praised by George III and William Blake, Füssli's most famous painting was his *Nightmare* (1781), a powerful vision of the mysterious and the subconscious. Producing work designed to arouse the imagination, Füssli painted visions that exposed the limited sway of social order and psychological balance and harmony, and depths in human experience which reason could not explain. Füssli's impact – his early work influenced Goethe – is a reminder that the painting of the 1780s cannot be seen simply in terms of

David's neo-classical history paintings. Füssli appealed to a definite taste in the period, as did his contemporary Franz Anton Mesmer, an Austrian doctor who rejected conventional science and medicine in favour of the notion of a universal fluid that conducted what he claimed was the lifeforce of magnetism. Mozart, who wrote the pastoral operetta *Bastien und Bastienne* for Mesmer (1768), offered in his last opera, *The Magic Flute* (1791), the portrayal of a world whose cosmology was Masonic and in which reason was magical. He was not alone in producing works of struggle, not equanimity.

Cosmopolitanism and artistic influences

The eighteenth-century polemic of cultural nationalism can be as misleading as that of stylistic or thematic exclusiveness. In practice, artists were more eclectic, often in painting adopting for each genre the style traditionally regarded as appropriate: a Dutch style for a still-life, an Italian style for a history picture, a French style in portraiture.[26] Certainly at the level of the elite, culture was cosmopolitan thematically, stylistically and in terms of artists and performers. There was more to cosmopolitanism than simple contacts, often personal or chance. It entailed a wider sense of shared values and commonalty of purpose that led Montesquieu, for example, to write of Europe as one large nation, with regions, and common interests. At the elite level there was a considerable public interest in developments elsewhere, one that was encouraged and met by the growth of the international cultural trade, particularly the book trade, by the republication of works in other countries, translations and artistic journalism. It was not only the works of leading French intellectuals that were translated into other languages. All sorts of books were translated, ranging from Combles on the cultivation of peaches to Chasles's realistic amorous fiction. In Russia in 1741–1800, 245 books were published that can be traced back to original English-language works by British authors. Not all translations were accurate or effective, particularly as they were often translated indirectly. Many of the English works translated into Russian had a French intermediary. The *Spectator* in a French version circulated across Europe. Furthermore, translators had a moral as well as a literary function, being expected to improve and modernise the text. However, they generally offered at least the substance of the work. Translations brought Newtonian physics to Italy and European mythological handbooks to Russia. The Russian dramatist Aleksandr Sumarokov (1718–77) first produced his adaptation of *Hamlet* in 1750.

'Cosmopolitanism' was aided by travel, patronage, the role of cultural intermediaries and the process of emulation. Travel helped to spread knowledge of present, as well as past, artistic developments among patrons. As the Grand Tour became fashionable, increasing numbers travelled for pleasure, particularly from Britain, Scandinavia, Poland and the Empire to France and Italy. While patrons toured for pleasure, artists travelled in order to acquire training and employment. The French authorities realised the importance of studying in Italy and most major artists spent some time in the French Academy in Rome. The Swedish architect Carl Cronstedt studied in France, Italy, Munich and Vienna between 1731 and 1737. Employment was an even bigger incentive to travel, either temporarily, in response to particular commissions, or for longer periods. The Nuremberg painter Carl Tuscher (1705–51) worked in Italy (1728–41), London (1741–3) and Copenhagen, as court painter (1743–51). Having studied in Rome in 1738–42, the French architect Jean-Laurent Legeay was appointed a professor at the Paris *Académie* before being appointed architect to Frederick II in 1754. Patronage was inspired by and sustained an elite cosmopolitan culture. Variations in the distribution of artists and performers were particularly marked in certain elite cultural forms, such as opera, and there was generally an additional sense that quality varied geographically and that certain places were characterised by innovative artists. This was exacerbated by the movement of many talented artists, either for training or employment. In addition, patrons often looked abroad when commissioning or purchasing works of art. In 1701 the Austrian aristocrat Johann von Liechtenstein asked the Florentine bronze-caster Massimiliano Soldani for reduced copies of the statues in the grand-ducal collection to be used as models for stone garden figures and to be kept in his gallery. Peter the Great recruited German scholars and scientists for the Academy of Sciences he founded.

The role of cultural intermediaries was facilitated by the appreciable number of foreigners who could be found in most major towns and by the cosmopolitan nature of most courts. Italians were well represented in a number of courts including Dresden, Madrid and Munich. In Vienna, too, various Italians established circles for intellectual exchange and served as a link between Austria and Anglo-French intellectual developments. Emulation and fashion were also significant. At the level of elite culture, particularly in the early decades of the century, there was a strong sense of inferiority in eastern, central and northern Europe (including Britain) to the cultural life and products of France and Italy. This sense of inferiority took a number of forms and had a variety of consequences, including the attempt to implant desired foreign fashions, practices and institutions, and the patronage of foreign artists. Russo-Polish cultural interdependence increased, the Ukraine continuing to serve as an important intermediary, but in addition, Russian links with Britain, France and the Empire grew rapidly. In the Balkans the Enlightenment, though limited in its impact, both represented and increased links with western and central Europe.

All the major stylistic and thematic changes of the century occurred on a European scale, though there were significant national variations and differences in chronology. Just as the baroque and rococo styles struck resonances, and Chinese and Turkish motifs were repeated across the continent, so the discussion of the arts in different countries tended to be similar and critical tendencies, whether towards sentimentality at mid-century or Romantic from the 1770s, were generally international in their scope. Thus the widespread use of the neo-classical style, based on the use of classical elements in order to produce what was judged a 'noble simplicity', reflected in part the international fame both of mid-century archaeological discoveries and of the writings of a number of theorists such as the French abbé Laugier's *Essai sur l'architecture* (1753) and the German Johann Winckelmann's *Thoughts on the Imitation of Greek Works* (1755).

Europe's cosmopolitan culture reflected the strength of artistic and intellectual movements in a number of countries. The most important were France and Italy and, to a lesser extent, Britain and the Empire, though clearly the perspective varied by country and art-form. The impact of Protestant north German culture was obviously greater in Denmark, where it considerably influenced the 'Golden Age' of painting there between 1770 and 1850, than in Iberia, where French and Italian influences were strongest. Technical innovations could also be a factor. At the beginning of the century Johann Böttger discovered kaolin, making it possible to produce a porcelain as hard as that imported from China. Establishing himself in Meissen (Saxony) in 1710, he helped to give the Empire a lead in the field, and caused a decline in interest in carved ivory.

Cosmopolitanism implied neither similar circumstances nor identical developments. It did, however, encourage eclecticism. Utilising the principles of the concerto, developed in Italy at the end of the seventeenth century, German composers added elements of their traditional qualities of counterpoint and polyphony, and of the French suite.[27] Italian influence was strongest in the fields of art, architecture and music, markedly weaker in that of literature. Italy was significant as a source of artists, and for the training and inspiration it provided to those from elsewhere, and, to a lesser extent, as a still wealthy society able to provide considerable patronage. The influence of ancient or modern, secular or religious Italy on foreigners could be profound. Gilles-Marie Oppenordt (1672–1742) developed his style in Rome in 1692–9, while supported by the French Academy. His first decorative works, altar designs for Notre Dame and Saint-Germain des Prés in Paris, were completely governed by Roman models, while his architectural work, as *Directeur Général des Bâtiments* to the duke of Orléans on the latter's Palais Royal, was heavily influenced by the architecture of Borromini and northern Italy. The movement of Italian artists and products was important, both in encouraging and supplying esteem for them elsewhere in Europe, and in providing models for artists elsewhere. In 1708 Prince Ferdinand of Tuscany commissioned a series of bronze reliefs from Soldani as a present for his German brother-in-law. Tourists and others purchased large numbers of Italian works, both old and contemporary, such as the views of Rome painted by Giovanni Paolo Pannini and etched by Giambattista Piranesi and those of Venice by Antonio Canaletto. A large number of Italians worked abroad, a process facilitated by political links with Austria and Spain. They could be found throughout Europe and were particularly influential in the first half of the century, especially in music. Developments in instruments and playing techniques were dominated by Italians in the first half of the century. The composer and harpsichord player Domenico Scarlatti (1685–1757), who served John V of Portugal, and from 1729 until his death worked at the Spanish court, released the keyboard music of his time from the sway of polyphony.

French influence was pronounced in a number of areas. France was less influential musically than Italy or the Empire, despite the efforts of musicians such as Jean-Philippe Rameau (1683–1764), whose *Traité de l'harmonie réduite à ses principes naturels* (1722) and *Nouveau système de musique théorique* (1726) laid the foundations of the modern theory of harmony and who was an innovator in the use of modulation. However, in architecture and painting France made a considerable impact. The impact of Versailles helped to encourage foreign patrons to turn to French architects. In contrast to the traditional Italian scheme of continuous suites of large rooms without any secondary smaller rooms, Robert de Cotte (1656–1735), a fashionable architect in Parisian court society, offered more convenient and intimate living arrangements. French architectural influence, particularly strong in the Empire, continued into the second half of the century. Legeay introduced neo-classicism in Prussia, Nicolas de Pigage

(1723–96) dominated architecture in the lands of the elector Palatine and Philippe de la Guêpière, succeeding Domenico Retti as court architect to Karl Eugen of Württemberg in 1752, met the ruler's demand to create ducal apartments in his palace of Stuttgart to rival the royal apartments at Versailles, and also built in the French style the rural pleasure retreats of Monrepos (1760–6) and Solitude (1763–7). Like their architect compatriots, numerous French painters worked abroad for long periods. Louis-Michel van Loo was made court painter in Madrid in 1737, his father Jean-Baptiste enjoyed a considerable success while in London in 1737–42, while Jean-Baptiste Leprince was extensively employed on decorative paintings for Russian imperial palaces in 1758-63, before attempting to make his paintings of Russian customs fashionable in Paris.

French cultural influence was not, however, primarily a matter of Frenchmen working abroad, even if that number was increased by Huguenot exiles and their descendants. Far more significant were the visits of foreign patrons and artists to Paris and their subsequent attempts to keep in touch with developments there, which have led, for example, to the observation that 'at times, the coincidences between Greuze's and Reynolds' works are so close that we feel that Reynolds, like most educated Europeans in the 1770s and 1780s, kept in constant touch with Greuze's prolific production of paintings and engravings'.[28] France led Europe in most fashions, including those in clothes, particularly for women, and behaviour. The morning levée and toilet was introduced into Britain from France, as was the umbrella. France's position in European fashion helped to encourage the demand for French products, whether tapestries in Portugal or clothes, hairdressers, cooks, food and wine in aristocratic circles in London. Parisian cabinet-makers and craftsmen set the highest standards for furniture. French cultural influence was increased by the spread of French as a language in European polite society and by the importance of French works in European intellectual and literary life. Among the foreign-language novels in late eighteenth-century Polish library catalogues, 83 per cent were French, 10 per cent English, 4 per cent German, 2 per cent Italian and 1 per cent Spanish. France replaced Spain and Italy as the major source of Polish religious literature. French influence in Poland increased during the period of Saxon monarchy when, as Augustus II, Augustus III and their Saxon ministers knew no Polish, they communicated in French. It increased again in the 1760s and 1770s when many French Jesuits fled to Poland and played a major role in Polish education. French supplanted

Latin as the language of Polish science and most English, Italian and Spanish works came to Poland in French translations.

In eastern Europe and Scandinavia, German culture was a significant influence, particularly in the courts and in the towns, where trade with the Empire and German merchants were both important. There were many Germans in the Russian court in the first half of the century, while in the 1730s and 1740s the Danish court was increasingly dominated by a German element as a result of a number of German marriages by the royal family, with a consequent reorientation of artistic taste. The accession of the Hanoverian dynasty in Britain did not have a dramatic cultural effect, because of the relatively small scale of royal patronage and the absence of a strong indigenous Hanoverian culture. In Britain the debate over foreign cultural influences was concerned generally with France and Italy. However, Britain, like much of the rest of northern Europe, was affected considerably by German musical developments. By the second half of the century the Empire was clearly the centre of European music. The Mannheim school of composers was responsible for the development from the Italian overture of the four-movement symphony, a musical form which, after being refined by Haydn and Mozart, was to dominate orchestral composition for more than a century. British influence abroad was strongest in intellectual life, literature and gardening. New English landscape gardens were adopted more readily because they were partly modelled on a truly cosmopolitan source, the classics; specifically, imagined Virgilian landscapes mediated through the paintings of Claude Lorraine and Poussin. The Adam style of interior decoration became influential in Paris in the 1780s, a period in which significant numbers of the French social elite were affected by anglomania, a phenomenon whose effects included an interest in horse-racing and a male fashion for English clothes.

Cosmopolitanism was not without its critics, though, in general, criticism was directed against specific cultural imports, rather than at the international dimension of culture. By the second half of the century many intellectuals were more willing to attack cultural borrowing and to discern and praise particular national cultures. Joseph II, who founded a German national theatre in Vienna in 1776, had been the dedicatee in 1769 of the *Hermannsschlacht*, a glorification of the struggle of the ancient Germans against Roman invasion, written by the poet Friedrich Klopstock. Klopstock, who produced much religious verse, particularly his Miltonic Messias (1780), 'sought in his *Oden* (1771) and his ... patriotic plays to replace the familiar classical myths by what he considered "Nordic" or "Germanic" topics'.[29] Foreign intellectual domination produced in reaction a growth of Russian patriotic sentiment, though this was directed against any foolish endorsement of all foreign fashions, rather than against the westernisation of Russian culture.

Language

Common languages were important in the definition of national cultures and as a means of communication for cosmopolitan culture. The trend towards national uniformity through the consolidation of major languages at the expense of lesser ones, served to make the common culture more accessible. However, much of the European population spoke minority languages, such as Basque, Catalan and Breton, or dialects that were frequently difficult to understand. There were numerous Italian dialects united only by their speakers' consciousness of themselves as *Latini*. The *langue d'oc* of southern France, a Romance language which itself took many forms, posed problems of comprehension for Parisians. To a certain extent the national languages acted as dialects of the cosmopolitan languages. The most important of these was Latin, the language in much of Europe of the church, the law and intellectual life. It was the *lingua franca* in much of eastern and southern Europe. Charles XII of Sweden's knowledge of Latin was good enough for him to use it for conducting negotiations in Poland. When Joseph II visited Transylvania in 1773 he often had to speak in Latin. Though Polish replaced Old Russian as the language of the administration and the courts in Lithuania in 1697, Latin remained the language of the courts in Poland. It was also the medium of Polish higher education and scholarship, though much less than in earlier periods. Most teaching at the Kiev Academy early in the century was in Latin and the language continued to be used for teaching there until the 1840s, while Gottlieb Bayer (1694–1738), a German appointed to the Russian Imperial Academy of Sciences, wrote most of his works in Latin. Latin was the language of administration for Hungary and the eastern provinces of the Habsburg Empire until 1784, when German replaced it. As in much of Europe, language was also an indicator of social position rather than a definition of nationhood, Latin in Hungary being favoured by the nobility. It was not until the 1780s, when Joseph II sought to spread the use of German, that the Hungarian nobility began to show much interest in the already strong Hungarian linguistic/literary reform movement.

By the closing decades of the century Latin was on the decline in eastern Europe for non-ecclesiastical purposes. In 1766 the

Codex Theresianus, a new legal code designed for all the German Habsburg territories, was not only drawn up in German, rather than Latin, but also used a not too technical vocabulary in order to make it more generally intelligible. Latin was dropped from the title of the catalogue of the Leipzig book fair in 1760. The military and treasury commissions established in Poland in 1764 used Polish.

Latin had already been generally supplanted in western Europe as a secular *lingua franca* by French during the reign of Louis XIV. French had become the language of court society, diplomacy and the arts. As it became more fashionable, increasing numbers felt it necessary to learn it and to be heard to use it. French became more important on France's borders, particularly in Lorraine, and in the Austrian Netherlands, where it was the major language of cultural trends and scientific thought. However, knowledge of the language was limited to the social elite and therefore most of the population had only a limited contact with this culture. Similarly, in the Empire, where French was fashionable, particularly in the court societies of Catholic Germany, its impact was socially limited. Frederick the Great regarded German as a barbaric language, preferring to use French, but he did little to encourage wider knowledge of the language. The spread of French helped the dissemination of French culture and ideas. Charles XII was able to read and listen to readings of the plays of Molière, Corneille and Racine. A 'French School' of poets in the second half of the century in Hungary imitated their French counterparts thematically and stylistically.

Though Latin and French were the two most important international languages, German was also of considerable significance in eastern and northern Europe. It was important in Denmark, Sweden where Charles XII wrote German very easily, and Russia, the monarchs of each of which ruled territories that had at least a German-speaking nobility. German was the language of the bureaucracy of Russia's Baltic provinces throughout the century. Though Peter the Great had contemplated introducing Dutch as an official language, none the less German was the most important foreign tongue during the period of early Russian westernisation. The Academy of Sciences' High School in St Petersburg, founded in the mid-1720s, used German and Latin until it changed to Russian in 1742. In the Habsburg Empire, German was the most important, though not the sole, language of administration and attempts were made to foster its use. Under Leopold I, fluent German was compulsory for army officers, while the process of 'Germanisation' that can be seen in the Habsburg dominions in the seventeenth century was continued.

Czech had been replaced by Latin and German in Bohemian scholarship, literature, higher education, administration and polite society, and these languages continued to be important. In 1720 the Bohemian Diet published its accession to the Pragmatic Sanction in German only. Joseph II sought to make German the language of administration, and to this end ordered its use and teaching in the growing educational system. In 1774 German was made the language of instruction in Bohemia's public elementary schools; in 1776 this was extended to most of the gymnasia (high schools); in 1780 Czech was no longer permitted in the gymnasia and after 1788 pupils seeking entry had to know German. In 1784 a university was established at Lvov in Galicia as a German-speaking centre and it did not become polonised until late in the following century. In the same year, Joseph decided that all lectures at Prague University should be in German, with the exception of those on law and theology, which were to continue in Latin. In 1782 Joseph had issued a patent for the Jews decreeing that after two years no document written in Hebrew or with Hebrew characters was to have any legal validity. Six years later he ordered that all ordinances for the kingdom of Bohemia should be printed in German only, though Czech was still permitted for local announcements.

Other languages were also spread with political assistance. In 1720 the Russian Senate limited the publication of church books in Ukrainian. Schools were established to russify the children of the Cossack elite, while, though German remained the language of most of the bureaucracy in the Baltic provinces, after Catherine II's reforms there, local schools were pressed to prepare their pupils for state service by teaching them Russian. Language reflected political links past and present and sustained cultural ties. Spanish was still commonly the language of official documents in Sicily until the 1760s, although the rule of the kings of Spain had ceased in the War of the Spanish Succession. The new nobility established in Wallachia and Moldavia by the Phanariot *hospodars* (provincial rulers owing allegiance to the Turkish sultans) spoke Greek. Constantin Brâncoveanu, *hospodar* of Wallachia from 1688 to 1714, generously sponsored Greek culture, revitalising a Greek academy in Bucharest and funding the foundation of printing presses in Bucharest and Snagov.

At times it is clear that language was intended as a political weapon, culture as a definition of allegiance. The Scottish Society for the Propagation of Christian Knowledge, founded in 1709, sought to deny an educational heritage to Gaelic and to extirpate the language. English was the sole language permitted both as the medium of instruction and for the conversation of the pupils in the schools the Society established in the Highlands. It was hoped through education and language to spread Calvinist doctrine and to assimilate the Highlands to anglophone Lowland Scotland. Against this, the Glasgow-based Highland Society, founded in 1727, promoted Gaelic, particularly by publishing in it. Churchmen and squires in Wales sought to suppress the Welsh language, as did the charity schools. The Reverend Griffith Jones (1683–1761) was much abused and denounced as a secret spreader of Methodism because from the 1730s he stressed the need to use Welsh as the medium of a popular literacy campaign and to catechise in it. He opened numerous schools and was partly responsible for the edition of the Bible and Prayer Book in Welsh issued by the Society for Promoting Christian Knowledge in 1746. The Church of Ireland was never able to overcome the language barrier that would have enabled it to increase its influence among native Catholics. In 1711 a scheme was put forward for the printing of an Irish New Testament, catechism, and Prayer Book, and the establishment in each parish of a Charter School to provide free instruction in the English language and Protestant doctrine. Despite support at the highest level, the plan came to nothing.

It would be mistaken, however, to see language primarily in terms of political power and cultural hegemony. Much was clearly a matter of the expansion of printing, and of intellectual and cultural interests, in both living and dead languages. Grammars and dictionaries were printed in increasing numbers, the first English–Portuguese dictionary and the first grammars of Dutch and Italian published in Portuguese appearing in the 1730s. J. B. Bullet (1699–1775) produced the most comprehensive 'Dictionnaire Celtique' yet published, as part of his *Mémoires sur la Langue Celtique* (Besançon, 1754–60), a work that also contained a history of the language and an etymological description of the areas of Europe with Celtic settlements.

If certain widely used languages remained important, knowledge of at least one of them being necessary in the senior ranks of many spheres of administrative, cultural and ecclesiastical life, there was also growing interest in national languages. This was a particular feature of the closing decades of the century, though a number of earlier rulers had been concerned about linguistic identity. Worried about the Swedish language, Charles XII attempted to find native words, frequently of dialect origin, for foreign expressions. In 1729 in the county of Nice, Victor Amadeus II placed government-appointed officials in charge of educational reform and partially replaced Latin with his administrative language, Italian. By the 1760s concern for vernacular languages had become more marked in some intellectual circles. Herder placed great weight on the distinct nature of each language as both a consequence and a sustainer of national identity. He claimed that every vernacular could be developed into a written language and used for both polite society and literary works, shaping the particular character of creative writing. Rejecting the widely held idea that a divine act was the primary impulse giving rise to speech, Herder presented language not as a universal system of rational signs, capable of being judged by abstract and universal standards and thus subject to hierarchical grouping, but as the evolutionary product of the experience of its speakers. This led him to display interest in folk works, as poetic productions true to the specific character of particular languages. In the *Critical Forests* (1769) Herder contrasted folksongs favourably with French literature. In his *Folksongs* (1778–9) he discussed what he claimed were true products of national culture.

Herder was not alone in finding vernacular languages worthy of intellectual attention. The Brothers Grimm, growing up at the end of the century, collected German folk tales. Across eastern Europe intellectuals devoted time to what had generally been regarded as the tongues of peasants, to languages that were primarily oral, with scant literary impact or treatment. In the Balkans intellectuals sought to reform and use vernacular languages in order to propagate new cultural ideas. Language was to serve to redefine the collective identity of peoples who lacked political independence or expression and, in doing so, was to act as a medium of cultural change: 1768, the year in which Father Marko Pohlin's Carniolan grammar was published, is usually given as the date of the beginning of the Slovene national revival, the comparable date for Bulgarian being 1762 when Paisij Xilendarski's Slavo-Bulgarian history was completed. Among the Serbs, who lacked independence, the church played a major role in keeping alive cultural identity and the memory of past greatness. However, the church and the writers of the period used an artificial literary language, Slavo-Serbian, close to church Slavonic, but not to the speech of the common people, who appear hardly to have understood it. In 1761 the Hungarian baron Lörintz Orczy organised a society for the purification of the language and took the French encyclopaedists as his model. György Bessenyei (1747–1811), 'the Hungarian Voltaire', a writer who consciously imitated Voltaire's way of life and sought to propagate his ideas, launched a project in 1781 for a Hungarian Academy of Science and Literature. The language issue became significant politically in Hungary, and there were demands in the early 1790s to make Hungarian the language of command in the army and a required subject in the schools. In the first half of the century in Poland numerous borrowings from French, German and Latin entered the language, but, thereafter, there was increased interest in linguistic integrity. Stanislaus Konarski (1700–73) sought the reform of the language. Polish linguistics became a distinct discipline, foreign borrowings were challenged, folklore and old Slav legends became fashionable, and in 1781 the first Polish encyclopedia was published. The first scholarly Russian grammar was published in 1757. Henrik Porthan (1739–1804), founder of modern studies in Finnish history and folklore, studied Finnish traditional literature and language.

In both Hungary and Bohemia Joseph II's support for German aroused opposition. Bohemian nobles 'were converted by the intellectuals' argument that the Czech language had been the hallmark of an independent and culturally renowned Bohemian Kingdom, and that a knowledge of Czech was a practical necessity for nobles in dealing with their serfs and other low subordinates'.[30] Such views characterised the published defences of the Czech language which were produced increasingly in later eighteenth-century Bohemia. These works extolled the antiquity of the Czech language and, by implication, nation, insisting upon their equality with other European languages and nations. Most of them were written in Latin or German. In 1791, at a ceremonial session of the Royal Bohemian Society of Sciences in Prague, Josef Dobrovsky asked Leopold II to protect Czech, protested against the government's policy of germanisation and stressed the utilitarian value of a multilingual empire. His appeal was translated into Czech and widely publicised. In 1793 a chair of Czech language and literature was established at the University of Prague. The first Czech-language newspaper appeared in 1719.

Linguistic consciousness was not restricted to languages that lacked government support. The century witnessed the development of a standard German literary language which was used by writers seeking to address all Germans, and to express artistic and philosophical ideas. Under Frederick William II (1786–97) the use of German revived at the Prussian court, while the dominance of French at the Academy of Sciences was challenged. English replaced Latin as the language of the English court records in the 1730s. In Russia, where there was a serious controversy over the origins of the people and the language, several writers developed a patriotic etymology. In a treatise published posthumously in 1773 Trediakovskii argued that foreign words taken from western European languages were endangering Russian, and suggested that Slavonic words or neologisms using

Slavonic roots should be employed instead. Italian intellectuals displayed increased interest in defining a common Italian language that could serve as the language of culture. Genovesi saw the expulsion of the Jesuits from the kingdom of Naples as an opportunity to create a co-ordinated educational system offering new scientific disciplines and teaching entirely in Italian. His plan was not adopted, though eventually local communities were instructed to open elementary schools, teaching Italian as well as Latin. The often piecemeal reorganisation of education in Catholic countries following the expulsion of the Jesuits tended to lead to a reduction in the role of Latin. Thus teaching in the Grand Collège en Ile de Liège, founded in 1773, was conducted by the secular clergy, and, though there was still a lot of Latin, French was dominant.

It would, however, be misleading to present the century as one of competing languages and emerging nationalism. Such an analysis is appropriate for certain areas and periods, but many of those who displayed an interest in the vernacular were themselves rooted firmly in cosmopolitan culture. Porthan's interest in Finnish culture did not prevent him from sharing Winckelmann's admiration for ancient Greece, while, as professor of rhetoric at Turku Åbo university, he taught Latin literature and language, defended its utility as a scholarly language, and taught trainee clerics the rules of classical rhetoric as an aid to preparing sermons. The leading Hungarian poets of the last decades of the century were the so-called French School, which followed the ideological content and verse forms of their French contemporaries. The profit motive also played a role. One of the leading publishers of Slavic books in the 1780s was the Leipzig printing house of Breitkopf.

At the elite level increased interest in vernacular languages did not lessen the impact of cosmopolitanism. At the popular level it is difficult to arrive at conclusions. Though opposition to foreigners, such as Catholic landlords and Jews in the western Ukraine, could be very pronounced, and language and dialect played a significant role in defining a sense of alienation, it is unclear whether linguistic consciousness became more pronounced and how dialects affected this consciousness. Most of the themes and issues of popular culture, whether wolves or stepmothers, do not appear to have been specific to particular peoples. Rather than different languages acting as barriers, common circumstances appear to have thrown up similar traditions. Werewolves appeared in Gascon and Livonian folklore. In much of France the period leading up to Christmas was considered peculiarly vulnerable to the activities of sorcerers. However, common beliefs, other than those taught by the churches, were not obvious to those shielded from cultural contacts, divided by language and generally restricted to an oral culture. For many of the literate and the travelled, a comparative interest in myths and beliefs entrenched an elite outlook, and a sense of distance from the masses. At the elite level, even when linguistic integrity and distinctions were stressed, knowledge of other languages was assumed and a common culture based on Christianity and the classics was propagated.

9 Science and Medicine

Though our century received the complimentary title of the 'century of philoso-
phy' from all sides, and although we have already preselected its epitaph:
Enlightenment!, many heads everywhere are seized by such sustained dizzi-
ness ... one quotes ghosts, sees through thick walls, consults with the deceased,
distils universal cures and preserves oneself eternally against death, one forges
diamonds, cooks up gold, carries the stone of wisdom in one's pocket, easily
conjures the moon down to earth, and diverts the earth from its orbit ... and the
originators of these miracles in no way collect gullible crowds at rural fairs;
no, Mesmer, Cagliostro and company find themselves surrounded by bejewelled
society.

(Catherine II, 1786)[1]

Some scientific enquirers were keen to develop and apply the
methods and insights which had brought about, in the late seventeenth century, the so-called Scientific Revolution: certain major
advances in discovering the operations of natural laws. For the
great majority of Europeans, however, such ideas and the standards of proof implied were little understood. The developments
in astronomy, mathematics and physics associated especially with
Isaac Newton (1642–1727) were resisted in some intellectual circles, particularly in France where the influence of the ideas of
Descartes (1596–1650) was very strong. The new science was
ignored by much of the population, and the new cosmology was
not accepted by all. In Viterbo in Italy, where there was a hot
spring, the local people thought that it was bottomless and
communicated with Hell. It was still widely believed that astrological anatomies and zodiacs were keys to character and guides
to the future, that extra-terrestrial forces intervened in the affairs
of the world, particularly human and animal health and the state
of the crops and weather, and that each constellation in the
zodiac presided over a particular part of man, guidance to this
process being provided by almanacs. Ptolemaic geocentrism continued important in this literature, while many almanac writers
boasted of being anti-Newtonian. Neither did scientific advances
necessarily challenge these traditional practices. Diego de Torres
Villarroel (1694–1770), professor of mathematics at Salamanca
from 1726, was criticised in 1770 by Campomanes for 'believing that his duties had been fulfilled in writing almanacs and

prognostications'. He had done so since 1719 and was interested in magic and the supernatural, and a defender of the value of astrology. Torres applied his mathematical and astronomical knowledge to his almanacs, but he also used them to refute the teaching of other sciences, denying the value of modern medicine in favour of the four humours.[2]

Popular conservatism was not the sole factor inhibiting the diffusion of new scientific ideas and methods. There was no simple 'correct' line of scientific development which led smoothly to modern conceptions of science. Unsound theories, like the phlogiston explanation of combustion, could lead to greater clarification of the issues involved, and were not simply worthless. A form of history of science was emerging which identified a mainstream tradition stressing observation, experiment and careful deduction of laws, but the very looseness of the processes involved made this difficult to apply in order to separate 'sound' from 'unsound' science. The sense of a great tradition, of a correct approach and of recent important breakthroughs in understanding light and gravitation gave a rough framework for what was and what was not scientific. Nevertheless, the creative tension in eighteenth-century science of experimentation and speculative systematisation did not foster simply one approach to any particular problem. Instead, a wide range of approaches was adopted and conclusions drawn. It was difficult to establish any individual interpretation in an age where standards of scientific proof were not always rigorous and the facilities for the necessary experimentation often absent. The amateur and commercial nature of much scientific activity possibly exacerbated the problem, though the world of scholarship was not free from serious error. The belief that man could come to understand much about himself and the world through his own reason and through empirical investigation had played a major role in the Scientific Revolution. However, science was a process, rather than a set of answers, and this belief encouraged not only the activities and acceptance of charlatans, but also the continued intertwining of metaphysics, theology, human interest and scientific thought and experimentation that had been so important in the previous century.

There was no shortage of charlatans, but in putting scientific interest and methods to personal profit, they also revealed the varied relationship of both of these to the widespread desire to understand and control the environment, at the individual level affecting education and health, and at the social level. This desire was only imperfectly catered for by existing formal institutions. The alchemist Saint-Germain enjoyed the favour of Louis XV. Frederick II's librarian Antoine-Joseph Pernety published a major alchemical dictionary in 1758. In 1715 Louis XIVs doctors were ready to try the remedies of itinerant quacks for his gangrene. The English quack-doctor Joshua Ward (1685–1761) gained tremendous popularity and a considerable fortune from 1734 and was patronised by George II, despite the fact that his remedies killed as many as they cured. In 1748 Frederick I of Sweden was treated by alchemists who claimed to know the secret of golden tinctures. Giuseppe Balsamo (1743–95), 'Count Cagliostro', began his career as an alchemist by seeking to transmute excrement, hair, herbs, minerals, urine and wood into gold in London in 1776–7. In Courland in 1778 he created an occult system called Egyptian Freemasonry, before establishing himself in St Petersburg as a clairvoyant, a holder of séances and a healer. His appeal was lessened in 1779 by the arrival of the cult of therapeutic magnetism, the invention of Franz Anton Mesmer. Interest in the 'exotic' and the 'monstrous' highlighted ambiguities in Enlightened thought.

Many scientists were interested in alchemy. The eminent British chemist Peter Woulfe (1727?–1803), who developed an apparatus for passing gases through liquids, also pursued alchemical investigations, fixing prayers to his apparatus. Nicholas-Philippe Ledru, who in 1783 established a clinic for the treatment of nervous disorders in Paris using electric shocks to treat epileptics, and was given the tide of Royal Physician by Louis XVI in 1784, was also interested in fortune-telling. The revolutionary Jean-Paul Marat published on heat, light and electricity, claimed to discover nervous, optical, igneous and electric fluids and dismissed the work of Newton.

The idea of direct divine intervention was not only held by the populace. Newton himself argued that God acted in order to keep heavenly bodies in their place. Jansenist miracles took place not in some obscure valley but in Paris, where in 1725 Voltaire witnessed the cure of a partial paralysis that was certified by the archbishop as a miracle. The idea that personal fault or the malevolent intentions of others were responsible for mishap proved difficult to dispel whatever the current teaching on cosmology, physics and medicine.

Medicine was a particular field of misapprehension because much about both body and mind was not understood. It was widely believed that masturbation was the specific cause of mental and physical diseases. Inadequate and inaccurate medical information, sexual titillation and the condemnation of sin combined in works such as *Onania, or the heinous sin of self-pollution, and all its frightful consequences in both sexes*. First published in London in 1708, it went through at least 19 editions, the 17th in

1756, and sold nearly 38,000 copies. Much of its information, such as the effect on the clitoris of masturbation, was anatomically or medically wrong.

Much scientific work advanced inaccurate theses that were contested in its own day but, as it often used principles of hypothesis and experimentation similar to those employed by its critics, were difficult to disprove. The weight of tradition was also still very important. For example, the argument that bile is responsible for the colour of human skin, advanced as a scientific fact by ancient writers, was repeated without experimental support by eighteenth-century scientists, including Buffon, Feijoo, Holbach and La Mettrie. This error was linked to false explanations, such as that of Marcello Malpighi (1628–94), professor of medicine in Bologna and the founder of microscopic anatomy, who believed that all men were originally white, but that the sinners had become black. The Italian scientist Bernardo Albinus proved to his own satisfaction in 1737 that Negro bile was black and in 1741 the French doctor Pierre Barrère published experiments demonstrating both this and that the bile alone caused the black pigment in Negro skin. This inaccurate theory won widespread acclaim, in part thanks to an extensive review in the *Journal des Savants* in 1742, and played a major role in the prevalent mid-century belief that Negroes were another species of man without the ordinary human organs, tissues, heart and soul. In 1765 the chief doctor in the leading hospital in Rouen, Claude Nicolas Le Cat, demonstrated that Barrère's theory was wrong. However, because the microscopes of the period were not strong enough to distinguish sharply within human skin tissue, Le Cat's alternative suggestion, based on microscopic experiments he had done with frogs, squids and other animals, was in fact inaccurate. In addition, like most good scientists of the period, he believed that animal spirits, not subject to the laws of physics and chemistry, pervade the hollow tubes of the nerves. None the less, Le Cat's work was experimentally and theoretically far in advance of that of Barrère and he was careful not to draw conclusions from exceptional cases. It is therefore striking that Le Cat was generally ignored and Barrère's arguments went on being cited favourably.[3]

Similar episodes could be discussed to illustrate the defects of the argument that eighteenth-century scientific activity, and experimentation in particular, necessarily advanced knowledge. John Needham (1713–81), the first Catholic cleric elected a fellow of the Royal Society of London (1747) and, subsequently, the first director of the Imperial Academy in Brussels, published in 1749 his experimental proof of the theory of spontaneous generation, the idea that inanimate matter could come alive, and thus that mutations and new creations of species were possible. Another Catholic cleric, the Neapolitan Spallanzoni, demonstrated the fallacy of Needham's experiment in 1760. A polymath, in the manner of a period where modern distinctions between branches of knowledge had little meaning, Needham also published on ants; the Alps; electricity, one of the great interests of the period; his correspondence with Voltaire on miracles; and, in 1761, a widely discussed, but speedily refuted, book that sought by the use of Chinese characters to interpret an Egyptian inscription. Another error that was refuted was the theory advanced by Newton and supported by Daniel Bernoulli concerning the hydro-dynamic aspects of the outflow of water through a hole at the bottom of a vessel. Newton subsequently accepted the criticisms of Giovanni Rizzetti.

Experimentation, even if designed to sustain established views, reflected a determination to expand on received information. Exploration played an important role, especially in botany, astronomy and geology. The collection of new species of plants and animals was a major interest of this period. Turgot sent two naturalists abroad. Charles III, who founded a Royal Botanical Garden in Madrid, also sent a scientific expedition to Spanish America in 1785 in order to discover plants with medicinal properties. The botanist Joseph Banks (1743–1820) sailed round the world with Captain James Cook and also collected plants on expeditions to Newfoundland and Iceland, succeeding George III's favourite the earl of Bute as director of the new gardens at Kew. Banks helped to make them a centre for botanical research based on holdings from around the world. He also played a role in the British acquisition of the botanical and zoological collections of the Swedish naturalist Carl Linnaeus (1707–78) who developed the comprehensive Latin binomial system for plants and animals, grouping both into genera and species. The Cook voyages – a microcosm of the Enlightenment – were important to a whole range of scientific activity (in addition to botany) adjudged useful to government.[4]

Linnaeus' career illustrates several aspects of eighteenth-century science. Interested in the acquisition of information, which led him to travel in Lapland collecting plants, he was also a systematiser whose theory was challenged by other scientists, especially Georges Louis Leclerc de Buffon and Albrecht von Haller. A professor who published in Latin in order to reach the scholarly community, he inspired a group of amateurs, the Linnean Society of London, founded in 1788 but without women fellows until the 1900s. Throughout Europe women were generally excluded from scientific work. Count Buffon (1707–88), the director of the Paris *Jardin des Plantes*, began in 1749 to publish a multi-volume *Histoire naturelle*, which achieved great popularity and was partly designed to replace what he saw as the arbitrary taxonomic classifications of Linnaeus.

Astronomical research also benefited from travel. In 1736 the French *Académie des Sciences* sponsored a journey to Lapland led by Pierre de Maupertuis and including the mathematicians Camus, Clairaut and Lemonnier. A degree of the meridian within the polar circle was measured in order to establish the shape of the earth, which was shown to be spheroid and slightly flattened at the Poles. Geological research, such as that of Guettard in the Puy de Dôme in 1751, threw doubt on the biblical view of the age of the earth and thus challenged traditional Christian teaching.

Though measurement played a major role in the experimentation of the period, there were important problems. It was difficult to make standard instruments and replicate laboratory results, and research in chemistry was hindered by the difficulty of quantifying chemical reactions. Good vulcanised tubing did not appear in Europe until the mid-1840s. The astronomer William Herschel (1738–1822), who was determined 'to take nothing upon trust', 'to carry improvements in telescopes to their utmost extent' and 'to leave no spot of the heavens unexamined', and who in 1781 found Uranus, the first planet discovered since antiquity, encountered numerous failures in 1773–4 in the construction of his first telescope. Classification was designed to aid research and various systems of measurement were introduced. Thermometers were produced by Celsius, Fahrenheit and Réaumur, each, however, using different scales, an example of the unco-ordinated nature of most scientific work in the period which was only partially counterbalanced by the extensive correspondence of the age.

The virtues of experimentation were widely praised in scientific circles. In works such as Condillac's *Traité des Systèmes* (1749), the *philosophes* condemned Descartes's ideal of *a priori* rationalist science, and though such reasoning continued to be very important, for example in psychology, experimentation was responsible for a number of major advances, such as those in chemistry and medicine. Stephen Hales (1677–1761), a clergyman like many of the scientists of the period, was typical in his wide-ranging interests. Besides inventing artificial ventilators and quantifying various aspects of plant physiology, Hales opened the way for a correct appreciation of blood pressure thanks to his conception of the living organism as a self-regulating machine, and his experiments. The surgeon John Hunter, who rebelled against the predominant European medical training of study of classical texts and refused to 'stuff Latin and Greek at the university', was typical of many of the leading surgeons of the period in his willingness to try new methods, even when the theoretical explanation was unclear. In his *Medical Sketches* (1786), John Moore discussed the transmission of impressions from one nerve to another, illustrated by the fact that eating ice-creams gives a pain in the root of the nose. He also described the effects of temporary pressure on the surface of a brain exposed by trepanning, from observation on a Parisian beggar, an apt image of some aspects of the Enlightenment.

Much of the experimentation conducted in provincial societies was designed to foster interest in accepted scientific principles, rather than to promote new knowledge. Nevertheless, medical research became more important. The appointment of physicians to the London charity hospitals turned them into centres of research and in Edinburgh the modernisation of the curriculum strengthened the role of hospital-based research. In England the training of surgeons was increasingly conducted in hospital schools rather than through apprenticeships. The major purpose of the Academy of Medicine, founded at Madrid in 1734, was to study medicine and surgery from observation and experience. The Spanish doctor Gaspar Casal (1679–1759) was the first to introduce in Spain the modern, empirical, symptomatic concept of illness. He used this method to describe the symptoms of pellagra and to differentiate it from scabies and leprosy.

More generally, medical care was increasingly understood in a secular context, with an emphasis on healing rather than on penitence and salvation. This concept dominated the influential *Memoirs on Paris Hospitals* (1788) by Jacques Tenon (1724–1816), a surgeon, hospital founder and member of the Paris Academy of Sciences who sought to apply Newtonian reason and mathematical analysis to hospital design, goals, and operation. Tenon's *Memoirs* were widely praised and were to be influential in hospital design the following century.[5]

A revolution in chemistry occurred towards the end of the century. During its closing decades, five gaseous elements were discovered and about a dozen gaseous compounds intensively investigated. Antoine Lavoisier (1743–94) 'set the science on a new footing, by stipulating a new working definition of the chemical element, by translating chemical affinities into numerical relations and by systematically rewriting the very language of the science'.[6] Chemistry was indeed created as a separate science, with a language and methodology that sought to distinguish it from alchemy. Lavoisier's *Méthode de Nomenclature Chimique* (1787) defined a system of quantification that could be used to facilitate comparative experimentation. Through his experiments, Lavoisier came to the conclusion that the weight of all compounds obtained by chemical reaction is equal to that of the reacting substances, a conclusion which he generalised as the law of conservation of mass in 1789. Lavoisier's systematisation of the chemistry of gases set the seal on one of the more successful areas of eighteenth-century chemical advance, the recognition that gases could be separated and identified, rather than being simply variants of 'air'. Joseph Priestley and Karl Scheele discovered what Lavoisier called oxygen. He also helped to discredit the theory of phlogiston, advanced by the German Georg Stahl (1660–1734) in 1697. Phlogiston was conceived of as an invisible, impalpable, weightless element found in various proportions in all combustible substances and given off in combustion and respiration. From 1763 it had been conceived of as having negative weight, something in itself no harder to accept than the equally little understood electrical and magnetic impalpable 'fluids'. Lavoisier himself was often wrong in his specific conclusions, for example the notion that oxygen was an acidifying principle.

The development of chemistry was not solely due to Lavoisier. In the Empire the number of academic posts and laboratories for chemistry and the number of chemists increased dramatically in 1720–80, thanks largely to government interest in promoting public health and industry. Whereas in 1720 most German chemists were practising medical doctors or teachers of medicine, by 1780 most worked in pharmacy, technology and the teaching of chemistry. Specialisation increased and chemists were more able and willing to conduct experimental research. The first German periodical devoted exclusively to chemistry, the *Chemische Annalen*, was founded by Lorenz Crell in 1778. The *Journal der Physik*, founded by F. A. C. Gren, followed in 1790.

In 1750 chairs of chemistry and physics were established in the University of Uppsala in Sweden, at the cost of chairs in poetry and oriental languages. In Britain the doctor William Brownrigg (1711–1800) formulated the concept of a multiplicity of chemically distinctive gases. Joseph Black (1728–99), professor of chemistry at Glasgow and later Edinburgh, discovered latent heat and first fixed the compound carbon dioxide. Henry Cavendish (1731–1810), a master of quantitative analysis, was in 1766 the first to define hydrogen as a distinct substance and in 1781 the first to determine the composition of water by exploding a mixture of hydrogen and oxygen in a sealed vessel. Joseph Priestley (1733–1804) discovered a number of gases and oxides and carried out experimental work on astronomy, electricity, optics and respiration. He also made considerable advances in the equipment for studying gases. The Swedish pharmacist Karl Scheele (1742–86) isolated a large number of new compounds in organic chemistry and discovered chlorine in 1774. Another Swede, Johann Wallerius, was the first holder of the chair of chemistry at Uppsala and has been termed the father of agricultural chemistry.

Two years after Cavendish's discovery, in 1776, that hydrogen is lighter than air, Black suggested it should be released into a bladder. Hydrogen was used as a lifting agent in a balloon commissioned by the French *Académie des Sciences* in 1783 and manufactured by the physicist J. A. C. Charles, who flew in it. Earlier that year the Montgolfier brothers had used hot air to send a balloon up to 6000 feet. The self-educated Joseph Montgolfier also used his ideas on the expansive power of heat to work on a heat pump, an ancestor of the internal combustion engine. The widespread interest in heat and motion led also to experiments with the industrial use of steam power and with steam locomotion, and to Meusnier's designs for cigar-shaped steerable balloons.

Much chemical research was directly intended for practical purposes. Thanks to the analysis of mineral spring waters by chemists and the development of techniques for making large amounts of carbon dioxide, it became possible in about 1780 to make artificial mineral waters on a commercial scale. The Edinburgh doctor Francis Home (1719–1813), who first called attention to croup as a distinct disease in 1765, tested water for bleaching and in 1756 published *Experiments on Bleaching*, which was translated into French and German and for which he was awarded a medal by the Trustees for the Improvement of Manufactures in North Britain.

However, the chemistry of such operations as brewing and iron-making was far from understood. The chemistry of industrial processes was still largely traditional, that is arrived at by a long process of local trial and error. In brewing the processes varied from region to region, with top- or bottom-fermentation and the evolution of local yeast strains. Some of these methods were doubtless better than others at excluding the contaminated air, but all were vulnerable, as the biochemistry was not yet understood. Pasteur's work on yeasts was not done until the 1850s, and enzymes were not discovered until the end of the nineteenth century. Consequently, when large-scale brewing began later in the eighteenth century, the hazards of sudden loss of huge and costly batches of porter were great. The big London brewers only used their fermentation vats in the winter, keeping the brew relatively safely bunged and stored in cask during the more dangerous summer months. Tanning of leather, a particularly widespread industry wherever meat slaughter for sufficient populations made it viable, was in something of the same state; processes were technically developed, but not capable of easy change and experimentation, since no distinction existed between the truly important and the accidental elements in the process. Iron-making also was largely unscientific, at least at the level of ordinary practice; deciding when to add the handful of sand to the furnace, when to tap the ore and how much blast to permit tended to be skilled judgements resting in the person of the workman. Dyeing was mainly with vegetable products, and often centred in local specialisms and processes, again with little possibility of improvement because of uncertainty about the active principles. Similarly, bleaching of cottons and linens was a long-drawn-out process which occupied much space and time, with comparatively little change over the century. In 1746 the English doctor John Roebuck (1718–94) revolutionised the manufacture of sulphuric acid, reducing it to a quarter of its former cost, by substituting leaden chambers for glass globes for the purpose of condensation. Sulphuric acid was used to replace natural acids such as soured milk in the bleaching of linen, but this was not widely applied and in any case was used only for vegetable fibres. Woollens were quicker to bleach with a mixture of washing in stale urine, and then 'stoving', which was effectively giving them a mild sulphuric acid bath by burning sulphur in a large closed chamber and letting the products condense over the cloth. There was little pressure to develop a complete understanding of the process, or to apply new methods. The Leblanc process for making sodium carbonate ('washing soda') from sodium chloride, invented by the French doctor Nicholas Leblanc (1742–1806), came only in 1790.

The growing prestige of science reflected the sense not only that it could have practical value, but also that, by increasing man's knowledge, it was worthy of praise. The English Dissenting Academies introduced the teaching of experimental science as a means of understanding the wisdom of God.[7] The *philosophes* praised science as an example of human creativity and extolled the achievements of contemporary and recent scientists. The public tributes of the French *Académie des Sciences* helped to establish an image of scientists as disinterested, passionless seekers after truth. Scientists such as Newton became a subject for the arts, the German painter Januarius Zick (1730–97) producing allegories of 'Newton and optics' and 'Newton and gravity'.

The prestige and value of science brought patronage and popularity. A number of rulers and aristocrats took a personal interest. The duke of Orléans, the regent, had his own chemistry laboratory. Peter I owned a planetarium, purchased scientific collections and in 1718 offered his subjects rewards for delivering human and animal monsters. He assured the public that such creatures were the result of natural causes, not of the 'devil who had no power over procreation'. Turgot was an able amateur scientist. A British tourist of the 1760s noted in Naples: 'The Prince of Sansevero who is a great chymist hath a great many curiosities of art that he himself hath performed all which he showed to us and explained with great politeness and gave us a book of all the curious effects of his art.'[8] George III was but one of many rulers who patronised astronomy, though, like most who showed an interest in the subject, he did not understand the complex mathematics that played an increasing role in it. Kaunitz was active in supporting scientific activity in Brussels.

Much government support was piecemeal and traditional in its concerns, such as public health and weapons technology. Nevertheless, the organisation of public institutions specifically for scientific research spread. They were far more focused than the universities and reflected the synergy of government interest and developing intellectual foci. In a continuation of a seventeenth-century trend, Academies of Science were established, as in Stockholm in 1739. Max III Joseph founded the Bavarian Academy of Sciences in 1759. In Parma a medical academy was founded in the Grand Hospital in 1751, to be followed by a medical journal. To a certain extent governments sought scientific advice, that of Louis XVI in pursuit of the traditional goals of better munitions and roads, a more productive agriculture and improved public health. The leading members of the *Académie des Sciences*, such as Borda and Perronet, were called on for technical assistance in subjects such as mathematics, navigation, engineering, cartography and the construction of canals. The physicist Charles Coulomb (1736–1806) became inspector of water in Paris and, after the Revolution, helped to introduce the new metric system of weights and measures, a standardisation that played a major role in encouraging the application of abstract and scientific ideas. Gaspard Monge (1746–1818), the founder of descriptive geometry, was appointed professor of hydraulics in Paris. New methods of measuring population were devised and applied by the French demographers Louis Messance, the abbé d'Expilly and the *intendant* Auget de Montyon. They showed that the widely held view that the population was declining was inaccurate. Terray, as controller-general

(1769–74), supported statistical investigations. In his *Recherches et Considérations sur la Population de la France* (1778) Montyon argued that policy should be based on statistical information. The French *Société Royale de Médecine*, established in 1778, developed out of a commission founded in 1776 to assemble information on epidemics and epizootics.

In 1776 Marsilio Landriani, an official in Lombardy, who had proposed the theory of eudiometry the previous year, was appointed to the chair of physics at the Brera Schools in Milan. Eudiometry, the study of the quality of the air, was proclaimed as a useful aid to the study of public health. In practice it was impossible in this period to measure the healthiness of the air, and the relationship between this healthiness and the respirability of the air, which could be tested by assessing the quantity of 'dephlogisticated' air, or oxygen, in samples was unclear. Despite governmental interest in public health, eudiometry proved a disappointment and was abandoned.

Scientists welcomed sponsorship, seeing state patronage as a way to have their disciplines publicly recognised and properly organised. However, the importance of these contacts should not be exaggerated. Though prominent in capital cities, where the institutionalisation of science in the shape of academies and learned societies was most obvious, they were of less importance elsewhere, although there were a large number of provincial academies in France. Much scientific work continued to be on an individual and amateur basis, although government support could be considerable where science was seen as potentially useful to the state.

In general, public awareness of science increased during this period. Bernard de Fontenelle (1657–1757), perpetual secretary of the French *Académie des Sciences*, helped to popularise scientific advances with a series of publications. In England a big market developed for scientific textbooks and works of popularisation, including books for women and even children. In Francesco Algarotti's *Il Newtonianismo per le Dame* (1737) the theories of light and gravitation were explained in a series of dialogues. It was translated into English in 1739. James Ferguson's *Astronomy explained on Sir Isaac Newton's Principles* (1756) achieved great success because he used familiar language, and was translated into German and Swedish. Museums of scientific apparatus and natural history were formed and scientific lectures developed. The middling orders in particular became consumers and, in some cases, producers of science. If science became fashionable and a matter of cultural status in some areas, the level of scientific knowledge was rarely profound and much of the interest was dilettante and restricted to display rather than theory. The mathematisation of science possibly made theories harder to grasp. Fontenelle claimed in the 1700s that beginners in mathematics had the ability, thanks to the development of the calculus, to solve problems easily which until that time had required great expertise, but much of the mathematical work of the century was incomprehensible to most of those with some interest in science. Instead it was the phenomena themselves that attracted attention because they appealed to the imagination as well as, or rather than, to the intellect. This was true of star-gazing, mesmerism and electricity.

Knowledge concerning electricity increased greatly during the century, from the construction in 1706 by Francis Hauksbee of the first machine to generate electricity, his *Physico-Mechanical Experiments* (1709) being soon translated into French and Italian, to the invention of the battery of cells and the dry pile in 1800 by Alessandro Volta, professor of physics at the University of Pavia. However, the process was not one of a simple advance of knowledge. Indeed the number of theories advanced to explain electrical phenomena help to explain the plausibility of Mesmer's ideas. There was disagreement over whether there existed one or two electrical fluids. In 1791 Luigi Galvani published the results of experiments which began with his observation of the effects of electricity on the muscles of a frog's leg in 1780. He advanced a theory of 'animal electricity', known as galvanism, which claimed that electricity is inherent in animal tissues, a view rejected by Volta who was concerned not only to win the professional assent of his fellow scientists, but also general public recognition.[9]

The clarification of the nature of electricity was an important example of the role of laboratory apparatus and the publicly-validated experimental process. Instruments such as the electrical machine produced new phenomena which stimulated the formation of new theories. If the experimental scientist accepted the results produced by his instruments, these could not scrutinise and measure much of nature. Nevertheless, considerable advances were made in a variety of fields. Typical of the inter-relationship between experimentation and application was the work of Chester Hall (1703–71), a lawyer whose study of the human eye convinced him that achromatic lenses were possible. His success in about 1733 in making them, laid the basis for an improvement in the performance of almost all optical instruments. In 1750 the optician James Ayscough published an account of the nature of spectacles, in which he recommended a tinted glass to reduce glare, and in 1755 an *Account of the Eye and the Nature of Vision*.

The effect of such research on the life of the ordinary people of the period is unclear. It has been suggested that in France both surgical cures for cataract and philosophical speculation demystified the difference between the blind and those with sight, though presumably not many patients were affected. Scientific discoveries and inventions often had only a limited effect on traditional practices, and this was not simply due to conservatism and to a lack of resources. In France, Antoine Parmentier and Antoine Cadet de Vaux sought to establish economic milling, the principle of gradual reduction, which, they argued, could revolutionise milling and baking. They attacked the blind routine and popular errors of accumulated experience, which they sought to transform through the establishment of new methods of production and thought, including scientific language. Their contemptuousness, remoteness and lack of interest in practical experience lessened their influence. Under Louis XIV the French government sought to establish naval shipbuilding on a theoretical basis, but 'mathematical description of the theoretical principles of *la manoeuvre*, the disposition of sails and the positioning of rudders, made not the slightest contribution to the improvement of warships. The actual construction of warships continued to be carried out after age-old practices by shipwrights who received their training by apprenticeship.' The Jesuit scientist Paul Hoste complained 'It is by luck that a good ship is built, for those who still make them are no better than those who build without knowing how to read or write,' though his explanation of why ships do not capsize was wrong. During the eighteenth century progress in French shipbuilding was not achieved by the investigation of mechanical principles, for 'the content of science moved ever farther away from the descriptive, ambiguous world of the shipbuilder, filled with limitation and constraints, toward a more extensive use of abstract concepts' defined by mathematics. Instead, it was the development of the profession of naval engineering with its combination of a general mathematical culture and the study of the old rules for building ships to find the best practice that was decisive.[10]

Alongside the advance of science, the value of practical experience continued to be appreciated by governments. In organising provincial societies of agriculture after 1760, the French minister, Bertin, instructed the *intendants* to select those with the relevant experience, rather than theorists. New scientific ideas and technological methods were most important in new areas of economic activity, but there were few of these. Many inventions incorporating new scientific ideas, such as that of the steam carriage by N. J. Cugnot in the 1770s, the first workable steamboat, demonstrated by the marquis de Jouffroy d'Abbans in 1783, or the pattern-weaving loom invented in 1747 by Jacques Vaucanson, did not lead to breakthroughs. Rather than society waiting for science in the shape of technological advance, the relationship was considerably more complex. New textile techniques were adopted more rapidly in Britain than in France. Steam power was mostly used in Britain, though it gradually spread to the continent.

Science did not only have an effect through technological developments. Intellectual advances gave some people a sense that certain aspects of the environment could be controlled or better understood. The desire to create a science of weather study was a major goal of agricultural societies, though weather forecasting made few advances until the nineteenth century. Statistics and probability theory developed. The *Ars Conjectandi* (1713) of Jacob Bernoulli (1654–1705), professor of mathematics at Basle, was the first major work on the theory. His nephew Daniel Bernoulli (1700–82), professor of mathematics at St Petersburg, and successively professor of anatomy, botany, physics and philosophy at Basle, and the formulator of the law of conservation of mechanical energy, applied statistics and probability calculus to determine the usefulness of inoculation. He examined the differential risk of dying from artificial or natural smallpox and in 1760 produced tables to demonstrate the advantage of inoculation in bringing to productive and reproductive maturity the maximum number of infants born and thus to preserve the investment made in bringing them up. Bernoulli also provided the first accurate calculations for the working of the heart, as well as studying the relationship between life and animal movement.

The marquis de Condorcet (1743–94), who contributed on mathematical subjects to the *Encyclopédie*, became perpetual secretary of the *Académie des Sciences* and supported Turgot's reforms and freedom of trade. He advanced probability theory (applying it outside the mechanical sciences) and wrote for a popular audience. In his *General Picture of Science, which has for its Object the Application of Arithmetic to the Moral and Political Sciences* (1783) Condorcet argued that a knowledge of probability, 'social arithmetic', allowed people to make rational decisions, instead of relying on instinct and passion. Condorcet was a great believer in the possibility of indefinite progress through human action, seeing the key in education. He believed that acquired characteristics could be inherited and thus that education would have a cumulative effect.

A concern with improving the lot of humanity characterised much scientific thinking in the closing decades of the century, such as that of Condorcet, Lavoisier and Mesmer. It was not necessarily atheistical, for most scientists believed that their work revealed God's majesty and purposes. The personal faith of scientists varied: Maupertuis claimed that the principle of 'least action' underlying the laws of motion demonstrated the existence of God. Stephen Hales was very specific about how his work revealed God's handiwork. Belief in Moses as a proto-scientist was widespread, for instance among the Oxford Hutchinsonians in the 1750s, and natural theology and Newtonian physics were interlocked from Boyle to Paley and beyond. The Swedish engineer Emanuel Swedenborg became a leading religious mystic.

Yet, whatever their personal faith, the work of many scientists made little specific reference to God. His intervention in the world he had created, allowed for by Newton, was increasingly restricted by the explanation of supposed anomalies. Geological discoveries and theories threw doubt on the biblical creation story, the universal flood and Old Testament chronology, while astronomical work challenged received notions of the universe and the idea that it was static. Much medical experimentation and psychological speculation placed little weight on the idea of the soul.

This was more important than the limited number of works which claimed that man was a machine, and denied the existence of the soul, the link between man and God which differentiated him, it was believed, from the animals. In his *L'Homme-Machine* (1748) La Mettrie abandoned the distinction between mind and matter and denied the existence of the soul. Baron d'Holbach, who wrote over 400 of the articles in the *Encyclopédie*, many of them on applied scientific topics, claimed in the *Système de la Nature* (1770) that man was simply a machine forced to act in certain ways and without either free will or a soul. In his *Philosophy in the Boudoir* (1795) the marquis de Sade denied the existence of the soul and argued that murder was natural and that no dividing line could firmly be drawn between live and dead (organically active) humans.

Few writers were atheists, but most studied man without much direct reference to divine teaching. John Locke's *Essay Concerning Human Understanding* (1690), argued that all knowledge consisted of ideas which originated in sensation. Psychological theories suggested that man, both as an individual and as a social being, could be improved by education and a better environment. Activity, rather than the passive acceptance of divine will and an unchanging universe, was stressed. The science of man had been 'internalised', the manner in which feelings shaped knowledge was of increasing concern and this greatly affected the literature of the period.[11] Interest in the origins of the species led a few thinkers towards the idea of evolution and there was debate over whether species were fixed, or could change and, if so, how. However, knowledge of pollination, hybridisation and developing creatures such as the polyp, impressed only a few theorists, principally Maupertuis who in his *Système de la Nature* (1751) advanced the idea of the mutation of species, the basis of organic evolution. Most writers clung to the notions of the fixity of individual species and of a static natural environment. Knowledge concerning human conception and the origin of man's characteristics, both as individuals and as a species, was still too limited to help to clarify theoretical speculation. Among scientists there was a reluctance to abandon the notion of a ladder of nature with species occupying fixed positions, and to probe the world of plant and animal breeders and their attempts to enhance particular characteristics.

The relationship between experimentation and theorisation was not always close or productive. Furthermore, theoretical advances were not always easy to apply. If by 1700 'matter theory had come to hinge not on the traditional four elements and on qualities but on particulars and short-range forces incorporating new laws of motion and principles of dynamic',[12] most crafts maintained traditional practices. The thinkers of the Enlightenment may have developed the concept of revolution in science but, outside the fields of chemistry and electricity towards the end of the century, there was little in the way of scientific revolution during the period. Possibly more important was the establishment of the idea that man could understand and influence his environment. The ideology of scientific advance was well developed by the end of the century, even if most people knew nothing of it and understood their lives, jobs and environment through the teaching of their predecessors.

10　International Relations

An overview

International relations absorbed the greatest amount of government attention in the states of the period. This was both traditional and understandable. Dynastic and national prestige, essential both for a sense of purpose and as a lubricant of domestic obedience, were gained principally through international success, and governments could hope to achieve tangible results in diplomacy. The international situation was both dangerous and unstable. The fate of victims could be political extinction, as in the case of Poland when partitioned, and the duchy of Lorraine when annexed. Rulers and ministers were obliged to keep an anxious eye on other powers. Thus foreign relations entailed both opportunities and threats, and much depended on diplomatic abilities and military skills. The personal nature of monarchies was never more evident than in the direct, often autocratic way in which diplomacy was intended to function: foreign policy-making was an attribute of sovereigns. A disadvantage of this, so far as the stability of the international scene was concerned, was that personal idiosyncrasies and dynastic considerations tended to predominate. They undermined attempts to systematise international relations in terms of a balance of power.

Two major elements in the international relations of the century were far from novel, and suggest that the period should be regarded as part of the 'early modern era', rather than a precursor of nineteenth-century diplomacy. They were the role of dynastic concerns and the continued habit of discussing relations in religious terms. A century after the French revocation in 1685 of the Edict of Nantes, that had hitherto guaranteed the rights of their Protestant minority (Huguenots), came the formation of the Fürstenbund (League of Princes) in 1785 by Frederick the Great of Prussia as a way to organise north German Protestant opposition to the emperor Joseph II. It would be misleading to ignore the significance of religious considerations in engendering hostility and, at least for contemporaries, explaining action. Much of this hostility stemmed from anger at the treatment of co-religionists in other countries, and this could often lead to diplomatic intervention, and resultant tension, as in the Palatinate in the late 1710s when a German religious war appeared imminent. In 1707 Charles XII of Sweden obliged the emperor Joseph I to restore to the Silesian Protestants their religious rights of 1648. Recalcitrant religious minorities, such as the Huguenots in the Cévennes mountains of France or the Hungarian Protestants, obtained some foreign assistance for their armed resistance in the 1700s. The religious situation in Europe was generally unstable in the first half of the century, particularly in the Empire, Poland and the Habsburg lands, in which Catholicism continued its advances of the previous century. Count Frederick Schönborn, imperial vice-chancellor 1705–34, sought to use imperial authority to further Catholic interests. In some respects Frederick the Great's invasion of the Austrian province of Silesia in 1740 represented the first significant Protestant counter-offensive in the Empire since the Thirty Years War, and Frederick certainly presented it as a move designed to help the Silesian Protestants. The confrontations and wars of the period were seen in religious terms by many commentators. The Austro-Spanish treaty of Vienna in 1725 was presented in Protestant Europe as a Catholic plot, visible evidence of an allegedly powerful, sinister conspiracy that supported the Jacobite pretender to the British throne and the Polish Catholics responsible for the so-called Thorn massacre of 1724, a judicial mass-execution that aroused outrage in Protestant Europe. This, and the Austro-French entente of the late 1730s, led to discussion of the need for a Protestant alliance. The Seven Years War was widely portrayed in propaganda as a religious conflict.

It was certainly true that the alliances of the period rarely conformed exactly to confessional lines. Though the leading English Jacobites were Anglican churchmen, the case for the House of Hanover was that it would secure the Protestant Succession. The alliance of Hanover, negotiated in 1725 to confront the new Austro-Spanish pact, linked Britain and Prussia to France, and, the following year, Prussia switched alliances to join Austria. Religion played no role in the War of the Polish Succession (1733–5), and if Prussia attacked Austria in the War of the Austrian Succession (1740–8), so also did Catholic Bavaria, France and Spain, while Britain came to Austria's defence. Sweden fought Prussia in the Seven Years War (1756–63). Count Osterman, the Russian foreign minister, observed in 1740 with reference to the Jülich–Berg succession dispute, 'religion is more talked of, than really minded in transactions of this kind'.[1]

It would be foolish, therefore, to exaggerate the significance of religious animosities in causing wars in this century, but it helps to account for the clergy's generally uncritical response to warfare, and that of many devout lay believers. The church played an important role in legitimating and inculcating the bellicose values of the political system, offering services both to secure divine intercession and of thanksgiving (*Te Deums*) that played such a major part in the pageantry of victory. As significant a source of pageantry, was the celebration of the royal hero as victor, part of a long European tradition of exalting majesty in its most impressive function, the display of power. This display ranged in style and form, from medals to the foundation of chivalric orders for the nobility under royal patronage, but it was a constant feature of the period. War was not the sole sphere in which such display could occur, but it was one that best served the aggressive dynastic purpose that lay at the heart of the political ideology of so many of the states of the period.

The dynastic theme in the diplomacy of the period, and in the attitudes that conditioned its formulation and execution, serves, like its religious counterpart, to link the eighteenth to the previous century. It has been argued that the early modern era witnessed the origins and growth of the modern impersonal state,[2] but insufficient evidence has been advanced to support the theory. Much of this theory is based on the writings of a small group of arguably unrepresentative thinkers, and the political practice of the age was still essentially monarchical in a traditional fashion across most of Europe. The crucial role of the monarch in most European countries, including Britain, throughout the eighteenth century, and the dynastic perspective of monarchical ambition, ensured a basic continuity in the conduct of international relations.

Clearly this perspective varied with individuals. Childless Frederick the Great (1740–86) was less obviously interested in dynastic affairs outside his immediate territories than Louis XV (1715–74) with his determination to support his son-in-law Don Philip in Parma.

Dynastic concerns did not exclude other interests. They did, however, remain a central feature of international relations. If proprietary dynasticism describes the attitude of most rulers to their countries it is not surprising that they were willing to use their resources for territorial gains. They did so in the setting of court cultures that were predisposed to war, regarding it as an heroic endeavour. Not all monarchs sought war, but most engaged in it at some time, a tendency possibly increased by a demographic structure that often led to young men succeeding to thrones.

Imbued with these bellicose values, monarchs faced a European situation made unpredictable and turbulent by the vagaries of dynastic luck. Both monarchs and peasants pursued land and heiresses. As wealth was primarily held in land, and transmitted through blood inheritance, it was natural at all levels of society for conflict to centre on succession disputes. Peasants resorted to litigation, a method that was lengthy and expensive, but the alternative was limited by state disapproval of private violence. Monarchs resorted to negotiation, but the absence of any effective adjudicating body and the need for a speedy solution once a succession fell vacant encouraged the decision to fight. Most dynasties, including the Bourbons in France, Spain and Naples, the Hanoverians, Romanovs and Vasas, owed their position to the willingness of past members of their family to fight to secure their claims to succession. Although peaceful successions of new dynasties did take place, war and inheritance were often two sides of the same coin.

The absence of effective adjudicating agencies was a significant cause of tension and conflict. The papacy had long ceased to be effective as a means for settling disputes among the Catholic powers. Protestantism had never created a comparable international agency. The first half of the century witnessed attempts to create a secular surrogate. The resort to international peace congresses as a means of tackling problems was a characteristic feature of the 1720s. The congresses of Cambrai and Soissons were linked to the development of a system of collective security involving reciprocal guarantees. Neither collective security nor the congresses, however, were particularly successful. They failed to produce a satisfactory solution to the problems affecting European relations, essentially because the irreconcilable interests of the major powers were made more apparent through the process of negotiation. The arbiter of disputes remained the battlefield.

European diplomacy 1700–21

The century began with two major wars, in western and northern Europe (Spanish Succession, 1701/2–13/14, and Great Northern War, 1700–21), shortly after two others, in the western and south-eastern parts of the continent (Nine Years War, 1688–97, and Austro-Turkish war, 1682–99), had finished. In sum, these wars placed a major strain on the political abilities of rulers and ministers, the financial resources of states and the personal lives of much of the population. They framed the history of Europe in the first half of the century. The wars comprehended a range of conflicts, and discussion of their causes, course, success and effects must vary greatly depending on the perspective adopted. Probably the most influential from the point of view of Europe's long-term development was the Great Northern War and, in particular, the resolution of a struggle between Charles XII of Sweden and the combined forces of Peter the Great of Russia, Augustus II of Saxony–Poland and Frederick IV of Denmark into a conflict between Charles and Peter, which the latter won decisively. However, the war that absorbed most attention was the War of the Spanish Succession. Frederick IV was forced to make peace in 1700, and until Charles XII invaded Saxony in 1706, the attention of Austria and much of the Empire was directed towards the war against Louis XIV.

Spanish Succession War

The attempt to avoid war over the Spanish Succession collapsed on the twin obstacles of Charles II's will and Austrian determination. When Charles II, the last Habsburg king of Spain, died childless in 1700 he left the whole of the possessions of the Spanish monarchy to Louis XIVs younger grandson, Philip, Duke of Anjou, with the proviso that, if he rejected the bequest and sought to partition the inheritance, it was then to be offered to the archduke Charles, younger son of Leopold I. The will was designed to elicit French support for the maintenance of the empire. Unwilling to lose the prize to the Austrians, Louis accepted the will for his grandson, expressing a clear preference for dynastic goals, for, by the now-discarded partition schemes of 1698 and 1700, France was to have gained part of the inheritance. Exhausted by the Nine Years War, pleased that France would gain no territory, and hopeful that Philip, now Philip V, would become a good Spaniard, politicians in England and the United Provinces were prepared to accept the will, despite the hesitation of their joint ruler William III of Orange.

Hostilities were begun in northern Italy by Leopold in 1701. The conflict began as a Bourbon–Habsburg struggle and, had it continued as that, it is difficult to see the latter succeeding. However, a marked deterioration in Anglo/Dutch–French relations in 1701–2, caused by fears of French commercial and territorial ambitions, led to a rallying of support to Austria. In 1701 Louis rejected Anglo-Dutch proposals that included assurances for their trade with Spain and her colonies, a Dutch barrier in the Spanish Netherlands, and compensation for Leopold. In September 1701 his stance led to the negotiation of the Grand Alliance between Austria, England and the United Provinces. This allocated Spanish possessions in Italy (Naples, Sicily, Sardinia and the Milanese-Lombardy) and the Spanish Netherlands to the Habsburgs, Spain and her colonies (Spanish America and the Philippines) to Philip V. England and the United Provinces were now tied to Austria, a link that was to cause them many difficulties.

Louis's recognition in 1701 of the son of the exiled James II of England as James III, a move reflecting sympathy, his belief in the divine right of succession and his wish to appear as a Catholic champion, further envenomed relations. Though William III died in 1702, English opposition to France, which he had sought successfully to establish, survived him, and in May 1702 the Grand Alliance declared war on Louis.

The War of the Spanish Succession was a complex struggle involving a variety of interests. For Pedro II of Portugal, seeking to gain land from Spain, or Victor Amadeus II of Savoy-Piedmont, seeking greater power in Italy, it was essentially an opportunity to benefit from the competing aims of the two alliances, to gain territory and prevent themselves from being wholly abandoned at the eventual peace treaty. For England, the Protestant Succession was involved, for the United Provinces the prevention of French proximity, and, for both, colonial and commercial considerations, especially West Indian trade. Different interests helped to ensure that diplomatic relations during the war were as complex as those during the years of peace, a common feature of all the wars during this period. However, wartime diplomacy was dependent also on strategic considerations and intertwined with the fortunes of war. Initially these were mixed, and France, supported by her Bavarian ally Max Emanuel, seemed poised to deliver a knockout blow to the Habsburgs. In 1704, as later, during the War of the Austrian Succession, in 1741–2, this was averted. At Blenheim on the Danube Anglo-Dutch forces under the duke of Marlborough and Austro-German units under Prince Eugene combined to rout the Franco-Bavarian army.

This sealed the pattern for the rest of the war: French troops were driven from the Empire, and French strategy became a matter of frontier conflict, a course of action that made it difficult for France to gain or retain allies. Bavaria, occupied and cruelly taxed by Austria, was not much of an advertisement for French power or a French alliance. The Bourbons were also driven from Italy: the alliance of Savoy-Piedmont was lost in 1703, the French were defeated by Victor Amadeus II and Eugene at Turin in 1706, and Naples was captured by the Austrians in 1707. Italy, a traditional field of French diplomacy and a vital part of the Spanish empire, was closed by Austrian power, albeit power supported by the English navy and by Savoy-Piedmont. Thanks to victories at Ramillies (1706) and Oudenaarde (1708) the French were driven from the Spanish Netherlands. The Grand Alliance had less success in attacking France itself or in conquering Spain. The Austrians preferred to devote their efforts to Italy and to suppressing the Hungarian revolt, exhaustion was beginning to affect the allies, and the defensive resources of France were not inconsiderable. Invasions of France, such as the drive on Toulon in 1707, were unsuccessful. In Spain the Anglo-Dutch-backed effort to establish Archduke Charles as Charles III failed. English dominance of the seas gave Charles, supported by the Mediterranean provinces, a chance, but Castile remained loyal to Philip, and Louis sent troops as military and political dominance of the peninsula eluded Charles.

As with all the wars of the period, negotiations for a peace continued during most of the conflict. Serious negotiations began in 1708. It was a measure of Louis XIVs desperation, in the light of the savage domestic pressures created by a long war, exacerbated by a crisis of famine and harsh weather, that in 1709 he was willing to cede the whole Spanish empire to Charles, and even to restore all he had taken in Alsace since 1648, including Strasbourg. These proposals came to nothing, as a result of Philip's unwillingness to accept them, and Louis's understandable refusal to accept the allies' demand that he should help expel his grandson led to the failure of these proposals. If successful, the proposals would have led to the apogee of Austrian Habsburg power and a vulnerable position for France. It is understandable that French propaganda in this period dwelt on the threat of the Habsburgs to the European system.

The projected terms of 1709 marked the highpoint of allied success. France succeeded in resisting Marlborough's attempts to break through her defences, while the overthrow of the Whig ministry in Britain (1710) and the succession of Charles, as Charles VI, to the Austrian lands in 1711, on the death of his brother Joseph I (emperor 1705–11) without sons, altered the international situation dramatically. The new British Tory ministry (1710–14) wanted peace and saw the means to be a compromise settlement with France, rather than support for a union of the Austrian and Spanish lands in the person of Charles. It was Anglo-French co-operation that led to the treaty of Utrecht (1713), a peace that ended the Spanish Succession War when Charles VI accepted it at Rastadt (1714).

Utrecht brought a partition of the Spanish empire that was particularly beneficial to Austria, Britain and the Bourbons. Philip V retained Spain and her empire outside Europe, while Charles VI's gains – Naples, Milan, Sardinia and the Spanish Netherlands – were now made for the benefit of Austria, and not for a cadet branch of the Habsburgs. The Dutch were allowed to garrison fortresses in what became the Austrian Netherlands, including several ceded by France. Victor Amadeus of Savoy-Piedmont received Sicily with a royal crown. Britain obtained Gibraltar, Minorca and commercial concessions from Spain, Nova Scotia and Newfoundland from France, and a position of international strength. Philip V renounced the French throne, the Protestant Succession in Britain was guaranteed, and the French agreed to expel the Old Pretender.

With hindsight, Utrecht appears as a major achievement, bringing peace and stability to much of Europe. The immediate reality was otherwise. The accession of George I to the British throne in 1714 and the return of the Whigs led to fear of an Anglo-French conflict, a suggestion made more plausible by the prospect of French support for the unsuccessful Jacobite risings of 1715 in favour of the Pretender. Philip V was not prepared to accept Utrecht, and his determination to regain Spain's Italian possessions led him to attack Sardinia in 1717 and Sicily in 1718. Nevertheless, whatever its imperfections, at least the settlement brought peace to western Europe in 1713–14. In the Baltic, conflict was not to cease until 1721.

Russia and the Great Northern War, 1700–21

While the western European powers founded great trading and colonial empires in the early modern period, the states of central and eastern Europe were involved in a bitter fight for survival. The struggle between the European states and the powers to the east has been a major theme in the history of the last millennium. The century between 1650 and 1750 was a crucial one in this struggle. It saw the definitive stemming of the Ottoman tide and the establishment of Russian hegemony in eastern Europe. The Turks were repulsed in the 1680s and 1690s by Austria and, to a lesser extent, Russia and Poland; the Russians entrenched themselves during the Great Northern War. By altering the political situation in eastern Europe, the Russian victory served to change the nature of the European international system. The tremendous natural resources of Russia, not least its population and its size, have tended to lead to the assumption that Russian success was inevitable. This is most clearly seen in the discussion of Russo-Swedish relations. For Peter the Great it was essential to defeat Charles XII and conquer Sweden's possessions on the eastern shore of the Baltic – Livonia, Estonia, Ingria – if he was to achieve his ambition of linking Russia to European developments. As Peter's reign was dominated by the Great Northern War, it is understandable that this struggle between Russia and Sweden should be seen as the pivotal conflict that determined Russian success. Sweden was so much poorer than Russia and its population so much smaller that it is easy to understand why many assume that the Swedish empire was doomed, its defeat by Peter inevitable.

This analysis is doubtful for several reasons. The very notion of inevitability is open to question and the determinism used to dismiss the fate of the Swedish empire is worrying. Historians have been too quick to employ the unhelpful concept of decline to categorise several states in the seventeenth and eighteenth centuries. Whatever its socio-economic fortunes, Spain, generally seen as in decline since the late sixteenth century, was still the largest empire in the world in 1700, as in 1800. The Turkish Empire, also seen as in decline since the late sixteenth century, took longer to disintegrate than the British Empire took to rise and fall.

The Swedish empire was never in the same class as its Spanish and Turkish counterparts, but similar caution is required in discussing its fate. It is easy to forget that in this period the gap, in terms of military strength, between the largest and the second-rank powers was much narrower than it was to be by the end of the eighteenth century. Furthermore, the challenge that the Swedes posed to Russia can only be understood by considering the general problem facing Russia: the inter-relationship of three powerful enemies, Sweden, Poland–Lithuania and the Turkish Empire. Peter did not invent the policy of a Russian drive to the west. It had been attempted by Ivan the Terrible in the 1560s and by Peter's father Alexis in the 1650s and in each case defeated, in large part by the Poles. The achievements of the Poles in the 1660s, when Russia, although winning the eastern Ukraine, failed to gain the western half, a territory she was not to annex until 1793, suggest that it is wrong to write off the Polish state as one inevitably bound to lose out because of its aristocratic and quasi-federalist political structure, one judged anarchic by the apologists of 'absolutism'. Just as historians have reassessed the vitality of the German political system – the Holy Roman Empire with its strong federalist element – so it is clear that Poland's strength in the late seventeenth century can be appreciated by those who are not influenced by the hindsight of future collapse and the prejudice of believing that only 'absolutist', states would succeed. There was little sign that Poland was to become a Russian satellite as it was to be from the 1710s.

The Ukrainian rebellion of 1648 and the consequent increase of Russian influence destroyed the regional balance of power and created in the Ukraine a vortex that drew in the great powers, helping to ensure that from the late 1650s until 1700 Russian foreign policy was dominated by the problem of the south. In 1686

Russia joined the anti-Turkish Holy League of Austria, Poland and Venice. Initially unsuccessful invasions of the Crimea in 1687 and 1689 and a failed siege of Azov in 1695 were followed by the fall of the latter to Peter in 1696 and an agreement with Austria in 1697 by which she was to continue the war until the Turks ceded Kerch, which gave Russia a window on the Black Sea. Peter's troops had already captured the Turkish forts at the mouth of the Dnieper. The entrances to the Balkans were being cleared.

However, Peter was abandoned by his allies in the treaty of Carlowitz of 1699 and his gains in the Russo-Turkish treaty in 1700, principally Azov, were not comparable with those of Austria or Venice: Hungary and the Morea in southern Greece. It is difficult to say what would have happened to Russian foreign policy had the war with Turkey continued. Peter's epic personal struggle with Charles XII has tended to divert attention from his great interest in his southern frontier, an interest that was to lead him to invade Moldavia in 1711, and to campaign in Transcaucasia and Persia in the last years of his reign. The lure of Constantinople was to be a major theme in eighteenth-century Russian foreign policy, one that owed much to a semi-mystical vision of Russia's role, that drew both on the theme of the Third Rome and on the idea of Russia as a Christian crusading power that would free the Balkans. Peter's enforced redirection of Russian ambitions towards the Baltic in 1700 served a more secular goal, the modernisation of Russia, as well as reflecting Peter's need to exploit the opportunities presented by alliance politics. The scheme for an attack on Sweden, developed by Frederick IV and Augustus II, offered Peter a limited role and few conquests compared to the great prospects of the recent Turkish war. Augustus appeared to benefit more, being allocated the promise of Livonia and hoping that victory against Sweden would enable him to increase royal authority in Poland. A more effective Poland was not a welcome prospect for Peter, whose small promised share of the Swedish empire revealed the restricted role then allocated to Russia in the international system.

Charles XII's military skill destroyed this diplomatic house of cards, producing as dramatic a defeat of a scavenging alliance as that which Austria was to inflict on her enemies in 1742. Luckily for Peter, Charles did not follow up his victory over the Russians at Narva (1700) by an advance into Russia. Instead, he turned south, invading Poland (1701). Augustus was defeated and a protégé of Charles, Stanislaus Leszcynski, was elected king. The creation of a Swedish–Polish bloc represented a major threat to Peter, one far more serious than the challenge posed by

Swedish control of the Baltic provinces. From 1701 Polish 'patriots', such as the army commander Jablonowski, pressed for co-
operation with Charles in order to regain the lands lost to Russia
in 1667, lands which succeeding kings of Poland on their election had sworn to reconquer. In the Swedish–Polish treaty of
1705 Charles promised to help in their reconquest. Stanislaus's
election thus threatened to undo the fragile territorial stability of
Russia's western and southern border. In addition, it opened up
the possibility of an alliance between Sweden, Poland and the
Turks. In 1699 Charles XII had encouraged the Turks to continue their war with Russia. It was fortunate for Peter that in the
1700s the Turks sought to avoid conflict with him, ignoring pleas
for assistance from the Tatars and the opportunity for intervention provided by the unpopularity of Peter's policies in
the Ukraine. Furthermore Charles, busy seeking to establish
Stanislaus in the quagmire of Polish politics, was not free to
attack Russia until 1708. However, the conflicting interests of
Russia and Sweden in Poland made peace between them impossible. Peter was fighting not only for his 'window on the west', for
which St Petersburg had been founded on the Gulf of Finland in
1703, but also to prevent Poland from becoming a Swedish client
state. Peter sent money and troops to the aid of Polish nobles
opposed to Charles; in 1707 he also supported the candidature
for the Polish throne of the Hungarian leader Rakoczi. A
Swedish invasion of Russia seemed the only way to end the
interminable Polish civil war. It led to Peter's crushing defeat of
Charles at Poltava in the Ukraine in 1709. This solved both the
Polish question and that of the Baltic provinces. Poltava led to
the effective end of the Swedish party in Poland. Leszcynski fled
to the Swedish base at Stettin and Augustus II was restored in
1710. In the same year, Russian troops overran Sweden's eastern
Baltic provinces, bar Finland.

At this moment of triumph, however, Peter miscalculated badly.
His determination to treat the Ukraine as Russian, rather than as
the buffer territory that the Turks wanted it to be, was exploited
by the anti-Russian party in Constantinople. In November 1710
the Turks declared war. Russian agents were sent to the Balkans
to organise risings, proclamations were issued urging the Balkan
Christians to revolt, and, in conscious imitation of Constantine
the Great, Peter had the Cross inscribed on his standards, with
the motto 'In this sign we conquer'. In 1711 the *hospodar* of
Moldavia, Demetrius Cantemir, signed a treaty with Peter agreeing to support him in return for recognition as hereditary prince
of Moldavia under Russian protection. Peter planned to cross the
Danube, but supply problems and the speedy movement of a large

Turkish army led to the Russian army being surrounded at the river Pruth and forced to ask for terms.

Though the defeat at the Pruth was not another Poltava, Peter was willing to abandon Livonia and recognise Leszcynski as king of Poland as the price of peace. In the end he was only made to accept the loss of Azov; not until the treaty of Kutchuk-Kainardji (1774) was Russia allowed to fortify Azov. Peter's failure to gain a window on the Black Sea and to become the dominant power in the eastern Balkans contrasted with his success in the Baltic. Had the Turkish Empire suffered serious defeat, a power vacuum might have been created in the Balkans and in Transcaucasia that would have sucked the Russians in, rather as they were sucked into Persian affairs in the early 1720s by the collapse of the Safavid dynasty. As it was, the continued vitality of the Turkish Empire served to thwart Peter, just as logistical problems and the victories of Nadir Shah were to end Russian occupation of the southern shores of the Caspian in 1732.

Although Peter failed to achieve his aims on his southern frontiers, he had more success in establishing himself as a European power. This was symbolised by the development of marital links with a number of German princely families reflecting Peter's prestige and helping to ensure his close involvement in German politics. The latter was also made necessary in 1714 when Charles XII left his Turkish exile and resumed his attempts to defend the Swedish empire. In response, Peter moved his troops westward. In 1716 he prepared to invade southern Sweden from Denmark and, that winter, quartered his troops on the German Baltic coast in Mecklenburg, neighbouring Hanover. This assertive stance led to divisions among the powers who had attacked Sweden after Poltava: Denmark, Hanover and Prussia. It was generally feared that the European system was threatened by Russian preponderance, and individual rulers, such as George I of Britain–Hanover, had particular quarrels with Peter. Other rulers, exhausted by the Spanish Succession and Northern wars, were both astonished and frightened by Peter's ability to go on fielding large forces. George I, concerned about Russian intervention in Mecklenburg, played the leading role in negotiating peace between Sweden and her western enemies, and in creating a powerful anti-Russian coalition, a process aided by Charles XII's death in Norway (1718). British diplomatic pressure helped ensure Peter's withdrawal from Mecklenburg in 1717, and in 1719 Austria, Hanover and Saxony signed a treaty aimed at driving Russian troops out of Poland. However, different views pulled the anti-Russian coalition apart in 1720.

The failure of the British attempt to create a *barrière de l'est* against Russia was both cause and effect of Peter's triumph. In diplomatic terms, this was sealed at the peace of Nystad in August 1721 and reflected in the frantic efforts of the European powers to win Russian support in 1725–6 during the confrontation between the alliances of Hanover and Vienna, and again in the 1740s in the early stages of the War of the Austrian Succession. Peter had solved both the Polish and the Swedish problems, and it was the inter-relationship between his successes that was crucial. Had Poland been a powerful active force in 1709 then Poltava would have been less crucial; a decade later she might have made the anti-Russian schemes a reality. It was Polish weakness that made possible both Peter's conquest of Sweden's eastern Baltic provinces and his retention of them, just as it permitted Russia to dominate the Ukraine, preventing its development into an independent state.

This helps to account for Russia's determination to retain influence in Poland, which was central to her diplomatic and military strategies. Because of it, plans to challenge Russia's control of her borderlands, such as those floated in Sweden in 1727 for an invasion of her former Baltic provinces, stood little chance of success. Helped by her preponderant international position in eastern Europe, Russia was able partially to integrate her Baltic and Ukrainian acquisitions. Victories in wars in Poland (1733–5) and against Sweden (1741–3) and, less clearly, against Turkey (1736–9) enabled Peter's successors to consolidate his gains, although it was not until Catherine the Great and the Russo-Turkish war of 1768–74, a war in which Polish events were again of great importance, that some of his southern schemes were realised. Securely in control of her borderlands, Russia was able to intervene with greater weight in European affairs. The march of her armies towards the Rhine in 1735 and 1748 helped to persuade France to end successive wars with Austria. By mid-century, Russian hegemony in eastern Europe was well established.

European diplomacy 1721–40

Philip V's determination to reverse Spain's loss of her Italian dominions was temporarily successful in 1717–18, but Anglo-French military pressure helped to force him to abandon his schemes and led to Victor Amadeus of Savoy-Piedmont losing Sicily to the emperor and receiving the less valuable Sardinia in return. In the 1720s Philip sought to gain by diplomacy what he could not obtain through war. The failure of negotiations, culminating in the unsuccessful international congress of Cambrai which met in 1724, to produce a satisfactory settlement of Philip's claims that the succession of his son by his second marriage, Don Carlos, to the Italian states of Parma, Piacenza and Tuscany be guaranteed adequately, led Spain to approach Austria, a diplomatic revolution in view of their recent enmity. This gave rise to the alliance of Vienna of 1725, which was matched swiftly by the alliance of Hanover, a league of Britain, France and Prussia.

The consequent cold war, comprising various diplomatic combinations, lasted until 1731, though hostilities were restricted to an unsuccessful Spanish siege of Gibraltar in 1727. The collapse of the Austro-Spanish alliance in 1729 was followed by that of the Anglo-French alliance (negotiated in 1716) two years later, when Britain unilaterally negotiated an alliance with Austria that closed French options by guaranteeing the Pragmatic Sanction. This was an arrangement, promulgated in 1719, by which the succession to the Austrian Habsburg territories was guaranteed to Maria Theresa, the eldest daughter of Charles VI who had no sons. The major role that the Pragmatic Sanction played in international affairs, as Austria made its guarantee by as many powers as possible a central feature in European diplomacy, illustrated the importance of dynastic considerations in setting the diplomatic agenda.

In 1731 the Austrian position seemed well established. Supported since 1726 by alliances with Prussia and Russia, Charles VI's position in eastern Europe was strengthened by Turkish concentration on the possibilities of Persian conquests, so that during the cold war of 1725–31, Austria did not have to worry about a war on two fronts. Divided forces had been a serious handicap during the Nine Years War and again, in the shape of a Hungarian rebellion, during the Spanish Succession War, and the diversion of Austrian resources to fight the Turks during the Austro-Turkish war of 1716–18 had encouraged Philip V in his Italian schemes. However, the Peace of Passarowitz (1718), which had granted Charles Little Wallachia (south-west Romania), Belgrade, and Serbia (north-central Yugoslavia), was not challenged in the 1720s or during the War of the Polish Succession (1733–5). In 1731 Britain and Spain allied with Charles, and their guarantees of the Pragmatic Sanction were followed by those of the Empire and the United Provinces. France appeared isolated, Austria triumphant, her self-confidence expressed in the splendid palaces and churches thrown up in contemporary Vienna.

The Austrian position was to be shaken in the War of the Polish Succession (1733–5). Touched off by Russian determination to retain influence in Poland and thus prevent the election of Stanislaus Leszcynski, now father-in-law of Louis XV, the conflict led to an attack by Louis, Philip V and Charles Emmanuel III of Sardinia on Russia's ally, Austria. Charles, deserted by Britain, Prussia and the United Provinces, bore the brunt of the struggle, losing the bulk of his Italian territories. The Spaniards conquered Naples in 1734. Nevertheless, Charles was able to maintain a presence in the peninsula, while Russia defeated both Stanislaus and a supporting French force. The war demonstrated the weakness of France's traditional eastern European allies, as neither Sweden nor Turkey was willing to intervene. In the subsequent peace, the Austro-Russian candidate, Augustus III of Saxony, was acknowledged as king of Poland, while Stanislaus and France were compensated with Lorraine, whose reversion, on the death of Stanislaus, was promised to France. Louis XV thus gained the duchy in 1766, the major acquisition of eighteenth-century pre-revolutionary France, and a valuable strategic gain. Duke Francis of Lorraine, who married Maria Theresa in 1736, received the following year the duchy of Tuscany, when the last of the Medici family died. Naples and Sicily were given to Don Carlos, Austria receiving in return Parma and Piacenza which Carlos had gained in 1731 on the death of the last of the Farnese. France recognised the Pragmatic Sanction.

The war was followed by an Austro-French entente that lasted until 1741. In some respects the late 1730s prefigured the post-1756 diplomatic world. Recognising the weakness of her traditional eastern European allies, and unwilling to support the pretensions of Spain in Italy or the Wittelsbachs in the Empire, France under the pacific Cardinal Fleury, first minister 1726–43, aligned herself with Austria, and their understanding restrained the ambitions of other states, particularly Spain. Anglo-Austrian relations were cool and Britain was forced to seek support with only limited success from Russia and Prussia.

Austria retained her alliance with Russia, which, however, compelled her to support the latter in conflict with the Turks (1737–9). The war went badly, culminating in the Peace of Belgrade (1739), which returned the town, Little Wallachia and Serbia to the Turks. They were never again to become part of the Habsburg patrimony. Though Austria had risen to become a major power in 1683–1718 through military victory, the defeats of 1733–9 provided ample warning of her vulnerability. The victories of earlier years had owed something to the international situation and, in particular, to her membership of powerful and successful coalitions. The mid-century wars were to underline the importance of diplomatic combinations.

European diplomacy 1740–63

If Austria seemed the fulcrum of European diplomacy in the summer of 1731, that place was occupied by France a decade later. Austria's apparent strength had owed much to her ability to gain the alliance of the other rising powers in Europe, Britain, Prussia, Russia and a resurgent Spain. A decade later she had to survive without their assistance. A major European war had for long been predicted over the Austrian succession. Plans for the partition of the Habsburg lands had been drawn up, and war was expected to follow the death of Charles VI.

The anti-Habsburg German coalition that the French warrior-diplomat Marshal Belle-Isle was to create in 1741 had been pre-figured in 1732 by France, Saxony and Karl Albrecht/Carl Albert of Bavaria, who had claims on the succession. However, the Austro-French entente of the late 1730s seemed to preclude such a conflict. The Bavarian envoy in Paris was reduced to speculating about the possible effects of the octogenarian Fleury's apparently imminent death. When Charles VI died in October 1740, Fleury assured the Austrian envoy that Louis XV would observe all his engagements with Austria. The cardinal's early plans were restricted to attempting to deny the imperial election to Francis of Lorraine, rather than to eternalise the glory of Louis XV by heeding Providence's call to re-establish a just European balance of power, as Karl Albrecht suggested. The invasion of the Austrian duchy of Silesia (modern south-west Poland) by Frederick the Great in December 1740 dramatically altered the situation, by substituting action for negotiation and by forcing other European powers to define their position. Frederick's invasion was not intended as the opening move of a major European war, a step that would precipitate attempts to enforce claims on the Austrian inheritance by the other powers. He hoped that Maria Theresa would buy him off by accepting his claims, and his invasion can be seen as much as the action of an opportunist, seeking to benefit from a temporarily favourable European situation, as the result of Prussian estrangement from Austria since 1733.

Frederick's opportunism can be regarded as a rash move, for although the conquest of Silesia proved relatively easy, its retention, in the face of persistent Austrian hostility, was to prove a major burden for the Prussian state. The French envoy in Berlin felt that Frederick had attacked carelessly, without either allies or negotiations to obtain them.[3] The attack on Austria was to some extent fortuitous. Frederick had earlier expressed more interest in his claims to the Rhenish duchies of Jülich and Berg and, just as he toyed with approaches from Britain and France, so he was clearly unsure where to direct his aggressive intentions. The markedly improvised nature of Prussian policy reflected the rapidly changing European situation. Anglo-Spanish hostilities – the War of Jenkins' Ear began in 1739 – seemed about to encompass France. Russian developments were arguably crucial in encouraging Frederick to attack, for the Tsarina Anna died three days before Charles VI, to be succeeded by the two-month-old Ivan VI and a weak and divided regency. The formation of the Austro-Russian alliance of 1726 had intimidated Frederick William I into abandoning the anti-Austrian alliance of Hanover, and fear of Russian attack had prevented him from executing his plans during the War of Polish Succession, but when the British envoy stressed Prussian vulnerability in February 1741, Frederick the Great replied that he was certain of Russia and therefore not worried about his other frontiers.[4]

Prussian aggression helped to precipitate a wider war. The failure of Austria either to defeat or to negotiate with Frederick led him to sign the treaty of Breslau with France in June 1741. Frederick agreed to support the imperial candidature of Karl Albrecht in return for a French guarantee of Lower Silesia and French promises of military assistance for Bavaria and diplomatic pressure on Sweden to attack Russia. What appeared to be a European system in flux led Spain and Saxony to join the anti-Austrian powers. In 1741 France arguably came closer to dominating Europe than any modern European state prior to Napoleon I's France. Russian diplomatic pressure on Frederick to desist from the invasion of Silesia was as unsuccessful as the attempt of George II of Britain to reconcile Austria and Prussia and create a powerful anti-French coalition. In November 1741 the Austrian envoy in Paris referred to France as having taken upon herself the distribution of kingdoms and provinces.[5] The Habsburgs lost Linz and Prague to invading forces and appeared prostrate, an impression reinforced by signs of support for Karl Albrecht in Bohemia and Austria.

And yet France failed. This was due to a variety of factors, including under-rated Austrian resilience, and the Russian refusal to enter the French system when in December 1741 a palace revolution brought Peter the Great's daughter, Elizabeth, to power. Frederick the Great betrayed his allies and signed a treaty with Austria (1742), the latter overran Bavaria, the Russians defeated France's ally Sweden, and the fall of the Walpole ministry led to a more aggressive British stance that was to produce hostilities with France (1743) and open war a year later.

French failure suggests that it was not possible for any one power to dominate Europe. Unable to do so militarily, she was forced, as was every other power considering a major conflict, to seek the assistance of others, but the very resort to war made it less easy to retain the support of allies. Powers that were willing to accept regular subsidies in peacetime, and in return promised support, proved only too willing to vary their policies to meet wartime exigencies. War made the position of second-rank powers more crucial, and, accordingly, it led to an increase in bids for their support, a significant corrosive of alliances that tended to lack any ideological, religious, sentimental, popular or economic bonds. The apparent collapse of Austrian power in 1741 and the willingness of France to encourage other powers to claim shares in the Austrian inheritance represented a great opportunity for the second-rank states, and it was one that they seized. However, France was unable to retain the alliance of all these powers once it became clear that Austria would not collapse. The appearance of two warring blocks inspired caution and ambition among the second-rank powers. Austrian military success led Karl Albrecht, who had been elected the Emperor Charles VII thanks to French support in 1742, to seek a settlement with Austria, a task accomplished by his successor in 1745. The prospect of Russian attack restrained Frederick the Great to some extent after 1742, while Philip V of Spain, and his successor Ferdinand VI sought to negotiate a separate peace, and Augustus III established a record in duplicity that should have gained him a reputation equal to that of Frederick.

The war brought territorial benefits for Frederick; for Charles Emmanuel III, who, as from the Polish Succession War, gained some of the Milanese; and for Don Philip, brother of Don Carlos and son-in-law of Louis XV, who acquired Parma and Piacenza. The schemes of the major powers were generally unsuccessful. The prospect that Austria would follow up her successes in 1742–3 by dominating the Empire and seeking to regain Silesia was ended when Frederick attacked her again in 1744 and forced Maria Theresa in the treaty of Dresden (1745) once more to recognise Silesia as Prussian. French schemes for an invasion of Britain in 1744–6 were unsuccessful, as was the Jacobite attempt in 1745 to reverse the Glorious Revolution. With Francis of Lorraine's election as emperor in 1745 and the Austro-Bavarian peace, hostilities largely ceased in Germany. Conflict in Italy was mostly inconclusive, the major schemes, particularly that for an Austrian reconquest of Naples, proving abortive. In 1745–8 French armies, under Marshal Saxe, overran the Austrian Netherlands, defeating the combined Austrian, British and Dutch army in a series of battles at Fontenoy (1745), Roucoux (1746) and Lawfeldt (1747). Defeat helped to lead to an Orangist coup in the United

Provinces in 1747, William IV reviving the authority once enjoyed by William III, after 45 years of republican control. However, he was no more able to stop the French army, and the prospect of the conquest of much of the United Provinces helped to lead them and Britain to push through peace with France despite the unwillingness of their Austrian ally. The treaty of Aix-la-Chapelle (1748) left Frederick in possession of Silesia, while France evacuated the Low Countries in exchange for regaining colonial losses.

The peace was to be followed by a number of diplomatic realignments. In 1752 Maria Theresa, Charles Emmanuel and Ferdinand VI jointly guaranteed each other's possessions, and thereafter Italy was substantially at peace until the French revolutionary wars began in 1792. This was due not to the end of local disputes, but to an international situation in which the major powers that had kept the peninsula in tumult for a quarter of a millennium no longer sought to do so. Crucial was the Austro-French alliance of 1756, the so-called Diplomatic Revolution, which helped to stabilise Italy, the Empire and the Low Countries by withdrawing great-power incitement and support for the disputes of local powers. This was most clearly seen in the Seven Years War (1756–63), the first major war for over 70 years in which Savoy-Piedmont neither participated nor benefited. Charles Emmanuel would have liked to participate, but the Austro-French alliance effectively removed the option.

The Diplomatic Revolution of 1756 was in no way inevitable for though the Anglo-Austrian and Franco-Prussian alliances were handicapped by differing aims and mistrust, Austria and France also had different views, as Count Wenzel von Kaunitz discovered in 1750–3 when, as Austrian envoy in Paris, he tried to further his scheme for an alliance. Kaunitz, who became chancellor in 1753, wished to end the Franco-Prussian alliance in order that Austria, whose ministry increasingly saw the recapture of Silesia as a priority and was reforming the Austrian finances and army accordingly, could attack Frederick. Her determination to outmatch the Prussian military establishment was a source of heavy financial pressure for Austria. However, the strengthening of Austria did not appeal to the French ministers of the early 1750s; they were suspicious of her and appreciated that Prussia could serve as a substitute for France's traditional allies in eastern Europe.

It was accident, rather than geopolitical determinism, that drove the two powers together. Unhappy with the Austrian response to requests for aid as she drifted into war with France over North American disputes, the British ministry sought to nullify the danger of a Franco-Prussian attack on George II's German principality, the vulnerable electorate of Hanover, by gaining the alliance of Russia. British success led Frederick, fearful of Russia, to reach an agreement with Britain for the neutralisation of Germany (Convention of Westminster, January 1756). This limited and tentative move towards Anglo-Prussian co-operation led to French disillusionment with Frederick and the negotiation of an Austro-French defensive alliance, the first treaty of Versailles (May 1756). Tsarina Elizabeth had seen the Anglo-Russian subsidy treaty as a means to get British support for war with Frederick, who had been opposing her schemes by, in particular, supporting Sweden, as in the Baltic crisis of 1749–50, and intriguing with the Turks. She reacted to the Anglo-Prussian agreement by ignoring Britain and planning to attack Frederick along with Austria. France did not wish to fight Prussia; Austria and Russia wished to, a policy sketched out in their alliance of 1746, and were planning for war to begin in 1757.

An increasingly desperate Frederick, aware of these plans, decided to try to thwart them by using his well-prepared army at once. In August 1756 he attacked Austria's ally, Saxony, which he saw as a potential base for Austrian attacks. This touched off a major conflict, not least by activating the defensive clauses of the Austro-French alliance. Louis XV's personal prestige was involved because Augustus III was the father-in-law of his own heir. In 1757, by the second treaty of Versailles, France agreed to pay Austria a subsidy and to maintain a large force in the Empire. The situation was a threatening one for Frederick, the disproportionate strength of his opponents and his vulnerability more akin to the situation that had confronted Charles XII in 1700 than that which had faced Maria Theresa in 1741. Like Charles, Frederick won early successes, particularly the crushing defeat of the French at Rossbach (1757), only to find that he could not achieve military victory and that the weight of his opponents' strength inexorably weakened his army, his state and, with them, his chance of sustaining the conflict. On a number of occasions Frederick sought a compromise peace, but without success; he was finally saved by the death of Elizabeth in 1762.

Her successor, Peter III, an admirer of Frederick, signed a peace with him, and Maria Theresa was forced to accept that she could not recover Silesia. At Hubertusburg in February 1763 the war ended on the basis of a return to the pre-existing situation, the *status quo antebellum*. Prussia had survived the challenge of war, though with the loss of something like 10 per cent of her population, and major physical and economic damage. It remained to be seen whether Frederick would be able to prevent another major conflict ensuing as rapidly as the Seven Years War had followed that of the Austrian Succession. There was no reason to predict in 1763 that Austria, Prussia and Russia would unite to partition Poland in 1772, and then again in the 1790s, or that the latter decade would witness them uniting against France.

European diplomacy 1763–93

'Denmark sweats horribly', a British diplomat remarked in 1762 when a Russian attack appeared imminent in support of the claims of Peter III to the Duchy of Holstein.[6] The succeeding three decades were to prove worrying for many minor powers. The aggressive energies and schemes of the major powers, which had been directed into conflict with each other during the mid-century wars, were, in subsequent decades, to concentrate on a competitive struggle for influence in the minor states and territorial gains from them. Despite the Austrian attempt to force the Dutch to accept the opening of the river Scheldt to navigation in 1784, and the Prussian invasion of the United Provinces in support of the Orangist Party in 1787, tension and conflict were concentrated in central and eastern Europe. There were several reasons for this. The western European powers were financially exhausted after the mid-century wars and also increasingly absorbed in colonial conflicts that distanced them to a certain extent from European continental disputes. French ministers stressed their continued interest in these disputes, their willingness to support allies and their ability to act. In 1784 the French finance minister, Calonne, told Frederick the Great's brother, Prince Henry, that France could assemble a field army of 60,000 in less than a fortnight and would do so to support their Dutch ally in the Scheldt dispute against their Austrian ally, Louis XVI's brother-in-law, the emperor Joseph II.[7]

However, many commentators doubted France's ability to act effectively. The financial burden of the Seven Years War, though difficult to calculate accurately, had been staggering. In 1753 the government had owed over 1360 million livres tournois as debt in securities, a figure that excludes much of the overall debt, especially the value of official posts that belonged to their holders. With negligible inflation, the comparable figure in 1764 was about 2350 million, a figure that totalled nearly two-thirds of annual agricultural and manufacturing output. The burden of the debt was such that France shifted from being a large to a small net supplier of peacetime investment capital. In 1777 Frederick the Great suggested that financial exhaustion constituted an insurmountable obstacle to any French attempt to oppose Austrian plans. He added that, because of her financial problems, France did not deserve to be considered a major power.[8]

Financial problems were significant. They helped to induce British ministries to respond cautiously to the demands of possible allies. Nevertheless, the effect of these problems should not be exaggerated. They neither prevented Britain from considering alliances nor France from attacking Britain in the War of American Independence. More significant was the diplomatic situation. Though there were tensions in Austro-French relations, increasingly so from 1778, when France refused to provide any help during the War of the Bavarian Succession, the two powers were none the less allied. When Joseph II prayed in 1774 for the success of Louis XVI's inoculation against smallpox, the Palatine envoy in Vienna suggested that it was possibly the first time that the Habsburgs had invoked Heaven for the preservation of a French monarch.[9] Frederick the Great's attempt to sow dissension between Austria and France achieved less success in the 1770s than it was to do in the 1780s. He might instruct his envoy in Paris in 1776 to stress Joseph's plans for Alsace and Italy, but, as he admitted the following year, the alliance was not without weight in French ministerial thinking.[10]

Austrian schemes at the expense of traditional French allies, such as Bavaria and Poland, were unpopular, but the alliance between the two powers reduced tension in the Low Countries, the Rhineland and Italy, thus helping to direct French attention to problems that seemed more immediate – colonial friction with Britain. The peaceful nature of French territorial expansion in Europe, the acquisition of Lorraine in 1766 and of Corsica two years later, reflected the role of the Austro-French alliance, if only in reducing tension between the two powers. This was matched by the Franco-Spanish alliance, which lasted from the third Family Compact of 1761 until the revolutionary wars. This alliance was of considerable importance in creating a dangerous situation for Britain during the American Revolution. It also helped to reduce tension in western Europe. Though the two powers were not without their differences, over their Pyrenean frontier in the 1770s for example, their relations were in general good, and it was not surprising that a diplomat could report of Frederick the Great in 1775, 'Spain, Portugal and Italy seldom occupy him farther than as subjects of raillery and table conversation.'[11]

Though the Corsicans, who bitterly resisted France's purchase of the island from Genoa in 1768, might not have agreed, the western European powers displayed scant interest in territorial expansion in Europe. They were not on Europe's 'open frontier' with Turkey, while there could be no agreement to partition areas of weak or unstable government. There was to be no partition of the United Provinces or the Rhineland to complement that of

Poland. Partly this was a matter of opportunity and possibly of differing traditions of political behaviour in eastern Europe, where the partition of Poland derived to a certain extent from the schemes for acquisitions from the Turks. There was also arguably space for gains in eastern Europe that would not bring rivals too close to areas deemed strategically crucial.

However, Russian assertiveness was more important in creating a different pattern in eastern Europe. Prussian hostility to Russia and Austria's limited interest in the views of her Russian ally had helped to limit her influence between 1726 and 1755, but Russia's major military role in the Seven Years War, which contrasted markedly with her modest part in the War of the Austrian Succession, and her successes in defeating Prussian armies helped to increase her importance. This was further enhanced by Prussian determination to avoid conflict after the ravages of the war and by Russian volatility in international affairs. In 1764 a Russo-Prussian alliance inaugurated the 'Northern System' of Nikita Panin, foreign minister from 1763, a scheme to maintain influence in the Baltic and eastern Europe by defeating French intrigues, controlling Poland and preventing the possibility of renewed Swedish aggression. In 1781 Catherine allied with Joseph II. Russian diplomatic independence kept other states waiting on Catherine's decisions. 'As long as Russia is coy towards Maria Theresa she will stick to Bourbon like a leech,' commented one diplomat in 1765.[12] This did not prevent other rulers from suggesting schemes to Catherine, such as the partition of Poland proposed by the Prussians, but it ensured that Russian approval was crucial. A former British diplomat noted in 1766, 'Russia alone would assure all our purposes, that single tie sufficient to counterbalance all other powers.'[13]

The 'Northern System' was essentially defensive, based on the wish of Catherine II to reform Russia after the Seven Years War and to protect Russian hegemony in eastern Europe. Events, as ever, did not conform to diplomatic schemes. Polish developments provided the prime element of unpredictability, though Sweden and Turkey were also to play a similar role by 1772. The first Polish crisis had been anticipated. Augustus III died in 1763, and in the following year, Catherine was able to secure the election of a former Polish lover, Stanislaus Poniatowski. Active Russian military intervention and the alliance of Prussia produced a speedy success that contrasted markedly with the more protracted intervention of 1733–5, produced by the previous election. Having reinforced what was effectively a protectorate over Poland, it was by no means probable that Russia would play a major role in partitioning the country within a decade.

This major shift in policy owed much to two elements that complicated Polish–Russian relations, the relationship with a wider international stage and the role of the Polish political nation. For most of the Saxon era (1697–1763) diplomatic relations with Russia had principally involved the magnates, while the majority of the nobility had been generally hostile to Russia. Polish politics, ever volatile, became more so as Poniatowski's attempts at reform increased tension. His proposal in 1766 to secure a definitive abolition of the *liberum veto*, and thus to strengthen the royal position, and his refusal to support Catherine's policies of extending the rights of Poland's Protestant and Orthodox religious dissenters, led to Russian military intervention. Catherine saw no reason why her policies of religious reform should not extend to her Polish protectorate.

Russian action provoked resistance among the Polish nobility, the Confederation of Bar being formed in 1768. Combined with its activities in the Crimea, a Turkish vassal state, the intervention of Russia in Poland seemed to threaten the destruction of the buffer zone between Russia and Turkey, a danger made more apparent when Russian troops pursuing Polish confederates violated Turkish territory. In 1768 the Turks declared war.

The war went badly for the Turks, the Russians destroying their fleet in 1770, and overrunning the Crimea, Moldavia and Wallachia. Russian success both led to the prospect of major territorial changes and aroused the fears and ambitions of other powers, particularly Austria and Prussia. A range of options seemed open, including an Austrian attack on Russia, a scheme propounded by Kaunitz, and Joseph II's very different favourite project, Austrian participation in the dismemberment of Turkey. Seeking to avoid war and keen to gain territory, Frederick the Great in 1771 promoted the idea of a partition of Poland, a scheme agreed to by Catherine and a few months later, despite the opposition of Maria Theresa, who thought it immoral, by Austria. In August 1772 the three powers settled their shares, while Russian military pressure led the Polish Diet to accept the partition the following year. The First Partition deprived Poland of almost 30 per cent of her territory and 35 per cent of her population. The Habsburgs gained the most populous share, Galicia, while Russia gained the largest, significant advances in Polish Livonia and White Russia, and Frederick gained Polish Prussia, and, thus, joined his dominions of Brandenburg and East Prussia.

The First Partition was not the only major change in the early 1770s. Gustavus III's coup in 1772 reintroduced absolutism to Sweden and royal direction to Swedish foreign policy. This dramatic failure of Russia's Northern System made Baltic affairs more volatile, for Gustavus was ambitious, and determined to gain territory, preferably the Danish possession of Norway. Russia had more success in the Balkans. Though the Pugachev revolt (a peasant–Cossack rising of 1773–4) and continued Turkish resistance forced Catherine to moderate her demands, the treaty of Kutchuk-Kainardji (1774) rewarded her with gains in the Caucasus and along the northern littoral of the Black Sea, on which freedom of navigation was gained, and with a measure of protection for the Orthodox in the Turkish Empire.

The treaty marked a major turning point in relations, and Russia was able to use it to make further gains that reflected and intensified her new position of superiority over the Turks. In 1783 Russia overran the Crimea. Russo-Turkish treaties in the period 1774–1804 awarded the former considerable advantages in Moldavia and Wallachia, including significant commercial and consular concessions, land grants and an effective veto over the Sultan's choice of *hospodars*. The effect of these changes was further to destroy Turkish buffer zones, to carry Russia nearer the heartlands of Turkish power and, by altering the balance of power in eastern Europe, to influence the attitudes of all other eastern European powers, particularly Austria.

The 1770s and 1780s witnessed a return to the Austrian aggression and expansionism of the first decades of the century. Under Joseph II, who became emperor and co-ruler with his mother Maria Theresa on the death of his father Francis in 1765, and who was sole ruler from 1780 to 1790, Austrian intentions were less narrow than they had been at mid-century, when attention had been devoted to the recovery of Silesia.

In the late 1770s the Bavarian succession offered the most inviting field for expansion, as the death of the elector Max Joseph III without children (1777) provided the opportunity for gains. Frederick the Great's determination to prevent this led to the War of the Bavarian Succession (1778–9), an inconclusive conflict made more so by the refusal of Joseph's ally, France, and Frederick's ally, Russia, to intervene militarily. However, both were opposed to significant Austrian territorial gains and this helped to lead Austria to acquire only a small area, the Innviertel, at the Peace of Teschen (1779).

Catherine's role, as co-mediator of the peace with France, represented Russia's growing status and significance in central European politics. It also led Joseph to seek Russia's alliance, a necessary step if the Russo-Prussian alliance was to be destroyed, and an apparent precondition for the success of his schemes. The successful negotiation of an understanding between the two powers in 1781 enabled Joseph to make a second attempt to gain Bavaria. In 1784–5 he pressed for the exchange of the Austrian Netherlands and Bavaria, but the scheme was defeated by opposition in the Empire, orchestrated by Prussia, by Russian lukewarmness and by French unwillingness to see a growth of Habsburg power in the Empire.

Joseph was thwarted in the Empire and also forced in 1784, under French pressure, to abandon his scheme to force the Dutch to accept the opening of the Scheldt, the closure of which was seen as an infringement of sovereignty and blamed for the economic weakness of the Austrian Netherlands. In 1781 Frederick the Great had pointed to the contrast between Joseph's vast projects and his limited success. Four years later the Spanish foreign minister, Count Floridablanca, told the French envoy that Joseph's aggressive character would sooner or later trouble the peace of all Europe with his wide-ranging ambitious schemes.[14] In the late 1780s, Joseph's energies were to be directed towards the Balkans. This was despite the opportunities for a war of revenge presented by the death of Frederick in 1786, regretted by Joseph as occurring 30 years too late.[15] The Russian alliance, and Russian aggression, led Joseph to concentrate on the Balkans. There was on his part a determination to match Russian gains, and a sense that decisive developments were at hand. Under the influence of her favourite Potemkin, who was interested in expansion to the south, Catherine was keen to gain further advantages from the Turks, and, according to Joseph, who visited her in the Crimea in 1787, she was dying to fight them again. The visit offered an impressive display of the benefits that could flow from acquisitions and the potential wealth of the region. Joseph was very impressed by his visit to the Russian Black Sea fleet base at Sevastopol, noting that the success of her schemes had exalted Catherine's imagination. Though the Austrians did not seek conflict with Turkey in 1787, the surprise Ottoman declaration of war on Russia that year, touched off by a number of minor disputes and by fear of Russian schemes, led Austria to come to the aid of her ally. Austrian operations in 1788 were disastrous, in marked contrast to the more predictable position-warfare of the Bavarian Succession War. Kaunitz warned in 1788 of the danger that Austria would lose her political and military reputation, and that Prussia would support the Turks. Joseph argued that Austria could not resist both Prussia and Turkey.[16]

The war, and the initial Austrian and Russian difficulties, had serious consequences, both domestic and international. The appearance of success, rather than the nature of policies, was crucial for states that wished to retain the initiative and discourage

opposition. Just as the French failure to protect their Dutch protégés from Prussian invasion in 1787 led to a serious loss of
domestic prestige and international respect, so Austria's problems led to fiscal difficulties and a fatal loss of reputation in the
face of rising domestic discontents. Russia's difficulties encouraged powers that hitherto had not dared to attack her to plan to
do so. A Russo-Turkish war had been the goal of the former's
opponents throughout the century, particularly Sweden, Poland
and Prussia. Frederick the Great had encouraged Turkey to attack
in mid-century. The failure of peace negotiations with Turkey in
1772–3 had played a major role in preventing Catherine from
acting against Gustavus III's French-backed coup in Sweden.

Gustavus's attack on Russia in 1788 threatened St Petersburg,
as Russia's northern provinces were only lightly defended. However, as the aggressor, Gustavus had violated his own constitution
of 1772, which required the concurrence of the Estates. The opposition of the aristocratic officer corps handicapped Gustavus, as
did the Anjala Confederation, a league of Finnish officers, remi-
niscent of the Polish aristocratic confederacies, who declared to
Catherine that they sought perpetual peace with Russia and
would not fight except in defence of their homeland. Yet, the
Confederation collapsed over the question of collaboration with
Russia, while threatened Anglo-Prussian military intervention led
Denmark rapidly to abandon her attack on Sweden. In the winter of 1789 Gustavus convened the Estates and profited from the
anti-aristocratic sentiments of the unprivileged orders to push
through an Act of Union and Security which greatly increased
royal authority and removed many of the remaining privileges of
the nobility. Russia's attempt to thwart this policy by supporting
the anti-royalist noble opposition in the Estates failed. The clear
relationship of domestic and international strength was displayed
by Gustavus's reasonable success in the rest of the war, which
led Catherine to conclude peace in 1790, without any Swedish
territorial gains, but with a recognition of the constitution of
1772 and a promise not to interfere in Swedish politics, a
promise fulfilled in the instructions to the new Russian mission
to Stockholm.

The Swedo-Russian conflict played a part in schemes for a
more extended confrontation with Russia. Gustavus himself had
recognised the wider importance of the struggle, negotiating a
subsidy treaty with the Turks (1789) and seeking an entente with
Poland, a country whose crown he considered seeking in the
winter of 1790–1. However, the strength of the developing anti-
Russian coalition depended on the plans of Britain and Prussia.
The Triple Alliance of Britain, Prussia and the United Provinces

(1788), which had stemmed from the Dutch crisis of the previous year, had become by 1790 an anti-Russian league. Concerned that Prussia would not benefit from possible Austro-Russian gains in the Balkans, Frederick William II's minister, Count Hertzberg, proposed in 1787–8 a complicated system of exchanges that would leave all gainers bar the Turks.

By 1789 discontent in the Austrian dominions and, in particular, revolt in the Austrian Netherlands, led Frederick William to plan war with Austria. Thanks to Joseph II, Austria had joined Poland in the ranks of European powers to be partitioned, creating a possible Austrian Succession war, without him even dying. Frederick William proposed to create independent states in the Austrian Netherlands and Hungary and negotiated alliances with Turkey and a resurgent Poland, where the international crisis had provided an opportunity for rejecting Russian protection and inaugurating a reform policy that included plans for a larger army.

Despite the massing of 160,000 Prussian troops in Silesia, Prussia accepted a settlement with Joseph's successor, Leopold II, that left the Austrian dominions intact. Leopold agreed to make no gains from the Turks, but Catherine's refusal to accept a similar settlement led Britain and Prussia to threaten her with war in early 1791. However, Russian determination and British hesitation led to a climbdown that destroyed the Anglo-Prussian alliance. Russia was left to fight Turkey without Swedish, Polish, Prussian or British intervention. The crisis of 1788–91 had been surmounted and in the Peace of Jassy (1792) Russia acquired the territory between the Dniester and Bug, an area that consolidated her position on the northern shores of the Black Sea and made the prospect of a Polish–Turkish alliance less credible. This prospect was to be extinguished by the Second and Third Partitions of Poland (1793, 1795), which destroyed the country and reflected Russia's dominance of eastern Europe after 1791, a dominance also seen in the Swedo-Russian alliance of 1791.

Gustavus III's eagerness to ally with Russia and Catherine's determination to regain control of Poland and destroy the Polish reform programme both arose from a common fear, that of the revolutionary hydra epitomised by France. The monarchs of the period were quite prepared to support revolutionary groups in the territories of their rivals, despite warnings, as when Spain joined France in assisting the American Revolution, that the example might be dangerous, the revolution contagious. Initially French developments at the end of the 1780s played little part in the international relations of the period. France had already revealed her unwillingness to assist her Austrian ally during the Bavarian Exchange and Scheldt disputes. Her inability or unwillingness to act had been displayed during the Dutch crisis of 1787, and, in the following year, French views on international relations, particularly on the fate of Turkey, were generally ignored. It was by no means clear in 1789 that within three years France was to repel a Prussian invasion and overrun the Austrian Netherlands. In late 1789 Joseph II had feared that France would invade the disturbed Austrian Netherlands, but his anxiety was to prove misplaced and Austrian authority was reimposed in the area in 1790. French weakness and the greater significance of events in eastern Europe ensured that it was only in 1791, when the latter were settled and when the revolutionary nature of French developments became increasingly apparent, that France became a central topic of European diplomacy. Any action to restore royal authority in France depended on a concert of powers, as Kaunitz pointed out in August 1791, but the Austro-Prussian reconciliation of that summer made this possible. Kaunitz saw this as a new political system that would astonish Europe as the Diplomatic Revolution had done. The stage was set both for the Second and Third Partitions of Poland and for the French Revolutionary Wars.

Conclusion

The protracted warfare of 1792–1815 involved more than a renewed bout of conflict, a repetition of the sustained warfare of 1618–59, 1688–1714 and 1740–63. It also entailed a consolidation of central governmental authority and power that had important implications for international relations. For most Europeans, 'internal' frontiers had been as significant as their international counterparts, and they had frequently been difficult to distinguish, both on the ground and on maps. These frontiers had crucial judicial and financial functions, especially in western Europe, with its denser and more historical fabric of jurisdictional authorities, and the accompanying vitality of local privilege. This mental world was not to change appreciably until the impetus, energy and focus that the French Revolution and the subsequent conflicts gave to nationalism altered the European political consciousness. Nationalism and war encouraged the consolidation of territorial sovereignty. This interacted with increasing state monopolisation of organised violence and greater precision in the mapping of frontiers. All were different facets of the consolidation and spread of governmental authority. The implementation of firm frontiers was bound up with the existence of more assertive states and growing state bureaucracies, which sought to know where exactly they could impose their demands for resources and where they needed to create their first line of defence.

11 Armies and Warfare

The crippled, limping, gun-laden protagonist, dependent on begging, in *Harlequin Returning from the Wars*, a mid-century work by the Florentine painter Giovanni Ferretti, was as realistic an image of war as the triumphal celebrations, mingling thanks to God and man, that greeted victory – celebrations in which many losers found it expedient to share. If, for most people, the state was more peripheral than the harvest or the conflict with disease, none the less the most significant impact of political society was war, the damage it could create, and the need to support it, through finance, recruitment and supplies. All societies were militarised, in the sense that armies were a significant government preoccupation, their financing, directly or indirectly, a major problem for both state and subject. Military affairs are thus worthy of attention because they reflect the aspirations and limitations of political action in a sphere which was deemed crucial.

Discussion has been greatly affected by two ideas. The first, that of a military revolution in the period 1560–1660, argued that tactical innovations required more training and larger, more permanent armies, resulting in a significant rise in their size and in the extent of government control over them. The second suggests that eighteenth-century warfare was characterised by operations that were limited in their nature and objectives, and marked by indecisive sieges and an avoidance of battle. In has also been argued that civilians were treated less harshly than in previous wars. This is linked to a widely held, yet inaccurate view, that international relations in the eighteenth century were indecisive, and that little of importance was at stake in them. Neither idea can be accepted without considerable hesitation. If an early-modern military revolution is to be discerned, and the concept should be approached with considerable scepticism, then it is possibly more appropriate to redirect it to the period after 1660. As far as French, Austrian, Prussian, Russian and English military developments are concerned this is certainly more appropriate. Montecuccoli, president of the Austrian war council 1668–80, was the key figure in seventeenth-century Austrian military developments, Louis XIV and Louvois his French counterparts. In terms of tactics and the size and permanence of armed forces, many of the key innovations of the century took place in the latter half. In place of converted merchantmen, navies came to rely almost exclusively on specialised vessels. Training became more important for troops and the use of bayonets, whether plug, ring or socket in type, was of great tactical significance. In place of a division between pikemen and musketeers, all infantrymen could be armed with the same weapon and infantry firepower increased. If attention is directed to the military changes of the late seventeenth century, then it is possible to see the early decades of the following period as a continuation in terms of the use and development both of the recently consolidated armed forces, such as the armies of Austria and Russia and the British navy, as well as of such innovations as the bayonet. For all of these reasons, it is clearly inappropriate to make a stark divide between the new century and the preceding period of military developments.

The early years of the century witnessed certain advances in weaponry, which essentially marked a continuation and spread of recent trends. Pikemen were phased out. The replacement of heavy and often unreliable matchlock guns with lighter and more rapid-firing flintlocks was continued, as was the introduction of the bayonet. Dramatic changes took place in Prussia and Russia. Frederick William I (1713–40) increased not only the size of the Prussian army, but also its readiness for action. He insisted on and personally supervised extensive training and regular manoeuvres. By 1740 when Frederick the Great came to the throne, the Prussian army was a major force with 83,000 troops and no shortage of weapons.

Russia

More dramatic were the changes in Russia, because of their scale, the fact that they occurred in wartime, making it possible to appreciate the effect at once, and because victories were won at the expense of Sweden, which had hitherto enjoyed a high military reputation. As with much else, Peter I's military reforms had been prefigured by his predecessors, including his father Alexis and the leading minister of the 1680s, Golitsyn. A comparison can justly be made with Prussia. The role of Frederick William I in laying the basis of Frederick the Great's achievements is a useful reminder of the need in Russian military history not to exaggerate the novelty of Petrine policies. That the pre- and early Petrine army was frequently unsuccessful, in the 1680s against the Tatars in southern Russia, in 1695, under Peter, against the Turks at the siege of Azov, and in 1700 against the Swedes at the battle of Narva, does not mean that Peter had to start completely afresh. Alexis recruited foreign officers and armed and organised troops on the western (non-Russian European) model, but in peacetime the army was run down and poorly trained.

A large standing army maintained out of tax revenues did not become a reality until Peter's reign. A major reorganisation of the army was carried out in 1699–1700. Regulations drawn up in 1698, and possibly written in part by Peter, emphasised the importance of regular armies, organised in a hierarchical fashion and maintained by training. In November 1699 Peter ordered the creation of 29 'new' (western) regiments. They were designed to be both permanent and regularly trained, and their novelty was expressed in part by their German-style uniforms. Peter therefore continued his father's rejection of dependence upon the noble cavalry of the feudal host, whose defects were castigated in *On the Conduct of the Army*, an essay in 1701 by Pososhkov. The crushing defeat at Narva led Peter to press ahead with his policy. Relying on the principle of conscription, in 1705, Peter introduced a system of general levies based upon a Swedish model. Every 20 taxable households were ordered to send one recruit and they were made responsible for his replacement if killed or incapacitated. This raised 45,000 troops. New regiments were created, 12 in 1705–7 alone, and by 1707 the army was about 200,000 strong. The practice of recruiting foreign officers continued.

Peter's military reforms extended to the navy. A fleet was constructed for the Azov campaign in 1696, foreign experts were imported and Russians sent abroad to learn shipbuilding. The subsequent development of the fleet reflected both Peter's personal enthusiasm for it, which led him to devote a lot of time to its details, and the need to challenge Sweden for control of the Baltic if Russia was to succeed in dislocating the structure of the Swedish empire and preventing a Swedish reconquest of her eastern Baltic provinces, lost to Russia in 1710. A naval academy and a large admiralty yard were constructed at St Petersburg and a school of navigation at Moscow. By Peter's death (1725) Russia had a fleet of 34 ships of the line and numerous galleys, and these played a major role in forcing Sweden to make peace in 1721.

Education was also an important theme in Peter's reforms. He founded artillery and engineering schools, while officers were trained by service as ordinary soldiers in the guards regiments. Peter insisted on progressing through the ranks himself and tried to ensure that no noble received a commission without some form of training. Peter's attempt to make state service a central focus for the aspiration of many led to the spread of uniforms, themselves a mark both of service and of the state's role in allocating rank. For the nobility military uniforms replaced gold-threaded robes as their principal dress, while Peter was the first monarch to require all Russian soldiers to wear specified uniforms. Under Peter the armed forces, particularly the army, replaced the Church, with which his relations were poor, as the lodestar of monarchical action and, to an extent, of national unity. Instead of a semi-sacral figure, Peter made the monarch a military leader and, if the nature of his successors from 1725 to 1796 – four women, one youth and only one adult male, Peter III, whose reign was very short – prevented the consolidation of this image, it did not permit a return to the earlier one.

In one particular respect the Petrine legacy was neglected. It was not until Catherine II rebuilt the fleet in the 1760s that Russia again became a significant naval power. Peter's successors did not, however, abandon his commitment to the army, and continuity was provided in leadership. Prince Menshikov, a general of obscure parentage who became the first head of the new War College, established in 1718–19 to direct military administration, was the most influential minister of Catherine I (1725–7). General Münnich, a German, who had entered Peter's service in 1721, was head of the War College 1732–41. Field-marshal Lacy, who joined the Russian army in 1700, commanded the victorious campaign against the Swedes in 1741–2. These generals retained the essentials of the Petrine system and delivered a series of victories between 1733 and 1742.

In the 1730s the Russians found, as Peter I had done, that the Turks were more difficult to defeat than the Poles or Swedes, a useful corrective to the modern view that Turkey was already 'the sick man of Europe'. As in 1711 the Russians entertained hopes of a rising of the Balkan Christians and of decisively pushing back the Turkish frontier. In practice, eastern Europe posed serious problems for military operations. Militarily there were two very different European theatres of operation. In the east, distances were vaster, logistics more of a problem, guerrilla or irregular warfare more common and it was more difficult to obtain a victory by reason of the distance that separated centres of power, the smaller role of fortifications and, arguably, the lower importance of settled agriculture. Despite the fall of Azov in 1736 and of Ochakov on the Black Sea in 1737, disease and logistical problems thwarted hopes of crossing the Dniester and invading the Balkans, and indeed, forced the abandonment of Ochakov in 1738. A successful invasion of Moldavia in 1739 suggested that the bold Russian plan would be realised, but it collapsed, like so many other bold military schemes of the century, not through military difficulties, but through the breakdown of the supporting diplomatic coalition, in this case a unilateral peace with the Turks made by Austria, which had been persuaded to enter the war in 1737.

Mid-century Prussia

If Russia was the most rapidly developing military power in the first 40 years of the century, the most prominent in mid-century was Prussia. As crown prince, Frederick the Great had criticised his father's neutrality in the War of the Polish Succession, fearing that inactivity in international relations would lead to Prussia losing ground to her neighbours, Saxony and Russia, and he had hoped in 1737–8 that a military solution would be found to the Jülich–Berg inheritance dispute in which Prussia was involved. His chance of glory was to come when his accession in 1740 was followed by the death of the emperor Charles VI and the consequent opening up of the succession to the Habsburg dominions, as several rulers refused to accept the attempt to pass the entire inheritance on to Charles's elder daughter, Maria Theresa. Frederick's military reputation was founded on his invasion of the Habsburg province of Silesia and his subsequent success in retaining it during the Silesian wars (1740–2, 1744–5), and during the Seven Years War (1756–63), when he had to defend himself against Austria, France, Russia, Sweden, and most of the German states.

Frederick's successes have been attributed in part to his tactical innovations and, in particular, to his use of oblique order as a variation upon the customary linear tactics of the age. He devised a series of methods for strengthening one end of his line and attacking with it, while minimising the exposure of the weaker end. This tactic depended on the speedy execution of complex manoeuvres for which well-drilled and disciplined troops were essential. But in practice it proved difficult to control troops once combat had begun, and the importance of these tactical innovations can be placed in perspective by considering other factors that helped to account for his success. In 1740 Austria was exhausted, her army in need of regeneration after her failure in the Turkish war of 1737–9. While during the Silesian wars Austria had to confront a number of other powers, including Bavaria, France and Spain, Frederick had no other enemy. In the 1740s, Austria's principal allies, Britain and Russia, refused to help her against Prussia, and the British pressed her repeatedly to direct her attentions against France. Furthermore, the Austro-Prussian campaigns were not easy triumphs. Surprise helped Frederick in his invasion of Silesia, but in the first battle, Mollwitz (1741), the Prussian cavalry was defeated and Frederick fled the battlefield, the eventual Prussian victory coming only as a result of a hard-fought infantry action. Battle casualties were higher on the Prussian side. This was repeated in the other major battle of the first war, Chotusitz (1742), a Prussian victory that was far from decisive and due more to discipline than tactics.

Military resilience reflected and was a significant cause of Austria's political survival in the early 1740s. A concentration on Frederick's invasion of Silesia has tended to distract attention from Austria's success in defeating the 1741 partition plan. It might be suggested that, but for British diplomatic pressure, the appeal of possible Italian conquests, and the overrunning of Bavaria in 1742, the Austrians would have reconquered Silesia, just as they drove the Bavarians and French out of Bohemia in 1742. A detailed study of diplomatic activity of the period reveals the opportunism and confusion that characterised what are too often seen as coherent and consistent strategies, and the same is true of an examination of many of the battles and campaigns of the period. An ability to react to developments is and was a feature of diplomatic and military skill, and this frequently appears to have been a key to Frederick's success. He was also greatly helped by his autocratic methods and by not needing to consult anybody.

Frederick's successes illustrated the strength of 'absolutism' as a political system when directed by an intelligent, strong-minded ruler who knew what he wanted. In contrast, mid-century military policy in Austria, France and Russia was handicapped by a lack of firm direction, factionalism, and government by council. These were due to the personalities of the rulers, two of whom were women with no experience of military affairs, while the third, Louis XV, lacked the requisite ability, and to the general absence of any effective substitute. This indicated one of the central political weaknesses of absolutism, the failure to provide an adequate alternative to poor leadership, a failure that often ensured that countries with an autocratic constitutional structure could be as prone to weaknesses, particularly factionalism, as those with a more open structure. It would, however, be foolish to deny that Frederick's grasp of war and of battle-winning techniques gave him a lead in military matters, and therefore, in combination with the aggressive nature of his policies, in political affairs. This was certainly the case up to 1757, when Frederick crushed the French at Rossbach, inflicting greater losses on a force that outnumbered his, before using the oblique attack to repeat the experience at Leuthen at the expense of the Austrians.

Mid-century reform in Austria and Russia

Prussian successes touched off a major burst of military reform in mid-century elsewhere in Europe as other powers strove to be able to imitate and thwart Frederick. Thus Austria responded to her defeats in the Silesian wars, while France, which had done well in its campaigns in the Low Countries in 1745–8, essentially perceived a need for reform only after her defeats in the Seven Years War. Had the French army in the interwar period (1748–56) matched Austrian developments or prefigured the reforms it was to experience after 1763, then it would no doubt have conducted itself better in the Seven Years War, as the Austrians did, with incalculable consequences, perhaps of a victory over Prussia that would have provided a vital accretion of prestige for the French *ancien régime*.

The most significant changes in the period occurred in Austria. In combination with the financial and administrative reforms carried out in this period by Haugwitz, they made Austria a formidable power prepared for war. The military reforms did not seek to copy those of Prussia, though they were designed to confront them. An important stimulus was the pressure for change within the Austrian army itself. Its training and equipment were improved. New drill regulations were issued in 1749 and a military academy opened at Wiener-Neustadt while Prince Liechtenstein reformed and improved the artillery. These changes were related to a longer-term trend in which the system of military entrepreneurship, of the private ownership of regiments, which had hampered the army's effectiveness and limited promotion prospects for good officers, was gradually dismantled. In 1722 Eugene had complained about the pressure to give regiments to young and inexperienced princes who ran them badly, thus losing good officers thwarted by their limited promotion prospects. Maria Theresa was convinced that the dominance of the army by the higher nobility, the group that had come to dominate military entrepreneurship, had ruined it. She sought to create a military establishment financed by regular taxation and commanded by loyal professionals. This entailed a reduction in the financial independence of the Estates and the military and financial role of the entrepreneurs. After 1744 opportunities for profit by the latter were restricted, while a definite attempt was made to widen the officer corps, in response to the specialised knowledge that was increasingly required, particularly in the artillery, and to the limited interest displayed by the higher nobility in such matters and in education in military academies. The Wiener-Neustadt academy was open to the sons of serving officers, a group that included commoners and minor nobles, while the engineers' academy was opened to pupils of all ranks.

The academies created the basis for a professionalised officer corps, producing a service nobility drawn from the middling and lower nobility. The military career was seen increasingly in Europe as a respectable pursuit, and not just as a mercenary trade or a part-time occupation for gentlemen. This could be related to the burgeoning of military literature from the 1720s, as officers sought to inform themselves. In time, service as an Austrian officer became bureaucratic in its nature, rewarded with prestige, security for old age and guaranteed employment, not lands and lordship. Promotion within the officer corps, previously largely controlled by regimental commanders, was gradually transferred to the government. The service-nobility nature of the Austrian officer corps was enhanced when the establishment of a political *modus vivendi* between the Habsburgs and the Hungarians after the rising of 1703–11 led to a significant influx of Hungarian and Slav aristocrats into the army.

Furthermore, Maria Theresa was determined to ensure the loyalty of the new professional officer group. She sought consistently to upgrade their self-image and social standing, ordering in 1751 that all officers were to be admitted to court. At first officers were ennobled individually for satisfactory service, but in 1757 she decreed that commoners with 30 years of meritorious service were to be raised to the hereditary nobility, ennoblement becoming an automatic result of service. After the Austrian victory over Prussia at Kolin in 1757, the empress founded the Military Order of Maria Theresa, a graduated scheme of decorations awarded to officers regardless of social rank or religion. This dynastic/state control over the concept of honour was one that was being attempted over much of Europe, not least because it helped with one of the major problems of the age, persuading the nobility to govern in the interest of the state. But it was particularly appropriate in the case of military officers. It represented an attempt to disseminate an idea of honour and rank arising from service rather than birth, one that was especially necessary in armies where it was essential to persuade aristocratic officers to take orders from men who were socially, though not militarily, their inferiors. In the case of Austria, it was linked with Maria Theresa's fairly effective suppression of duelling in the army.

The mid-century also witnessed Russian military reforms. Though Shuvalov's proposals of 1753–8 for a Higher Military Department or School, to provide a sound knowledge of the mechanics and principles of war, came to nothing, the Military Commission created in 1755 produced new regulations for the infantry and cavalry and also for the Cossacks. The infantry code, published in 1755, stipulated Prussian-style tactics. In 1756 the artillery held a number of long exercises which built up their speed and accuracy; in 1757 it was reorganised and in the late 1750s received a series of new pieces. These reforms gave the Russian army in the Seven Years War a greater fire-power and the artillery a sound professional basis.

The mid-century reforms in the Austrian and Russian armies had an appreciable effect in the Seven Years War, creating a very difficult military situation for Frederick the Great in contrast to that in the Silesian wars. The Austrians had already grasped the principles of Prussian strategy and tactics, interior lines and oblique order, and they benefited from a new emphasis on the scientific development of military technique. The Austrian medium artillery balanced mobility and fire-power effectively and was to be copied by Frederick and the French. In 1758 the Austrian general staff was established and Austrian operations were to be characterised by improved supplies and flexibility in the field. The Austrian use of dispersed columns helped to produce successes against Prussia in 1758–9.

Prussia also suffered from the vast improvement in Russian tactics. By 1759 the Russians had come to grips with tactical innovations made further west, and their use of field artillery contributed to victory over the Prussians at Paltzig (1759). The Russian artillery had already displayed a clear superiority over the Prussian at Gross-Jägersdorf (1757). This Russian victory, in common with the fighting power of the Russian infantry at the indecisive battle of Zorndorf (1758) and the Austro-Russian success at Kunersdorf (1759), helped to give Frederick a permanent fear of the Russians, one that he attempted to assuage by disparaging remarks about them, but which conditioned his policies for the rest of his life. These Russian military successes were not just flashes in the pan. They were followed by a temporary seizure of Berlin (1760) and by the capture of Colberg and Schweidnitz (1761), which threatened the destruction of Frederick's territorial position. Russian military success against Prussia was impressive, more prestigious than victories against Poland, Sweden and Turkey. It was the counterpart of the country's economic, administrative and diplomatic developments: both the product of them and the way in which western Europe was made most conscious of them. The war witnessed further developments in the Russian army. The adoption of more flexible means of supply helped to cut the baggage train of the field army, making it less like that of an oriental host. The daily rate of march increased, crucial in an army operating at such a distance and when the political situation dictated the need for victory before Russia's system of alliances disintegrated. The army made progress in the use of light troops and field fortifications, the handling of battle formations, and the reorganisation of the artillery. By the end of the war, the Russian army was the most powerful in Europe; its ability to campaign successfully in the Empire was displayed in a conflict with a power, Prussia, that had itself at Rossbach overthrown the image of western European military superiority.

After the Seven Years War

The decades after 1763 were spent in digesting the lessons of the Seven Years War, particularly as there was no major military confrontation in western and central Europe, other than the short and inconclusive War of the Bavarian Succession (1778–9), until the outbreak of the French revolutionary wars in 1792. The most significant changes were made by Prussia and France. During the Seven Years War, Frederick responded to Austrian and Russian strength with a number of innovations. He used artillery as a key to open deadlocked battlefronts, distributed cannon among the battalions of infantry, and made use of howitzers, with their arching trajectory, for offensive purposes. These artillery-based tactics were not simply a response to the growing potential of a military arm that derived from technical improvements and economic capacity. They also reflected the military problem posed in particular by the successful use of positions in the North Bohemian and Moravian hills by the Austrian field-marshal Daun. Diversionary attacks were used to break up hilltop defensive concentrations. Austrian and Russian defensive positions, as at Kunersdorf, did not crumble before the oblique order. Frederick also used light infantry, but the Prussians, afraid of desertion, did not like to employ infantry out of sight of their officers.

These developments proved inadequate in 1778 when the Austrian field-marshal Lacy was able to use massive concentrations of defensive forces in the Bohemian hills to thwart Frederick's bold plan for the conquest of Bohemia. The war was a logistical triumph for Austria, although one that exhausted the treasury, helping to produce pressure for peace, and was a military disaster for Frederick. The Prussian army was ravaged by dysentery and desertion, unable to gain the advantages of surprise and speed. It was mainly luck that the terms of the Peace of Teschen (1779) represented a diplomatic success for Frederick. The war revealed serious weaknesses in the Prussian army: the absence of sufficient supplies; demoralised infantry; undisciplined cavalry; poor medical services; an inadequate artillery train. Chance prevented a serious defeat in the Bavarian Succession War, a defeat that might have made the rapid collapse of the Prussian military machine and state before Napoleon in 1806 less surprising.

Reform in the French army

The crushing French defeat by Frederick at Rossbach in 1757 was a serious humiliation for a country that prided itself on its army. It helped to inspire a major movement for military reforms. In part, this entailed a re-equipment of the army with improved weapons. A new musket was introduced in 1777. Under the direction of Gribeauval, the French artillery was made more mobile and generally improved. Artillery was one sphere in which governments welcomed the opportunities presented by technical progress. In the 1760s Gribeauval introduced both a new sight and a screw device for altering elevation accurately. His combination of powder and shot increased the rate of fire. These mechanical innovations were complemented by improved training, including schools for artillery officers. They were also matched by new developments in other fields. In place of static linear tactics, there was discussion of the use of attacking columns. In his *Essai général de tactique* (1772) Guibert advocated living off the land in order to increase the speed of operations. Others pressed the virtues of irregular warfare, leading in 1788 to the establishment of light infantry battalions as distinct units. The divisional system evolved in France from 1759, eventually giving commanders the means of controlling much larger armies than the 60,000–70,000 which had been considered the maximum in the middle of the century.

Many of the developments of this period, including the deployment of new artillery, only came to maturity in the 1780s. As grave financial problems and, possibly groundless, fears of Prussian forces ensured that France did not implement her threats to prevent the Prussian invasion of the United Provinces in 1787, the success of the *ancien régime* French army in adopting new ideas was not tested until 1792, when the special circumstances of the French Revolution make comparison difficult. In several respects, the army of revolutionary France was a product of pre-revolutionary changes. Even if its former commander-in-chief, Louis XVI, was executed, Gribeauval's guns remained standard. Napoleon, who was taught to use them, also read Guibert. The regular army was disrupted through desertion and emigration, but it played a major role in the successes of 1792. These have often been ascribed to revolutionary enthusiasm, but weight has also to be placed on military capability. The French navy had also developed considerably towards the close of the *ancien régime*. Under Marshal Castries, who was minister of the marine in 1780–7, the conscription, organisation and administration of the navy were reformed, armaments and vessels standardised, naval colleges founded and harbours improved. The vitality and strength of *ancien régime* military arrangements in this period were also shown by the revolutionary wars, which were no easy triumph for the French. Both the Austrians and the Russians fought well, despite the substantial manpower available to France.

Continuing problems

A stress on change and reform tends to make the period appear one of continual improvement. In practice, as with other aspects of government activity, what is striking is the extent to which action was generally taken in response to failure, and the manner in which reorganisation was so often necessary or felt to be so. Armies proved a good example of the clash between aspiration and reality that is such an obvious feature of the administration of the period, and were possibly the most crucial instance of this, given their importance and the value attached to them. One of the principal problems that was not solved was desertion. This arose from the element of compulsion in recruitment and the poor treatment of soldiers. Supply difficulties were also a striking feature of campaigns in this period. The French army that invaded Spain in 1719 had not been improved during the demobilisation that had followed the War of the Spanish Succession. Supplies were a particularly serious problem for offensive operations, shortages hitting the Spaniards in Lombardy in January 1734, while in that year the French armies on the Rhine and Moselle suffered from a lack of provisions, and their colleagues in Lombardy delayed the start of the campaign because of a lack of forage. Operations denuded whole areas, making it harder to obtain supplies. Most supplies had to be moved on carts and were thus dependent on the roads. This exposed armies to one of the least effective areas of eighteenth-century government, road maintenance, and thus to the depredations of the weather. For example, the French Moselle offensive of 1734 was delayed by poor roads and bad weather, the cannon becoming stuck in the mud.

Sickness, like poor roads, was an area in which governments appeared nearly helpless in the face of a hostile environment.

The threat of disease, in common with supply and transportation problems, encouraged units to stay in winter quarters, a practice which, though by no means an invariable rule, reduced the tempo of military activity without any equivalent cut in its cost. Another sphere in which it is necessary not to exaggerate change is the effectiveness of the weaponry. Numbers and discipline were placed at a premium by their limited accuracy.

A significant problem affecting training was the condition of the troops. The very slow spread of barracks, an expensive device, ensured that troops were frequently quartered among the civilian population. Units of the Hungarian army were housed in peasant dwellings, because barrack construction started late there and proceeded slowly. In Russia it was not decided to house all Moscow's soldiers in barracks until 1765. This policy made it harder to train troops and even to develop a distinctive military attitude. It also made relations with civilians and their attitudes to soldiers a serious problem.

Recruitment

Recruitment was also a difficult problem, one that was exacerbated by the prevalence of desertion. There was no uniformity in recruitment practices. The principal categories were 'voluntary' and 'compulsory', the latter either conducted in an organised fashion or quite arbitrarily. The importance of voluntary service varied considerably, but its existence reflected the appeal of the military life for many. For petty nobles it provided a career; for many soldiers it represented an escape from the burdens of civilian life, or the constraints of local society on young adult males. A valuable source of voluntary enlistment, matching what happened in many spheres of civilian life, were the sons of soldiers and sailors, providing, for example, most of the recruits for the French engineers in the first half of the century.

Military service was particularly valuable for exiles, providing opportunities for advancement that they would otherwise be deprived of. The openness of *ancien régime* society to useful exiles, such as Huguenots (French Protestants) in Protestant Europe or the Jacobite diaspora in Catholic countries, was one of its distinctive features. It was of particular significance in military affairs, with large numbers of Irishmen going into the French army and Scottish Jacobites being recruited for the Russian navy. Not all those who served foreign rulers were lifelong exiles. Many responded to traditional links – Scots in the service of the United Provinces, Germans in that of Venice, Swiss in that of France – and most reflected a specialised form of the typical migration of the century, the move towards areas of greater opportunity, migration in search of social mobility. In military terms this entailed a move to countries with substantial military forces, and was thus a counterpart of the relationship between regions of centralised and decentralised power.

The use of foreign soldiers was popular with many rulers. In the case of officers and skilled soldiers, such as gunners, they might be recruited for their expertise. British and Dutch naval officers found posts in the Russian fleet. Foreign troops were felt to be more reliable politically, particularly in the event of domestic disorder. Encapsulating what could be the isolating effect of military life, their use avoided the problem of arming the population. However, the willingness of governments to arm the people is more striking than their occasional hesitation. Training in the use of arms was given to what must have appeared the most unreliable members of the community, often criminal in their background. Russian peasants belonging to the patrimony of the crown were allowed to hand over vagrants, landless labourers and other unwanted members of their villages to the army as a first stage in meeting their conscription quota. The willingness of governments to arm the poor and the marginal members of the community is an interesting indication of their confidence in the essential stability of the social order, as mirrored in the armed forces, and in the ability of discipline to direct action and attitudes. This was a view that was to be vindicated by the infrequency of army and naval mutinies.

Conscription was the alternative to voluntary enlistment. Across much of Europe it was conducted in an arbitrary fashion, the very antithesis of bureaucratic practice. A classic instance of this was the British navy, recruited with the assistance of force in the shape of the press-gang. Though the formation of a reserve of seamen was proposed, nothing came of it, and the most important section of the British armed forces continued to be dependent on a recruitment system that was not only arbitrary, but also only partially successful. On numerous occasions naval preparations and operations were handicapped by a lack of sailors. Possibly there was no better option. The French and Spanish registration of potential sailors led to evasion and a shortage of seamen. As with so much else, the ability to conceive a system was not matched by the capacity to make it work. The Russians used conscription with only limited success, force proving an unsuccessful way to teach marine skills.

Methods similar to the press-gang were frequently used in European armies. A major consequence was serious desertion. Partly in response to their drawbacks as well as to the need for larger armies or for sustaining a certain size of force in the face of the attrition produced by long wars, various states experimented with more systematic methods of recruitment. These conscription systems were furthest developed in central and eastern Europe, possibly reflecting the greater authority of governments in these regions and their greater indifference to personal liberties. To work effectively, these systems entailed considerable regulation of the population, which could only be achieved by means of the co-operation of the nobility, the local arm of government across most of Europe. As the bulk of the officer corps was drawn from the same group, recruitment fitted into the same command structure. Governments regulated and benefited from this system and it was less dangerous for them than the older practice of nobles raising mercenary bands and directing them as they pleased.

The system also had hidden costs, leading to a degree of inflexibility and underlining the aristocratic control of the army. Behind the systems of conscription and the militarist patina that they gave to society, with their passes, registers, annual inspections, musters, lists, and numbers painted on houses, was the constant reality of aristocratic domination of society. The Danish ordinance of 1701 reintroducing a militia system based on conscription tied the conscript to a specific locality during his six years of service, giving landowners opportunities to apply pressure on troublesome peasants. The largest system of conscription was that established in 1705 in Russia, where serfdom lessened the scope of voluntary enlistment. Service was lifelong in the first half of the century, for 25 years thereafter. Manpower was summoned for the army and navy by proportional levies on the male population liable for service. The clergy were exempted and local and occupational concessions freed specified groups. Wealthy peasants could buy themselves out. The system was not extended to White Russia, the Baltic provinces and the Ukraine until the reign of Catherine II. Possibly the large numbers of troops that could be raised through conscription explains why the Russians, though keen to recruit foreign officers, did not make a practice of hiring foreign mercenary troops.

In Prussia a cantonal system was established between 1727 and 1735. Every regiment was assigned a permanent catchment area around its peacetime garrison town, from where it drew its draftees for lifelong service. The name of every duty-bound male was entered on a roll at birth, though there were a large number of exemptions. These covered the nobility, localities such as Berlin, and workers deemed important, such as apprentices in many industries and textile workers. The regiments were required to be up to strength only for the few weeks of the spring reviews and summer manoeuvres. For the rest of the year the native troops were allowed to return home to their families and trades, while even when at the garrison town they were allowed to pursue civilian occupations. In a similar fashion artillery horses were registered and then distributed among the peasantry, their care secured by inspections. The system was extended to Silesia in the 1740s. It worked reasonably well, providing a stable and predictable link between regiments and reserves of manpower in specific areas. The Prussian cantonal system led to a high military participation rate among the population. It also provided a manpower pool deep enough to allow some selectivity, while generating significant parish and regional solidarity in companies and regiments and encouraging a sense of feudal obligation among the officers.

In 1762 Frederick II of Hesse Cassel divided his territory on the Prussian model into recruiting cantons, one for each regiment. Recruiting by force was prohibited, and exemptions were given either by the payment of taxes or by occupation. The major towns were exempt as were propertied farmers, taxpayers, apprentices, salt-workers, miners, other important workers, domestic servants and students. Eligible men were listed and checked annually. Military service entailed the analysis, stratification and surveillance of society.

In 1730, a peacetime year, Hesse had one in nineteen of the population under arms. France and the Habsburg territories neither required such a proportion, because their reserves of manpower were larger, nor could they have obtained it. Uniformity in the Habsburg military system was lessened by the privileges of particular areas, especially Hungary. In 1781 Joseph II introduced a system of conscription to Austria and Bohemia.

Native French forces were raised voluntarily, in the case of the regulars, and by conscription, in that of the militia. The recruitment of volunteers was handled by officers, generally nobles, who recruited in their seigneury of origin. The militia sometimes served as a source for the regular army. In 1706–12 this compulsory transfer was achieved by the drawing of lots, helping to make militia service very unpopular. It was affected by exemptions and these were maintained vigorously. The 1743 proposal to extend the militia to Paris led to widespread concern and the production of critical handbills. Exemptions were permitted on occupational grounds to the benefit of those employed in trade, manufacturing and public functions. As very few peasants were exempt, most recruits were rural in origin. Although desertion was a major problem, the French system worked well in mobilising large numbers for the army in time of war, a vital political resource. In the early 1750s the section of the regular army staffed by French soldiers, 130,000 men, was only slightly more than 0.5 per cent of the population. The Seven Years War took the army to about 540,000 French soldiers, while non-French forces rose from 40,000 to 70,000, recruited mainly from Switzerland. Numbers fell greatly with post-war demobilisation.

Including the navy, men under arms at any one moment during the war totalled 2.5 per cent of the population, while the need to replace losses ensured that in total nearly a million Frenchmen, about 4 per cent of the pre-war population, served. This was achieved with relatively minor economic effects, suggesting that recruits were men whose labour could be reallocated with least difficulty, thanks to the significant underemployment of the population in rural areas. For some, military service operated as a form of migration comparable to that of movement to the towns. Thus the failure of the French to establish a conscription system identical with that of Prussia or Russia reflected the success of their own methods, itself a testimony to the size of the population of western Europe. This was further underlined by the ineligibility on health grounds of much of the population. The French army drew its troops from the age group 16–40, recruiting first among unmarried males. Between a quarter and a half of this group were ineligible because they were infirm or too short, the latter often a product of nutritional deficiencies.

Recruitment was not helped by the harshness of military life. The behaviour of soldiers, the attitude towards them of some officers, a group with whom they had little social affinity, the prevalence of desertion and the need for drill led to discipline that was often savage. The limited effectiveness of the weapons of the period ensured that both troops and warships had to come close to the enemy in as large numbers as was possible. This was a frightening experience: the enemy could be seen clearly and the noise of the battlefield was terrifying. The complicated loading drill for the weapons of the period required the conditioning of soldiers to repeat them under stress. The effect of weapon fire depended on the standard of fire discipline. Drill and discipline were therefore military necessities, on both land and sea. In war, casualty rates were often high, over half in some Cossack units that fought the Swedes in the 1700s. The chance of survival of Prussian soldiers in the Seven Years War has been estimated as only one in fifteen.

Peacetime service was less dangerous, but the desire to prepare troops for future conflict was not always matched by care for them. The debilitating effect of peace was stressed frequently by commentators, particularly military ones who disliked peacetime economies and the lessened stress on training. Peacetime life could be boring for soldiers. Pay was a problem during both war and peace and British sailors, who suffered from low pay, often in arrears and reduced by discounts, were not alone in having their morale affected.

However, it is important not to exaggerate the miseries of military life. The military were a section of the community which governments needed and cared for, albeit at a basic level. Their basic sustenance was provided in peacetime. In the 1720s every French soldier in Roussillon received daily about 1 kilogram of bread, 500 grams each of vegetables and meat, 25 of fat and 1 litre of wine or beer. Discipline in practice was not always as savage as in theory, a common feature of the law enforcement of the period, which was often tempered and episodic. In the Prussian army a relatively small number of hard cases received a disproportionate number of the most severe punishments. The most vivid accounts of the system's horrors were likely to be composed by critics. Though force played a role in the British navy, particularly in recruitment, sailors were part of a trained unit whose operational effectiveness reflected morale rather than coercion. Russian discipline, however, appears to have been more savage, possibly due to the practice of treating soldiers as possessions of their officers and the fact that service divorced them from their native communities.

There were also some signs of improvements in the treatment of soldiers as the century progressed. Russian regulations for officers issued in the 1760s emphasised the need for positive motivation in the process of transforming peasants into soldiers. Training often seems to have generally created a bond not only between soldiers, but also between troops and their officers. In 1765 France created invalidity pensions. Ex-soldiers were provided with a pension and allowed to live in a residence of their choice, the first true attempt by the monarchy to provide old soldiers with the possibility of gaining an honourable place in society. It is true that French policy towards veterans and the administration of the Hôtel des Invalides in Paris displayed paternalism, favouritism and the effects of social privilege, that reforms and financial expedients were inconsistently applied and that occasional royal visits and the distribution of largesse could not satisfy the needy veterans. The Invalides catered only for a minority of officers and men. It was not until the pension law of 1790 that all veterans of the same rank received equitable treatment based on length of service.

However, pre-revolutionary policy towards ex-soldiers did reflect humanitarian considerations. These were also displayed in the French navy in the 1780s. In 1781 pay and bonuses were increased, travelling expenses for recruits introduced and the decision taken to award half-pay to injured novice sailors who could no longer earn their living. In 1782 the government assumed the responsibility for lodging naval conscripts before their assignment and began work on a naval hospital at Toulon. In 1784 Castries issued a regulation dealing with food for the navy. He insisted that the flour should be of the finest quality, the wine of good stock and that the sailors were to receive pork and beef. In the same year, he reformed the system of naval conscription and ordered expenses and the provision of lodgings for those on their way to duty. The size and regularity of pension payments were improved, and naval discipline was eased. In 1786 Castries projected an increase in the number of hospitals, as well as higher salaries for doctors and surgeons, and he raised the overall number of medical officers in the ports. The ordinances of 1786 reflected the fruitful fusion of regulation and science that characterised some of the most progressive legislation of the period. Castries also issued specific orders for washing down the ships with cleansing agents. He established a standard uniform for the first time and took steps to ensure that ships were equipped with medicines and with foodstuffs necessary for recuperating sailors. Castries also instigated research by the Royal Society of Medicine in Paris on the preparation and preservation of foodstuffs on board ship, the nutritional requirements of seamen, ship ventilation, and the treatment of a number of illnesses.

There was little time to implement Castries' programme before the Revolution. More generally, many *ancien régime* reforms in the treatment of soldiers and sailors, such as the Dutch measures of the early 1730s to improve conditions for sailors, or those of 1741 to limit typhus, were of little effect. In his last illness Frederick the Great declared: 'In the course of my campaigns all my orders relating to the care of the sick and wounded soldiers have been badly observed.'[1] However, the reforms demonstrate the need to avoid any idea that the position of troops, any more than that of peasants, was uniform, their treatment always bleak. The fighting qualities of the armies and navies that confronted the forces of revolutionary France did not stem simply from discipline or belief in their cause. They also reflected a professionalism born of training and responsible treatment.

Warfare and the militarised society

The belief that the French Revolution inaugurated a new age of total war is linked with the idea that warfare under the *ancien régime* was limited in its aims, methods and effects upon civilians.

It has been argued that lack of state finances and the limited capacity of the industrial base drastically restricted the size and range of action of armies; that wars waged by these armies had to be, and were, reduced in scope, goals and financial effects, and that these limitations were related to a system of international relations based on the concept of the balance of power in which no significant changes occurred. These arguments are open to serious question. The conduct of military operations frequently reflected the desperate issues at stake in wars. Armies aimed to win, while civilians were often acutely affected by conflict. The heavy expenditure on the armed forces had a direct or indirect effect upon the entire community. If wars rarely produced the complete defeat of an enemy, that did not prevent the achievement of victory.

The argument that war was relatively 'civilised' and had little impact on the civilian population can be countered by consideration of guerrilla action. Regular troops were harassed by guerrillas in Piedmont, Dauphiné and Spain in the 1690s and in a large number of areas, including Bavaria, Hungary and the Tyrol, in the 1700s. There was intensive Polish guerrilla warfare against the Swedish invaders in 1703–4, while in 1707 Swedish demands for food in the Masurian woods region of Poland led to guerrilla warfare. Guerrillas played a considerable role in Iberian operations during the War of the Spanish Succession. Marshal Berwick, who led the Franco-Spanish invasion of Portugal in 1704, was surprised by the weakness of organised resistance, but equally amazed by the vigour of the peasants in attacks on his communications and in fighting back in the villages. Their success in exacerbating his supply problems played a major role in inducing Berwick to retreat. Guerrillas were used by both sides during the operations in Spain. Exactions by Saxon garrisons led to widespread popular support for a rising by Polish aristocrats in 1715. In 1744 over 5000 peasants were used by Charles Emmanuel III of Savoy-Piedmont in irregular operations against a Franco-Spanish invasion force. They were of particular importance in cutting supply lines. Earlier in the War of the Austrian Succession, there had been partisan warfare in Bavaria and Bohemia. In 1747 the Genoese patriotic rising against Austria led to partisan warfare by local peasants and the use of workers' brigades. Priests were trained to fight, while women worked on the fortifications. Guerrilla warfare is not always easy to define, but its existence calls into question the habit of typecasting eighteenth-century military operations in terms of the predictable combat of regular units. It also suggests that it is necessary to consider the question of popular political consciousness. Guerrilla warfare was often inspired by exactions, but that does not mean that they necessarily defined this consciousness.

If some aspects of European society were militarised, others were not; but when the fiscal consequences of military expenditure, including subsequent debt burdens, are considered, for the bulk of the population government demands stemmed from military concerns. The extent to which this expenditure produced results varied. Much was devoted to the peacetime maintenance of troops who supported government authority. In war, armies were capable of considerable achievements, as Peter I demonstrated by acquiring a Baltic coastline and Frederick the Great showed by gaining and holding Silesia. The basic possibilities of military action, however, were restricted by technological constraints, particularly in terms of mobility and firepower, and the absence of any superiority comparable to that which separated European from some non-European peoples was a factor preventing the seizure of European hegemony by any one state. Though weaponry improved, there was no technological breakthrough and no fundamental alteration in the nature of war. As a result, successful military powers were able to operate without altering their economic system or developing a sophisticated industrial capacity. Though armies and war were important, military pressure for economic and technical change was limited.

Naval warfare

A similar picture obtained in naval warfare. Technical developments did not overcome the fundamental limitations of the vessels. Tactical innovations were limited. Nevertheless, it was possible to plan for and obtain victory. Most states displayed some interest in developing naval power, but, generally, less than that devoted to their armies. This reflected the restricted colonial aspirations of most countries, the difficulty of turning naval superiority to international advantage and the greater value attached, socially, politically and internationally, to armies.

Ships remained, technically, wooden vessels dependent on the wind and requiring large crews that posed problems of supply. All these limitations constrained operations, not least the difficulty of securing sufficient manpower when large ships had crews of from around 500 to 1000. Warships were expensive to build and the investment of effort and money that they represented and the time that they took to construct and equip, generally several years, encouraged tactics aimed at avoiding their loss. Ships were also expensive to maintain, their wooden bottoms being prone to damage from barnacles and worms. In addition, rigging and masts were vulnerable to the elements. The consequent restriction on winter campaigns was more pronounced than that affecting armies, while the limitations produced by bad weather and adverse winds had no equivalent in land warfare. They had a serious effect on many naval operations, such as the British attempt to send a fleet to the West Indies in 1740, and the possibility of poor weather and adverse winds had to be continually considered in naval planning.

The principal innovations of the period could not overcome these severe constraints. Copper sheathing reduced the difficulties caused by barnacles, weeds and the teredo worm and the consequent loss of speed. Pioneered by the British, it had been generally adopted in their fleet by the 1770s. By the following decade the same fleet was equipped with the carronade, a new short-barrelled gun that was very effective at close quarters and required a relatively small crew. It was used with great effect against the French at the battle of the Saints in 1782. Improvements in signalling methods helped to ease the difficulties of operational command. Towards the end of the century there developed the idea of 'breaking the line', rather than keeping an unbroken line of ships parallel to that of the enemy, which was a more defensive formation. Nevertheless, as with land conflict, naval warfare in the early 1780s had more in common with that of a century earlier than with that of a hundred years later.

The constraints affecting naval warfare did not preclude clear victory. Though some battles, such as the Anglo-French encounters off Malaga (1704) and Toulon (1744), were indecisive, others had important results, both strategically and politically. The British destruction of the Spanish fleet off Cape Passaro (1718) crippled the attempt to conquer Sicily, while the destruction of the French fleet at Lagos and Quiberon Bay (1759) ruled out a French invasion of Britain in support of the Jacobites. Correspondingly, the failure of the navy, hampered by the wind, to destroy the French fleet in the English Channel in 1744, forced the British to keep a large force in Channel waters during the following years to prevent a French invasion, an obligation that limited the possibilities of colonial operations.

The belief, held vigorously by some British politicians, that naval superiority would produce international hegemony or, at least, security, was mistaken. Privateering, the *guerre de course*, could not produce victory, but, as used by the French against the British, it could counteract the economic effects of maritime dominance. It proved very difficult to limit privateering. Warships were unable often to maintain blockading stations in poor weather, while convoying used up naval power and restricted maritime sailing options. Though naval power was a crucial element in colonial struggles, it did not necessarily produce victory, as the British discovered in the West Indies in the early 1740s. In European affairs, it was of less value. The 140 shots fired during a naval bombardment of Copenhagen in 1700 hit only one building and one ship. Frederick William I of Prussia, fearful of Russia, told a British diplomat in 1726, 'as to your fleet, it is of no manner of service to me'. Two years later, the duke of Parma was reported as claiming, 'he did not fear the English, for their fleet could not come to him at Parma'. In 1727 the Austrian chancellor Count Sinzendorf mocked the capacity of the British navy, declaring 'several houses shelled in Naples or Palermo will not settle the affair'. Three years later, he doubted the capacity of the states joined by the treaty of Seville, France, Britain, Spain and the United Provinces, to harm the Austrian position in Italy, on the ground that 'landings could not be considerable and the fleets could only burn a few houses'.[2]

The obstacles encountered in amphibious operations during the century revealed much of the technical and supply problems confronting eighteenth-century warfare in general. The operations of the period lacked the sustained firepower and continual support that air-power, specialised landing and support crafts, warships capable of indirect fire and ships not dependent on favourable winds have subsequently produced. Landings were slow; it was difficult to ship sufficient wagons and horses; adequate intelligence about navigation problems and enemy defences was generally lacking and there was a serious shortage of transport ships. As a result, the most successful operations were generally small-scale raids, such as those mounted by Russian galley-borne troops against Sweden in the closing stages of the Great Northern War. Although there were important successes, such as the Swedish invasion of Denmark in 1700 and the French of Minorca in 1756 and Egypt in 1798, attempts at a more sustained kind of intervention were frequently unsuccessful, and on some occasions, such as the French operation to relieve Danzig in 1734, disastrous. Similarly, efforts at combined operations, such as the Austrian invasions of Provence in 1707 and 1746 supported by the British navy, had only limited success.

These difficulties were part of a broader failure of naval power. When British ministries thought of using naval power as a central plank in the anti-Russian coalitions that they constructed in 1720–1 and 1791, they realised that it would have little military impact. The swing in the European balance of power towards Austria, Prussia and Russia, and their general lack of interest in oceanic and colonial affairs, particularly after Charles VI disbanded the Ostend Company in 1731, lessened the political relevance of naval superiority.

Furthermore, this superiority was difficult to maintain. British success and French concentration on privateering ensured that by the end of the War of the Spanish Succession, Britain was the leading naval power, the United Provinces being no longer able to compete, and not needing to, as a result of the Anglo-Dutch diplomatic entente that lasted from 1688 to 1756. British naval dominance was most clearly displayed in the late 1710s and 1720s. However, the development of the French and Spanish navies under Maurepas and Patino altered the situation in the 1730s and changed the naval balance of power. When France and Spain were allies, as in 1733–5 and 1740–8, British options were seriously limited, and British success for much of the Seven Years War was due to Spanish neutrality (1756–61). Even then the naval situation was serious for Britain. The attempt to relieve the British garrison in Minorca when the French invaded in 1756 failed.

In both Britain and France, the two leading naval powers, there was disagreement over whether or not to concentrate on naval forces, a debate intertwined with one over the respective merits of continental and colonial strategies. Until the mid 1760s Britain attempted to combine both. Troops were sent to the continent in the Wars of the Spanish and Austrian Succession and the Seven Years War. However, despite the continental interests of George I and II as electors of Hanover, the army was seen as an addition to, not a substitute for, naval power. French commitment to naval power was less sustained. In the early 1750s Rouillé and Machault directed a building programme designed to expand the fleet, but it was destroyed during the Seven Years War, only to be rebuilt by Choiseul in the 1760s. Combined with a growing Spanish fleet, the French were able to challenge Britain's naval mastery during the War of American Independence. The large French fleet of the late 1770s, with its well-built ships and relatively sophisticated conscription system, represented a considerable achievement of the French *ancien régime*. The French utilised new scientific ideas, such as the work of Euler on fluid resistance and floating bodies, in their naval construction, just as Castries was to use them in naval medical matters. The French achievement was matched by the programme of British naval building during the war, which by 1782 had given Britain, despite her lack of allies, clear naval superiority and which put her in a very good position during the conflict with revolutionary France that began in 1793. Each war set a new record for the size of the British fleet, establishing a target for the next generation, made possible by the rise in national prosperity, particularly in population and the merchant marine.

Navies revealed in a pointed fashion many of the problems that faced warfare in this period. The difficulty of obtaining supplies while at sea made logistics a more formidable problem. Desertion could make ships dangerous to operate. Ships had a limited life-span. Naval administration was often rigid and apparently inefficient. British ships in the 1750s were built and fitted on a random basis. The Navy Board of the period was opposed to innovations in working practices in the dockyards. Yet it would be foolish to neglect the administrative achievements of the period. Whatever its other problems, the press-gang was a cheap, easy and flexible system to operate. Thus naval operations reveal the achievements and limitations of the governments and societies of the period. Which of these is stressed must be partly a subjective matter. Although in 1762 British ships were able to help capture Manila from Spain, a city on the other side of the world, they were still at the mercy of the sea and the winds. It might be possible to man, equip and supply large squadrons, but in 1740 typhus savaged the British fleet and in 1741–3 the Swedish navy was effectively put out of action by serious epidemics that owed much to insanitary conditions and inadequate supplies. Such problems increased the unpredictability of military affairs and thus the volatility of the international situation.

Conclusion

Alongside an understanding of the limitations of European military machines, it is also important to consider the potential of force, range and organisation that they represented, a potential that gave them an increasing advantage over many non-European forces. Governments that adopted only a minor role in social welfare played a much greater part in aspects of society focusing on military capability. This was not only true of European states, but their greater relative effectiveness owed much to more insistent practices of governmental intervention and also to the development of a culture in which planning and the measurement, understanding and control of time and space played a greater role. These cultural and psychological attitudes and procedures enabled the Europeans to take particular advantage of technological changes. Attempts to standardise weaponry, for example, reflected an understanding of the value of uniformity and predictability and an ability to plan for them. Europeans were also increasingly better able to analyse and systematise military practices and to consider new options, including seeing war in its political and social contexts.

12 Europe and the Outer World

To devote much space to colonies and trans-oceanic conflict in any work on eighteenth-century Europe might be held to reveal a western European bias, as the eastern European states did not have a trans-oceanic presence of note. It was the case, however, that expansion outside Europe was of significance, politically, economically and culturally, not only for the maritime powers, or for those countries, including in particular, Russia, that were to some extent frontier states. The diplomatic inter-relationship of states also ensured that conflict or peace outside Europe could affect other European powers. Peter the Great's campaigns against Persia in the early 1720s helped to keep the peace in the Baltic; the Spanish expeditionary force of 1732 attacked Oran in North Africa and not, as had been feared, the island of Sardinia or Austrian Italy. The outbreak of Anglo-French hostilities in North America in 1754 helped to precipitate the Diplomatic Revolution by leading the British to step up diplomatic efforts to prevent an attack on Hanover. The financial strain caused by intervening in the War of American Independence was partly responsible for France's weak position in European diplomacy in 1787–9.

The economic benefits of extra-European possessions and trade could also be extremely significant in international relations. They brought profits, and, although not always, improved the fiscal strength of governments. This enabled a number of powers, principally Britain, France, Spain and the United Provinces, to pay subsidies to other European states, which could be of considerable importance in affecting both peacetime diplomacy and the durability and strength of alliances in wartime. These subsidies, being paid in cash, provided a crucial basis for the raising of loans. In 1703–13 Anglo-Dutch subsidies represented approximately an addition of 25 per cent to the Savoyard budget. Spain paid Charles Albert of Bavaria nearly 2 million livres annually in order to support his challenge to Maria Theresa in the War of the Austrian Succession. Both Britain and France spent £1–2 million annually in subsidies to other powers during the same war. The recipients of British subsidies included Austria, Hanover,

Hesse-Cassel, Sardinia and Russia, and of French included Bavaria, Sweden and the Spanish prince Don Philip, while those of the United Provinces went to Austria and Saxony. In the early 1750s the British paid subsidies to Bavaria and Saxony and, during the Seven Years War, they paid for Hanoverian and Hessian troops and for the equivalent of 19 per cent of Frederick the Great's war costs. In 1757–62 France paid Austria the equivalent of £450,000 annually, while Austria paid Russia a smaller sum.

The general movement of money between governments in the form of subsidies was thus one from west to east, from maritime to continental Europe. There were exceptions to this pattern. The Turks were ready to subsidise powers opposed to Russia, particularly Sweden, and an Austro-Turkish agreement of 1771, aimed against Russian penetration of the Balkans, led to a small subsidy to Austria. Nevertheless, the overwhelming impression is of a movement from maritime to continental Europe, one that would have been more marked if all the sums promised had been paid and stronger if merely a fraction of all the subsidies sought had been granted. The movement of money was not simply due to the commercial strength of the maritime states. Western Europe was more populous, wealthy and agriculturally developed than any comparably sized region between the Elbe, the Aegean and the Urals. However, the ability to move funds internationally reflected in part the commercial strength and sophistication of societies that were able to raise large sums of cash; and this owed something to their trans-oceanic commerce.

The fiscal and economic impact of extra-European activity was not restricted to government finance. Trade brought a number of goods to European countries, the subsequent distribution of which, domestically or through re-export, brought wealth. By supplying new products or providing existing ones at a more attractive price or in new forms, oceanic trade both satisfied and stimulated consumer demand. This process was not restricted to the western littoral of the continent, but was spread throughout Europe by mercantile activity that responded to markets encouraged by both demand and emulation. If falling prices and greater availability of extra-oceanic goods, such as sugar or calicoes, were significant, so also were the varied means, including the development of the press and other advertising media, by which fashions could be encouraged and retail services publicised. Publications did not only spread news of new fashions or encourage the idea that it was better to drink tea or coffee than alcohol. They also offered views on the societies, religions and cultures of distant areas and on their actual or potential relationship with those of Europe.

Europe and the non-European world

These views were extremely varied, and a large number of factors were involved in establishing perceptions of these areas and in the subsequent discussion of them. The nature of the distant society, its religion, political and social organisation and wealth, was of importance, as were the colour and physiognomy of the population and the ease with which unchallenged and interesting information could be obtained. The interests, commercial, strategic and religious, of European powers were of significance, as was the extent to which these interests could be secured. The attitude of writers to these interests was of importance, as could be seen clearly in the case of slavery. Furthermore, attitudes were often dependent on national preferences. It was relatively easy for a British or Dutch writer to condemn trans-oceanic Catholic proselytism.

The cultural influence of distant areas was often dependent on the extent to which they could be used by writers to make comments on their own countries. As a source of motifs, distant areas, particularly the Orient, were important, but artistically their impact was not generally significant. If European settlers absorbed to a small extent the local styles, devices and instruments in architecture and music, these were of limited consequence in Europe. In contrast, many writers were willing to create and use a literary image of particular distant societies. In part, this was based on knowledge of their practices and, to a less extent, literature. Confucius was available in translation. Sir William Jones, who made his reputation translating Persian works in the 1770s, producing a *Grammar of the Persian Language* in 1771, mastered Sanskrit in the following decade, and translated several Hindu classics. Founding the Bengal Asiatic Society in 1784, he studied Indian languages, literature and philosophy.

Yet most European intellectuals, particularly in the first half of the century, had only a very limited knowledge of distant cultures, and very few had travelled outside Europe. Dependent for their knowledge on the writings of others, they could be misled by inaccurate information, such as the Patagonian giants reported by John Byron on his circumnavigation of 1764–6, or unduly influenced by particular impressions. The island of Tahiti in the Pacific, described by the French explorer Bougainville and his British counterpart Cook, was presented as an earthly paradise, a Garden of Eden without Christianity. This seductive portrayal of innocent children of nature was true only in part, but it served to challenge conventional European views and to help in the redefinition of what was considered to be natural behaviour.

The cult of the noble savage, whether found in the South Seas, among the North American Indians, or located in the myths of national history, such as the primitive Goths, was but one instance of the use of comparison as a form of judgement. Though certain writers employed fantastical journeys, such as to the moon and Lilliput, most relied on contemporary societies that, supposedly, could be reported objectively and which anyway were known to exist. The Orient was the most important region, at least in the first half of the century. Africa and the Pacific were mostly unknown to Europeans, as was the interior of North America. They did not appear to contain developed societies and cultures comparable to those of southern and eastern Asia. In central and southern America the native societies had been brought under Spanish control, the Mayas of the Yucatán being finally conquered in the 1690s. When Voltaire presented a perfect native South American society in his fantastical novel *Candide*, published in 1759, his Eldorado had to be located on a plateau surrounded by unscalable mountains and reached by his hero only after 24 hours on an underground river. In contrast, Persia, India and China, particularly the last, had long been perceived as impressive societies. The use of the wise Oriental commenting on European civilisation, and thus serving as an acceptable mouthpiece for the author's criticisms of it, had long been familiar and was to be employed by writers such as Lyttelton and Montesquieu, who published letters supposedly from a Persian in Europe to a compatriot at home in 1735 and 1721 respectively. At the beginning of the century, Russia could be so used, and it was a measure of the perceived Europeanisation of the country that it lost this role.

The Orient was unsettling and stimulating precisely because it presented developed civilisations that seemed equal or superior to that of Europe and owed nothing to what were regarded by Europeans as central to modern civilisation, particularly Christianity and the religious framework of morality. The vitality of medieval Islam had long ensured that the achievements and ideology of Christian Europe were seen as relative, and that the pluralistic nature of world civilisation had been grasped. However, in contrast to Islam, Chinese society was not Judaic in its origin nor obviously dominated by revealed religion and monotheistic theology. The comparative challenge it could be made to pose was indicated by Voltaire's *Essai sur les Moeurs* (1756), which continued the writer's campaign to scour history and the world in order to establish standards by which contemporary France could be judged.

The eighteenth century witnessed a gradual shift away from the Orient as a point of reference for European writers. Though

Usbek and Rica, the two Persian visitors in Montesquieu's *Lettres Persanes* (1721), could serve to comment on Pope Clement XI as a 'conjurer who makes people believe that three are only one; that wine is not wine and bread not bread', a sweeping attack on transubstantiation, Persia was in decline, and the 1720s were to be a decade when the chaos caused by civil war in Persia was widely reported in the European press. The capital, Isfahan, was occupied by the Afghans in 1722 and the Safavid dynasty extinguished by Nadir Shah in 1736. Ottoman defeats between 1683 and 1718 reduced Turkish prestige. Turkey was believed to be in decline and the ambivalent Turkish stance towards Christian Europe, in particular the borrowing of military technology and experts by sultans such as Selim III, reduced its possible usefulness as a source of alternative values. The obvious weakness of the Mughal empire, particularly after the death of Aurangzeb in 1707, made India seem weak and in disorder. Japan and Korea were in self-imposed isolation. Only China appeared politically powerful. Between 1680 and 1760 the Manchu dynasty conquered Taiwan, Outer Mongolia, Tibet, the Amur region, eastern Turkestan, Tsinghai and south-eastern Kazakhstan, a formidable amount of territory that brought rule over a large number of non-Chinese peoples. Nevertheless, China participated in the general lessening of approval that marked European intellectual attitudes towards the Orient in the second half of the century. The weaknesses of Oriental powers were increasingly seen, and they were regarded as especially stagnant domestically, unable to offer the intellectual dynamism and respect for the individual that were sought by European commentators.

The relative shift in interest from the Orient first to the Pacific islanders, in their supposed 'state of nature', and then to the civilised, and yet reputedly free and egalitarian, American settlers who rebelled against George III, was a response both to a general shift in sensibility and to the tyranny of fashion that increasingly influenced informed circles. Just as not all 'progressive' writers had praised China, so doubts were expressed about the paradisaical qualities of Tahiti and the Potomac. The Hessian soldiers sent to fight the Americans were not alone in their conviction that the American treatment of their slaves formed a hypocritical contrast with their claims of the equality of man. Nevertheless, for many, America came to occupy the place of China, Christian Schubart writing in his *Deutsche Chronik* in 1777 'Oh, you beloved America, you are still the hobbyhorse upon which we journalists can canter at ease.' American independence was obviously important as a concrete example of the possibility of a completely fresh start, a citizens' army and a written constitution. It offered an exciting perspective, bringing change and democracy from the realms of utopian fancy, revealing the weakness of the old order and showing that internal strife could produce radical reform, rather than simple anarchy. Independent America was not the equivalent of China in offering a potential comparison with European civilisation. The American War of Independence, the greatest trans-oceanic military commitment by any European power in the century, was a civil war not only within a political entity, the British Empire, but also within the Christian European community. Far from broadening the knowledge of other civilisations, it could be taken to be an alternative model for Europe.

If the wider world was of political, economic and cultural significance for Europe, the extent of its impact varied. Much clearly was outside the perception of most of the population. If silver was in short supply, not everyone could relate this to the need to finance the negative balance of trade with the Orient that led, for example, to average annual bullion exports thither from Amsterdam of 3 million florins in 1721–6. Economically, the impact was obviously greatest on areas making goods for distant markets or consuming products from them. Politically it was the frontier and, particularly, the major maritime powers that were most affected. Nevertheless, this varied considerably. Though it was to be pregnant with future consequences, expansion into Siberia and Central Asia had only a limited effect on Russia, especially as Peter the Great's successors continued his direction of Russian attention and intentions towards the west and south. Territorially Russia expanded. The cession of the Amur valley to China by the treaty of Nerchinsk (1689) was not reversed until 1858, but gains were made on Russia's southern frontier and more settlements established in Siberia. Omsk was founded in 1716 and Petropavlovsk on the Kamchatka peninsula, a region slowly acquired during the century, in 1740. Native peoples were slowly brought under control. The New Siberian Islands in the Arctic were discovered towards the end of the century. But Russian penetration of Central Asia remained limited. The Kazakh nomads to the east of the Caspian were nominally vassals, but the area was not fully dominated militarily until the 1850s. The Khanates of Bukhara, Khiva and Kokand were not to be conquered until the second half of the nineteenth century.

While Central Asia represented a formidable military problem, Alaska posed serious logistical difficulties. A project for a Russian colony in California had been discussed in the 1730s, but it was to be Alaskan fur that brought the Russians further east. In 1724 Peter the Great ordered the Dane Vitus Bering to discover a serviceable sea route from Siberia to North America, and sailing from Kamchatka in 1728, Bering enlarged public knowledge of an earlier exploration of the strait separating Asia from America that now bears his name. In 1741 Bering and Chirikov explored the Alaskan coast and subsequently a Russian company was formed which established fur-trading stations along the coast and on the nearby islands. This led to the nearly complete extermination of the sea-otter, Steller's sea-cows and of the native Aleutian population. As the sea-otter became scarcer, the Russians moved south along the west coast of North America, leading Spain, which laid claim to the area, to make forestalling moves in the late 1780s. Similar extermination of native populations and wildlife had marked other episodes of European expansion. The dodo, a bird found on the Indian Ocean islands of Mauritius and Réunion, became extinct in 1681 as a result of being killed for food and the eating of its eggs by pigs introduced by the Europeans.

Russia may have missed an opportunity to become a major Pacific power in the eighteenth century, though there were formidable obstacles to such an ambition. Siberia operated as a greater barrier than major oceans such as the Atlantic. The distances were formidable, the climate ferocious and the Siberian rivers flowed north–south and were ice-bound for months on end, as was the coast. Demographically, Siberia was only a minor part of Russia, and the return of the granary of the Amur valley to China restricted its development possibilities. Immigration was limited and, including the native peoples, the population was only about 600,000 by the end of the century. If war with China was not a realistic possibility for Russian rulers busy with Sweden, Poland and Turkey, nevertheless relatively little effort was devoted to Pacific and North American exploration. Furs were not as valuable as gold, and it was understandable that the government took the practical step of leaving most of the exploitation of the area to local initiative and to a trading company.

The Russian attitude was mirrored to a certain extent by that of Denmark. The inhospitability of its possessions of Greenland and Iceland and their limited value, except for whale fishing, led Danish kings to devote their energies to gains in neighbouring Holstein, and Danish merchants to seek profits in the Canton trade with China. Nevertheless, the Danes were not solely guided by profit. Danish missionaries spread Protestantism in India and Greenland, while Christian VI financed an expedition to explore the interior of Egypt in 1737–8. Other powers proved slow to seize opportunities overseas. This arose from a feeling that colonies were less useful and valuable than trading stations, as well as from the cost of overseas exploration and settlement, the resistance of native peoples, and the absence in many areas of push and pull factors in terms of emigration and resources that could be profitably exploited. The combination of insufficient demand and limited opportunity was responsible both for the restricted nature of European conquest and settlement overseas, compared with the following century, and for the unequal distribution of what did occur.

The resistance of already established powers, either native peoples or successful conquerors, was of considerable significance. The Portuguese empire was particularly affected by this. The discovery of gold in the Portuguese colony of Brazil, first in Minas Gerais and subsequently in the Cuiaba, Goias and Mato Grosso regions, led to a major movement of population into the interior, both from Brazil and from Portugal itself. In contrast, the rest of the overseas empire was both short of settlers and faced with more serious opposition. In 1693–5 the attempt by the Portuguese to expand their influence in south-east Africa was defeated by the Bantus. In 1698 their leading base in East Africa, Mombasa, fell to the Omani Arabs, who, possessing muskets and artillery, posed a military threat far greater than that of the Amerindian tribes of Brazil. Retaken in 1728, Mombasa, and the attendant suzerainty over the Swahili islands and states of East Africa, were lost again in 1729. Goa on the western coast of India was an exposed settlement with very few Portuguese settlers. In alliance with the British of Bombay, the Goan forces were unable in 1721 to capture the principal base of the Angria family, formidable Maratha corsairs who challenged the Portuguese naval position in Indian waters as did the well-gunned Omani warships. In 1737–40 Goa was involved in a disastrous war with the Maratha confederation. Portuguese lands north of Bombay were lost and Goa only escaped occupation by paying a large indemnity.

The Portuguese were not the only power to encounter serious resistance. The Spaniards met with significant resistance from the Araucanians of central Chile. Louis XIV's intervention in Siam (Thailand) in the 1680s had been unsuccessful, and both the British and the French were repulsed when they sought to benefit from the Burmese civil war in the 1750s. In 1741 the Bey of Tunis seized the offshore island of Tabarca which the French had purchased from the Lomellino family, defeated a French counter-attack and sacked the French Africa Company's base at Cap Nègre.

A major problem confronting the European powers was the vitality and aggressive expansionism of many non-European states. It was not always a case of European powers competing to exploit the weakness of overseas states; although these were often divided, some were powerful, and divisions among both European and non-European powers could produce alliances between them. The Afghans intervened in both Persia and India. In the latter, struggles between the local princes played a far larger role than European activity in the first half of the century, and the Anglo-French conflict in mid-century southern India was waged substantially as auxiliaries to local princes.

Native resistance to political control could be matched by a limited European drive to establish settlements. Though the Dutch explorer Abel Tasman had explored Fiji, New Zealand, Tasmania and Tonga in the mid-seventeenth century, the Dutch East India Company was not interested in establishing the value of these discoveries. Spanish settlement of northern New Spain was restricted and slow. Military governments were established in Texas (1718), Sinaloa (1734), New Santander (1746) and California (1767). Los Angeles was not settled until 1769, interest in the coast further north in the 1780s was largely a response to fears of British and Russian activity, and by the end of the century, the population of California was much less than 10,000.

On the other hand, expansion in some areas was considerable. North America provided an example both of the expansion of British trading bases, in the Hudson's Bay region, and of the settlement of large numbers, in the Thirteen Colonies on the Atlantic seaboard, the latter growing in the face of opposition by the Indians and by other European powers, in this case France and Spain. The Hudson's Bay Company, set up in 1670 and granted monopoly rights to fur-trading in northern Canada, ran its affairs like most companies enjoying an exclusive trade with little government supervision and only limited support. Its history illustrates the influence of war on European overseas activity. Sporadic hostilities with the French in 1683–1713 led to no dividend being paid in 1690–1718. In the 1690s no regular English troops were sent to help and only in 1696–7 did naval vessels reinforce the Company's ships. Awarded to Britain at the Peace of Utrecht of 1713, the Company's bases competed with those of French Canada. Until about 1730 competition was noticeable only at the southern edge of the Bay, but in the 1730s and 1740s the French expanded from the Great Lakes past the Lake of the Woods (Fort Saint-Charles, 1732) and Lake Winnipeg (Fort Maurepas, 1734) and on to the Saskatchewan river (Fort La Jonquière, 1751). The line of French posts lay across the canoe routes to Hudson's Bay. They were clearly aimed at the British. In 1743 the minister of the marine, the ministry that ran French colonies, ordered his Canadian subordinates to prevent the British from using Hudson's Bay as a base for establishing posts on the Great Lakes, cutting the communications between the French colonies of Canada and Louisiana and possibly finding a route to the Pacific. In response to this and to domestic criticism, the British Company adopted a more energetic attitude to exploration and expansion after 1750 and began constructing posts away from the Bay.

The Hudson's Bay Company provided an example of the primarily commercial interests of a privileged company concerned to maintain and develop its privileges and profits. This produced criticism of its effectiveness in upholding national interests in the face of French competition and of its lack of interest in expanding into the interior, criticism that led in 1749 to a parliamentary enquiry, and in 1752 to an unsuccessful attempt by London merchants to obtain trading privileges in Labrador. Other privileged companies, such as the British Royal Africa Company, faced similar criticism. Their monopolies aroused anger in those excluded from their benefits, principally the merchants of secondary ports. Demands for governmental assistance, such as those from the British Royal Africa Company, were resented. The poor financial state of the Dutch West India Company and the heavy cost of its West African operations led it to depend on government subsidies. Some critics argued that these companies were too concerned with their profits to risk them by expansion, either by increasing the volume of trade and thus lowering prices, or by adding to their overseas territorial interests and thus increasing costs. The directors of the Dutch East India Company were criticised on both counts.

In contrast to the Hudson's Bay Company, the British North American colonies expanded at a tremendous pace, although this created serious political problems. The population quintupled to well over a million between 1675 and 1740 and its growth continued thereafter. Settlement spread geographically both westward and in the gaps between the coastal enclaves. Numerous towns were founded, including Baltimore (1729), Richmond (1733) and Charlottesville (1744). There was a significant expansion of settlement to the south, whence rice and cotton were exported to Europe. Carolina was divided into North and South in 1713, Georgetown being founded in 1735 and Charlotte in 1750. Georgia was established in 1732, Savannah being founded the following year.

The British North American colonies were settlement colonies, inhabited by large numbers of Europeans, although appreciable numbers of negroes were also brought in, largely to work the plantations. By 1740 two-thirds of the population of South Carolina were slaves, a figure that made it more like the British West Indian colonies than those of northern British America.

By 1740 five out of six people living in the British West Indies were slaves; in 1789 there were 50,000 whites, 10,500 free coloureds and 465,000 slaves. In the French West Indies there were nearly 55,000 whites in 1788, at least as many coloureds and 594,000 slaves. In contrast, the province of New York was five-sixths white in 1738. The British, unlike the French, were happy to allow other Europeans to settle in their colonies, although rights for Catholics were limited. Driven by economic difficulties or religious persecution and lured by hopes of opportunity and freedom, many Germans migrated to the New World. The arrival of Protestant refugees from the archbishopric of Salzburg in the 1730s was one example of the manner in which expansion overseas affected areas of Europe that were far from maritime in their interests or traditional connections.

Immigration of both whites and negroes and disease helped to increase the preponderance of non-native people on the eastern seaboard, as it did in the West Indies. Yellow fever was brought from Africa, while smallpox wiped out half of the Cherokee in the late 1730s. The principal division in European overseas expansion was that between regions where Europeans were numerous, if not a majority, and those where they were an obvious minority. Essentially this was a division between the western and the eastern hemisphere. The distinction is clear if the possessions of particular states are considered. Spanish settlement in and exploitation of the Philippines was far less than that of Mexico or Peru, a contrast that owed much to climate, the absence of bullion in the former, and Spanish determination that the trade of the islands should be subordinated to the Spanish imperial economic system. The Portuguese colonies in Africa and Asia were less populous than Brazil.

Europeans preponderated in the eastern hemisphere only in a few areas. One which experienced the shift from trading station to settlement colony was the Cape of Good Hope. Founded in 1652 to supply the ships of the Dutch East India Company en route to the Indian Ocean, the colony expanded with scant support from the Company. Whereas the Company withdrew its trading base in Natal at Delagoa Bay in 1730, settlers, attracted by well-watered lands and a temperate climate, moved out from the Cape. The Hottentots and Bushmen did not offer effective resistance and by 1760 the Orange river had been crossed. It was not until the Boers (Dutch settlers) came into contact with the Xhosa, a migrating Bantu people, in 1779 that the situation changed. Few other areas in the eastern hemisphere had a climate suitable for European settlement and agriculture. New Zealand was not settled until the following century and the British decision in 1786 to found the colony of New South Wales at Botany Bay in Australia was primarily taken for strategic reasons and to provide a penal establishment. In January 1788 the first settlement was founded and named Sydney.

Demographically, the European world was the western hemisphere and Europe, an Atlantic world. The Pacific and Indian oceans were too distant to trade with easily for other than high-value goods; emigration thither in large numbers was not practical; local states were more powerful; and there was no basis for a large slave economy comparable to the large number of slaves transported from West Africa and Angola to work in the plantations of the western hemisphere.

Distance was less of a problem in the Atlantic world. The English Atlantic 'shrank' between 1675 and 1740 as a result of significant improvements, such as the development of postal services, and the invention of the helm wheel, which dramatically increased rudder control on large ships. The number of transatlantic voyages was doubled in this period and the number of ships that extended or ignored the 'optimum' shipping seasons also increased on several major routes. Average peacetime passages from England to Newfoundland were 5 weeks, from the eastern Caribbean colonies to England 8 weeks, and from Jamaica to England 14.[1] In contrast, the voyage round the Cape of Good Hope between Lisbon and Goa usually took 6 to 8 months in either direction, as did the crossing from Manila to Acapulco, the route followed by the Manila galleon that was authorised to trade between the Philippines and Mexico. The population of Spanish America in 1800 totalled 16.9 million, of whom 3.3 were white, 0.8 Negroes, 5.3 coloureds and 7.5 Indians. The population of North America, though smaller, was dominated by whites.

Territorially the western hemisphere witnessed major changes in this century, both among the European powers and between them and the native peoples, but these were largely in North America. In Central and South America Spanish control remained paramount with the principal exception of Brazil. The Dutch colonised Surinam as a plantation economy. Voltaire had Candide visit it and meet a Negro who told him, 'Those of us who work in the factories and happen to catch a finger in the grindstone have a hand chopped off; if we try to escape, they cut off one leg. Both accidents happened to me. That's the price of your eating sugar in Europe.... Dogs, monkeys, and parrots are much less miserable than we are. The Dutch ... who converted me, tell me every Sunday, that we are all children of Adam,' the last a reference to Christian hypocrisy.[2] The French made a major effort to settle neighbouring Cayenne in the 1760s, but most of the settlers died of tropical diseases. Portugal and Spain clashed over their competing interests to the north of the Plate estuary, but, in general, they co-existed peacefully and South America was probably the most stable continent with a sizeable population, although the Indians may not have appreciated the point. The West Indian islands were mostly under European control, although the native Caribs retained their position in northern St Vincent and resisted an attempt to extend British plantations there in 1771–2, while the Maroons of Jamaica, runaway slaves, defeated British attempts to subdue them in the 1730s and were granted land by treaties in 1738–9. In North America the Indians near the European colonies were increasingly brought under their control, leading to a series of bitter conflicts, but the major territorial shifts were between the European powers, even if the territories ceded, such as Louisiana transferred by France to Spain in 1763, were only partially controlled.

In the eastern hemisphere territorial changes between the European powers were less marked. When France was defeated by Britain in the struggle for influence in India in mid-century, this did not entail the transfer of large areas of territory. Similarly in West Africa gains such as that of Senegal, taken from the French by Britain in 1758 and returned in 1783, were essentially those of coastal slaving stations. There was little attempt to penetrate into the interior because of the climate, the dominance of trade by the coastal stations, and the strength of the local states, especially Asante and Dahomey. Guadja Trudo of Dahomey used powder and shot in 1727 to conquer the major slaving port of Whydah, where Brazilian tobacco was exchanged for slaves of Sudanese origin to the profit of the Dutch. In Africa and elsewhere territorial claims were often no guide to real power. The French annexation of Madagascar in 1768 had little impact. The island was not controlled from the posts of Fort Dauphin and Ile Ste Marie, though the French had staked a claim to a possible base on the route to the Orient.

The hesitation of European powers to expand territorially was fully seen in the Orient, where policy was controlled, in the case of the British and Dutch, not by royal officials but by trading companies. Although the Dutch had bases in Sumatra, Borneo and the Celebes, Java was the only major island on which they were a territorial power. This power was in opposition to the wishes of the Directors in Amsterdam, but came about in response to the massive expansion in the cultivation of coffee after the plant was introduced to the local chiefs by the Dutch in 1707. Javan peasants under the control of local chiefs served the same function as negro slaves in the western hemisphere. The spread of Dutch control was gradual and entailed conflict, both with some of the local chiefs and with the Chinese population, over 10,000 of whom were slaughtered in 1740. Chinese economic influence in the Philippines, much of which was under Spanish control, also led to tension, and moves towards expulsion of the Chinese were made in 1709, 1747, 1755, 1763 and 1769. In 1763, 6000 Chinese were reputedly massacred for participating in an anti-Spanish Filipino conspiracy.

In India Britain became a territorial power in mid-century. The perception of Britain's role and capacity changed dramatically in the 1760s and 1770s, with the servants of the East India Company, whose private army had risen from 3000 in 1748 to 69,000 in 1763, thinking of the conquest of China. Bengal, Bihar and Orissa were brought under British control after the victories of Plassey (1757) and Buxar (1764). The Northern Circars were added in the late 1760s, Benares and Ghazipur in 1775. Whereas France had challenged Britain in India in the mid-century conflicts, her impact was more limited in the War of American Independence, despite the vigour of Suffren's naval campaigns. Britain's principal rivals were native, the Marathas, and Haidar Ali and Tipu Sultan, rulers of Mysore, and the serious difficulties she encountered with them in the 1780s and 1790s revealed the problems of intervening in local disputes. Colonial conflict also proved, like its European counterpart, a major fiscal strain. Following the defeat and death of Tipu in 1799 when Seringapatam was stormed, Britain became the major territorial power in southern India.

The balance sheet of European expansion therefore reveals significant gains, particularly once the hesitation about territorial expansion in many circles is grasped. In 1800 most of the world's population had never seen a European, and penetration of Africa, Asia and Australia was limited. Japan, with its population of about 30 million, was isolated, unwilling to trade with Europeans except through a small artificial island in Nagasaki harbour. In much of the eastern hemisphere the major conflicts did not involve Europeans. In 1739 Nadir Shah, who had seized power in Persia, destroyed the Mughal army, seized Delhi and massacred the inhabitants, while in Africa the expansion of Islamic proselytism led to a series of major holy wars in the 1790s. European powers were the only ones able to operate around the world, but the benefits of maritime power were often only commercial and their impact on the land empires episodic.

Exploration

The balance sheet of exploration showed a similar maritime slant. After the great 'discoveries' (as far as the Europeans were concerned) of 1480–1630, the remainder of the seventeenth century had not been an age of major maritime 'discoveries', with the important exception of those of Tasman. The following century was the great age of Pacific exploration. Organised by governments and executed by warships, the expeditions had a variety of purposes, including the discovery of a north-west passage from the Pacific to the Atlantic and the investigation of a large southern continent believed, on the authority of ancient writers, to extend north of the Tropic of Capricorn in the southern Pacific. The South Seas were seen as a possible source of great wealth. In 1721–2 the Dutch explorer Roggeveen 'discovered' Easter Island and some of the Samoan islands. In 1767 a British naval officer, Samuel Wallis, 'discovered' many islands in the Pacific, including King George the Third's Island, better known as Tahiti, by following a route chosen for reasons of exploration, not for the furtherance of British trade or the pursuit of that of Spain. The collaborative international observation of Venus's transit across the sun in 1769, which involved 151 observers from the world of European science, took another British officer, James Cook, to Tahiti whence he conducted the first circuit and charting of New Zealand and the charting of the east coast of Australia. Here in 1770 Cook landed in Botany Bay and claimed the territory for George III. In 1772–5 Cook's repeated effort to find a great southern continent, including the first passage of the Antarctic circle, failed. New Caledonia was 'discovered' by him, as in 1777 was Hawaii, while in 1778 he proved that pack ice blocked any possible northwest passage from the Atlantic to the Pacific north of North America. The French explorers Bougainville and La Pérouse also explored much of the Pacific, the former circumnavigating the globe in 1767–9. These explorations owed much to governmental support, technical developments, particularly John Harrison's invention of an accurate chronometer to measure latitude, and an ability to keep crews and ships at sea for long periods. One of Harrison's chronometers was used by Cook.

The mapping of the reverse side of the earth was one of the great European achievements of the century. Accounts of exploration, for example of Cook's voyages or Dalrymple's *Collection of Voyages to the South Seas* (1770–1), were very popular. The initial political and economic, as opposed to scientific, effects were limited, and the consequences, including the Europeanisation of Australasia, were not to become apparent until the following century. However, exploration increased the gap between the maritime power and range of the leading European powers and those of non-European powers, and ensured that the imperial sway that was to be brought to the native peoples of the Pacific was European.

Land exploration was less dramatic than the probing of the Pacific, due largely to less government support and interest and to the weakness of the maritime powers in the face of the hostile environment and peoples of many regions. Much of the interior of North America was explored by the British, French and Spaniards, though the first crossing of the continent from the Atlantic to the Pacific by a white man was not made until 1792–3 by Alexander Mackenzie. Mackenzie, building on the 'discoveries' of Pond and Hearne, had earlier followed the river subsequently named after him, to the Arctic. The Spaniards Escalante and Dominguez explored Utah and Colorada in 1776, while French explorers, such as St Denis, Tisne, La Harpe, Bourgmont and the Mallets, explored part of the vast Louisiana territory in the first half of the century. Much of South America and Africa were not explored until the following century, though James Bruce 'rediscovered' the source of the Blue Nile in 1770, and Mungo Park 'discovered' the course of the Niger in 1796. Exploration brought information of new animals and plants, such as those that Joseph Banks found when he accompanied Cook. It stimulated enquiry and discussion concerning the environment and the nature of society. It offered Europeans a leap in knowledge that further increased their obvious advantages over most other societies. It is not surprising that for many this gap was marked by a lack of respect for the achievements of other cultures.

The colonial struggle

The enormous wealth that colonies did, or could, or were believed, to bring was a major reason for European interest in them. One contemporary estimate valued France's domestic exports at £11.5 million in 1787, while the exports from its colonies to France averaged over £8.25 million between 1784 and 1790.[3] It was not surprising that overseas trade was seen as a solution for national indebtedness, or that so many individuals pressed to share in the wealth it created. Its expansion and protection were seen as worthwhile objectives of government activity. Governments encouraged the production of colonial goods, the French supporting the development of cotton production in Louisiana in the 1730s. Trade and production had to be protected. In European waters this was not necessary in peacetime, except with regard to the Barbary States. They required naval scrutiny, for example from France 1736–9, and/or diplomatic conciliation, Venice signing treaties with Algiers, Morocco, Tripoli and Tunis in 1763–5. Outside Europe greater lawlessness, competing claims and difficulties of supervision helped to produce in many areas, such as

West Africa and Nova Scotia, a situation of tension with periodic outbreaks of fighting. Elsewhere in the colonies peacetime relations between European powers were generally good.

In West Africa the basic issue at stake was the exploitation of the slave trade, though other products, such as gum, were also important. The difficulty of maintaining exclusive rights to the trade of sections of the coast helped to cause conflict. In 1724 a French naval force seized the Dutch base of Arguin in an area where they claimed exclusive commercial privileges. In 1723 the Portuguese destroyed the British Royal Africa Company's factory at Cabinda; in 1725 the Company complained about French action on the Guinea Coast and in 1728 Dutch attacks upon its ships led to the dispatch of naval assistance. In 1723 Walpole wrote of the dispute between the governor of Bombay and the Indian agents of Britain's ally Portugal, 'It amounts to no less than open hostilities committed on both sides'.[4] In these cases colonial competition did not undermine the alliance of the powers concerned. This became more difficult for Britain as public awareness of colonial issues and sensitivity to them increased during the century.

The eighteenth century saw what has been called the Second Hundred Years War. Britain and France were in active competition throughout the century in colonial trade and acquisition. Some governments, such as those of Orléans, Walpole and D'Aiguillon, were less enthusiastic than others about colonial confrontation. The British ministry resisted opposition pressure in 1730 to take an aggressive stance over competing claims to St Lucia, while assurances were exchanged over the Gambia in 1772–3. Efforts were made to end North American border disputes in the early 1750s, and, with some success, to settle Indian differences in the mid-1780s. None of these ministries, however, was able to do more than negotiate short-term agreements, and many of the negotiations, such as those of the early 1750s, proved abortive.

Successful negotiations of colonial issues tended to be held only at the end of wars, but the hurry that marked most peace congresses, as powers tried to beat their allies in settling their specific interests first, made many peace settlements unsatisfactory. The Peace of Utrecht (1713) left significant Anglo-French disputes unresolved in North America and the West Indies, and it was largely the alliance of the two governments in 1713–14 and 1716–31 and their relative lack of interest in colonial matters that prevented more serious disputes in this period. In 1729 Anglo-Spanish and in 1748 Anglo-French disputes in the Americas were referred to commissioners who met without appreciable success. In 1783 there was little easing of tension over Indian rivalries, while Anglo-French commercial issues were postponed to separate negotiations, and the French were forced to threaten punitive measures against British exports in 1785 in order to oblige the Pitt ministry to negotiate seriously. The sole Anglo-French treaty that solved most colonial disputes for a while was the Peace of Paris of 1763. This was partly because it dealt with British, French and Spanish interests only, while the role of colonial issues in creating tension in the early 1750s meant that they occupied a prominent place in the negotiations. The completeness of British colonial and naval victory in the Seven Years War (1756–63), rather than the quality of the peace settlement, deterred Choiseul from attempting to challenge the terms at once. None the less, they inspired a desire for revenge.

Whatever the attitude of home governments, it was difficult to prevent colonial rivalry. Merchants, settlers and many colonial governors proved willing to risk conflict to attain their goals, and they played major roles in pushing Britain and Spain and Britain and France towards war in 1739 and 1755 respectively. The commercial concessions in the Spanish empire obtained by the British at Utrecht both transgressed Spanish imperial mercantile policies and plans and were exploited, often illegally, in order to further British commercial penetration. Spanish determination to increase the profits of their American trade clashed with British interloping, especially as the Spanish commercial system involved carefully regulated trade dominated by the needs of peninsular Spain. Relations were further exacerbated by frontier disputes between Spanish Florida and the new colony of Georgia and by British subjects cutting logwood on the coast of Honduras. Diplomatic attempts to find a solution, initially successful, failed in 1739 as a result of Spanish firmness and the limited options left to the British ministry by domestic agitation and ministerial divisions.

The resulting War of Jenkins' Ear lasted until 1748. It had been embarked on with high hopes in Britain, where the Spanish American empire was regarded as vulnerable and ready to rebel. These hopes, comparable to those which launched France and Sweden against Austria and Russia respectively two years later, were to be cruelly disappointed. Though Porto-Bello fell in 1739, the ability of Spain to defend its empire had been underestimated. Her land fortifications were part of a successful effort to harness the geography of the West Indies. Tropical diseases, particularly yellow fever, reduced the effectiveness of regular troops unfamiliar with the region and increased the relative value of fortifications and the colonial militia. In 1740–2 the British forces in the West Indies lost over 70 per cent of their strength. In 1762, when they took Havana, they lost a third of their troops to yellow fever and malaria. The percentage was even greater in the British force sent to the Caribbean in 1796. As Spanish naval weakness tended to leave the initiative to the British in the West Indies, it is clear that tropical disease and the Spanish defensive system helped to compensate for the naval inferiority of the Bourbons and their decision to devote most of their resources to conflict in Europe, where Spain concentrated in 1741–8 on the acquisition of an Italian principality for Don Philip.

The continued ravages of disease, despite some medical advances, indicated that eighteenth-century European science and organisation, while capable of charting the Pacific, could not meet the ecological challenge of the Tropics. Though scurvy had been recognised as a problem of diet, little was known about the cause or transmission of the major military and tropical diseases and this hindered efforts at prevention or cure. Body lice and a fly-carried bacillus were not recognised as the carriers of typhus and dysentery respectively, while mosquitoes were not seen as the vectors of malaria and yellow fever. A medical regime of blood-letting was unable to provide cures.

Disease and local resistance helped to end British hopes of overthrowing the Spaniards in the Caribbean, and the failure to seize Cartagena in 1741 was a cathartic experience. Thereafter in the 1740s the prospect of hostilities widening to include war with France kept most of the British navy in European waters. Colonial rivalry did not at this point play much part in the drift to war between Britain and France, although tension was evident in a number of areas including North America. French governmental concern in the 1730s and early 1740s in the western hemisphere focused, however, on possible British gains from the Spaniards in the Caribbean rather than on controlling the empty lands to the west of the Appalachian mountains and of the British colonies. Wealth, not land, was at stake.

British intervention in the War of Austrian Succession led to conflict with France in 1743, war being declared the next year, when France prepared for an invasion of Britain in support of the Jacobites, an attempt that had to be abandoned because of Channel storms and the British navy. Although the British planned an attack on Quebec, colonial hostilities with France were restricted substantially to the capture of the major French fortress of Louisbourg on Cape Breton Island by a force substantially consisting of New England militia (1745) and the loss of the British East India Company's trading station at Madras (1746).

Louisbourg was designed to guard the eastern approaches to New France (Canada). Both France and Spain, with bases such as Havana, tried to compensate for naval weaknesses by using fortified bases to command crucial sea lanes. Louisbourg, after its return at the treaty of Aix-La-Chapelle (1748), fell again to the British in 1758, which demonstrated the failure of this strategy. Although more than £2 million had been spent since the work of fortification began in 1720, the garrison in 1745 was only 1300, a force inadequate to defend it against major seaborne or land operations. The value of the command of the sea was revealed both in Britain's two captures of Louisbourg and in the subsequent demolition of the fortress, completed by the end of 1760.[5] The British were also helped by the relative freedom from disease of Canada compared with the Caribbean. French hopes that disease would dislodge the besieging forces in 1758 proved misplaced, although the French expedition sent to recapture Louisbourg in 1746 was savaged by scurvy, fever and smallpox, compelling the abandonment of the scheme.

Disease was not the sole reason for the contrast between the defensive strengths of French and Spanish America. Demography was also important. Whereas Spanish America was populous, the mainland French colonies were not. In contrast to British America, immigration was not greatly encouraged and European settlement was restricted to the French. As a result, the two principal French colonies were poorly populated. By the end of 1720 the population of Louisiana was only 4000, including nearly 1000 soldiers. Much of the population had been transported for criminal offences and there were very few women. The surrounding Indians were not always friendly, as the campaigns against the Chickasaw in the 1730s testified. Canada had only about 56,000 inhabitants in 1740 compared with nearly a million in British America. This had a direct military impact in the shape of a smaller militia.

The demographic imbalance between French and Spanish America was related to their respective economies. The French West Indian colonies of Martinique, Guadeloupe and Saint-Domingue were important producers of plantation goods, particularly sugar, supplying 43.3 per cent of European imports in the 1780s, comparable to the Spanish islands, such as Cuba, which exported tobacco, sugar and hides. However, the French mainland colonies were not sources of great wealth. Canadian fur was not equivalent to Mexican sugar, dyestuffs, cacao and, in particular, silver. In 1800 Mexico, with a population little more than that of the United States (6:5 million), was recording exports worth as much.

Economic factors alone cannot explain why France, the most densely populated major European colonial power, had so little overseas emigration. Instead, most French migration was internal. Canada and Louisiana were less attractive than the British colonies to immigrants because of the centralised and authoritarian nature of French colonial government and because the firm Catholicism of the colonies did not welcome migrants inspired to migrate by religious nonconformity. Opportunities to acquire land and autonomy were also less than in the British colonies, and the climate was a factor.

Colonial disputes played a much bigger role in Anglo-Bourbon relations in the second half of the century. It was not inevitable that another war should begin so soon after that of the Austrian Succession. Britain, France and Spain had not done well enough in the war to encourage them to begin again; they were exhausted and their governments did not seek war. The issue that had led Britain into conflict, the supposed threat to the European system represented by French victories over Austria, had been resolved. Furthermore, there was little sign in 1748 that France intended to attack Austria again. The Anglo-French alliance of 1716 had followed hard on the heels of a major conflict, and although there was no reason in 1748 to believe that such an alliance was imminent, there was equally no reason why Anglo-French relations should not have developed as Anglo-Spanish ones were to do. The peace of 1748 had failed to settle Anglo-Spanish commercial differences, much to the disgust of the British Opposition, but these were negotiated peacefully by the two powers, and a commercial treaty was signed in 1750. Britain and Spain enjoyed reasonably close relations in the early 1750s and, when war broke out between Britain and France in 1754, Spain remained neutral.

French ministers did not want war but they were nevertheless determined to maintain their colonial position. The governors of Canada sought to prevent the westward expansion of the British colonies by constructing a chain of forts from Canada to Louisiana. The disputes in America were made more serious by the belief of the British ministry that they were faced not with frontier disputes, but with a French plan to weaken fatally the British position in America, and that it was necessary to act vigorously in order to show the French that they should abandon their plan.

In the early 1750s the British colonists were active in arousing alarm over French encroachments. The ministry's room for manoeuvre was restricted by Opposition pressure on a divided government. Border hostilities in 1754 were followed in 1755 by a British attack on French ships sailing to Canada. Though war was not declared until the following year, both powers continued hostile acts, the British navy seizing all French ships they could find on the open seas. The French foreign minister claimed that the British, in order to satisfy ambitions of conquest, sought to destroy in the New World the balance of power which, he argued, was as important there as in Europe.[6]

Anglo-French maritime and colonial hostilities were more significant in the Seven Years War (1756–63) than in the preceding conflict. The early stages of the war were particularly unsuccessful for Britain. Minorca was lost (1756), Hanover overrun (1757), and the early stages of the conflict in Canada were far from successful, particularly in the light of the contrast in the size of the armies. Greater French interest in Canada had led to an increase in the size of the garrison of Louisbourg to 2500 regulars, with a supporting naval squadron; but the British expedition intended to attack the fortress in 1757 included 12,000 troops, and a force of 13,000 seized it the following year. In 1759 the French planned an invasion of Britain. If they had succeeded, judgements of the policies of the leading British minister, William Pitt, and of the wisdom of Britain's war with France, might have differed radically from the praise they received that year. However, French fleets were defeated at Lagos and Quiberon Bay; had it been otherwise, Pitt would have been criticised for dispersing British strength outside Europe. Choiseul's invasion plan was unrealistic, in so far as it anticipated significant Jacobite support, and it is unlikely that the regular forces that were intended to invade Essex from Ostend and the Clyde from Brest could have conquered Britain. But the landing of a regular force, several times greater than the Jacobite army which had invaded England from Scotland in 1745, would have posed serious problems.

The war witnessed a considerable improvement in British fortunes. By February 1759 the navy had a record strength of 71,000 men. In 1756 a good supply system for the British army in North America was established and the campaign of 1760 was a logistical triumph. British amphibious forces succeeded in capturing all the major overseas centres of the French empire except New Orleans: Louisbourg and Goree (1758), Guadeloupe and Quebec (1759), Montreal (1760), and Martinique (1762). The new king of Spain, Charles III, signed an alliance with France, the Third Family Compact, in 1761, a serious defeat for British diplomacy, and Britain and Spain fought a brief war in 1762. The British conquest of Havana and Manila indicated that success had not left the ministry when Pitt resigned in 1761. His criticism of the terms of the Peace of Paris of 1763 had little impact in the face of widespread satisfaction with the terms and general eagerness for peace shown by a country that was finding it increasingly difficult to finance the conflict. Guadeloupe, Martinique, St Lucia and Goree were returned to France, and there were concessions over Newfoundland fishing rights, but the return of Minorca to Britain and the recognition of Britain's gains in Canada, Senegal, the West Indies (Grenada, Tobago, Dominica, St Vincent) and India amounted to an impressive British triumph. There was clearly no longer a colonial and maritime balance of power between Britain and France.

The thirty years between the Peace of Paris and the declaration of war by Revolutionary France on Britain on 1 February 1793 witnessed several dramatic changes of fortune in the relations between the two powers. Triumphant in 1763, Britain used gunboat diplomacy with success over the next couple of years to defend her position. Thereafter, domestic stress, associated particularly with the Wilkesite troubles and ministerial instability, helped to produce a confused and weak policy in the later 1760s which encouraged the assertive schemes of Choiseul, and led in particular to an irresolute response to the French annexation of Corsica in 1768. The Falkland Islands crisis of 1770, in which Britain threatened war when Spain expelled a British settlement, led France to the brink of war in support of her ally. But Choiseul was dismissed and the Bourbons backed down. D'Aiguillon, who became foreign minister in 1771, was interested in the idea of a reconciliation with Britain, particularly as he was concerned about the need to resist what he saw as the threat of Russian power to the European system. Though this view was also held by some British ministers, suspicion of French intentions and concern about the domestic response dissuaded them from heeding the French approach.

Anglo-French relations were dominated from 1775 until 1783 by the issue of how far France was to benefit from British difficulties with her American colonies. As elsewhere, long-standing diplomatic grievances and more immediate opportunities for action were interdependent. The new French ministry of 1774 was less inclined than D'Aiguillon to heed British wishes, but it would no more have risked war with Britain than Louis XV had over the Falklands in 1770, or than Britain had been prepared to do over Corsica in 1768, had it not been for American developments. These served to weaken Britain far more than Jacobitism had done, though, as with that case, the French ministry was hesitant about giving open support, not least because the French were waiting for their naval strength to increase. Until the news of the British defeat at Saratoga in October 1777 reached Europe, French assistance was unofficial. By February 1778 France and the American rebels had signed a treaty of alliance. British and French envoys were withdrawn the following month and hostilities began that summer. Spain, whose naval assistance was crucial to France, entered the war in 1779, largely in order to make territorial gains, particularly Gibraltar, while Britain declared war on the United Provinces in 1780 in order to prevent them from supplying her enemies.

Britain's defeat in the war was not as serious as it could have been. The Franco-Spanish attempt to invade England in 1779 was abandoned. The Americans did not manage to conquer Canada, the Spaniards failed at Gibraltar and the French in India, and at the battle of the Saints in 1782 Rodney saved Jamaica and the reputation of British naval power. Nevertheless the loss of the Thirteen Colonies was a serious blow and Britain's prolonged failure against the Americans influenced European opinion. Her defeat was seen in the terms of the treaty of Versailles (1783). American independence was recognised, Spain regained Florida, lost in 1763, and Minorca, and France recovered Senegal and Tobago. The war represented not only a military success for France, but also a diplomatic one, as Britain had been isolated in the conflict.

It has been argued that there was no need for a European ally to divert Bourbon attention, that French resources were not fully convertible to naval purposes, that parity in naval effectiveness between the British and the Bourbons was attained in the second half of 1781, and that by 1782 Britain's general superiority at sea was established. Nevertheless, the surrender of Lord Cornwallis's outnumbered army at Yorktown in Virginia in October 1781 was also a defeat for British naval power. The French fleet was able to help George Washington's American army by blockading Cornwallis, because too many British warships were elsewhere. Britain was not operating with an adequate margin of strength.

Although the issue of naval strength was crucial to British security and her ability to maintain her efforts overseas, the failure to suppress the American rebellion was decided on land. The outcome showed the difficulty of achieving success in a civil war against a determined enemy, the problems facing any attempt to achieve military victory in this period, and the limitations of a maritime power in conflict with a land-based foe. Yorktown led to a political shift in Britain, where financial strain, popular discontent and defeat produced a loss of confidence in the North ministry. Opposition politicians determined to end the war came to power in 1782, to the delight of the heavily indebted French government, which was increasingly preoccupied with the expansion of Russia.

Defeat led to ministerial instability in Britain in 1782–4. Many feared that the rebellion in America would be followed by another in Ireland, and that France would seize India. A perceptive commentator, asked in 1780, when law and order broke down in London at the time of the anti-Catholic Gordon Riots, to suggest which European country would probably experience revolution before the end of the decade, might well have replied Britain rather than France. Lord Mountstuart observed in 1781, 'last year the whole Kingdom was in arms, destruction threatened the capital and universal ruin was expected'.[7] In the immediate post-war period Britain remained isolated, her approaches for an alliance rejected by Austria, Prussia and Russia, her attempt to divide the United Provinces from France unsuccessful. This position was reversed in 1787, when France proved unable to protect her Dutch protégés from a British-supported Prussian invasion. Thereafter, France, afflicted by domestic crisis and fiscal chaos, lost influence, failing in 1790 to support adequately its Spanish ally when the latter clashed with Britain in the Nootka Sound incident, a dispute over territorial and trading rights on the west coast of Canada. In 1790–1, British politicians contemptuously debated the fate of France. Although many were concerned about the subversive consequences of French Revolutionary propaganda and the French example in Britain, few anticipated that in 1792 France would succeed in defeating a counter-revolutionary invasion, overrun the Austrian Netherlands and threaten the United Provinces.

European colonies

The American War of Independence was the most dramatic example of the clash between European governments and their overseas settlers, which became increasingly apparent in the second half of the century. This clash reflected the determination of the former to retain control and to profit from their colonies, particularly by controlling their trade. No eighteenth-century colonists were granted representation in European legislatures until after the Revolution, when the French colonies were admitted to the National Assembly. The majority of the officials in the settlement colonies were appointed by the home governments. They were generally natives of Europe and products of their patronage systems, a blow to the interests and aspirations of colonists. Tension between home governments and colonists was not continuous. Links were generally close and many colonists were recent immigrants dependent on their home countries for military assistance and part of an economic system that was organised to supply European needs. Colonial newspapers were frequently dominated by news of the mother country. Tension tended to be most marked when military assistance was least required, for example, in Spanish America, and in British America after the conquest of Canada, and where the economy, as in both these areas, was more powerful and self-sufficient than it was, for example, in the West Indian colonies, which depended heavily on the sale of colonial products in Europe. The Dutch agricultural settlers in South Africa were as relatively heedless of their European masters as the British North American settlers pressing to expand into areas reserved by London for the Indians.

Eighteenth-century government entailed the dissipation of authority over distance, and colonies provided only one instance of this, but the strategic, financial and commercial issues and opportunities involved ensured that governments often put more effort into overcoming the effects of colonial distance than they did with many regions in their European dominions. Governmental pressure was facilitated and made more apparent by the preponderantly urban nature of colonial settlement, a situation that owed much to the use of native peoples or slaves as the agricultural workforce in many areas, and to the importance of overseas trade in the colonial economies. Philadelphia had grown to about 25,000 people by 1760, less than eighty years after its foundation. Older established towns, such as Bahia, Mexico City and Lima, helped to give colonial society an urban stamp, with incalculable consequences for its politicisation.

Governmental pretensions were strongest in the field of commerce, in which regulation was used to further mercantilist ends. The British Navigation System obliged colonists to supply Britain with goods that she could not produce herself at the same time as they were given a monopoly of the British market and were obliged to use their own or British ships for their trade. Other colonial powers, such as France and Portugal, devised similar systems. Spain's trade with Spanish America was directed from Cadiz. Pombal founded chartered companies to monopolise the trade of the Amazon region and of north-east Brazil, their exclusive privileges affecting not only British merchants but also Brazilian interests. These systems encountered resistance, not least from European traders excluded from their privileges. It would be mistaken to argue that all colonists resented and opposed the commercial regulations. Just as, in Europe, central government demands and initiatives met with a measure of local support, and, in different parts of the world, such as Java, various groups willingly co-operated with European intruders, so, in the European colonies, there was co-operation with as well as resistance to home governments. Rather than suggesting any inevitable clash, it is necessary to explain why the process of reaching and endlessly redefining a consensus that underlay and often constituted government in this period broke down in some areas. In northern India the British initially adapted themselves to the social system as they found it, conciliating the local elites of Muslim service gentry and Hindu merchants and benefiting from their power. This mutually profitable relationship lasted until the following century when attempts were made to control and change society in India.

In the American colonies many problems stemmed from the fact that the powerful section of the population was European, part of a political community that was united as well as divided by the Atlantic. If American interests could lead colonists to clash with their home governments over the division of the profits and responsibilities of the Atlantic trading systems, European ideas could provide them with justifications for resistance. The abortive plot of 1787 to expel the Portuguese and declare Goa a republic was inspired by those Goan clergy who had returned from France with radical ideas. The Republican conspiracy in Minas Gerias in Brazil in 1789 similarly failed.

In Spanish America the clash between *peninsulares* (natives of Spain) and *creoles* (Spaniards born in America) was exacerbated by the Bourbon reforms of the eighteenth century, pragmatic devices by officials concerned to maximise governmental revenues rather than the expression of a new enlightened ideology. Spanish reforms generally ignored *creole* aspirations. Senior officials were mostly *peninsulares*. Administrative reorganisation led to the creation of new territorial units and of non-venal *intendancies*. Although the Latin American wars of liberation were not to begin until the following century, and owed much to the Napoleonic subjection of Spain in 1808, separatist feeling was already developing in eighteenth-century South America.

The collapse of the first British overseas empire, and British recognition of the loss of its most populous territory in 1783, owed as much to disagreements over the nature of the colonial bond as to specific colonial grievances. The role of imperial issues in the cause and conduct of the Seven Years War and its fiscal consequences helped to make America an important topic of British governmental concern, and thus of political debate thereafter. Keen to make the colonists contribute more to the cost of their defence, the government sought both to increase taxation by the Stamp Act of 1765, and to improve the effectiveness of commercial regulations. These attempts clashed with traditional lax enforcement, associated smuggling to non-British territories, and the sense that the levying of taxation for revenue purposes by a Parliament that included no colonial representatives was a dangerous innovation. A sense of shared community with Britain had for long been matched by one of particular interests, shown for example by Maryland and Virginia which tried to encourage local shippers by giving them preferential treatment over the British.

American opposition to the new fiscal regime led to mob violence, which the colonial authorities failed to control, despite the deployment of naval and military forces. Force was inappropriate. Troops were used for tasks for which they had no particular training and the navy was unable to police the entire coastline, lacked sufficient small vessels, and was able to concentrate ships in Boston harbour and along the New England coast in 1774–5 only by abandoning the rest of the coast to virtually unregulated trade. As Joseph II was to discover in the late 1780s, force was no substitute for consensus, and the military effort required to suppress disaffection posed serious political, military and financial problems.

Although only a minority of the American colonists wished for independence when real hostilities began in 1775, the strength of separatist feeling within this minority was such that compromise on terms acceptable to the British government and British political opinion appeared increasingly unlikely. When, for example, Americans subscribed to resolutions rejecting tea drinking, in response to the Tea Act of 1773 facilitating sales of East India Company tea, and went on to dump some of the tea in Boston harbour, they were publicly rejecting in a highly charged atmosphere the structure and rationale of empire. The issue could no longer be discussed in purely British mercantilist terms. The emptiness of the imperial ethos for many was revealed in the paranoia and the symbolic and practical acts of defiance that led to a spiral of violence. In 1776 a congress of colonial representatives at Philadelphia declared the colonies independent. Their search for foreign, particularly French, support, typical of the European rebellious movements of the century, helped to internationalise the struggle, and to make compromise more difficult.

Slavery

The European origin of the rebels aided them in obtaining support from other European powers, and indeed from British opposition circles, to an extent that non-white rebels would not have received. In much of the world European colonisation was based on the enslavement or expropriation of native peoples and the importation of slaves. The slave trade was most clearly developed in the supply of Africans to the American plantations. Slavery was neither invented by Europeans, nor in the eighteenth century did they monopolise it. West and East Africa yielded large numbers to Arab slave traders who supplied the Muslim world, while the enslavement of Africans by Europeans was dependent on the co-operation of African rulers such as the kings of Dahomey. In British North America, Indian tribes, particularly the Cherokee, owned Negro slaves from early colonial days and they were important to Cherokee civilisation and prosperity. Nevertheless, the Europeans greatly expanded their Atlantic slave trade during the century. The Christian churches had adapted to colonial slavery, displaying, for example in Goa, East Africa and the Philippines, little interest in the training of native ministries.

By the end of the century European criticism of slavery was growing, with the rise of sentimentalism and of new religious sensibilities. In the 1780s the already existing strong criticism of the slave trade by intellectuals, such as Raynal, bore fruit in the foundation of campaigning associations, the British Society for Effecting the Abolition of the Slave Trade (1787) and the French Société des Amis des Noirs (1788). These societies used the methods of public political action of the period, such as meetings and subscriptions, and benefited from the existence of the press, which enabled them to reach out to a constituency whose knowledge of national issues had not hitherto been regular. On 7 April 1789 the *Leeds Intelligencer* reported the collection of £18 for supporting the application to Parliament for repeal of the trade 'raised by voluntary contributions in a small part of the high end of Wensleydale.... The contributors (being chiefly farmers) were informed of the injustice and inhumanity of the slave trade by pamphlets circulated previous to the collection.' The tone of the campaign was moral and didactic and, like many Enlightenment campaigns, it was fired by a self-righteous conviction that it would ultimately succeed. Sierra Leone was founded in 1787 by British abolitionists as a colony for free Negroes. In 1794 the Convention emancipated the slaves in France's Caribbean possessions. Britain abolished the slave trade in 1807, emancipation following in 1833.

In many senses the abolitionist movement was a considerable European achievement, that had to be imposed on other slaving societies by force. This was essentially a nineteenth-century achievement, and Mercier's description in *L'An 2440* of a monument in the Paris of the future depicting a coloured man, his arms extended, a proud look in his eye, surrounded by the pieces of twenty broken sceptres, and atop a pedestal reading 'Au vengeur du nouveau monde', was utopian. The newly-independent Americans signally refused to emancipate their slaves.

Conclusion

The late eighteenth-century agitation for abolition revealed that, in an age when European peoples were extending their sway, attitudes towards other peoples were complex, and a sense of fellow humanity, always present in the Christian message, was not absent. This sense of fellow humanity was not uniform and it was predicated on European cultural assumptions. Foreign cultures were intellectually categorised in European terms, presented in dictionaries and grammars. The imagined Orient affected policy more than the experience of the Orient. The *philosophes* agreed with colonial administrators as to the need to civilise savages, as native peoples were all too often depicted. The development of a concept of just wars in the independent United States of America, in which it was essential to seek alternative means of resolving conflicts before embarking on war, was of scant assistance to the Indians.

On the other hand, non-white subjects of European powers who were not slaves were increasingly granted civil rights if they were prepared to adopt European practices such as Christianity. There was a movement from economic exploitation to closer connections and to notions of responsibility. In 1761 Asian and East African Christian subjects of the Portuguese crown were given the same legal and social status as Portuguese whites on the grounds that subjects should not be distinguished by colour. It was made a criminal offence for whites to insult coloured subjects. Repeated in 1763, these regulations were given teeth when new officials were sent to Goa in 1774 with instructions to favour Indian clerics. Pombal explicitly cited the classical Roman model of colonisation. Citizenship was to bring equality. If there was no question of giving Hindus, Muslims, Buddhists, Negroes and Mulattos equal status, that was little different from the position in Europe where the rights of heterodox Christians or of Jews were generally limited. If the drive for emancipation and equality was predominantly legal and did not extend to economic opportunities and circumstances, this was again similar to the moves against serfdom in Europe. Economic equality did not hold the same place on the moral agenda, a circumstance understandable in the light of the ideology and social assumptions of the age.

If new issues, such as emancipation and colonial independence, were to become increasingly prominent towards the end of the century, they did not alter the essential governmental, political and commercial nature of trans-oceanic activity. This was still seen as essentially competitive and for Britain the crucial rival power was France. Other states had and did feature, but the role of France had become more prominent as the century progressed. The Dutch had become increasingly unable to take major independent initiatives and British concern about them, as about the Spaniards, was centred on their willingness to support France. Russia was a powerful force in European diplomacy, but her trans-oceanic activities were limited to her growing position on the Alaskan coast. Most rumours of and schemes for Russian colonial expansion, whether in Madagascar, California in the 1730s, or North Africa in 1774 were unfounded or unsuccessful. The same was true of the majority of plans for action by other powers, such as the 1747 scheme, supported by Grand Duke Francis of Tuscany, for the dispatch of three warships to the Indian coast. The fate of the Balkans and of the Near East, which was to excite so much concern the following century and to put Britain into opposition with Russia, was not a major issue until the Ochakov crisis of 1791. In so far as it excited British concern earlier, this centred on the possibility of France gaining commercial concessions, bases, such as Crete, and a foothold on the route to India.

As with much else, the extent and rate of change in Europe's impact on the outside world was less than was to be the case the following century. Nevertheless, there were important shifts, especially the British maritime and colonial defeat of France and the creation of the United States of America. Both were to help frame the nineteenth-century world and were to be particularly important to the nature of power in the West.

13   Government and Administration

The nature of government in this period, its objectives and achievements, can be approached from a number of angles. Much of the discussion has revolved around the notion of Enlightened Despotism or, as it is sometimes described, Enlightened Absolutism. This suggests that many governments, particularly in the second half of the century, were influenced in the formulation and implementation of their policies by ideas associated with the Enlightenment and that government became a means to implement an Enlightenment agenda. The validity of this concept has been much debated, which is scarcely surprising as it shares the ambiguity and amorphousness that characterises the very notion of the Enlightenment itself. Furthermore, Enlightened Despotism is sometimes discussed in a manner that implies that states or governments were in some fashion separate from and acting upon society. Such a view, which was indeed sometimes taken, tends to lead to a presentation of government and society in adversarial terms and to treat the disparity between policies and their implementation accordingly.

The discussion of Enlightened Despotism commonly centres on two questions, namely how far governments were motivated by Enlightenment ideas and how far the principal impetus was provided by the fiscal exigencies dictated by military preparedness as well as the costs and debts arising from conflict. The latter question has the virtue of not presenting government as in easy command of a range of options. The governments of the period can indeed be best understood in terms of the problems that faced them and their limited room for action. It is also necessary, however, to appreciate that governments were not separated from society and that administrations were not united forces bound together by a common purpose. The century witnessed the coining of the term bureaucracy, by the French economist Gournay, but governments were not characterised by an ethos or methods akin to those understood by the term today. Though patronage and clientage, departmental feuds and corruption play a significant role in modern governments they were far more important in the eighteenth century.

The nature of government in the period was such that a concentration on the administration and its officials can be misleading. Service to the sovereign was not simply discharged by officials. Government was the function and privilege of a large number of individuals and institutions who were guided by their own conventions and ideas, both traditional and reforming. This posed a political problem for central government in the event of non-co-operation, but it also vastly extended its range. The relationship is best described, not simply in terms of antagonism and conflict, but as a persisting pattern of definition and compromise, that was closely related to the linked notion of good kingship.

Such an interpretation is given added force by a reassessment of absolutism, the term most frequently used to describe the methods and aspirations of most of the monarchical states in the late seventeenth and early eighteenth century. Until recently, such states were generally seen as powerful entities characterised by rulers who dictated policy and dispensed with representative assemblies, central governments that sought to monopolise power and coerce opponents, and the growth of centralising institutions, such as the court, the standing army and the bureaucracy. However, a detailed examination of the governing practices of early eighteenth-century states suggests that this assessment is misleading. The power of rulers was limited in three significant respects: resistance to the demands of the central government; the often tenuous control of the rulers over governments; and constraining attitudes towards the proper scope of monarchical authority. The first is readily apparent. The habit of obedience towards authority was tempered by the number of authorities claiming obedience and, in particular, by a stubborn determination to preserve local privileges that helped to ensure that the focus of authority was often a local institution or a sense of locality, rather than a distant ruler. This was exacerbated by the general failure of dynasticism to provide an ideological sanction for unity comparable to that which nationalism was arguably to offer in the following centuries.

The power of central government was also limited. The number of trained officials was commonly limited, communications were poor, most governments short of money and, in a generally pre-statistical age, it was difficult to obtain adequate information. Thus the most effective way to govern was in co-operation with those who wielded social power and with the institutions which had local authority. Behind the façade of power, the imposing palaces built in imitation of Versailles, and the larger armies, rulers were dependent on local institutions and sought the co-operation of the influential. This was particularly the case in the larger states. The stress placed on Louis XIV's use of *intendants*, officials sent to the provinces by the central government, can hide the fact that they had to co-operate with local institutions, such as the provincial *parlements*, and that much power remained with the governors of provinces, commonly major aristocrats. The scope of Prussian government did not extend to the estates of the nobility. In practice, absolutism tended to mean seeking to persuade the nobility to govern in the interests of the ruler, a far from novel objective. It was only in small states, such as Denmark, Savoy-Piedmont and Portugal, where it was easier for strong rulers, such as Victor Amadeus II of Savoy-Piedmont, to supervise government personally, that the connotations of the term absolutism become appropriate. Even then the difficulties of coping with factionalism in the bureaucracy and of inculcating notions of state service and efficient administration were considerable. Furthermore, over most of Europe clear hostility to the idea of despotism, and conventions of acceptable royal behaviour, limited the possibilities for monarchical action by setting restrictive parameters of consent, although the constitutional expression of the latter varied. Monarchy was expected to operate against a background of legality and tradition, and this made new initiatives politically hazardous and administratively difficult.

A stress on the problems facing rulers and on the co-operative nature of government provides the best basis from which the government initiatives of the period can be assessed. The extent to which these initiatives should be seen as reforms is questionable. A desire to alter institutions and social practices was fairly common in government and intellectual circles. It ranged from attempting to change social conventions, such as the feeling that engaging in certain economic activities compromised aristocratic status, to seeking to create a more effective administrative system. Such reforming aspirations were by no means a novel feature of the period, and many looked back to the desire for a well-ordered state imbued with mercantilist principles that had already become well entrenched in government circles in the previous century. Though the opponents of reform were, and still sometimes are, stigmatised frequently as selfish protectors of particular interests who failed wilfully to appreciate the interests of society, such an analysis ignored the ambiguity of reform. Instead of reform being the cutting edge of the modern state, most administrative agencies were not particularly effective, but, instead, represented fresh and unpopular fiscal demands and novel interventions in existing social and government practices that were frequently more responsive to local interests and needs. Partly as a result, reform was frequently unpopular and ineffective, and the repetition of laws was a measure of this failure. Government thus had a political dimension even in states whose constitutional arrangements would suggest a limited role for politics. The role of patronage and factionalism in government, the nature of administrative practice and the importance of the administration in the distribution of the wealth raised by taxation helped both to erode the notional barriers between government and politics and to force constant supervision of the government upon the ruler. The monarch was generally the only person in a position to solve the disputes that arose. The fusion of government and politics was related to the large degree to which the administrative, judicial and political powers of central organs of government overlapped or merged. Governments sought to legislate as well as administer; the two actions were not necessarily seen as separate, but were linked, not least in the habit of legislating through judicial decisions and administering through judicial agencies. The nature of government in this period, in particular its political benefits and costs, helps to explain why what might appear as administrative problems and abuses, open to reform and remedy, were often an integral aspect of government.

Public order, crime and law

Government was expected to protect people and their property, provide justice and suppress disorder. Monarchs swore to do so when crowned, and institutions of both central and local government were supposed to control crime and enforce the law. Civil obedience, however, was not widely ingrained. Furthermore, organised crime was a major problem in many areas and its repression was often brutal. Deterrence through execution or corporal punishment, rather than incarceration, was generally favoured, imprisonment being seen as an expensive method commonly used principally for those who were suffering civil action, in particular, debtors. Travellers' accounts referred frequently to the bodies of criminals exposed in public places.

The extent of crime is difficult to evaluate, not least because of uncertainty as to how the percentage reported varied. It has been argued, for example, that crime was seriously under-reported in south-western France, and the same was also likely to be the case elsewhere, not least because the absence of insurance lessened the need to report theft. Contemporaries certainly believed that crime was not constant and this prompted attempts to suppress it, such as the campaign against highwaymen near Hamburg in 1764. Crime seems to have risen after wars were ended, presumably because armed men accustomed to fight were demobilised without adequate provision in a labour market in which unemployment and underemployment were chronic. Banditry was a major problem in Spain after the end of the War of the Spanish Succession.

Certain regions were also noted for organised crime. Generally these were areas where policing was limited, frequently with an inhospitable terrain, often mountainous frontier regions where smuggling could be remunerative. Louis Mandrin operated on the Savoy–French frontier, before being seized by the French in 1755 on Savoyard territory and executed. Dealers in contraband salt infested the Duchy of Parma in 1767. Banditry was fairly constant in many rural regions, such as Calabria, Apulia, Sicily and Jülich. Its intensity tended to vary.

It would, however, be misleading to suggest that banditry was only a problem in marginal or remote areas. Most highways were affected by it, those in Austria for example, particularly so in 1776. Banditry was a serious problem both in the wealthy United Provinces and in the county of Lippe, a small German principality unable to afford effective policing and reliant from mid-century on military patrols that did not become effective until about 1800.[1] Equally, it would be wrong to argue that everyone was terrified by crime. The Bavarian foreign minister claimed in 1781 that Dutch press reports of crime in the electorate were exaggerated, that only one robbery had taken place on a highway in the first nine months of the year, and that only eleven robbers had been executed in the same period.

Governments were more concerned about banditry and large-scale organised crime than about violence between individuals or attacks on property. Their essential response was the use of police and military units. Attempts to alter social behaviour, such as Victor Amadeus II's banning of the bearing of arms in Sicily, where the level of banditry and vendetta angered him, failed. Police forces were generally very small. Most watchmen or guards were employed by towns or rural parishes, and were generally part-time, poorly armed and unable to deal with major outbreaks of crime. Centralised police forces were also commonly small. The French *maréchaussée* was only about 3000 strong. It could serve as a useful supplement to the rural law enforcement system, but it was too weak to achieve significant results in, for example, the surveillance and control of vagrants. Absence of sufficient personnel, funds and sources of information have been blamed for its failure to control adequately rural society in Guyenne and Auvergne. In the *généralité* of Limoges in 1777 there were only about 250 men in the *maréchaussée* and one company of disabled soldiers available for policing. Yet, both in Guyenne and in Lower

Normandy, there was a growing local acceptance of the role of the *maréchaussée*.

In Russia, endemic banditry in both towns and countryside was matched by inadequate policing. In 1722 Peter I had to reinforce the police in Moscow with troops. There was no national police force. In 1762 Peter III placed the chief of police of St Petersburg in charge of police forces elsewhere, but in 1764 Catherine II returned control to provincial governors. Her remodelling of local administration in 1775 assigned rural police responsibilities to a land commissar, generally a noble elected by his peers. The police in the major towns were not always satisfactory. When the police in Novgorod were accused of corruption, Jakob Sievers, the provincial governor from 1764 to 1781, blamed the absence of salaries, the lack of efficient organisation and the failure to ensure clear subordination to a superior authority. Rural areas were left essentially to their own devices.

There were moves towards more effective or centralised policing. The *lieutenance de police* in Paris founded in 1667 was reorganised in 1701. In Austria, Joseph II sought to transfer some control from town councils to the central government, while the government of Bavaria tried to organise a force in the 1780s. In Turin the police kept a close eye on gatherings, inns and strangers. In England locally controlled forces coped with crime, but new initiatives were made. John Fielding, an active JP (Justice of the Peace), organised mounted police patrols in and around London in the 1750s. In 1785 a bill was introduced in parliament to create a single centrally controlled force for London, in place of the existing local ward and vestry constables and watchmen. Though it was defeated, due to fears about the consequences for liberty, and opposition from local interests, similar legislation was passed for Dublin by the Irish Parliament in the following year. Claiming that corporate liberties might be violated by the equivalent of a standing army, the corporation opposed the new force without success and a local rate was introduced to pay for it, while the force, unlike the parochial watchmen, was given arms.

The treatment of suspected criminals, once apprehended, varied greatly. Capital or corporal punishments or transportation were commonly favoured rather than imprisonment. Many British criminals were sent to America to be indentured servants. Many from France and Italy became galley oarsmen, in France housed in hulks and working in the dockyards. Bandits were sometimes offered military service, as by Genoa in 1755. Deterrence was seen as crucial. It led to public punishment, prisoners being placed in the stocks, or in Russia returned to the scene of their crime in order to be whipped. British publications such as the *Newgate Calendar*, while glamourising some criminal 'heroes', also tended to emphasise their remorse and repentance. Punishments were often harsh, whipping with rods being a preferred method in Brussels. In Russia in the 1730s the death penalty was mandatory for state crimes and for felonies, including murder, rape, arson, counterfeiting, the embezzlement of state funds, theft for the fourth time, not reporting taxable individuals to census-takers, and converting Russians to another faith.

Signs of a less harsh attitude have been detected. Although the number of capital offences increased greatly in England, the number of those hanged in London was far lower in the late eighteenth than in the early seventeenth century. From about 1750 the public nature and severity of capital punishment in Amsterdam changed appreciably, and there is evidence of incarceration being used instead of public pain. In Paris and the region under the *Parlement* of Paris, death sentences were not common and one in four was commuted. At least seven magistrates had to concur before a severe punishment was imposed.[2]

In Toulouse, however, the few criminals who were caught were punished with great severity. Servants who committed crimes were treated in an exemplary fashion, being branded and sent to the galleys. New ideas of tolerance and humanity appear to have had little effect on law enforcement in a town in which murder and arson were common. More generally, severe punishment was seen as a means to repair the breach in order and society caused by crime. It appeared as a ritual purification of evil. Torture was a consequence of the limited value of detective work for serious crimes, of the influence of legal precedent, and of a mental world where the use of torments to elicit the truth did not appear incredible or wrong.

An obvious change was the abolition or diminished use of torture as a means for establishing guilt in much of Europe. Its unreliability for getting at the truth, and its cruelty, were prolaimed by many writers including Voltaire and the Italian Cesare Beccaria, whose *Dei Delitti e Degli Pene* (*Of Crimes and Punishments*) appeared in 1764. Christian Thomasius, professor of jurisprudence at Halle (1690–1728), called for the abolition of trials for witchcraft and of torture and for a law based on reason. The use of judicial torture was ended in Sweden, Prussia, Saxony, Denmark, the Habsburg dominions and France between 1734 and 1788. In part, this reflected technical developments in judicial methods, in particular the lessened need for confessions and an increasing willingness to rely on circumstantial evidence. In part, however, a moral opposition to torture appears to have played a role. In 1764 Kaunitz suggested to Count Cobenzl, the chief minister in the Austrian Netherlands,

the abolition of two of our criminal laws against which humanity has complained for several centuries in all the states of Europe: these are torture and branding ... Both show how little legislators have appreciated the value of men. It is possible to correct them before believing oneself obliged to destroy them. Useful employment in prisons could replace branding. Other judicial methods could supplant torture.[3]

It is important, however, to stress the extent of the opposition to such schemes. Kaunitz's suggestion elicited no response until 1766, when the Grand Council decided to retain both torture and branding. In 1771 this council persisted in regarding torture as necessary. Many of the deputies elected to the Legislative Commission in Russia in 1767 considered torture essential as a deterrent and a source of confessions. Keen to gain immunity from torture and corporal punishment, the Russian nobility did not wish this privilege extended to others. The French *parlements* succeeded in resisting the abolition of torture until the 1780s. Torture to secure a confession was not abolished until 1780, torture after conviction to secure the names of possible accomplices until 1788. Attempts to abolish torture in Lombardy were unsuccessful under Maria Theresa, while the consultative process that preceded abolition in the bulk of the Habsburg dominions in 1776 revealed support for torture from the provincial governments of Upper and Lower Austria, Bohemia and Moravia and the supreme court. In Russia and Spain, it was not abolished until early in the following century, although in the 1790s in Spain there was less reliance on torture, as well as an emphasis on the proportionality of penalties.

Most crime did not fall into the categories judged serious. It is possible that the great majority of the population, the peasantry, settled their own problems without recourse to judicial agencies. Furthermore, in much of Europe, judicial authority over most cases was wielded not by royal courts but by those of individuals and institutions that enjoyed jurisdictional powers as a result of their functions and privileges. Seigneurial justice was important in many areas and frequently active, while privileged corporations, such as town councils or guilds, enjoyed judicial powers that reflected and enhanced their authority, and could also be a source of profit. In much of Europe the judicial authority of the crown was restricted to particular places, such as highways, specific crimes like treason and a carefully designated appellate jurisdiction. Thus in the region of Sarlat in south-western France, cases of theft were still largely handled at the level of the seigneurial courts and according to traditions of popular redress and conciliation in the 1760s, 1770s and 1780s.

The efficiency of courts, both royal and private, is difficult to gauge. Civil litigation could be slow and expensive, the latter a consequence of the remuneration of officials by means of fees paid by litigants. This was a customary feature of *ancien régime* administration whether it was royal, ecclesiastical, seigneurial or corporate. Though this method of remuneration served to transfer a portion of the cost of the institution to the consumer, it also discouraged the latter from bringing suits to court.

There is some evidence nevertheless that the use of legal redress in civil disputes increased. In France, where a contrast has been discerned between the law, seen as enforcing abstract rights, and mediation, aimed at restoring harmony in a particular community, clerical mediators appear to have been appealing to the law increasingly, and in Languedoc more disputes were brought before the courts and fewer handled informally. In Surrey, where an appreciable percentage of prosecutions were initiated by labourers or servants, it has been suggested that the law governed and served all social groups. Despite such evidence, it would be misleading to suggest that the norms of institutional justice were accepted generally. Feuds, attempts to enforce particular norms of behaviour and to gain social goals, eluded control by the authorities and were prevalent in many areas. Crime literature presented in a heroic light prominent criminals such as the English highwaymen or the French bandit leaders Mandrin and Louis-Dominique Cartouche. It is difficult to assess popular attitudes towards both the law and its enforcement. Perceptions of acceptable behaviour appear to have varied socially and regionally, but, rather than interpreting the law as a source and sphere of social antagonism, it is more appropriate to suggest that elite and popular perceptions often overlapped. Changes in crime patterns varied regionally. The material insecurities of life appear to have led some to violence, and in the Tuscan village of Altopascio crime has been related directly to the material condition of the criminal, an increase being discerned in years of deprivation. There was an uneasy balance between general lassitude and episodic activity and severity in the enforcement of the law by the usually weak police forces, who were placed under special stress in periods of dearth.

Some attempts were made at judicial reform. The powers and activities of seigneurial courts were increasingly restricted and regulated. Laws were codified, though the process was slow and success was only partial. In 1686 the Swedish Estates authorised a commission for the codification of Swedish law, most of which dated from the Middle Ages and much of which was inapplicable or only partly intelligible. Despite the support of Charles XII, progress was slow, but the jurist Gustav Cronhielm drafted a code in the 1720s which the Estates debated thoroughly in 1731 and 1734.

The *Code of 1734* remains the basis of modern Swedish law. In Prussia new legal codes included the *Codex Fridericianus* of 1749.

In Sweden, as elsewhere, the pressure for codification preceded the Enlightenment and derived essentially from the confusion of the law. In their search for clarification, many jurists rejected the idea that past laws had a sacrosanct character and, instead, pressed for a legal code that would accord with the development of society, particularly away from the disciplinary role of the church, and that could be used to direct that development. In Dutch and Neapolitan jurisprudence the notion of natural law was modified, the law increasingly regarded as a 'Newtonian' science of human nature, aimed at ascertaining what laws, morals and norms nature must necessarily produce. Many writers traditionally designated as Enlightenment intellectuals were convinced that judicial norms played a creative role in social life, and envisaged a legislative and judicial ideal that replaced traditional precepts and practices with what they construed to be an exemplary and logical system.

Such notions proved too ambitious. Louis XIV had never attempted a fundamental reform of the legal system and France remained with several different systems. Pressure for codification and judicial reform did increase in France in the second half of the century. Several writers, reasoning from first principles, advocated geometrically equal jurisdictions, a simplified court hierarchy, streamlined legal procedures, a single rational code of law and the abolition of venal office-holding and traditional perquisites, both of which were fundamental in French judicial institutions. In 1771 the chancellor Maupeou introduced a number of major changes. He established new courts in six towns within the jurisdiction of the old *Parlement* of Paris, with power to determine cases that hitherto had had to be judged in the capital. A new supreme jurisdiction was also established in both Normandy and Languedoc. These *conseils supérieurs* represented an attempt to create roughly equal areas of jurisdiction. In these *conseils* and in the remodelled *parlements*, though not in the lower courts, Maupeou dispensed with the sale of office. Judges received salaries, but no fees. The new courts were criticised as corrupt and incompetent, though it was essentially the political changes following the accession of Louis XVI in 1774 that led to the reversal of the reforms and the dismissal of Maupeou. Although fundamental changes did not come until the Revolution, when the *parlements* were abolished and the laws codified, in 1786–8 the criminal law was reformed and a measure of judicial reform introduced.

In many other countries change was also limited. An attempted reform of the Neapolitan courts failed in 1735, as did moves

towards legal codification in the 1740s. In the Danubian principalities there were sporadic attempts to codify the local laws. In
Poland where, because there was no government law enforcement agency, plaintiffs carried out verdicts, the practice of 'head-
money' remained the normal means for settling cases of assault
and murder, until changes were introduced in 1764. Interest in
legal codification increased in Poland in the second half of the
century. Nobles from the Milanese provinces annexed by Victor
Amadeus II refused to serve in his army after he tried to apply
Piedmontese law to them. Differences remained between the legal
systems of Piedmont and Savoy, although they had long been
ruled by the same dynasty. Similarly, after Frederick the Great's
conquest, Prussian common law had only a limited validity in
Silesia. In 1745, Pompeo Neri was instructed to revise the Tuscan
legal code. In his report of 1747, Neri proposed a reorganisation
of the laws, but this was rejected.

Elsewhere, change was more conspicuous. Philip V's military
victories allowed him to alter the Spanish situation fundamentally. In 1707 the political privileges of Aragon and Valencia were
abolished, Castilian law was introduced and high courts established on the Castilian model. In 1715 a high court was established in Majorca when Philip conquered it from his rival for the
Spanish throne, and in 1718 Majorcan civil law was abolished. In
1716, under the *Nueva Planta* (New Plan), it was forbidden to
employ the Catalan language in the administration and courts of
Catalonia. Catalan usages and forms were abolished and Castilian
law and practices introduced.

However, these regulations were not enforced in a fashion likely
to produce standardisation. It was decided in 1711 and 1716 that
Aragonese and Valencian civil cases were not to be judged by
Castilian law unless the crown intervened. The *Nueva Planta*
stated that Catalan law was to be preserved for matters dealing
with the family, property and the individual. Civil and mercantile
law remained exclusively Catalan and, until the early nineteenth
century, Catalan criminal law remained important. In Navarre
and the Basque region the local laws and courts were preserved.

Military strength also helped the Austrians to alter arrangements in Little Wallachia, which they ruled between 1718 and
1739, limiting noble and clerical judicial rights and regulating
labour services. Elsewhere in the Habsburg dominions attempts
to introduce judicial changes in the early decades of the century
were largely unsuccessful. Joseph I set up commissions to codify,
revise and unify the statutory laws of Moravia and Bohemia.
Active mainly in 1709–10 and in the early 1720s, these commissions were based on the Estates. They drafted only one of the

envisaged nine sections of the new code, that concerned with constitutional law, which stressed the rights and privileges of the Estates.

Important changes were not achieved until the reign of Maria Theresa. In 1747, Gabriele Verri redrafted the Milanese laws and, two years later, the Austrian and Bohemian chancelleries were abolished. The judicial and administrative functions of central government were separated, and changes accordingly were made in the provinces; the Senates of Justice of the provincial governments being replaced by appeal courts attached to the Department of Justice. A comparable separation did not occur in Baden until 1790, when an attempt was made to create an independent judiciary. Austrian changes in 1749 facilitated legal codification. The codification of civil law began in 1753, the decision being taken to co-ordinate the existing provincial laws and supplement them where necessary by the natural law, rather than to introduce a completely new legal system based on reason alone. The codification was not completed until 1811. Traditional attitudes, particularly that of provincial particularism, remained strong. Far from supporting legislation for all her dominions, the president of the Department of Justice told Maria Theresa that it was more prudent to introduce new laws in one province only and then extend them if successful. The empress retained much Polish law in Galicia, while the judicial organisation of the Austrian Netherlands retained its essential characteristics.

Maria Theresa's second son, Leopold, made major changes in Tuscany, where he was grand duke from 1765 to 1790, and where Beccaria's ideas were of considerable influence. In his *Of Crimes and Punishments* (1764), Beccaria had emphasised the value of prevention and called for consistency in sentencing and a rational and utilitarian approach to justice. In Tuscany, the appointment of judges was reformed, the imprisonment of debtors abolished, the publication of judgments instituted and precise regulations for sentencing and the conduct of cases introduced. In 1786 the death sentence was abolished and the accused's right of defence recognised.

Joseph II was more enthusiastic about standardisation than his mother. In 1784 he wrote to Kaunitz:

> I have found in Lombardy a major change for the better since my last visit there 15 years ago.... I have ordered the government to see in what manner they can adapt the principles established in the German provinces to local circumstances. The most important aim is certainly to improve and accelerate the administration of justice, which has certainly greatly improved in Germany as a result of the principles introduced there.[4]

In 1787, a penal code was issued, based on the principle of equality before the law. Both clear and concise, it abolished the death sentence. In the same year, Joseph made an ambitious attempt completely to reorganise the judicial system in the Austrian Netherlands. On his visit there he had decided that the existing system was chaotic with over 600 different tribunals and an excessive number of lawyers. Joseph wished to increase efficiency and to end particular interests. He personally played a major role in the new plans, which decreed the suppression of the seigneurial system of justice and of the traditional courts and their replacement by 64 regional courts under the central direction of a council in Brussels that was to be appointed by the emperor himself. The response was unenthusiastic, Joseph's plans, being seen as a fundamental infringement of the constitution. The Council of Brabant, the leading judicial body in the province, argued that Joseph had exceeded his authority and refused to register the decree as law. The incident revealed the political sensitivity of judicial issues, and the role of law and judicial institutions in representing and defining a sense of corporate, particularly provincial, identity.

In 1700 Peter I established a commission to codify Russian law. The accompanying manifesto declared that 'the administration of justice should, in all types of cases, be equal for people of all types of ranks in the Muscovite realm, from the highest to the lowest'. However, the commission was ineffective, as were others set up in 1714 and 1720. Peter issued detailed regulations to try to eliminate the arbitrary administration of justice, but his new court system did not last. The courts of appeal were abolished in 1727. Elizabeth and Catherine II both failed to codify the law, and its administration was handicapped further by the absence of sufficient trained and responsible officials and judges. In the Baltic provinces, however, Catherine was more successful, largely because there were more nobles accustomed to playing an active administrative role, and local customary law was replaced by the laws of the Russian empire.

The codification of laws and the increase in government authority were not necessarily sources of improved justice, however the latter is to be assessed. Individual rulers and others wielding judicial power could abuse it. In 1713 Eberhard Ludwig of Württemberg ordered the immediate execution of two Stuttgart women who had shouted obscenities at him and his mistress. The Privy Council, however, refused to interrupt the prescribed course of justice. If in some areas, such as the Prussian Rhineland, the judicial system was reasonably efficient, this was as much due to the training and ethos of the legal personnel as to the government's supervision. A concentration on legislation and administrative innovation would suggest that many governments were introducing change successfully, and in some spheres it is possible to point to improvements. The Piedmontese municipal reforms, for example, served to unify different codes.

Yet the general impression is of limited success. Many innovations proved difficult to introduce. The Tuscan penal code of 1786, illuminated by humanitarian ideas, saw the reclamation of the criminal as the prime objective of penal action, but it had only limited effect. Joseph II's penal code of 1787 was abandoned after his death. The delays of most courts led a number of rulers to use extraordinary jurisdictions in order to achieve their ends.

In France the royal government was handicapped by the independence, formalism and disputes of the courts, though the *lettre de cachet* could be used for imprisonment without trial. *Lettres de cachet* were not solely a means of state repression. Many were requested by individuals in order to remove troublesome members of their own families. Bitterly criticised by some writers and gradually abandoned in the mid 1770s, it was none the less a contrast to the cumbersome character of the judicial system, which often enabled suspects to disappear. The court of the *Prévôt* of the *Maréchaussée*, with its swift procedure and absence of appeal, revealed the government's determination to regulate the non-sedentary population – vagabonds, vagrants, brigands and deserters – whose mobility challenged the capacity of the ordinary courts and the local police.

Policing and judicial agencies both faced formidable challenges. As with much administration in this period, one can point to both success and failure. If secular authorities commonly had more success than their ecclesiastical counterparts, who often found it very difficult to discipline dissident clerics and parishioners, they also faced more serious problems. Two general conclusions can be advanced. Policing agencies responded to what was urgent or particularly violent, and a certain equilibrium that offered a reasonable amount of peace tended to reign, but this did not free the population from fear and the need to consider their own defence, while the agencies ignored the non-observance of much of the law.

Secondly, by drawing attention to changes in law and judicial administration from 'the late seventeenth century (at least) we will have to search for explanations that do not depend on the immediate influence of Enlightenment rationality or on the social consequences of the Industrial Revolution'.[5] These changes illustrate a notable feature of *ancien régime* government. Traditional concerns and respect for the past were combined with a willingness to consider new initiatives, many of which had been discussed or attempted before. In common with current circumstances, the past therefore did not necessarily dictate only one set of options. Judicial institutions could respond to problems, Courts of Requests being founded in England to get people to pay their debts at a time when the central common-law courts were pricing themselves out of business. Important initiatives could also be taken, as by the Paris police or by the Yorkshire magistrates in the early 1780s, who led the moves for the increased regulation and policing of the bulk of the population. The efficiency of policing and the quality of judicial action across most of Europe are topics that are still essentially obscure. Possibly as a result insufficient attention has been devoted to the ability of institutions to develop on their own account and excessive weight has been placed on regulation and intervention by rulers.

Fiscal problems

Nothing is so perverse as mankind is about Taxes, all like Expence and yet nobody is for the means.

(Joseph Yorke, British envoy at The Hague)[6]

Many individuals and most institutions were in debt in eighteenth-century Europe. Peasants borrowed seed-corn, equipment and money to pay their rent and taxes. Institutions borrowed to pay taxes, purchase privileges and finance their activities. The resulting burdens were often considerable. Apulia in Italy was not the only region where increasing fiscal demands upset the fragile mechanisms of rural credit, worsening the situation of the peasantry. St Petersburg was not the only town unable to cover the expenditure that a discharge of its legal commitments would have entailed. In 1724–7, the first four years of the collection of the poll tax in Russia, arrears in the towns amounted to 64 per cent of assessment. The precarious nature of Munich's city finances led to very few major building works being undertaken. When in mid-century the Ludwigsbrücke, a stone bridge replacing an earlier one, was built it had to be financed by means of loans and an unpopular tax on beer. Some institutions could not cope. The Scottish university of St Andrews sold one of its three constituent colleges, St Leonard's. Other institutions and individuals survived crises only by heavy borrowings and increased debts.

At all levels, debt led not only to a financial burden that mortgaged the future, but also to a loss of autonomy in decisions. Sovereign powers tended to have substantial debts, both because of the considerable discrepancies between the income and expenditure of most of them, and because they were in the best position to borrow, from their own subjects and from foreigners. The debts of some states were considerable. Those of Augustus II of Saxony–Poland reached the equivalent of about 35 years' revenue. In 1747 it was calculated that half the revenues of the Milanese were pledged to cover interest on debts. Portuguese government salaries and pensions were ten years in arrears in 1773 and the pension payments for 1773 were not settled until 1786.

In the case of some powers it is clear that the pressures of war finance and debts were principally responsible for their fiscal difficulties. Plans to reduce the debts of the duchy of Holstein were abandoned in 1752 when the funds were earmarked instead for military expenditure. Money was the sinews of war, and war largely shaped the demands for fiscal revenue. If the morale of the Spanish troops invading Naples in 1734 was high because they had been paid on time, desertion was for other rulers a consequence of inadequate funds. French naval expenditure rose from 20 million livres in 1774 to 200 million in 1778, as France prepared for war with Britain.

It is not surprising that most attempts to alter financial arrangements took place during or after wartime. In 1715 the Swedish minister Görtz planned a new financial system and the creation of a national debt. In 1750 the French foreign minister claimed that, apart from Spain, all the powers which had taken part in the recent War of the Austrian Succession had had to continue their wartime taxation policies in order to deal with their debts. In that year, Charles Emmanuel III of Savoy-Piedmont sought to renegotiate his debts at a lower rate of interest, while in 1749 Ensendada had begun his attempt to alter the traditional Spanish tax structure in favour of a comprehensive tax. In 1763 the diplomat Joseph Yorke observed that 'the regulating the finances seems to be the principal occupation, and I see no court yet which has been able to hit upon a plan in any way palatable to the people or profitable to itself'.[7]

It would be misleading to suggest that financial problems were simply the consequence of war, financial reforms only a preparation for more conflict. Frederick the Great was generally successful in avoiding deficit financing. Many of the heavily indebted rulers, such as the margraves of Ansbach and Bayreuth in the 1750s or the prince-bishop of Freising in the 1780s, played little part in international affairs and incurred only small military expenditure. Conspicuous consumption, in particular on court life and building works, placed a major strain, as on the finances of the electorate of Cologne in the 1740s and of Bavaria in the

1780s. Furthermore, the granting, generally to courtiers, of pensions, annual payments that did not take the form of salaries, could create additional problems, as in Bavaria in the early 1720s and Savoy-Piedmont in the early 1780s. Expenditure was a problem not least because in most states there were inadequate budgetary controls and financial planning. In 1748 Frederick the Great contrasted the wealth of France with the disorder of its badly administered finances: there was no central bank, funded debt or consolidated revenue fund and the budgetary process was limited. In Russia under Catherine II the procurator-general directed revenue collection and the treasuries, but he lacked the institutional means to investigate the appropriateness of expenditure and the political strength to control military costs. Catherine remained the arbiter for the allocation of funds.

Income was a serious problem. All states have and had limited resources, but the capacity of eighteenth-century states to tap these was seriously restricted, while the very nature of the economic system posed serious problems. Average productivity and wealth were low, not all activities were integrated into the money economy, and agriculture, the principal source of wealth and employment, was subject to marked variations in profitability. In 1740 the Dutch government was opposed to the idea of increasing taxes because of the extent of popular misery. The extensive crop failures in France in 1770 and the consequent economic and financial crisis have been held responsible for the government's support for reform and their attempt to increase taxes in 1771. In the 1780s a number of bad French harvests cut tax revenues and hit government finances, already weakened by the cost of intervention in the War of American Independence.

If the nature of the economic system created serious problems, some states were more successful in raising their revenues than others. Although inflation played a part, the net revenue of the Russian government rose from 19 million roubles in 1769 to 40 million in 1795. Portuguese government revenues rose from over 9 million cruzados in 1716 to an annual average of 15 in 1762–76. Danish revenues increased by about 50 per cent between 1770 and 1800. Certain increases can be attributed to extraneous circumstances. Acquisitions in Europe by a number of states, including Austria, France, Prussia, Savoy-Piedmont and Russia, could be important, a benefit from military expenditure, although never equal to the cost. Foreign subsidies could also be significant, particularly in wartime, although not only then. Benefits from colonial territories could be appreciable. The public revenues of New Spain yielded 8 million pesos in 1769, 20 million in 1800, the royal tobacco monopoly of New Spain being especially profitable.

These sources could be crucial in giving states the additional revenues to enable them to attempt specific initiatives, especially in international relations. Nevertheless, they rarely compared with the yield from domestic taxation. Even Portugal, which gained considerably from Brazilian gold, obtained more from these taxes.

Tax systems varied greatly, even within the same country. Though taxes generally fell on similar sources of income, the relative importance of these sources varied, as did exemptions from taxes, methods of assessment and collection, and the relationship between central government and the collectors. Depending on which facet is studied, the states can be grouped variously. In addition, there was no common pattern of change, or any commonly agreed ideal structure. Taxation can be divided by source of revenue essentially into taxes falling on land, individuals or households, trade and articles of general consumption.

Taxes falling on land, such as the land-tax in England or the *taille* in France, suffered from problems of assessment, exemption and political control. Assessments were often out of date or dependent on the valuation of the owner. Surveys and new assessments were commonly undertaken in the face of considerable resistance, as in Luxemburg and the county of Namur in the Austrian Netherlands in the 1760s and 1770s. In the former, the nobility mounted strong opposition to the attempt to make them and the clergy pay more. Fearful of arbitrary taxation, the *parlements* thwarted an attempt in 1763 to introduce a general cadaster of land-ownership that might serve as the basis for a more orderly and centralised system of taxation in France. Many European landowners enjoyed full or partial exemptions. Collection was sometimes, as in Bohemia in the 1700s, under the control of the Estates. The consent of such institutions was often required if such taxes were to be increased. When in 1764 Karl Eugen of Württemberg proposed a graduated property tax based on a survey of assets, the money to be collected by ducal officials and to go directly to the military chest, the scheme was rejected. Nevertheless, in some states, particularly Prussia and the Habsburg dominions, exemptions were restricted and yields increased. Reforms in the Milanese and Silesia were linked to land surveys. In 1777 the periodic reassessment of all taxable lands was decreed in France.

Taxes on individuals and households, such as the Russian poll tax and the French *capitation*, were dependent on accurate information, which was frequently lacking. Until the 1730s Transylvanian taxes were assessed in *portals*, groups of about nine households. Changes introduced in 1730 and 1750 replaced this assessment by a poll tax. This shift has been seen both as a reflection of the increased efficiency of administrative methods and as a change that brought the government into direct contact with individual producers.[8] Victor Amadeus II carried out a census in Sicily for tax purposes. In 1718 Peter I decreed a poll tax, to replace the current system of basing direct taxation on the household or the plough. This required a new census, which was initially slow and inaccurate, but a revision, which began in 1721, helped to improve its accuracy, and in 1724 the new tax began to be levied. It was collected by military officers and the money was sent directly to military units. Arrears and peasant flight were a major problem and in 1731 severe penalties for non-payment were imposed. Troops were billeted on debtors. The tax was not extended to the Ukraine, Belorussia, and the Baltic provinces until 1783. In the Ukraine the tax led to the Cossacks and the peasants being tied to the land. In Livonia there was serious rioting in 1783–4 in response to the introduction of the tax. The poll tax was the largest single source of Russian government income, amounting to about 30 per cent of the total, and the only tax paid directly to the government by the serfs of landowners. Other peasants and townspeople paid a supplement, designed to correspond to the income obtained by landowners from their peasants. This was increased in 1760, 1769 and 1783, in part to reflect military expenditure. Old Believers paid a double poll tax. The revenue raised from the poll tax increased appreciably during the century: less than 6 million roubles in 1763, it averaged between 21 and 23 million in 1784–93.

Though in Russia nobles and clerics were exempt, in 1746 a graduated poll tax was introduced in Austria which everyone paid. In the same year, the Estates of Bavaria rejected a proposal from the elector for a similar tax. The 1740s were a decade of fiscal innovations, due to the costs of the Austrian Succession War and the debts arising from it. However, in 1748 the Estates of the province of Holland rejected the idea of a graduated poll tax, and, instead, determined to continue their reliance on excises. Four years earlier, the province's leading minister had argued:

> that every branch either of revenue, or consumption, is already so charged in this province, that any augmentation of taxes upon the one is experienced to produce near an equivalent diminution in the produce of the taxes upon the other: – that any new imposition would determine numbers of its inhabitants to quit it: – that whatever treasures there may be in private coffers, the state was already so completely mortgaged, that it had nothing left to pawn for the use, or loan of them.[9]

Taxes falling upon articles of general consumption, excises, were easier to assess and collect than taxes on land or people, and exemptions from them were less common. The importance of indirect taxation varied. The government monopoly of tobacco, established by Philip V in Spain in 1701, became a major source of revenue. The revenue from the sale of salt and liquor rose from 19 per cent of the total Russian state revenue in 1724 to 29 per cent in 1769.[10] Indirect taxes were useful because their yield was tied to the level of exchange of the taxed commodity, with the significant exception of contraband. They were hidden in the sale price of the product, and paid in cash at the time of purchase. In general they were less controlled by representative institutions than direct taxes.

The yield of excises was reduced by contraband supplies. New ones were introduced with difficulty. In 1754 a plan to impose new taxes on salt and tobacco in the Austrian Netherlands was formulated, but the government moved very cautiously. Duties on salt were increased in 1764, but the Estates of Brabant contested the right to increase the duty, and though Count Cobenzl, more concerned about the response of the people than that of the Estates, determined to ignore the complaints and to accustom the people to the taxes, the governor, Charles of Lorraine, forced him to accept a compromise, which damaged Cobenzl's reputation. The Cider Excise of 1763, a tax upon cider and perry made in Britain, encountered considerable opposition and was repealed in 1766. It was easier to introduce new taxes in the wake of fundamental political changes, such as the change of dynasty in Spain. In 1707 Castilian taxes were introduced into Aragon and by 1713 the province was beginning to make an appreciable contribution to Spanish financial needs. Because excises were generally imposed on items of mass consumption, they tended to be a significant burden on the poor. Salt taxes, such as the French *gabelle*, were much resented. In Sicily the easiest tax to collect was the flour excise, which, like the customs, was farmed out.

Many governments also sought to impose taxes on items that could be regarded as luxuries. Colonial goods were especially favoured, because they had to be imported and were therefore both easier to tax and a drain on the balance of payments, and because they were widely seen as luxuries. Frederick the Great altered the burden of consumption taxes towards the wealthy, ending the excises on flour and malt, and introducing steep import duties on tobacco and coffee.

In 1724 most of the existing British customs duties on coffee, tea, chocolate and coconuts were replaced by a tax on their domestic consumption. All dealers and retailers had to register with the excise officials, who enjoyed both inspection and summary judicial powers, and whose responsibility for beer and malt taxation ensured a nationwide presence. As a result of the legislation of 1724, the annual revenue from the commodities rose by £120,000, while re-exports increased. Walpole's proposals to extend these arrangements to wine and tobacco in 1733 provoked a furious political row, and the ministry had to abandon the scheme. After the Seven Years War the British government sought to ease the burden of its debts and reaffirm parliamentary authority in American affairs by imposing a number of duties, including those on stamped paper (Stamp Act, 1765) and on glass, paper, lead, and tea imported into the American colonies (Townshend Acts, 1767).

The burdens produced by the War of American Independence (1775–83) forced British and French ministers to re-examine their states' finances. In 1783 Vergennes, the French foreign minister, pressed for the introduction of new taxes on luxury objects on the grounds that such dues could easily be borne.[11] Two years later the second earl of Fife blamed 'the horrid American war' for the increased levy in William Pitt the Younger's budget on the employers of manservants and the new tax on employers of female servants.[12] In 1784 taxes were imposed in Britain on pleasure-horses, hackney coaches, shooting certificates, bricks, tiles, candles, linens, calicoes, men's hats, gold and silver plate and ladies' ribbons; 1785 brought new taxes on, among other things, post-horses, gloves, retail shops, coachmakers' and pawnbrokers' licences, gun-dogs, sporting guns and new carriages; 1786 added perfumes and powders, particularly hair powder, and in 1789, when the unpopular shop tax was repealed, taxes on pleasure- and racehorses, carriages and a number of stamp duties were increased. The background to Pitt's budgets was a reluctance to tax the poor excessively.

The theoretically fully-regulated nature of several European countries in this period has led to their being described as well-ordered police states.[13] In comparison, Pitt's budgets might suggest that Britain should be seen as a comprehensively taxed state, but the necessary perspective is that of a debt of over £240 million. Though taxes as a percentage of national income rose from 12.9 in 1780 to 15.1 in 1790, they did not exceed 20 per cent until the first years of the following century.[14] An income tax was not introduced until 1798, when wartime needs called for far more than traditional expedients. Indeed Pitt's budgets in the 1780s were singularly conservative. He 'preferred to raise his balance in the budget from a wide variety of sources, rather than by a simpler and more comprehensive attack on the main yardsticks of wealth'.[15]

Pitt's attempts to increase Britain's foreign trade in the 1780s reflected his perception of it as a source of wealth. In accordance with the ideas of Adam Smith's *Wealth of Nations* (1776), which Pitt praised in the House of Commons in 1792, the ministry sought to help British trade by reducing the regulation of commerce. However, many states during the century saw trade rather as a source of customs revenue. In Naples, for example, exports were taxed more heavily than imports, fiscal opportunity dominating economic policy. A comparable lack of interest in the economic effects of taxation characterised the reports on foreign systems commissioned by the French government in the 1760s. Customs revenues were valuable, not least because they were relatively easy to collect and could serve readily as collateral for loans. In 1701 Charles XII of Sweden was able to borrow 750,000 florins from the United Provinces on the security of Riga's tolls.

Customs revenues also suffered from smuggling, peculation and exemptions. Victor Amadeus II was able to double the customs revenue from Palermo by taking steps against corruption. In Naples contraband in silk was limited in 1751 when the government drastically reduced ecclesiastical immunities. Silk production on church lands had been exempt from duties and clerics were not subject to the civil courts. Thirty years later French merchants established at Palermo defended their privileges in the face of an attempt to tax them for the benefit of local roadworks. Pressed by the French envoy at Naples, the government pointed out that other immunities, such as those enjoyed by cardinals and by the Order of Malta, were being ended.[16]

The list of means used to raise revenues could easily be extended. Honours and offices were sold; and governments pressed for funds, such as Denmark in 1715 and Venice in 1743, resorted to this expedient. In the province of Holland, where tax posts and postmasterships were sold, this source of revenue was itself taxed until 1800. In the Austrian Netherlands fees were exacted from officials, including judges, upon appointment, and although Maria Theresa was aware of the problems springing from this fiscal device, she never thought the circumstances propitious for abandoning it. Lotteries were set up, as in the Austrian Netherlands in mid-century, and the French used tontines, that of 1759 raising a capital of 46 million livres. In a tontine, in return for a non-refundable contribution, the interest paid to investors rose as members of their age group died, but the French government was handicapped in setting profitable levels of return by the primitive level of actuarial statistics. The revenues from royal lands could be appreciable, and were an important reason for the financial strength of the Prussian government. However, most royal estates had been granted away. Peter I thus lost nearly half of those of the Russian crown. Debasing the coinage was a desperate expedient, used by Frederick the Great during the Seven Years' War. In the same conflict, Karl Eugen of Württemberg did the same, as well as selling government posts, establishing a compulsory lottery and extorting forced loans from his officials. The printing of money helped Catherine II to finance her wars, though with inflationary consequences.

Borrowing

The varied sources of income employed by the governments of Europe did not, in general, suffice, and it proved necessary to resort to borrowing. One British diplomat wrote from Turin in 1780:

> taxes are laid as heavy as the land can bear, and unless resources are sought for an increase of trade, to augment the revenues of the customs, the king of Sardinia will find himself at a loss to know how to go on without borrowing money.[17]

Governments borrowed abroad as well as at home. The United Provinces, Switzerland and Genoa were major sources of international loans, their bankers able to tap extensive European networks that spanned national and religious borders. In 1746 Augustus III of Saxony–Poland was offered Swiss and Frankfurt loans to help Saxon credit. In 1765 the Dutch banking house of Clifford arranged a 10 million guilder loan to the Danish crown. An appreciable portion of the British national debt was held by foreign investors. In 1724, 12 per cent of the Bank of England stock was thus held, most of it in Dutch hands. Financial shifts could therefore have far-reaching consequences. The crash of two leading Dutch banking houses in 1763 was due in part to Frederick II's attempt to restore sound money after his wartime debasement of the currency. Changes in the French government's debt in 1770 hit the Genoese. A lot of credit was also raised domestically, not least by the expedient of making payments in bills rather than in cash. These generally traded at a discount, as high as 15–20 per cent for those paid to the naval workmen at Toulon in the autumn of 1757. A year later, the French naval debts were reckoned at over 42 million livres, and in 1759 the navy spent another 20 million more than it received, leading to a collapse in its credit system. In the same war, the British government borrowed about 37 per cent of the £83 million it spent. In the following war almost half the British costs incurred in the conflict were covered by borrowing. Annual public expenditure in Britain rose from £10.4 million in 1775 to £29.3 million by 1782, £114.6 million was spent in 1776–82 and the national debt rose from £127 million (1775) to £232 million (1783). Owing to debt servicing, peacetime expenditure after each war was higher than the pre-war level. Austria also borrowed heavily to pay for the Seven Years War.

Though borrowing was important to both Britain and France, the money was raised in different fashions. The funded national debt based on the Bank of England enabled British ministries to borrow large sums at low rates of interest. Whereas in the early 1690s the government was paying up to 14 per cent for long-term loans, the rate of interest fell to 6–7 per cent in 1702–14, 4 per cent in the late 1720s, at or below 3 per cent in the late 1730s, and, after a wartime rise, to 3.5 per cent in 1750. The system was not without its problems. An anonymous writer, who, in 1813, praised the introduction of income tax as an attempt to equalise revenue and expenditure, claimed:

> From the period of the complete introduction of the funding System ... to the close of the American War, the object of our measures of finance during war appeared to be only to provide for the immediate expenses of the year, by borrowing such sums as were necessary for any extraordinary charge incurred, and by imposing such taxes as might meet the interest of the loan, leaving to the period of peace the consideration of any provision for the repayment of debt; and this being attempted at irregular periods and on no permanent system, was never carried into effectual execution; the total amount of debt redeemed between the Peace of Utrecht [1713] and the close of the American war [1783] being no more than £8,330,000.[18]

Possibly the funds invested in the national debt might have played a more beneficial economic role if invested elsewhere. Government borrowing was not for productive expenditure, but for war, though the economic benefits of conquests must not be discounted. The general benefit to the economy of low rates of interest on government debt and to the political system of a funded national debt were considerable. The British financial system was not, however, without its problems in other spheres. Much of the work of the Exchequer was still conducted according to medieval forms and the efficiency of the treasury and revenue departments was found wanting during the American war, leading to reform in the post-war period.

The British government was not alone in being able to borrow at low rates of interest. The Dutch government was also able to do so, and the province of Holland borrowed at 2 per cent in 1753. Other governments were not so fortunate. In Naples an attempt was being made in 1749–51 to redeem certain revenues and to cut interest rates on the debt from 7 to 4 per cent, but it encountered considerable opposition. In contrast the Austrians were generally successful after the Seven Years War in reducing their interest rates from 5–6 to 4 per cent. In Hungary a similar conversion in 1774 was achieved, substantially thanks to the sequestration of Jesuit assets. French government finances were intertwined with those of the private financiers whose loans, often short-term, enabled the government to function. Major bankers, such as Samuel Bernard, Isaac Thellusson and the Pâris brothers, played a crucial role, but they ensured that the national finances were heavily influenced by private individuals. Projects for a national bank from Bernard and John Law in 1709 and 1715 respectively were rejected because of the suspicion that such a bank would be dominated by a single individual. Law's bank did become a state bank for a while, but the eventual collapse of his schemes discredited the notion. As for most French finance ministers, reform entailed reducing expenditure, rather than seeking to create financial institutions, the influence of private financiers persisted until the Revolution. There was no consolidated revenue fund and the treasury's authority and knowledge were limited. Nevertheless, efforts were made to lessen the influence of the financiers. The finance minister Terray, described by one observer in 1770 as 'in an inextricable labyrinth',[19] undertook a partial bankruptcy that year and restricted the role of private enterprise in government finance. Necker sought to strengthen the treasury, though he paid for the American war by borrowing and in general did little to reform government finances.

The role of financiers in the management of French governmental finances exemplified the importance of private individuals and consortia in financial administration. This was marked in the case of tax farming, which was important in a number of states, particularly for the collection of indirect taxes. Tax farming offered a source of credit, and underlined the symbiotic relationship of governments and certain financial interests. In some states it was of little consequence or replaced by direct administration, as in late seventeenth-century England. The largest Polish industrial enterprise, the salt mines near Cracow, were run until 1737 by Saxon financiers who thus recouped their loans to the royal treasury. In 1737 this tenancy agreement was replaced by direct royal control. In Castile the tax farmers resisted the loss of their privileged position, but in 1749 the Royal Treasury began to administer directly all its tax revenues, leading to substantial gains. The Milanese tax farm was abolished in 1770.

In other countries tax farming spread. In 1715 the Swedish customs duties were farmed for the sake of the advance payment. Tuscan revenues were farmed in 1740–68. Austrian tobacco revenues were definitely farmed from the 1730s, Bohemian and Austrian stamp duties, transit dues and tobacco revenues and Austrian customs duties from 1765 until the mid-1770s, and the Moravian drink excise from 1771 to 1778. Frederick the Great farmed out payments in kind in East Friesland, and in 1766 farmed the excise duties, hitherto levied by local authorities, employing officials from the French tax farm, though on terms less favourable than they received in France. The Company of General Farmers, the consortium of financiers who leased the collection of French indirect taxes, on the eve of the Revolution had sole responsibility for the salt and tobacco taxes, and was employing or organising over 30,000 agents. The company served increasingly after 1749 as a source of credit and capital for the government, and as a mechanism for making payments. It illustrated the potential for administrative efficiency in the period. Although the system of taxes it collected was very confused, the company, unhampered by venal offices, was very efficient in collecting them. It was not, however, particularly popular and the *cahiers* drawn up in Roussillon were not alone in their complaints.

'There is a difficulty, if not an impossibility of speaking with any precision upon the subject of French finance' an anonymous writer complained in 1772.[20] The nature of financial administration, especially the limitations of the information available and the role of non-government bodies, ensured that such a claim could be advanced for most countries. It is not surprising therefore that the habitual response to financial difficulties was the attempt to reduce expenditure and to increase the yield of existing taxation, rather than to introduce a new system. The former was particularly apparent in the aftermath of wars, when most governments tried to regularise their affairs. Savoy-Piedmont was still seeking in 1755 to lessen its debts from the Austrian Succession War by continuing wartime rates of taxation and by 'an economy that prevails throughout'. The last of the Medici grand dukes of Tuscany, Gian Gastone, who ruled from 1723 to 1737, ended many of the pensions (annual payments made regardless of age) granted by his predecessor. At his accession in 1759, Charles III of Spain declared that he would cut the royal household and increase the army and navy.

Alongside such traditional expedients, numerous attempts were made to introduce major financial changes. As with mercantilist projects to improve aspects of the economy and thus increase the yield of taxation, many of these remained blueprints, were only partially introduced, or were far from completely successful. However, they are important indications of the willingness of certain rulers and ministers to consider important changes in a sphere involving both government effectiveness and social privilege. These attempts were not restricted to the second half of the century. Rather than being treated as an aspect of that ambiguous entity described as Enlightened Despotism, they can be seen throughout the century. Indeed, far from being a question of who was to pay for Enlightened Despotism, financial projects centred rather on the more traditional costs of preparing for and fighting wars and servicing the subsequent debt.

For example, Peter I's reign was a period of new financial devices, such as the College of Revenue created in 1719: and important initiatives, such as Louis XIV's capitation tax, were launched elsewhere. In his early years as emperor, Charles VI made a determined attempt to improve Austrian finances. In 1713 all the local Austrian revenue offices were ordered to produce an exact schedule of their debts and accounts; in 1714 a reform of the treasury was proposed, the 'idea that separate sections would deal with one class of business for the whole empire, rather than (as previously) with all types of business for a single province, was clearly stated',[21] and moves were made to establish a state banking mechanism. Christian Schierendorf, a treasury official, suggested a central Diet (Estates) for all the hereditary lands, and the institution of an income tax. However, as in Spain and Russia, most of the projects of the first two decades of the century were either not implemented or unsuccessful. Similarly, in the two decades after peace was negotiated in 1713, the Dutch search for new kinds of taxation in order to reduce crippling debts was generally unsuccessful. The second Great Assembly of 1716–17, called, like its predecessor in 1651, to consider political and financial changes, achieved virtually nothing in the face of bitter inter-provincial wrangling.

The period 1725–48 was not one of major financial changes. War engrossed the attention of many of the states for much of the time, while most of the monarchs and leading ministers of the period were not interested in such changes: Fleury in France, Catherine I, Peter II and Anna in Russia, Charles VI in his later years in Austria and Philip V in his later years in Spain. The financial crises in France, Britain and the United Provinces in 1720–1 also discouraged experimentation. New initiatives were not always successful. Under regulations issued in 1733, all Russian colleges (ministries) collecting state revenue were instructed to send their accounts to the College of Audit, but by 1769, 53,170 accounts remained unsettled due to lack of staff, while the Salt Board, which had not submitted accounts since 1735, stated that it was unable to cope with the accounts coming from 600 places where the sale of salt took place.

Reforms were introduced in several countries in mid-century. The late 1740s were particularly important in Austria and Spain. In both, the need for more tax revenues, together with the centralising tendencies of some ministers, resulted in a number of schemes, such as the Gaisruck Commission's investigation of Lower Austrian towns. Haugwitz's changes in Austria were based upon a realisation of the inadequacy of existing institutions and practices to raise the funds necessary for war with Prussia. Tax reforms were introduced in the Austrian Netherlands and Lombardy. In the province of Flanders the inequitable distribution of taxes resulting from the domination of the Estates by the clergy and the towns of Ghent and Bruges was reformed in 1754.

The Seven Years War led to the postponement of financial changes planned in a number of areas, such as the province of Brabant in the Austrian Netherlands, but the cost of the conflict forced most participants to consider financial reform seriously in the post-war years. This was true both of major powers such as Britain, and minor states such as Baden. Thomas, Freiherr von Fritsch, the ennobled son of a Leipzig publisher, played a major role in the re-establishment of devastated Saxony. The Saxon government, heavily influenced by urban mercantile and banking circles, concentrated on economic development, rather than on the army or the attempt to retain the dynastic link with Poland. In the latter in 1764 the Diet appointed a Commission of Finance to create a general customs system, a plan thwarted by Frederick the Great who wanted to keep Poland weak. The Portuguese treasury, entrusted in 1761 by Pombal with the supervision of all public accounts, was relatively efficient and effective.

The financial policies of the major powers can be regarded in a number of lights. No other major state could emulate Prussia, where Frederick the Great, who had inherited a state treasury of 10 million thalers in 1740, left more than 51 million to his successor in 1786. Both sums reflected the benefits of periods of peace, but they were also due to the strong internal position of the Prussian ruling house. If other major states were heavily indebted, that did not prevent them from continuing to operate at home and to act in an aggressive fashion abroad. It is possible to present, for example, French finances in the period 1763–78 in a calamitous light, but the extent of the financial crises should not be exaggerated and the budgetary situation faced by, for instance, Turgot in 1774 was not too disastrous. Though Terray failed to balance the budget, in 1771–4 he increased revenues by about 40 million livres, cut the deficit and halved the anticipations on future income, establishing a policy of ministerial control over spending that prevailed until 1781.

Military expenditure and wars from 1778 hit the finances of Britain, France, Spain, Austria and Russia. The opposition of the privileged to higher and progressive taxes helped to force Spain to resort to loans. Faced with a serious liquidity crisis, Joseph II energetically promoted major tax changes designed to ensure an equitable taxation of nobility and peasantry. His attempt to tax agricultural production introduced in 1783 was opposed by most of the Council, while the Bohemian and Austrian chancellery under Count Leopold von Kollowrat implemented it slowly. If most of the *ancien régime* states were heavily indebted, that did not mean that they were necessarily bankrupt. The bankrupt position of France in 1788 was an unusual one for a major state. Britain's debt was greater per capita than France's, but it was funded and thus less of a problem. By 1789 the French government was using 60 per cent of its revenues just to pay the interest on its debts.

The ability of most states to go on borrowing was striking, and their financial difficulties in the mid-1780s did not prevent Austria and Russia from fighting the Turks, or most of Europe from waging a cruelly expensive war with revolutionary France. In part this reflected the resources released by the general tendency throughout the century towards the legalisation, unification, centralisation, commercialisation and funding of public debt. Provided political confidence was maintained, deficit financing became easier and cheaper. If wars and their consequences posed major financial problems, the same has also proved true for modern states with their far wealthier economies and vastly greater bureaucracies.

Regions on the margins of authority

One of the major problems confronting the rulers and governments of many European states was their relationship with regions where their authority and/or power were especially circumscribed. The nature of the problem varied greatly and was understandably less serious for minor states. In Portugal there was no real problem and the reigning dynasty, the Braganza, were not foreigners. In all large states, however, the problem existed, particularly with respect to regions gained through conquest and dynastic succession in which local privileges and a sense of separate identity had been preserved. Yet, this was not invariably the case.

The Swedish region of Ingria was conquered by Peter I during the Great Northern War, later becoming the province of St Petersburg. During the war most of the landowners left or were expelled and Peter, acknowledging no prior right of ownership, began settlement and development policies accordingly. Such policies were common only in eastern Europe, in cases of colonial expansion, and in the wake of rebellions which had been suppressed without negotiation, such as the Jacobite rising in the Scottish Highlands in 1745–6. This was followed by the abolition of hereditable jurisdictions, and an attempt to use the confiscated estates of the rebels to fund a programme of economic modernisation. The construction of roads, bridges and harbours and the improvement of education were designed to integrate the Highlands into the rest of the country. Most of the improving schemes proved to be ill-conceived and in 1784 the estates were returned to the pardoned owners or their heirs.

Scotland was regarded as important in London primarily in so far as it was a security threat. The claims of the exiled Stuarts were supported by many Scots in the risings of 1715 and 1745. In addition, the union of Scotland and England in 1707 led to Scottish representation in Parliament and thus increased the interest of ministers in ensuring that Scottish elections were managed to their satisfaction. There were some attempts to bring Scotland more firmly within a unified political and administrative system. These failed, partly because of opposition from Scottish politicians, but, more, because for most of the century the ministers in London never maintained sufficient interest to implement a coherent Scottish policy. First ministers, such as George Grenville in 1763–5, did not understand conditions in Scotland and encountered difficulties over Scottish patronage. In general, the government preferred to entrust the management of Scottish affairs to local politicians whom they could trust, such as the earl of Islay, later third duke of Argyll, from the 1730s until his death in 1761, and Henry Dundas for most of the 1780s and 1790s. Gradually the Scottish ruling class developed a British and imperial outlook and many Scots served in the British army in the second half of the century, though the evolving relationship was not without its tensions.

Anxiety about Scotland definitely eased in the second half of the century. In contrast, Ireland, in which Stuart supporters had been crushed in the early 1690s and in which there was no rising in 1715 or 1745, remained a serious problem for British politicians. Much of the army was based in Ireland and, though some success was achieved by managing the government through local politicians, known as Undertakers, the parliament in Dublin created numerous difficulties. George, fourth viscount Townshend, the lord lieutenant in 1767–72, resided there constantly, instituting a new system of direct management of the government, but failing to assuage mounting resentment about the political and constitutional dependence of Ireland on Britain. Resentment of the economic subordination was also very strong. Tension increased during the American War of Independence and, in the face of growing unrest and the fear that the Volunteer movement, a citizens' militia formed in Ulster in 1778, would lead to a rebellion, the Tudor legislation, which had placed the Dublin parliament under the control of the Privy Council in London, was repealed in 1782, and the parliament was granted full powers of initiative and legislation. In the same year the British parliament repealed the Declaratory Act of 1719, which had underlined its claim to legislate for Ireland and that of the British House of Lords to act as a final court of appeal in Irish cases. After a further Renunciation Act in 1783, the influence of the royal representative, the lord lieutenant, was nearly the sole means left for keeping the legislative programmes of the two islands in step. During the regency crisis of 1788–9 caused by George III's ill-health, the Irish parliament adopted a position contrary to that of London, inviting the future George IV to assume the royal functions without conditions. In ceding to the Dublin parliament the sort of rights demanded, without success, by the American colonists before their rebellion, the London parliament appeared to have created an unstable relationship. Wales, in contrast, presented no difficulties during the century, while in 1765 the sovereignty of the Isle of Man was purchased from the duke of Atholl for £70,000 and an annuity.

Though regional feeling was strong in France, separatist sentiment was weak. Cries of 'Long Live our Emperor' greeted Joseph II in 1777 as he passed through Lorraine, annexed to France only in 1766, on his way to Paris. In Franche-Comté, conquered in 1674 in the face of considerable local opposition, French patriotism spread, due less to the royal government, which was seen as oppressive, than to the prestige of French intellectual and artistic life. After about 1740 the advantages of being with France were obvious, though assimilation with France was still restricted in 1789 essentially to the nobility and the educated urban groups. French replaced Flemish in Dunkirk and French Flanders. In Corsica Genoese authority had been limited since the uprising of 1729, and a constitution and government had been devised that was praised by the *philosophes*. The island was sold by Genoa to France in 1768 and French troops were sent by Choiseul to conquer it. Praised by Boswell, Dumouriez, Rousseau and Voltaire, the Corsican peasant militia was nevertheless defeated by 1769. The island was then incorporated into France, Estates being created that gave a controlling voice to the nobility, those enobled by the French crown.

French administrators, influenced by physiocratic ideas, proposed the *Plan Terrier*, a blueprint for the social and economic development of the island. Already, in 1761, Choiseul had suggested that administrative reform and road construction would lead to a considerable revenue from Corsica.[22] French rule was not universally popular, the forcible enlistment of sailors for the navy in 1780 leading some to flee to Italy, but no demand for Corsican independence was heard before the spring of 1793.

The general absence of separatism did not mean that regional feeling in France was weak. A strong sense of regional identity, privileges and history existed. Discourses in the Academy of Pau in south-western France revealed a militant provincialism, expressed in bold defences of the autonomy of the province of Béarn and of the reputation of Henry of Navarre. Regional identity was sustained by provincial institutions, such as *parlements* and Estates. The variegated nature of French administration, without uniformity in taxation, local laws and local government, both reflected and encouraged a sense of regional identity. This variety extended into many spheres. Alsace and Artois fell outside the jurisdiction of the king's premier surgeon.

Disputes arose from the varied nature of different institutions and from a sense of provincial particularism. The latter helped to lead the *conseil souverain* of Arras, the leading law court in Artois, to oppose the *Parlement* of Paris. In the *pays d'états*, the most important of which were Brittany, Burgundy, Languedoc and Provence, taxes were levied only with the consent of the Estates, and new central government demands were particularly strongly resisted. In Brittany there were sporadic tax revolts against the capitation tax in 1719–20, the *vingtième* was only established in the 1750s after considerable compromise with local views, and in the 1760s a violent conflict over taxation arose between the *Parlement* of Rennes and the provincial commandant, the duke d'Aiguillon. The duke's demands for compulsory labour for road-building also led to objections. Brittany was by far the most important example of regional particularism in France. A large province, only incorporated into France in 1532, with a separate language in half the province, it had the only really powerful provincial Estates, which were often backed up by the *Parlement* of Rennes. The abolition of provincial privileges in 1789 proved divisive in Brittany.

Aside from legal manifestations of provincial particularism, royal authority was also challenged by illegal opposition. Officials in Roussillon found little local support for their struggle with smugglers in the early 1770s and the army argued that local complicity made it impossible to pursue bands in the interior. If in some areas central government activities aroused opposition, they could also develop links within the country. Schemes such as that of the early 1760s to use wood from the western Pyrenees for masts for the navy helped to increase a sense of interdependence. Nevertheless, provincial sentiment remained strong and a major element in the political crisis of the late 1780s was support for federalist schemes and opposition to centralisation. Jean de Boisgelin, the cardinal-archbishop of Aix and president of the Estates of Provence, which were re-established in their old form in 1787, envisaged self-government for all provinces and cities. At the Assembly of Notables in 1787, he pressed for provincial autonomy and a national body of provincial representatives to advise the king and approve certain laws. By 1789 the president of the *Parlement* of Lorraine was advocating the collection and appropriation of taxes by provincial governments. Such ideas were doubtless a measure of the general perception of both crisis and a need for radical change, but they also suggest the range of political ideas held in *ancien régime* France.

Philip V's success in the War of the Spanish Succession enabled him to limit regional privileges in Spain and he introduced *intendants* to serve as a new link between central and local government. But provincial particularism was not destroyed. Local elites were able to determine the implementation of some central government schemes; opposition in southern Spain, for example, frustrated the agrarian reforms of Charles III. Historical and jurisdictional circumstances, and the rule of much of the peninsula by distant foreign monarchs helped to ensure that much of Italy enjoyed a considerable measure of autonomy. This was particularly true of frontier areas. The valley of Oulx, granted to Savoy-Piedmont at the treaty of Utrecht, was treated like an autonomous region. Even a ruler as determined to reduce regional autonomy as Victor Amadeus II did not seek to bring uniformity to his dominions.

Nevertheless, a general tendency during the century towards greater central authority in Italy can be discerned. In Savoy, the royal administration succeeded both in providing for the redemption of seigneurial dues and in increasing the tax paid by the nobility. In the Val d'Aosta in 1757–8, Charles Emmanuel III of Savoy-Piedmont transferred duties and powers from the

Conseil des Commis, the executive body of the Estates, to royal delegates. The scope of Piedmontese law was extended, obligatory taxes decreed, which effectively neutralised the Estates, and the office of *intendant* was introduced. In 1759–73 the courts and administration of the island of Sardinia were changed in order to integrate the island into the rest of the Savoyard dominions. Several feudal jurisdictions were suppressed, the independence of the religious orders was limited, and universities were established at Cagliari and Sassari in order to educate officials for local administration. The Venetian attempt to make the Uskok warriors in their Dalmatian territory pay taxes led them to rebel in 1704. In 1763 Tillot, the leading minister in the duchy of Parma, organised a small expedition against Mezzano, an episcopal fief whose population resisted integration with the duchy. In 1767–8 he took similar police measures over the Corti di Monchio, a mountainous region on the Parmesan–Tuscan frontier, where the privileges and immunities of the local ecclesiastical lord had also created difficulties, the area containing many deserters and smugglers.

The Habsburgs ruled much of Italy after the Peace of Utrecht (1713), but Charles VI claimed to have inherited these lands as rightful king of Spain, not to rule them by right of conquest. He administered them through the traditional Spanish Council of Italy, now based in Vienna but still with Spanish and Italian members. Charles recognised the privileges of Naples in 1713, 1717 and 1720 and did little to alter the administration or to limit noble privileges, both there and elsewhere in Italy. His financial demands were, however, unpopular and may have contributed to the general support of the Milanese nobility and senior clergy for the Savoyard administration of the duchy in 1733–6. The general absence of local assistance in Italy for Charles during the War of the Polish Succession (1733–5) was striking.

Under Maria Theresa a major attempt was made to increase government power in the Milanese. This reflected her financial problems, the widespread interest in reform in Vienna and, possibly, the greater prospect of successful change in Habsburg Italy after the loss of Naples and Sicily with their strongly entrenched nobility. In 1749 the sale of offices was forbidden and payments were fixed for services performed by officials. In 1755 the criterion for membership of municipal administrations was changed from noble status to wealth. The land survey of the Milanese was completed and in 1760 the system of self-assessment for taxation was replaced by that of official assessment. Under Count Gian Pallavicini, governor 1750–3, and Count Karl Firmian, minister plenipotentiary from 1759, the power and ambitions of the central government increased appreciably. Although local government was left in the hands of local citizens, a measure of uniformity and centralisation was introduced. The Council of Italy was abolished in 1757. Milanese revenues appear to have doubled between 1749 and 1783. Although Joseph II alienated the patrician reformers in Milan by replacing the traditional administrative and judicial system in 1786 with new administrative units and courts and a new code of law, these changes were accepted without violence.

The situation was less favourable in the other Habsburg territories that were not part of the so-called hereditary dominions. As in the case of the French in Corsica, the vitality of *ancien régime* government and its willingness to create new administrative structures were best exemplified in a conquered region where they were essentially lacking. It was then that the essential assumptions and processes of consensus and compromise that underlay the constitutions and government of the period were least appropriate and necessary. When held by the Austrians in 1718–39, Little Wallachia was administered by a military governor. The fiscal system was reorganised, requiring an accurate census. This was resisted by the undertaxed nobility who concealed the number of their serfs, causing the census figures to fall by over 40 per cent in 1724. As a result, their privileges and their influence in the administration were reduced, leading to a reversal in the 1727 census of the fall recorded in 1724. The judiciary ceased to be simply an agent of noble power. Though the social hierarchy and the notion of privilege were both preserved, the Austrians succeeded in transferring power from local to central government.

Major changes were also attempted on the Military Frontier in Croatia and southern Hungary, which was investigated by Joseph, duke of Hildburghausen, in 1737. He condemned both the traditional system of elected captains and loosely constituted military units and the maladministration of the Inner Austrian Estates, and argued that the population should be placed under strict military command. Opposition from all concerned and the outbreak of war with the Turks led to the shelving of the scheme, but Maria Theresa reorganised the Military Frontier and the local forces, transferring control from Inner Austria to a newly-created Military Directory, headed in 1744–9 by Hildburghausen. This led to mutinies in 1744, 1746, 1750, 1751 and 1755 when the concession of the appointment of local inhabitants to two-thirds of the commissions in the Frontier regiments was granted in order to ease tension. An administrative reform programme was introduced in Transylvania in 1761–4. The pace of reform was stepped up there in the 1780s.

Count Anton Pergen, the first Austrian governor of Galicia, the area gained from Poland in 1772, argued in 1773 that local poverty and customs made it imprudent to launch hasty reforms, a view supported by Maria Theresa and by Kaunitz, who suggested treating the province like the Austrian Netherlands. This argument was dismissed by Joseph II, who in 1776 had the separate department that had been created to administer the province absorbed into the Austro-Bohemian chancellery. Although Habsburg claims to the province derived from their possession of the crown of Hungary, Joseph was opposed to its becoming part of Hungary, as that would have preserved the financial and political privileges of the numerous nobility. Joseph followed a policy of centralisation in Galicia, designed both to integrate it into the other Habsburg possessions and to increase its revenues. Administrative boundaries were redrawn, common coinage, weights and measures introduced, the corporate powers of the nobility abolished, and a mass of regulations issued, many of which were ineffective and unpopular. In 1790 the local nobility drew up the *Charta Leopoldina*, a proposal for provincial autonomy, which was rejected by Leopold II. Bukovina, gained from the Turks in 1775, was placed under military administration, though few benefits were derived from this very poor region.

In the Austrian Netherlands, Hungary and Transylvania, Habsburg plans conflicted with traditional assumptions and local institutions and privileges, the latter confirmed by the Habsburgs in documents such as the *Diploma Leopoldinum*, which provided the basis for relations with Transylvania between 1691 and 1843. Under Charles VI there was no attempt to end provincial and municipal privileges in the Austrian Netherlands, but local opposition to central government financial demands led to much urban unrest, and in 1719 Brussels was occupied by 10,000 troops. Military force ended rioting in the towns and it proved possible to finance a permanent military establishment of about 20,000 men. In the late 1710s Charles VI pressed for the reorganisation of the financial administration and for the keeping of adequate accounts. After 1719 retrenchment and the sale of offices helped to reduce the debt.

The resignation in 1724 of Prince Eugene, governor since 1716, and in 1725 of his deputy, the marquis de Prié, was followed by a return to the tradition of rule by a resident member of the royal family, Charles VI's sister, Maria Elizabeth, and local privileges and semi-autonomy were respected until the 1750s. In 1757 the Austrian Netherlands Council at Vienna, an institution that often favoured the region when acting as its intermediary with the rest of central government, was suppressed and its authority transferred to the chancellery. The Austrian Netherlands made a substantial contribution to the cost of the Seven Years' War (1756–63), but demands thereafter for greater revenues and increased loans caused tension. In the 1760s attempts to introduce a land survey in the province of Luxemburg and to make the nobility and clergy pay more taxes were opposed by the Estates and the nobility. In 1766 an Austrian official complained that 'the provincial Council does not know how many villages there are. The publication of regulations is neglected to an incredible extent and, if they are published, little attempt is made to implement them.'[23] The plan for Luxemburg was finally implemented in the 1770s, but it was not until Joseph's personal rule in the 1780s that fundamental changes in the region were introduced. In 1781 Joseph ordered an increase in its revenues; in 1787 comprehensive administrative and judicial changes were decreed, without consultation, and in 1789 Joseph introduced permanent taxes in the provinces of Hainault and Brabant and dissolved the latter's Estates. The 1787 decrees were rescinded that year by the Brussels authorities, as the result of a powerful protest movement, but resistance to those of 1789 was met by force. This led to a successful uprising, and the abandonment of Joseph's policies did not prevent the creation of a Belgian republic in January 1790. A successful Austrian invasion the next winter was followed by the attempts of Leopold II and Francis II to re-create a working relationship. In 1793 Francis endorsed de-centralisation, establishing a council at Brussels with members from the region. The military successes of revolutionary France rendered the arrangements immaterial, but they indicated the extent to which Joseph II's successors rejected his policies.

A similar process occurred in Hungary, a kingdom that was hereditary in the Habsburg line and that included, outside modern Hungary, Slovakia and Croatia. Under the diploma of Ferdinand II of 1622, the ruler was obliged to observe the laws, administer justice, heed the grievances of the Estates and respect the latters' right to choose a Palatine. Attempts by Leopold I to increase his authority led to a number of rebellions, the last of which, the Rakoczi rising, was ended in 1711 by the Peace of Szatmár. This acknowledged the Habsburg hereditary rights, but also, as in the earlier compromise of 1681, Hungary's constitutional self-government and traditional privileges, including noble tax-exemption. The reign of Charles VI (1711–40) brought few government changes. Calls from the exiled Ferenc Rakoczi and his son Josef to rebel during Austro-Turkish wars were ignored and the Diet of 1723 accepted the idea of female succession. The office of Palatine was left vacant from 1731, a royal appointee, Francis of Lorraine, from 1736 Charles's son-in-law, acting in his place.

In offering support to Maria Theresa, the Diet of 1741 was able to insist on the filling of the post and on the exemption of the nobles and of the Catholic clergy from paying taxes and customs, a privilege Charles VI had failed to change in 1723 and 1729. Hungarian troops contributed much to the Habsburg effort in the Austrian Succession and Seven Years Wars, though no Hungarian was placed in a leading position in the high command. Though the Diet's prerogatives were strengthened in 1741, they were to be challenged by Maria Theresa. The Diet of 1751 voted increased taxes for three years only, but they continued to be collected until the next Diet of 1764–5, when they led to protests. The Diet also rejected government proposals to increase taxes and to replace the noble obligation to serve in the feudal levy by a tax to be paid by nobles and clergy. From 1765 the Diet was prorogued and the office of Palatine left vacant until 1790. Having failed to secure the Diet's co-operation in reform, Maria Theresa made some changes by royal order alone but, unwilling to call another Diet or to risk major changes, she was unable to reform the tax system and to obtain additional military assistance during the war of the Bavarian Succession.

Joseph II, in contrast, sought major changes, refusing to submit to separate coronations, and thus confirm privileges, in Bohemia and Hungary. Seeking more power, as well as units dictated by geographical and demographic convenience,[24] Joseph reorganised the system of Hungarian provincial administration in 1785, and, initially, his new arrangements worked. In the first general levy, that of 1787, two-thirds of the recruits demanded were under arms by the end of the year, despite complaints about the unconstitutional nature of his procedures, his refusal to summon the Diet and his arbitrary decision to employ the feudal levy outside Hungary. Joseph's hold over Hungary weakened as a result of the military failures of the war with Turkey that began in 1788, and also of his increasing ill-health. This provided an opportunity for noble opposition to increase and, in the face of a noble revolt, Joseph revoked most of his edicts in January 1790. This did not quell Hungarian anger and those elected to the Diet in 1790 called for effective self-government. In addition, there were some calls for a separate army, for annual Diets and the restoration of the elective nature of the monarchy. As in the Austrian Netherlands, Leopold's conciliatory tactics, divisions

among his opponents, the widespread wish to re-create an acceptable relationship, fear of social disorder and Austrian military
intervention, 11 regiments marching in in 1790, led to a compromise. The privileges of the Estates, the role of the Diet, and
the separate status of Hungary were accepted, alongside Habsburg
hereditary rights and the crown's prerogatives.

Austria's rival, Prussia, had fewer problems with regional
autonomy, still less with separatism, but provincial particularism
was fairly strong, which was scarcely surprising as the disjointed
territories denoted by the term Prussia were very different and
lacked a common history and tradition. In 1740 the Cleves
Estates unsuccessfully sought to restrict official posts to local
nobles. Prussian administration was, however, responsive to local
circumstances. The General Directory, an institution created in
1723 by Frederick William I to supervise military, police and
financial matters, was arranged on a territorial basis, with a number of provincial boards under it. Their heads were given a large
measure of responsibility. The instructions drawn up for the
General Directory in 1748 included variations for the western
provinces, while Silesia was not placed under it at all. Its provincial administration came under the direct control of the king,
reflecting his concern about this important conquest and his irri-
tation with the bureaucratic forms of the Directory.

Though sensitive to the varied nature of his territories,
Frederick the Great was determined to maintain his control.
After he acquired East Friesland in 1744, he abolished the
prince's privy council and issued a new list of *Drosten*, local nobles
with some police and military responsibilities, altering their position to bring it more into line with Prussian government elsewhere. Distance, however, made supervision difficult. Daniel
Lentz, given charge of the provincial government in 1748, was
ordered to execute his instructions as he saw fit, and Frederick
did not visit the province until 1751.

The federal nature of the government of Poland–Lithuania
provided many opportunities for the expression of regional particularism. Poland and Lithuania each had a crown army and a
set of officials. In contrast, both the Swedish and the Russian
empires were reasonably centralised. This was especially the case
with Sweden after her losses in the Great Northern War (1700–
21). Finland, a poorly-populated and vulnerable borderland, had
only a weak voice in the Swedish Diet.

The Russian nobility had, by the standards of the age, a
national rather than a provincial orientation, a consequence of the
scattering of their properties over central Russia, their strong traditions of service and the relative weakness of provincial identity

in the traditional Muscovite lands. When Peter I conquered Sweden's Baltic provinces in 1710–11, he left their administration with its powerful elements of self-government substantially unchanged. In the Ukraine, by contrast, Peter sought to limit the autonomy of Ivan Mazepa, *hetman* from 1687 until 1709. Fears about the tsar's plans caused Mazepa to turn to Charles XII in 1708, which then led to a substantial increase in the Russian military presence and a reign of terror. After the end of the Great Northern War, Peter directed his attention to the Ukraine, creating in 1722 a College to govern the region, ordering the establishment of Russian law and placing the Ukraine under the jurisdiction of the Senate, the body he had founded in 1711 to handle internal affairs. Marriage into Russian rather than Polish families was encouraged. Large numbers of Ukrainian Cossacks were sent to work on Peter's construction projects, and many of them died.

After Peter's death his policy was reversed in 1727, the Ukrainian College abolished, the *hetmanate* restored and Ukrainian affairs transferred to the College of Foreign Affairs. A Ukrainian code of rights was drawn up in the 1730s and completed in 1743, but was never promulgated. The *hetmanate* lapsed in 1734, to be restored in 1751. In 1754 the Senate abolished the border between Russia and the Ukraine, closing the customs posts. In 1763 the *hetman* drafted a petition requesting that the *hetmanate* be made hereditary and pressing for effective autonomy. In response, Catherine II abolished the *hetmanate* in 1764, replacing it with a College. She felt that all regions in the empire ought to send deputies to the Legislative Commission of 1767, though the elections in the Ukraine were marked by demands for autonomy. In 1782 the Russian provincial administrative system was extended into the Ukraine with a total disregard for historical links and the College was abolished. Catherine similarly implemented her domestic reforms throughout her territories, the Russian administrative and judicial reforms of 1775 being introduced in 1778 in the lands acquired in the First Partition of Poland.

The size of the Russian empire made the enforcement of government wishes difficult. Troops ordered from Moscow in February 1772 to suppress trouble among the Yaik Cossacks did not arrive on the Yaik until June. Nevertheless, frontier areas were more under central control than in the Turkish Empire. The principles and policies of centralisation and uniformity that were adopted in Russia reflected the strength of the central government and helped to increase its control. If government policy, especially in the case of the Ukraine, was far from consistent, that was due in part to the political context of policy, and, in particular, the role of personal links. The last *hetman* was the brother of the tsarina Elizabeth's lover and presumed morganatic husband, and the *hetmanate* was restored for him in 1751. If the tendency of most of the states of the period was towards centralisation, this was affected by the unpredictability, both in policies and in their implementation, consequent upon the influence wielded by monarchs.

Government agencies

To suggest that the attitudes and actions of government servants might have posed one of the most important problems for the rulers of the period might appear paradoxical, particularly as a stress on the beneficial consequences of the increased size and centralisation of the administrations of the early modern period is well established in much of the historiographical literature. The introduction of royal officials supposedly sent to govern the provinces, such as the *intendants* of seventeenth-century France, has occupied a historiographical role akin to that of the introduction of mobile field artillery. Nevertheless, as it becomes increasingly apparent that it is misleading to reify the states and governments of the period, so more attention can be devoted to the attitudes and actions of officials whose loyalties were not generally directed to any abstract notion of the state. A centralised state model of allegiance was usually absent or weak. The practical power of officials was increased by the imperfect and often episodic character of the supervision they received. When Victor Amadeus II arrived in Sicily in 1713, he was the first ruler of the island to do so since 1535. Ireland, Scotland and Wales were not visited by their ruler on any occasion during the century. The same was true for much of England and France. Francis of Lorraine visited his grand duchy of Tuscany only once during his reign (1737–65). At the ministerial level there was often a lack of continuity and supervision. Ministers were frequently transient figures or concerned with court intrigue. Thanks to there being 24 French ministers of finance between 1715 and 1789, the permanent officials enjoyed considerable power. The experience of such officials helped to keep them in their posts even when they did not own them.

At the level of central government, commentators frequently suggested that there were insufficient men of ability from whom ministers and senior officials could be chosen. Such claims were, for example, advanced in Spain in 1750 and in Savoy-Piedmont in the early 1780s. The shortage of enough men of ability appears to have been a particular problem in Russia and it lay behind Peter I's concern with education and training.

Corruption was a widespread problem in European governments, reflecting the importance of tax revenues as a form of ready wealth, proprietary attitudes towards posts and the general practice of paying officials by allowing them to retain part of the proceeds of their positions. Peter I was appalled at the scale of Russian corruption and created special inspectors to deal with it, and eventually a network of procurators, parallel to the local administration, under a procurator-general. It proved very difficult to reduce corruption. Corrupt practices reflected strongly developed administrative attitudes and their more important beneficiaries were commonly individuals of social prominence and administrative or political power. In Tuscany most of those who were guilty were nobles annually diverting moderate sums in order to finance an appropriate lifestyle. The Medici grand dukes did not crack down on such officials as they did not want to anger the nobility, but Francis of Lorraine, who tried to introduce a more impersonal, bureaucratic and centralised style of government, refused to accept the argument that families suffered when their individual members were convicted of crime. The vigorous enforcement of the laws against corruption proved to have real limits, because the grand duke was dependent on the co-operation of his servants.[25]

In the Armagh district of Ireland the Cust family used the local collectorship of taxes so as to end up as substantial rentiers in the area. The unacceptable level of Henry Cust's corruption led to his losing his post in 1761, but he suffered no social or financial penalty and in 1769 was appointed high sheriff of Armagh. The effectiveness of the Russian procuracy was limited by the interchangeability of its personnel with local administration, a practice later restricted by Prince A. A. Vyazemsky who, in 1764, replaced a procurator-general dismissed for embezzlement. However, the procuracy suffered from a shortage of qualified people and many procurators took bribes and abused their powers. Louis XVI's brother, the count of Artois, went massively into debt largely as a result of financial mismanagement and speculation by his council.

Corruption was but one aspect of an administrative ethos for which the connotations of the term bureaucracy are inappropriate. Administrative organisations reflected the values and methods of the social system. Many posts were hereditary in families, frequently because, as in France, they were owned by them. Vast sums of money – possibly four times the annual revenue of the crown in France in 1722 – were tied up in this system of venality.[26] This was not necessarily as inefficient as was once imagined. Family pride could be a spur to competence, and there was also a measure of hereditary expertise. More generally, appointment and promotion often resulted from social rank, patronage and inheritance, rather than from educational qualifications or objectively assessed merit. Social assumptions, the role played by patronage, the political importance of administrative posts and the opportunities for gain, both legal and illegal, helped to ensure that senior posts were occupied by men of rank. This could lead to a situation where those who wielded authority and the power for change were gentlemen amateurs, frequently without vocation or aptitude, rather than professional experts. The expert assistants were generally too humble in status to be able to push through changes, particularly in a society and administrative ethos where precedent commanded both respect and legal authority. Prussian administration was commonly held to be a model of efficiency, but though more cohesive than its counterparts in other countries, and with reasonably professional structures and a speedy conduct of business, recruitment was still greatly influenced by patronage, friends and relations being helped even if incompetent. Frederick the Great's attempts to make the somewhat unwieldy administration more efficient and more responsive to his wishes failed, and as a result, he sought to by-pass existing institutions and, especially after 1763, to create new administrative departments and arrangements directly answerable to himself, as with the excise in 1766.

Throughout Europe officials saw themselves as office-holders rather than employees; they worked within constraints imposed by political rather than legal responsibility for their actions, and authority and power were dispersed, rather than concentrated. This helped to encourage disputes between officials. In the localities governments operated through different agents whose mandates were often unclear and whose activities became caught up in the existing maze of local government and social relationships. Conflicts such as those over trade at Trieste in the 1760s between the Austrian Council of Commerce and the Treasury, which supervised the customs and excise, were all too common. Disputes between central and local government officials and agencies were but one aspect of the differences of interest and opinion that divided most authorities, secular and ecclesiastical, central and local, in this period. They could have detrimental consequences, the paralysing rivalry between institutions in the French diocese of Rennes, for example, not ceasing even during food crises.

Disputes should be treated as an integral feature of any system of government, especially one where privilege and precedent played such a major role, rather than as a feature peculiar to the period. Because most authorities were involved in disputes, the actions of central government agencies could often affect the fortunes of other authorities. This both gave a certain weight to their actions, helping to ensure that they were generally supported by at least some party in every dispute, and led the authorities and groups outside central government to attempt to develop links within it and to play a role in the personal, factional and institutional jockeying for position that lay behind the façade of central government. Royal officials and merchants in Troyes in France asked for, and in 1773 obtained, a royal edict to resolve their dispute over the government of the town. The intertwining of the disputes within central government and those elsewhere constituted one of the central features of the administrative history of the period and can be seen as an important aspect of its 'political' history.

Politically this intertwining had the advantage for central government that it provided it with allies and ensured that the focus of many disputes it became involved in was local. For example, the problems surrounding the building of new roads near Auch and Pau in south-western France primarily involved conflicts between local groups, opposition to central government being less important. However, the intertwining made it more difficult to push through changes in the face of recalcitrant officials and local authorities.

The *intendants* of Louis XV and XVI spent longer in particular *généralités* than those of Louis XIV and were therefore less dependent on the patronage of any individual minister. They became more integrated members of local society and more willing to adopt local views. However, they still moved around several provinces or returned to Paris to the royal councils. Many of the *intendants* were opposed to the changes proposed by Necker's first ministry. *Intendants*, like many other royal officials, were allowed to appoint their subordinates and they generally did so from local families: for example the Paillot family in Troyes provided the local subdelegate throughout the century. Such positions, though not hereditary, tended to run in families.

Similar differences characterised other administrations. The inability of the Neapolitan government to supervise local customs offices led to their corruption and domination by local interests. The royal commission sent to the Danish possession of Iceland in 1770–1 received numerous complaints about the injustices of local officials and the burdens exacted by landlords. Icelandic officials guarded their interests, particularly their tax exemptions, held most church and crown lands as fiefs, belonged to the families that possessed most of the privately owned land, and prevented the redress of peasant grievances. The position in

Iceland lends substance to Frederick William I of Prussia's injunction, in his instructions written for his heir in 1722, that the officials responsible for royal domains should not be employed in their areas of origin.

Difficulties with local government and royal officials in the provinces also explain the preference of many rulers, such as Catherine II, for special commissions, which appeared to be the answer of governments such as Russia's to the lack of qualified personnel for local administration and the only means to achieve any degree of centralisation. Peter I found it very difficult to select nobles suitable for provincial government or to get appointees to go to their posts. The activities of the Colleges engaged in financial administration were handicapped by the failure of local government bodies to submit their accounts and therefore Peter used the army to improve the responsiveness of local administration. Throughout Europe attempts to introduce changes also encountered the problem of the inveterate distrust of central government by local interests, which tended to treat it as an alien body that was expensive, corrupt and too large, and whose aspirations and policies were dangerous.

If local administration was often unresponsive to the instructions of rulers and ministers, the same was also true of many of the institutions of central government. Royal courts were an essential, though increasingly less central, feature of the administrative system, and also the focus of political struggles which affected the aims, conduct and personnel of government. Given the structures and attitudes of both courts and society it was essentially the case that in large states 'absolute' monarchs could succeed in achieving only a precarious balance among rival factions. Rulers often appeared to have only a limited control of court politics and central government policies. The central administration of Prussia during the reign of Frederick I (1688–1713) was characterised by the influence of favourites, vacillating policies, corruption, intrigue not controlled by the ruler, and the perception of monarchical weakness.

The calibre and interests of individual monarchs were unpredictable, and it was difficult for them to ensure continuity in policy between reigns. They could not readily institutionalise change. The importance of the attitude of individual rulers represented a powerful element of discontinuity that encouraged those unhappy about patronage and policies to look forward to the accession of the heir to the throne, the reversionary interest. This led Peter I to have his son Alexis, who opposed his westernisation policies and had fled Russia, brought back, tried and killed in 1718.

Many rulers were also inconsistent in their implementation of policies. A tension between the regularisation of power through the establishment of agreed administrative procedures and the personal intervention of the monarch was characteristic of the states of the period. Furthermore, the limited authority of government institutions in a system where court favour was crucial, power not necessarily based upon tenure of a formal office, and only the monarch could arbitrate effectively in disputes, forced rulers to act. A continued display of royal favour was necessary for the maintenance of the authority of ministers, institutions and edicts. Many ministers fell, as Tanucci did in Naples in 1776, because they lost the support of the monarch or his relatives. Peter I himself decided many issues that should have been reserved for the Colleges, and he was responsible for co-ordination among the Colleges and for the general planning of policy. Posts became influential because favourites filled them, royal favour qualified the autonomy of institutions and the procedures for appointment and promotion, and those close to the ruler, such as Alexis Makarov, private secretary to Peter I and Catherine I, enjoyed considerable influence.

The dominance of patronage and factionalism and the vulnerable position of most ministers encouraged them to favour relatives and clients. The situation was also exacerbated by the apparent policy of some rulers, such as Charles VI, Peter I, and Louis XIV, to allow the continuance of factionalism because it ensured that they received varied advice and increased their power.

Even when rulers were in control of their courts and ministers secure of their position, the institutions and personnel of central government frequently proved unresponsive to their demands, particularly if these entailed change. Charles XII was not alone in feeling that his administrators lacked sufficient dedication. Dissatisfaction with the operation of central government was responsible for a number of fundamental reorganisations, such as those carried out by Peter I and Frederick William I. However, it is important not to exaggerate the extent to which monarchs sought to reorganise central government, or to fall for the fallacy that change equalled reform and that monarchs who failed to attempt to execute major administrative changes deserve castigation. There were good political reasons for doubting the feasibility of change, sound administrative explanations for querying the possibility of improvement. The general absence of sweeping administrative changes in *ancien régime* France was matched elsewhere, as in the Prussia of Frederick the Great and in Georgian England, both generally regarded as successful states.

Winning consent: the process of government

The problems of government were not restricted to financial difficulties, the maintenance of law and order, unreliable officials,
factional politics and unresponsive local communities. Religious
and ecclesiastical issues could create many problems, as could
political disorder. These difficulties were not peculiar to national
governments. Major institutions and landlords faced similar
problems, as they strove to reconcile traditional practices and
assumptions with the desire to achieve specific goals. The
Glengary estate in Scotland, in which timber was cut down illegally by tenants in 1769, was not the only large estate that found
it difficult to control the activities of dependants. Supervision was
made difficult for all institutions by the relatively small size of
their staff. The bureaucracy of the grand duchy of Tuscany num-
bered only 1335 in 1765, the Spanish naval ministry employed
about 20 people in Madrid in 1750 and 30–35, including clean-
ers, in 1790. In 1800 the British Foreign Office had only eleven
clerks, the War Office only six.

Responding to such problems and to different suggestions
about policy and contrasting expectations as to how to put into
practice notions of good kingship, rulers sought in large measure to govern by eliciting consent and through winning the co-
operation of those who wielded power and authority in their
states. The circumstances in which this process took place varied
greatly, principally due to different constitutional and institutional situations, the skill of individual monarchs, their ministers
and those with whom they dealt. Political contingencies were also
crucial, not least the problems confronting monarchs and their
aspirations. Although the circumstances varied, the search for
consent and co-operation is a central theme of the period. To a
certain extent it has been overshadowed by a historiographical
stress on disagreements and conflict, on how the *ancien régime*
did not work, rather than on how it did. This can be seen especially in discussion of the relations between monarchs and representative institutions. A conflict between the two has been
generally assumed, and thus the institutions, Diets, Estates and
parliaments, have been regarded as satisfactory from the monarchical point of view, if weak, in abeyance or non-existent.

There is little doubt that certain monarchs adopted this view.
The claims of some institutions to political authority and administrative power created difficulties, and in a number of countries
the monarchs allowed them to lapse. The French foreign minister Torcy rejected the notion of summoning the Estates General
in 1712: he argued that 'instances in the past have shown that

such sorts of assemblies have nearly always produced trouble, and the last Estates General, held in 1614, led to civil war...as the Estates General has not been convoked for nearly a century it has in effect been abolished'.[27] Indeed, it was to meet only in 1789 and then as a measure of desperation. The *parlements* were much more important in eighteenth-century France. The Diet of Baden was not convened during the century and had not met since 1626. The Portuguese *Cortes* did not meet between 1698 and 1820, despite the fact that the *Cortes* of 1697–8 agreed to an increase in taxation. Cosimo III of Tuscany convened the Senate only once. In Württemberg, where the Estates granted direct taxes and, using their own officials, supervised their collection, there were a number of serious disputes with dukes determined to raise more money. In one such in 1764, when a tax revolt led to the use of troops and to the intervention of the Aulic Council, a court of the Empire, Duke Karl Eugen allegedly declared 'I am the State.'[28]

In Württemberg the Estates survived for a number of reasons. These included the fortuitous death of dukes, the dukes' unpopularity after 1733 when a Catholic succeeded, the strong constitutional and institutional position of the Estates, particularly their role in the collection of taxes, and the protection provided by the constitution of the Empire, imperial institutions and the willingness of other powers to intervene. Elsewhere in Europe the survival of representative institutions was not generally a consequence of their successful defiance of rulers, but rather, of their value in eliciting support and of respect for their constitutional role. Among the large states, representative institutions were most powerful in Britain, Poland, Sweden and the United Provinces, but they were also of considerable importance in the Habsburg territories, much of the Empire, and in some provinces of France. They were either absent or ineffective in most of Italy, Spain and Russia, though Catherine II tried to set up an Estates structure.

Possibly the best example of the role of Estates in increasing the power of a state was the importance of parliamentary support in the establishment and maintenance of the British funded national debt. This was both the source of the British government's financial strength and flexibility and the product of the co-operation between crown and political society that was expressed in the constitutional position of Parliament and the policies of successive ministries. Although not to the same extent, other representative institutions served as sources of strength and foci of co-operation. They were most important when their powers to grant taxes were matched by their responsibility and ability to collect them. Politically this helped to ensure their continued existence, for it meant that the Estates could operate as a branch of executive government, and thus if co-operation was obtained, extend the power of the ruler. Representative institutions in the Habsburg lands could be very important. In the Bohemian lands the Diets legislated actively, collected taxes and regulated economic affairs, health and police measures. Joseph I, emperor from 1705 to 1711, often praised the Bohemian Estates to his ministers, and, despite his reputation as a monarch who wished to limit the powers of the Estates, he deferred to their rights and therefore abandoned plans both for a universal excise that would have been collected by royal officials and for updated land registers in the Tyrol and Lower and Upper Austria. The creation of a permanent executive body by the Bohemian Estates in 1714 further strengthened their position. Rather than unify the Estates of the hereditary lands, in order to equalise the basis of direct taxation as was suggested in 1714, Charles VI preferred to negotiate with them separately, as he also did when it came to settling his succession in the early 1720s. Count Lothar Königsegg, appointed governor of the Austrian Netherlands in 1714, was instructed to change as little as possible.

Under Maria Theresa the administrative role of the Estates declined to a certain extent, though royal indebtedness and the use of the credit of the Estates increased their political weight in certain respects during and after the Seven Years War. The nature of the relationship between central government and Estates varied by province, issue and official. Co-operation continued to be an important theme. Estates and their officials were the characteristic executants of government policy and should be seen as part, rather than a rival, of government. Issues involving Estates often divided central government, a result, in part, of the links of clientage and patronage that rule out any easy separation of central from local government. A dispute in 1723 over the right to collect taxes in the province of Hainault in the Austrian Netherlands led the duke of Aremberg, on behalf of the Estates, to use his influence in Vienna in order to have the government in Brussels overruled. Joseph II's more autocratic temper and his appreciation that it would be difficult to obtain the support of the Estates for his policies, led him to adopt a harsh attitude towards them. Though he supported the creation of a Galician Diet at Lvov, its power was seriously restricted and all taxation remained under royal control. Leopold II favoured an executive, rather than a legislative, role for the Estates.

In Prussia the Estates continued to discharge certain functions, but they were scarcely equal partners with the rulers. In his 1722 instructions for his heir, Frederick William I insisted that East

Prussia must remain firmly under royal control and that government there by the Estates must not re-emerge. Frederick the Great had little time for Estates, writing in 1772 that he would sooner attempt the labours of Hercules than try to make a Swedish Diet listen to reason. The Estates of the distant western provinces of Prussia, particularly Cleves, enjoyed most power.

In neighbouring Saxony, in contrast, the Estates retained the majority of their prerogatives, especially in financial affairs, and they influenced the elector's privy council. In the semi-autonomous Saxon possession of Lusatia the Estates exercised a considerable degree of self-government. A similar variety characterised the situation in Italy. The constitutional position of the rulers of Piedmont was not restricted by institutions comparable in their power to the Sicilian Parliament, Milanese Senate, or Mantuan *Congregazione*, all of which served to defend the interests of the privileged. The Estates of Savoy, Piedmont and Nice had all ceased to meet before the century began. The Milanese Senate, a legal body dominated by the local nobility, had its jurisdiction increased in 1770–1 when the public administration of Lombardy was reorganised, but in 1786 it was abolished when Joseph reorganised the duchy afresh.

In France the situation was complex. Whereas only few provinces had Estates, representative assemblies, all of France was divided among 12 and, after the acquisition of Lorraine, 13 *parlements*. As with most *ancien régime* institutions their organisation reflected particular regional circumstances and was far from uniform. The most important, in terms of political and legal importance and area of jurisdiction, was that of Paris. *Parlements* were 'sovereign' courts of law, final courts of appeal which had to register laws for them to take effect and had a right to criticise them through remonstrances. Conflict between the monarchy on the one hand and some provincial Estates and *parlements* on the other has attracted considerable attention, and it led many contemporaries and certain historians to think primarily in terms of competing views and of institutional opposition to royal power and authority. In 1754 Frederick the Great contrasted Prussia and France: 'We do not have here vexatious priests and obstinate *Parlements*.'[29] Louis-Sébastien Mercier argued in the *Journal des dames* in 1775 that only the firmness of the *parlementaire* magistrates had historically saved France from despotism. Louis XV himself thanked Charles III in 1771 for his concern at the maintenance of Louis' authority at a time of 'domestic embarrassments caused by my *Parlements*' and for 'his generous offer of help, if it was necessary, in coping with the disobedience of the badly intentioned'. The following year Louis saw Gustavus III's coup in Sweden as a victory for monarchical authority and compared it to his own position.[30] In contrast, on the *parlements'* side in late eighteenth-century France, there was much talk of *le despotisme ministériel*, the despotism of the ministers. In 1764 the *Parlement* of Paris warned Louis XV against those who, it alleged, sought to substitute a despotic and absolute government for a monarchical one.

There were indeed a number of serious clashes between the government and the Estates and *parlements*. The Estates of Brittany resisted the authority of Versailles, and in mid-century there was also an important clash over the levying of taxes in Languedoc, though this was a relatively minor affair compared with the trouble in Brittany. Between 1673 and 1713 Louis XIV did not visit the *Grand-Chambre* of the *Parlement* of Paris and his solemn receptions for its delegates came to be defined as acts of extreme generosity on his part. 1673 was Louis's last *lit de justice*, an occasion when the king in person instructed the *Parlement* to register a law. In excluding Philip V from the French succession, Louis subverted the basic principles of dynastic and legal succession, while in 1714 he further legally promoted his bastards to the status of princes of the blood, adding them to the order of succession. Neither act was carried out in a *lit de justice*, 'the association of Crown and *Parlement* symbolised by the *lit de justice* in the Grand-Chambre of the Palais de Justice was severed'.[31]

Louis's death was followed by a change in arrangements. In 1715 the *Parlement* of Paris set aside Louis XIV's will, which limited the power of the regent, Orléans, and, in return, Orléans revoked the law of 1673 and allowed the *Parlements* again to remonstrate before registering laws. Nevertheless, in 1718 Orléans had the right to remonstrate defined more stringently and in 1720 the *Parlement* of Paris was exiled to Pontoise. As in the administrative sphere, the reaction against Louis XIV's policies had been short-lived. Orléans effectively reversed his earlier policy. The issue of *parlementaire* power remained relatively unimportant in the provinces until mid-century, and the *Parlement* of Paris created comparatively few difficulties except in 1730–2. The position of the Jansenists then proved a contentious source of constitutional dispute. In January 1731 Louis XV replied to remonstrances from the *Parlement* of Paris by describing the *Parlement* as simply an instrument by which the monarch made known his orders. *Parlementaire* decrees on ecclesiastical issues were annulled by the king and the Parisian judges went on strike. Louis refused to grant an audience to hear the grievances of the *Parlement*. In 1732 growing tension led to a judicial strike and, when the *Parlement* refused to register a disciplinary declaration, despite a *lit de justice*, to the exile of many members. The scale of the crisis should not be exaggerated. It was resolved at the end of the year when the exiles were recalled and the disciplinary declaration withdrawn. The root cause of the dispute was ecclesiastical, rather than constitutional. Many of the leading speakers in the *Parlement* were inspired by religious not constitutionalist fervour: Pucelle, Titon and Fornier de Montagny were all noted visitors at St-Médard. The *Parlement* had condemned to be burnt the *Judicium Francorum*, a revised version of a radical pamphlet which had appeared during the Fronde and attributed to the *Parlement* of Paris, which it claimed represented the nation and had the duty of watching over the people's interest, rights and prerogatives which it had never possessed.

The next few years were relatively free of disagreement. In 1733 the remonstrances against the levying of the wartime tax, the *dixième*, were moderate in tone. The introduction of the *vingtième* tax in 1749 led to renewed protests. Calling for reduced government spending and lower taxes, the *Parlement* of Paris sought to give responsibility for overseeing financial policy to the sovereign courts. However, it was ecclesiastical issues that again proved most contentious. In the case of the *Parlement* of Paris, they led in the 1750s to three interruptions of ordinary justice, two exilings of magistrates and one mass resignation of offices. *Lits de justice*, effective in financial disputes, proved ineffective in ecclesiastical affairs. The importance of these disputes is contested. On the one hand a mid-century crisis, pregnant with future consequences, has been discerned:

> Just as Gallican–Jansenist denunciations of episcopal despotism antedated the denunciations of particular monarchical acts as despotic, so the breakdown of the distinction between the despotic and the absolute occurred first in an ecclesiastical context and then spread to relations between king and subjects in other domains…beneath parliamentary-Jansenism's ritual appeal to the 'prince' in sacerdotal–imperial relations it is more accurately the power of the Parlement and behind it the nation that is half-consciously being invoked.[32]

On the other hand, it has been suggested that the evidence for thinking that the *parlementaires* either asserted or implied some notion of national sovereignty is both 'scant and ambiguous', that there was a 'fundamental but precarious, unity about French political life', and 'a tendency for both sides to resolve conflicts by negotiation'.[33] In 1770–1 negotiations broke down. A serious clash with the *Parlement* and the refusal of the latter to yield to Louis XV's wishes led to the exile of the judges and the so-called Maupeou Revolution, named after the chancellor who carried through the remodelling of the *parlements*.

The crisis produced a fierce debate in which sides were taken and opponents denigrated. Writers supporting Maupeou claimed that the *parlements* were attempting to subject the nation to a hereditary aristocracy and that their infringements on monarchical power were matched by their irresponsibility, hostility to the church and indifference to public welfare. They were specifically criticised for miscarriages of justice, a refusal to reform the laws and the judicial system, and collaboration with monopolists to increase the price of bread. The defenders of the *parlements*, in turn, presented them as the protectors of the people against arbitrary government and, stressing the divergence between rule by law and rule by the king, pressed the need for a society under the rule of law where the government operated within the framework of a fixed constitution protected by an independent judiciary.[34]

The virulence of the public debate is possibly misleading. The government succeeded in persuading large numbers of judges to co-operate in the new courts, and, despite the charges of ministerial despotism, did not abolish the right of registration and remonstrance and did not create a new government order. Louis XV in effect sought to make the existing system work with less dispute. The contention of the early 1770s was, anyway, eased by the chance which solved many eighteenth-century disputes, the accession of a new monarch and the accompanying changes in patronage, policy and expectations. Louis XVI, who succeeded in 1774, dismissed Maupeou and reversed his changes, in accordance with the advice of the new controller-general, Turgot, who thought he could carry out his reform programme without serious obstruction from the *parlements*. A *lit de justice* ended the *Parlement* of Paris's opposition to Turgot's policies, and between 1774 and 1786 this *Parlement* was more circumspect and docile than it had been since the 1740s. In part, this can be attributed to their experience of Maupeou's policies, but, in part, it may also have owed something to the impact of a new reign and new ministers as well as to the successes of the American war. The tax increases of the early 1780s passed with great ease, though they were relatively few as Necker financed the war by loans. Certain of the provincial *parlements* were more fractious, opposing both the *intendants* and the government's fiscal demands, but such episodic clashes were far from new and the *parlements* of Louis XVI's early years were divided both individually and collectively.

It is easy to concentrate on prominent moments of dispute and to lose sight of less spectacular practices and periods of co-operation. The *parlements* and the Estates offered the crown important support in the judicial, financial and administrative spheres. The

Parlement of Paris's administrative decrees helped to ensure the supply of food and firewood to the capital, to maintain hygiene in public places and to regulate guilds, hospitals and prisons. These functions were shared with the lieutenant-general of police in Paris and with the *intendants* outside Paris.[35] Voltaire was scornful, claiming that when the *Parlement* of Paris ceased operating in 1753–4, the police carried on, the markets were conducted in an orderly fashion, and that conciliation and arbitrators replaced the judges. Though the variegated and multiform nature of French administration ensured that any one agency or official was less crucial than in certain other states, Voltaire under-rated the role of the *Parlement*. The sovereign courts, especially the *parlements*, exercised and supervised a wide range of administrative responsibilities based on their legal and police powers.

In Provence the *Parlement* of Aix played a major role in 1720 in organising resistance to the spread of the plague from Marseilles. Though calm in the 1730s, that *Parlement* opposed the fiscal demands of Louis XV's later years, beginning with the *vingtième*. In return for its eventual support, the *Parlement* obtained certain of its other demands, including the regulation of army requisitions and the suppression of a tax on the export of olive oil. This indicates the reality of compromise and concession that underlay so many of the disputes of the period. Public statements of discontent were intended to elicit concessions from the government, not to rally mass support. In Provence this process was eased by the links that bound the *Parlement* to the royal government. These were symbolised by Jean-Baptiste des Gallois de La Tour, who was both *intendant* of the province and first president of the *Parlement*. He was succeeded in both posts by his son Charles who was *intendant* in 1744–71 and 1775–90 and first president from 1748. Charles stressed that it was possible to be both a good subject and a good Provençal. His support of the liberty of the *Parlement* and his opposition to Maupeou led to his being replaced as *intendant* by the latter, but all the other royal ministries were prepared to accept his attitude. In Brittany a similar practice of compromise reflected the strength of regional institutions and led to the central government enjoying less power than in the provinces near Paris but, at the same time, ensured that order was maintained and the requests of central government heeded for much of the period. The interim commission of the Breton Estates became permanent by mid-century and raised most of the taxes, especially those which affected the privileged orders. The commission relied on the local contacts of its members, who worked out the allocation of the new taxes with the peasant notables of each parish. On the one hand, this kept down taxes, which were much lower than in the rest of France. On the other, taxes were collected and the creditworthiness of the Estates added further value to their co-operation. When in the 1760s the provincial commandant, the duke d'Aiguillon, clashed with the *Parlement* of Rennes over new taxes the consequent political dispute and disruption of the provincial government provided a salutary reminder of the value of co-operation. Except in Brittany, and in other provinces in 1787–8, the Estates gave the government very little trouble.

Co-operation between the central government and the *parlements* and Estates was made more difficult by the related problems in agreeing what were the best interests of society and in maintaining relationships of mutual respect and confidence, problems that were most acute when new fiscal demands were raised and enforced. Thus, the cost of the Seven Years War could erode confidence in Brittany. The extent of these failures should not be exaggerated. Differences over political objectives and methods were scarcely unique to eighteenth-century France. They should be regarded as an integral, not an extraneous, aspect of government in a society where the limited institutional expression of political issues ensured that they were contested in an administrative context. In addition, it was not simply central government that was affected by judicial resistance and covert obstruction. These were the normal methods by which the institutions of *ancien régime* France contested unwelcome demands from any higher authority. It is only if central government is assumed to have required and sought uncontested power and authority that the *parlements* and Estates can be presented as dangerous obstacles.

This was, however, not the objective of a monarchy that sought to respect the law, neither was it practical in the absence of other institutions that might serve, however imperfectly, to present and represent views and interests that the central government had to consider. There was no common constitutional form for the European monarchies of the period, no ideal model to which they sought to approximate. To condemn France because the *parlements* and Estates occupied a position that did not exist in Russia would be foolish. The process of judgement is difficult and often anachronistic and there are a range of perspectives among which it is difficult to choose. Should the strength of the state or the interests of the subjects be stressed, and how are these to be defined? If strength is seen to arise from co-operation between monarchs and the propertied orders, then intermediate institutions can be presented as an important, though not a necessary, condition of this co-operation.

Enlightened despotism

The problem of establishing acceptable relations between monarchs and their powerful subjects was not restricted to the question of defining relations with representative institutions. Even in countries where these were important, they did not sit continually and many lacked executive agencies. In addition, many of them contained and represented only a section of those who wielded social and local government power. The need for the rulers to establish good relations with these individuals reflected not only their power, but also the non-existence in most of Europe of any comprehensive system of central government administration of the localities. Resources of both manpower and money were lacking. It proved difficult to solve these problems.

Peter I tried to establish a well-organised hierarchical service of paid officials for Russian provincial administration, but his success was limited, and after 1727 only a handful of the higher officials received salaries from public funds, a situation that encouraged corruption. Russian provincial administration suffered from a lack of sufficient trained personnel. This helped to limit the impact of reforms, such as those of Catherine II. These reforms did not involve any major break, as they brought little change in the personnel of local government, personal abilities and attitudes and training being left largely unaltered.

It would be wrong to suggest that the principal limitation on royal control was resources. If, instead, most rulers are seen as primarily concerned both to preserve the systems of government they had inherited and to increase their effectiveness, then their essential political and administrative problem can be regarded as one of seeking to maintain or create a satisfactory consensus and working relationship with the socially powerful, rather than the imposition of a new system of government. Far from ranking rulers by their success in envisaging, creating and maintaining new systems, it is better to make a subtle assessment of their skill in administering what was there already. This should not be based on any assumption that states should have been developing in a standard fashion or that rulers should have been planning and acting in a certain manner.

Raynal wrote in the *Historie des deux Indes* (1770) that the best government was that of a just and enlightened despot. In his *Observations on the Life of Jan Zamoyski* (1785) Stanislaus Staszic spoke of an Enlightened Despotism as being acceptable for Poland. The term Enlightened Despotism was used in the nineteenth century to describe the government of many European states in the decades before the French Revolution. Like the

Enlightenment, it is an idea that poses many problems of definition. The so-called Enlightened Despots, a group whose most
prominent members were Catherine II, Joseph II, Frederick the
Great, Gustavus III, Charles III and Leopold of Tuscany, later
Leopold II of Austria, mostly followed a number of policies that
were praised widely by many of the leading intellectuals of the
period. This was particularly true of their attacks on clerical
power and privileges, their espousal of religious toleration, their
legal reforms, especially legal codification and the abolition of
torture, and their interest in educational reform. However, many
of these policies had been supported by rulers earlier in the century, or indeed in earlier periods, who have never been associated with the Enlightenment. To a certain extent, the burst of
reforms that characterised the period 1763–89 in much of Europe
represented a resumption, after the wars of 1733–63, of earlier
policies or of an earlier concern about particular problems. The
reign of Peter I and the early years of those of Charles VI, Philip
V and Frederick William I had seen a major interest in wide-
ranging administrative reform, and Peter's efforts to change
Russian society were ambitious. Frederick William I and Peter I
were supporters of religious toleration. Many of the rulers of the
period had sought to improve education and had clashed with
the Church. A quest for data upon which informed decisions
could be made can be seen in such measures as the land surveys
of the period. Trained administrators, some the products of new
institutions such as the University of Halle, founded in 1694,
were used by the rulers of the early decades of the century and, in
so far as the phrase 'enlightened government' means much, these
individuals were enlightened by the standards of the age, though
not committed to any specific body of ideas.

The timing of the major reform initiatives of the century is
instructive. They tended to follow periods of major warfare, and
probably represented a response both to the problems, especially
financial, revealed by these conflicts and to the opportunities for
improvement and change presented by peace. It would be wrong
to suggest that each period of reform was similar. That of 1763–
89 saw more interest in serfdom and the position of the peasantry and a greater determination to limit the role of the church
in certain spheres, such as censorship, rather than the wish to
control the church characteristic of earlier periods. Nevertheless,
because less attention has been devoted to the reforms earlier in
the century, especially to their supporters and their intellectual
origins, it is difficult to determine the extent to which those of
1763–89 should be regarded as new. The participation and influence of intellectuals appears more prominent in the later period,

but it is by no means clear that the reforms of this age should be attributed to them, or that they were more successful than those earlier in the century. Reforming policies appear to have been most successful in 1763–89 in some, though not all, of the smaller states such as Denmark, certain of the Italian principalities, especially Tuscany and Parma, and some of the German ones, such as Baden, Trier and the bishopric of Münster. These states did not generally maintain large armies or pursue aggressive foreign policies. In the case of Portugal, under Pombal, the Enlightenment coincided with the struggle of an old power to be great again, by adopting and adapting self-consciously the techniques its government believed their competitors had used to surpass Portugal.[36] However, the ability of some of the rulers of the small states to implement reforms was not new. This had also been the case earlier in the century, as in Savoy-Piedmont under Victor Amadeus II.

The rule of the Enlightened Despots has been described as being marked by the spirit of system and by a relative absence of respect for precedent and privilege. In place of the particular loyalties and rights that typified the corporate nature of society, the Enlightenment offered a universal perspective based on rational assessments derived from first principles. This analysis is inaccurate. The Enlightenment was no more outside and opposed to society than were the Enlightened Despots or governments. Just as the attitudes of intellectuals were divided, far from consistent and often equivocal in the face of what some described as abuses, so the Enlightened Despots in the formation and execution of their policies respected privilege and precedent far more than is generally appreciated. This was not surprising as the rulers in general sought both to co-operate with the socially powerful and to pursue what was practical. Far from praising abstract notions, in 1786 Joseph II condemned fools who produced systems on paper. Choiseul criticised d'Alembert for being vain enough to think that 'the events of this world revolve around the opinion of his head'. In 1791 George III was told by the French envoy that it was appropriate for the Revolutionary government to abolish feudal rights in Alsace: 'for the sake of public utility, governments should seek administrative uniformity. The King of England argued that such uniformity could exist only in small states, and that in kingdoms as big as France any attempt to introduce it would create problems'.[37]

It has been argued that 'where the power of traditional institutions was less well-established or simply less important, either in the overseas possessions of the western European states or in newly-acquired territories within Europe, the enlightened intentions of the governments were much clearer and their achievements rather greater'.[38] French policies in Corsica, Habsburg government in Galicia, and reforms in the Spanish and Portuguese colonies have all been presented in this light. There is considerable force in this argument, but it must be presented not as evidence that rulers were able to carry out in some areas what they did not dare attempt elsewhere although they would have liked to; but rather as an indication that attempts were made to introduce major changes when they were felt to be necessary because the basis for co-operation with the local elite was weak.

This was most clearly the case in conquered regions and in some colonies. Such a situation was not, however, restricted to the second half of the century. The Austrians made a major effort to change the government and society of their conquest of Little Wallachia, but this helped to ensure that the local elite provided them with no assistance when the Turks reconquered the province. Victor Amadeus sought administrative reform when he arrived in his new possession, Sicily, in 1713 and sent officials from Turin to help his viceroy, Count Annibale Maffei, implement his policy. He had little success and the local elite offered little resistance to the Spanish invasion of 1718.

The notion of enlightened government creates considerable difficulties. It is not easy to define, and entails subjective criteria. It is, for example, by no means clear that it is useful to treat as anachronistic political systems such as that of Poland, that failed to correspond to these criteria. If Enlightened Despotism is to be redefined as enlightened government, then not only are the central figures, many of the monarchs of the second half of the century, to be displaced, but it is also by no means clear how such a vague notion is to be confined and why it should not be applied to all government in the period, whether of a diocese, corporation or estate. One common characteristic was more active government, as measured, for example, by the number of decrees issued. This was readily apparent during the reign of Joseph II. The number issued for Austria, Bohemia and Galicia increased six or seven times under Joseph.[39]

Another difficulty with the notion of enlightened government is that it fails to place sufficient weight on the different nature of the states and societies of the period and the varying circumstances of their rulers. Although many contemporary commentators discerned common themes in the policies of many of the rulers, differences were also stressed. If attention is directed to the various problems of individual rulers as the cause of their policies, rather than some common Enlightenment agenda, then it is most appropriate to stress both the different circumstances of the rulers and the role of expedients in their reaction to them. Clearly, certain common attitudes characterised their reactions, but it is by no means clear that these were either new or sufficiently important to merit particular attention.

Many intelligent men both inside and outside government criticised and opposed the policies of the rulers generally described as Enlightened Despots and policies commonly regarded as enlightened. To write off the critics of such policies as reactionaries concerned only with their privileges would be wrong. There were important debates over most of the major issues of the period and informed opinion was not always to be found on one side of such debates. Abstractions such as the Enlightenment, Enlightened Despotism and enlightened government dissolve under scrutiny, to reveal a world in which issues were far from clear, compromise was common and rulers were often primarily trying desperately to cope with their immediate problems, or, if they were planning for the future, were more interested in foreign policy than domestic reform.

14 Ideology, Politics and Reform

Political thought

The political thought of this period is amorphous and difficult to assess. It is by no means clear what was most influential and representative. There is a temptation to concentrate on theoretical writings, on what was obviously 'political thought' and on works that were radical in intention and tone, or that might seem to prefigure or even act as a spur to later developments, especially the Revolution and progressive nineteenth-century thought. However, it is important to remember that much political thinking was expressed in ethical, religious and judicial terms, indeed can best be understood as an aspect of these spheres of intellectual activity, rather than as a consciously independent intellectual tradition. Much about political reflection was traditional, and any concentration on new or radical elements within it may distort it. In addition, it is far from obvious whose views should be regarded as important. Rather than examining the ideas of theorists and intellectuals, it is possibly more appropriate to consider those of the men and women who wielded power, whose views are likely to have been a mixture of received opinions. These too are not always easy to assess. If some monarchs, such as Frederick the Great, wrote a certain amount of reflective material, most did not, and it is by no means clear whether what was produced was a faithful representation of their views or was written for effect.

Any consideration of the opinions of those who wielded power reveals a range of influences and a more complex pattern than would be suggested by a concentration on the works of a small number of writers. Political figures borrowed from a number of traditions and were far from consistent in the views they advanced. Gustavus III of Sweden was not the only ruler who wavered between different outlooks. In 1790, as he considered a monarchical crusade against revolutionary France, Gustavus observed 'I am myself a democrat'.[1] To a certain extent, fashionable new notions were cited in defence of often conflicting, established positions, without bringing much change to the latter. In the case of the *Parlement* of Paris, 'their fundamental position, which had not changed substantially over the centuries, was not changed either by their citing of Montesquieu, or for that matter, later, of Rousseau. But in seeking a contemporary appeal, which meant recourse to shifts in emphasis and new meanings for old words, their stance appeared to alter'.[2] Many political writers were inconsistent, an understandable result of the different traditions they sought to reconcile, of changes in circumstances and of the difficulty of applying general precepts to particular problems and of considering the situation in a number of countries. Thus, the response of many French writers to Poland, to Russian intervention there and to the exercise of power in eastern Europe in general, differed from their attitude to French politics. An example of altering views is offered by the French physiocrat Le Mercier de la Rivière, who in his *L'Ordre Naturel et Essentiel des Sociétés Politiques* (1767), called for legal despotism, an all-powerful monarch to govern in accordance with natural law. He claimed that public education and freedom of expression would reveal to the subjects the 'evident' underlying principles of the social order and thus lead them to support the legal despot. The work aroused the interest of such rulers as Catherine II, Leopold of Tuscany, Karl Friedrich of Baden and especially the future Gustavus III, who thought it should cause a 'revolution in thinking'.[3] Gustavus commissioned Le Mercier de la Rivière to write his *De l'Instruction Publique* (1775), and was duly praised in it for granting 'true liberty' to Sweden, but the work put forward different views from those in his earliest book. The concept of legal despotism was abandoned and more stress was placed on the duties and limitations of monarchical authority.

Theoretical discussion offered a perspective from which different societies could be judged. Thus the contrast between monarchy and despotism, monarchical rule in accordance with, or in defiance of, the natural laws that were held to cause, shape and spring from man's social organisation, could be seen as universally valid. However, the attempt to apply these universal judgements to particular countries, to determine, for example, whether a ruler was despotic, was fraught with difficulties, not least because in order to understand political behaviour, it had to be approached in terms of the specific institutions, traditions and practices of individual states. A failure to do so often led to serious misunderstandings.

Nevertheless, many commentators did seek to present European developments in terms of common themes. The *philosophes* were acutely concerned about the progress of their ideas outside France, not least because many found foreign rulers more willing patrons than Louis XV. The French 'Patriots' opposed to Maupeou's

1771 changes saw them as part of a general European trend, linking them in particular to Gustavus III's coup of 1772 against the
government of the Swedish Estates, and the policies of Johann
Friedrich Struensee in Denmark. Struensee was a German doctor
who became the lover of the queen and, controlling royal policy
from 1770, reorganised the Danish government, offending much
of the nobility before he was removed in a coup in 1772. British
writers compared the Parliament of Westminster and the *Parlement*
of Paris when the latter challenged royal policies, and French
politicians were also conscious of the analogy.

Though many writers did discern and present common themes,
most rulers and politicians appear to have thought of domestic
politics in rigidly national terms. There was no universally
accepted view of the nature of royal power. The practice of
regarding the situation elsewhere and seeking to further a common interest accordingly was well developed in religious and
diplomatic terms, but not in economic, social, constitutional and
government issues. Intervention in the domestic affairs of another
state was commonly undertaken for diplomatic reasons, rather
than in response to any ideological views. Thus Russia sought to
keep monarchy weak in Poland and Sweden, France and Spain
helped the American rebels against Britain, and France offered
aid in the mid-1780s to the Dutch 'Patriots' challenging the power
and influence of William V of Orange. This situation did not alter
until the early 1790s when contrasting hopes and fears concerning the progress of revolutionary movements outside France
encouraged a greater willingness to intervene in other countries
for ideological reasons. In common with the churches, the
supporters of the Revolution claimed a universal applicability
for their teachings, but, in contrast to the established churches,
they did not consider themselves bound in a matrix of rights,
privileges and institutions that would enable them to co-exist,
albeit often with considerable difficulty, with other beliefs.

Traditional views dominated the political thought of most sections of society, in so far as these can be assessed, just as they
influenced the activities and inter-relationships of most institutions and the suppositions of most of those who wielded power
or sought to influence or control its exercise. These traditional
views centred on the maintenance of established institutions,
practices and conventions, but they reflected more than simply
the preservation of privilege. They derived from a set of beliefs
that stressed the value of the past, seeing it as a source of legitimacy. Privileges and rights were not simply a form of property. They were also felt to express an appreciation of value and
a basic justice. Agreements issued in the past, rather than the

consent of present subjects, were the basis of authority. In institutional terms they established the legal basis on which authority was exercised and by which it could be judged. The communities in the northern Jura which rebelled against the absolutism of the prince-bishops of Basle in 1726–40 invoked agreements nearly 200 years old. In the eyes of some theorists the past was the setting for the creation of organised society by means of original contracts, through which people had actually or notionally surrendered their freedom and that of their descendants to act as they chose in an anarchic society without laws and therefore without rights, in order to create a sovereign power that could maintain law and thus preserve rights. This abstract reference to a past constitutionalism had less relevance than the living constitutionalism provided by the maintenance of traditional privileges. This was fortified by the reiteration of such privileges during the succession procedures for new leaders, not simply rulers, but also officials at every level of corporate society, such as mayors and guild-masters.

This reiteration represented a confirmation of a living contract in which authority was seen to represent a legal conduct that respected the privileges of others. This was most obviously presented in the *capitulations*, the list of restrictions, accepted by many new rulers. These were particularly important in the Empire and Poland. In the Habsburg lands, the Estates of every province offered homage to the new sovereign, who, in return, guaranteed its laws. Gaspard Thaumas de la Thoumassière, professor of French law at Bourges under Louis XIV, was not alone in arguing that provincial customs implied a contractual relationship between a monarch and a province.

Respect for privileges conditioned the policies of most rulers and the manner in which they were discussed. The Edict of Marly of 1707, for example, established in theory uniform national standards for medical education and regulation in France, but it carefully respected the existing prerogatives of the corporations. Any infringement of privileges could be denounced as an illegal tampering with rights in a political culture that generally distinguished between monarchy and despotism by reference to the policies and apparent attitudes of the ruler, rather than his constitutional position. In 1779 when Lenoir, the Parisian lieutenant-general of police, published an ordinance imposing a new code of recruitment and accountability on the Parisian grain-brokers, which insisted that they act like public servants, he was criticised for a despotic action and his ordinance was attacked as a violation of natural law. The stress on privileges helped to ensure that most of those who sought change claimed, as Gustavus III did, to be re-establishing lapsed practices and constitutions.

Respect for the past did not necessarily entail monarchical sentiments. Indeed, an important feature of the European tradition was the very varied nature of its governmental legacy. Republicanism offered a distinct set of constitutional arrangements and institutions; its classical and modern language and conventions provided a basis for judging the policies of contemporary monarchs. Diderot used the anti-monarchical sentiments of Tacitus in order to criticise modern rulers, and, in the *Voyage de Hollande* (1774), praised the United Provinces as a country of liberty. The *philosophe* Helvétius, a believer in the essential mental equality of all men and in the role of environmental conditioning, expressed a preference for republican institutions in his *De l'Esprit* (1758). In his article on Geneva in the *Encyclopédie*, D'Alembert praised the Genevan practice of burying the dead in a cemetery outside the city, and pointed out that the government rarely used the rack.

Republics and republicanism might have such lessons to offer but did not, however, generally pose a radical challenge. Republicanism existed in a number of ways, but republican states were usually aristocratic and conservative, and most of their intellectuals advocated a traditional constitutionalism. Marco Foscarini, who produced an encyclopaedic study of Venetian culture in 1752 and was to become Doge in 1763, was heavily influenced both by classical models, and by his Jesuit mentors, and was completely aloof from the contemporary debates of the *philosophes*. For most political commentators, republics became less important, a measure of their weakness and decline and of the decreasing favour with which they were generally viewed. Republican governments were accused of being selfish, exclusive and obscurantist. Proposals for reform were defeated in both Genoa and Venice. Britain, rather than the relatively and apparently declining United Provinces, was contrasted with France. In his article in the *Encyclopédie* on republics, Jaucourt claimed that their citizens could enjoy less freedom than the subjects of a monarchy. In 1781 Gustavus III observed:

> The *philosophes* who enthuse over the name of a republic should look at the actual state of the United Provinces. They will see that our customs and the art of war of this century no longer allow these sorts of governments to enjoy the resources that the ancient republics possessed; that since large permanent armies and fleets have been established, a republic which will not dare to compete, for fear of losing its domestic liberty, runs the risk of losing her independence, respect and glory.[4]

Republicanism revived as an issue in the 1770s and 1780s. The creation of an independent United States of America indicated that a new republic could be created, that it could defeat a powerful monarchy and encapsulate Enlightenment ideas. The new state also demonstrated that republicanism did not offer a model only for cities and small states. The Dutch Patriot movement also sought to revive the republic. Republican sentiment contributed to the ferment of political thought that characterised much of Europe in the 1780s. However, it is important to note the traditional nature of most republican views. In the United Provinces, unlike in America, it was possible to seek to adapt the existing system of government, rather than to create a new one. The election of militia officers from the citizenry in the United Provinces was not a novel demand.

Even if rulers acted in a despotic manner, most commentators were unhappy with the idea of rebellion. Notions of national sovereignty were poorly developed in most countries, and little constitutional role was left for the nation, except as represented by the monarch. The extensive authority of monarchs was accepted even by many of their critics, though not in Hungary and Poland where the concept of nobility as nation was strong. The notion of authority being legitimate because it came from God remained deep-rooted, for example in the ideas of Louis-Adrien La Paige (1712–1802), a Parisian lawyer who was a major mid-century Jansenist writer, but to La Paige the king was constrained by his obligation to respect institutions, such as *parlements*, that also had rights.[5]

If divine authority was one source of legitimate power, legal conduct and consent, it was but part of the set of assumptions that constituted paternalism. Notions of paternalism and patriarchalism were widespread at all levels of society and they influenced the response to royal authority. In so far as evidence survives concerning the attitudes of rank-and-file Russian nobles, they expressed a preference for personal and paternal notions of authority. Traditional popular concepts of the king as father of his people and protector of his subjects were reiterated frequently. These notions had a symbolic force that is difficult to assess. Russian court festivals ascribed the metamorphosis of evil into good to the accession of a monarch to the throne. For his coronation in 1775 Louis XVI revived the ceremony of 'touching for the king's evil', laying hands on over 2000 scrofulous individuals in order to use his distinctive royal powers to effect a cure. On the other hand, the ceremony had not been performed in France since 1738, and in Austria sacramental kingship was not favoured by Joseph II. Some monarchs, such as

Frederick the Great, preferred to present themselves as bureaucratic monarchs, servants rather than fathers of the people. Nevertheless, there is little doubt that paternalist and patriarchal views were widely held in Europe. Proprietary notions of royal authority accorded with social customs that gave husbands considerable power and authority over their wives, parents over their children. They also created a bond for those who otherwise had little to expect from the political system. This was brought out clearly in periods of disorder when royal intervention was sought by rioters. Thus in Madrid in 1766, a mob shouting 'Long Live the King', appealed to the traditional royal prerogative of dispensing justice.

An appeal to royal paternalism and patriarchalism could still entail criticism of royal policies. It offered a prescriptive model of royal conduct without any obvious explanation of how the king was to be persuaded to observe it, other than by appealing to his good nature. In Louis XIV's last years a group, among whom Chevreuse, Fénelon, Saint-Simon and Beauvillier were prominent, pressed for a government and society based upon Christian ideals. Their aspirations and plans required an absolute monarch willing to modify the government. They hoped that a revival of co-operation between king and people could be obtained by re-creating traditional consultative institutions, but they still wished to retain ultimate power in the hands of a paternalist king. Appeals to rulers as fathers of their people frequently involved criticisms of royal officials. And yet there is little doubt that notions of paternalism and patriarchalism constituted the 'political thought' of many and that they offered an image of the monarch which left little role for disobedience. God, rather than man, would bring new rulers.

The extent to which peasants were royalists is unclear. Most presumably had only a faint notion of national issues. Nevertheless, there are suggestions that in some regions the peasantry looked to the crown as a source of assistance. During the so-called Age of Liberty (1719–72), many of the Swedish peasants were royalists. In 1723, the Estate of Peasants helped Frederick I in his unsuccessful attempt to enlarge his prerogatives. In 1743 a rising by the peasants of Dalarna against the Diet revealed their royalism with the cry 'better one king than the rule of many'. The importance of pretenders in major Russian revolts is an indication of the royalism of peasant political attitudes. Joseph II's real and still more his reputed attitudes towards serfdom led some Habsburg peasants to see him as a saviour, though his religious policies seemed to many to be a breach of the good kingship they sought.

Another sphere of political thought in which conservative notions were dominant was that of relations between particular communities: local, ethnic and religious. Though some writers might enunciate the idea of the nation, there is little doubt that loyalty to particular communities and the habit of conceiving of loyalties primarily in terms of them, were widespread. A concentration on the works of French writers, especially the *philosophes*, possibly leads to an under-rating of this, for they were mostly metropolitan in their interests and national or international in their commitments. In much of Europe, however, the attitudes of local communities to central government, to each other, and to their internal issues, were the prime constituent of politics and thus, of political thought. A strong sense of locality characterises much of the writing of the period and underlies the political attitudes expressed. The Dominican priest Father Cresp, who wrote a history of the city of Grasse in Provence in 1762, expressed a veneration for the king and a marked Gallicanism alongside his local patriotism.

It is appropriate that the major writer whose work was most conducive to local liberties, the Frenchman Charles-Louis Secondat, baron de la Brède et de Montesquieu (1689–1755), himself was a provincial office-holder, having in 1716 inherited a senior post in the *Parlement* of Bordeaux. He drafted a proposal for the re-establishment of provincial Estates as a partial remedy for France's problems, claiming that those provinces which had retained them were the most prosperous in the country. Montesquieu's work, like that of the other writers of the period, should not be seen in isolation. The early eighteenth century witnessed a debate in France between those who supported what was termed the 'royal thesis' and those who advanced the 'thesis of the nobility'. This debate revolved around different interpretations of French constitutional history, but it was also felt to have contemporary relevance. Montesquieu's major work *L'Esprit des Lois* (The Spirit of the Laws), published in 1748 in Geneva, was in some respects a reply to the abbé Jean-Baptiste Dubos's best-seller of 1734, the *Histoire critique de l'établissement de la Monarchie française*, which argued that the royal authority of the Bourbons represented a return to the situation under the Franks after a long period of noble usurpation.

In contrast, Montesquieu based his assessment of constitutional arrangements and political action on the distinction between despotism and other forms of government. The traditional typology of government, inherited from Aristotle and Polybius, had presented the categories of monarchy, aristocracy and democracy. Offering instead the categories of despotism, monarchy and republic, subdivided into democracy and aristocracy, Montesquieu claimed that the most important distinction was that between despotism and other governments and that, compared with despotism, both monarchy and republic were good forms and might be termed moderate. The quality of these systems rested on their motivating ethos and on their particular institutions. As he had already made clear in his *Lettres Persanes* (*Persian Letters*), published in 1721, Montesquieu had inherited the argument advanced by critics of Louis XIV that freedom led to prosperity, arbitrary power to desolation, and followed the practice of applying this argument to France. Montesquieu, like most writers, presented his political arguments in a wider ethical frame: 'Arbitrary theological moral codes, domestic autocratic rule and lack of freedom in relations between the sexes, oppressive religious institutions, absolute and authoritarian government, and the subjugation of one people by another, all are detested by Montesquieu as manifestations of unquestioned, unlimited, and unaccountable power'.[6] For Montesquieu, despotisms were animated and motivated by baser human drives, particularly fear, ambition and lust, while monarchies were characterised by honour and republics by love of country. Monarchies were distinguished from despotisms by the moderation of the rulers' goals, the restraint of their methods, the legal nature of their authority and actions and the consequent privileges of those who wielded power under the monarchs. These privileges ensured both that they did not tyrannise those under their authority and that they could act as a restraint on the power of the sovereign. Thus intermediate bodies between monarchs and subjects could serve a vital function. Their existence was both the consequence and the guarantee of the legal actions of government. Just government therefore entailed a constitutional pluralism that sought to resolve competing interests through co-operation. For Montesquieu, this constitutional balancing was more important than any specific set of arrangements. He had a strong sense of the constant changes brought about by time in the fortunes of states and the delicate balance between rulers and intermediate powers, and believed that human society, far from being constant, was affected by environmental circumstances such as climate, and social forces such as education, religion, legal and fiscal systems, population size and military institutions.

L'Esprit des Lois was a great success, frequently reprinted and widely discussed. In its first eighteen months it was reprinted 22 times. Montesquieu's attempt to reduce the diversity of governments to order and to bring coherence to political and constitutional discussion accorded with the systematising and schematising spirit of the age. A prominent member of the Bordeaux *Académie*, in which he played a major role in the discussion of scientific experiments and theories, Montesquieu appeared to offer a science of human society. His specific preference for law-abiding governments, mixed constitutions and a separation of government functions among different bodies also accorded with views fashionable in the period. He praised the constitutions of states whose virtues were often more apparent to foreigners than to their own citizens. *L'Esprit des Lois* acclaimed Scandinavia as the home of European liberties, while the separation of powers (executive, legislative and judiciary) in Britain, where Montesquieu had lived in 1729–31, was applauded, despite considerable criticism of the corrupt nature of the British political system by Opposition writers, such as Bolingbroke. Montesquieu's restatement of the traditional concept of mixed government accorded with the views of many contemporaries. For example, the Swedish political thinker Johan Montin, also writing in the 1740s, claimed that governments must conform to the attitudes and needs of their subjects and that they should balance order with freedom. Montesquieu acknowledged his debt to Grotius and Pufendorf, influential seventeenth-century proponents of the school of natural law. Because *L'Esprit des Lois* accorded so well with widely held views, it is difficult to distinguish between its great popularity and its influence. In contrast, Rousseau's *Contrat social* (*Social Contract*), with its preference for direct democracy and the 'general will', rather than for intermediate institutions and sectional interests, was not a great success when it appeared in 1762. *L'Esprit des Lois* was quoted by Beccaria and clasped by Leopold of Tuscany in his portrait by Batoni. Although placed on the Index by the pope in 1751, the book was influential throughout Christian Europe. Montesquieu's ideas rapidly became popular in Hungary, a Latin translation of *L'Esprit des Lois* being sold as early as 1751 in Bratislava. The arguments and vocabulary of the book were invoked by the *Parlement* of Paris, words such as liberty and society making their first significant appearance in the remonstrances of the 1750s and 1760s. Of the 526 articles in the first part of Catherine II's 'Instruction' of 1767 for the deputies to the Legislative Commission, 294 were taken from *L'Esprit des Lois*, though Catherine adapted Montesquieu's arguments to accord with her own views and the particular problems of governing Russia. In 1764 Scheffer, strongly influenced by Montesquieu, proposed to balance the power of the Swedish Diet by increasing that of the crown. Choiseul was not alone in believing in the need for rulers to submit to laws jointly made by the people and their established magistrates. In 1790 the marquis de Noailles,

French ambassador in Vienna, told Kaunitz that a despotic monarchy had never existed because a monarchy was a state whose head 'se dirige par les loix' [directs himself in accordance with the laws]'.[7]

Montesquieu's arguments, however, were not without theoretical problems. Also they had only a limited relevance to the actual conduct of government and were not welcomed by all who considered them. In common with natural-law theorists, 'he gave moral force to what he took to be the principles of human nature and used these values, these natural laws (in both the descriptive and the normative senses of the term) as fundamental criteria for evaluating institutions and regimes'.[8] This led Montesquieu to assume that freedom was good and the rule of law preferable, although, in the preface to *L'Esprit des Lois*, disclaiming any intention of censuring any established institution, he stated that he would offer a dispassionate analysis. Montesquieu's methodology was empirical and functionalist, concerned with evidence and observation, and the combination of this with his moralist's assumptions was more optimistic than practical. The criteria he offered for judging legal actions and for distinguishing between monarchies and despotisms were vague.

Furthermore, Montesquieu's arguments had only limited value for the rulers of the period. In his *De la Politique* (*Of Politics*) of 1725, he condemned selfishness and deceit in government and diplomacy, arguing that they were immoral and futile. Such an approach accorded with the dominant characteristic of much political theorising in the period, being more concerned with the ethics and nature of power than its problems. The concept of separation of powers was not without its difficulties and Montesquieu provided little guidance as to how consent was to be obtained for major changes. It is possible to sympathise with Gustavus III's 1771 observation that the Swedish Diet was 'no pleasant spectacle for any but cosmopolitan philosophers', and to appreciate Kaunitz's complaint in 1750 that the Council of Brabant 'thought themselves interpreter and judge of the laws, even arbiter of the rights and prerogatives of the crown, and sought only to realise the dangerous system of an intermediate power between ruler and the subjects set out by Montesquieu in his *L'Esprit des Lois*'.[9]

The problem of obtaining consent, of organising the political consensus and co-operation within society that all believed to be necessary, in such a way that it facilitated, rather than inhibited, change, was tackled by a number of writers, including Rousseau and Le Mercier de la Rivière. Jean Jacques Rousseau (1712–78), the son of a Genevan watchmaker, was an outsider who was a contributor to the *Encyclopédie*, but became disillusioned with the world of the Parisian *philosophes*. He wrote a number of works that challenged fashionable views, and it is not surprising that their reception was mixed. Voltaire came to regard him as a traitor to the *philosophes*. In two essays written in competitions for the *Académie* of Dijon, a form of patronage and source of fame that was becoming increasingly important, Rousseau examined the relationship between man in his natural state and natural forces, and modern society. In the *Discourse on the Sciences and the Arts* (1749) he claimed that science, technology and culture corrupted society, transforming self-reliance into decadence, and that progress was a delusion. In the *Discourse on Inequality* (1755) Rousseau argued that the development of society added to the differences between individual humans that were natural, new inequalities, especially those related to what he termed the 'fatal' concept of property. For Rousseau, unlike Thomas Hobbes, the state of nature was peaceful and innocent, society the cause of division, strife and the corruption of human nature and natural passions. In two popular didactic works, *La Nouvelle Héloïe* and *Émile*, published in 1761–2, Rousseau argued that moral sense or sensibility was crucial to human conduct and, therefore, education, and asserted the importance of virtue and spiritual awareness, thus diminishing the relative importance of the *philosophes'* central theme, the role of reason.

Rousseau was pessimistic about the causes and consequences of social organisation, and yet also believed that once humans existed in civil society it was possible to develop their best, that is natural, features through creating the right context, especially through an education that took note of what he claimed were their natural virtues. In his *Contrat social* (1762), Rousseau no longer presented the state of nature in as optimistic a light as in his *Discourse on Inequality*. Instead he argued that it was through becoming a social being that man could realise his true nature. However, the form of society was crucially important to the success of this process. Writers before Rousseau who had discussed the idea of a social contract had argued that though sovereignty derived its authority from the consent of the people in a social contract, this agreement, usually ascribed to the remote past, led to a transfer of sovereignty from the people to the ruler. Rousseau stated that no transfer need or should take place, because people could be free if their individual moral will was subsumed in a general will stemming from their retention of sovereignty, 'sovereignty, being nothing other than the exercise of the general will, can never be alienated; and the sovereign, which is simply a collective being, cannot be represented by anyone but itself – power may be delegated, but the will cannot be'.[10] Though he considered the conduct of administration by all the citizens as impractical, he regarded their legislative sovereign power as important and as the source of their willing obedience and thus of the authority of the state.

Nevertheless, Rousseau had a pessimistic view of the capability of most men and advocated a supreme intelligence to create a constitution, presented significantly in a scientific image, 'the lawgiver is the engineer who invents the machine'.[11] Far from being optimistic, Rousseau claimed that the system created would naturally be in a situation of stress, because the governing agency entrusted with administrative authority would seek to increase its power. To ease his pessimistic vision, Rousseau resorted to religion. The persuasive powers of lawgivers are attributed to their ability 'to attribute their own wisdom to the Gods; for then the people, feeling subject to the laws of the state as they are to those of nature, and detecting the same hand in the creation of both man and the nation, obey freely and bear with docility the yoke of the public welfare'.[12] The book concludes with a chapter on civil religion, in which Rousseau praised the joining of divine worship to a love of the law, criticised Christianity for failing to propagate the necessary civic virtues, and called for a civil religion subordinate to the sovereign that would teach the necessary 'sentiments of sociability, without which it is impossible to be either a good citizen or a loyal subject'.

Rousseau's writings pointed to a number of different, sometimes conflicting, conclusions and were interpreted in various fashions by contemporaries and the generation of the Revolution. Disagreement has persisted, not least over the issue as to whether the notions of the general will and the lawgiver had totalitarian implications. It is not surprising that they were thus understood by some of the revolutionaries, such as Maximilien Robespierre. Rousseau disparaged most sources of authority. In the *Contrat social* he condemned monarchy, Christianity, intermediary institutions and the untutored people. In his scheme for a constitution for Corsica, the only country fit to receive laws according to the *Contrat social*, Rousseau expressed a preference for government by an aristocracy of merit. In his considerations on the government of Poland he argued that it represented a distortion of praiseworthy ideals and condemned the 'tumulte démocratique'. In practical terms, Rousseau thought the people required leadership, leadership which could direct the general will, and compensate for their propensity to be misled. As, for him, the general will 'is always rightful and always tends to the public good', and 'if the general will is to be clearly expressed, it is imperative that there should be no sectional associations in the state',[13] the legitimacy of dissenting views and sectional interests was clearly limited. The combination of the notion of the public good, the creation of an ideal republic by the legislator's will, and the critical view of existing institutions and of the public, was a heady one in revolutionary circumstances and was to prove so in France in the 1790s. It could seem to justify both the dictatorship of the self-selected just and their radical use of power in order to transform society. Rousseau offered one course for the achievement of consent: the general will, civic religion and, 'in order that the social pact shall not be an empty formula...the commitment...that whoever refuses to obey the general will shall be constrained to do so by the whole body'.[14] The *Contrat social* was clearly utopian in pre-revolutionary Europe, not only because of its hostility to the Christian churches, but also because Rousseau offered not only a new justification for decisive action by the sovereign body, but also a new location for sovereignty. The *Contrat social* was scathing at the expense of monarchs and monarchies.

The writings of the physiocrats, such as François Quesnay (1694–1774) and the marquis de Mirabeau (1715–89), took greater note of current political realities. They offered a functionalist view, one that advocated reforms in order to create a more prosperous and efficient society. Such notions were not new. John Law had pressed for uniformity in laws, customs and taxes and the equality of all under the law. The marquis d'Argenson, French foreign minister 1744–7, argued that such an equality would increase French power, and he condemned what he claimed was the principal obstacle, the role of the nobility. The physiocrats called for a legal despotism, the monarch being guided by the divinely created natural laws and seeking to ensure their observance, especially the 'natural order' of free economic activity. This entailed unfettered property rights and opposition to privileged groups. There was therefore a fundamental contradiction within physiocracy between the preservation of a powerful monarchy and complete economic freedom. Anne-Robert Jacques Turgot, a contributor to the *Encyclopédie* and an *intendant* who was controller-general in 1774–6, admired the physiocrats. Opposed to privilege, he believed that the *parlements* represented only sectional interests, and that the French government had to be reorganised so that it could be more effective in tapping the resources of society for public welfare. The public interest lay in decisions conformable to reason and thus to natural laws, and consent for such decisions would be more readily obtained by means of a national education system inculcating civic virtue and a hierarchy of provincial representative assemblies based on property-holders.

Notions of legal despotism were based on the idea of the proper use of authority and on the anger of some writers with existing representative assemblies because they apparently did not foster national interests and thus represent the people. They were essentially optimistic in that they believed that a wise prince would be able to discern correctly national interests and would submit freely to the rule of law. They reflected that strong strain of belief in monarchs as political redeemers which can be seen in works like Lord Bolingbroke's *Idea of a Patriot King* (1749), which called for a monarch powerful enough to override parties.

These views were tested by the actions of monarchs. George III's accession in 1760 had been greeted with considerable optimism, but the king found that he was expected by many politicians to obey a set of unwritten conventions that dictated his choice of ministers. The fourth duke of Devonshire, a member of the inner Cabinet, argued that George should retain his grandfather George II's ministers:

> the Duke of Newcastle had united with him the principal nobility, the moneyed men and that interest which had brought about the Revolution, had set this Family [the Hanoverian dynasty] on the throne, and supported them in it, and were not only the most considerable party but the true solid strength that might be depended on for the support of government ... they were infallibly the people that the king must trust to for the effectual support of his government.

George had different views. Having made his favourite, lord Bute, first minister in 1762 and seen him fail to retain his position in the face of bitter domestic opposition, George complained to the French ambassador in 1763 about

> the spirit of fermentation and the excessive licence which prevails in England. It was essential to neglect nothing that could check that spirit and to employ firmness as much as moderation. He was very determined not to be the toy of factions as his father had been and his fixed plan was to establish his authority without breaking the law.[15]

The ambiguity of a number of constitutional points, such as the collective responsibility of the Cabinet and the degree to which the monarch had to choose his ministers from those who had the confidence of Parliament, exacerbated a political struggle that was essentially a commonplace of monarchical regimes, the efforts of a new ruler to take control of the government. It was not until the end of the decade that George found, in the person of Lord North, a satisfactory minister who could control Parliament. George's attempt helped to spawn a critical political literature that condemned his alleged despotic attitudes and policies, a literature that influenced the American response to the government's plan to increase its American revenues. In 1783–4 George engineered the fall of the Fox–North ministry and supported that of the younger Pitt, although it lacked a parliamentary majority.

In their reforms in France in the early 1770s, Maupeou and Terray ignored the argument that the *parlements* were the natural protectors of the people against arbitrary rule and revealed no interest in creating institutions to fulfil this need. Joseph II planned for reform through despotism. A fundamental principle of his *Rêveries*, written in 1763, was the need for 'an absolute power in order to be able to do good for the state'. Joseph stressed the importance of abasing and impoverishing the aristocracy, 'as it is not helpful to have small kings and great subjects who live at their ease without thinking of the state's needs. All men owe the state their services … it is not possible for a state to be happy nor for a sovereign to do great things if they are restrained by the rules, statutes and oaths which the provinces regard as their protection.' In 1789 Joseph informed the Estates of Brabant, 'I do not need your consent to do good'.[16] When Maria Theresa died in 1780, Joseph refused to be crowned in Bohemia and Hungary, both because he did not wish to be bound by the coronation oaths and as a mark of his opposition to the disparate nature of his inheritance and the consequent particularism. Joseph's policies were denounced as despotic by many, including some who had supported reforms. August Schlözer, a professor at Göttingen University who had advocated physiocratic ideas, condemned Joseph's policies in the 1780s as despotic and his journal, the *Staatsanzeiger*, supported the Hungarians who opposed Joseph, many of whom were Schlözer's ex-students or correspondents. Viennese newspapers referred to Joseph as a tyrant in 1786.

The preamble of Gustavus III of Sweden's new constitution, issued after his coup in 1772, declared that the king had tried 'to promote the advancement, strength, and welfare of this realm, as well as the improvement, safety, and happiness of our loyal subjects … the present situation of the country requires an unavoidable amendment of the Fundamental Laws, adapted to the above-mentioned salutary purpose'. The constitution of the Swedish Age of Liberty was dismissed, 'under the name of the blessed Liberty, several of our fellow-subjects have formed an Aristocracy, so much more intolerable, as it hath been framed under licentiousness, fortified by self-interest and severities, and finally supported by foreign powers, to the detriment of the whole society'. The new constitution declared 'the greatest abhorrence to a king's despotic power' and the need for 'a king in power, but bound to the law', though the crucial argument was one common to the *Contrat social*, namely the suspicion of traditional intermediary institutions, 'an Aristocratic government of many, to the detriment of the whole society'.[17] After Gustavus failed to win widespread support at his first Diet under the new constitution, that of 1778–9, where his proposed religious and penal reforms were criticised, it is not surprising that he displayed little interest in his constitutional limitations. In 1788 he attacked Russia, despite the constitutional prohibition on offensive war without the consent of the Estates. The following year, in co-operation with the non-noble Estates, Gustavus enlarged his powers with the Act of Union and Security. In the same year, the main thrust of radical propaganda in France was that the king should ally with the Third Estate against the nobility. In contrast to Gustavus, Louis XVI had to be forced to move in this direction. Gustavus, however, was as dissatisfied with particular constitutional settlements as were Louis's critics. In 1792 he planned another coup to establish a new constitution with a reorganised legislature.

The policies of certain of the rulers in the second half of the century and the currency enjoyed by ideas of a legal despotism might suggest that the greater semblance of ideological cohesion in the first half of the century (at least in comparison with the second half), with the emphasis on the role of the aristocracy, especially when represented in Estates, was under stress. Any emphasis on a matching rise of political radicalism would support such a view. Scepticism is necessary on both counts. Radicalism in this period is not a simple or unitary phenomenon. How far support for abstract notions such as the equality of man should be seen as anything other than rhetorical flourishes is open to question. Belief in an essential equality rarely led to support for egalitarian policies. A 'radical Enlightenment', centred on a number of anti-clerical English and Dutch writers in the first half of the century, has been discerned,[18] but the size of the group was tiny and it is possible that its radicalism has been exaggerated. Utopian writing, as ever, provided an opportunity for presenting different models of society. *Le Naufrage des Isles flottantes, ou Basiliade* (1753), by Morelly, purported to be a translation of an Indian work. Claiming that reason and instinct could be assimilated, it argued that individual desire could be harmonised with collective need by means of a communal life system. Aside from opposing private property, the work also propounded vegetarianism, as good for health and virtue. Two years later appeared another work attributed to Morelly with the significant title of *Code de la nature, ou le véritable Esprit de ses Loix* (*Nature's code, or the true spirit of her laws*, 1755). This advocated communal self-sufficiency and ownership of tools and products, the abolition of financial remuneration and equal education. The abbé Mably, in his *Doutes proposés aux philosophes économistes* (1768), similarly attacked private property.

More influential than such pictures of a better society was the attempt to create better individuals represented by Freemasonry, with its aspiration to educate and improve members through reason and mystical practices and its rejection of the comprehensive authority and teachings of the churches. Freemasonry began in Britain, where the Grand Lodge was established in 1717. The first German lodge was founded in Dresden in 1733. Freemasonry spread rapidly on the continent through the first half of the century, despite the opposition of the Catholic Church, which condemned it, and hostile moves by a number of states, principally Catholic but sometimes Protestant, such as the canton of Berne in 1745. This opposition possibly played a role in the limited support for Freemasonry in Iberia and much of Italy. The first lodge in Vienna, opened in 1742, was closed a year later, although by the end of the 1740s lodges were given a grudging assent in the Habsburg lands, and the first lodge in Bohemia was founded in Prague in 1749. The first lodge in Catholic Mainz, opened in 1765, was closed two years later.

Freemasonry exemplified certain of the characteristics of the age. It was far from uniform in its practices, being divided into a number of systems. Its values reflected the attempt to resolve some of the conflicting aspirations of the period, especially the cult of reason and the appeal of the mystical, esoteric and secret. Its organisation was similarly an uneasy mix of hierarchy and equality. Freemasons professed brotherhood, benevolence and a belief in a Supreme Being. Their religious rituals offered a mysticism that differed from that of Christianity, and Freemasonry was not restricted to the members of any one church. Many leading political, social and intellectual figures were Freemasons, including Robert Walpole, Sonnenfels, Voltaire, Montesquieu, Helvétius, Herder, Lessing and Goethe, as were several rulers, such as Ferdinand of Brunswick, Frederick the Great, Gustavus III and Peter III. It was especially popular in Britain, France, and in Russia in the early decades of Catherine II's reign until Catherine turned against it in late 1779. That year there were more than 2500 Freemasons in Russia, including most of the leading nobles. In 1789 there were about 700 lodges in France. In Hesse-Cassel, where the first lodge was founded in Marburg in 1743, four new lodges were founded in Cassel during the reign of Frederick II (1760–85). Their membership of over 200 included Frederick, most of his senior officials and many of the leading nobles. The majority of members in the two Transylvanian lodges (the first founded in 1767) and the one in Bukovinia were officials or in the army.

Freemasonry was seen by some as a subversive movement, and in the 1790s it was blamed for the Revolution. Austrian bourgeois members were given swords to wear in meetings so that they appeared equal to aristocratic members. Most lodges, however, did not extend their belief in the equality of Freemasons to a wish to make all thus equal. The aristocratic membership of numerous lodges, many of which admitted only nobles, doubtless facilitated this process, for nobles were accustomed to a language of equality among themselves that neither extended to non-members nor compromised the differences between members of the order. Most lodges excluded women and Jews. The Transylvania and Bukovinia lodges included Saxons, Hungarians, Germans, Catholics, Lutherans, Calvinists and Greek Orthodox, but no Jews, women or peasants. Far from being radical, many European lodges appear to have been essentially sociable. In Toulouse, most Freemasons were devout Catholics, as concerned with precedence, ritual and hierarchy as any other corporate body. If some Dutch lodges in 1787 were pro-Patriot, others were firmly Orangist. There were few Masonic atheists or republicans in any monarchical country, and no evidence that their beliefs arose from their Masonry, nor can their membership of a secret subgroup within society demonstrate that they were at odds with that society. Despite the papal bulls of 1738 and 1751, many French clergy were Freemasons. In Strasbourg the canon-counts of the chapter belonged to the Candeur Lodge and 5 per cent of the membership of the Toulouse lodges were clerics. In Bordeaux numerous local clergy had Masonic links. Regular (monastic) clergy also participated.

Masonic ideas, the belief in man's ethical autonomy, capacity for moral improvement and common rationality, the exclusiveness and yet universal pretensions, had potentially radical connotations. However, Freemasonry was no more radical in practice than several other aspects of European thought in this period, such as the republican tradition or the community of Christian believers. Rather than concentrating on the possible implications of theories or the fears of opponents, it is more appropriate to consider the actions of supporters. In 1777, when Kaunitz recommended action against Charles of Lorraine, the governor of the Austrian Netherlands, who was attending lodges openly, Joseph II came to his uncle's defence, writing of the lodges that 'their innocence is recognised by all sensible persons in society'.[19] Nevertheless, Maria Theresa subsequently sought to suppress the lodges in this area, while in 1785, suspicious of possible links with Prussia, Joseph placed the lodges in the Habsburg lands under police supervision. Lodges were ordered to produce membership lists quarterly, a step that led many Freemasons to resign.

The 1780s saw an increase in concern about the possible radical consequences of Freemasonry, a concern that stemmed essentially from fears aroused by the Bavarian Illuminati. This was one of a number of quasi-masonic organisations that arose, reflecting the popularity of the masonic form and ideal and the absence of any effective supervisory body to control a movement that was both universal and prone to schism. While the Freemasons were increasingly divided between a number of organisations, of which the most important were the Lax and the Strict Observances, two important secret movements emerged. The Rosicrucians, who claimed, like the Freemasons, medieval and older antecedents, practised cabalism, astrology and sorcery. They were most influential in the 1780s both at the court of Frederick William II of Prussia, who was a member, and in Russian Masonic circles which came under their influence. The Russian Rosicrucians were directed from Berlin, Novikov publishing occult and Rosicrucian works in Russia, and attempts were made to recruit the heir to the throne, Grand Duke Paul. Already concerned about the Freemasons, Catherine II was worried about the possibly revolutionary sympathies of the secret societies, and in the early 1790s their activities were limited, Novikov being imprisoned without a formal trial in 1792.

The Illuminati were founded in Bavaria in 1776 by an Ingolstadt academic, Adam Weishaupt, in order to 'help reason gain supremacy'. Weishaupt hoped to influence rulers to use the schools and churches to educate the people in order to foster a number of concepts associated with some Enlightenment circles, such as natural religion, although most of the rank-and-file members did not share his bold plans. Many of the members were nobles and officials and some were clergymen, and though the movement preached the reduction of social barriers, it practised social segregation in appointing to senior positions in the Order. The suspicions the Illuminati engendered arose not so much from their beliefs, which were more utopian than revolutionary, as from their secrecy and their deliberate attempt to increase their influence in Bavaria, a state which was generally resistant to fashionable opinion. Just as the Rosicrucians were seen in Russia as representing Prussian interests and the Freemasons in Naples were regarded from 1775 as opposed to Tanucci, so the Illuminati were viewed in Bavaria as supporters of Joseph II, who shared their anti-clerical views and wished to take over the state. In 1785 all secret societies, including the Freemasons and Illuminati, were banned by Karl Theodor of Bavaria and in 1787 evidence that purported to demonstrate a plot by the latter was published. The Bavarian foreign minister wrote of 'that abominable sect, which directly seeks to destroy religion and healthy morals and to overthrow the thrones of rulers'.[20] Officials who were members were dismissed and the treatment of the Illuminati revealed the fears and recourse to police action and persecution that characterised several of the states of the period.

In an age bred on notions of conspiracy, it is not surprising that Freemasonry and other movements aroused acute fears. They did so in part precisely because so many of their adherents were prominent members of society, or were believed to be so. The principal domestic threat to the states of the period was seen to lie not in social or political revolution by those excluded from the privileges of rank, but in conspiracies by those who enjoyed power and influence: rulers, officials and nobles. Rebellion by the excluded could be suppressed, even if it was on the scale of the Pugachev rising. In contrast, coups such as those of Gustavus III in 1772, and to a lesser extent, 1789, and the so-called Maupeou Revolution of 1771 in France, and major alterations of policy by rulers or royal favourites such as Struensee in Denmark, led to important constitutional and political changes. In this context it is easy to appreciate why the views of the elite and developments that might change them should give rise to concern.

It is also clear how unhelpful rigid terms such as conservatism and radicalism are in this setting. Clearly much depended on the nature of the individual political system. If the wish by members of the elite to alter the terms of the relationships of power and authority within any given system is considered, then it is possibly inappropriate to use the words 'conservative' and 'radical'. Most constitutions were unwritten, a set of agreements and conventions that reflected contrasting traditions and gave rise to conflicting assumptions. Far from this being the product of a 'failure' to create clearly defined constitutional monarchies, it was the consequence of the existence within each society of several sources of power and the need to define their authority accordingly. As the definition varied by state, attitudes that in one country might seem radical could in another be seen as conservative.

The wish to overthrow political systems in contrast must be seen as radical, but a striking feature of the period is the limited nature of effective radicalism. The views of the vast majority of the indigent are obscure, not least because of the illiteracy of many of them, but there is little evidence of a widespread revolutionary consciousness. Much popular action involved opposition to what was seen as the unfair exercise of power by, for example, raising prices, increasing tithes or enclosing common lands, rather than any attempt to challenge the lineaments of authority. Popular demonstrations, such as the gatherings of the 'popolo' outside the Pitti Palace in Florence in 1710–11, crying out for 'Bread and Work' and singing menacing songs, were a common, though by no means invariable, response to periods of hardship and episodes of apparent misgovernment. The 'political thinking' they represented and gave voice to was essentially traditional, revolving around notions of good kingship and good lordship, and there is little sign that it changed during the period.

At all social levels, there was no need to develop a new ideology in order to justify opposition, violent action or revolution. The inheritance of political, social, ethical and religious beliefs and conventions that can be described as political thought was a very heterogeneous one. It included notions that were potentially subversive, such as the distinction between a tyrant and a monarch, and conventions that justified resistance. There was much literature in the 1700s criticising Louis XIV, a lot of it produced by Huguenots. Such writing circulated inside as well as outside France. In Toulouse, for example, many critical pieces appeared illegally. One, of 1711, compared Louis XIV and Nero, the values of classical republicanism serving, as so often, as a basis for hostile remarks.

The contemporary Rakoczi rising in Hungary rejected the direction of Habsburg policy and appealed to a traditional sense of national identity and liberties. In 1704 the rebels addressed a proclamation to foreign observers, justifying their rebellion in terms of the inviolability of the contractual agreement between the ruler and his subjects and the right of subjects to resist unjust rulers. In 1705 a rebel assembly at Szécsény formed a Confederation of Hungarian Estates for Liberty and called for the re-establishment of lost liberties. In 1707 the Habsburgs were formally dethroned. The attitudes that were to lead to opposition to Joseph II and the arguments that were to be advanced to justify it were present already in the early 1700s. Frederick the Great's description of the ruler as 'the first servant of the state' can be traced back to antiquity.

Traditionalism in political argument was a common feature of the period, unsurprisingly so in the light of the time-honoured issues that gave rise to dispute, especially new fiscal devices and relations between central governments and the localities, the relatively fixed nature of administrative and political structures, institutions and conventions, particularly those associated with the position of the monarch, and the widespread respect for precedent. A memorandum of 1765 noted 'The Tyroleans ... do not easily submit to new impositions, and sometimes threaten that if they are ill used they will throw themselves under the protection of their friends the Swiss', who had won independence from Habsburg rule. A habitual complaint was voiced in Turin in 1781, 'The People murmur openly at the want of economy of the Court'.[21]

Many themes in political debate were far from new. The recovery of the 'Gothic constitution', supposedly overlain by absolutism, was a commonplace of pre-Revolutionary debate in France. Especially at the level of elites, the political arguments that were advanced also took note of theoretical developments, quoting and paraphrasing, not always accurately, the views of such writers as Montesquieu. In France there were increasing references to concepts of individual liberty and the rights of the nation. The radical Patriot pamphleteers who attacked the Maupeou government in the early 1770s used Rousseau extensively, quoting at length from the *Contrat social*. There is little evidence, however, that these writings changed attitudes, and most of the opposition to the Maupeou Revolution stressed corporate pride and the legitimacy of the *parlements*' judicial rights. The preamble to the manifesto renouncing the allegiance of the Austrian Netherlands to Joseph II, drawn up in October 1789 by Hendrik van der Noot, included passages from the work of the French materialist philosopher and *encyclopédiste*, baron d'Holbach, but it was based on the 1581 resolution renouncing allegiance to Philip II.

At the popular level, it could be suggested that tensions increased in periods of economic distress, without implying that they were simply due to them, and that increasing population pressure and general failing living standards led to a rise in tension from the 1760s. What was possibly crucial was not the depth of a particular crisis, but the sense that crisis was imminent and that human agents were responsible. In much of Europe 1709 was a year of chronic food shortage and near famine but, as in the difficult years of the early 1740s, there was relatively little collective protest, possibly because people were too weakened by hunger to engage in violent physical activity. The attempt by the French government, under physiocratic influence, to reorganise the grain trade in the 1760s and 1770s increased the habit of ascribing harvest difficulties to human agencies, both because of the actual consequences of the policy and because writers, both pro- and anti-government, encouraged the notion that human intervention could and did affect the situation. Turgot's free-trade regulations of 1774, ending the need for producers to sell in particular markets, were blamed for rising grain prices in 1775 and this led to widespread riots in which grain was seized and forcibly sold at what was regarded as a just price, a practice known as *taxation populaire*. Certain French newspapers blamed European food shortages on government policies and the greed of the wealthy.

Yet, such views were not new, and the principal problems posed by food shortages, indigence, disorder and a fall in government revenues, were also far from novel. If the French political crises of the early 1770s and the 1780s coincided with periods of economic difficulty and were doubtless exacerbated by them, it is worth noting that other states survived severe periods without comparable political crises. The financial and public order consequences of economic crises called for good leadership and a relatively united elite response. It was the absence of these that led to serious difficulties in France in the late 1780s, rather than the economic crisis itself. The British traveller and doctor John Moore wrote of Frederick the Great's Prussia, 'A government, supported by an army of 180,000 men, may safely disregard the criticisms of a few speculative politicians, and the pen of the satirist.'[22] He could have added food riots and peasant uprisings, but not serious division among the elite.

When elite views are considered, it is apparent that the notion of ideological cohesion in the first half of the century and of a subsequent increase in tension faces serious difficulties. If all could agree that power had to be wielded justly and could only thus be exercised properly, there was nevertheless wide room for disagreement over the propriety of particular policies. The German poet and academic Christoph Wieland presented in his political novel, dedicated to Joseph II, *Der goldene Spiegel* (1772) an enlightened monarch ruling his model state in tranquillity and prosperity and governing in a constitutional fashion. Like most writers, he gave little thought to the problems of war and finance. The importance of the concept of justice made suspicion concerning the motives of monarchs, ministers and institutions important. It also made it difficult to accommodate new government requirements, and, therefore, to help tackle crucial problems such as finance. These difficulties existed at the beginning of the period and made the task of achieving co-operation between central governments and elites a troublesome one.

Politics

The spirit of sedition and discontent is general.
(Hanoverian envoy in St Petersburg, 1718)[23]

The cabals and intrigues... not only filled the town and the palace but the whole country, every party wishing to name the successor.
(British envoy in Turin on the ill health of the first minister, 1781)[24]

I hate all reforms.

(Second earl of Fife, 1792)[25]

Even though many of the channels and arenas of modern demo-cratic politics, such as elections, assemblies and parties, existed only in parts of Europe, it would be wrong to dismiss the notion of political activity in this period. Politics, the struggle for and exercise of power, existed at many levels. In addition, even in states that lacked any mechanism, however imperfect, for obtain-ing the views of those who were not in government, the idea of public opinion existed, even if the definition of the public whose views were of interest was often so limited as to prohibit public politics. In 1746 the Senate of Venice forbade political discus-sion. In Russia people were not allowed to assemble in public or private without the permission of the police and all announce-ments not approved by them were banned.

Where political views could be expressed, they were supervised. The most important method was censorship. The scope and effectiveness of this varied greatly. It was extremely lax in Britain and the United Provinces, where most works that were not markedly seditious or anti-religious could be published. Though censorship was stricter elsewhere, there was an easing of regula-tions in the second half of the century in a number of states including Austria. The list of condemned works placed on the Index by the papacy became a poorer guide to what Catholics could not obtain. In France, where 'the authorities allowed, encouraged, and indulged in abuses of the law',[26] Malesherbes was in charge of censorship in the 1750s and early 1760s and he was tolerant, permitting the publication of critical works by, among others, Diderot.

The comparative decline of censorship helped to facilitate the growth of the periodical press, both newspapers and journals. The English Licensing Act lapsed in 1695. The first successful London daily newspaper began publication in 1702, and by the end of 1792 there were 16 daily papers published in the capital. The annual sale of newspapers in England in 1713 was about 2.5 million. The figures for 1750, 1775 and 1801 were 7.3, 12.6 and 16 million. There were 57 German newspapers published in 1701, 94 in 1750, 126 in 1775, and 186 in 1789. The press increased in circulation and numbers of titles in countries where it was already established, such as France and the United Provinces, and spread to other states. Though readership was primarily urban, peasants read newspapers especially in Germany where papers such as the *Bole aus Thüringen* (*Messenger from Thuringia*: 1788–1816) were produced especially for them. The quantity of news and information provided was considerable, and the press played a major educational role. The *Deutsche Zeitung für die Jugend und ihre Freunde* (*German Newspaper for the Young and their Friends*) used footnotes to explain where places mentioned were and to discuss institutions such as the *Parlement* of Paris (14 July 1786), provided biographical details, for example an obituary of Frederick the Great, and described events abroad, such as, in 1786, the trial of Warren Hastings and the Diamond Necklace affair in Paris.

Though in some states newspapers occasionally criticised governments bitterly and were condemned accordingly, the *Nouvelles Ecclésiastiques* being denounced by the archbishop and *Parlement* of Paris in 1731–2 and the *Duende de Madrid* (1735–6) investigated by the Spanish government, it would be wrong to present the press, or the culture of print in general, as hostile to authority. Print was a medium not a message, but if there was any general bias it was, with conspicuous and numerous exceptions, towards those values summarised by the term Enlightenment, values endorsed and pursued by many monarchs and officials. Outside France, Britain and the United Provinces, many newspapers owed their foundation to official support. The bi-weekly *Mannheimer Zeitung* was both founded in 1767 and transformed into a four-times-a-week paper in 1792 with the backing of the elector Palatine. Governments sought to use print to diffuse acceptable new ideas and educate the population and also took advantage of its capacity for more pointed political propaganda.

Arguably the major change in the period was the sheer number of publications embodying some elements of a new stance. The quantity and range of reading matter altered. There was a general infiltration of more detached and critical views of social arrangements, a greater entrenchment of comparative perspectives that drew on the Orient, the ancient world and utopias, and a far greater dissemination of published works. This represented a change of viewpoint towards more numerous and more open speculation.

The greater awareness of the possibilities of print was part of a more widespread concern to influence public opinion, the opinion of those interested in politics. Public opinion developed as a category in political thought, although there was uncertainty about what constituted such opinion and about its impact on high politics. The open discussion of many political issues became more important and acceptable in most states. The publication of proclamations, manifestos and declarations, though far from new, increased during the century. In periods of tension, such as the 1730s in Britain and the early 1770s in France, the production of favourable material was actively sponsored by political groups and attempts were made to enlist the support of those who were not formerly represented in the political system. Their views could also be expressed and wooed in songs, demonstrations and placards. These could be very hostile to the government and therefore were sometimes illegal, as in Paris in the 1750s and 1770s and Amsterdam in 1754. In Dresden in 1750 posters were secretly put up attacking the bad administration of the Saxon finances. In Parma the year before, new taxes had been condemned in a similar fashion. The burning in effigy of unpopular ministers such as Walpole and Maupeou, and the development of political clubs and dinners, were features of the public world of politics in periods of tension.

A high level of political activity was not generally sustained, and a striking feature of the public politics of the period in most states is its episodic and reactive nature. It was most marked and government concern about it was strongest when new policies were introduced in sensitive areas, such as new taxes, the regulation of the grain trade and the redefinition of relations between central government and regions with strong particularist traditions. It is not surprising that public opinion often appeared opposed to the pretensions and policies of central governments. However, it is more accurate to see public opinion as hostile to change, both because of its unsettling effect and because of the specific innovations proposed.

Public politics was most sustained in states with powerful representative institutions where a relatively large number of people were directly represented: Britain, the United Provinces, Sweden and Poland. Despite the complaints of Opposition spokesmen, the British political system was not solely a matter of patronage and corruption. As there was never enough patronage to satisfy all the claims made upon the government, it was a dangerous tool, engendering expectations and encouraging politicians, both within and outside government, to strive to increase their influence. The role of patronage and corruption should not be exaggerated even in Scottish constituencies and those with small electorates, both generally held to be corrupt. Their electors often displayed considerable independence and some Opposition MPs were always elected. Common interests and the need for organisation, both to win elections and to further views once elected, encouraged the development of political groupings. In country seats gentlemen of a given persuasion subscribed to support their cause electorally. In London in the 1710s political clubs super-vised electoral efforts. The foundation of political and quasi-political groups was further encouraged by the importance of a number of ad hoc issues and by the role that the political system permitted for lobbying and extra-parliamentary activity. Thus the successful agitation for the repeal of the 1763 cider excise involved the circulation of petitions, subcommittees reporting to a large standing committee, and salaried clerks. The success-ful opposition of various local interest groups to Pitt's unpopu-lar fustian tax of 1784 led to the development of a General Chamber of Manufactures. Successful lobbying in and out of Parliament thwarted Pitt's Irish Trade proposals of 1785. The Yorkshire Association, a movement for constitutional and politi-cal reform, pressed unsuccessfully in 1780 for more frequent elections and consequently, it was hoped, more responsive and less easily corrupted representatives. The association, with its county committees and conferences of delegates, created its own national political structure.

The extent to which the major political groups of the period should be called parties is a matter of controversy. It is arguable that British eighteenth-century political parties lacked, to some degree, an identifiable national leadership, an organised con-stituent membership and a recognised corpus of policy and prin-ciple around which to cohere and which could serve to link local activists to national activity. The relationship between political behaviour in the localities and at Westminster varied widely, both over time and with reference to the type and size of constituency. Not all constituencies were dominated by two-party politics, and in some, divisions within one of the parties were paramount. The centrally directed planning that characterised the Foxite cam-paign for the general election of 1790 was unprecedented. Lacking the institutional organisation of their modern counterparts, eigh-teenth-century parties were essentially organised in terms of fam-ily interests in many of the localities. The role of family interests was particularly prominent in Scotland. Proposals such as that of the earl of Findlater to the earl of Kintore in 1780, that they should co-operate to overthrow the electoral influence of the duke of Gordon, were a staple of political activity.

Two political parties, the Whigs and the Tories, can be clearly distinguished in the first half of the century, though the Whigs, during their long period in office in the reigns of George I (1714–27) and George II (1727–60) were often divided between those in and out of office. As some of the Tories were Jacobites (supporters of the exiled Stuart dynasty), the party was regarded as disloyal by many, including crucially George I and George II, and the Tories suffered proscription, being excluded from most senior posts in government, the armed forces, the judiciary and the Church. The effective collapse of the Jacobite option at the battle of Culloden (1746), the mid-century process of seeking to conciliate and comprehend opponents within ministerial ranks, and the expectations concerning the future behaviour of the heir to the throne, first Frederick, Prince of Wales, and then the future George III, along with the actual behaviour of the latter, helped to produce major changes in the political system. The cohesion and identity of the Tories were seriously compromised, and the two-party system was replaced in the 1760s by a number of essentially personal political groups, the rivalries of political leaders and the changing preferences of George III making the situation very unstable.

As much as any ruler who did not have to face a powerful representative institution, George was determined to reject the politics of faction, to thwart the efforts of unacceptable politicians to force their way into office. As did other rulers, George found it most difficult to create acceptable relationships with senior political figures at his accession, when he had to persuade politicians who had had a good working relationship with his predecessor, and those who had looked for a dramatic change, to adjust to the wishes of a new monarch, and when the country encountered major problems. The first difficulty was largely responsible for the ministerial instability of the 1760s and was not resolved until Lord North became first minister in 1770. The second, in the shape of a lack of confidence in the ministry to win the American war, led to the fall of North in 1782 and a period of marked ministerial and constitutional instability until Pitt the Younger, a first minister enjoying royal support, won the 1784 general election, beginning a period of stable government under his ministry that lasted until his resignation in 1801.

The Swedish Diet of 1680 increased the power of the crown at the expense of the Estates and the aristocratic Council of State. Charles XI and Charles XII were absolutist rulers. Charles XII breached constitutional conventions in 1697 by swearing no coronation oath, giving no Accession Charter and placing the crown on his head himself. He never summoned the Estates and his policies overrode the law and aroused discontent. In the province of Livonia some of the nobility, arguing that, as their ancestors had called in the Swedes, the Estates had the right to veto any changes in the government, gave their allegiance to Augustus II of Saxony–Poland in 1699, in return for his guarantee of Livonian autonomy and freedom of (Protestant) worship. In Sweden the reaction against Charles XII's policies led, after his death without an heir in 1718, to the creation of a parliamentary regime, the constitutions of 1719 and 1720 giving power to the Estates in the so-called Age of Liberty.

Lasting until overthrown by Gustavus III in 1772, this political system was characterised by strife between the four Estates (nobility, clergy, burghers, peasants) and by a struggle for power from the 1730s between two parties known as the Hats and the Caps. By the early 1740s the parties had become effectively organised and by the 1750s they were continuing to operate during the intervals between meetings of the Estates. The parties disseminated propaganda and sponsored tours of the provinces by active politicians, and carefully organised their members who were elected to the Estates. Though there was no mass politics, the electorate, with whom sovereign power lay, was relatively large. The parties and party system of the period have been described as modern 'even if the pattern of franchise and representation was dictated by the increasingly anachronistic four-estate system', though with the important exception 'that organisation on the level of the local constituency (except for Stockholm) and the ability of the parties to dominate electoral contests on that level were either rudimentary or nonexistent'.[27] The parties were patronage structures divided by their quest for office and their attitude to foreign policy, rather than representative of any fundamental divisions in society. The high aristocracy and the old and new nobility were equally divided among the two parties, while, in each, many of the senior members belonged to a small number of families tightly linked by intermarriage.

The Swedish Age of Liberty came to an end in 1772 for different reasons than the ending of Polish independence with the partitions (1772–95) and the collapse of Dutch internal peace in the mid-1780s. However, the political institutions of each of the states were affected by corruption, the demands of sectional interests and the difficulties of operating the constitutional systems in order to devise acceptable policies, as well as by partisanship and increasing popular disillusionment and discontent. In Sweden many of the nobles, worried about the views of the other Estates, connived at Gustavus's coup, but the political system was also weakened by unpopularity, being regarded as venal and arbitrary. France supported the coup.

The Polish constitution, with its elective monarchy and Diet that placed a stress on unanimity by the principle of the *liberum veto*, made it difficult for any monarch to increase his power and compensate for the weakness of the central government. Provincial government was run by dietines – assemblies of nobles.

Rulers were obliged to win the support of some of the greater nobility and of their private armies, administrative systems and patronage networks, the sources of most power in the state. Shifts occurred in the relationship between the king and the greater nobility as in 1750 when Augustus III, instead of balancing the gift of posts to his allies the Czartoryski family, and his rivals the Potockis, awarded them to the former. These, rather than changes in governmental policy, were the crucial developments in Polish politics.

This process involved rulers in struggles among the nobility and compromised their wish to increase their authority. In addition, the nobles' search for patronage and support was not constrained by national boundaries. They were willing to seek and accept foreign support. In combination with Russian military strength, this ensured that the last Polish king, Stanislaus Poniatowski (1764–95), had either to co-operate or to compete with his former lover Catherine II, to whom he owed the throne, if he wished to rule. Poniatowski sought to reform the constitution and strengthen government institutions, but his schemes eventually were both vitiated by foreign intervention and helped to provoke it. The establishment of a Permanent Council in 1775 increased the effectiveness of the central government. The postal service, police and financial administration were reorganised in the 1770s and 1780s. The constitution of 3 May 1791 provided for a hereditary monarchy and a strengthened executive and abolished the *liberum veto*. An army of 100,000 was stipulated and local commissions of Law and Order and of Civil and Military Affairs were decreed to provide the basis of a stronger administration.

It is not clear how this would have affected Poland, but it was unacceptable to Catherine, and Russian troops invaded in May 1792, shortly after revolutionary France declared war on Austria. The old Polish constitution was reimposed, but the weakness of Catherine's Polish protégés, Russian and Prussian desire for territory and their fear that Jacobinism would take root in Poland led to the Second Partition in 1793. The rest of Poland became a Russian protectorate, the reduction of the Polish army to 15,000 men helping to provoke a revolt in 1794. Its suppression was followed by the extinction of an independent Poland with the partition of the remaining territory (1795).

In the same year the French overran the United Provinces, bringing independent Dutch republicanism to an end, because when the country was refounded as an independent state after the Napoleonic wars its constitution was monarchical. The new king, William I, was the son of William V of Orange, who as stadtholder of all of the provinces of this federal state (1751–95), had represented the monarchical component of its mixed government. Constitutionally a stadtholder was the servant of the provincial Estates, who elected him and from whom he received his commission. Generally without any formal role in the legislative process, a stadtholder shared executive power with the Estates. Under William III, stadtholder of most of the provinces between 1672 and 1702, William IV, stadtholder of all of them from 1747 until 1751, and William V, his son, the stadtholder appointed many urban magistrates and certain provincial officials from lists submitted by the local authorities. Assistance from about fifty locally-based lieutenant-stadtholders permitted William V to run a fairly comprehensive system of political influence that was powerful across most of the country: in the 1770s over all bar rural Friesland and certain of the leading towns of Holland, especially Amsterdam. As the prince of Orange, besides being stadtholder of all or most of the provinces, was normally appointed captain- and admiral-general of the state, he was also influential in military affairs, though the size of the forces and sometimes their conduct, especially that of the navy, were under the control of the representative institutions: the provincial Estates and their federal institution, the Estates General.

For much of the century Dutch history could be presented as a clash between the Estates and the stadtholders, but the situation was more complex. In several provinces there was considerable co-operation between them, and strong opposition to the position and pretensions of the Orange family was concentrated in the province of Holland. Though bitterly divided, this was the wealthiest and most powerful province, and it played the major role in the reaction that followed the death of William III without children in 1702. His five stadtholderates were left vacant and, when William IV was elected to the first of these, Gelderland, in 1722, the others adopted formal resolutions not to alter their existing form of government. It was only 25 years later that he was elected by them, and made captain- and admiral-general and that all the posts were made hereditary in his family, so that his death in 1751, with an infant heir, was not followed by a reaction comparable to those that had followed the deaths of William II (in 1650) and William III.

This transformation was due to popular disillusion with the evident corruption of the ruling oligarchies and their inability to deal with national problems, and to the international situation in 1747 when, as in 1672, a French invasion led to a rallying to the prince of Orange, seen as the saviour of the country. Popular riots and British support for William IV led to a collapse of will among his opponents. Among the mass of the people, for example the sailors, dockers and carpenters of Amsterdam and Rotterdam, the Orange cause was popular. Political consciousness was not restricted to those who had a stake in the oligarchical political system. The changes of 1747 were followed not only by attacks on the houses of tax farmers and excisemen, but also by agitation by bourgeois urban groups, such as the *Doelisten* of Amsterdam and their Leiden counterparts, for less oligarchic municipal government.[28] As in Britain, traditions of political activity, a comparatively permissive attitude towards political debate on the part of government, and a political press, ensured that the public world of politics was not restricted to those who were formally represented in the political system. In addition, throughout Europe many who were not thus represented in national politics could play a role, formally or informally, in the local political worlds of town, village and corporate and communal institutions.

The constitutions of countries were often a poor guide to the nature and concerns of their governments. In all states public opinion had to be taken into account by government and political figures. The French government was not alone in using informers to report on opinion in the capital city. In Florence in 1739, and probably in most other years as well, the government sent spies to coffee-houses and other public places to report on what was being said. Similarly, even in monarchical states with powerful representative assemblies, the royal court was an essential forum of politics and source of political activity and division. Politicians sought to use the decisions of the assemblies to influence court attitudes. As most states were monarchies, it is not surprising that royal favour was crucial and that government policies were generally viewed in the light of the royal support they were known or believed to enjoy. Political groups commonly centred on senior members of the royal family and circle. Thus the Neapolitan courtiers who intrigued against Tanucci in the 1770s were led by the queen. Ministers had to be courtiers.

The role of policy in the politics of the period related essentially to issues of patronage and foreign policy, the latter being linked often to the former. A recent study of the Russian elite in the early decades of the century noted that

> operating on the fundamental premise that all power rested ultimately in the autocrat, elite politics during this period centred on the competition for position, influence, and imperial favour between patronage groups based on kinship and patron–client relations. These groups rarely evaluated one another in terms of policy issues; rather their political world was divided into 'friends' and 'enemies'.[29]

Thus, in the political crisis of 1730 following the sudden death of Peter II, when Anna was only accepted as tsarina upon conditions, and these conditions were then reversed, the issue at stake was less the nature of the Russian constitution than the identity of those who would wield power. The Supreme Privy Council demanded that Anna should rule with the advice of the Council and not make war or peace, marry, name a successor, grant titles or estates, make use of state revenues and make senior appointments without their consent. These demands have been seen by some as designed to create a noble oligarchy, but the opposition to them was led by prominent aristocrats excluded from power. There was no tradition of common action and neither a leadership nor an institutional framework that could provide noble cohesion. If the power of the Russian nobility was effectively represented throughout the century by groups of individual families, linked by kinship and patronage, these families sought imperial favour and had to operate in a political world made insecure by the mortality of monarchs, uncertainty over the succession and the role of favourites. Throughout Europe knowledge about the views of the sovereign and links to him were crucial. Power rested on circumstances as much as on institutions.

Two qualifications to the picture of elite politics centring on the source of patronage – the monarch – with few issues bar the disposal of patronage, can be suggested. Towards the end of the century, some monarchs arguably became less patrimonial in their attitudes. In contrast to Maria Theresa, who had made no distinction between affairs of state and dynastic concerns, Joseph II insisted on carefully distinguishing between state finances and his own private property. The institutionalisation of pensions, so that they were no longer dependent on the grace of a monarch, could be regarded in the same light as could the stress by rulers such as Frederick the Great on service to the state by all, including the monarch. Officials in certain states such as Baden began to argue that they should administer them in the interests of the general welfare. The benefit of the community, rather than monarchical *gloire*, played a large role in official propaganda. However, the importance of the notion of service to the state was already apparent in several countries at the beginning of the century, especially in Russia where Peter I used phrases such as 'common interest' and 'common interest of the state'. In practice, authority remained personalised in all monarchies, the clear patterns of bureaucratic behaviour having little impact in the senior ranks of central governments, where factionalism, patronage and the peremptory intervention of the monarch remained important. Those in the top four ranks in the Russian Table of

Ranks in the early decades of the century referred to their years in public affairs as 'service' or 'service to the sovereign', and not as 'government service' or 'state service'.

The second qualification relates to the extent to which the interest of some rulers in what were in their eyes reforms, but should possibly be more impartially described as changes, created a politics of issues by arousing a range of opposition, even from those not normally well informed, concerning the policies of central government, and producing topics of contention that could not be resolved by the methods used to deal with patronage disputes. The major source of discontent arose from attempts by rulers to increase the share of the national resources they obtained through taxation by raising tax rates, ending exemptions, improving the information available on sources of wealth and intervening in economic affairs. This was a problem both in major states and in minor ones, such as the prince-bishopric of Münster in the 1770s. The financial imperative also played a large role in administrative reorganisation and in redefining relations with representative and other institutions. Thus, the maintenance of privilege and the retention of liberties were at stake. In some situations, such as that of Hungary in the late 1780s, the pace of change sought by the central government and the circumstances affecting the response to its demands were such that the political nation, those interested and involved in politics, was dominated by the issue of how to respond to the changes, but more usually the response was patchy and affected by cross-currents of patronage, particularism and other disputes. This did not reflect any failure to grasp the systematic reform programmes of the governments of the period, but, rather, arose from the ad hoc nature of government actions. The improvised and relatively unsystematic quality of government policies and their implementation is clear even for leaders usually credited with seeking major changes, such as Joseph II and Pombal, and for those whose internal power was considerable, such as Frederick the Great. Developments could be very uneven both geographically and between different branches of administration. The attitude of individual states was often inconsistent, because governments were under conflicting pressures, were tempted to follow lines of least resistance, and were directed by ministers who did not share the same views and whom only firm royal leadership could unite. The attitude of the French government to the *parlements* and to its financial problems was a classic instance of this. One reason for Maupeou's confrontation with the *parlements* in 1770 was the wish to undermine Choiseul's chances of obtaining taxes for war with Britain.

Pombal was in a stronger position in Portugal in the 1760s than either Choiseul or Maupeou were in France, and his policies could be radical, as with his expulsion of the Jesuits, secularisation of the Inquisition, education reform and commercial strategies, but many had to be modified to suit local circumstances. Although when Pombal was able to give problems his complete attention the government performed with efficiency and achieved results, such oversight was not always possible. Furthermore, dependent on royal support, Pombal confronted the central problem that faced *ancien régime* reformers, that of perpetuating the reforms he had initiated. When José I died in 1777, Pombal's position became untenable.

Although across Europe the results achieved by government were generally less than the aspirations for change, and the declared goals were frequently misleading, the process of innovation was itself important. For whatever reason, past arrangements were declared unsatisfactory and effectiveness was held to lie in remodelling and novelty. If the principal intentions of governments – international strength and internal stability and co-operation – were generally traditional and their commitment to existing social systems was strong, the methods by which many sought to achieve their aims involved the disruption of traditional practices and the modification of established methods. Administrative and financial innovations were not a new departure, but, in several states, the pace of change increased in the first half of the century, possibly in response to the major strains produced by the wars of the period 1688–1721. The extent to which new departures produced a sense of dislocation, uncertainty and grievance varied. *Ancien régime* Europe was less static, stagnant and uniform than it might appear, and yet many of its cultural and social suppositions testified to a strong commitment to the principles of tradition and stability. The balance between acceptance and discontent, co-operation and opposition, varied by individual and group and depended on circumstances, including the political skill of the ruler in matching his policy with the assumptions, expectations, resources and problems of his subjects and with their institutions. As a result, there was no common government or political response to particular difficulties or periods that have been discerned as years of crisis, such as 1768–74. If there was a dynamic relationship between the specific situations which stimulated attempts to introduce changes and the ideas which shaped these initiatives, it varied depending on national circumstances and political skills.

There are signs of a widespread, if often slight, increase in the size and activity of central governments. This was certainly the tendency, though from very different bases, in Russia, Poland, Prussia, Austria, Spain, Britain and France. Prussia was transformed under Frederick William I into what was, by the standards of the age, a well-organised and efficient state. The number of officials grew in most large states, the administrative aspect of government becoming more important than its judicial function. The 'progressive replacement of administrator-judges by administrator-technicians and managers was one of the essential characteristics of the administrative monarchy. Until mid-century the word administration was only used in French as part of a phrase but thereafter it began to be used to denote a combination of agents, officers, procedures and public interest objectives.'[30] The creation of a separate bureaucratic caste with its own service values opposed to local vested interests has been discerned in the Milanese and Vienna under Joseph II.

The widespread increase in the effectiveness with which both new and traditional government methods were applied in the large states, combined with economic growth, accounted for the greater strength of these states in terms of financial and military power. Co-operation between rulers and elites also played a crucial role in this process and this aspect of government and politics invalidates any analysis that sees the century in terms of greater state power over society. This was applicable, and then only in part, to countries ruled by foreign governments. Instead, the underlying social and political realities of partnership in government and the control of society between rulers and the elite explain not only why an increase in the power of many states took place, but also why it did not lead in general to acute political strife, especially in countries with a succession of able monarchs. The relationship was a complex one, requiring sensitivity and management. To a certain extent, the problems that affected two of the largest states, France and the Habsburg dominions, in the late 1780s reflected the absence of adequate leadership. Joseph II tried to provide too much leadership, and Louis XVI did not offer enough. The breakdown of co-operation between rulers and elites created not only serious issues of constitutional and political conduct, but also the need for institutions and practices through which political interests could be expressed and gain support. In Hungary, the Austrian Netherlands and France a new political world was created, one where public politics played a major role and where constitutional innovation was increasingly seen by some as necessary and acceptable. Nevertheless, a profound ambivalence about the notion of legitimate opposition and the practice of politics as an acceptable struggle for influence between competing interests was inherited from the pre-revolutionary political culture. These were still stigmatised as factious and disruptive, if not conspiratorial. The ideal of unity persisted, as did the belief that it could be obtained, given good will. The harshness with which those of dissident opinions were to be treated in most of Europe in the 1790s was a product not only of the fears and enthusiasms of the period, but also of earlier attitudes.

15   The Revolutionary Crisis

The coming of revolution

The Hague is like Paris in the time of the Fronde.

(British envoy in The Hague, 1787)[1]

Popular assemblies were dangerous only when Princes did not know how to manage them; and on my remarking that the manner of transacting the business of the Swedish Diet, in a committee in which His Majesty could overawe and direct debates, was a particular advantage to him, he replied that this would be a great disadvantage to Louis XVI.

(British envoy in Stockholm reporting comments of Gustavus III, March 1792)[2]

In the last chapter, features that reflected and sustained stability earlier in the century, such as the importance of co-operation in the political system, the limited influence of radicalism, and the dominance of traditional patterns of beliefs, views, expectations and practices, are stressed. More generally, trade and the spread of the money economy are seen as compatible with privilege, rather than as necessarily sapping the *ancien régime*. It is reasonable then to ask why a major revolution brought war, disorder and fear to much of Europe in the 1790s. The French Revolution, whose beginning is commonly dated to the storming of the Bastille, the Parisian fortress-prison that symbolised arbitrary royal power, on 14 July 1789, was only the most prominent challenge to established authority in the last two decades of the century. Other important episodes included the political strife in Geneva in 1781–2, the rebellions against Joseph II in the Austrian Netherlands and Hungary, and the Irish rebellion of 1798. In Russia, there were major disturbances in 1796–8; urban and peasant uprisings that were attributed to the impact of radical ideas.

If the 1770s are included, then the Pugachev rising in Russia, the American Revolution, and the peasant revolts in some of the Habsburg dominions can be added as major challenges to established authority. The Bavarian envoy in Vienna wrote in 1775, 'it appears that the spirit of revolt has become universal'.[3] The number and seriousness of the rebellions of the period have led to it being described as an Age of Revolutions. Discerning

507

common themes in the varied rebellions, some scholars have argued that they were related, all aspects of a 'democratic revolution' or an 'Atlantic revolution' against the authority and power of the privileged.[4]

This argument can be questioned on a number of grounds. Certain other periods of three decades also witnessed major challenges to established authority. The half century 1720–70 saw few serious violent internal challenges to the rulers of the period, although George II's power was seriously shaken by the Jacobite rising in Scotland in 1745–6. However, the years 1688–1715 included, before 1700, a successful coup supported by an invasion in England, civil war in Scotland and Ireland, and an uprising in Catalonia; and, after 1700, civil war in Poland and Spain, a Jacobite rebellion in Scotland, and major uprisings in Hungary, Moldavia, the Ukraine and the Cévennes region of France. The Hungarian rising against Joseph II was no more serious than that of 1703–11. Comparable features have been discerned in some of the clashes of the earlier period,[5] although arguably these claims are no more persuasive than those for the 'Atlantic revolution' in the last decades of the century.

Archduke Albert, the husband of Joseph II's sister Maria Christine, appointed with her as joint governor-general of the Austrian Netherlands in 1780, in succession to her uncle Charles of Lorraine, wrote from Brussels in 1787 that 'the number of religious enthusiasts and those whose heads are heated with notions of patriotism is very great' and referred to 'this age of delirium and universal frenzy'.[6] This was far from being the case, although authorities everywhere were apprehensive that discontent would turn into rebellion. There was some loss of institutional confidence, but most European regimes were resilient enough to survive. Much of Europe was not affected by insurrections in the last decades of the century. This was true, for example, of Scotland, most of the Empire, most of Italy and Switzerland, and Iberia. In addition, many disturbances and disputes can be seen best as aspects of any complex eighteenth-century society, rather than as evidence of an Age of Revolution. In the case of England, the major disturbance of the period, the Gordon Riots in London in 1780, was largely a violent anti-Catholic demonstration spawned by alcohol and bigotry, rather than radicalism. Similarly, Cardinal Boncompagni, the governor of Bologna in the 1780s, was unpopular with the local nobles for traditional reasons: because he had introduced papal troops into the town and made changes in its government. The coup that removed Struensee in Denmark in 1772 was an example of violent court politics, rather than a product of national political consciousness.[7]

It has been argued recently that 'the crisis of the *Ancien Régime* was precisely and fundamentally one of outworn institutions whose inertial power was the force impeding the reforms that were eagerly sought both by *philosophes* and by those who were experiencing the realities of a changing economic life'.[8] How far this argument is appropriate for France is unclear: most of the leading ministers of the 1780s, especially Necker, Calonne and Brienne, were far from averse to innovation. The thesis is inappropriate for much of Europe. The Danish economic and social reforms of 1786–97, such as the limitation of landlord rights over peasants in 1786–8, are evidence of the vitality of *ancien régime* government in this period. The 1780s were a decade of administrative change in a number of states, including Britain, and where crisis occurred, it was more commonly a violent response to governments and rulers seeking change and believed to be desirous of more. This was the case with America in the 1770s, Hungary and the Austrian Netherlands in the 1780s, and Sweden, where Gustavus III was assassinated by disaffected nobles in 1792. Much depended on how change was sought. In America, Hungary, the Austrian Netherlands and Sweden consultative bodies tended to be excluded and innovation thus seemed despotic, in means if not end. In France an attempt at consultation was forced on government and then mishandled.

If the rebellions and disturbances of the period are seen as the consequence of economic difficulties or social structures, then it is appropriate to ask why these did not create disorder in other areas suffering from comparable difficulties and confronting similar issues. The crucial distinguishing feature could rather be seen as one of political circumstances and government skill, which would qualify the idea of a general crisis. In addition, many of the issues causing social tension were scarcely new. In most of Europe, such as Iberia, Piedmont, England, the Empire and Switzerland, the entrenched oligarchies continued to remain relatively homogeneous. There were groups knocking on the doors of power, some of whom were willing to appeal for French support in the 1790s, but there is little sign that they were especially numerous or that their opposition betrayed profound social tensions. In Piedmont professional and non-noble townsmen expanded their landowning during the century, but it does not appear that this caused marked social tension. In France there was less homogeneity among what was a larger elite than that in Piedmont, and signs of a less close correlation between wealth, status, power and nobility in France than existed in other large states, such as Austria; but, if so, and such features are difficult to compare, this was not new, and there is also evidence of the emergence of a society of 'notables' offering such correlation.

Opposition to the rebellions of the period was not limited to those in authority. Loyalist movements, whether in America in 1775–83, England from 1792, or Naples in 1794 and 1799, could attract considerable support. In the Austrian Netherlands, the Tyrol, Portugal, Russia and Spain, opposition to the French invasion took on the aspect of a religious crusade, capable of mobilising popular opinion on a wider scale than the revolutionaries were able to do. Many of the nobles leading the Hungarian opposition to the Habsburgs changed their attitude because of their fear of the possibly contagious consequences of the French Revolution. In May 1792 in the Diet the nobility offered military and financial aid to support the war against France. The extent of loyalist and counter-revolutionary sentiment throughout Europe suggests that the impact of radical ideas and revolutionary pressures, social, economic and political, was less universal, automatic and popular than the notion of a general crisis would suggest.

The language of ministerial tyranny, popular virtue and the justice of rebellion circulated widely. The earl of Selkirk wrote to a fellow Scottish peer in 1787: 'Lord Cathcart stands now a candidate solely upon ministerial interest, and in real opposition to the endeavours of the many Peers who are striving to rescue the Peerage of Scotland from the most disgraceful subjection and oppression of Ministerial Tyranny, under which they have been sunk so long.' But he went on to ask for his support in an election, not a revolution.[9] Initially the French Revolution appealed strongly to the aristocratic opposition in Sweden, which saw it primarily as the overthrow of a royal despotism. However, opponents of Gustavus III's alleged despotism did not need to look abroad to justify their position. The traditions of Swedish representative and aristocratic constitutionalism provided an appropriate vocabulary and ideology. Gustavus's assassin defended himself at his trial by accusing the king of having violated his contract with the nation. His young noble supporters espoused social equality and popular sovereignty and praised the French Revolution. The bulk of the noble opposition, however, did not share these views and were shocked by the assassination.

Traditional political assumptions and arguments were also prominent in other countries where rebellions took place. In Hungary and the Austrian Netherlands national and provincial liberties were foremost, and radical ideas, although present, received little support: 'the majority of the politically active residents of Brussels identified their interest with the preservation of the ancient regime. A few intellectuals espoused the Jacobin cause, but they could not make a revolution on their own'.[10] In the duchy of Limburg, where Joseph II's Edict of Toleration had proved very welcome to the large Protestant population, the Austrian reconquest was popular, and the Austrians rewarded the liberation from what they called the 'Brabant tyranny' of the rebels by strengthening Third Estate representation in the Estates. Despite the loss of their fiscal immunity, the Luxemburg nobles rallied to the Habsburgs in the crisis.

In Britain and America, it was not inappropriate that those who opposed George III's governments in the 1760s and early 1770s saw themselves as preserving traditional liberties, although in America the situation changed as a consequence of the failure to settle the crisis, and new freedoms were asserted. After the gain of legislative independence by the Dublin Parliament in 1782, extra-parliamentary agitation in Ireland was of limited importance for the rest of the decade. This reflected the weak and divided nature of this agitation and the recovery by the British government from the precarious position that had led it to concede this independence. The Irish agitation, demands and methods of the 1790s reflected, as in a number of other countries, the effects of the French Revolution, although the circumstances resulting from the military challenge of France were arguably more important than her revolutionary ideology, and the French invasion force in Ireland during 1798 was disgusted to discover itself the ally of a fervently Catholic population.

Municipal autonomy, federal republicanism and hostility to the House of Orange were powerful political and constitutional traditions in the United Provinces, and municipal coups, urban disorder and the creation of unofficial citizen militias were customary means of procedure in periods of instability. Opposition to William V, especially in light of his ambiguous stance during the Fourth Anglo-Dutch War (1780–3), and traditional republican sentiment, combined to produce the Patriot movement of the 1780s. As with the agitation of the late 1740s, its main support came from the lesser bourgeoisie, and not from the wealthy urban oligarchs, the Regent class. The Amsterdam Regents were interested in limiting the power of the stadtholder but, like their colleagues elsewhere, were unhappy about the direction of the movement. Bourgeois Free Corps were formed to lend force to the overthrowing of Orangist municipal and provincial governments. William's constitutional rights in numerous municipalities and provinces were abolished and the prince had to leave The Hague in September 1785.

Rather than seeking to create a unitary state, the Patriots sought to follow the American example of republican federalism with an extension of political rights, although, at a meeting of the national federation of Free Corps in Utrecht in 1786, the idea of a representative assembly of the whole 'Netherlands People' was discussed. Dutch political thought and action had changed. Whereas during the 1747 Orangist restoration there had been scant interest in reforms at a level above that of the individual province, in the 1780s there was more understanding of a national political culture and a mass participatory politics.

Like the Americans, the Dutch Patriots faced substantial internal opposition and received French political and financial support. However, the opposition was stronger than in America, the Patriots being weak in a number of provinces, and the French promise of military assistance proved an illusion in 1787. In addition, the Patriot movement had not sufficient time in which to establish itself, and when foreign intervention came, it took the form of the hostile Prussian army, one of the most professional armies in Europe, its invasion based on her neighbouring Rhenish provinces, while no other states distracted Prussia. She was supported by Britain with a naval mobilisation, pressure on France not to act, and intervention in Dutch politics. The Free Corps proved no bar to the Prussians. Many Patriots fled abroad and the Orange order was restored, guaranteed in 1788 by a Triple Alliance with Britain and Prussia.

External action also proved decisive in both Geneva and Liège. In Geneva agitation against the ruling oligarchy was far from new. In 1782 the non-citizen residents seized power, although taking great care to maintain the established institutions and to respect legal procedures.[11] This had little effect on the neighbouring powers that guaranteed the constitution. Although Zürich abstained, France and Berne, joined by Sardinia, besieged the city and re-established the old constitution. In Liège, where the bourgeoisie had seized power in 1789 during an economic depression, Prussian troops restored the old constitution in 1790.

Demands from those excluded from power were not restricted to these areas. They were an established part of municipal politics throughout Europe. The Common Council of London had often sought to restrict the authority of the Aldermen. In Capodistra, a town in Venetia, an attempt in 1769–71 by the 'people', supported by some dissident nobles, to gain representation in the council, controlled by a small oligarchy, was resisted and failed due to the unrelenting attitude of the Venetian government. The events in Geneva, the United Provinces and Liège in 1781–90 were not unprecedented. They reflected traditional tensions and aspirations in these areas. However, the majority of large European towns did not experience comparable developments.

The notion of a widespread 'Democratic Revolution' of which events in France formed only a part can be questioned. Nevertheless, the struggle for American Independence did have a major impact in Western Europe. Although far away, it was cast in universal terms. Furthermore, the success of the American Patriots suggested that change was not only possible and desirable, but could also be achieved through violence. Far from revolution leading simply to anarchy, it could create something that was new and worthwhile.

Crisis in France

Without a doubt the consequences of the French Revolution, its success in creating a new constitutional, political, ideological and religious order, in defeating domestic and foreign opponents, and in bringing change to other states, were of fundamental importance in European history. That does not make the origins of the Revolution of comparable importance and uniqueness. It is not surprising that nearly all German newspapers devoted more space in 1789 to the Austro-Turkish war than to events in France. Many of the problems affecting France in the late 1780s were far from novel or unique. Earlier crises in eighteenth-century France also entailed appeals to public opinion, ministerial instability, court faction and unpredictable outcomes. Earlier in the century, the classic ministerial techniques of negotiation, bluff and raising the stakes could also swiftly convert confrontation into crisis. Royal brinkmanship had always risked a slide into ever deeper chaos. The collapse of the political regime in the summer of 1789 can therefore be explained in traditional terms, but that was not true of what replaced it. The escalation of domestic political conflict in 1789 was out of proportion to the gravity of the issues.

The political impetus for constitutional redefinitions and innovations in France in the mid-1780s came largely from the government. Serious financial problems led many ministers to support the idea of constitutional change in return for help in coping with them. An Assembly of Notables comprised of leading figures nominated by Louis XVI assembled in February 1787, but refused to accept the proposals from first Calonne and then Brienne that the taxation system be reorganised, and that both a universal land tax, and provincial assemblies elected by landowners, be introduced. Instead, influenced by suspicion of the crown fabricating and remodelling institutions to suit its purposes, that stemmed from the Maupeou coup of 1771, the Notables sought government economies, and assemblies that were virtually autonomous, instead of being simply bodies for consultation and collaboration. They insisted on the calling of an Estates General, which had last met in 1614, and also on the opening of government finances through annual publication of the budget and accounts.

By the end of 1787 political opposition ensured that the streamlined absolutist monarchy envisaged by reforming ministers was no longer an option, and economic and fiscal problems ensured that a multi-layered crisis developed: of the economy, and of state finance and credit-worthiness, and of the very process of government.[12] The political failure of the Calonne and Brienne ministries to devise an acceptable political and financial solution led to a governmental loss of initiative and the decision in August 1788 to postpone problems until an Estates General could be convoked in May 1789.

Possibly no acceptable solution could have been devised. It was difficult to take those who had little if any experience of the problems of central government into either confidence or a limited degree of partnership, and to persuade them to employ their new-found role in coping with difficult circumstances. It was far easier for them to press demands for greater power, and to voice the suspicions and fears that arose from the divided court, unstable ministries and rapidly changing policies of the period. Possibly the situation would have been eased had France gained international prestige, but the humiliating *débâcle* of her Dutch policy in 1787 was followed by diplomatic neglect, most conspicuous in the failure to prevent the outbreak of war between her allies, Austria and Turkey. Had France fought the Prussian invaders of the United Provinces and lost in 1787, then the crisis could have come sooner, although it might have been easier to adopt financial palliatives in wartime. Joseph II harmed his internal position by his defeats at the hands of the Turks in 1788. However, the success of the Austrian army in 1789 laid the basis for Leopold II's successes in negotiating peace and resolving internal problems. The contrast in October 1789 between the delirious celebrations with which the Viennese greeted the news of the capture of Belgrade and the forced transfer of Louis XVI and the court from Versailles to Paris after the invasion of the palace of Versailles, is a reminder of the political value of success and the way in which it was easier to obtain through victory than through internal policies.

Louis XVI was not helped by his inability to manage court faction, including difficulties with his brothers and his cousin, the duke of Orléans, the premier prince of the blood. The radical Orléans (Philippe Égalité) helped to undermine Louis's position and was eventually to vote for his execution. From the other extreme, one of Louis's brothers, the count of Artois, opposed any diminution of monarchical authority. The serious divisions in the royal family helped to weaken the court, another traditional theme. The monarchy had also been tarnished by a series of scandals, especially Marie-Antoinette's involvement in the fraudulent Diamond Necklace Affair of 1785–6.[13]

The elections to the Estates General early in 1789 increased political participation, tension and expectations. In each electoral district the three orders (Clergy, Nobles, Commoners) separately drew up *cahiers de doléances*, lists of grievances which they wanted redressed. They sought to clarify the constitutional nature of the French monarchy and its relationship with the legal rights of its subjects. Guaranteed rights, representative government, a reformed church, and taxation only by consent were clear demands, and the political pivot of the new order was to be the powers of an Estates General and of provincial Estates, both of which were to meet regularly. Decentralisation was a central demand, but radicalism was limited: separation of powers, not republicanism, was sought, and there was little interest in the abolition of the nobility, monasticism, urban and provincial privileges and tithes.

Nevertheless, the content of the *cahiers* was less important than their existence. From a financial crisis, the whole governmental and political structure was called into question. The Estates General was expected to reform the state in conjunction with the monarchy. The elections and the *cahiers* created new links between an emerging public political world in the localities and the metropolitan arena of national politics. Local deliberations on national political concerns took place against a collapse in many areas of government authority. Serious economic difficulties played a major role in the breakdown of order in many towns and in much of the countryside in 1789, creating a threatening and violent context that made the control of military forces and stores a more critical issue as the crisis escalated. Peasant disturbances created pressure for the abolition of feudal dues without indemnity.

The summer of 1789

When the Estates General convened at Versailles on 5 May 1789, it reflected the distribution of political power in France. There were no peasants or artisans among the representatives of the

Third Estate and only 1 per cent were manufacturers. In contrast, 12 per cent were merchants, 25 per cent lawyers and 43 per cent office-holders. Whether the Estates General could have produced an acceptable constitution is unclear. There was much good will in the spring of 1789 towards creating a new political understanding, but the government was unable to work with it. Lacking political skill and an understanding of developments outside the court, Louis XVI failed to grasp the opportunity to create and guide a new consensus, possibly an unattainable goal, though arguably some other monarchs would have made a better effort.

Louis's opening speech was interrupted by repeated cries of *Vive le Roi*. In the first session, Necker pressed the case for reform, but division between the three orders, especially over the voting arrangements between the Noble and Third Estates, replaced good will and optimism by suspicion and fear. Division over the issue of common voting, a measure that would lessen aristocratic influence and that was supported by Necker but not pushed strongly enough by him, or separate voting, by Estate, which would enable the Clergy and Noble Estates to outvote the Third Estate, was serious from the outset. The Third Estate refused to accept the system of orders, and on 10 June 1789 voted for the common verification of credentials.

Heady oratory, pressure of circumstances and a growing sense of crisis led the Third Estate on 17 June to declare themselves the National Assembly and to claim a measure of sovereignty as the only elected representatives of the people. The government countered by planning a 'Royal Session' to reassert the authority of Louis XVI. The preparatory prohibition of any meetings by the Estates, however, led the angry deputies, wrongly concluding that a dissolution was intended, to assemble on 20 June in an indoor tennis-court and to pledge themselves not to disperse until reform was complete and the constitution of France was clarified. Eventually held on 23 June 1789, the Royal Session was a failure. Support for the king was ebbing, Louis XVI's preferred reforms were too late, and the Third Estate refused to disperse. Louis backed down, while public order collapsed in Paris. On 27 June the king bowed to the crisis and instructed the Clergy and Noble Estates to join the National Assembly. It became clear that constitutional reform would not be painlessly achieved. The Estates General were fulfilling royal fears, while Louis XVI's apparent shifts of attitude increased concern about his intentions.

Political crisis coincided with a food shortage. Midsummer was always a period of difficulty in the eighteenth-century economy: the period before the new harvest was that in which food stocks were at their lowest, concern and rumours about the food supply at their most acute. After the poor harvest of 1788, grain prices climbed in the second half of 1788 and continued to do so into 1789. Necker had sought to employ governmental controls over the grain trade in order to keep the volatile population of Paris quiet: it was affected by widespread unemployment in the industrial sector and had already rioted on 27–8 April 1789. This led to shortages in other provinces, producing bread riots across northern France in May 1789, and although the situation was eased by imports, uncertainty led to stockpiling. On 14 July the price of grain peaked in Paris, and the Bastille was seized in an outburst of popular action. In the countryside, peasants refused to pay seigneurial dues and tithes and began to attack *châteaux*.

Grain prices were only one factor in the cauldron of mounting chaos. On 11 July Necker was dismissed by Louis and replaced by a ministry under Breteuil whose intentions are unclear. Traditionally it has been argued that Louis intended to reassert royal authority by force, only to be forestalled by rebellion in Paris, but it has been suggested that Breteuil sought a settlement to the crisis through negotiations with the National Assembly.[14]

These tentative negotiations were rendered redundant by the popular uprising in Paris. Anger at the Royal Session combined with anxiety about the troops massing near Paris. On the night of 12–13 July, 40 of the 54 customs-posts around the city were burnt down. After the Bastille was violently seized on 14 July, during a search for weapons designed to help resist military attack, Louis was advised that he could not rely on his troops to suppress the Parisians, who had rallied to the support of the National Assembly. Even the military deserted the crown. On 17 July his brother, the count of Artois, the leading opponent of reform, later Charles X, left Versailles for the frontier. The same day, Louis visited the Hôtel de Ville to announce that Necker had been recalled the previous day, and that troops were withdrawing from Paris.

It was widely believed that this marked the success, and thus end, of the revolution. However, the thwarting of the royalist 'counter-revolution' and the return of Necker brought neither order nor stability. The pressure for change was too great. The National Assembly, now in charge, began preparing a new constitution. As the taste for reform became stronger, ideas and practices that were central to the *ancien régime* were challenged and destroyed. On 4 August the National Assembly, against the background of widespread peasant violence against their masters in the 'Great Fear', abolished all feudal rights and dues, advancing an ideal of the polity based on the nation itself as a source of equity, a dynamic that required and made possible the replacement of the practice and ethos of privilege by laws common to all. The Declaration of the Rights of Man and the Citizen promulgated on 26 August claimed that men were free and equal in rights, that social distinctions could only be founded on common utility, that the purpose of all political association was the preservation of the rights of man, and that the law was the expression of the general will.[15] The principles of the new order were presented in universal terms.

It is difficult to avoid the thought that if Gustavus III had been in the position of Louis, with forces near Paris in the summer of 1789, he would have acted more effectively. On the other hand, Gustavus was assassinated in an aristocratic conspiracy in 1792, the widespread dissatisfaction with current circumstances that had helped Gustavus in Sweden in 1772 handicapped Louis in 1789, while gaining control of Paris was both more difficult than doing likewise with Stockholm and, in 1789, less the key to effective control over the entire country. The collapse of established authority in France had already made it harder to control.

It was this collapse and the length and intensity of the resulting crisis that was to encourage the development of novel political positions, the radicalisation of the situation, and the participation of many who had not hitherto been accustomed to political office and activity. These reflected not only the opportunities to seize power afforded by the collapse of the prestige and mechanisms of established authority, but also the need to produce solutions to the real and imaginary problems of the period, to re-create authority, and to give force to the new constitution. This proved difficult, and the disorders of 1789 continued: 'Pre-existing problems, such as discontent in the army or religious animosities, acquired a new intensity and form in the highly politicized atmosphere created by the Revolution ... the Revolution ... readily allowed the definition of localized controversies and opposing interests in political terms.'[16] In Lyons, for example, it allowed the silk weavers to attempt to settle scores with the silk merchants.[17] In other places, such as Nîmes, the Revolution gave new life to old rivalries between Protestants and Catholics. More generally, artisans and peasants came to play a role in the political crisis.

The Revolution and its course were not the inevitable consequences of the situation in pre-revolutionary France. Many writers and political figures had felt for some time that major changes were necessary,[18] and many of the ideas of the revolutionary period had been anticipated during the previous decades. However, an obvious feature of much contemporary political commentary in the late 1780s and early 1790s is the sense of unpredictability and the perception both within and outside France that her future was uncertain. If contemporaries ascribed much to political circumstances and chances, it is reasonable to take note of their views, bearing in mind that countries with similar social and economic situations did not experience a revolution other than as a consequence of French conquest. Arguably the failure of military forces, foreign and domestic, to defeat the revolutionaries was the most important distinguishing feature of the early years of the French Revolution, the reason why it did not join so many other European political episodes in oblivion, as with, for example, the contemporary attempt to use a new constitution to create a new, reformed and stronger Poland. Had the duke of Brunswick, the commander of the Prussian army invading France in 1792, pressed on successfully when he encountered strong resistance at Valmy it is difficult to know what would have happened.

The October Days to Varennes, 1789–91: Failure to compromise

I am going to write private truths which might be unpleasant for a royal eye. If this country ceases to be a monarchy it will be entirely the fault of Louis XVI. Blunder upon blunder, inconsequence upon inconsequence, a total want of energy of mind accompanied with personal cowardice have been the destruction of his reign. In this last affair [the Flight to Varennes] ... he ought to have effected his plan or perished in the attempt ... It has always been the fate of this unfortunate monarch that whenever the enemies of his government have begun to suffer in the public opinion he has adopted some measure which has reinstated them ... foreign forces would ... serve only to unite the country still stronger against him and would compel the French to form a good government, who, if left to themselves, would have frittered it away into a nondescript metaphysical permanent anarchy or rather ochlocracy [mob rule]'.

(Earl Gower, British envoy, 1 July 1791)[19]

As ever in a monarchical society, the views of the monarch were an important 'circumstance'. Louis XVI's reluctance to accept reform, including his refusal to assent to the Declaration of the Rights of Man, focused uncertainty and mistrust, leading, in a Paris still affected by bread shortages, to the 'October Days'. Rumours of preparations for a counter-revolution led a Parisian crowd, including many women, to march on Versailles on 5 October 1789. They were determined to bring Louis to Paris. After the Queen's apartments were stormed by a section of the crowd, the king, under pressure, went to the Tuileries Palace in Paris next day. Versailles was abandoned, and, with the volatile metropolis ever more the centre of politics, royal authority and power were exploded. As yet, there was no solid alternative. The aristocratic constitutionalism which had helped to undermine the reforming aspirations of the Calonne and Brienne ministries in 1787–8 appeared increasingly redundant.

The rapid speed of changes in France and the absence of sufficient time, trust and shared views to permit the development of stable constitutional conventions and techniques of parliamentary management, helped to keep the relationship between the royal government and the National Assembly unsettled, but so, also, did differences over policy. Above all, there was a crucial lack of trust, a justified sense that, if he was able to dispense with it, Louis XVI would not accept the dominant role of the Assembly. This greatly weakened attempts to create a liberal monarchy with a constitution similar to that of Britain.

Royal powers were eroded. On 22 May 1790 the National Assembly resolved that the king could not declare war without its approval. There was also continued pressure on social and other privileges and practices. The guilds were abolished in 1789. On 16 August 1790 the *parlements* were replaced by a national system of law courts with elected judges.

The effects of violence and upheaval, the processes of politicisation, especially being involved in a process of change and, also, the formation of political groups, and the need to solve problems of state finance, church reform and administrative and judicial reform, all led to an interacting progression of change and further politicisation. Nevertheless, the Revolution was not a homogeneous and unilinear movement, and instead, developed in fits and starts. By the first anniversary of the storming of the Bastille, many deputies were opposed to further reform and instead more concerned to consolidate and institutionalise gains already achieved. Leadership seemed firmly in the hands of 'moderate' elements: 'the spring and summer of 1790 marked the rise to prominence of the Society of 1789, whose principal objective was to work with the monarchy and bring the Revolution to a close'.[20] The marquis of Lafayette, a liberal aristocrat who had been elected vice-president of the National Assembly and commander of the newly constituted Paris National Guard in July 1789, played a major role in limiting the power of the radicals and charting a moderate path for the Revolution.[21] After the Great Fear, the peasants had been dispersed by the *Gardes Nationales* with considerable effectiveness.

Although a few of the deputies in the National Assembly, such as Sieyès and Volney, had been greatly influenced by radical political ideas, the earlier impact of the radical Enlightenment on the working assumptions of the majority had been limited.

Instead, radical ideas spread as a consequence of the Revolution. This owed much to the extent to which there was a clear social character to many of the factional alignments. The conservative groups were dominated by the privileged, and socio-cultural divisions among the deputies, especially between the nobility and the bourgeoisie,[22] helped to focus and sustain political perceptions. Nevertheless, the absence of a powerful radical ideological drive at this stage of the Revolution is apparent. It is possible that a constitutional monarchy would have been viable if Louis XVI and the conservative aristocracy had been willing to support it. The Flight to Varennes of June 1791 exposed the flaw in the constitutional monarchy, but there were also important differences over policy that were not restricted to Louis and the conservative aristocracy.

These differences focused on the Church. Church property was nationalised and the Civil Constitution of the Clergy of 12 July 1790 made the Church akin to a branch of the civil service and brought sweeping change to an institution that rested its legitimacy on continuity and distinctiveness. Changes included a salary scale and residence requirements for the clergy, a rationalisation of the ecclesiastical map, complementing the replacement of secular provinces by departments, and election of clerics by the laity. Episcopal powers were to be exercised in conjunction with an advisory council. Many of the bishops held liberal political views and had been prepared to co-operate in the National Assembly's work of constitutional reform. Some clerics sympathised with the removal of the governmental role of the papacy in the Civil Constitution. Many clerics, however, rejected the Civil Constitution, often because they were guided by their parishioners. Thus the clerical response in part was an early indicator of opinion at the parish level moving away from the Revolution because it was tampering with religion. Clerical protests led the Assembly on 27 November 1790 to impose an oath on the clergy to support the new order, with dismissal as the penalty for refusal. This divisive step helped undermine support for the Revolution in many parts of rural France.[23]

Disenchantment with and concern about his position within France, and pious outrage at the church reforms, led Louis XVI to heed the advice from his wife and others that he should flee. He intended to escape to Montmédy in Lorraine, near the frontier with the Austrian Netherlands and in an area where the military commander, the marquis of Bouillé, was willing to offer protection, and then to pursue a negotiated restoration of his authority. The emperor, Leopold II, was initially cool about his brother-in-law's plight, but his attitude changed as the situation within France deteriorated, and as it became clear that Louis would try to flee, thus forcing a crisis. If Louis escaped, it would place him in a better position to demand help for counter-revolution, from both within and outside France.

Louis escaped from the Tuileries on the night of 20–21 June 1791, but was recognised at Sainte-Ménehould on the evening of 21 June and stopped at Varennes. Although 100 soldiers subsequently arrived to assist his flight, they were outnumbered by a large and hostile crowd. Louis refused to try to fight his way out, although his troops offered do so. Louis was returned to Paris, the problem of a monarch out of sympathy with developments in his country unsolved. The flight prompted the emergence of republicanism, especially in Paris, and encouraged the radical press to become more extreme and to reject any argument that the revolutionary process should be ended.

From Varennes to War, 1791–2

Tension within France rose as a consequence of the international response to Louis's unsuccessful flight. On 6 July 1791 Leopold II issued the Padua Circular, an appeal to Europe's rulers for concerted action to restore the liberty of the French royal family. Frederick William II joined Leopold on 27 August 1791 in issuing the Declaration of Pillnitz, which was intended to give added force to the principles of the Padua Circular. Louis himself had little choice but to accept formally the new constitution on 13 September 1791. It replaced the National Assembly by a Legislative Assembly that shared power with the king.[24] This did not greatly ease international tension. Instead, signs of French aggression and apparent instability kept the situation volatile. These included the annexation of the Papal territory of Avignon in September, growing calls for war against Austria and the German protectors of the *émigrés* (those who had fled France), and the distrust between Louis XVI and the new Legislative Assembly which followed his vetoing of the decree against the *émigrés* passed on 9 November 1791.

These steps also helped to undermine chances of compromise within France.[25] There were already serious points in dispute. The reform of the Church was a particularly divisive issue, as was the franchise. Radical opposition to the narrow franchise in the 1791 constitution had led to the massacre of the Champs de Mars in July 1791 when Lafayette and the National Guard, operating at the behest of the moderates in the National Assembly, suppressed radical agitation. This engendered fresh hostility. In the autumn of 1791, although they remained important, moderate politicians, such as Lafayette, became less influential, and this further encouraged a move towards more radical positions and a more divided political situation within France. Distrust, both within France and in relations with Austria, helped to lead to war. The declaration of war on Leopold's successor, Francis II, on 20 April 1792, was presented as the just defence of a free people and supported by politicians who hoped that a successful war would rally support for constitutional royalism within France, and by others, pro- and anti-royalist, who imagined that success or failure would serve their ends, by leading to the defeat of the Revolutionaries or by discrediting the monarchy. The republican propagandist Jacques Pierre Brissot and other Girondin leaders sought war as a means to unite the country behind them, with Louis either included in this new unity or clearly identified as its opponent.

The Second Revolution, 1792

The course of the war played a major role in bringing down Louis and the 1791 constitution. The conflict did not initially go well for the French, and on 21 May Frederick William II of Prussia declared war on France. Louis's dismissal on 13 June 1792 of the Girondin ministers appointed on 10 March helped to radicalise his opponents. Marseilles' volunteers marched into Paris on 30 July, singing the *Chant de guerre pour l'armée du Rhin*, the *War Song* now known as the *Marseillaise*, written by Rouget de Lisle. Such volunteers were keen to fight against the enemies of the Revolution, and, increasingly, ready to identify them with the royal occupants of the Tuileries. The creation of the notion of a sovereign will – the Revolutionary people – to which opposition was illegitimate encouraged fervour and the use of force. Five days earlier, the Prussian commander, the duke of Brunswick, issued a declaration setting out the aims of Frederick William II and Francis II – the re-establishment of Louis's legislative authority – and warning that Paris would be subject to exemplary vengeance if the king was harmed.

News of the declaration caused outrage in Paris, helping precipitate the crisis on 10 August in which the radicals seized power and the Tuileries was stormed. The 1791 constitution was overthrown, the monarchy was suspended by the Legislative Assembly, and on 13 August 1792 Louis was in effect imprisoned in the Temple keep. The theory, and, to a limited extent, practice of popular sovereignty was thrust to the fore. Direct action undercut the claims of Assembly and monarchy alike to embody national sovereignty. Revolutionary politicians proved best able to channel and exploit such action. The Legislative Assembly was replaced in September by a National Convention theoretically elected by universal manhood suffrage.

Earlier that month, the surrender of frontier fortresses to the advancing Allied forces had exacerbated paranoia in Paris, leading to the September Massacres there as prisoners were slaughtered for alleged treason. On the 2nd and 3rd all but two of Paris's prisons – full of those arrested on suspicion of treason – were broken into and makeshift tribunals were erected. There were acquittals, but on 2–7 September 1100 to 1400 people were killed. Most were politically innocuous, many common criminals. Over 200 priests were killed. The Massacres helped to stir up European opinion against the Revolution.

Terror at home was followed by a dramatic shift in the military situation. The Prussian advance on Paris was blocked by larger French forces at Valmy on 20 September, Brunswick retreated, and by the end of November Savoy, the Austrian Netherlands and much of the Rhineland had been overrun by French armies. On 19 November the National Convention passed a decree declaring that the French people would extend fraternity and assistance to all peoples seeking to regain their liberty, a principle that was subversive of all international order. Eight days later, Savoy was incorporated into France. The pace and pressure of frenetic change did not abate. On 3 December the decision was taken to try Louis XVI. On 15 December a decree to ensure that the *ancien régime* be swept away in territories occupied by French forces was promulgated. Elections were to be held to create a new order, but the electorate was restricted to adult men ready to swear an oath to be 'faithful to the people and the principles of liberty and equality'. It was anticipated that people thus 'freed' would support and seek 'union' with France.

Absorbed by the trial of Louis XVI, the strains of which made compromise in foreign policy very difficult, and affected by the rhetoric and experience of success, the French government failed to appreciate the impact of its policies and statements on neutral powers, especially Britain and the United Provinces. Negotiations with them in the winter of 1792–3 were hampered by mutual suspicion and incompatible views and principles. Louis was guillotined on 21 January 1793, and by 7 March the National Convention had declared war on Britain, the United Provinces and Spain.

From the Republic to the Terror, 1792–4

French declarations and the debates they sprang from reflected the application of philosophical idealism to domestic government and to international relations. The new society that was being advocated and created in France was designed to burst the mould of the traditional territorial state. The universal aspirations of French policy revealed an unwillingness to compromise with other states. As a result, France was at war for the rest of the decade and this was to be as important in changing France and Europe as the earlier course of the Revolution.

The political context of French Revolutionary warfare provided a frenetic energy to the conduct of war by France. In August 1793 the Revolutionary government issued the *levée en masse*: the entire population could be obliged to serve in the war and all single men between 18 and 25 were to join the army. The distinction between the volunteer professional army and the conscript militia had in effect been ended. Such powers of conscription were not new in Europe, and, particularly as a result of draft avoidance and desertion, it anyway proved difficult to raise the numbers that had been anticipated. However, the armies raised were both larger than those deployed by France hitherto that century, and enabled her to operate effectively on several fronts at once, to sustain casualties and to match the opposing forces of much of Europe. The French war effort owed much to the combination of a large population and a mobilisation of resources made possible by the extension of government power. In 1793–4 alone, nearly 7000 new cannons and howitzers were cast by the French. A large powder factory was founded at Grenelle capable of producing 30,000 pounds of gunpowder daily.

The French had mass and system. The new logistics brought about by the partial abandonment of the magazine system helped the aggressive style of war – both in strategy and in tactics – of Revolutionary armies able to rely on numbers and enthusiasm. Enthusiasm is an intangible factor. It has been argued that the French soldiers were better motivated, and hence more successful and better able to use the new methods. Revolutionary zeal had greatly declined by 1797.[26] Nevertheless, initially at least, Revolutionary enthusiasm does seem to have been an important element in French capability. It was probably necessary for the greater morale needed for effective shock action, for crossing the killing ground produced by opposing fire. Patriotic determination was also important to counter the effects of the limited training of the early Revolutionary armies.

Enthusiasm was important for more than tactics. The outbreak of war increased the paranoia of French public culture and helped the Revolutionaries to associate themselves with France. They demonised their opponents. Waging war by the brutalisation of subjects and the despoliation of foreigners produced resources. The exploitative nature of French rule abroad led to a crucial increase in resources that complemented France's domestic mobilisation, but the exploitation helped to limit the popularity of the Revolution outside France. This encouraged rebellion, and also created within France an atmosphere of expediency in which it became easier for a general to reach for power.[27]

There had been rapid advances earlier in the century, for example in late 1733 by the Russians into Poland and the French into northern Italy. Nevertheless, the pace of war, or in scientific terms, the volume of force, speeded up in the 1790s. If, by 1748, the French under Saxe had overrun the Austrian Netherlands, that had taken several years campaigning. In 1792, although the initial French attempts to invade the Austrian Netherlands failed, an invasion in November met with overwhelming success, and it fell in a month.

Helped by local hostility to the radicalism and expropriations of the French conquerors, the Austrians regained the Austrian Netherlands after their victory at Neerwinden the following year (18 March 1793); but, by the end of 1794, the French had again conquered it. They had also driven the Spaniards out of Roussillon and made gains in Catalonia. Having triumphed in the Austrian Netherlands, the French went on to overrun the United Provinces: in January 1795 Amsterdam was captured.

The superiority in French numbers was important both in battles, such as Valmy (20 September 1792), Jemappes (6 November 1792) and Wattignies (15–16 October 1793), and in offensives, as in Roussillon. Tactics were also important. The characteristic battlefield manoeuvre of French Revolutionary forces, and the best way to use the mass of new and inexperienced soldiers, most of whom went into the infantry, was the advance in independent attack columns. This was best for an army that put an emphasis on the attack. Column advances were more flexible than traditional linear formations and rigid drill. The French combination of mobile artillery, skirmishers and assault columns was potent, an original and disconcerting ad hoc combination of tactical elements matched to the technology of the times and the character of the new republican soldier.

The politics of revolution ensured that systems of command differed from those of the *ancien régime*. There was a more 'democratic' command structure, at least at battalion level. The social gap between non-commissioned officers and their superiors was less than hitherto. At the strategic level, the greater number and dispersal of units meant that command and co-ordination skills became more important, and the French benefited from young, energetic and determined commanders. Careers were open to talent, commanders including Jean-Baptiste Jourdan, a former private, Lazare Hoche, a former corporal, and Napoleon Bonaparte, initially a junior artillery officer from the recent acquisition of Corsica. Those who failed, or were suspected of treachery, were executed. Eight days after the outbreak of war, one French army murdered its unsuccessful commander, Théobald Dillon. Other generals followed. Houchard was even executed for achieving only moderate success at Dunkirk in 1793. Punishment and politicisation ensured that the generals were willing to accept heavy losses among their troops.

Initial confusion was followed by a measure of organisation, as the government struggled to equip, train, feed and control the new armies. This owed much to Lazare Carnot, head of the military section of the Committee of Public Safety. War led to administrative rationalisation, although the process was heavily politicised, not a matter of abstract bureaucratic reform. The process of forming the new armies and using them with success was instrumental in the transition from a royal army to the nation in arms. The way was open for the ruthless boldness that Napoleon was to show in Italy in 1796–7.[28]

The course of the Revolutionary Wars helped mould politics within France, as also did the pace of radicalism and successive searches for order and stability. The Girondins fell in June 1793 as the more radical Montagnards seized power. Based in Paris, especially in the Jacobin Club, the Montagnards competed for power with another radical group, the Hébertistes. Already the principal institutions of revolutionary violence had been established: the Revolutionary Tribunal on 10 March 1793 and the Committee of Public Safety on 6 April. These institutions were focused by the strains of foreign and civil war and by paranoid fears of betrayal. Dictatorship seemed necessary. Once the leading Montagnard, Maximilien Robespierre, a minor provincial lawyer, had been elected to the Committee in July 1793, it launched a fully fledged Terror. This was radical, both in its objectives and in its lower-class connotations, although the cause of the people was also employed to keep them in order. The Montagnards were apt to decry all obstacles as the work of nefarious enemies of the Revolution. The press was curbed, while the Revolutionary Tribunal of Fouquier Tinville handed out summary justice.[29] Victims included revolutionaries no longer deemed sufficiently radical or reliable, especially Girondins and, in the spring of 1794, the supporters of Jacques Hébert and Georges Danton. Danton had become disenchanted with the Terror, while Hébert sought its extension. The Hébertistes were purged in March 1794. Danton and others, like Camille Desmoulins, accused of 'indulgence' were purged the following month.

Royalists were also the target for action, especially in western France where a rising in the Vendée was triggered by attempts to enforce the conscription law of 23 February 1793. Initial success led to brutal repression, including widespread atrocities against non-combatants. There were no limitations in the application of the Terror in the west. In the Vendée, as elsewhere, revolts, like the Terror itself, owed much to local rivalries[30] that were no longer contained by the political conventions of the *ancien régime* and were, instead, exacerbated by the pressures of Revolutionary change. Change was particularly strongly felt in religion and public ideology, as de-christianisation became a central aspect of state policy. On 10 August 1793 the government staged a Festival of Unity and Indivisibility in Paris: Hérault de Séchelles, the president of the Convention, paid tribute to the fecundity of Nature in front of a massive crowd. This was the apogee of a turning to a romanticised Nature as the centre of a religious cult of identity. 'Liberty trees' were a more mundane product of the same tendency. In order to change values, the government sought to encourage state-supported primary education. This was seen as an important means to lessen the influence of the Church. Some success was achieved, and there is evidence that in certain towns, such as Rouen, the majority of children went to school in 1794.

Moves against the Church encouraged hostility to the new order. The 1792–4 ban on Christian practice and the limited toleration permitted in 1795 were unpopular but, nevertheless, took their toll on active and public religious commitment among men in particular. They also had the new patriotism in which to express their beliefs. The army served as a coercive agency of de-christianisation, while, in contrast, women played a major role in sustaining Christianity, both in France and elsewhere in Europe. In some regions, such as the Yonne, the Revolution encouraged strong lay piety. There were illegal celebrations of religious festivals, religiously inspired riots, for example to seize church buildings and religious buildings, and petitions on behalf of religion. In March 1795 the crowd of Auxerre, which was not a centre of royalism, opened the cathedral for worship.[31] In other regions, such as the Vendée, strong piety was linked to more explicitly anti-Revolutionary violence and to support for royalism.

Provincial opposition was not only mounted by Royalists. The purge of the Girondins led in 1793 to a series of revolts, especially in southern France, termed 'Federalist' by the Revolutionaries. Those in Bordeaux and Marseilles were swiftly repressed, but the opposition in Lyons and Toulon was fierce. These revolts overlapped with counter-revolutionary activity, and much of western and southern France was in a state at least close to insurrection from 1792. Particular disturbances arose from a background of widespread instability.

Neither the French nor other people were trusted by the Revolutionary government. Between the creation of the National Convention in September 1792 and its dissolution in the autumn of 1795, no legislative elections took place in France; only at the local level were a few assemblies convened for municipal and judicial purposes. Apart from the abortive Constitution of 1793, the Convention was not prepared to let the people have a direct say in whom they elected as their deputies. Elections offered the possibility of democracy, but the elites thwarted this process with a two-tier procedure intended to filter out popular elements.[32] Instead, the electorate was given an opportunity to participate in two constitutional referenda.

From Thermidor to Napoleon: The failure of the Liberal Republic, 1794–9

Terror achieved its purpose of inspiring fear, but on 27 July 1794 the prospect of fresh purges by Robespierre led to the coup of 9 Thermidor (named from the month in the Revolutionary calendar). Robespierre was overthrown and executed by opponents in the Convention,[33] and a less radical government put in place. The Paris Jacobin Club was closed in November 1794, its provincial branches the following August. The Chénier Law of 1795 brought fresh restrictions on the press, and was followed by the Stamp Duty of 1797. The National Guard, which had been radical from the summer of 1792, became the force of propertied order and helped defeat popular uprisings in 1795. Alongside political reaction, there was a cultural turning towards elitism and against the possibility of a popular culture posed during the Revolution. From 1794 the elite became more clearly the focus of subsidised art and architecture, a process that culminated with the apotheosis of Napoleon.[34] There was also with the Directory a return to fashions in clothes, in reaction to the compulsory virtue and sobre uniformity of the Terror.[35]

Once free of the dominant Committee of Public Safety, the National Convention remained the representative body until it dissolved itself on 2 November 1795 in order to make way for a new constitution and regime, that of the Directory. Although a bicameral legislature and a system of checks and balances were created, real power rested with the five Directors who composed the executive. Domestically, the Directory offered stability. Paris was no longer swayed by the radical *sans-culottes* and the treaty of

La Jaunaye of 17 February 1795 had reduced tension in the Vendée, although peace was not restored for many years.

Continued foreign war, however, prevented any real stability in France. The Directory believed foreign war necessary in order to support the army, to please its generals, and, for these and other reasons, to control discontent in France, not least by providing occupation for the volatile generals, whom they found it difficult to manage. The views and ambitions of many of the generals were not limited to the conduct of war, and many were contemptuous of civilian authority and involved in politics. Pichegru played a role in the 1797 Fructidor coup, by which the Directory purged the chamber of many Royalist deputies and returned to a Jacobin style of politics.

Interest in peace was not pursued with great energy. The Alsatian Jean François Reubell, who was the most influential of the Directors in foreign policy, sought a peace that would guarantee what were presented as natural, and therefore rational, frontiers: the Rhine and the Alps. Such frontiers appeared a counterpart to the redrawing of boundaries within France, as long-lasting provinces were replaced by the new departments and their supposedly more rational boundaries. This rationalisation entailed a significant expansion of French power into Germany and the Low Countries, and was also unpopular in the occupied territories, whose people were exploited in order to pay for the war. Aside from dealing with the massive deficit inherited from the monarchy, the Directory had to support the war. The issue of *assignats* – paper money – had not solved the problem, because the Revolutionary regime could not control its debts. The *assignats* lost value in the face of serious inflation.

Victories led to pressure for further conquest, in order to satisfy political and military ambitions and exigencies. The French did not push all before them. The Austrians proved tough opponents, especially in the Austrian Netherlands in 1793 and Germany in 1796. The Russians were to show impressive staying-power and fighting-quality, both in 1799 and subsequently. Further afield, Napoleon Bonaparte's victories over the Mamelukes in Egypt in 1798 are a less than complete account of French effectiveness. It is as pertinent to note the failure of French forces to recapture newly-independent Haiti in 1802–3: 40,000 French troops, including Napoleon's brother-in-law Charles Leclerc, died, the vast majority as a result of yellow fever.

The French were driven out of Haiti by Jean-Jacques Dessalines, who proclaimed himself Emperor Jacques I. This lesser-known imperial counterpart of Napoleon indicated that, in Haiti, as elsewhere, the successful use of force was crucial to power. That was certainly demonstrated in France in 1799 by Napoleon. The conduct of the war had created an atmosphere of expediency in which it became easier for him to mount a coup.

Napoleon, the new commander of the French Army of Italy, had developed in 1796 the characteristics of his generalship: self-confidence, swift decision-making, rapid mobility, the concentration of strength, and, where possible, the exploitation of interior lines. Victory by French columns over outnumbered defenders at Mondovi (27 April 1796) knocked the king of Sardinia out of the war. At Lodi (10 May), Bassano (8 September), Arcola (15–17 November) and Rivoli (14 January 1797), Napoleon's ruthless boldness and ability to manoeuvre on the battlefield brought victory over the Austrians, and associated Napoleon with military success.

Meanwhile, France remained politically unstable. The political 'centre', the base of the Directory, was divided and under challenge from both left and right, and instability was accentuated by both elections and conspiracies. In the coup of 18 Fructidor (4 September 1797), the two moderate Directors were removed by their more assertive colleagues. This 'Second Directory' denied the constitutional Royalists gains made in the elections of March 1797. The different prospects offered by a Royalist France had already been thwarted by the failure of attempts to overthrow the Directory in 1795.[36]

The Directory also had to continue supporting the burdens of war. Defeated, Austria was obliged to accept the treaty of Campo Formio on 18 October 1797, which left France the leading power in Italy and Germany. This was not, however, the end of French activity. Military convenience, lust for loot, the practice of expropriation, ideological conviction, the political advantages of a successful campaign, and strategic opportunism, all encouraged aggressive action, as with the occupation of Venice in 1797, the Papal States in February 1798 and Piedmont in December 1798, and the invasion of Switzerland in February 1798 and Egypt in July 1798.

This aggression encouraged the creation of the Second Coalition in 1799, with Austria, Britain, Naples, Portugal, Russia and Turkey opposed to France. With Poland partitioned out of existence and Russia at peace with Turkey, the Russians were able to intervene effectively in Western Europe. In 1799 a Russian army under Suvorov advanced into northern Italy, the first time that the Russians had operated there. The French were driven back across the Rhine and expelled from most of Italy and Switzerland, but plans to overthrow the Republic and restore the Bourbons exaggerated the scope of the divided Coalition's power.

The Directory was able to rally France, helped by the failure of their opponents to disrupt seriously the French home base, but it was discredited by division, and unpopular. A change seemed necessary. Stability was also threatened by the political process. Under the Directory, the electoral apprenticeship was greater than had been the case under the Convention. The franchise remained very broad, and in two of the annual elections that were held the level of participation was reasonably high. Political parties played a role, although there was considerable reluctance to endorse their existence. The greater role of elections in the political process encouraged governmental intervention, much of which was crude. The elections of 1798 produced a large group of radical deputies, only for the Directory to annul many of the results. The ethos and practice of participatory politics threatened the stability of elite power, and helped make the Directory appear unsettled. This both encouraged its overthrow and was a major reason why the bourgeois turned to Napoleon: he safeguarded, if not political freedom, at least the status and power challenged by elections and electioneering.[37]

On 18–19 Brumaire 1799 (9–10 November), the Directory was replaced in a coup by the Consulate with Napoleon as First Consul. Within France, his rise to power, which in 1804 culminated when he crowned himself Emperor, consolidated the objectives of the Directory by marking the end of political and social radicalism. The Revolution had been defeated – the opposition of the Jacobin deputies to Brumaire was fruitless – and the way was open for a reconciliation with much of the old order within France. Abroad Napoleon showed a singular unwillingness to accept compromise, a desire, at once opportunistic, brutal and modernising, to remould Europe, a cynical exploitation of allies, and a ruthless reliance on the politics of expropriation, that prevented international stability. Thanks largely to Napoleon, the nineteenth century began under the shadow of war.

Conclusion

The significance of the French Revolution is a subject of bitter dispute. Traditional views centre on a social theory of revolution and, in particular, the supposedly revolutionary rising bourgeoisie. Revisionist interpretations play down the existence of social tension, and stress, instead, the radicalising role of the collapse of political authority. They also tend both to adopt a narrative approach, in which there is a focus on political action and divisions and the role of chance, and to stress the extent of Revolutionary disruption and violence.[38] Recently, there have been attempts to revive interest in the role of social divisions in causing and affecting the crisis,[39] and also an emphasis on the modernising aspirations of the Revolution and its extension of a measure of participation in politics and government.[40]

The general theme of much recent work, nevertheless, is the limited appeal of the revolutionary programme once aristocratic constitutionalism had been replaced by a degree of social and religious radicalism. The challenge to established privilege did not only affect the obviously privileged. Regional privileges, corporate and communal rights, and traditional cultural norms were shattered or tested, as with the threat to medical independence posed by the unsuccessful attempt to create a system of government-sponsored universal health care.[41]

The attack on religion was particularly serious. If European rulers such as Joseph II had limited the wealth and authority of the Catholic Church, none had assaulted Christian beliefs and practices to the extent of the Revolutionary government. As the superficiality of 'de-christianisation' and the vitality of religious faith in eighteenth-century Europe are increasingly appreciated, so the limited appeal of the Revolutionary message as it developed in France can be more readily grasped.

Why then was France different? Why was the *ancien régime* overthrown there, producing republicanism and the Terror in the short-term, and deep-seated and long-lasting divisions in the country's subsequent history? The collapse of the monarchy at the end of the 1780s is the first point. It created a vacuum that unleashed a bitter struggle for power and allowed aspirations to flourish that would otherwise have been contained. The elections for the Estates General and the *cahiers* produced great hopes and fears, to which were added the economic crisis of food shortage and unemployment. The coincidence of the political and economic crisis in the summer of 1789 was crucial in unleashing tensions and crystallising ideas.

After the dramatic events of 1789, there was a failure to compromise. Far from adopting a deterministic approach and implying that the course of the Revolution and the fall of the monarchy were inevitable, there were turning points and contingencies, especially the divisive topic of church reform, the issuing of paper money, the attitude of the king and the outbreak of war. These were the essential reasons for the failure to compromise that wrecked the 1791 settlement that many hoped would end the Revolution.

With the war the Revolution entered a new phase. As France was plunged deeper into a military crisis that showed no signs of ending rapidly, and the central government became more

extreme, opposition in the country to the Revolutionary government grew. These circumstances encouraged the recourse to
Terror in 1793–4. In this exceptional situation, still more extreme
ideas and movements arose, until the reaction of Thermidor. Yet
the divisions that were deepened by the Terror, plus the continuation of the war, made it virtually impossible to establish successfully any sort of stable liberal regime after 1795. As a
consequence, the outcome of 1799 was always likely, although it
might have been a stronger form of civilian rule rather than that
of Napoleon. In some respects he was the last of the 'Enlightened
Despots', the culmination and extension of ideas and practices of
state-directed change. The nature of his rule – one based on force
not hereditary right – was excused for many by the 'conservative'
dimension of his regime, certainly its conservatism in comparison
with that of the Convention. Napoleon's commitment to war,
however, and his inability to accept lasting compromise in international relations ensured that his achievements and impact were
to be conditioned by the experience of war.

Epilogue

1789 was not an especially good year for the people of Turin. The population figures, published the following January, showed that deaths had exceeded births that year by 55 per cent, in part due to an epidemic of measles. Despite immigration from rural areas the town's population had fallen. Its foundling hospital received over 500 children, presumably because their parents had died or could not cope with them. The government was similarly confronted by traditional problems. The large number of abuses in the administration of communal properties, despite the regulations of 1775, led to the establishment of a council to deal with the problem. Victor Amadeus III was greatly concerned about military matters, leading in early 1790 to Genoese fears of an attack. There were few signs that the established order was soon to be disrupted and Nice and Savoy overrun in 1792 by the armies of Revolutionary France, though in the summer of 1790 the peasants on the lands of Prince Carignan near Turin rose against tax demands, while the government backed up with arrests its prohibition of public discussion of politics and its limitation of the newspapers permitted to circulate. However, these restrictions were hardly novel: Turin had long been known as a rigorously policed city where the free expression of opinion was restricted.

Elsewhere in Europe the situation was largely unchanged. Governments were more concerned in 1789–90 with the possibility that Prussia would attack Austria and Russia with British support than with events in France. The Habsburg position appeared precarious in Hungary and the Austrian Netherlands. Catherine II was increasingly absorbed with developments in Poland. Although some commentators thought that France would achieve stability and greater strength under a constitutional monarchy, most were as convinced of French weakness in 1790 as they had been since the collapse of her Dutch policy in 1787. Her failure in 1790 to support Spain effectively in her colonial confrontation with Britain over Nootka Sound simply confirmed these views. There was little sense in 1790 that revolutionary views would be contagious or could be spread by France. Burke did not publish his *Reflections on the Revolution in France*, with its warnings of dangers in store, until November and initially his attitude was an unusual one.

The radicalism of the views of some of the supporters of the Revolution was clear. Alongside the title of the Paris newspaper *Postillon Extraordinaire*, in June 1790, was the declaration: 'No more Princes, No more Dukes, No more Counts, No more Masters'. Such calls meant little as yet to the people of the rest of Europe. For most of them, as in 1799, life was a struggle similar to that of their grandparents, often conducted in the same place and in the same occupation. For most, in 1789, as in 1799, there was insufficient food, especially that rich in protein, labour was arduous and the consequences of injury or disease serious if not always fatal. Consolation, for most, was provided by their religious beliefs and by the intermediary role of the churches. This was true in 1789 and 1799, despite the attempts in France to replace Christianity by new forms of civic religion.

As yet, both in 1789 and a decade later, the bulk of the population was untouched by the developments that were to change the lives of their descendants. The technological and organisational changes summarised by the phrase Industrial Revolution were still restricted in their impact. The major transformations in theoretical and applied science and technology in most fields, whether transportation, the generation and distribution of power, medicine, contraception or agricultural yields, were yet to come. The wealth had not yet been created that would make it feasible to suggest that man's lot on earth could be substantially improved.

The legislation issued in Revolutionary France brought no real improvement for the poor because the country lacked the wealth and tax base to support an effective and generous national welfare system. Without economic growth, the secular philosophies of change and improvement were flawed, and it is not surprising that most radical thinkers in the eighteenth century were sceptical about the appeal of their views to the bulk of the population. Whatever their stated belief in the sovereignty of the people might be, they were hostile to what they viewed as popular superstition and conservatism. In 1793 Saint-Just, a prominent member of the Committee of Public Safety, stated that 'men must be made what they should be'.[1] It is not surprising that their imposed public virtue had only limited appeal. Besides being impractical, it was largely irrelevant to the problems of most people.

The impact of the Revolution should not be exaggerated. Its radicalism exhausted and discredited, France swiftly reverted to order and then monarchy, first Napoleonic and then, from 1814, Bourbon. Revolutions elsewhere in Europe in the 1790s were suppressed or forced to depend on French military assistance. Napoleon's reordering of the map of Europe was based on his army, not on popular consent. France achieved many of its military successes as a state that exemplified diverse features that numerous pre-revolutionary European rulers and ministers had sought to introduce, although Napoleon pushed ideas for change further than they had done. Far from proving corrupt and decadent caricatures, as revolutionaries had hoped, the *ancien régime* states and societies proved remarkably resilient. Never as inflexible as the term *ancien régime* might suggest, they did more than survive. France and revolution were resisted and in the end defeated. The major changes of the following century were to take place in societies still heavily influenced by privilege and faith.

Notes

ABBREVIATIONS

Add.   Additional Manuscripts
AE   Paris, Archives des Affaires Étrangères
BL   London, British Library
Bod.   Oxford, Bodleian Library
CP   Correspondance Politique
CRO   County Record Office
Munich   Munich, Bayerisches Hauptstaatarchivs
PRO   London, Public Record Office, State Papers

1 HOSTILE ENVIRONMENT

1. BL. Add. 61684, f. 94.
2. J. Komlos, *Nutrition and Economic Development in the Eighteenth-Century Habsburg Monarchy: An Anthropometric History* (1989).
3. W. H. McNeill, *Plagues and Peoples* (1979), pp. 225–6.
4. New Haven, Beinecke Library, Osborn Shelves C 467 vol. 2, no. 41.
5. D. Roche, *The People of Paris: An Essay in Popular Culture in the Eighteenth Century* (1987).
6. C. W. Ingrao, *The Hessian Mercenary State: Ideas, Institutions, and Reform under Frederick II, 1760–1785* (1987), pp. 91–2.
7. D. R. Weir, 'Family Income, Mortality, and Fertility on the Eve of the Demographic Transition: A case study of Rosny-sous-Bois', *Journal of Economic History* (1995).
8. W. G. Monahan, *Year of Sorrows: The Great Famine of 1709 in Lyon* (1993).
9. T. Kjaergaard, *The Danish Revolution, 1500–1800: An Ecohistorical Interpretation* (1995).
10. J. Kington, *The Weather of the 1780s over Europe* (1988).
11. S. Clark, *Thinking with Demons: The Idea of Witchcraft in Early Modern Europe* (1997).
12. J. B. Twitchell, *The Living Dead: A Study of the Vampire in Romantic Literature* (1981).
13. T. Kavanagh, *Enlightenment and the Shadow of Chance: The Novel and the Culture of Gambling in Eighteenth-Century France* (1993).
14. AE. CP. Angleterre 265, f. 18, 24.

2 ECONOMIC FRAMEWORK

1. PRO. 80/123, Thomas Robinson to George Tilson, 22 Sept.
2. See, most recently, S. Ogilvie and M. Cerman (eds), *European Proto-Industrialization* (1996).
3. S. Ogilvie, *State Corporatism and Proto-Industry: The Württemberg Black Forest, 1580–1797* (1997).
4. Gloucester CRO, D2002 F1, travel journal of John Mitford, 1787.

3 THE WHEELS OF COMMERCE

1. BL. Stowe 791, p. 15.
2. Bod. MS. Eng. Misc., f. 54, 01.
3. I. Blanchard, *Russia's 'Age of Silver': Precious-Metal Production and Economic Growth in the Eighteenth Century* (1989).
4. Aylesbury CRO, D/GR/6/7.
5. J. L. Rosenthal, *The Fruits of Revolution: Property Rights, Litigation and French Agriculture, 1700–1860* (1992).
6. A. Miller, *Letters from Italy* (1776), 1, p. 83.
7. T. Frängsmyr, J. L. Heilbron and R. E. Rider (eds), *The Quantifying Spirit in the Eighteenth Century* (1990).
8. J. P. Mackey, *The Saxon Post* (1978), p. 14.
9. New Haven, Beinecke Library, Osborn Shelves C 455, 41/66.
10. BL. Add. 35540, f. 177.
11. M. C. Lowe, 'The Development of the Portuguese Postal Service', *Stamp Lover*, 84 (1992), p. 136.

4 SOCIETY

1. A. Walker, *Ideas Suggested on the Spot in a Late Excursion* (1790), p. 108.
2. E. C. Musgrave, 'Women in the Male World of Work: The Building Industries of Eighteenth-Century Brittany', *French History* (1993).
3. M. D. Sheriff, *The Exceptional Woman: Elisabeth Vigée-Lebrun* (1997).
4. P. H. Amann, 'French Sharecropping Revisited: The Case of the Lauragais', *European History Quarterly* (1990), p. 344.
5. M. Jackson, *New-Born Child Murder* (1996).
6. H. Barker and E. Chalus (eds), *Gender in Eighteenth-Century England: Roles, Representations and Responsibilities* (1997); R. Shoemaker, *Gender in English Society, 1650–1850: The Emergence of Separate Spheres?* (1998).
7. Aylesbury CRO, Saunders deposit, Pickersgill to sister, April 1761.
8. A. Ribeiro, *Fashion in the French Revolution* (1988).
9. F. Bluche and J. F. Solnon, *La véritable hiérarchie sociale de l'ancienne France: Le Tarif de la première capitation, 1695* (1983).
10. Paris, Bibliothèque Victor Cousin, Fonds Richelieu 33, f. 30.
11. D. Roche, *The Culture of Clothing: Dress and Fashion in the Ancien Régime'* (1994).
12. K. Verdery, *Transylvanian Villagers: Three Centuries of Political, Economic and Ethnic Change* (1983), p. 151.

13. P. G. M. Dickson, *Finance and Government under Maria Theresa, 1740–1780* (2 vols, 1987), I, p. 122.
14. G. Astoul, 'Solidarités paysannes au pays des croquants au XVIIIe siècle', *Annales Historiques de la Révolution Française* (1998).
15. P. Jones, *The Peasantry in the French Revolution* (1990); C. Ramsay, *The Ideology of the Great Fear: The Soissonnais in 1789* (1991).
16. J. Scott, *Weapons of the Weak: Everyday Forms of Peasant Resistance* (1985); Y. M. Berce, *Revolt and Revolution in Early Modern Europe* (1987); A. Walthall, *Social Protest and Popular Culture in Eighteenth-Century Japan* (1986).

5   TOWNS

1. BL. Add. 58213, f. 216.
2. G. Rozman, *Urban Networks in Russia, 1750–1800, and Premodern Periodization* (1976), p. 243.
3. B. Lepetit, *The Pre-Industrial Urban System: France, 1740–1840* (1994).
4. J. de Vries, *European Urbanization, 1500–1800* (1984).
5. T. Margadant, *Urban Rivalries in the French Revolution* (1992); M. L. Kennedy, *The Jacobin Clubs in the French Revolution: The Middle Years* (1988).
6. Chelmsford CRO, D/DM 01/19.
7. G. von Proschwitz (ed.), *Gustave III par ses lettres* (1986), p. 70.
8. C. R. Friedrichs, *Urban Society in an Age of War: Nördlingen, 1580–1720* (1979).
9. M. Sonenscher, *The Hatters of Eighteenth-Century France* (1987).
10. W. D. Edmonds, *Jacobinism and the Revolt of Lyon, 1789–1793* (1990).
11. A. Young, *Travels during the Years 1787, 1788 and 1789* (1794), I, p. 151.
12. M. Lindemann, *Patriots and Paupers: Hamburg, 1712–1830* (1990).
13. BL. Add. 35355, ff. 154–9.
14. A. Farge and J. Revel, *Rules of Rebellion: Child Abductions in Paris in 1750* (1992).
15. T. M. Adams, *Bureaucrats and Beggars: French Social Policy in the Age of the Enlightenment* (1990).
16. D. G. Troyansky, *Old Age in the Old Regime: Image and Experience in Eighteenth-Century France* (1989); J. Imbert (ed.), *La Protection sociale sous la révolution française* (1990); O. H. Hufton, *Women and the Limits of Citizenship in the French Revolution* (1992).
17. P. Harsin, *Les Relations Extérieures de la Principauté de Liège* (1927), pp. 229–30.

6   FAITH AND THE CHURCHES

1. BL. Add. 12130, f. 66.
2. AE. CP Autriche 358, f. 315.
3. R. W. Olson, *The Siege of Mosul* (1975), p. 73.
4. PRO. 94/112, Keene to Delafaye, 9 July 1732; Aylesbury CRO, D/LE E2 no. 5.
5. AN. KK. 1400, pp. 2–3.

6. Bod. Ms. Eng. Misc., f. 54, f. 161; G. Adams, *The Huguenots and French Opinion, 1685–1787: The Enlightenment Debate on Toleration* (1991).
7. T. P. Power, *Land, Politics and Society in Eighteenth-Century Tipperary* (1993).
8. AE. CP Rome 538, f. 11.
9. BL. Stowe 791, p. 122.
10. Bod. MS. Eng. Misc., f. 54, f. 53.
11. R. L. Gawthrop, *Pietism and the Making of Eighteenth-Century Prussia* (1993).
12. W. R. Ward, *The Protestant Evangelical Awakening* (1992).
13. B. R. Kreiser, *Miracles, Convulsions and Ecclesiastical Politics in Early Eighteenth-Century Paris* (1978), pp. 215–16.
14. G. Bremner, 'Jansenism and the Enlightenment', *Enlightenment and Dissent* (1984), p. 6.
15. Paris, Bibliothèque Nationale, n.a. fr. 486, f. 91.
16. Munich, Bayr. Ges. Berlin 176, f. 16, Cardinal Antici to Palatine envoy in Berlin.
17. D. Beales, *Joseph II: In the Shadow of Maria Theresa* (1987), p. 168.
18. G. Addy, *The Enlightenment in the University of Salamanca* (1966), p. 118.
19. M. Ozouf, *Festivals and the French Revolution* (1988).

7 ENLIGHTENMENT

1. BL. Stowe 791, pp. 127–8.
2. W. Hubatsch, *Frederick the Great* (1975), p. 107.
3. D. W. Freshfield, *The Life of Horace Benedict De Saussure* (1920), p. 99.
4. G. von Proschwitz (ed.), *Gustave III par ses lettres* (1986), pp. 33–4.

8 CULTURE AND THE ARTS

1. R. W. Berger, *A Royal Passion: Louis XIV as Patron of Architecture* (1994).
2. S. J. Klingensmith, *The Utility of Splendor: Ceremony, Social Life, and Architecture at the Court of Bavaria, 1600–1800* (1993).
3. W. G. Kalnein and M. Levey, *Art and Architecture of the Eighteenth Century in France* (1972), p. 176.
4. C. B. Johnson, 'A Documentary Survey of Theater in the Madrid Court during the First Half of the Eighteenth Century' (PhD, Los Angeles, 1974), pp. 277–8.
5. J. Lough, *Paris Theatre Audiences in the Seventeenth and Eighteenth Centuries* (1957), p. 231.
6. C. J. Herber, 'Economic and Social Aspects of Austrian Baroque Architecture', *Eighteenth-Century Life*, 3 (1977), pp. 117–18.
7. C. B. Bailey, 'Aspects of the Patronage and Collecting of French Painting in France at the End of the Ancien Régime' (D.Phil., Oxford, 1985), pp. 31–5.

8. E. Lilley, 'On the Fringe of the Exhibition: A Consideration of some Aspects of the Catalogues of the Paris "Salons"', *British Journal for Eighteenth-Century Studies*, 10 (1987).
9. T. E. Crow, *Painters and Public Life in Eighteenth-Century Paris* (1985).
10. J. Whaley, *Religious Toleration and Social Change in Hamburg, 1529–1819* (Cambridge, 1985), p. 177.
11. J. M. Black, *The British and the Grand Tour* (1985), p. 211.
12. H. C. Robbins Landon and D. W. Jones, *Haydn: His Life and Music* (1988).
13. A. Braham, *The Architecture of the French Enlightenment* (1989).
14. R. M. Isherwood, 'Popular Musical Entertainment in Eighteenth-Century Paris', *International Review of the Aesthetics and Sociology of Music*, 9 (1978), pp. 308, 295.
15. S. Pedersen, 'Hannah More meets Simple Simon: Tracts, Chapbooks, and Popular Culture in Late Eighteenth-century England', *Journal of British Studies*, 25 (1986), p. 87.
16. R. A. Schneider, *Public Life in Toulouse, 1463–1789: From Municipal Republic to Cosmopolitan City* (1990).
17. J. A. Sharpe, *Early Modern England* (1987), p. 285.
18. J. Devlin, *The Superstitious Mind: French Peasants and the Supernatural in the Nineteenth Century* (1987), p. 218.
19. J. M. Black, *The English Press in the Eighteenth Century* (1987), p. 262.
20. L. Hughes, 'Ablesimov's Mel'nik: A Study in Success', *Study Group on Eighteenth-Century Russia Newsletter*, 9 (1981), p. 31.
21. R. Scribner, 'Is a History of Popular Culture Possible?', *History of European Ideas*, 10 (1989), pp. 175–91; T. Harris (ed.), *Popular Culture in England, c. 1500–1850* (1994), pp. 1–27.
22. W. C. Shrader, 'Some Thoughts on Rococo and Enlightenment in Eighteenth Century Germany', *Enlightenment Essays*, 6 (1975), pp. 61–2.
23. A. M. Wilson, *Diderot* (New York, 1972), p. 463.
24. H. Honour, *Neo-classicism* (1968), p. 21.
25. P. Conisbee, *Painting in Eighteenth-Century France* (1981), p. 8.
26. M. Webster, *Johann Zoffany* (1976), p. 8.
27. P. Drummond, *The German Concerto: Five Eighteenth-Century Studies* (1980).
28. R. Rosenblum, 'Reynolds in an International Milieu', in N. Penny (ed.), *Reynolds* (1986), p. 48.
29. V. Lange, *The Classical Age of German Literature* (1982), p. 50.
30. J. F. Zack, 'The Czech Enlightenment and the Czech National Revival', *Canadian Review of Studies in Nationalism*, x (1983), p. 22.

9 SCIENCE AND MEDICINE

1. L. Hecht, 'Cagliostro in Russia', *Eighteenth-Century Life* (1975), p. 75.
2. G. M. Addy, *The Enlightenment in the University of Salamanca* (1966), p. 112.
3. G. S. Rousseau, 'Le Cat and the Physiology of Negroes', *Studies in Eighteenth-Century Culture* (1973).
4. J. Gascoigne, *Sir Joseph Banks and the English Enlightenment* (1995); N. Jardine, J. A. Secord and E. C. Spary (eds), *Cultures of Natural History* (1996).

5. J. Tenon, *Memoirs on Paris Hospitals*, edited by D. B. Weiner (1996).
6. R. Porter and M. Teich (eds), *Revolution in History* (1986), p. 309.
7. J. H. Brooke, *Science and Religion: Some Historical Perspectives* (1991).
8. Bod. MS. Add. A 366, f. 60.
9. J. Mertens, 'Shocks and Sparks. The Voltaic Pile as a Demonstration Device', *Isis* (1998).
10. J. Pritchard, 'From Shipwright to Naval Constructor', *Technology and Culture* (1987), pp. 7, 9, 19–20.
11. G. S. Rousseau, 'Nerves, Spirits, and Fibres: Towards Defining the Origins of Sensibility', in A. Giannitreppani (ed.), *The Blue Guitar* (1976), p. 147.
12. Porter and Teich, *Revolution in History*, p. 301.

10 INTERNATIONAL RELATIONS

1. PRO 91/26, Edward Finch to Lord Harrington, 1 Nov. 1740.
2. J. H. Shennan, *The Origins of the Modern European State, 1450–1725* (1974), *Liberty and Order in Early Modern Europe: The Subject and the State, 1650–1800* (1986).
3. AE. CP Prusse 115, Valory to Amelot, 3 Jan. 1741.
4. PRO 90/49, Dickens to Harrington, 4 Feb. 1741.
5. PRO 107/50, Wasner to Zöhrern, 1 Nov. 1741.
6. BL. Add. 58213, f. 86.
7. J. Flammermont (ed.), *Les Correspondances des agents diplomatiques étrangers en France avant la Révolution* (1896), p. 115.
8. Ibid., p. 102.
9. Munich, Bayr. Ges. Wien 702, Ritter to Beckers, 29 June 1774.
10. Flammermont (ed.), *Les Correspondances*, pp. 100, 102.
11. BL. Add. 24161, f. 205.
12. BL. Stowe 261, f. 98.
13. BL. Add. 57928, f. 190.
14. AE. CP Espagne 616, f. 119.
15. A. Beer (ed.), *Joseph II, Leopold II und Kaunitz: Ihr Briefwechsel* (1873), p. 240.
16. Ibid., pp. 422, 420.

11 ARMIES AND WARFARE

1. C. Duffy, *The Military Life of Frederick the Great* (1986), p. 335.
2. J. M. Black, 'The British Navy and British Foreign Policy in the First Half of the Eighteenth Century', in J. M. Black and K. Schweizer (eds), *Essays in European History* (1985), p. 43.

12 EUROPE AND THE OUTER WORLD

1. I. K. Steele, *The English Atlantic, 1675–1740: An Exploration of Communication and Community* (Oxford, 1986).
2. Voltaire, *Candide* (1759), ch. 19. See J. M. Postma, *The Dutch in the Atlantic Slave Trade, 1600–1815* (1990).

3. M. Duffy, *Soldiers, Sugar and Seapower: The British Expeditions to the West Indies and the War against Revolutionary France* (Oxford, 1987), p. 7.
4. PRO. SP. 43/4, f. 159.
5. R. McNeill, *Atlantic Empires of France and Spain: Louisbourg and Havana, 1700–1763* (1986).
6. AN. K. 1351 no. 88.
7. BL. Add. 36803, f. 81.

13   GOVERNMENT AND ADMINISTRATION

1. F. Egmond, *Underworlds: Organized Crime in the Netherlands, 1650–1800* (1993); P. Nitschke, *Verbrechensbekämpfung und Verwaltung. Die Enstehung der Polizei in der Graftschaft Lippe, 1700–1814* (1990).
2. R. M. Andrews, *Law, Magistracy, and Crime in Old Regime Paris, 1735–1789, I: The System of Criminal Justice* (1994).
3. G. de Boom, *Les Ministres Plénipotentiaires dans les Pays-Bas Autrichiens* (1932), pp. 239–40.
4. Beer (ed.), *Joseph II, Leopold II und Kaunitz* (1873), p. 164.
5. J. M. Beattie, *Crime and the Courts in England, 1660–1800* (1986), p. 621.
6. BL. Add. 58213, f. 226.
7. BL. Add. 58213, f. 300.
8. Verdery, *Transylvanian Villagers*, p. 92.
9. PRO. 84/406, f. 230.
10. J. P. LeDonne, 'Indirect Taxes in Catherine's Russia, I: The Salt Code of 1781', *Jahrbücher für Geschichte Osteuropas*, 23 (1975), p. 161.
11. Paris, Bibliothèque Nationale, n.a. fr. 6498, f. 300.
12. Aberdeen University Library, Tayler papers 2226/34/6.
13. M. Raeff, *The Well-Ordered Police State: Social and Institutional Change through Law in the Germanies and Russia, 1600–1800* (1983).
14. P. Mathias, *The Transformation of England* (1979), p. 118.
15. J. Ehrman, *The Younger Pitt: The Years of Acclaim* (1969), p. 255.
16. Paris, Archives Nationales, AN. KK. 1393, 10 Feb. 1781.
17. BL. Add. 37083, f. 10.
18. Anon., *Outlines of a Plan of Finance* (1813), p. 1.
19. Bury St Edmunds CRO, Grafton papers 423/325.
20. PRO. 109/87, memoir of 28 Sept. 1772.
21. J. Stoye, 'Emperor Charles VI: The Early Years of the Reign', *Transactions of the Royal Historical Society* (1962), p. 67.
22. AE. CP Espagne 532, f. 43.
23. de Boom, *Ministres Plénipotentiaires*, p. 106.
24. R. J. W. Evans, 'Frontiers and National Identities in Central Europe', *International History Review* (1992), p. 492.
25. C. Waquet, *Corruption: Ethics and Power in Florence, 1600–1770* (1991).
26. W. Doyle, *Venality: The Sale of Offices in Eighteenth-Century France* (1996).
27. PRO. 78/154, ff. 318–19.
28. H. P. Liebel-Weckowicz, 'The Revolt of the Württemberg Estates', *Man and Nature: Proceedings of the Canadian Society for Eighteenth Century Studies*, II (1984), p. 116.

29. *Politische Correspondenz*, x, 235.
30. M. E. Boutaric (ed.), *Correspondance secrète inédite de Louis XV* (2 vols, 1866), I, pp. 146–7, 181–2.
31. S. Hanley, *The Lits de Justice of the Kings of France* (1983), p. 328.
32. D. Van Kley, *The Damiens Affair and the Unraveling of the Ancien Régime'*, *1750–1770* (1984), pp. 201–2.
33. J. M. J. Rogister, 'Parlementaires, Sovereignty, and Legal Opposition in France under Louis XV', *Parliaments, Estates and Representation*, 6 (1986), pp. 27, 31.
34. D. Echeverria, *The Maupeou Revolution* (1985), p. 138.
35. B. Stone, *The Parlement of Paris, 1774–1789* (1981), p. 16.
36. K. Maxwell, *Pombal: Paradox of the Enlightenment* (1995).
37. AE. CP Ang. 579, f. 314.
38. H. M. Scott, 'Whatever Happened to the Enlightened Despots?', *History* (1983), p. 257. The best introduction to the subject is H. M. Scott (ed.), *Enlightened Absolutism: Reform and Reformers in Later Eighteenth-Century Europe* (1990).
39. P. G. M. Dickson, 'Monarchy and Bureaucracy in Late Eighteenth-Century Austria', *English Historical Review* (1995), pp. 351–4.

14 IDEOLOGY, POLITICS, REFORM

1. H. A. Barton, 'Late Gustavian Autocracy in Sweden', *Scandinavian Studies*, 46 (1974), p. 280.
2. J. H. Shennan, 'The Political Vocabulary of the Parlement of Paris in the Eighteenth Century', *Diritto e Potere nella Storia Europea* (1982), p. 94.
3. H. A. Barton, 'Gustav III of Sweden and the Enlightenment', *Eighteenth-Century Studies*, 6 (1972), p. 3.
4. G. von Proschwitz (ed.), *Gustave III par ses lettres* (1986), p. 213.
5. J. M. J. Rogister, 'Louis-Adrien La Paige and the attack on *De l'esprit* and the *Encyclopédie* in 1759', *English Historical Review*, 92 (1977), p. 534.
6. D. B. Young, 'Libertarian Demography: Montesquieu's Essay on Depopulation in the *Lettres Persanes*', *Journal of the History of Ideas*, 36 (1975), p. 681.
7. AE. CP Autriche 359, f. 204.
8. D. B. Young, 'Montesquieu's Methodology', *The Historian*, 44 (1981), p. 41.
9. Barton, 'Gustav III', p. 9; de Boom, *Les Ministres Plénipotentiaires*, p. 81.
10. M. Cranston (ed.), Rousseau, *The Social Contract* (1968), II, p. i.
11. Ibid., II, p. vii.
12. Ibid., II, p. vii.
13. Ibid., II, p. iii.
14. Ibid., I, p. vii.
15. P. D. Brown and K. W. Schweizer (eds), *The Devonshire Diary* (1982), pp. 54, 60; AE. CP Angleterre 450, f. 337.
16. D. Beales, 'Joseph II's *"Rêveries"'*, *Mitteilungen des Österreichischen Staatsarchivs*, 33 (1980), pp. 155, 151.

17. W. Coxe, *Travels into Poland, Russia, Sweden, and Denmark* (3rd edn, 1787), IV, pp. 429–30, 446.
18. M. Jacob, *The Radical Enlightenment: Pantheists, Freemasons and Republicans* (1981).
19. R. Forrest, 'Freemasons in Transylvania, 1767–1790', *Consortium on Revolutionary Europe: Selected Papers, 1997* (1998), pp. 34–42; D. Beales, *Joseph II* (1987), p. 486.
20. Munich, Bayr. Ges. Wien 730, Vieregg to Hallberg, 14 Aug. 1787.
21. BL. Add. 35501, f. 14, 37082, f. 64.
22. John Moore, *A View of Society and Manners in France, Switzerland and Germany* (1779), II, p. 188.
23. Bod. Ms. Fr. d. 35, f. 5.
24. BL. Add. 36803, f. 62.
25. Aberdeen University Library, 2226/131/903.
26. W. Hanley, 'The Policing of Thought: Censorship in Eighteenth-century France', *Studies on Voltaire* (1980), p. 295.
27. M. Metcalf, 'The First "Modern" Party System?', *Scandinavian Journal of History* (1977), p. 287.
28. H. L. A. Dunthorne, 'Prince and Republic: The House of Orange in Dutch and Anglo-Dutch Politics during the First Half of the Eighteenth Century', *Studies in History and Politics*, 4 (1985), pp. 19–34.
29. B. Meehan-Waters, *Autocracy and Aristocracy* (1982), p. 159.
30. B. Barbiche, 'The Genesis and Development of the Administrative Monarchy in France', *Proceedings of the Western Society for French History* (1984), p. 246.

15   THE REVOLUTIONARY CRISIS

1. Merton College Oxford, Malmesbury papers, James to Gertrude Harris, 21 Aug. 1787.
2. BL. Add. 46822, f. 226.
3. Munich, Bayr. Ges. Wien 702, 7 June 1775.
4. See Godechot, Palmer and Venturi items in bibliography.
5. See Frey in the bibliography to chapter 14 and Subtelny in the bibliography to chapter 13.
6. Beer, *Joseph II, Leopold II und Kaunitz*, p. 485.
7. T. Munck, 'The Danish Reformers', in H. M. Scott (ed.), *Enlightened Absolutism: Reform and Reformers in Later Eighteenth-Century Europe* (1990), p. 252.
8. L. G. Crocker, 'Interpreting the Enlightenment: A Political Approach', *Journal of the History of Ideas* (1985), p. 217.
9. Aberdeen University Library, Keith of Kintore papers, bundle 229, 28 Nov. 1787.
10. J. L. Polasky, *Revolution in Brussels, 1787–1793* (1987), pp. 269, 271.
11. J. D. Candaux, 'La Révolution Genevoise de 1782', *Études sur le XVIIIe Siècle* (1980), p. 92.
12. V. R. Gruder, 'Class and Politics in the Pre-Revolution: The Assembly of Notables of 1787', in E. Hinrichs et al., *Vom Ancien Régime zur*

Französischen Revolution (1978), pp. 227–8, 231: V. R. Gruder, 'A Mutation in Elite Political Culture: The French Notables and the Defense of Property and Participation, 1787', *Journal of Modern History* (1984), p. 633; P. M. Jones, *Reform and Revolution in France: The Politics of Transition, 1774–1791* (1995).

13. R. Browne, 'The Diamond Necklace Affair Revisited', *Renaissance and Medieval Studies* (1989); S. Maza, *Private Lives and Public Affairs: The Causes Célèbres of Prerevolutionary France* (1993).

14. M. Price, 'The "Ministry of the Hundred Hours": A Reappraisal', *French History*, 3 (1990), pp. 317–39.

15. J. M. Roberts (ed.), *French Revolution Documents* (1966), p. 172.

16. S. F. Scott, 'Problems of Law and Order during 1790', *American Historical Review* (1975), pp. 887–8.

17. W. D. Edmonds, *Jacobinism and the Revolt of Lyon, 1789–1793* (1990).

18. Echeverria, *Maupeou Revolution*, p. 299.

19. Gower to Lord Grenville, Foreign Secretary, 1 July 1791, BL. Add. 59021 f. 1. See, more generally, J. Hardman, *Louis XVI* (1993).

20. T. Tackett, *Becoming a Revolutionary: The Deputies of the French National Assembly and the Emergence of a Revolutionary Culture, 1789–1790* (1996), p. 273.

21. B. M. Shapiro, *Revolutionary Justice in Paris, 1789–1790* (1993).

22. H. B. Applewhite, *Political Alignment in the French National Assembly, 1789–1791* (1991).

23. T. Tackett, *Religion, Revolution and Regional Culture in Eighteenth-Century France: The Ecclesiastical Oath of 1791* (1986).

24. C. J. Mitchell, *The French Legislative Assembly of 1791* (1988).

25. A more optimistic account is offered in M. P. Fitzsimmons, *The Remaking of France: The National Assembly and the Constitution of 1791* (1994).

26. For a revisionist critique of the Revolutionary armies, S. P. Mackenzie, *Revolutionary Armies in the Modern Era* (1997).

27. T. C. W. Blanning, *The French Revolutionary Wars, 1787–1802* (1996).

28. H. G. Brown, *War, Revolution and the Bureaucratic State: Politics and the Army Administration in France, 1791–1799* (1995).

29. K. M. Baker (ed.), *The Terror* (1994).

30. M. Crook, *Toulon in War and Revolution: From the Ancien Régime to the Restoration, 1750–1820* (1992).

31. S. Desan, *Reclaiming the Sacred: Lay Religion and Popular Politics in Revolutionary France* (1990).

32. Crook, *Elections in the French Revolution: An Apprenticeship in Democracy, 1789–1799* (1996).

33. M. Lyons, 'The 9 Thermidor: Motives and Effects', *European Studies Review* (1975).

34. C. Hesse, *Publishing and Cultural Politics in Revolutionary Paris, 1789–1810* (1991); J. A. Leith, *Space and Revolution: Projects for Monuments, Squares and Public Buildings in France, 1789–1799* (1991).

35. A. Ribeiro, *Fashion in the French Revolution* (1988).

36. M. Lyons, *France under the Directory* (1975).

37. Crook, *Elections*.

38. For example, Blanning and Doyle items in bibliography.
39. For example, G. Lewis, *The French Revolution: Rethinking the Debate* (1993).
40. I. Woloch, *The New Régime: Transformations of the French Civic Order, 1789–1820s* (1994).
41. D. B. Weiner, *The Citizen-Patient in Revolutionary and Imperial Paris* (1993).

EPILOGUE

1. N. Hampson, *The French Revolution and Democracy* (1983), p. 17.

Select Bibliography

This is not a comprehensive bibliography. Preference has been given to works in English and to books as these are more accessible. The bibliographies of the recent works cited should be consulted for a fuller guide to the available literature.

General works

P. Ajello et al., *L'Età Dei Lumi* (1985).

M. S. Anderson, *Historians and Eighteenth-Century Europe, 1715–1789* (1979).

M. S. Anderson, *Europe in the Eighteenth Century* (3rd edn, 1987).

J. M. Black and R. Porter (eds), *A Dictionary of Eighteenth-Century World History* (1994).

A. Cobban (ed.), *The Eighteenth Century* (1969).

W. Doyle, *The Old European Order, 1660–1800* (2nd edn, 1992).

O. Hufton, *Europe: Privilege and Protest, 1730–1789* (1980).

New Cambridge Modern History vols 6–8.

I. Woloch, *Eighteenth-Century Europe: Tradition and Progress, 1715–1789* (1982).

John W. Yolton et al. (eds), *The Blackwell Companion to the Enlightenment* (1991).

Austria and the Habsburg lands

D. Beales, *Joseph II, vol. I: In the Shadow of Maria Theresa, 1741–80* (1987).

T. C. W. Blanning, *Joseph II* (1994).

W. W. Davis, *Joseph II: An Imperial Reformer for the Austrian Netherlands* (1974).

P. G. M. Dickson, *Finance and Government under Maria Theresa, 1740–1780* (1987).

C. W. Ingrao, *In Quest and Crisis: Emperor Joseph I and the Habsburg Monarchy* (1979).

C. W. Ingrao, *The Habsburg Monarchy, 1618–1815* (1994).

R. J. Kerner, *Bohemia in the Eighteenth Century* (1932).

B. K. Kiraly, *Hungary in the Late Eighteenth Century* (1969).

D. McKay, *Prince Eugene of Savoy* (1977).

E. Palmenji (ed.), *A History of Hungary* (1975).

H. E. Strakosch, *State Absolutism and the Rule of Law* (1967).

F. Szabo, *Kaunitz and Enlightened Absolutism, 1753–1780* (1994).

E. Wangermann, *The Austrian Achievement, 1700–1800* (1975).

Balkans

B. Jelavich, *A History of the Balkans* (1983).
W. H. McNeill, *Europe's Steppe Frontier, 1500–1800* (1964).
T. Naff and R. Owen (eds), *Studies in Eighteenth Century Islamic History* (1997).
P. F. Sugar, *Southeastern Europe under Ottoman Rule, 1354–1804* (1983).

Britain

T. Bartlett, *The Fall and Rise of the Irish Nation: The Catholic Question, 1690–1830* (1992).
J. M. Black (ed.), *Britain in the Age of Walpole* (1984).
J. M. Black (ed.), *British Politics and Society from Walpole to Pitt, 1742–1789* (1990).
J. M. Black, *The Politics of Britain, 1688–1800* (1993).
I. R. Christie, *Wars and Revolutions: Britain, 1760–1815* (1982).
L. Colley, *Britons: Forging the Nation, 1707–1837* (1992).
S. J. Connolly, *Religion, Law and Power: The Making of Protestant Ireland, 1660–1750* (1992).
P. Langford, *A Polite and Commercial People. England, 1727–1783* (1989).
B. Lenman, *Integration, Enlightenment, and Industrialization: Scotland, 1746–1832* (1981).
T. W. Moody and W. E. Vaughan (eds), *Eighteenth-Century Ireland, 1691–1800* (1986).
R. Porter, *English Society in the Eighteenth Century* (1982).

The Empire (Germany)

T. C. W. Blanning, *Reform and Revolution in Mainz, 1743–1803* (1974).
J. Breuilly (ed.), *The State of Germany: The National Idea in the Making, Unmaking and Remaking of a Modern Nation-State* (1992).
J. G. Gagliardo, *Germany under the Old Regime, 1600–1790* (1991).
M. Hughes, *Early Modern Germany, 1477–1806* (1992).
H. Holborn, *A History of Modern Germany, 1648–1840* (1982).
C. W. Ingrao, *The Hessian Mercenary State: Ideas, Institutions and Reform under Frederick II, 1760–1785* (1987).
J. J. Sheehan, *German History, 1770–1806* (1989).
J. A. Vann and S. W. Brown (eds), *The Old Reich: Essays on German Political Institutions, 1495–1806* (1974).
J. A. Vann, *The Making of a State: Württemberg, 1593–1793* (1984).
P. H. Wilson, *War, State and Society in Württemberg, 1677–1793* (1995).

France

P. R. Campbell, *Power and Politics in Old Regime France, 1720–1745* (1996).
J. B. Collins, *The State in Early Modern France* (1995).
P. Goubert, *The Ancien Régime* (1973).
J. Hardman, *Louis XVI* (1993).

E. Le Roy Ladurie, *The Ancien Régime: A History of France, 1610–1774* (1996).

H. Méthivier, *Le Siècle de Louis XV* (1966).

J. H. Shennan, *Philippe, Duke of Orléans: Regent of France, 1715–1723* (1979).

D. Sturdy, *Louis XIV* (1998).

Italy

D. Carpanetto and G. Ricuperati, *Italy in the Age of Reason, 1685–1789* (1987).

J. Georgelin, *Venise au Siècle des Lumières* (1978).

H. Gross, *Rome in the Age of Enlightenment* (1990).

N. Jonard, *Milan au Siècle des Lumières* (1974).

G. Symcox, *Victor Amadeus II. Absolutism in the Savoyard State, 1675–1730* (1983).

F. Venturi, *Italy and the Enlightenment* (1972).

S. J. Woolf, *A History of Italy, 1700–1860: The Social Constraints of Political Change* (1979).

Poland

N. Davies, *God's Playground* (1981).

J. F. Fedorowicz (ed.), *A Republic of Nobles* (1982).

J. Lukowski, *Liberty's Folly: The Polish–Lithuanian Commonwealth in the Eighteenth Century, 1697–1795* (1991).

L. Wolff, *Inventing Eastern Europe: The Map of Civilization on the Mind of the Enlightenment* (1994).

Prussia

L. and M. Frey, *Frederick I* (1984).

W. Hubatsch, *Frederick the Great: Absolutism and Administration* (1976).

H. C. Johnson, *Frederick the Great and his Officials* (1976).

H. Rosenberg, *Bureaucracy, Aristocracy and Autocracy: The Prussian Experience, 1660–1815* (1958).

Russia

M. S. Anderson, *Peter the Great* (1995 edn).

E. V. Anisimov, *The Reforms of Peter the Great* (1993).

E. V. Anisimov, *Empress Elizabeth: Her Reign and Her Russia, 1741–1761* (1995).

P. Avrich, *Russian Rebels, 1600–1800* (1972).

R. Bartlett and J. M. Hartley (eds), *Russia in the Age of Enlightenment* (1990).

P. Dukes, *The Making of Russian Absolutism, 1613–1801* (2nd edn, 1990).

R. Jones, *The Emancipation of the Russian Nobility, 1762–1785* (1973).

C. S. Leonard, *Reform and Regicide: The Reign of Peter III of Russia* (1993).

I. de Madariaga, *Russia in the Age of Catherine the Great* (1981).

I. de Madariaga, *Catherine the Great: A Short History* (1990).
R. E. McGrew, *Paul I of Russia, 1754–1801* (1992).
M. Raeff, *Plans for Political Reform in Imperial Russia, 1730–1905* (1966).

Scandinavia

H. A. Barton, *Scandinavia in the Revolutionary Era, 1760–1815* (1986).
R. M. Hatton, *Charles XII of Sweden* (1968).
D. G. Kirby, *Northern Europe in the Early Modern Period. The Baltic World, 1492–1771* (1990).
M. Roberts, *The Age of Liberty. Sweden, 1719–1772* (1986).

Spain and Portugal

R. Herr, *The Eighteenth Century Revolution in Spain* (1958).
H. Kamen, *The War of Succession in Spain, 1700–15* (1969).
J. Lynch, *Bourbon Spain, 1700–1808* (1989).
K. Maxwell, *Pombal: Paradox of the Enlightenment* (1995).

United Provinces

W. P. Te Brake, *Regents and Rebels: The Revolutionary World of an Eighteenth-Century Dutch City* (1989).
J. Israel, *The Dutch Republic: Its Rise, Greatness, and Fall, 1477–1806* (1994).
M. C. Jacob and W. W. Mijnhardt, *The Dutch Republic in the Eighteenth Century: Decline, Enlightenment, and Revolution* (1992).
E. H. Kossmann, *The Low Countries, 1780–1940* (1978).
H. H. Rowen, *The Princes of Orange* (1988).
S. Schama, *Patriots and Liberators: Revolution in the Netherlands, 1780–1813* (1977).

1   HOSTILE ENVIRONMENT

J. Alexander, *Bubonic Plague in Early Modern Russia* (1980).
L. Bonfield et al. (eds), *The World We Have Gained* (1986).
L. W. B. Brockliss and C. Jones, *The Medical World of Early Modern France* (1997).
M. Drake, *Population and Society in Norway, 1735–1865* (1969).
M. W. Flinn, *The European Demographic System, 1500–1820* (1981).
D. V. Glass and D. E. C. Eversley (eds), *Population in History* (1965).
D. V. Glass, *Numbering the People: The Eighteenth-Century Population Controversy and the Development of Census and Vital Statistics in Britain* (1973).
K. Hastrup, *Nature and Policy in Iceland, 1400–1800* (1990).
T. D. Kendrick, *The Lisbon Earthquake* (1956).
F. F. Mendels, *Industrialization and Population Pressure in Eighteenth-Century Flanders* (1981).
L. P. Moch, *Moving Europeans: Migration in Western Europe since 1650* (1993).

D. Porter and R. Porter, *Patient's Progress: Doctors and Doctoring in Eighteenth-Century England* (1989).

J. D. Post, *Food Shortage, Climatic Variability, and Epidemic Disease in Pre-industrial Europe: The Mortality Peak in the Early 1740s* (1985).

M. Ramsey, *Professional and Popular Medicine in France, 1770–1830* (1988).

J. C. Riley, *The Eighteenth-Century Campaign to Avoid Disease* (1986).

G. B. Risse, *Hospital Life in Enlightenment Scotland* (1986).

R. I. Rotberg and T. K. Rabb (eds), *Population and Economics* (1986).

J. Soderberg, *A Stagnating Metropolis: The Economy and Demography of Stockholm, 1750–1850* (1991).

G. D. Sussman, *Selling Mother's Milk: The Wet-Nursing Business in France, 1715–1914* (1982).

G. Vigarello, *Concepts of Cleanliness: Changing Attitudes in France since the Middle Ages* (1988).

D. Winch, *Malthus* (1987).

E. A. Wrigley and R. S. Schofield, *The Population History of England, 1541–1871* (1981).

2   THE ECONOMIC FRAMEWORK

M. Berg, *The Age of Manufactures: Industry, Innovation and Work in Britain, 1700–1820* (1985).

W. J. Callahan, *Honor, Commerce and Industry in Eighteenth-Century Spain* (1972).

Cambridge Economic History of Europe, vols v and vi (1977, 1966).

C. Cipolla, *The Industrial Revolution* (1973).

P. Clendenning, 'The Economic Awakening of Russia in the Eighteenth Century', *Journal of European Economic History* (1985).

L. M. Cullen, *Economic History of Ireland since 1660* (1972).

M. J. Daunton, *Progress and Poverty: An Economic and Social History of Britain, 1700–1850* (1996).

R. Floud and D. McCloskey (eds), *The Economic History of Britain since 1700* (1981).

E. F. Hecksher, *An Economic History of Sweden* (1954).

P. T. Hoffman, *Growth in a Traditional Society: The French Countryside, 1450–1815* (1996).

P. Hudson, *The Industrial Revolution* (1992).

A. Kahan, *The Plow, the Hammer, and the Knout: An Economic History of Eighteenth-Century Russia* (1985).

H. Kisch, *Prussian Mercantilism and the Rise of the Prussian Silk Industry* (1968).

J. Komlos, *Nutrition and Economic Development in the Eighteenth-Century Habsburg Monarchy. An Anthropometric History* (1989).

P. Kriedte, 'Demographic and Economic Rhythms: The Rise of the Silk Industry in Krefeld in the Eighteenth Century', *Journal of European Economic History* (1986).

W. Kula, *An Economic Theory of the Feudal System: Towards a Model of the Polish Economy, 1500–1800* (1976).

J. R. Lampe and M. R. Jackson, *Balkan Economic History, 1550–1950* (1982).

D. S. Landes, *The Unbound Prometheus: Technological Change in Europe since 1750* (1969).

P. Musgrave, *The Early Modern European Economy* (1999).

S. C. Ogilvie and M. Cerman (eds), *European Proto-Industrialization* (1996).

E. Pawson, *The Early Industrial Revolution. Britain in the Eighteenth Century* (1979).

R. Price, *An Economic History of Modern France, 1730–1914* (1981).

D. R. Ringrose, *Spain, Europe, and the 'Spanish Miracle', 1700–1900* (1996).

B. H. Slicher van Bath, *The Agrarian History of Western Europe, AD, 500–1850* (1962).

B. H. Slicher van Bath, 'Eighteenth-Century Agriculture on the Continent of Europe: Evolution or Revolution', *Agricultural History* (1969).

J. K. J. Thomson, *Clermont-de-Lodève, 1633–1789. Fluctuations in the Prosperity of a Languedocian Cloth-Making Town* (1982).

J. de Vries, *The Economy of Europe in an Age of Crisis, 1600–1750* (1976).

C. Wilson and G. Parker (eds), *An Introduction to the Sources of European Economic History, 1500–1800* (1979).

3   THE WHEELS OF COMMERCE

A. Attman, *Dutch Enterprise in the World Bullion Trade, 1550–1800* (1983).

R. Bonney (ed.), *Economic Systems and State Finance* (1994).

F. Braudel, *The Wheels of Commerce* (1982).

F. W. Carter, *Trade and Urban Development in Poland: An Economic Geography of Cracow, from its Origins to 1795* (1993).

P. Chorley, *Oil, Silk and Enlightenment* (1965).

J. Clark, *La Rochelle and the Atlantic Economy during the Eighteenth Century* (1982).

D. Eltis, *Economic Growth and the Ending of the Transatlantic Slave Trade* (1987).

E. Fox-Genovese, *The Origins of Physiocracy: Economic Revolution and Social Order in Eighteenth-Century France* (1976).

W. O. Henderson, *Studies in the Economic Policy of Frederick the Great* (1963).

S. Kaplan, *Provisioning Paris* (1984).

V. Kula, *Measures and Men* (1986).

J. T. Lindblad, *Sweden's Trade with the Dutch Republic, 1738–1795* (1982).

N. McKendrick et al., *The Birth of a Consumer Society: The Commercialization of Eighteenth-Century England* (1982).

R. L. Meek, *Precursors of Adam Smith, 1750–1775* (1973).

J. A. Miller, *Mastering the Market: The State and the Grain Trade in Northern France, 1700–1860* (1998).

D. D. Raphael, *Adam Smith* (1985).

J. C. Riley, *International Government. Finance and the Amsterdam Capital Market, 1740–1815* (1980).

H. L. Root, *The Fountain of Privilege: Political Foundations of Markets in Old Régime France and England* (1994).

C. Sargentson, *Merchants and Luxury Markets: The Marchands Merciers of Eighteenth-Century Paris* (1996).

T. J. Schaeper, *The French Council of Commerce, 1700–1715* (1983).

A. Smith, *An Inquiry into the Nature and Causes of the Wealth of Nations* (1976 edn, by W. Todd).

M. Sonenscher, *Work and Wages: Natural Law, Politics and the Eighteenth-Century French Trades* (1989).

R. L. Stein, *The French Sugar Business in the Eighteenth Century* (1988).

R. Szostak, *The Role of Transportation in the Industrial Revolution: A Comparison of England and France* (1991).

K. Tribe, *Governing Economy: The Reformation of German Economic Discourse, 1750–1840* (1988).

4 SOCIETY

(a) General

S. Cavallo, *Charity and Power in Early Modern Italy: Benefactors and their Motives in Turin, 1541–1789* (1995).

A. Farge, *Fragile Lives: Violence, Power and Solidarity in Eighteenth-Century Paris* (1992).

R. and E. Forster (eds), *European Society in the Eighteenth Century* (1969).

R. Herr, *Rural Change and Royal Finances in Spain at the End of the Old Regime* (1988).

T. Le Goff, *Vannes and its Region* (1981).

B. McGowan, *Economic Life in the Ottoman Europe: Taxation, Trade and the Struggle for Land, 1600–1800* (1981).

P. B. Munsche, *Gentlemen and Poachers: The English Game Laws* (1981).

S. Ogilvie and R. Scribner (eds), *Germany: A New Social and Economic History* (1996).

J. A. Sharpe, *Early Modern England: A Social History, 1550–1750* (1987).

E. P. Thompson, *Customs in Common* (1991).

W. E. Wright, *Serf, Seigneur and Sovereign: Agrarian Reform in Eighteenth-Century Bohemia* (1966).

(b) Women and Families

H. Cunningham, *Children and Childhood in Western Society since 1500* (1995).

C. Fairchilds, *Domestic Enemies: Servants and their Masters in Old Regime France* (1984).

G. L. Gullickson, *Spinners and Weavers of Auffay: Rural Industry and the Sexual Division of Labour in a French Village, 1750–1850* (1986).

O. Hufton, *The Prospect Before Her: A History of Women in Western Europe, I: 1500–1800* (1995).

E. Jacobs (ed.), *Women and Society in Eighteenth-Century France* (1979).

S. C. Maza, *Servants and Masters in Eighteenth-Century France* (1983).

J. V. H. Melton, *Absolutism and the Eighteenth-Century Origins of Compulsory Schooling in Prussia and Austria* (1988).

M. Okenfuss, *The Discovery of Childhood in Russia: Education and Childhood under Peter the Great: The Evidence of a Slavic Primer* (1989).

L. Pollock, *Forgotten Children: Parent–Child Relations from 1500–1900* (1983).

D. W. Sabean, *Power in the Blood: Popular Culture and Village Discourse in Early Modern Germany* (1984).

M. E. Wiesner, *Women and Gender in Early Modern Europe* (1993).

(c) Nobility

J. V. Beckett, *The Aristocracy in England, 1660–1914* (1986).

P. Camporesi, *Exotic Brew: Hedonism and Exoticism in the Eighteenth Century* (1992).

J. Cannon, *Aristocratic Century: The Peerage of Eighteenth-Century England* (1984).

G. Chaussinand-Nogaret, *The French Nobility in the Eighteenth Century* (1985).

S. Clark, *State and Status: The Rise of the State and Aristocratic Power in Western Europe* (1995).

J. Dewald, *The European Nobility, 1400–1800* (1996).

P. Dukes, *Catherine the Great and the Russian Nobility* (1967).

H. A. Ellis, *Boulainvilliers and the French Monarchy: Aristocratic Politics in early Eighteenth Century France* (1988).

O. Hufton, 'The Seigneur and the Rural Economy in Eighteenth-Century France', *Transactions of the Royal Historical Society* (1979).

G. E. Mingay, *The Gentry: The Rise and Fall of a Ruling Class* (1976).

H. M. Scott (ed.), *The European Nobilities in the Seventeenth and Eighteenth Centuries* (1995).

(d) Peasantry

J. Alexander, *Autocratic Politics in a National Crisis: The Imperial Russian Government and Pugachev's Revolt* (1969).

J. Blum, *Lord and Peasant in Russia from the Ninth to the Nineteenth Century* (1961).

J. Blum, *The End of the Old Order in Rural Europe* (1978).

J. C. Gagliardo, *From Pariah to Patriot: The Changing Image of the German Peasant, 1770–1840* (1969).

P. Higonnet, *Pont-de-Montvert: Social Structure and Politics in a French Village, 1700–1914* (1971).

P. M. Jones, *Politics and Rural Society: The Southern Massif Central c. 1750–1880* (1985).

E. Le Roy Ladurie, 'The French Peasantry in the Eighteenth Century', *The Consortium on Revolutionary Europe. Proceedings* (1975).

F. McArdle, *Altopascio: A Study in Tuscan Rural Society, 1587–1784* (1978).

T. Munck, *The Peasantry and the Early Absolute Monarchy in Denmark* (1979).

J. Pallot and D. J. B. Shaw, *Landscape and Settlement in Romanov Russia, 1613–1917* (1990).

T. Scott (ed.), *The Peasantries of Europe from the Fourteenth to the Eighteenth Centuries* (1998).
T. F. Sheppard, *Lourmarin in the Eighteenth Century: A Study of a French Village* (1971).
K. Verdery, *Transylvanian Villagers* (1983).

5 TOWNS

P. Benedict, 'More than Market and Manufactory: The Cities of Early Modern France', *French Historical Studies* (1997).
G. Bossenga, *The Politics of Privilege: Old Regime and Revolution in Lille* (1991).
T. Brennan, *Public Drinking and Popular Culture in Eighteenth-Century Paris* (1988).
C. Fairchilds, *Poverty and Charity in Aix-en-Provence, 1640–1789* (1976).
C. R. Friedrichs, *The Early Modern City, 1450–1750* (1995).
J. Hittle, *The Service City: State and Townsmen in Russia, 1600–1800* (1979).
P. M. Hohenberg and L. H. Lees, *The Making of Urban Europe* (1985).
R. A. Houston, *Social Change in the Age of Enlightenment: Edinburgh, 1660–1760* (1994).
O. H. Hufton, *The Poor of Eighteenth-Century France, 1750–1789* (1974).
C. Jones, *The Charitable Imperative: Hospitals and Nursing in Ancien Régime and Revolutionary France* (1989).
C. Lis, *Social Change and the Labouring Poor: Antwerp, 1770–1870* (1986).
R. B. Litchfield, *Emergence of a Bureaucracy: The Florentine Patricians, 1530–1790* (1986).
K. Norberg, *Rich and Poor in Grenoble, 1600–1814* (1985).
D. Roche, *The People of Paris* (1987).
G. Rozman, *Urban Networks in Russia, 1750–1800* (1976).
R. A. Schneider, *Public Life in Toulouse, 1463–1789: From Municipal Republic to Cosmopolitan City* (1990).
R. A. Schneider, *The Ceremonial City: Toulouse Observed, 1738–1780* (1995).
M. Sonenscher, *The Hatters of Eighteenth-Century France* (1987).
R. M. Schwartz, *Policing the Poor in Eighteenth-Century France* (1988).
J. P. Spielman, *The City and the Crown: Vienna* (1993).
N. Todorov, *The Balkan City, 1400–1900* (1982).
J. de Vries, *European Urbanization, 1500–1800* (1984).
S. Woolf, *The Poor in Western Europe in the Eighteenth and Nineteenth Centuries* (1986).

6 FAITH AND THE CHURCHES

N. Aston, *The End of an Elite: The French Bishops and the Coming of the Revolution, 1786–1790* (1992).
F. Baker, *John Wesley and the Church of England* (1970).
D. D. Bien, *The Calas Affair* (1960).
C. Brown, *The Social History of Religion in Modern Scotland* (1987).

W. J. Callahan and D. Higgs (eds), *Church and Society in Catholic Europe of the Eighteenth Century* (1979).
W. J. Callahan, *Church, Politics and Society in Spain, 1750–1874* (1984).
J. Cracraft, *The Church Reforms of Peter the Great* (1971).
G. R. Cragg, *The Church in the Age of Reason, 1648–1789* (1960).
G. L. Freeze, *The Russian Levites: Parish Clergy in the Eighteenth Century* (1977).
R. L. Gawthrop, *Pietism and the Making of Eighteenth-Century Prussia* (1993).
D. Hempton, *Methodism and Politics in British Society, 1750–1850* (1984).
P. T. Hoffman, *Church and Community in the Diocese of Lyon, 1500–1789* (1984).
N. Hope, *German and Scandinavian Protestantism, 1700–1918* (1995).
J. Israel, *European Jewry in the Age of Mercantilism* (1985).
D. van Kley, *The Jansenists and the Expulsion of the Jesuits from France, 1757–1765* (1975).
D. van Kley, *The Religious Origins of the French Revolution: From Calvin to the Civil Constitution, 1560–1791* (1996).
B. R. Kreiser, *Miracles, Convulsions, and Ecclesiastical Politics in Early Eighteenth-Century Paris* (1978).
J. McManners, *French Ecclesiastical Society under the Ancien Régime: A Study of Angers in the Eighteenth Century* (1964).
J. McManners, *Death and the Enlightenment* (1981).
K. A. Papmehl, *Metropolitan Platon of Moscow* (1983).
T. Tackett, *Priest and Parish in Eighteenth-Century France* (1977).
J. Whaley, *Religious Toleration and Social Change in Hamburg, 1529–1819* (1985).

7   ENLIGHTENMENT

A. O. Aldridge (ed.), *The Ibero-American Enlightenment* (1971).
J. L. Black, *G. E Müller and the Imperial Russian Academy* (1986).
J. Bloch, *Rousseauism and Education in Eighteenth-Century France* (1995).
L. W. B. Brockliss, *French Higher Education in the Seventeenth and Eighteenth Centuries* (1986).
H. Brunschwig, *Enlightenment and Romanticism in Prussia* (1975).
H. Chisick, *The Limits of Reform in the Enlightenment: Attitudes towards the Education of the Lower Classes in Eighteenth-Century France* (1981).
A. Curran (ed.), *Faces of Monstrosity in Eighteenth-Century Thought* (1997).
R. Darnton, *Mesmerism and the End of the Enlightenment in France* (1967).
R. Darnton, *The Business of Enlightenment: A Publishing History of the Encyclopédie, 1775–1800* (1979).
'The Enlightenment and the National Revival in Eastern Europe', *Canadian Review of Studies in Nationalism*, special issue (1983).
P. Gay, *Voltaire's Politics* (1969).
P. Gay, *The Enlightenment, An Interpretation* (1967–9).
A. Goldgar, *Impolite Learning: Conduct and Community in the Republic of Letters* (1995).

N. Hampson, *The Enlightenment* (1968).

N. Hans, *New Trends in Education in the Eighteenth Century* (1951).

A. Hertzberg, *The French Enlightenment and the Jews: The Origins of Modern Anti-Semitism* (1990).

U. Im Hof, *The Enlightenment* (1994).

M. C. Jacob, *The Radical Enlightenment* (1981).

J. B. Knudsen, *Justus Möser and the German Enlightenment* (1986).

J. Lough, *The Encyclopédie* (1971).

J. A. McCarthy, *Crossing Boundaries: A Theory and History of Essay Writing in German, 1680–1815* (1989).

G. Marker, *Publishing, Printing, and the Origins of Intellectual Life in Russia, 1700–1800* (1985).

H. T. Mason, *Voltaire* (1975).

H. T. Mason, *French Writers and their Society, 1715–1800* (1985).

D. Outram, *The Enlightenment* (1995).

R. R. Palmer, *The Improvement of Humanity: Education and the French Revolution* (1985).

R. Porter and M. Teich (eds), *The Enlightenment in National Context* (1981).

H. de Ridder-Symoens (ed.), *A History of the University in Europe, II: Universities in Early Modern Europe, 1500–1800* (1996).

T. J. Schlereth, *The Cosmopolitan Ideal in Enlightenment Thought* (1977).

R. Scruton, *Kant* (1982).

J. O. Urmson, *Berkeley* (1982).

F. Venturi, *Utopia and Reform in the Enlightenment* (1971).

H. Vyverberg, *Human Nature, Cultural Diversity, and the French Enlightenment* (1989).

A. M. Wilson, *Diderot* (1972).

8 CULTURE AND THE ARTS

J. M. Black, *The British Abroad: The Grand Tour in the Eighteenth Century* (1992).

D. Charlton, *New Images of the Natural in France* (1984).

R. Chartier, *The Cultural Origins of the French Revolution* (1991).

T. Christensen, *Rameau and Musical Thought in the Enlightenment* (1993).

P. Conisbee, *Painting in Eighteenth-Century France* (1981).

P. Conisbee, *Chardin* (1985).

T. E. Crow, *Painters and Public Life in Eighteenth-Century Paris* (1985).

T. E. Crow, *Emulation: Making Artists for Revolutionary France* (1995).

N. Elias, *Mozart: Portrait of a Genius* (1993).

F. Furet and J. Ozouf, *Reading and Writing: Literacy in France from Calvin to Jules Ferry* (1982).

J. Grieder, *Anglomania in France, 1740–1789* (1985).

H. Hatzfeld, *The Rococo: Eroticism, Wit and Elegance in European Literature* (1972).

D. Heartz, *Haydn, Mozart and the Viennese School, 1740–1780* (1995).

G. L. Hersey, *Architecture, Poetry and Number in the Royal Palace at Caserta* (1983).

H. Honour, *Neo-classicism* (1968).

R. M. Isherwood, *Farce and Fantasy: Popular Entertainment in Eighteenth-Century Paris* (1986).

T. D. Kaufmann, *Court, Cloister and City: The Art and Culture of Central Europe, 1450–1800* (1995).

V. Lange, *The Classical Age of German Literature, 1740–1815* (1982).

J. A. Leith, *The Idea of Art as Propaganda in France, 1750–1799* (1965).

M. Levey, *Painting and Sculpture in France, 1700–1789* (1983).

J. Lough, *Paris Theatre Audiences in the Seventeenth and Eighteenth Centuries* (1957).

R. Muchembled, *Popular Culture and Elite Culture in France, 1400–1750* (1985).

W. Roberts, *Jacques-Louis David, Revolutionary Artist: Art, Politics, and the French Revolution* (1989).

M. F. Robinson, *Opera before Mozart* (1968).

C. Rosen, *The Classical Style: Haydn, Mozart, Beethoven* (1976).

R. Rosenblum, *Transformations in Late Eighteenth-Century Art* (1969).

D. P. Schroeder, *Haydn and the Enlightenment: The Late Symphonies and their Audience* (1990).

L. Senelick (ed.), *National Theatre in Northern and Eastern Europe, 1746–1900* (1991).

P. Stewart, *Engraven Desire: Eros, Image, and Text in the French Eighteenth Century* (1992).

S. Taylor (ed.), *The Theatre of the French and German Enlightenment* (1979).

Twilight of the Medici: Late Baroque Art in Florence, 1670–1743 (1974).

C. Verba, *Music and the French Enlightenment: Reconstruction of a Dialogue, 1750–1764* (1993).

S. West (ed.), *Italian Culture in Northern Europe in the Eighteenth Century* (1998).

9 SCIENCE AND MEDICINE

G. N. Cantor, *Optics after Newton* (1983).

A. Cunningham and R. French (eds), *The Medical Enlightenment of the Eighteenth Century* (1990).

L. Daston, *Classical Probability in the Enlightenment* (1988).

A. Donovan, *Antoine Lavoisier: Science, Administration and Revolution* (1993).

M. E. Fissell, *Patients, Power and the Poor in Eighteenth-Century Bristol* (1992).

R. Fox (ed.), *The Culture of Science in France, 1700–1900* (1993).

J. Gascoigne, *Science in the Service of Empire: Joseph Banks, The British State and the Uses of Science in the Age of Revolution* (1998).

C. C. Gillispie, *Science and Polity in France at the end of the Old Regime* (1981).

C. S. Gillmor, *Coulomb and the Evolution of Physics and Engineering in Eighteenth-Century France* (1971).

D. Goodman and C. Russell (eds), *The Rise of Scientific Europe, 1500–1800* (1991).

H. Guerlac, *Newton on the Continent* (1981).

R. Hahn, *The Anatomy of a Scientific Institution: The Paris Academy of Sciences, 1666–1803* (1971).

T. L. Hankins, *Science and the Enlightenment* (1985).

R. W. Home, *Electricity and Experimental Physics in Eighteenth-Century Europe* (1992).

K. Hufbauer, *The Formation of the German Chemical Community* (1982).

L. J. Jordanova, *Lamarck* (1984).

J. Konvitz, *Cartography in France, 1660–1848* (1987).

J. E. McClellan, *Science Reorganized: Scientific Societies in the Eighteenth Century* (1985).

R. Porter, *The Making of Geology: Earth Science in Britain, 1660–1815* (1979).

G. S. Rousseau and R. Porter (eds), *The Ferment of Knowledge: Essays in the Historiography of Eighteenth-Century Science* (1980).

C. Russell, *Science and Social Change, 1700–1900* (1983).

L. Schiebinger, *The Mind has No Sex? Women in the Origins of Modern Science* (1989).

10 INTERNATIONAL RELATIONS

P. P. Bernard, *Joseph II and Bavaria* (1965).

J. M. Black, *Natural and Necessary Enemies: Anglo-French Relations in the Eighteenth Century* (1986).

J. M. Black, *The Rise of the European Powers, 1679–1793* (1990).

J. M. Black, *The Failure of a Great Power: French Foreign Policy, 1661–1815* (1999).

A. C. Carter, *Neutrality or Commitment: The Evolution of Dutch Foreign Policy, 1667–1795* (1975).

J. R. Dull, *A Diplomatic History of the American Revolution* (1985).

A. W. Fisher, *The Russian Annexation of the Crimea, 1772–1783* (1970).

H. H. Kaplan, *The First Partition of Poland* (1962).

H. H. Kaplan, *Russia and the Outbreak of the Seven Years War* (1968).

D. McKay and H. M. Scott, *The Rise of the Great Powers, 1648–1815* (1983).

S. P. Oakley, *War and Peace in the Baltic, 1560–1790* (1993).

H. Ragsdale (ed.), *Imperial Russian Foreign Policy* (1993).

K. Roider, *Austria's Eastern Question, 1700–1790* (1982).

P. W. Schroeder, *The Transformation of European Politics, 1763–1848* (1994).

11 ARMIES AND WARFARE

M. S. Anderson, *The War of the Austrian Succession* (1995).

T. M. Barker, *Army, Aristocracy, Monarchy: Essays on War, Society, and Government in Austria, 1618–1780* (1982).

J. M. Black, *Culloden and the '45* (1990).

J. M. Black, *European Warfare, 1660–1815* (1994).
J. M. Black, *Britain as a Military Power, 1688–1815* (1998).
J. M. Black (ed.), *European Warfare, 1453–1815* (1999).
J. R. Bruijn, *The Dutch Navy of the Seventeenth and Eighteenth Centuries* (1993).
D. Chandler, *The Art of Warfare in the Age of Marlborough* (1976).
J. Childs, *Armies and Warfare in Europe, 1648–1789* (1982).
A. Corvisier, *Armies and Societies in Europe, 1494–1789* (1979).
C. Duffy, *The Army of Frederick the Great* (1974).
C. Duffy, *The Army of Maria Theresa* (1977).
C. Duffy, *Russia's Military Way to the West* (1981).
C. Duffy, *The Military Experience in the Age of Reason* (2nd edn, 1998).
P. Englund, *The Battle of Poltava: The Birth of the Russian Empire* (1992).
M. P. Gutman, *War and Rural Life in the Early Modern Low Countries* (1980).
J. Glete, *Navies and Nations: Warships, Navies and State Building in Europe and America, 1500–1860* (1993).
J. L. Keep, *Soldiers of the Tsar: Army and Society in Russia, 1462–1874.*
B. K. Kiraly and G. E. Rothenberg (eds), *War and Society in East Central Europe* (1979).
W. H. Pintner, 'The Burden of Defense in Imperial Russia, 1725–1914', *Russian Review* (1984).
J. Pritchard, *Louis XV's Navy, 1748–1762* (1987).
N. A. M. Rodger, *The Wooden World: An Anatomy of the Georgian Navy* (1986).
D. Showalter, *The Wars of Frederick the Great* (1996).
P. H. Wilson, *German Armies: War and German Politics, 1648–1806* (1998).
R. E Weigley, *The Age of Battles* (1991).

12   EUROPE AND THE OUTER WORLD

B. Bailyn and P. D. Morgan (eds), *Strangers within the Realm: Cultural Margins of the First British Empire* (1991).
J. M. Black, *War and the World, 1450–2000* (1998).
J. Hemming, *Red Gold: The Conquest of the Brazilian Indians* (1978).
D. Howse (ed.), *Background to Discovery: Pacific Exploration from Dampier to Cook* (1990).
P. Lawson, *The East India Company: A History* (1993).
P. J. Marshall, *Bengal: The British Bridgehead, Eastern India, 1740–1828* (1988).
P. J. Marshall and G. Williams, *The Great Map of Mankind: British Perceptions of the World in the Age of Enlightenment* (1982).
J. C. Miller, *Way of Death: Merchant Capitalism and the Angolan Slave Trade, 1730–1830* (1989).
G. S. Rousseau and R. Porter (eds), *Exoticism in the Enlightenment* (1990).
B. L. Solow (ed.), *Slavery and the Rise of the Atlantic System* (1991).

13   GOVERNMENT AND ADMINISTRATION

T. M. Adams, *Bureaucrats and Beggars: French Social Policy in the Age of the Enlightenment* (1991).

J. M. Beattie, *Crime and the Courts in England, 1660–1800* (1986).

C. B. A. Behrens, *Society, Government and the Enlightenment: The Experiences of Eighteenth-Century France and Prussia* (1985).

R. Bellamy (ed.), *Beccaria: On Crimes and Punishments and Other Writings* (1995).

J. F. Bosher, *French Finances, 1770–1795* (1970).

J. F. Bosher, 'Current Writing on Administration and Finance in Eighteenth-Century France', *Journal of Modern History* (1981).

I. A. Cameron, *Crime and Repression in the Auvergne and the Guyenne, 1720–1790* (1982).

J. A. Carey, *Judicial Reform in France before the Revolution of, 1789* (1981).

F. L. Carsten, *Princes and Parliaments in Germany* (1959).

J. B. Collins, *The State in Early Modern France* (1995).

R. A. Dorwart, *The Administrative Reforms of Frederick William I of Prussia* (1953).

R. van Dülmen, *Theatre of Horror: Crime and Punishment in Early Modern Germany* (1990).

W. J. Gleason, *Moral Idealists, Bureaucracy, and Catherine the Great* (1981).

V. R. Gruder, *The Royal Provincial Intendants* (1968).

T. E. Hall, 'Thought and Practice of Enlightened Government in French Corsica', *American Historical Review* (1965).

J. D. Hardy, *Judicial Politics in the Old Regime: The Parlement of Paris during the Regency* (1967).

D. Hickey, *Local Hospitals in Ancien Régime France: Rationalization, Resistance, Renewal, 1530–1789* (1997).

R. A. Kann and Z. V. David, *The Peoples of the Eastern Habsburg Lands, 1526–1918* (1984).

N. Landau, *The Justices of the Peace, 1679–1760* (1985).

J. H. Langbein, *Torture and the Law of Proof in Europe and England in the Ancien Régime* (1977).

J. P. LeDonne, *Absolutism and Ruling Class: The Formation of the Russian Political Order, 1700–1825* (1991).

H. Liebel, *Enlightened Bureaucracy versus Enlightened Despotism in Baden, 1750–1792* (1965).

A. Maczak, *Government and the Governed in Pre-Industrial Europe* (1989).

P. Mansel, *The Court of France* (1988).

G. T. Matthews, *The Royal General Farms in Eighteenth Century France* (1958).

B. Meehan-Waters, *Autocracy and Aristocracy: The Russian Service Elite of 1730* (1982).

R. Mousnier, *The Institutions of France under the Absolute Monarchy, 1598–1789* (1979, 1984).

A. R. Myers, *Parliaments and Estates in Europe to 1789* (1973).

C. Peterson, *Peter the Great's Administrative and Judicial Reforms* (1979).

M. Raeff, *The Well Ordered Police State: Social and Institutional Change through the Law in the Germanies and Russia, 1600–1800* (1983).

S. G. Reinhardt, *Justice in the Sarladis, 1770–1790* (1991).

J. C. Riley, *The Seven Years War and the Old Regime in France* (1986).

R. Ruff, *Crime, Justice and Public Order in Old Regime France* (1984).

H. M. Scott (ed.), *Enlightened Absolutism: Reform and Reformers in Later Eighteenth-Century Europe* (1990).

J. H. Shennan, *The Parlement of Paris* (1968).

P. Spierenburg, *The Spectacle of Suffering: Executions and the Evolution of Repression* (1984).

B. Stone, *The Parlement of Paris, 1774–1789* (1981).

O. Subtelny, *Domination of Eastern Europe. Native Nobilities and Foreign Absolutism, 1500–1715* (1986).

F. A. Szabo, *Kaunitz and Enlightened Absolutism, 1753–1780* (1994).

E. C. Thaden, *Russia's Western Borderlands, 1710–1870* (1984).

E. P. Thompson, *Whigs and Hunters* (1975).

J. C. Waquet, *Corruption: Ethics and Power in Florence, 1600–1770* (1991).

M. R. Weisser, *Crime and Punishment in Early Modern Europe* (1979).

14   IDEOLOGY, POLITICS, REFORM

K. Baker, *Condorcet* (1975).

K. Baker (ed.), *The Political Culture of the Old Regime* (1987).

D. Bell, *Lawyers and Citizens: The Making of a Political Elite in Old Regime France* (1994).

J. M. Black, *Pitt the Elder* (1992).

R. Browning, *Political and Constitutional Ideas of the Court Whigs* (1982).

R. Censer and J. D. Popkin (eds), *Press and Politics in Pre-Revolutionary France* (1987).

I. R. Christie, *Stress and Stability in Late Eighteenth-Century Britain* (1984).

M. Cranston, *Philosophers and Pamphleteers: Political Theorists of the Enlightenment* (1986).

H. Dippel, *Germany and the American Revolution, 1770–1800* (1977).

D. Echeverria, *The Maupeou Revolution* (1985).

K. Epstein, *The Genesis of German Conservatism* (1966).

A. Farge, *Subversive Words: Public Opinion in Eighteenth-Century France* (1994).

L. and M. Frey, *Societies in Upheaval: Insurrections in France, Hungary, and Spain in the Early Eighteenth Century* (1987).

S. Hanley, *The Lit de Justice of the Kings of France* (1983).

J. Hardman, *French Politics, 1774–1789* (1995).

R. Harris, *Politics and the Rise of the Press: Britain and France, 1620–1800* (1996).

R. D. Harris, *Necker: Reform Statesman of the Ancien Régime* (1979).

M. C. Jacob, *Living the Enlightenment: Freemasonry and Politics in Eighteenth-Century Europe* (1991).

D. van Kley, *The Damiens Affair and the Unraveling of the Ancien Régime. Church, State, and Society in France, 1750–1770* (1984).

R. Masters, *The Political Philosophy of Rousseau* (1968).

J. W. Merrick, *The Desacralization of the French Monarchy in the Eighteenth Century* (1990).

J. Money, *Experience and Identity. Birmingham and the West Midlands, 1760–1800* (1977).

A. Murdoch, *The People Above: Politics and Administration in Mid-Eighteenth Century Scotland* (1980).

A. Pagden (ed.), *The Languages of Political Theory in Early Modern Europe* (1986).

J. G. A. Pocock, *Virtue, Commerce and History* (1985).

M. Price, *Preserving the Monarchy: The Comte de Vergennes, 1774–1787* (1995).

D. Ransel, *The Politics of Catherinian Russia: The Panin Party* (1975).

P. Riley, *The General Will before Rousseau* (1986).

M. Roberts, *Swedish and English Parliamentarism in the Eighteenth Century* (1973).

G. Rudé, *Paris and London in the Eighteenth Century: Studies in Popular Protest* (1970).

R. Shackleton, *Montesquieu* (1961).

J. N. Shklar, *Men and Citizens: A Study of Rousseau's Social Theory* (1969).

D. Stone, *Polish Politics and National Reform, 1775–1788* (1976).

A. Strugnell, *Diderot's Politics* (1973).

R. M. Sunter, *Patronage and Politics in Scotland, 1707–1832* (1986).

J. Swann, *Politics and the Parlement of Paris under Louis XV, 1754–1774* (1995).

R. Wokler (ed.), *Rousseau and Liberty* (1995).

15 THE REVOLUTIONARY CRISIS

K. M. Baker (ed.), *The Terror* (1994).

P. P. Bernard, *From the Enlightenment to the Police State: The Public Life of Johann Anton Pergen* (1991).

T. C. W. Blanning, *The French Revolution: Class War or Culture Clash* (1998).

J. F. Bosher, *The French Revolution* (1988).

M. Crook, *Napoleon Comes to Power: Democracy and Dictatorship in Revolutionary France* (1998).

W. Doyle, *The Origins of the French Revolution* (1988).

W. Doyle, *The Oxford History of the French Revolution* (1989).

W. D. Edmonds, *Jacobinism and the Revolt of Lyon, 1789–1793* (1990).

A. Forrest, *The French Revolution* (1995).

A. Forrest and P. M. Jones (eds), *Reshaping France: Town, Country and Region during the French Revolution* (1991).

J. Godechot, *France and the Atlantic Revolution of the Eighteenth Century* (1965).

H. Gough, *The Terror in the French Revolution* (1998).

N. Hampson, *Will and Circumstance: Montesquieu, Rousseau, and the French Revolution* (1983).

R. D. Harris, *Necker and the Revolution of 1789* (1986).

P. Higonnet, *Class, Ideology and the Rights of Nobles during the French Revolution* (1981).

L. A. Hunt, *Politics, Culture and Class in the French Revolution* (1984).

D. Johnson (ed.), *French Society and the Revolution* (1976).

P. M. Jones, *Reform and Revolution in France: The Politics of Transition, 1774–1791* (1995).

P. M. Jones (ed.), *The French Revolution in Social and Political Perspective* (1996).

J. Klaits and M. Haltzel (eds), *The Global Ramifications of the French Revolution* (1994).

C. Lucas, *Rewriting the French Revolution* (1991).

R. R. Palmer, *The Age of the Democratic Revolution* (1961).

J. L. Polasky, *Revolution in Brussels, 1787–1793* (1987).

J. Popkin, *A Short History of the French Revolution* (1995).

J. M. Roberts, *The Mythology of the Secret Societies* (1972).

D. M. G. Sutherland, *France, 1789–1815: Revolution and Counter-Revolution* (1985).

F. Venturi, *The End of the Old Regime in Europe, 1768–1776: The First Crisis* (1989).

F. Venturi, *The End of the Old Regime in Europe, 1776–1789* (1991).

E. Wangermann, *From Joseph II to the Jacobin Trials* (2nd edn, Oxford, 1969).

Index

Frederick II, king of Prussia (the
Great) – *continued*
and the silk industry 63
on the Swedish clergy 204
and taxes 96–7, 177, 178, 434
and trade 83, 84
and Turkey 349
Frederick IV, king of Denmark 84,
327
Frederick, Prince of Wales 497
Frederick V, king of Denmark 268
Frederick William I, king of Prussia
5, 86, 96, 98, 123, 303, 375
and the army 354
and the French Revolution 522,
523
and the General Directory 447
and government 453, 454, 457–8,
465, 505
and the towns 173
Frederick William II, king of Prussia
350, 488
free trade 82, 85, 87–8, 491
Freemasonry 486–8, 489
French language 299
French Prophets 225
French Revolution 351, 507, 513–34,
535–7
and the arts 281–2
and the Assembly of Notables
513–14
Champ de Mars massacre 522
and the Church 521, 522; de-
christianisation policy 220,
528, 533
and church buildings 275
clashes between town and country
180
and the Directory 529–32
and the Enlightenment 254
and the Estates General 514,
515–16
and food shortages 516–17
and Ireland 511
and the Jews 217
and loyalist sentiment in Europe
510
and the National Assembly 516,
517–18, 520, 521
and the nobility 133
and the October Days 519–20
and the peasantry 152, 156
and political thought 469, 471,
481, 489
and poor relief 196–7
and radicalism 520–1
revisionist historians on the 532–3

September massacres (1792) 524
and the Terror 527–9, 534
Thermidor reaction 529, 534
French Revolutionary Wars 362,
363–4, 400, 402, 499, 510, 519,
523, 524, 525–7
and the Directory 530–2
and Napoleon 535, 536–7
Friedrich Karl of Mainz 156, 265
Füssli, Johann Heinrich 291–2

Gabaléon de Salmour, Count Joseph
137
Gainsborough, Thomas 284
Galiani, Ferdinando 10–11
Galli-Bibbiena, Ferdinando 287
Galvani, Luigi 218
galvanism 318
gardens, landscape gardening
270–1, 297
Gay, John, *Beggar's Opera* 278
Geddy, John 35
Geneva 175, 188, 189, 506, 512
Genoa 535
bankers 431
nobility 128–9
rebuilding of 190
and reform 473
rising (1746) 188–9
Genovesi, Antonio 150, 198, 304
George I, king of Britain 265, 268,
330, 334, 376, 496
George II, king of Britain 21, 266,
308, 339, 341–2, 376, 496, 511
and the Jacobite rising 508
George III, king of Britain 291, 382,
392, 439
and astronomy 316
on government 466
and political thought 483–4
and politics 497
George IV, king of Britain 439
German cultural influence 295, 297
German Imperial Free Cities 166,
188
German Imperial Free Knights 129
German language 299–300, 303
German states (Empire)
agricultural improvements 40–1
and *capitulations* 472
and the Enlightenment 255–6,
257–8, 259
Freemasonry 486
and the French Revolutionary Wars
530
and international relations 323–4
and the Jesuits 232–3

590 *Index*

CPSIA information can be obtained at www.ICGtesting.com
Printed in the USA
LVOW090937171111

255270LV00004B/3/P